**HOLT** Eastern Hemisphere

# PEOPLE, PLACES, AND CHANGE

## An Introduction to World Studies

**HOLT, RINEHART AND WINSTON**

A Harcourt Education Company

**Austin** • Orlando • Chicago • New York • Toronto • London • San Diego

# THE AUTHORS

**Prof. Robert J. Sager** is Chair of Earth Sciences at Pierce College in Lakewood, Washington. Prof. Sager received his B.S. in geology and geography and M.S. in geography from the University of Wisconsin and holds a J.D. in international law from Western State University College of Law. He is the coauthor of several geography and earth science textbooks and has written many articles and educational media programs on the geography of the Pacific. Prof. Sager has received several National Science Foundation study grants and has twice been a recipient of the University of Texas NISOD National Teaching Excellence Award. He is a founding member of the Southern California Geographic Alliance and former president of the Association of Washington Geographers.

**Prof. David M. Helgren** is Director of the Center for Geographic Education at San Jose State University in California, where he is also Chair of the Department of Geography. Prof. Helgren received his Ph.D. in geography from the University of Chicago. He is the coauthor of several geography textbooks and has written many articles on the geography of Africa. Awards from the National Geographic Society, the National Science Foundation, and the L. S. B. Leakey Foundation have supported his many field research projects. Prof. Helgren is a former president of the California Geographical Society and a founder of the Northern California Geographic Alliance.

**Prof. Alison S. Brooks** is Professor of Anthropology at George Washington University and a Research Associate in Anthropology at the Smithsonian Institution. She received her A.B., M.A., and Ph.D. in Anthropology from Harvard University. Since 1964, she has carried out ethnological and archaeological research in Africa, Europe, and Asia and is the author of more than 300 scholarly and popular publications. She has served as a consultant to Smithsonian exhibits and to National Geographic, Public Broadcasting, the Discovery Channel, and other public media. In addition, she is a founder and editor of *Anthro Notes: The National Museum of Natural History Bulletin for Teachers* and has received numerous grants and awards to develop and lead in-service training institutes for teachers in grades 5–12. She served as the American Anthropological Association's representative to the NCSS task force on developing Scope and Sequence guidelines for Social Studies Education in grade K–12.

# CONTENT REVIEWERS

**Robin Datel**
*Instructor in Geography*
*California State University,*
*Sacramento*

**David Dickason**
*Professor of Geography*
*Western Michigan University*

**Dennis Dingemans**
*Professor of Geography*
*University of California, Davis*

**Robert Gabler**
*Professor of Geography*
*Western Illinois University*

**Jeffrey Gritzner**
*Professor of Geography*
*University of Montana*

**W. A. Douglas Jackson**
*Professor of Geography, Emeritus*
*University of Washington*

**Robert B. Kent**
*Professor of Geography*
*and Planning*
*University of Akron*

**Kwadwo Konadu-Agyemang**
*Professor of Geography*
*and Planning*
*University of Akron*

**Nancy Lewis**
*Professor of Geography*
*University of Hawaii*

**Bill Takizawa**
*Professor of Geography*
*San Jose State University*

# EDUCATIONAL REVIEWERS

**Patricia Britt**
*Durant Middle School*
*Durant, Oklahoma*

**Marcia Caldwell**
*Lamar Middle School*
*Austin, Texas*

**Marcia Clevenger**
*Roosevelt Junior High School*
*Charleston, West Virginia*

**James Corley**
*Durant Middle School*
*Durant, Oklahoma*

**Maureen Dempsey**
*Spring Creek Middle School*
*Spring Creek, Nevada*

**Jean Eldredge**
*Teague Middle School*
*Altamonte, Florida*

**Cindy Herring**
*Old Town Elementary School*
*Round Rock, Texas*

**Lois Jordan**
*Pearl/Cohn Comprehensive*
*High School*
*Nashville, Tennessee*

**Kay A. Knowles**
*Montross Middle School*
*Montross, Virginia*

**Wendy Mason**
*Corbett Junior High School*
*Schertz, Texas*

**Rebecca Minnear**
*Burkholder Middle School*
*Las Vegas, Nevada*

**Jane Palmer**
*District Supervisor for*
*Social Studies*
*Sanford, Florida*

**Sandra Rojas**
*Adams City Middle School*
*Commerce City, Colorado*

**JoAnn Sadler**
*Curriculum Supervisor*
*Buffalo City Schools*
*Buffalo, New York*

**Celeste Smith**
*Crockett High School*
*Austin, Texas*

**Frank Thomas**
*Crockett High School*
*Austin, Texas*

**Susan Walker**
*Beaufort County School District*
*Beaufort, South Carolina*

**Field Test Teachers**
**Ricky A. Blackman**
*Rawlinson Road Middle School*
*Rock Hill, South Carolina*

**Lisa Klien**
*Daniels Middle School*
*Raleigh, North Carolina*

**Deborah D. Larry**
*Garland V. Stewart Middle School*
*Tampa, Florida*

**Linda P. Moore**
*Cramerton Middle School*
*Cramerton, North Carolina*

**Earl F. Sease**
*Portage Area School District*
*Portage, Pennsylvania*

**Christi Sherrill**
*Grier Middle School*
*Gastonia, North Carolina*

**John W. Watkins, Jr.**
*Clark Middle School*
*East St. Louis, Illinois*

---

**Editorial**
Sue Miller, *Director*
Robert Wehnke, *Managing Editor*
Diana Holman Walker, *Senior Editor*
Holly Norman, *Project Editor*
Daniel M. Quinn, *Senior Editor*
Sue Minkler, *Assistant Editorial*
*Coordinator*
Gina Rogers, *Administrative Assistant*

**Pupil's Edition**
Andrew Miles, *Editor*
Jarred Prejean, *Associate Editor*

**Teacher's Edition**
Lissa B. Anderson, *Editor*
Suzanne Hurley, *Senior Editor*

**Technology Resources**
Annette Saunders, *Editor*

**Fact Checking**
Bob Fullilove, *Editor*
Jenny Rose, *Associate Editor*

**Copy Editing**
Julie Beckman, *Senior Copy Editor*

**Text Permissions**
Ann B. Farrar,
*Senior Permissions Editor*

**Art, Design and Photo**
**Book Design**
Diane Motz, *Senior Design Director*
Candace Moore, *Senior Designer*
Mercedes Newman, *Designer*

**Image Acquisitions**
Joe London, *Director*
Tim Taylor,
*Photo Research Supervisor*
Stephanie Morris,
*Photo Researcher*
Michelle Rumpf,
*Art Buyer Supervisor*
Coco Weir, *Art Buyer*
Julie Kelly, *Art Buyer*

**Design Implementation**
The GTS Companies

**Design New Media**
Susan Michael, *Design Director*
Kimberly Cammaerata, *Design*
*Manager*
Grant Davidson, *Designer*

**Media Design**
Curtis Riker, *Design Director*

**Cover Design**
Jason Wilson, *Designer*

**Pre-press and**
**Manufacturing**
Gene Rumann,
*Production Manager*
Nancy Hargis,
*Production Supervisor*
Vivian Hess,
*Administrative Assistant*
Clary Knapp,
*Production Coordinator*
Rhonda Farris, *Inventory Planner*
Kim Harrison, *Manufacturing*
*Coordinator, Media*

# HOLT

# PEOPLE, PLACES, AND CHANGE

CONTENTS

**UNIT 2** **Gaining a Historical Perspective** . . . . . . . . . . . . . . . . . . . **96**

*Notes from the Field*

## UNIT 3 Europe

 **UNIT 4**

# Russia and Northern Eurasia

# UNIT 5 Southwest Asia . . . . . . . . . . . . . . . . . . . . . . 374

**Notes from the Field**

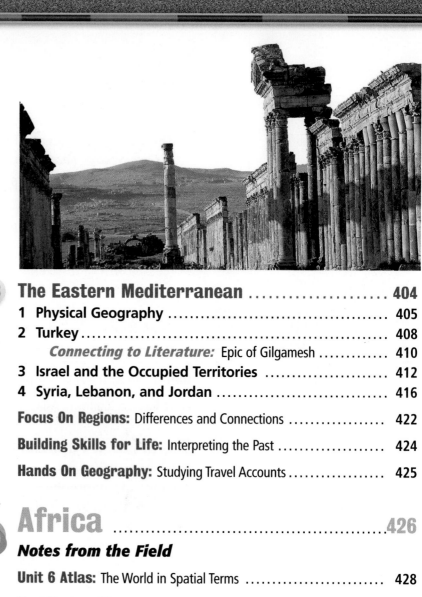

UNIT **6** Africa ................................................. 426

**Notes from the Field**

# UNIT 7 East and Southeast Asia ....532

*Notes from the Field*

# UNIT 8 South Asia .................................. 610
### *Notes from the Field*

UNIT 9

# The Pacific World and Antarctica

# FEATURES

# FEATURES

## BUILDING SKILLS FOR LIFE:

## HANDS on GEOGRAPHY

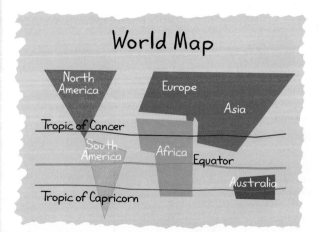

## MAPS

# FEATURES

# DIAGRAMS, CHARTS, and TABLES

# FEATURES

## DIAGRAMS, CHARTS, and TABLES *continued*

# How To Use Your Textbook

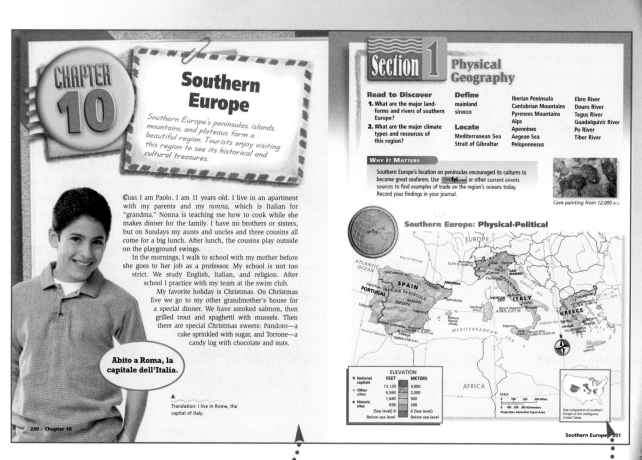

**An interview** with a student begins each regional chapter. These interviews give you a glimpse of what life is like for some people in the region you are about to study.

**Chapter Map** The map at the beginning of Section 1 in regional chapters shows you the countries you will read about. You can use this map to identify country names and capitals and to locate physical features. These chapter maps will also help you create sketch maps in section reviews.

# Use these built-in tools to read for understanding.

**Read to Discover** questions begin each section of *Holt People, Places, and Change.* These questions serve as your guide as you read through the section. Keep them in mind as you explore the section content.

**Why It Matters** is an exciting way for you to make connections between what you are reading in your geography textbook and the world around you. Explore a topic that is relevant to our lives today by using CNNfyi.com .

**Define and Locate** terms are introduced at the beginning of each section. The Define terms include terms important to the study of geography and to the region you are studying. The Locate terms are important physical features or places from the region you are studying.

**Interpreting the Visual Record** features accompany many of the textbook's rich photographs. These features invite you to analyze the images so that you can learn more about their content and their links to what you are studying in the section. Other captions ask you to interpret maps, graphs, and charts.

**Our Amazing Planet** features provide interesting facts about the region you are studying. Here you will learn about the origins of place-names and fascinating tidbits like the size of South America's rain forests.

**Reading Check** questions appear often throughout the textbook to allow you to check your comprehension. As you read, pause for a moment to consider each Reading Check. If you have trouble answering the question, review the material that you just read.

# Use these tools to pull together all of the information you have learned.

**Critical Thinking** activities in section and chapter reviews allow you to explore a topic in greater depth and to build your skills.

**Homework Practice Online** lets you log on to the HRW Go site to complete an interactive self-check of the material covered.

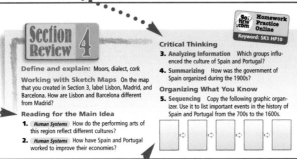

**Reading for the Main Idea** questions help review the main points you have studied in the section.

**Graphic Organizers** will help you pull together important information from the section.

**Building Social Studies Skills** activities help you develop the mapping and writing skills you need to study geography.

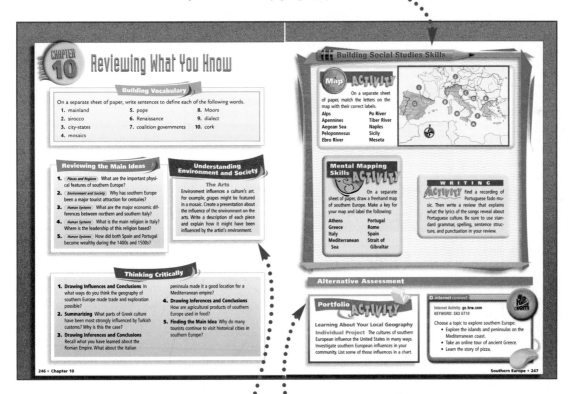

**Understanding Environment and Society** activities ask you to research and create a presentation expanding on an issue you have read about in the chapter.

**Portfolio Activities** are exciting and creative ways to explore your local geography and to make connections to the region you are studying.

# Use these online tools to review and complete online activities.

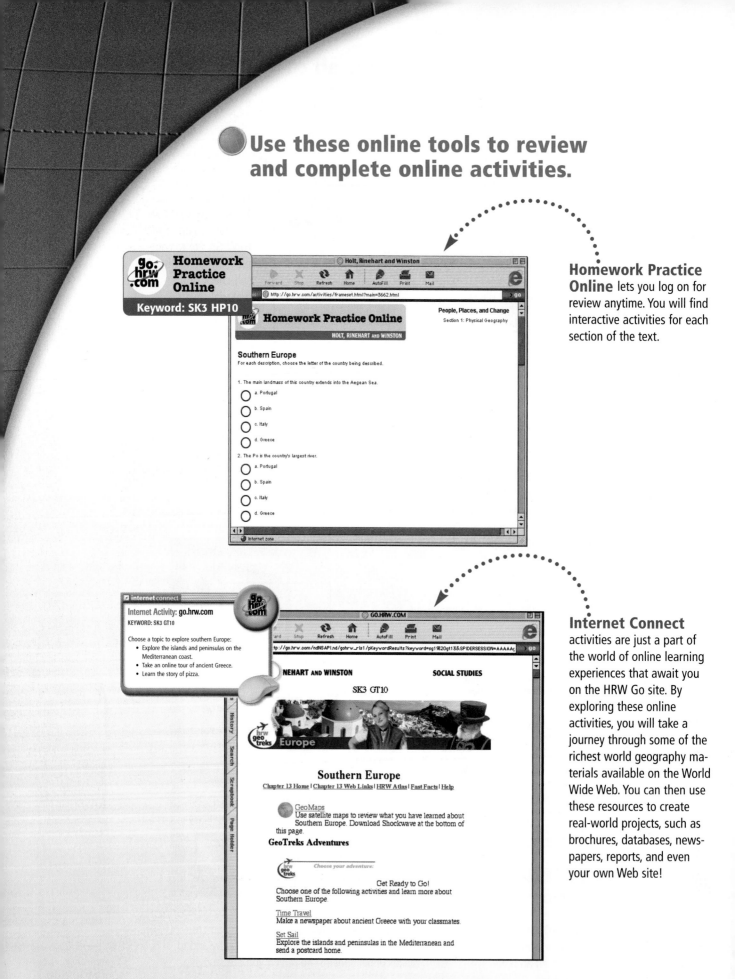

**Homework Practice Online** lets you log on for review anytime. You will find interactive activities for each section of the text.

**Internet Connect** activities are just a part of the world of online learning experiences that await you on the HRW Go site. By exploring these online activities, you will take a journey through some of the richest world geography materials available on the World Wide Web. You can then use these resources to create real-world projects, such as brochures, databases, newspapers, reports, and even your own Web site!

# Why Geography Matters

*Have you ever wondered. . .*

*why some places are deserts while other places get so much rain? What makes certain times of the year cooler than others? Why do some rivers run dry?*

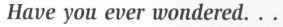

Maybe you live near mountains and wonder what processes created them. Do you know why the loss of huge forest areas in one part of the world can affect areas far away? Why does the United States have many different kinds of churches and other places of worship? Perhaps you are curious why Americans and people from other countries have such different points of view on many issues. The key to understanding questions and issues like these lies in the study of geography.

## Geography and Your World

All you need to do is watch or read the news to see the importance of geography. You have probably seen news stories about the effects of floods, volcanic eruptions, and other natural events on people and places. You likely have also seen how conflict and cooperation shape the relations between peoples and countries around the world. The Why It Matters feature beginning every section of *Holt People, Places, and Change* uses the vast resources of **CNN fyi.com** or other current events sources to examine the importance of geography. Through this feature you will be able to draw connections between what you are studying in your geography textbook and events and conditions found around the world today.

*The* **CNN fyi.com** *Web site*

*My fall semester project, growing a garden*

## Geography and Making Connections

When you think of the word *geography,* what comes to mind? Perhaps you simply picture people memorizing names of countries and capitals. Maybe you think of people studying maps to identify features like deserts, mountains, oceans, and rivers. These things are important, but the study of geography includes much more. Geography involves asking questions and solving problems. It focuses on looking at people and their ways of life as well as studying physical features like mountains, oceans, and rivers. Studying geography also means looking at why things are where they

are and at the relationships between human and physical features of Earth.

The study of geography helps us make connections between what was, what is, and what may be. It helps us understand the processes that have shaped the features we observe around us today, as well as the ways those features may be different tomorrow. In short, geography helps us understand the processes that have created a world that is home to more than 6 billion people and countless billions of other creatures.

## Geography and You

Anyone can influence the geography of our world. For example, the actions of individuals affect local environments. Some individual actions might pollute the environment. Other actions might contribute to efforts to keep the environment clean and healthy. Various other things also influence geography. For example, governments create political divisions, such as countries and states. The borders between these divisions influence the human geography of regions by separating peoples, legal systems, and human activities.

Governments and businesses also plan and build structures like dams, railroads, and airports, which change the physical characteristics of places. As you might expect, some actions influence Earth's geography in negative ways, others in positive ways. Understanding geography helps us evaluate the consequences of our actions.

# ATLAS
## CONTENTS

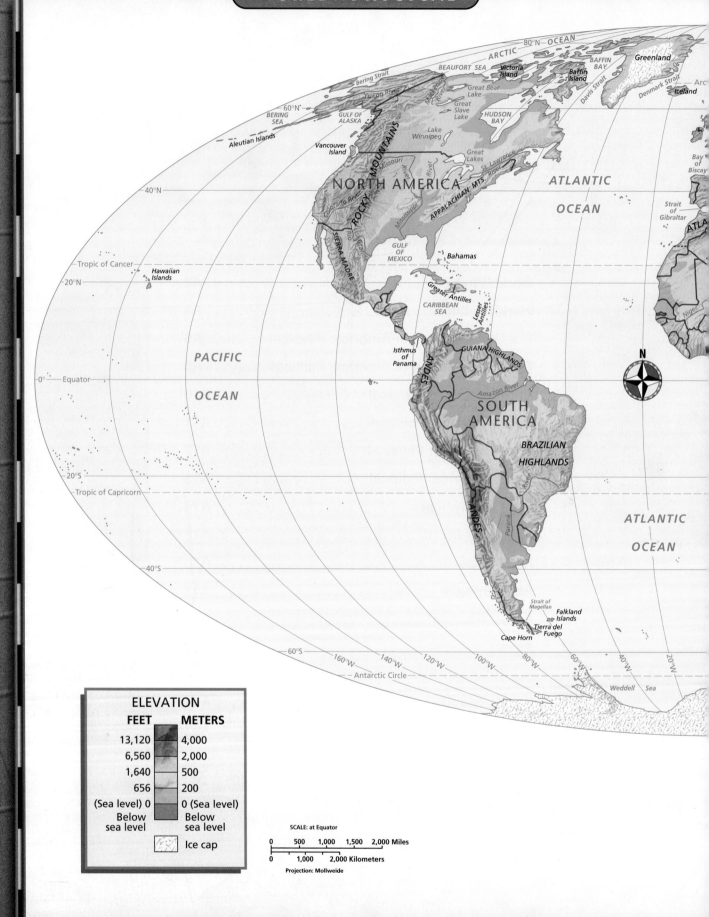

ARCTIC OCEAN
80°N

BEAUFORT SEA
Victoria Island
BAFFIN BAY
Greenland

Great Bear Lake
Baffin Island
Denmark Strait
Iceland
Arc

Bering Strait
Yukon River
Mackenzie River
Great Slave Lake
HUDSON BAY
Davis Strait

60°N
BERING SEA
GULF OF ALASKA

Aleutian Islands

Vancouver Island

Lake Winnipeg
Great Lakes
St. Lawrence River
Bay of Biscay

NORTH AMERICA
40°N
APPALACHIAN MTS.
ATLANTIC OCEAN
Strait of Gibraltar
ATLA

ROCKY MOUNTAINS
Colorado River
Missouri River
Mississippi

SIERRA MADRE
Rio Grande
GULF OF MEXICO

Tropic of Cancer
Hawaiian Islands
20°N
Bahamas

Greater Antilles
CARIBBEAN SEA
Lesser Antilles

Niger

PACIFIC
Isthmus of Panama
GUIANA HIGHLANDS

ANDES

OCEAN
Amazon River

0° Equator
SOUTH AMERICA

N

BRAZILIAN
HIGHLANDS

River

20°S
Tropic of Capricorn

ANDES
Paraná
ATLANTIC

40°S
OCEAN

Strait of Magellan
Falkland Islands
Tierra del Fuego
Cape Horn

160°W 140°W 120°W 100°W 80°W 60°W 40°W 20°W
60°S
Antarctic Circle

Weddell Sea

## ELEVATION

| FEET | | METERS |
|---|---|---|
| 13,120 | | 4,000 |
| 6,560 | | 2,000 |
| 1,640 | | 500 |
| 656 | | 200 |
| (Sea level) 0 | | 0 (Sea level) |
| Below sea level | | Below sea level |
| | Ice cap | |

SCALE: at Equator

0   500   1,000   1,500   2,000 Miles

0        1,000        2,000 Kilometers

Projection: Mollweide

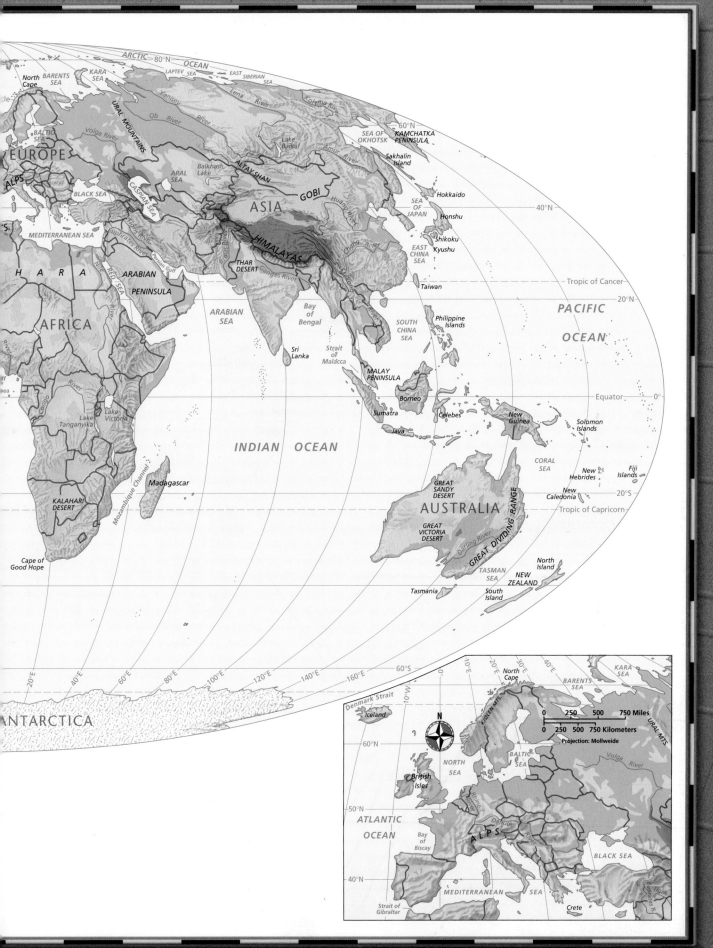

ARCTIC 80°N OCEAN

North Cape
BARENTS SEA
KARA SEA
LAPTEV SEA
EAST SIBERIAN SEA

EUROPE
BALTIC SEA
URAL MOUNTAINS
Ob River
Yenisey River
Lena River
Kolyma River

SEA OF OKHOTSK
KAMCHATKA PENINSULA

60°N

ALPS
BLACK SEA
CASPIAN SEA
ARAL SEA
Balkhash Lake
Lake Baikal
ALTAY SHAN
Amur River
Sakhalin Island

MEDITERRANEAN SEA
ASIA
GOBI
Hokkaido

SEA OF JAPAN
Honshu
40°N

Tigris River
Euphrates River
Persian Gulf
HIMALAYAS
Huang River
Chang River
Shikoku
Kyushu

EAST CHINA SEA

HARA
Nile River
ARABIAN PENINSULA
THAR DESERT
Ganges River
Mekong River
Taiwan
Tropic of Cancer

AFRICA
RED SEA
ARABIAN SEA
Bay of Bengal
20°N

PACIFIC OCEAN

Congo River
Sri Lanka
Strait of Malacca
SOUTH CHINA SEA
Philippine Islands

Lake Tanganyika
Lake Victoria
MALAY PENINSULA
Borneo
Celebes

Equator 0°

INDIAN OCEAN
Sumatra
Java
New Guinea
Solomon Islands

Madagascar
Mozambique Channel
CORAL SEA
New Hebrides
Fiji Islands

KALAHARI DESERT
GREAT SANDY DESERT
New Caledonia
20°S

AUSTRALIA
GREAT DIVIDING RANGE
Tropic of Capricorn

GREAT VICTORIA DESERT
Darling River

Cape of Good Hope
TASMAN SEA
North Island
NEW ZEALAND

Tasmania
South Island

20°E 40°E 60°E 80°E 100°E 120°E 140°E 160°E 60°S

ANTARCTICA

North Cape
KARA SEA
10°E 20°E 30°E 40°E
BARENTS SEA

Denmark Strait
Iceland
N
SCANDEN MTS.
URAL MTS.

0 250 500 750 Miles
0 250 500 750 Kilometers
Projection: Mollweide

60°N
NORTH SEA
BALTIC SEA
Volga River

British Isles
Rhine River

ATLANTIC OCEAN
50°N
Danube River
ALPS

Bay of Biscay
BLACK SEA

40°N
MEDITERRANEAN SEA
Strait of Gibraltar
Crete
Euphrates R.

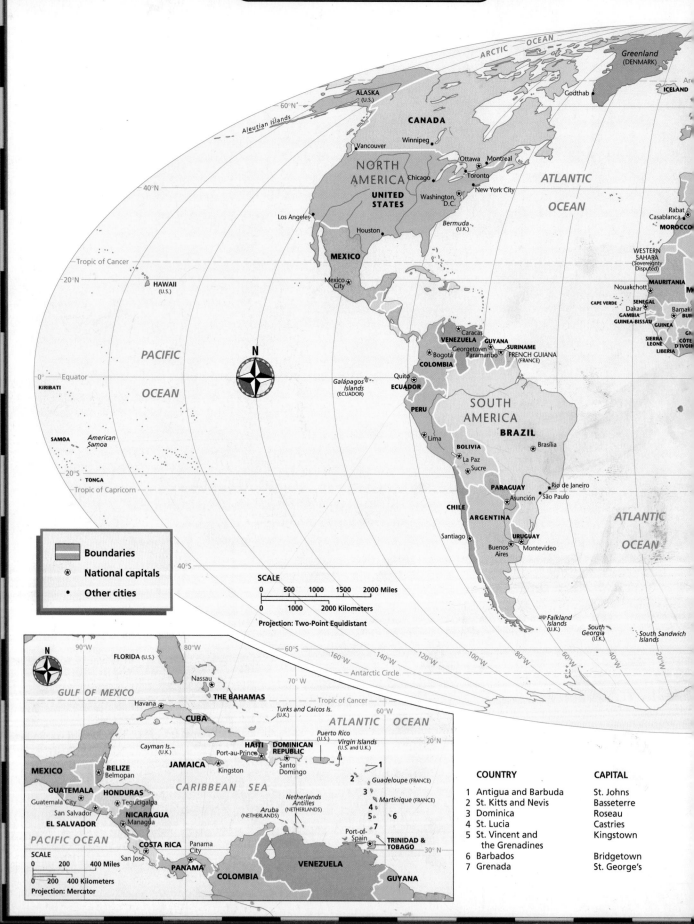

ARCTIC OCEAN

Greenland (DENMARK)

Godthab

ICELAND

ALASKA (U.S.)

60°N

Aleutian Islands

CANADA

Vancouver    Winnipeg

NORTH AMERICA

Ottawa   Montreal

Chicago

Toronto

New York City

ATLANTIC OCEAN

40°N

UNITED STATES

Washington, D.C.

Rabat
Casablanca

MOROCCO

Los Angeles

Bermuda (U.K.)

Houston

WESTERN SAHARA (Sovereignty Disputed)

Tropic of Cancer

MEXICO

MAURITANIA

20°N

HAWAII (U.S.)

Nouakchott

CAPE VERDE    SENEGAL
Dakar    Bamako
GAMBIA    BU
GUINEA-BISSAU    GUINEA

Mexico City

Caracas

VENEZUELA    GUYANA    SURINAME
Georgetown    Paramaribo    FRENCH GUIANA (FRANCE)

SIERRA    CÔTE
LEONE    D'IVOIRE
LIBERIA

PACIFIC

Bogotá

COLOMBIA

0°    Equator

KIRIBATI

Galápagos Islands (ECUADOR)

Quito
ECUADOR

OCEAN

PERU

SOUTH AMERICA

BRAZIL

SAMOA    American Samoa

Lima

Brasília

BOLIVIA

La Paz
Sucre

20°S    TONGA

Rio de Janeiro

Tropic of Capricorn

PARAGUAY

Asunción    São Paulo

ATLANTIC

CHILE

ARGENTINA

URUGUAY

OCEAN

Santiago

Buenos Aires    Montevideo

N

Boundaries

National capitals

Other cities

40°S

SCALE
0    500    1000    1500    2000 Miles
0    1000    2000 Kilometers
Projection: Two-Point Equidistant

60°S

Falkland Islands (U.K.)

South Georgia (U.K.)

South Sandwich Islands

160°W    140°W    120°W    100°W    80°W    60°W    40°W    20°W

Antarctic Circle

90°W    80°W

N

FLORIDA (U.S.)

70°W    60°W

GULF OF MEXICO

Nassau

THE BAHAMAS

Tropic of Cancer

Havana

CUBA

Turks and Caicos Is. (U.K.)

ATLANTIC OCEAN

20°N

Cayman Is. (U.K.)

HAITI    DOMINICAN
Port-au-Prince    REPUBLIC

Puerto Rico (U.S.)

Virgin Islands (U.S. and U.K.)

1

MEXICO

BELIZE
Belmopan

JAMAICA

Kingston

Santo Domingo

Guadeloupe (FRANCE)

2

GUATEMALA

HONDURAS

CARIBBEAN    SEA

3

Guatemala City

Tegucigalpa

Netherlands
Antilles
(NETHERLANDS)

Martinique (FRANCE)

San Salvador

NICARAGUA

Aruba
(NETHERLANDS)

4

EL SALVADOR

Managua

5    7    6

PACIFIC OCEAN

COSTA RICA

Panama City

Port-of-
Spain

TRINIDAD &
TOBAGO

SCALE
0    200    400 Miles
0    200    400 Kilometers
Projection: Mercator

San José

PANAMA

VENEZUELA

30°N

COLOMBIA

GUYANA

| COUNTRY | CAPITAL |
|---|---|
| 1 Antigua and Barbuda | St. Johns |
| 2 St. Kitts and Nevis | Basseterre |
| 3 Dominica | Roseau |
| 4 St. Lucia | Castries |
| 5 St. Vincent and the Grenadines | Kingstown |
| 6 Barbados | Bridgetown |
| 7 Grenada | St. George's |

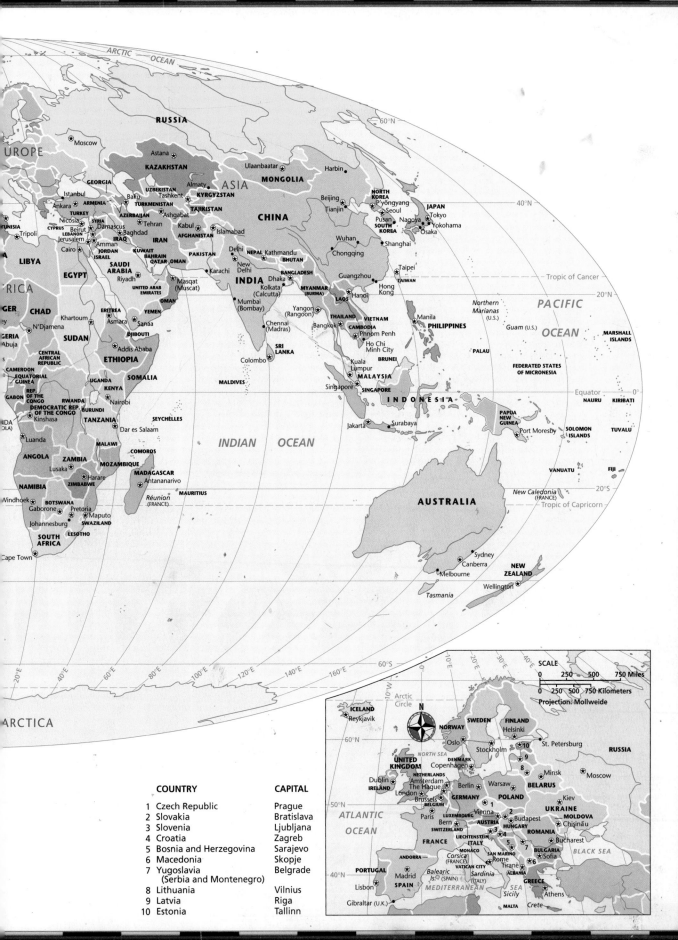

ARCTIC OCEAN

RUSSIA

Moscow

EUROPE

KAZAKHSTAN

Astana

Almaty
Tashkent
UZBEKISTAN
KYRGYZSTAN
TURKMENISTAN
TAJIKISTAN

Ulaanbaatar

MONGOLIA

ASIA

Harbin

Beijing
Tianjin

CHINA

Wuhan

Chongqing

Shanghai

NORTH KOREA
P'yŏngyang
Seoul
Pusan
SOUTH KOREA

JAPAN
Tokyo
Nagoya
Yokohama
Osaka

40°N

60°N

GEORGIA
Istanbul
Ankara
ARMENIA
TURKEY
Baku
AZERBAIJAN
Tehran
Ashgabat
Kabul
Islamabad
AFGHANISTAN
PAKISTAN
Delhi
New Delhi

Nicosia
CYPRUS
SYRIA
Beirut
LEBANON
Damascus
Baghdad
IRAQ
IRAN
Amman
JORDAN
Jerusalem
ISRAEL
Cairo
KUWAIT
BAHRAIN
QATAR
OMAN
UNITED ARAB EMIRATES
Masqat (Muscat)
Karachi

NEPAL
Kathmandu
BHUTAN
BANGLADESH
Dhaka
Kolkata (Calcutta)
MYANMAR (BURMA)

Guangzhou
Hong Kong

Taipei
TAIWAN

Tropic of Cancer

20°N

TUNISIA
Tripoli

LIBYA

EGYPT

SAUDI ARABIA
Riyadh

YEMEN
Sanaa

ERITREA
Asmara
DJIBOUTI

INDIA
Mumbai (Bombay)

Chennai (Madras)

SRI LANKA
Colombo

MALDIVES

Yangon (Rangoon)
THAILAND
Bangkok
LAOS
Hanoi
VIETNAM
CAMBODIA
Phnom Penh
Ho Chi Minh City

Manila
PHILIPPINES

Guam (U.S.)

Northern Marianas (U.S.)

PACIFIC OCEAN

MARSHALL ISLANDS

AFRICA

CHAD
N'Djamena
Khartoum
SUDAN

NIGER
NIGERIA
Abuja

CENTRAL AFRICAN REPUBLIC

CAMEROON
EQUATORIAL GUINEA
GABON
REP. OF THE CONGO

ETHIOPIA
Addis Ababa

SOMALIA

UGANDA
KENYA
Nairobi

RWANDA
BURUNDI
DEMOCRATIC REP. OF THE CONGO
Kinshasa
TANZANIA
Dar es Salaam

SEYCHELLES

BRUNEI

Kuala Lumpur
MALAYSIA
SINGAPORE
Singapore

PALAU

FEDERATED STATES OF MICRONESIA

INDONESIA

Jakarta
Surabaya

PAPUA NEW GUINEA
Port Moresby

Equator

SOLOMON ISLANDS

NAURU

KIRIBATI

TUVALU

0°

ANGOLA
Luanda

ANGOLA
ZAMBIA
Lusaka

MALAWI

COMOROS

MOZAMBIQUE
MADAGASCAR
Antananarivo

INDIAN OCEAN

NAMIBIA
Windhoek
BOTSWANA
Gaborone
ZIMBABWE
Harare

SWAZILAND
Pretoria
Maputo
Johannesburg
SOUTH AFRICA
LESOTHO

Réunion (FRANCE)

MAURITIUS

AUSTRALIA

New Caledonia (FRANCE)

VANUATU

FIJI

20°S

Tropic of Capricorn

Cape Town

Sydney
Canberra
Melbourne

NEW ZEALAND

Tasmania

Wellington

20°E    40°E    60°E    80°E    100°E    120°E    140°E    160°E    60°S

ANTARCTICA

| COUNTRY | CAPITAL |
|---|---|
| 1 Czech Republic | Prague |
| 2 Slovakia | Bratislava |
| 3 Slovenia | Ljubljana |
| 4 Croatia | Zagreb |
| 5 Bosnia and Herzegovina | Sarajevo |
| 6 Macedonia | Skopje |
| 7 Yugoslavia (Serbia and Montenegro) | Belgrade |
| 8 Lithuania | Vilnius |
| 9 Latvia | Riga |
| 10 Estonia | Tallinn |

SCALE
0   250   500   750 Miles
0   250   500   750 Kilometers
Projection: Mollweide

ICELAND
Reykjavik

Arctic Circle

N

NORWAY
Oslo

SWEDEN
Stockholm

FINLAND
Helsinki

St. Petersburg

RUSSIA

60°N

NORTH SEA

DENMARK
Copenhagen

10

9

8

Minsk

BELARUS

Moscow

UNITED KINGDOM
Dublin
IRELAND
London

NETHERLANDS
Amsterdam
The Hague

GERMANY
Berlin

POLAND
Warsaw

Kiev

UKRAINE

50°N

ATLANTIC OCEAN

Brussels
BELGIUM
LUXEMBOURG
Paris
FRANCE

1
Vienna
AUSTRIA
Bern
SWITZERLAND
LIECHTENSTEIN

2
Budapest
HUNGARY

3
4
5
7

MOLDOVA
Chişinău

ROMANIA
Bucharest

6
BULGARIA
Sofia

BLACK SEA

ANDORRA

PORTUGAL
Lisbon

Madrid
SPAIN

Corsica (FRANCE)
Balearic Is. (SPAIN)

MONACO
SAN MARINO
ITALY
Rome
VATICAN CITY
Sardinia (ITALY)

ALBANIA
Tirane

GREECE
Athens

40°N

MEDITERRANEAN

Sicily

SEA

MALTA

Crete

Gibraltar (U.K.)

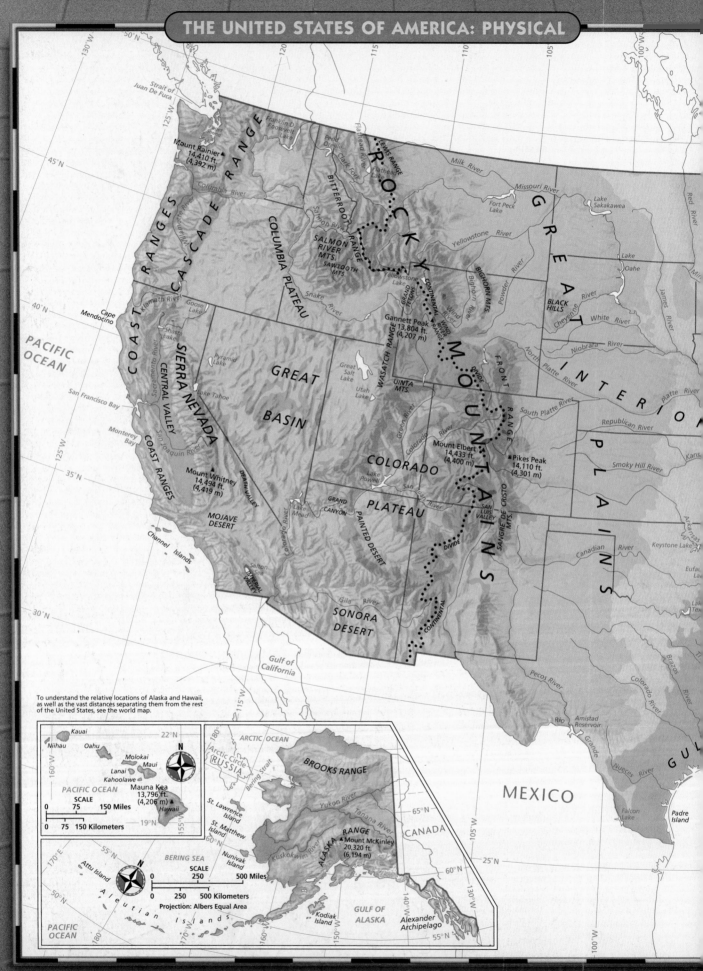

To understand the relative locations of Alaska and Hawaii, as well as the vast distances separating them from the rest of the United States, see the world map.

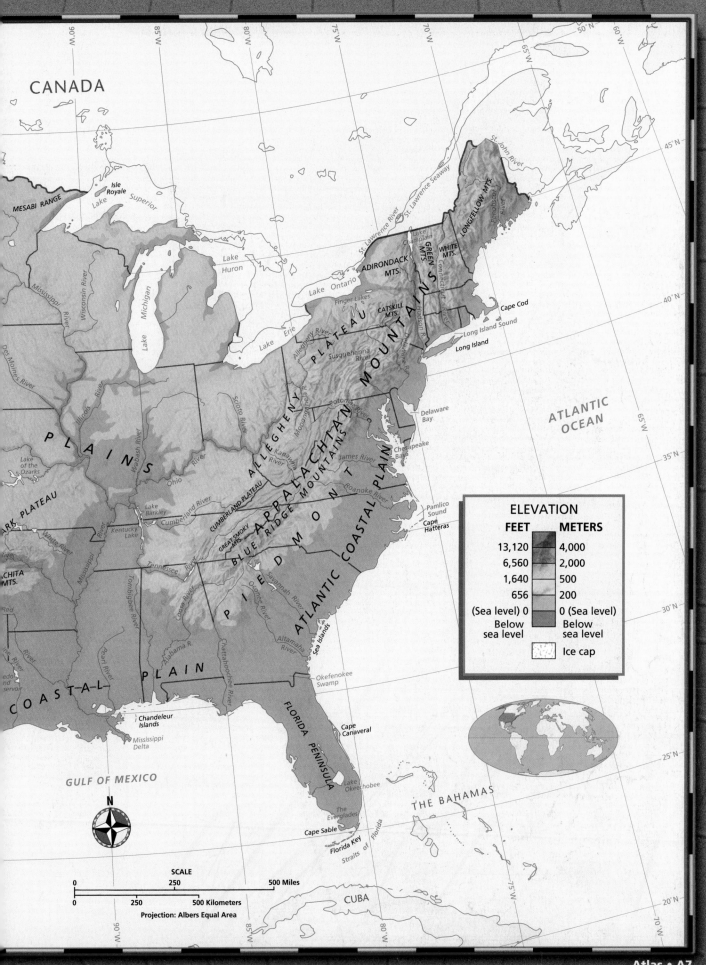

CANADA

MESABI RANGE
Isle Royale
Lake Superior
Lake Michigan
Lake Huron
Lake Ontario
Lake Erie

Mississippi River
Wisconsin River
Des Moines River
Illinois River
Wabash River
Ohio River
Scioto River
Allegheny River
Susquehanna River

P L A I N S

Lake of the Ozarks
OZARK PLATEAU
White River
Lake Barkley
Kentucky Lake
Cumberland River
Tennessee River
Mississippi River
Tombigbee River
Coosa River
Oconee River

OUACHITA MTS.
Red River

ALLEGHENY PLATEAU
APPALACHIAN MOUNTAINS
CUMBERLAND PLATEAU
GREAT SMOKY MTS.
BLUE RIDGE MOUNTAINS

ADIRONDACK MTS.
Finger Lakes
CATSKILL MTS.
Delaware River
Lake Champlain
GREEN MTS.
WHITE MTS.
LONGFELLOW MTS.
St. Lawrence Seaway
St. Lawrence River
St. John River
Penobscot River
Connecticut River
Hudson R.

Cape Cod
Long Island Sound
Long Island

P I E D M O N T
Potomac River
Monongahela R.
Kanawha River
James River
Roanoke River
Savannah River
Altamaha River

A T L A N T I C   C O A S T A L   P L A I N

Delaware Bay
Chesapeake Bay
Pamlico Sound
Cape Hatteras

ATLANTIC OCEAN

Sea Islands

Chattahoochee River
Alabama R.
Pearl River
Chandeleur Islands
Mississippi Delta

C O A S T A L   P L A I N

Okefenokee Swamp

GULF OF MEXICO

FLORIDA PENINSULA
Cape Canaveral
Lake Okeechobee
The Everglades
Cape Sable
Florida Key
Straits of Florida

THE BAHAMAS

CUBA

## ELEVATION

| FEET | | METERS |
|---|---|---|
| 13,120 | | 4,000 |
| 6,560 | | 2,000 |
| 1,640 | | 500 |
| 656 | | 200 |
| (Sea level) 0 | | 0 (Sea level) |
| Below sea level | | Below sea level |

Ice cap

N

SCALE
0      250      500 Miles
0      250      500 Kilometers
Projection: Albers Equal Area

PACIFIC OCEAN

WASHINGTON
Olympia ★
Seattle
Tacoma
Spokane
Strait of Juan de Fuca
Puget Sound
Franklin D. Roosevelt Lake

Portland
Salem ★
Eugene
OREGON
Columbia River

IDAHO
Boise ★
Snake River

Pend Oreille
Flathead Lake

MONTANA
Helena ★
Fort Peck Lake
Billings
Yellowstone
Missouri River
River

NORTH DAKOTA
Bismarck ★
Fargo
Red River

SOUTH DAKOTA
Pierre ★
Lake Oahe
Sioux Falls
Minne...

Cape Mendocino
Goose Lake
Shasta Lake
Sacramento River

Pyramid Lake
Reno
Carson City ★
Lake Tahoe
NEVADA

WYOMING
Yellowstone Lake
Casper
Cheyenne ★

NEBRASKA
Platte River
Omaha
Lincoln ★

Oakland
San Francisco
San Francisco Bay
Sacramento ★
Stockton
Modesto
San Jose
Monterey Bay
San Joaquin R.
Fresno

Great Salt Lake
Salt Lake City ★
Utah Lake
Provo
UTAH

COLORADO
Denver ★
Colorado Springs
Green River

KANSAS
Topeka ★
Arkansas River
Wichita
Missou...

CALIFORNIA
Bakersfield
Las Vegas
Lake Mead
Colorado River

Lake Powell

Los Angeles
Long Beach
Channel Islands
Anaheim
Santa Ana
San Diego
Salton Sea

ARIZONA
Phoenix ★
Gila River
Tucson

NEW MEXICO
Santa Fe ★
Albuquerque
El Paso
Canadian River
Keystone Lake
Tu...
OKLAHOMA
Oklahoma City ★
Eufaula Lake
Amarillo

Lubbock
Lake Texor...
Abilene
Fort Worth
Dallas
TEXAS
Odessa
Pecos River
Waco
Colorado River
Brazos River
Austin
San Antonio
Rio Grande
Amistad Reservoir
Corpus Christi
Laredo
Padre Island
Houst...

Gulf of California

MEXICO

To understand the relative locations of Alaska and Hawaii as well as the vast distances separating them from the rest of the United States, see the world map.

Kauai
Niihau
Oahu
Honolulu ★
Molokai
Lanai
Kahoolawe
Maui
HAWAII
PACIFIC OCEAN
Hawaii
N

SCALE
0    75    150 Miles
0    75    150 Kilometers

ARCTIC OCEAN
Arctic Circle
RUSSIA
Bering Strait
Nome
St. Lawrence Island
St. Matthew Island
Nunivak Island
Yukon River
Fairbanks
CANADA
ALASKA
Anchorage
Kodiak Island
GULF OF ALASKA
Juneau ★
Alexander Archipelago

N
SCALE
0    250    500 Miles
0    250    500 Kilometers
Projection: Albers Equal Area

BERING SEA
Attu Island
Aleutian Islands
PACIFIC OCEAN

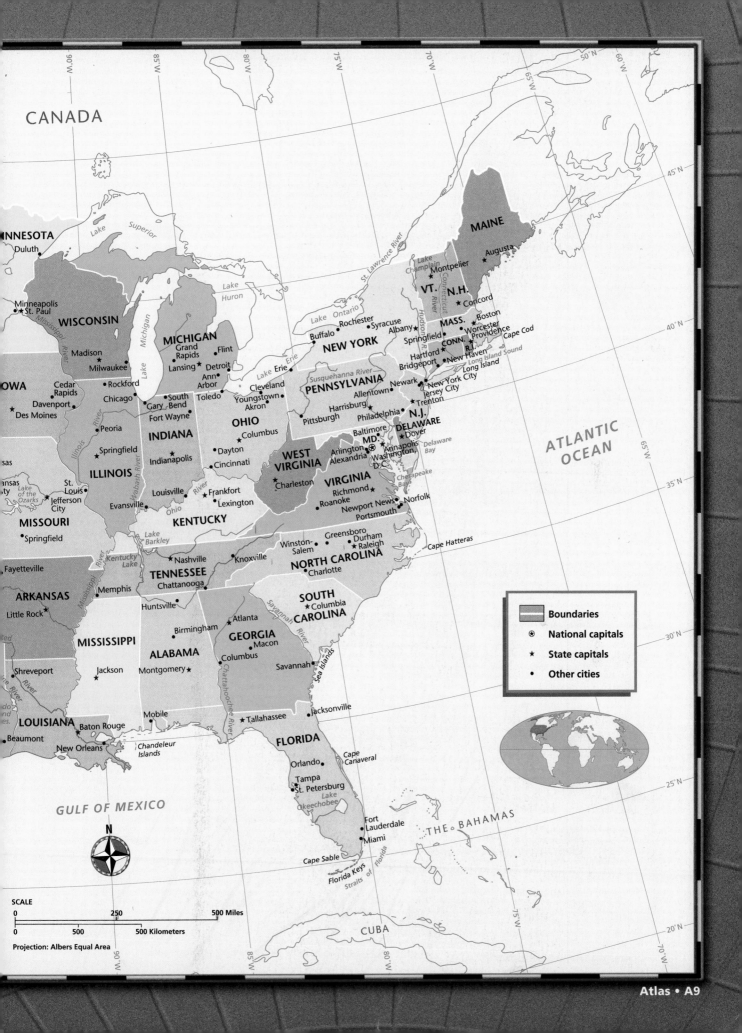

CANADA

MINNESOTA
Duluth

Minneapolis
St. Paul

WISCONSIN
Madison ★
Milwaukee

IOWA
Cedar Rapids
Davenport
Des Moines

MICHIGAN
Grand Rapids
Lansing ★
Flint
Detroit
Ann Arbor

Lake Superior
Lake Michigan
Lake Huron
Lake Erie
Lake Ontario

Rockford
Chicago
Gary
South Bend
Fort Wayne
Toledo
Cleveland
Youngstown
Akron

Peoria

ILLINOIS
Springfield ★

INDIANA
Indianapolis ★

OHIO
Columbus ★
Dayton
Cincinnati

St. Louis
Jefferson City ★

KANSAS

Lake of the Ozarks

MISSOURI
Springfield

Fayetteville

ARKANSAS
Little Rock ★

Evansville

Louisville
Frankfort ★
Lexington

KENTUCKY

Ohio River

Kentucky Lake

Lake Barkley

Nashville ★

TENNESSEE
Chattanooga

Knoxville

Memphis

Huntsville

MISSISSIPPI
Jackson ★

ALABAMA
Birmingham
Montgomery ★

Shreveport

LOUISIANA
Baton Rouge ★
Beaumont
New Orleans

Chandeleur Islands

GULF OF MEXICO

St. Lawrence River

MAINE
Augusta ★

Lake Champlain

Montpelier ★
VT.
N.H.
Concord ★

MASS.
Boston ★
Worcester
Providence
R.I.
Springfield
Hartford ★
CONN.
New Haven
Bridgeport

Buffalo
Rochester
Syracuse
Albany ★

NEW YORK

Hudson R.
Connecticut River

Cape Cod

Long Island Sound
Long Island

Newark
New York City
Jersey City

Susquehanna River

PENNSYLVANIA
Allentown
Harrisburg ★
Pittsburgh
Trenton ★
Philadelphia
N.J.

Baltimore
DELAWARE
Dover ★
MD.
Annapolis ★
Arlington
Alexandria
Washington, D.C. ⊛

Delaware Bay

WEST VIRGINIA
Charleston ★

VIRGINIA
Richmond ★
Roanoke
Newport News
Portsmouth
Norfolk

Chesapeake Bay

Greensboro
Durham
Winston-Salem
Raleigh ★

Cape Hatteras

NORTH CAROLINA
Charlotte

SOUTH CAROLINA
Columbia ★

Atlanta ★

GEORGIA
Macon
Columbus

Savannah

Savannah River

Chattahoochee River

Sea Islands

Mobile

Tallahassee ★
Jacksonville

FLORIDA

ATLANTIC OCEAN

Orlando
Cape Canaveral

Tampa
St. Petersburg

Lake Okeechobee

THE BAHAMAS

Fort Lauderdale
Miami

Cape Sable

Florida Keys

Straits of Florida

CUBA

Legend:
- Boundaries
- ⊛ National capitals
- ★ State capitals
- • Other cities

SCALE
0    250    500 Miles
0    500    500 Kilometers

Projection: Albers Equal Area

N

90°W  85°W  80°W  75°W  70°W  65°W  60°W  50°N  45°N  40°N  35°N  30°N  25°N  20°N

# NORTH AMERICA: PHYSICAL

# NORTH AMERICA: POLITICAL

EUROPE

ASIA

ARCTIC OCEAN

North Pole

ICELAND

Arctic Circle

Queen Elizabeth Islands

Ellesmere Island

Greenland (DENMARK)

Denmark Strait

BEAUFORT SEA

Banks Island

Point Barrow

ALASKA (U.S.)

Yukon River

Victoria Island

Baffin Bay

Cape Farewell

Anchorage

GULF OF ALASKA

Kodiak Island

Great Bear Lake

Mackenzie River

Baffin Island

Davis Strait

St. Lawrence Island

Nunivak Island

BERING SEA

Bering Strait

Alexander Archipelago

Juneau

Queen Charlotte Islands

Great Slave Lake

Peace River

Southampton Island

Coats Island

Mansel Island

Hudson Strait

LABRADOR SEA

Hudson Bay

PACIFIC OCEAN

Vancouver Island

Edmonton

CANADA

Lake Winnipeg

Calgary

Vancouver

Seattle

Portland

Columbia River

Winnipeg

Cape Mendocino

Snake River

Missouri River

Minneapolis

Lake Superior

Lake Michigan

Lake Huron

Ottawa

Toronto

Lake Ontario

Lake Erie

Anticosti Island

St. Lawrence R.

Newfoundland

St. Pierre and Miquelon (FRANCE)

Prince Edward Island

GULF OF ST. LAWRENCE

Cape Breton Island

Quebec

Montreal

Boston

Cape Cod

New York City

Philadelphia

Baltimore

Washington, D.C.

ATLANTIC OCEAN

Milwaukee

Detroit

Chicago

Cleveland

Columbus

San Francisco

San Jose

Salt Lake City

Great Salt Lake

Denver

Platte River

Kansas City

Indianapolis

St. Louis

Ohio R.

Norfolk

Cape Hatteras

Los Angeles

San Diego

Tijuana

Phoenix

Colorado River

UNITED STATES

Memphis

Red River

Mississippi River

Atlanta

Birmingham

Bermuda (U.K.)

Dallas

Jacksonville

Austin

San Antonio

Houston

New Orleans

Cape Canaveral

Tropic of Cancer

Rio Grande

Monterrey

GULF OF CALIFORNIA

GULF OF MEXICO

Florida Keys

Miami

Nassau

THE BAHAMAS

Turks and Caicos Islands (U.K.)

Straits of Florida

Havana

CUBA

Puerto Rico (U.S.)

San Juan

ST. KITTS & NEVIS

ANTIGUA & BARBUDA

Guadeloupe (FRANCE)

DOMINICAN REPUBLIC

MEXICO

Guadalajara

Mexico City

Puebla

Balsas R.

Mérida

Cayman Is. (U.K.)

HAITI

Kingston

JAMAICA

Santo Domingo

Port-au-Prince

Virgin Is. (U.S., U.K.)

Martinique (FRANCE)

ST. LUCIA

ST. VINCENT AND THE GRENADINES

Netherlands Antilles (NETHERLANDS)

DOMINICA

BARBADOS

GRENADA

CARIBBEAN SEA

Belmopan

BELIZE

GUATEMALA

Guatemala City

HONDURAS

Tegucigalpa

NICARAGUA

Managua

San Salvador

EL SALVADOR

Aruba (NETHERLANDS)

Panama Canal

TRINIDAD AND TOBAGO

San José

Panama City

COSTA RICA

PANAMA

SOUTH AMERICA

Equator 0°

## Legend

- ▭ Boundaries
- ⊛ National capitals
- • Other cities

N

SCALE

0    500    1000 Miles

0    500    1000 Kilometers

Projection: Azimuthal Equal Area

CENTRAL AMERICA

CARIBBEAN SEA

Panama Canal

GULF OF PANAMA

Margarita Island

Tobago
Trinidad

Orinoco River Delta

N

ATLANTIC OCEAN

Lake Maracaibo

LLANOS

Cauca River

Meta River

Orinoco River

Angel Falls

GUIANA

Devil's Island
Cape Orange

▲ Mount Tolima
18,425 ft. (5,616 m)

Magdalena River

HIGHLANDS

Malpelo Island

Caquetá River

Rio Negro

Amazon River Delta

Mount Chimborazo
20,561 ft. (6,267 m)

GULF OF GUAYAQUIL

Japurá River

AMAZON

Amazon River

Equator 0°

Galápagos Islands

Putumayo River

Juruá River

Amazon

BASIN

Tapajós River

Tocantins River

Ucayali River

Purus

Madeira River

Xingu River

River

Parnaíba River

Mount Huascarán
22,205 ft. (6,768 m)

ANDES

BRAZILIAN

Mamoré River

Beni River

Ancohuma Peak
20,958 ft. (6,388 m)

MATO GROSSO
PLATEAU

Araguaia River

HIGHLANDS

10°S

PACIFIC OCEAN

Lake Titicaca

Lake Poopó

Pilcomayo River

São Francisco

Desaguadero River

CHACO

Paraguay River

BRAZILIAN
PLATEAU

20°S

Tropic of Capricorn

ATACAMA DESERT

San Ambrosio Island

San Félix Island

ANDES

Salado River

Paraná River

Uruguay River

Tropic of Capricorn

Juan Fernández Islands

Mount Aconcagua
22,834 ft. (6,960 m)

Rio de la Plata

30°S

ATLANTIC OCEAN

Salado River

PAMPAS

Colorado River

GULF OF SAN MATÍAS

Chiloé Island

PATAGONIA

CHONOS ARCHIPELAGO

GULF OF SAN JORGE

Cape Tres Puntas

Bahía Grande

Strait of Magellan

Falkland Islands

South Georgia Islands

TIERRA DEL FUEGO

CAPE HORN

SCALE

0    250    500    750    1,000 Miles

0    250    500    750    1,000 Kilometers

Projection: Azimuthal Equal Area

# SOUTH AMERICA: POLITICAL

CENTRAL AMERICA

CARIBBEAN SEA

**N**

ATLANTIC OCEAN

Barranquilla
Cartagena

Caracas

**VENEZUELA**

Lake Maracaibo

Orinoco River

Georgetown
Paramaribo

**GUYANA**

Cayenne

Medellín

Bogotá

**SURINAME**

FRENCH GUIANA (FRANCE)

Malpelo Island (COLOMBIA)

**COLOMBIA**

Cali

Rio Negro

Amazon River

Equator 0°

Quito

**ECUADOR**

Guayaquil

Galápagos Islands (ECUADOR)

0° Equator

Amazon River

Belém

**BRAZIL**

Marañón River

**PERU**

Ucayali River

Trujillo

Recife

São Francisco River

Callao

Lima

10°S

Salvador

PACIFIC OCEAN

Lake Titicaca

**BOLIVIA**

Brasília

Arequipa

La Paz

Lake Poopó

Sucre

Belo Horizonte

20°S

**PARAGUAY**

Campinas

São Paulo

Rio de Janeiro

Tropic of Capricorn

Tropic of Capricorn

Asunción

Curitiba

Paraguay River

San Ambrosio Island (CHILE)

San Félix Island (CHILE)

Paraná River

Uruguay River

Pôrto Alegre

**CHILE**

Córdoba

Juan Fernández Islands (CHILE)

ATLANTIC OCEAN

30°S

Valparaíso
Santiago

Rosario

**URUGUAY**

Buenos Aires

Montevideo

Río de la Plata

**ARGENTINA**

| | Boundaries |
|---|---|
| ⊛ | National capitals |
| • | Other cities |

40°S

SCALE

0    250    500    750    1000 Miles

0  250  500  250  1000 Kilometers

Projection: Azimuthal Equal Area

Strait of Magellan

Falkland Islands (U.K.)

Tierra del Fuego

South Georgia Island (U.K.)

50°S

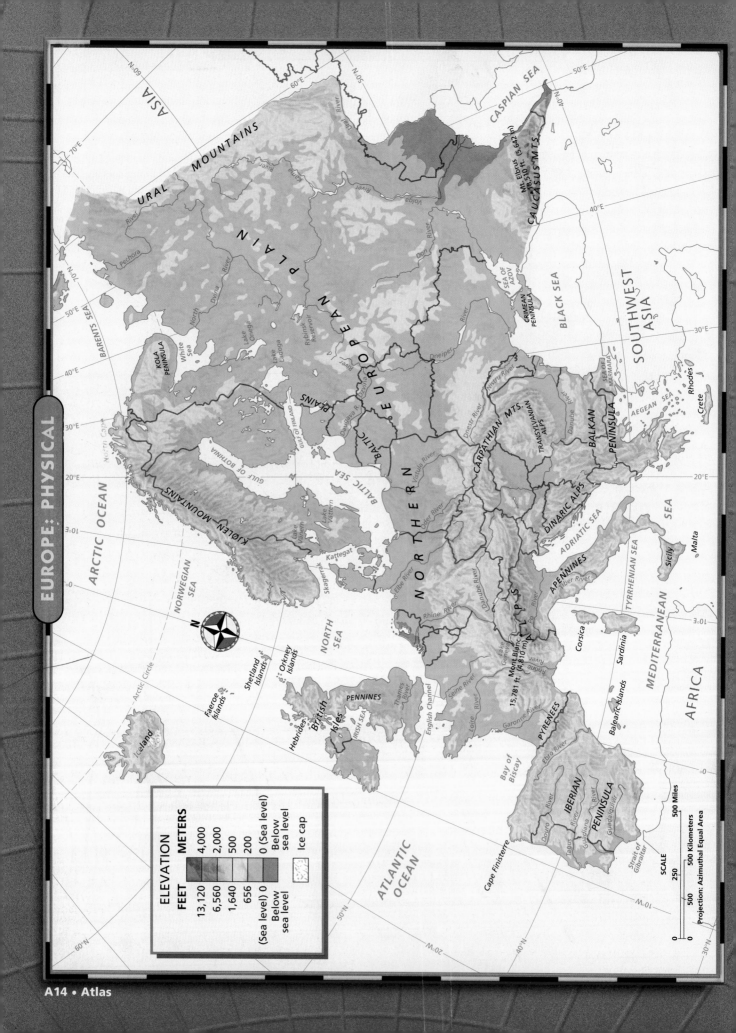

ASIA

URAL MOUNTAINS

URAL

Pechora River

BARENTS SEA

KOLA PENINSULA

White Sea

Dvina River

North

Lake Onega

Lake Ladoga

Rybinsk Reservoir

NORTHERN EUROPEAN PLAIN

Volga River

River

Don River

CASPIAN SEA

Mt. Elbrus (5,642 m) 18,510 ft.

CAUCASUS MTS.

SEA OF AZOV

CRIMEAN PENINSULA

BLACK SEA

SOUTHWEST ASIA

NORTH CAPE

KJØLEN MOUNTAINS

NORWEGIAN SEA

GULF OF FINLAND

BALTIC PLAINS

Daugava River

Dnieper River

Dnestr River

Nistru River

CARPATHIAN MTS.

TRANSYLVANIAN ALPS

Danube River

SEA OF MARMARA

AEGEAN SEA

Rhodes

Crete

ARCTIC OCEAN

Lake Vänern

Lake Vättern

GULF OF BOTHNIA

BALTIC SEA

Oder River

Vistula River

NORTHERN

BALKAN PENINSULA

DINARIC ALPS

ADRIATIC SEA

SEA

Kattegat

Skagerrak

Elbe River

Rhine River

APENNINES

Tiber River

TYRRHENIAN SEA

Sardinia

Sicily

Malta

Iceland

Arctic Circle

Faeroe Islands

Shetland Islands

Orkney Islands

NORTH SEA

British Isles

Hebrides

IRISH SEA

PENNINES

Thames River

English Channel

Seine River

ALPS

Lake Geneva

Mont Blanc (4,810 m) 15,781 ft.

Rhône River

Po River

Corsica

MEDITERRANEAN

AFRICA

Loire River

Garonne River

Bay of Biscay

PYRENEES

Ebro River

IBERIAN PENINSULA

Guadiana River

Guadalquivir River

Cape Finisterre

Douro River

Tagus River

Strait of Gibraltar

Balearic Islands

ATLANTIC OCEAN

N

SCALE
0      250    500 Miles
0      500    500 Kilometers
Projection: Azimuthal Equal Area

60°N

70°E

60°E

50°E

40°N

50°N

40°E

30°E

20°E

10°E

0°

10°W

20°W

30°N

40°N

50°N

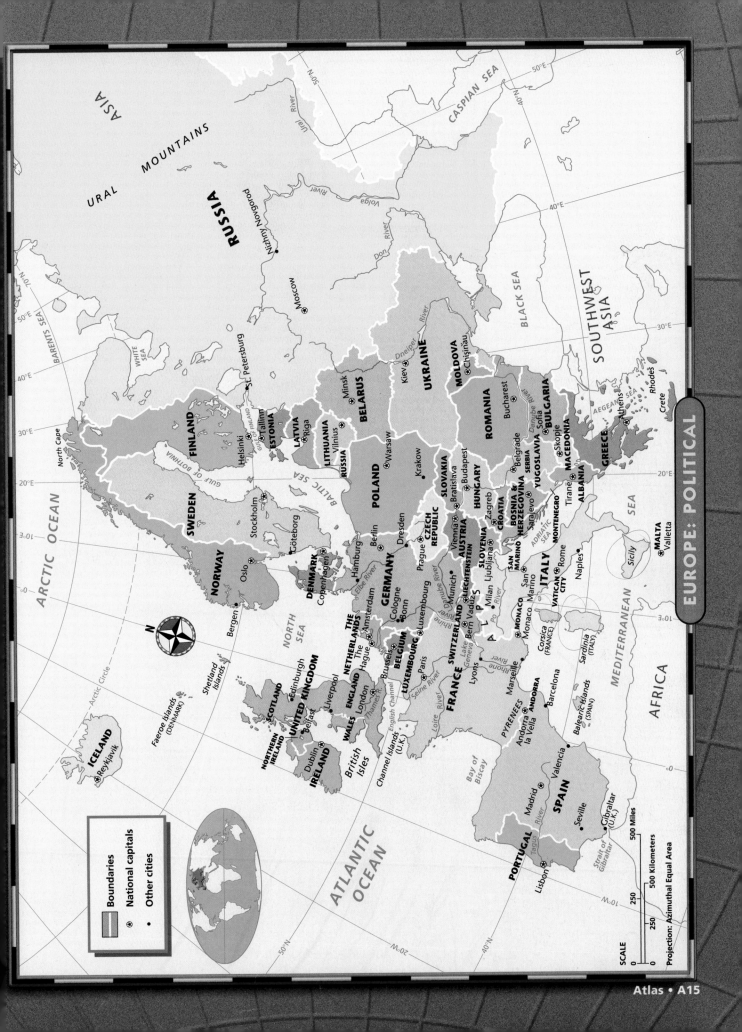

EUROPE: POLITICAL

**Boundaries**
⊛ National capitals
• Other cities

SCALE
0       250       500 Miles
0       250       500 Kilometers
Projection: Azimuthal Equal Area

ELEVATION

| FEET | METERS |
|------|--------|
| 13,120 | 4,000 |
| 6,560 | 2,000 |
| 1,640 | 500 |
| 656 | 200 |
| (Sea level) 0 | 0 (Sea level) |
| Below sea level | Below sea level |

Ice cap

PACIFIC OCEAN

NORTH AMERICA

Aleutian Islands

KAMCHATKA PENINSULA

CENTRAL RANGE

KOLYMA MTS.

CHERSKIY RANGE

VERKHOYANSKIY RANGE

STANOVOY MOUNTAINS

Aldan River

Lena River

Shilka

Amur River

GREATER KHINGAN RANGE

SEA OF OKHOTSK

Sakhalin Island

Kuril Islands

Hokkaido

Honshu

SEA OF JAPAN

Korea Strait

Shikoku

Kyushu

Okinawa

Ryukyu Islands

Taiwan

EAST CHINA SEA

YELLOW SEA

BOHEA HILLS

NORTH CHINA PLAIN

CHINA

GREAT WALL

QIN LING

Huang River

Chang River

GULF OF TONKIN

Hainan

SOUTH CHINA SEA

Luzon

Luzon Strait

Philippines

Mindanao

MOLUCCAS

CELEBES SEA

Celebes

BANDA SEA

New Guinea

MAOKE MOUNTAIN

ARAFURA SEA

AUSTRALIA

Tropic of Cancer

Wrangel Island

New Siberian Islands

North Land

TAYMYR PENINSULA

CENTRAL SIBERIAN PLATEAU

Lower Tunguska River

Angara River

SAYAN MOUNTAINS

Lake Baikal

Yablonovy Range

MONGOLIAN PLATEAU

GOBI

ALTAI SHAN

TIAN SHAN

KUNLUN MOUNTAINS

PLATEAU OF TIBET

Mount Everest 29,035 ft (8,850 m)

HIMALAYAS

Ganges River

Brahmaputra River

Mekong River

INDOCHINA PENINSULA

Chao Phraya River

GULF OF THAILAND

MALAY PENINSULA

Strait of Malacca

Sumatra

Bangka

Borneo

JAVA SEA

Java

BERING SEA

BARENTS SEA

Franz Josef Land

Novaya Zemlya

KARA SEA

LAPTEV SEA

Yenisey River

Ob River

Irtysh River

WEST SIBERIAN PLAIN

S I B E R I A

KAZAKH UPLANDS

Lake Balkhash

TARIM BASIN

TAKLIMAKAN DESERT

HINDU KUSH

Indus River

INDO-GANGETIC PLAIN

THAR DESERT

DECCAN PLATEAU

Godavari River

WESTERN GHATS

EASTERN GHATS

Sri Lanka

Bay of Bengal

Irrawaddy River

Andaman Islands

ANDAMAN SEA

Nicobar Islands

Mentawai Islands

UST'URT PLATEAU

KYZYL KUM

TURAN LOWLAND

KARA-KUM

Syr Darya

Amu Darya

GREAT SALT DESERT

CASPIAN SEA

CAUCASUS MTS.

Mount Ararat 16,945 ft (5,165 m)

ANATOLIAN PLATEAU

Cyprus

ZAGROS MTS.

SYRIAN DESERT

AN-NAFUD

SINAI PENINSULA

Tigris River

Euphrates River

PERSIAN GULF

Strait of Hormuz

GULF OF OMAN

RUB' AL-KHALI

Socotra Island

GULF OF ADEN

ARABIAN SEA

Lakshadweep Islands

Maldives

INDIAN OCEAN

URAL MOUNTAINS

Ural River

EUROPE

BLACK SEA

SEA OF AZOV

Bosporus

MEDITERRANEAN SEA

RED SEA

AFRICA

Equator

N

SCALE

| 0 | 500 | 1,000 Miles |
| 0 | 500 | 1,000 Kilometers |

Projection: Modified Oblique Conic

170°W
180°
170°E
160°E
150°E
140°E
130°E
120°E
110°E
100°E
90°E
80°E
70°E
60°E
50°E
40°E
30°E

80°N
70°N
60°N
50°N
40°N
30°N
20°N
10°N

Tropic of Cancer
Equator

10°S
Arctic Circle

140°E
130°E
120°E
110°E
100°E
90°E
80°E
70°E
60°E
50°E
40°E

ASIA: POLITICAL

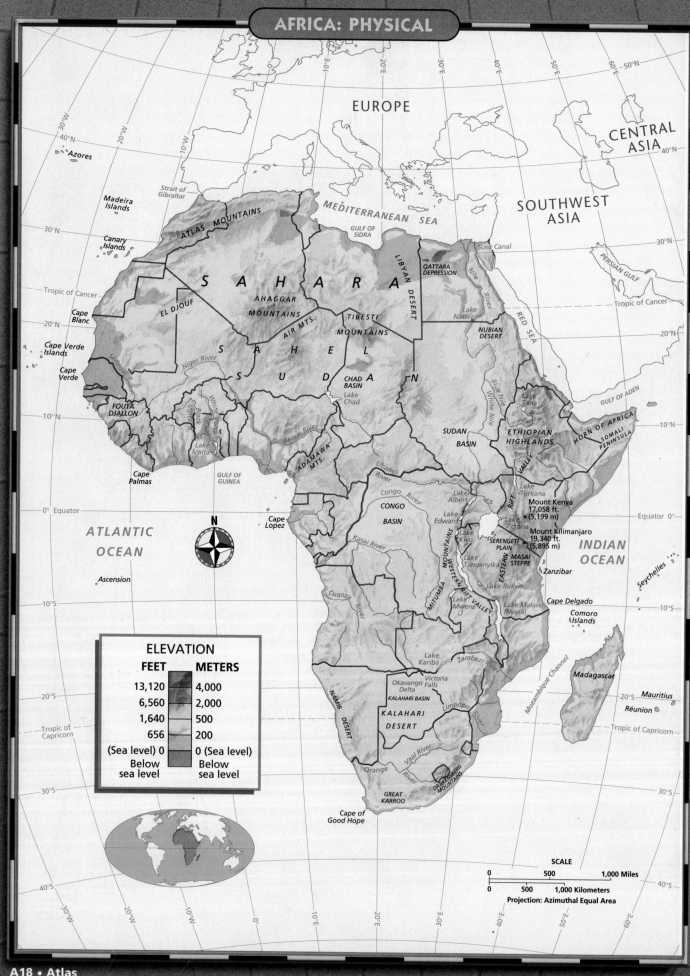

# AFRICA: PHYSICAL

EUROPE

CENTRAL ASIA

SOUTHWEST ASIA

MEDITERRANEAN SEA

ATLAS MOUNTAINS

Strait of Gibraltar

Azores

Madeira Islands

Canary Islands

Cape Blanc

Cape Verde Islands

Cape Verde

SAHARA

EL DJOUF

AHAGGAR MOUNTAINS

AIR MTS.

TIBESTI MOUNTAINS

LIBYAN DESERT

GULF OF SIDRA

QATTARA DEPRESSION

Suez Canal

Nile River

Lake Nasser

NUBIAN DESERT

RED SEA

GULF OF ADEN

SAHEL

SUDAN

CHAD BASIN

Lake Chad

Senegal R.

Niger River

FOUTA DJALLON

Black V.

White Volta

Lake Volta

Benue River

ADAMAWA MTS.

GULF OF GUINEA

Cape Palmas

Cape Lopez

Ubangi River

Congo River

CONGO BASIN

Kasai River

Blue Nile

White Nile

Lake Tana

ETHIOPIAN HIGHLANDS

HORN OF AFRICA

SOMALI PENINSULA

SUDAN BASIN

RIFT VALLEY

Lake Turkana

Mount Kenya 17,058 ft. (5,199 m)

Lake Albert

Lake Edward

Lake Kivu

Lake Victoria

MITUMBA MOUNTAINS

WESTERN RIFT VALLEY

EASTERN RIFT VALLEY

Lake Tanganyika

SERENGETI PLAIN

MASAI STEPPE

Mount Kilimanjaro 19,340 ft. (5,895 m)

Zanzibar

Lake Rukwa

Cape Delgado

Seychelles

Cuanza River

Lake Mweru

Lake Malawi (Nyasa)

INDIAN OCEAN

ATLANTIC OCEAN

Ascension

Comoro Islands

Lake Kariba

Zambezi River

Victoria Falls

Okavango Delta

KALAHARI BASIN

Mozambique Channel

Madagascar

Mauritius

Réunion

NAMIB DESERT

KALAHARI DESERT

Limpopo River

Vaal River

Orange River

GREAT KARROO

DRAKENSBERG MOUNTAINS

Cape of Good Hope

Cape Palmas

N

Equator

Tropic of Cancer

Tropic of Capricorn

## ELEVATION

| FEET | | METERS |
|------|---|--------|
| 13,120 | | 4,000 |
| 6,560 | | 2,000 |
| 1,640 | | 500 |
| 656 | | 200 |
| (Sea level) 0 | | 0 (Sea level) |
| Below sea level | | Below sea level |

## SCALE

0    500    1,000 Miles

0    500    1,000 Kilometers

Projection: Azimuthal Equal Area

# AFRICA: POLITICAL

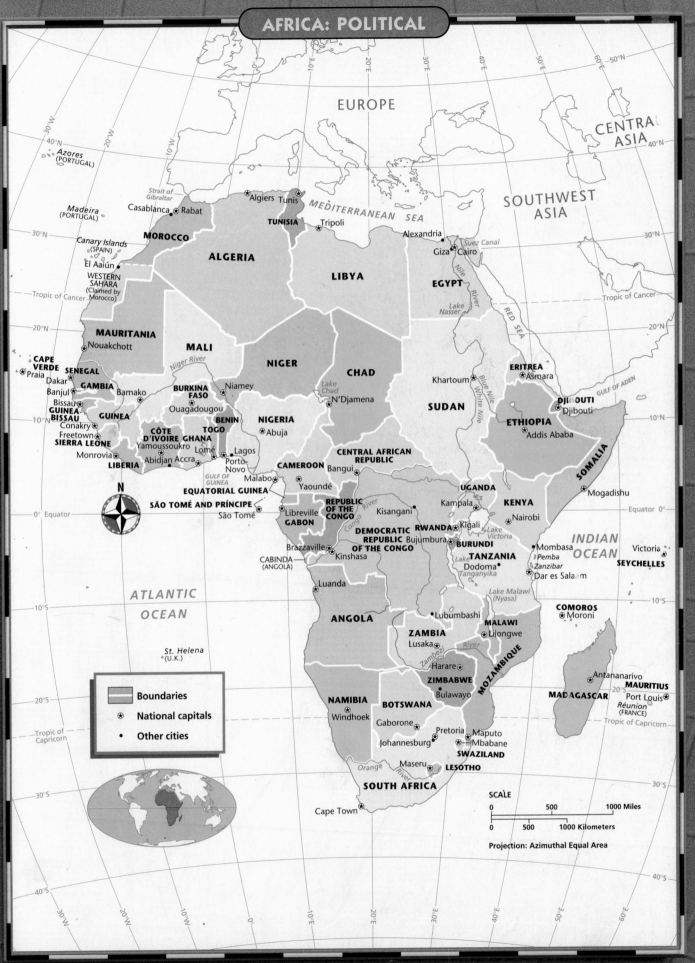

EUROPE

CENTRAL ASIA

SOUTHWEST ASIA

MEDITERRANEAN SEA

Strait of Gibraltar
Algiers  Tunis
Casablanca  Rabat
TUNISIA  Tripoli
MOROCCO
Alexandria
Giza  Cairo
Suez Canal

Madeira (PORTUGAL)

Azores (PORTUGAL)

Canary Islands (SPAIN)
El Aaiún
WESTERN SAHARA (Claimed by Morocco)

ALGERIA

LIBYA

EGYPT

Lake Nasser

Nile River

RED SEA

Tropic of Cancer

MAURITANIA
Nouakchott

MALI

NIGER

CHAD

Khartoum

Blue Nile
White Nile

ERITREA
Asmara

GULF OF ADEN

DJIBOUTI
Djibouti

CAPE VERDE
Praia

SENEGAL
Dakar

GAMBIA
Banjul

Bissau
GUINEA-BISSAU

GUINEA
Conakry

SIERRA LEONE
Freetown

Monrovia
LIBERIA

Bamako

Niger River

BURKINA FASO
Ouagadougou

Niamey

NIGERIA
Abuja

N'Djamena

Lake Chad

SUDAN

ETHIOPIA
Addis Ababa

SOMALIA

Mogadishu

CÔTE D'IVOIRE  GHANA
Yamoussoukro
Abidjan  Accra

BENIN
TOGO
Lomé
Porto-Novo

Lagos

GULF OF GUINEA

Malabo

CAMEROON
Bangui

CENTRAL AFRICAN REPUBLIC

EQUATORIAL GUINEA

SÃO TOMÉ AND PRÍNCIPE
São Tomé

Yaoundé

UGANDA
Kampala

KENYA
Nairobi

REPUBLIC OF THE CONGO
GABON
Libreville

Congo River

Kisangani

DEMOCRATIC REPUBLIC OF THE CONGO

RWANDA
Kigali

Bujumbura
BURUNDI

Lake Victoria

Brazzaville
Kinshasa

CABINDA (ANGOLA)

TANZANIA
Dodoma
Dar es Salaam

Lake Tanganyika

Zanzibar
Pemba
Mombasa

INDIAN OCEAN

Victoria
SEYCHELLES

Luanda

Lubumbashi

Lake Malawi (Nyasa)

COMOROS
Moroni

ATLANTIC OCEAN

St. Helena (U.K.)

ANGOLA

ZAMBIA
Lusaka

MALAWI
Lilongwe

MOZAMBIQUE

Zambezi River

Harare

ZIMBABWE
Bulawayo

Antananarivo
MADAGASCAR

MAURITIUS
Port Louis
Réunion (FRANCE)

NAMIBIA
Windhoek

BOTSWANA
Gaborone

Pretoria
Johannesburg

Maputo
Mbabane
SWAZILAND

Orange River
Maseru  LESOTHO

SOUTH AFRICA

Cape Town

N

Boundaries

National capitals

Other cities

Equator

Tropic of Capricorn

SCALE
0    500    1000 Miles
0    500    1000 Kilometers

Projection: Azimuthal Equal Area

INDIAN OCEAN

TIMOR SEA

CORAL SEA

GREAT BARRIER REEF

GREAT DIVIDING RANGE

PACIFIC OCEAN

TASMAN SEA

NEW ZEALAND

North Cape

North Island

Auckland
Hamilton

Wellington

Cook Strait

Christchurch

SOUTHERN ALPS
Mount Cook
12,349 ft
(3,764 m)

Dunedin

South Island

Stewart Island

Tropic of Capricorn

Cape York

CAPE YORK PENINSULA

GULF OF CARPENTARIA

Flinders River

Cloncury

QUEENSLAND

Rockhampton
Bundaberg
Brisbane
Gold Coast

GREAT ARTESIAN BASIN

Sydney

NEW SOUTH WALES

Canberra
AUSTRALIAN CAPITAL TERRITORY
Mount Kosciusko
7310 ft. (2,230 m)

Lachlan River

Darling River

Wagga Wagga

Murray River

VICTORIA

Melbourne
Geelong

Ballarat

Bass Strait

Launceston

Hobart

TASMANIA

ARNHEM LAND

Darwin

NORTHERN TERRITORY

MACDONNELL RANGES
Alice Springs

AUSTRALIA

SOUTH AUSTRALIA

Lake Eyre
(52 ft [16 m]
below sea level)

Port Pirie

Adelaide

Kangaroo Island

Great Australian Bight

KIMBERLEY RANGE

GREAT SANDY DESERT

GIBSON DESERT

GREAT VICTORIA DESERT

WESTERN AUSTRALIA

Laverton

HAMERSLEY RANGE

Broome

North West Cape

Carnarvon

Geraldton

Perth
Fremantle

SCALE: At Equator

0       250       500 Miles

0    250    500 Kilometers

Projection: Lambert Conformal Conic

ELEVATION

| FEET | METERS |
|---|---|
| 13,120 | 4,000 |
| 6,560 | 2,000 |
| 1,640 | 500 |
| 656 | 200 |
| (Sea level) 0 | 0 (Sea level) |
| Below sea level | Below sea level |

⊛  National capital
★  State/territorial capitals
•  Other cities

170°E
160°E
150°E
140°E
130°E
120°E
110°E
180°
10
10°S
20°S
30°S
40°S
50°S

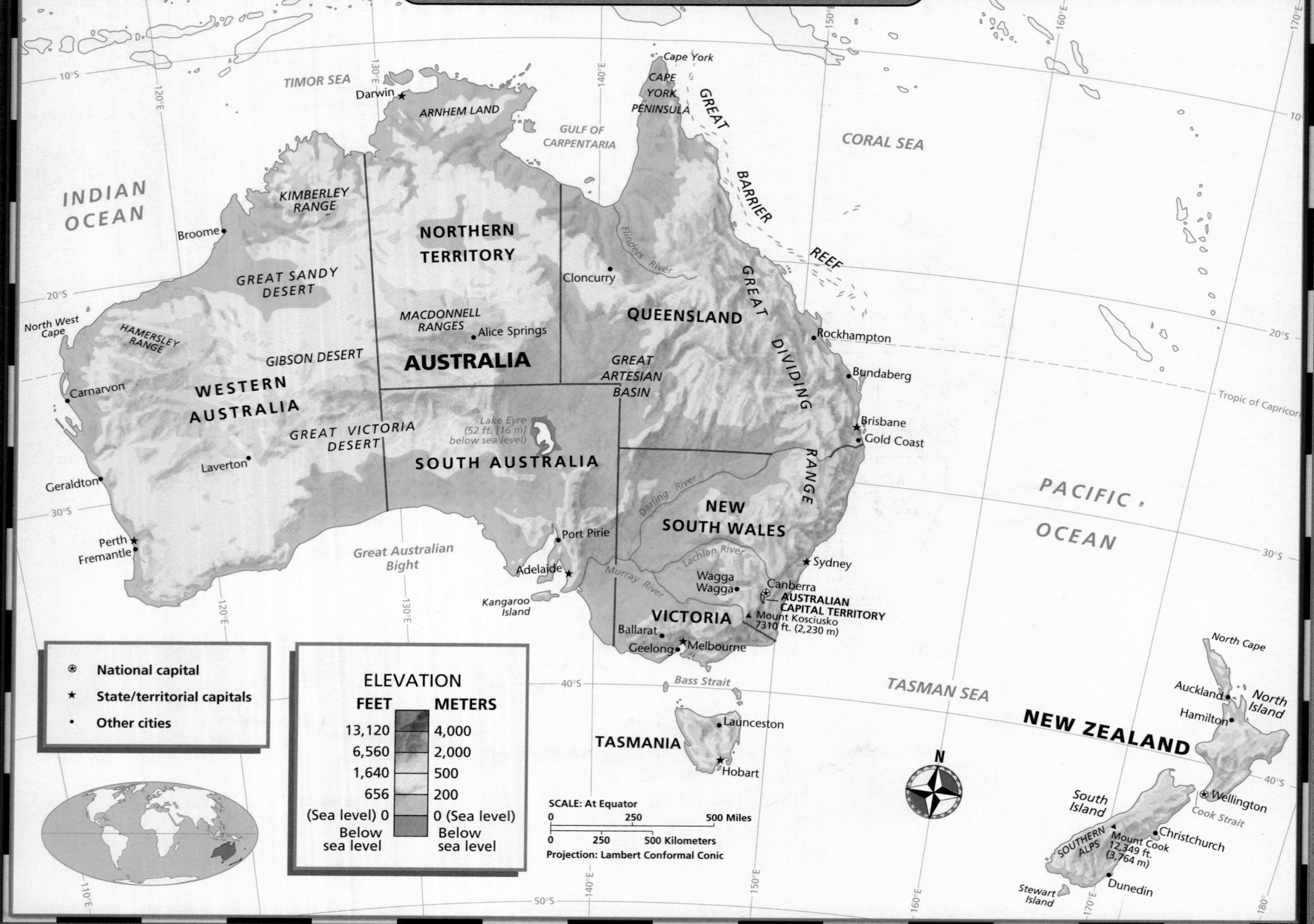

NORTH AMERICA

NORTH PACIFIC OCEAN

ASIA

JAPAN

Bonin Islands (JAPAN)

Volcano Islands (JAPAN)

Northern Marianas (U.S.)

Guam (U.S.) • Agana

PHILIPPINE SEA

SOUTH CHINA SEA

PALAU ⊛ Koror

FEDERATED STATES OF MICRONESIA

Truk Is.

MICRONESIA

Palikir ⊛

Eniwetok I.

MARSHALL ISLANDS

Wake Island (U.S.)

Kwajalein Island

⊛ Majuro

Gilbert Islands ⊛ Tarawa

Midway Island (U.S.)

Johnston Island (U.S.)

Hawaiian Islands

Hawaii (U.S.)

Kingman Reef (U.S.)

Palmyra Island (U.S.)

Washington Island

Fanning Island

Howland I. (U.S.)

Baker I. (U.S.)

Jarvis I. (U.S.)

McKean I.

Gardner

Phoenix Islands

KIRIBATI

Starbuck Island

Manihiki Island

POLYNESIA

Marquesas Islands (FRANCE)

Tuamotu Archipelago (FRANCE)

French Polynesia

Society Islands (FRANCE)

Tahiti (FRANCE)

Papeete

Cook Islands (NEW ZEALAND)

Rarotonga Island

Tubuai Islands (FRANCE)

Rapa Island (FRANCE)

Pitcairn (U.K.)

Pitcairn Island

Ducie Island

Easter Island (CHILE)

Tropic of Cancer

Equator 0°

Tropic of Cancer

International Date Line

TUVALU

Funafuti

NAURU

Yaren ⊛

SOLOMON ISLANDS

Honiara ⊛

Guadalcanal I.

Tokelau (N.Z.)

SAMOA

American Samoa

Apia Pago Pago

Wallis & Futuna (FRANCE)

FIJI

Suva ⊛

TONGA

Nuku'alofa ⊛

Niue (N.Z.)

MELANESIA

VANUATU

Espiritu Santo I.

Malekula I.

Port-Vila

New Caledonia (FRANCE)

Noumea ⊛

Loyalty Islands (FRANCE)

Norfolk Island (AUSTRALIA)

Kermadec Islands (NEW ZEALAND)

SOUTH PACIFIC OCEAN

NEW ZEALAND

Chatham Islands (N.Z.)

Bounty Islands (N.Z.)

Auckland Islands (NEW ZEALAND)

TASMAN SEA

AUSTRALIA

PAPUA NEW GUINEA

Port Moresby ⊛

New Guinea

Bismarck Archipelago

CORAL SEA

TIMOR SEA

ARAFURA SEA

Christmas Island (AUSTRALIA)

INDIAN OCEAN

N

SCALE

1000 Miles

1000 Kilometers

500

500

0

0

Projection: Mercator

Boundaries

⊛ National capitals

• Other cities

PACIFIC ISLANDS

Atlas • A21

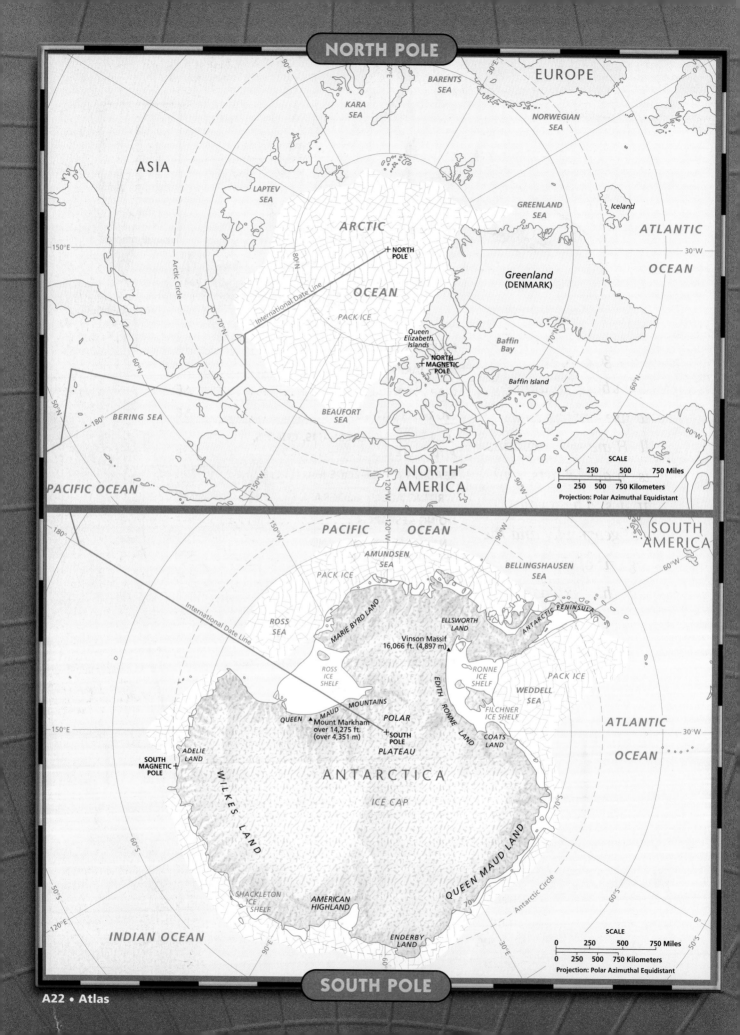

EUROPE

BARENTS
SEA

KARA
SEA

ASIA

LAPTEV
SEA

GREENLAND
SEA

Iceland

NORWEGIAN
SEA

ATLANTIC

150°E

Arctic Circle

ARCTIC

90°E

80°N

NORTH
POLE

30°W

OCEAN

OCEAN

70°N

Greenland
(DENMARK)

International Date Line

60°N

70°N

PACK ICE

Queen
Elizabeth
Islands

Baffin
Bay

NORTH
MAGNETIC
POLE

50°N

180°

BERING SEA

60°N

150°W

BEAUFORT
SEA

Baffin Island

60°N

PACIFIC OCEAN

120°W

90°W

NORTH
AMERICA

SCALE

0    250    500    750 Miles

0  250  500  750 Kilometers

Projection: Polar Azimuthal Equidistant

180°

PACIFIC    OCEAN

SOUTH
AMERICA

150°W

120°W

90°W

AMUNDSEN
SEA

BELLINGSHAUSEN
SEA

60°W

PACK ICE

ROSS
SEA

MARIE BYRD LAND

ELLSWORTH
LAND

ANTARCTIC PENINSULA

International Date Line

Vinson Massif
16,066 ft. (4,897 m)

ROSS
ICE
SHELF

RONNE
ICE
SHELF

PACK ICE

EDITH RONNE LAND

WEDDELL
SEA

MAUD MOUNTAINS

POLAR

FILCHNER
ICE SHELF

ATLANTIC

150°E

QUEEN

Mount Markham
over 14,275 ft.
(over 4,351 m)

SOUTH
POLE

COATS
LAND

30°W

SOUTH
MAGNETIC
POLE

ADELIE
LAND

PLATEAU

OCEAN

ANTARCTICA

WILKES LAND

ICE CAP

70°S

60°S

SHACKLETON
ICE SHELF

AMERICAN
HIGHLAND

QUEEN MAUD LAND

50°S

120°E

INDIAN OCEAN

90°E

ENDERBY
LAND

70°S

60°S

Antarctic Circle

30°E

60°S

SCALE

0    250    500    750 Miles

0  250  500  750 Kilometers

Projection: Polar Azimuthal Equidistant

# SKILLS HANDBOOK

*Studying geography requires the ability to understand and use various tools. This Skills Handbook explains how to use maps, charts, and other graphics to help you learn about geography and the various regions of the world. Throughout this textbook, you will have the opportunity to improve these skills and build upon them.*

## CONTENTS

## GEOGRAPHIC Dictionary

- globe
- grid
- latitude
- equator
- parallels
- degrees
- minutes

- longitude
- prime meridian
- meridians
- hemispheres
- continents
- islands
- ocean

- map
- map projections
- compass rose
- scale
- legend

# MAPPING
## THE EARTH

### The Globe

A **globe** is a scale model of Earth. It is useful for looking at the entire Earth or at large areas of Earth's surface.

The pattern of lines that circle the globe in east-west and north-south directions is called a **grid**. The intersection of these imaginary lines helps us find places on Earth.

The east-west lines in the grid are lines of **latitude**. These imaginary lines measure distance north and south of the **equator**. The equator is an imaginary line that circles the globe halfway between the North and South Poles. Lines of latitude are called **parallels** because they are always parallel to the equator. Parallels measure distance from the equator in **degrees**. The symbol for degrees is °. Degrees are further divided into **minutes**. The symbol for minutes is ′. There are 60 minutes in a degree. Parallels north of the equator are labeled with an *N*. Those south of the equator are labeled with an *S*.

The north-south lines are lines of **longitude**. These imaginary lines pass through the Poles. They measure distance east and west of the **prime meridian**. The prime meridian is an imaginary line that runs through Greenwich, England. It represents 0° longitude. Lines of longitude are called **meridians**.

Lines of latitude range from 0°, for locations on the equator, to 90°N or 90°S, for locations at the Poles. See **Figure 1**. Lines of longitude range from 0° on the prime meridian to 180° on a meridian in the mid-Pacific Ocean. Meridians west of the prime meridian to 180° are labeled with a *W*. Those east of the prime meridian to 180° are labeled with an *E*. See **Figure 2**.

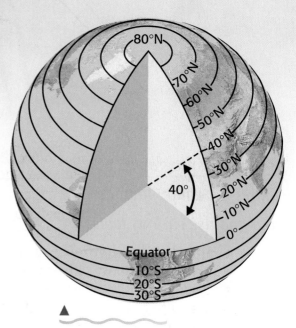

**Figure 1:** The east-west lines in the grid are lines of latitude.

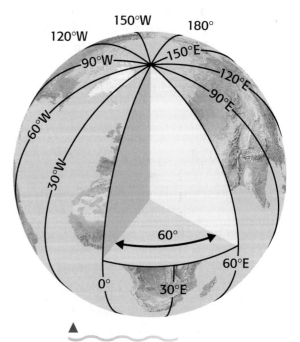

**Figure 2:** The north-south lines are lines of longitude.

## NORTHERN HEMISPHERE

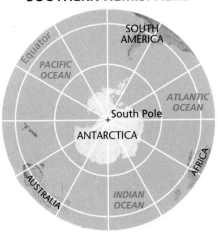

Figure 3: The hemispheres

## SOUTHERN HEMISPHERE

## EASTERN HEMISPHERE

## WESTERN HEMISPHERE

The equator divides the globe into two halves, called **hemispheres**. See **Figure 3**. The half north of the equator is the Northern Hemisphere. The southern half is the Southern Hemisphere. The prime meridian and the 180° meridian divide the world into the Eastern Hemisphere and the Western Hemisphere. The prime meridian separates parts of Europe and Africa into two different hemispheres. To prevent this, some mapmakers divide the Eastern and Western hemispheres at 20° W. This places all of Europe and Africa in the Eastern Hemisphere.

Our planet's land surface is organized into seven large landmasses, called **continents**. They are identified in **Figure 3**. Landmasses smaller than continents and completely surrounded by water are called **islands**. Geographers also organize Earth's water surface into parts. The largest is the world **ocean**. Geographers divide the world ocean into the Pacific Ocean, the Atlantic Ocean, the Indian Ocean, and the Arctic Ocean. Lakes and seas are smaller bodies of water.

## YOUR TURN

1. Look at the Student Atlas map on page A4. What islands are located near the intersection of latitude 20° N and longitude 160° W?

2. Name the four hemispheres. In which hemispheres is the United States located?

3. Name the continents of the world.

4. Name the oceans of the world.

# MAPMAKING

**A** **map** is a flat diagram of all or part of Earth's surface. Mapmakers have different ways of showing our round Earth on flat maps. These different ways are called **map projections**. Because our planet is round, all flat maps lose some accuracy. Mapmakers must choose the type of map projection that is best for their purposes. Many map projections are one of three kinds: cylindrical, conic, or flat-plane.

**Figure 4:** If you remove the peel from the orange and flatten the peel, it will stretch and tear. The larger the piece of peel, the more its shape is distorted as it is flattened. Also distorted are the distances between points on the peel.

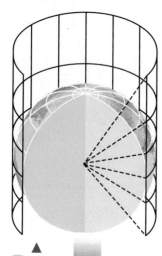

**Figure 5A:** Paper cylinder

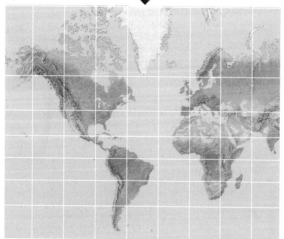

**C**ylindrical projections are designed from a cylinder wrapped around the globe. See **Figure 5A**. The cylinder touches the globe only at the equator. The meridians are pulled apart and are parallel to each other instead of meeting at the Poles. This causes landmasses near the Poles to appear larger than they really are. **Figure 5B** is a Mercator projection, one type of cylindrical projection. The Mercator projection is useful for navigators because it shows true direction and shape. The Mercator projection for world maps, however, emphasizes the Northern Hemisphere. Africa and South America appear smaller than they really are.

**Figure 5B:** A Mercator projection, although accurate near the equator, distorts distances between regions of land. This projection also distorts the sizes of areas near the poles.

Conic projections are designed from a cone placed over the globe. See **Figure 6A**. A conic projection is most accurate along the lines of latitude where it touches the globe. It retains almost true shape and size. Conic projections are most useful for areas that have long east-west dimensions, such as the United States. See the map in **Figure 6B**.

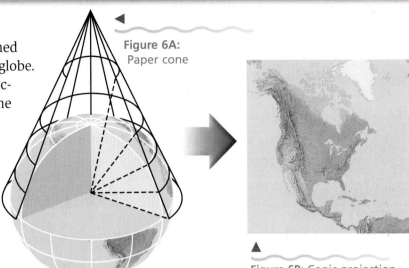

**Figure 6A:** Paper cone

▲
**Figure 6B:** Conic projection

**F**lat-plane projections are designed from a plane touching the globe at one point, such as at the North Pole or South Pole. See **Figures 7A** and **7B**. A flat-plane projection is useful for showing true direction for airplane pilots and ship navigators. It also shows true area. However, it distorts true shape.

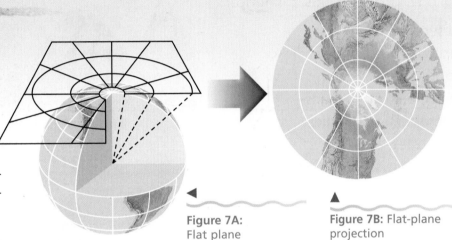

◄
**Figure 7A:** Flat plane

▲
**Figure 7B:** Flat-plane projection

**T**he Robinson projection is a compromise between size and shape distortions. It often is used for world maps, such as the map on page 76. The minor distortions in size at high latitudes on Robinson projections are balanced by realistic shapes at the middle and low latitudes.

## YOUR TURN

1. What are three major kinds of map projections?
2. Why is a Robinson projection often used for world maps?
3. What kind of projection is a Mercator map?
4. When would a mapmaker choose to use a conic projection?

# MAP ESSENTIALS

In some ways, maps are like messages sent out in code. Mapmakers provide certain elements that help us translate these codes. These elements help us understand the message they are presenting about a particular part of the world. Of these elements, almost all maps have directional indicators, scales, and legends, or keys. **Figure 8**, a map of East Asia, has all three elements.

A directional indicator shows which directions are north, south, east, and west. Some mapmakers use a "north arrow," which points toward the North Pole. Remember, "north" is not always at the top of a map. The way a map is drawn and the location of directions on that map depend on the perspective of the mapmaker. Maps in this textbook indicate direction by using a **compass rose** 1. A compass rose has arrows that point to all four principal directions, as shown in **Figure 8**.

**Figure 8: East and Southeast Asia—Physical**

Mapmakers use scales to represent distances between points on a map. Scales may appear on maps in several different forms. The maps in this textbook provide a line **scale** 2. Scales give distances in miles and kilometers (km).

To find the distance between two points on the map in **Figure 8**, place a piece of paper so that the edge connects the two points. Mark the location of each point on the paper with a line or dot. Then, compare the distance between the two dots with the map's line scale. The number on the top of the scale gives the distance in miles. The number on the bottom gives the distance in kilometers. Because the distances are given in intervals, you will have to approximate the actual distance on the scale.

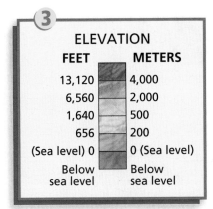

**ELEVATION**

| FEET | | METERS |
|---|---|---|
| 13,120 | | 4,000 |
| 6,560 | | 2,000 |
| 1,640 | | 500 |
| 656 | | 200 |
| (Sea level) 0 | | 0 (Sea level) |
| Below sea level | | Below sea level |

**T**he **legend** ③, or key, explains what the symbols on the map represent. Point symbols are used to specify the location of things, such as cities, that do not take up much space on a large-scale map. Some legends, such as the one in **Figure 8**, show which colors represent certain elevations. Other maps might have legends with symbols or colors that represent things such as roads. Legends can also show economic resources, land use, population density, and climate.

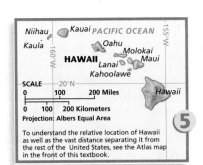

Size comparison of Canada to the contiguous United States

**P**hysical maps at the beginning of each unit have size comparison maps ④. An outline of the mainland United States (not including Alaska and Hawaii) is compared to the area under study in that chapter. These size comparison maps help you understand the size of the areas you are studying in relation to the size of the United States.

**I**nset maps are sometimes used to show a small part of a larger map. Mapmakers also use inset maps to show areas that are far away from the areas shown on the main map. Maps of the United States, for example, often include inset maps of Alaska and Hawaii ⑤. Those two states are too far from the other 48 states to accurately represent the true distance on the main map. Subject areas in inset maps can be drawn to a scale different from the scale used on the main map.

## YOUR TURN

Look at the Student Atlas map on pages A4 and A5.

1. Locate the compass rose. What country is directly west of Madagascar in Africa?

2. What island country is located southeast of India?

3. Locate the distance scale. Using the inset map, find the approximate distance in miles and kilometers from Oslo, Norway, to Stockholm, Sweden.

4. What is the capital of Brazil? What other cities are shown in Brazil?

# WORKING

## WITH MAPS

The Atlas at the front of this textbook includes two kinds of maps: physical and political. At the beginning of most units in this textbook, you will find five kinds of maps. These physical, political, climate, population, and land use and resources maps provide different kinds of information about the region you will study in that unit. These maps are accompanied by questions. Some questions ask you to show how the information on each of the maps might be related.

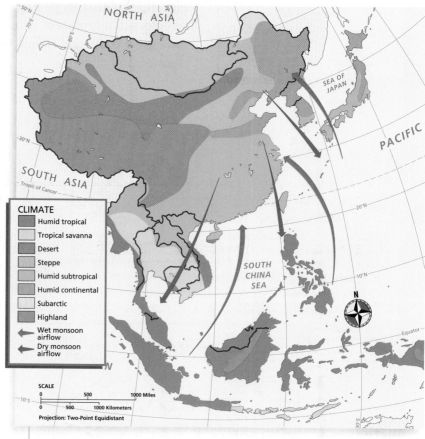

▲

**Figure 9:** East and Southeast Asia—Climate

Mapmakers often combine physical and political features into one map. Physical maps, such as the one in **Figure 8** on page S6, show important physical features in a region, including major mountains and mountain ranges, rivers, oceans and other bodies of water, deserts, and plains. Physical-political maps also show important political features, such as national borders, state and provincial boundaries, and capitals and other important cities. You will find a physical-political map at the beginning of most chapters.

Mapmakers use climate maps to show the most important weather patterns in certain areas. Climate maps throughout this textbook use color to show the various climate regions of the world. See **Figure 9.** Colors that identify climate types are found in a legend with each map. Boundaries between climate regions do not indicate an immediate change in the main weather conditions between two climate regions. Instead, boundaries show the general areas of gradual change between climate regions.

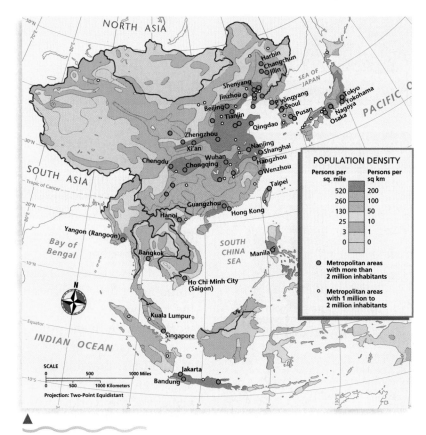

Figure 10: East and Southeast Asia—Population

POPULATION DENSITY

| Persons per sq. mile | Persons per sq km |
|---|---|
| 520 | 200 |
| 260 | 100 |
| 130 | 50 |
| 25 | 10 |
| 3 | 1 |
| 0 | 0 |

● Metropolitan areas with more than 2 million inhabitants

○ Metropolitan areas with 1 million to 2 million inhabitants

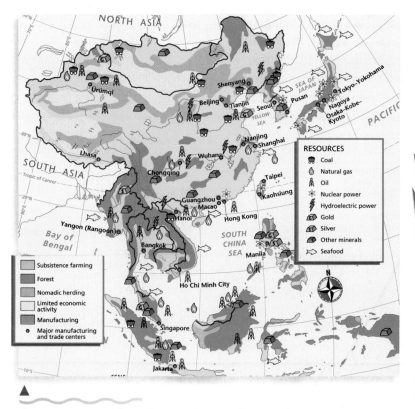

Figure 11: East and Southeast Asia—Land Use and Resources

RESOURCES

- Coal
- Natural gas
- Oil
- Nuclear power
- Hydroelectric power
- Gold
- Silver
- Other minerals
- Seafood

- Subsistence farming
- Forest
- Nomadic herding
- Limited economic activity
- Manufacturing
- ● Major manufacturing and trade centers

**P**opulation maps show where people live in a particular region. They also show how crowded, or densely populated, regions are. Population maps throughout this textbook use color to show population density. See **Figure 10**. Each color represents a certain number of people living within a square mile or square kilometer. Population maps also use symbols to show metropolitan areas with populations of a particular size. These symbols and colors are shown in a legend.

**L**and Use and Resources maps show the important resources of a region. See **Figure 11**. Symbols and colors are used to show information about economic development, such as where industry is located or where farming is most common. The meanings of each symbol and color are shown in a legend.

## YOUR TURN

1. What is the purpose of a climate map?

2. Look at the population map. What is the population density of the area around Qingdao in northern China?

3. What energy resource is found near Ho Chi Minh City?

# USING
## GRAPHS, DIAGRAMS, CHARTS, AND TABLES

**B**ar graphs are a visual way to present information. The bar graph in **Figure 12** shows the imports and exports of the countries of southern Europe. The amount of imports and exports in billions of dollars is listed on the left side of the graph. Along the bottom of the graph are the names of the countries of southern Europe. Above each country or group of countries is a vertical bar. The top of the bar corresponds to a number along the left side of the graph. For example, Italy imports $200 billion worth of goods.

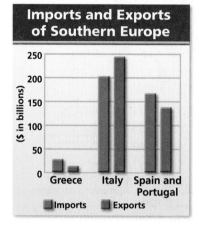

Figure 12: Reading a bar graph

**O**ften, line graphs are used to show such things as trends, comparisons, and size. The line graph in **Figure 13** shows the population growth of the world over time. The information on the left shows the number of people in billions. The years being studied are listed along the bottom. Lines connect points that show the population in billions at each year under study. This line graph projects population growth into the future.

Figure 13: Reading a line graph

**A** pie graph shows how a whole is divided into parts. In this kind of graph, a circle represents the whole. The wedges represent the parts. Bigger wedges represent larger parts of the whole. The pie graph in **Figure 14** shows the percentages of the world's coffee beans produced by various groups of countries. Brazil is the largest grower. It grows 25 percent of the world's coffee beans.

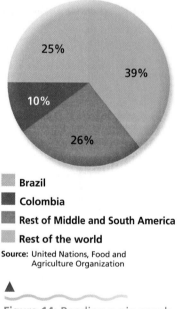

**Source:** United Nations, Food and Agriculture Organization

Figure 14: Reading a pie graph

**A**ge structure diagrams show the number of males and females by age group. These diagrams are split into two sides, one for male and one for female. Along the bottom are numbers that show the number of males or females in the age groups. The age groups are listed on the side of the diagram. The wider the base of a country's diagram, the younger the population of that country. The wider the top of a country's diagram, the older the population.

Some countries have so many younger people that their age structure diagrams are shaped like pyramids. For this reason, these diagrams are sometimes called population pyramids. However, in some countries the population is more evenly distributed by age group. For example, see the age structure diagram for Germany in **Figure 15**. Germany's population is older. It is not growing as fast as countries with younger populations.

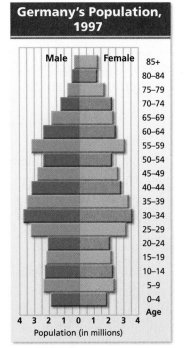

**Source:** U.S. Census Bureau

**Figure 15:** Reading an age structure diagram

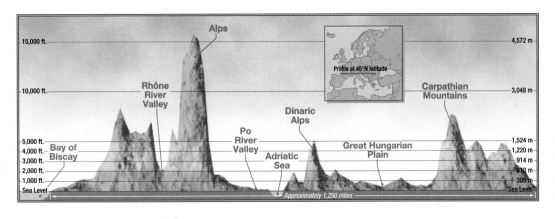

**Figure 16:** Reading an elevation profile

**E**ach unit atlas includes an elevation profile. See **Figure 16**. It is a side view, or profile, of a region along a line drawn between two points.

Vertical and horizontal distances are figured differently on elevation profiles. The vertical distance (the height of a mountain, for example) is exaggerated when compared to the horizontal distance between the two points. This technique is called vertical exaggeration. If the vertical scale were not exaggerated, even tall mountains would appear as small bumps on an elevation profile.

In each unit and chapter on the various regions of the world, you will find tables that provide basic information about the countries under study.

The countries of Spain and Portugal are listed on the left in the table in **Figure 17**. You can match statistical information on the right with the name of each country listed on the left. The categories of information are listed across the top of the table.

Graphic organizers can help you understand certain ideas and concepts. For example, the diagram in **Figure 18** helps you think about the uses of water. In this diagram, one water use goes in each oval. Graphic organizers can help you focus on key facts in your study of geography.

Time lines provide highlights of important events over a period of time. The time line in **Figure 19** begins at the left with 5000 B.C., when rice was first cultivated in present-day China. The time line highlights important events that have shaped the human and political geography of China.

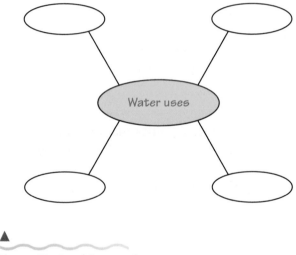

## Spain and Portugal

| COUNTRY | POPULATION/ GROWTH RATE | LIFE EXPECTANCY | LITERACY RATE | PER CAPITA GDP |
|---|---|---|---|---|
| Portugal | 9,918,040 0.1% | 73, male 79, female | 90% (1995) | $14,600 (1998) |
| Spain | 39,167,744 0.1% | 74, male 82, female | 97% (1995) | $16,500 (1998) |
| United States | 272,639,608 0.9% | 73, male 80, female | 97% (1994) | $31,500 (1998) |

**Sources:** Central Intelligence Agency, *The World Factbook 1999; The World Almanac and Book of Facts 1999*

Figure 17: Reading a table

Water uses

Figure 18: Graphic organizer

### Historical China: A Time Line

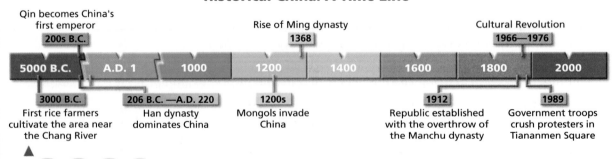

Qin becomes China's first emperor
**200s B.C.**

Rise of Ming dynasty
**1368**

Cultural Revolution
**1966—1976**

| 5000 B.C. | A.D. 1 | 1000 | 1200 | 1400 | 1600 | 1800 | 2000 |

**3000 B.C.**
First rice farmers cultivate the area near the Chang River

**206 B.C. —A.D. 220**
Han dynasty dominates China

**1200s**
Mongols invade China

**1912**
Republic established with the overthrow of the Manchu dynasty

**1989**
Government troops crush protesters in Tiananmen Square

Figure 19: Reading a time line

## Corn: From Field to Consumer

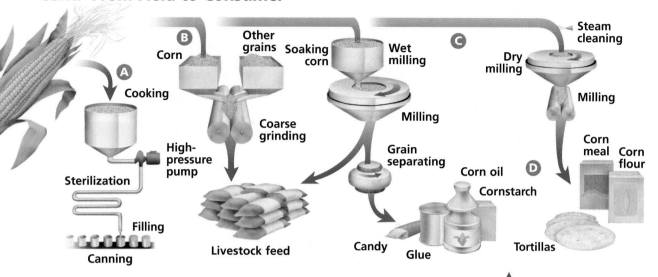

▲ **Figure 20:** Reading a flowchart

**A** Corn can be processed in a variety of ways. Some corn is cooked and then canned.

**B** Corn is ground and used for livestock feed.

**C** Corn also might be wet-milled or dry-milled. Then grain parts are used to make different products.

**D** Corn by-products, such as cornstarch and corn syrup, are used to make breads, breakfast cereals, puddings, and snack foods. Corn oil is used for cooking.

**F**lowcharts are visual guides that explain different processes. They lead the reader from one step to the next, sometimes providing both illustrations and text. The flowchart in **Figure 20** shows the different steps involved in harvesting corn and preparing it for use by consumers. The flowchart takes you through the steps of harvesting and processing corn. Captions guide you through flowcharts.

## YOUR TURN

1. Look at the statistical table for Spain and Portugal in Figure 17. Which countries have the highest literacy rate?

2. Look at the China time line in Figure 19. Name two important events in China's history between 1200 and 1400.

3. Look at Figure 20. What are three corn products?

# READING

## A TIME-ZONE MAP

The sun is not directly overhead everywhere on Earth at the same time. Clocks are set to reflect the difference in the sun's position. Our planet rotates on its axis once every 24 hours. In other words, in one hour, it makes one twenty-fourth of a complete revolution. Since there are 360 degrees in a circle, we know that the planet turns 15 degrees of longitude each hour. (360° ÷ 24 = 15°) We also know that the planet turns in a west-to-east direction. Therefore, if a place on Earth has the sun directly overhead at this moment (noon), then a place 15 degrees to the west will have the sun directly overhead one hour from now. During that hour the planet will have rotated 15 degrees. As a result, Earth is divided into 24 time zones. Thus, time is an hour earlier for each 15 degrees you move westward on Earth. Time is an hour later for each 15 degrees you move eastward on Earth.

By international agreement, longitude is measured from the prime meridian. This meridian passes through the Royal Observatory in Greenwich, England. Time also is measured from Greenwich and is called Greenwich mean time (GMT). For each time zone east of the prime meridian, clocks must be set one hour ahead of GMT. For each time zone west of Greenwich, clocks are set back one hour from GMT. When it is noon in London, it is 1:00 P.M. in Oslo, Norway, one time zone east. However, it is 7 A.M. in New York City, five time zones west.

## WORLD TIME ZONES

As you can see by looking at the map below, time zones do not follow meridians exactly. Political boundaries are often used to draw time-zone lines. In Europe and Africa, for example, time zones follow national boundaries. The mainland United States, meanwhile, is divided into four major time zones: Eastern, Central, Mountain, and Pacific. Alaska and Hawaii are in separate time zones to the west of the mainland.

Some countries have made changes in their time zones. For example, most of the United States has daylight savings time in the summer in order to have more evening hours of daylight.

The international date line is a north-south line that runs through the Pacific Ocean. It is located at 180°, although it sometimes varies from that meridian to avoid dividing countries.

At 180°, the time is 12 hours from Greenwich time. There is a time difference of 24 hours between the two sides of the 180° meridian. The 180° meridian is called the international date line because when you cross it, the date and day change. As you cross the date line from the west to the east, you gain a day. If you travel from east to west, you lose a day.

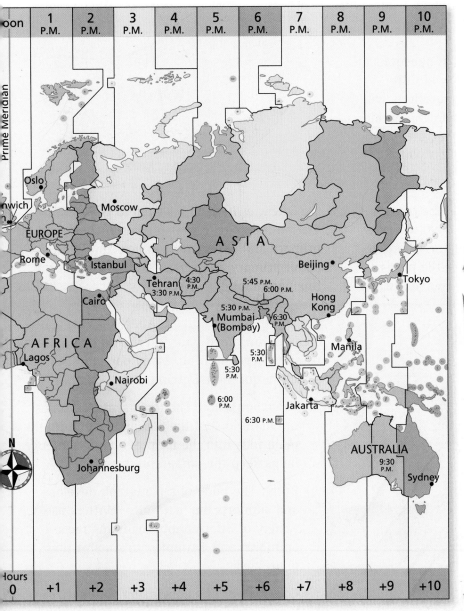

## YOUR TURN

1. In which time zone do you live? Check your time now. What time is it in New York?

2. How many hours behind New York is Anchorage, Alaska?

3. How many time zones are there in Africa?

4. If it is 9 A.M. in the middle of Greenland, what time is it in São Paulo?

# WRITING
## ABOUT GEOGRAPHY

**W**riters have many different reasons for writing. In your study of geography, you might write to accomplish many different tasks. You might write a paragraph or short paper to express your own personal feelings or thoughts about a topic or event. You might also write a paper to tell your class about an event, person, place, or thing. Sometimes you may want to write in order to persuade or convince readers to agree with a certain statement or to act in a particular way.

You will find different kinds of questions at the end of each section, chapter, and unit throughout this textbook. Some questions will require in-depth answers. The following guidelines for writing will help you structure your answers so that they clearly express your thoughts.

**Prewriting** Prewriting is the process of thinking about and planning what to write. It includes gathering and organizing information into a clear plan. Writers use the prewriting stage to identify their audience and purpose for what is to be written.

### The Writing Process

- Proofreading and Publishing
- Prewriting
- Evaluating and Revising
- Writing a Draft

Often, writers do research to get the information they need. Research can include finding primary and secondary sources. You will read about primary and secondary sources later in this handbook.

**Writing a Draft** After you have gathered and arranged your information, you are ready to begin writing. Many paragraphs are structured in the following way:

- **Topic Sentence:** The topic sentence states the main idea of the paragraph. Putting the main idea into the form of a topic sentence helps keep the paragraph focused.

- **Body:** The body of a paragraph develops and supports the main idea. Writers use a variety of information, including facts, opinions, and examples, to support the main idea.

- **Conclusion:** The conclusion summarizes the writer's main points or restates the main idea.

**Evaluating and Revising** Read over your paragraphs and make sure you have clearly expressed what you wanted to say. Sometimes it helps to read your paragraphs aloud or to ask someone else to read them. Such methods help you identify rough or unclear sentences and passages. Revise the parts of your paragraph that are not clear or that stray from your main idea. You might want to add, cut, reorder, or replace sentences to make your paragraph as clear as possible.

**Proofreading and Publishing** Before you write your final draft, read over your paragraphs and correct any errors in grammar, spelling, sentence structure, or punctuation. Common mistakes include misspelled place-names, incomplete sentences, and improper use of punctuation, such as commas. You should use a dictionary and standard grammar guides to help you proofread your work.

After you have revised and corrected your draft, neatly rewrite your paper. Make sure your final version is clean and free of mistakes. The appearance of your final version can affect how your audience perceives and understands your writing.

## Practicing the Skill

1. What are the steps in the writing process?
2. How are most paragraphs formed?
3. Write a paragraph or short paper about your community for a visitor. When you have finished your draft, review it and then mark and correct any errors in grammar, spelling, sentence structure, or punctuation. At the bottom of your draft, list key resources—such as a dictionary—that you used to check and correct your work. Then write your final draft. When you are finished with your work, use pencils or pens of different colors to underline and identify the topic sentence, body, and conclusion of your paragraph.

# DOING
## RESEARCH

Research is at the heart of geographic inquiry. To complete a research project, you may need to use resources other than this textbook. For example, you may want to research specific places or issues not discussed in this textbook. You may also want to learn more about a certain topic that you have studied in a chapter. Following the guidelines below will help you plan and complete research projects for your class.

**Planning** The first step in approaching a research project is planning. Planning involves deciding on a topic and finding information about that topic.

- **Decide on a Topic.** Before starting any research project, you should decide on one topic. If you are working with a group, all group members should participate in choosing a topic. Sometimes a topic will be assigned to you, but at other times you may have to choose your own. Once you have settled on a topic, make sure you can find resources to help you research it.

- **Find Information.** In order to find a particular book, you need to know how libraries organize their materials. Libraries classify their books by assigning each book a call number that tells you its location. To find the call number, look in the library's card catalog. The card catalog lists books by author, by title, and by subject. Many libraries today have computerized card catalogs. Libraries often provide instructions on how to use their computerized card catalogs. If no instructions are available, ask a library staff member for help.

Most libraries have encyclopedias, gazetteers, atlases, almanacs, and periodical indexes. Encyclopedias contain geographic, economic, and political data on individual countries, states, and cities. They also include discussions of historical events, religion, social and cultural issues, and much more. A gazetteer is a geographical dictionary that lists significant natural physical features and other places. An atlas contains maps and visual representations of geographic data. To find up-to-date facts, you can use almanacs, yearbooks, and periodical indexes.

References like *The World Almanac and Book of Facts* include historical information and a variety of statistics. Periodical indexes, particularly *The Reader's Guide to Periodical Literature*, can help you locate informative articles published in magazines. *The New York Times Index* catalogs the newspaper articles published in the *New York Times*.

You may also want to find information on the World Wide Web. The World Wide Web is the part of the Internet where people put files called Web sites for other people to access. To search the World Wide Web, you must use a search engine. A search engine will provide you with a list of Web sites that contain keywords relating to your topic. Search engines also provide Web directories, which allow you to browse Web sites by subject.

**Organizing** Organization is key to completing research projects of any size. If you are working with a group, every group member should have an assigned task in researching, writing, and completing your project. You and all the group members should keep track of the materials that you used to conduct your research. Then compile those sources into a bibliography and turn it in with your research project.

In addition, information collected during research should be organized in an efficient way. A common method of organizing research information is to use index cards. If you have used an outline to organize your research, you can code each index card with the appropriate main idea number and supporting detail letter from the outline. Then write the relevant information on that card. You might also use computer files in the same way. These methods will help you keep track of what information you have collected and what information you still need to gather.

Some projects will require you to conduct original research. This original research might require you to interview people, conduct surveys, collect unpublished information about your community, or draw a map of a local place. Before you do your original research, make sure you have all the necessary background information. Also, create a pre-research plan so that you can make sure all the necessary tools, such as research sources, are available.

**Completing and Presenting Your Project** Once you have completed your research project, you will need to present the information you have gathered in some fashion. Many times, you or your group will simply need to write a paper about your research. Research can also be presented in many other ways, however. For example, you could make an audiotape, a drawing, a poster board, a video, or a Web page to explain your research.

## Practicing the Skill

1. What kinds of references would you need to research specific current events around the world?
2. Work with a group of four other students to plan, organize, and complete a research project on a topic of interest in your local community. For example, you might want to learn more about a particular individual or event that influenced your community's history. Other topics might include the economic features, physical features, and political features of your community.

# ANALYZING
## PRIMARY and SECONDARY SOURCES

When conducting research, it is important to use a variety of primary and secondary sources of information. There are many sources of first-hand geographical information, including diaries, letters, editorials, and legal documents such as land titles. All of these are primary sources. Newspaper articles are also considered primary sources, although they generally are written after the fact. Other primary sources include personal memoirs and autobiographies, which people usually write late in life. Paintings and photographs of particular events, persons, places, or things make up a visual record and are also considered primary sources. Because they allow us to take a close-up look at a topic, primary sources are valuable geographic tools.

Secondary sources are descriptions or interpretations of events written after the events have occurred by persons who did not participate in the events they describe. Geography textbooks such as this one, as well as biographies, encyclopedias, and other reference works, are examples of secondary sources. Writers of secondary sources have the advantage of seeing what happened beyond the moment or place that is being studied. They can provide a perspective wider than that available to one person at a specific time.

## How to Study Primary and Secondary Sources

1. **Study the Material Carefully.** Consider the nature of the material. Is it verbal or visual? Is it based on firsthand information or on the accounts of others? Note the major ideas and supporting details.

2. **Consider the Audience.** Ask yourself, "For whom was this message originally meant?" Whether a message was intended for the general public or for a specific private audience may have shaped its style or content.

3. **Check for Bias.** Watch for words or phrases that present a one-sided view of a person or situation.

4. **Compare Sources.** Study more than one source on a topic. Comparing sources gives you a more complete and balanced account of geographical events and their relationships to one another.

## Practicing the Skill

1. What distinguishes secondary sources from primary sources?
2. What advantages do secondary sources have over primary sources?
3. Why should you consider the intended audience of a source?
4. Of the following, identify which are primary sources and which are secondary sources: a newspaper, a private journal, a biography, an editorial cartoon, a deed to property, a snapshot of a family vacation, a magazine article about the history of Thailand, an autobiography. How might some of these sources prove to be both primary and secondary sources?

# CRITICAL THINKING

*The study of geography requires more than analyzing and understanding tools like graphs and maps. Throughout* Holt People, Places, and Change, *you are asked to think critically about some of the information you are studying. Critical thinking is the reasoned judgment of information and ideas. The development of critical thinking skills is essential to learning more about the world around you. Helping you develop critical thinking skills is an important goal of* Holt People, Places, and Change. *The following critical thinking skills appear in the section reviews and chapter reviews of the textbook.*

**Summarizing** involves briefly restating information gathered from a larger body of information. Much of the writing in this textbook is summarizing. The geographical data in this textbook has been collected from many sources. Summarizing all the qualities of a region or country involves studying a large body of cultural, economic, geological, and historical information.

**Finding the main idea** is the ability to identify the main point in a set of information. This textbook is designed to help you focus on the main ideas in geography. The Read to Discover questions in each chapter help you identify the main ideas in each section. To find the main idea in any piece of writing, first read the title and introduction. These two elements may point to the main ideas covered in the text.

Also, write down questions about the subject that you think might be answered in the text. Having such questions in mind will focus your reading. Pay attention to any headings or subheadings, which may provide a basic outline of the major ideas. Finally, as you read, note sentences that provide additional details from the general statements that those details support. For example, a trail of facts may lead to a conclusion that expresses the main idea.

**Comparing and contrasting** involve examining events, points of view, situations, or styles to identify their similarities and differences. Comparing focuses on both the similarities and the differences. Contrasting focuses only on the differences. Studying similarities and differences between people and things can give you clues about the human and physical geography of a region.

*Buddhist shrine, Myanmar*

*Stave church, Norway*

**Supporting a point of view** involves identifying an issue, deciding what you think about it, and persuasively expressing your position. Your stand should be based on specific information. When taking a stand, state your position clearly and give reasons that support it.

**Identifying points of view** involves noting the factors that influence the opinions of an individual or group. A person's point of view includes beliefs and attitudes that are shaped by factors such as age, gender, race, and economic status. Identifying points of view helps us examine why people see things as they do. It also reinforces the realization that people's views may change over time or with a change in circumstances.

**Identifying bias** is an important critical thinking skill in the study of any subject. When a point of view is highly personal or based on unreasoned judgment, it is considered biased. Sometimes, a person's actions reflect bias. At its most extreme, bias can be expressed in violent actions against members of a particular culture or group. A less obvious form of bias is a stereotype, or a generalization about a group of people. Stereotypes tend to ignore differences within groups.

*Political protest, India*

Probably the hardest form of cultural bias to detect has to do with perspective, or point of view. When we use our own culture and experiences as a point of reference from which to make statements about other cultures, we are showing a form of bias called ethnocentrism.

**Analyzing** is the process of breaking something down into parts and examining the relationships between those parts. For example, to understand the processes behind forest loss, you might study issues involving economic development, the overuse of resources, and pollution.

**Evaluating** involves assessing the significance or overall importance of something. For example, you might evaluate the success of certain environmental protection laws or the effect of foreign trade on a society. You should base your evaluation on standards that others will understand and are likely to consider valid. For example, an evaluation of international relations after World War II might look at the political and economic tensions between the United States and the Soviet Union. Such an evaluation would also consider the ways those tensions affected other countries around the world.

**Identifying cause and effect** is part of interpreting the relationships between geographical events. A cause is any action that leads to an event; the outcome of that action is an effect. To explain geographical developments, geographers may point out multiple causes and effects. For example, geographers studying pollution in a region might note a number of causes.

*Ecuador rain forest*

*Cleared forest, Kenya*

*Drought in West Texas*

*Dallas, Texas*

**Drawing inferences and drawing conclusions** are two methods of critical thinking that require you to use evidence to explain events or information in a logical way. Inferences and conclusions are opinions, but these opinions are based on facts and reasonable deductions.

For example, suppose you know that people are moving in greater and greater numbers to cities in a particular country. You also know that poor weather has hurt farming in rural areas while industry has been expanding in cities. You might be able to understand from this information some of the reasons for the increased migration to cities. You could conclude that poor harvests have pushed people to leave rural areas. You might also conclude that the possibility of finding work in new industries may be pulling people to cities.

**Making generalizations and making predictions** are two critical thinking skills that require you to form specific ideas from a large body of information. When you are asked to generalize, you must take into account many different pieces of information. You then form a main concept that can be applied to all of the pieces of information. Many times making generalizations can help you see trends. Looking at trends can help you form a prediction. Making a prediction involves looking at trends in the past and present and making an educated guess about how these trends will affect the future.

*Communications technology, rural Brazil*

# SKILLS

Like you, many people around the world have faced difficult problems and decisions. By using appropriate skills such as problem solving and decision making, you will be better able to choose a solution or make a decision on important issues. The following activities will help you develop and practice these skills.

## Decision Making

**Decision making** involves choosing between two or more options. Listed below are guidelines to help you with making decisions.

1. **Identify a situation that requires a decision.** Think about your current situation. What issue are you faced with that requires you to take some sort of action?

2. **Gather information.** Think about the issue. Examine the causes of the issue or problem and consider how it affects you and others.

3. **Identify your options.** Consider the actions that you could take to address the issue. List these options so that you can compare them.

4. **Make predictions about consequences.** Predict the consequences of taking the actions listed for each of your options. Compare these possible consequences. Be sure the option you choose produces the results you want.

5. **Take action to implement a decision.** Choose a course of action from your available options, and put it into effect.

## Problem Solving

Problem solving involves many of the steps of decision making. Listed below are guidelines to help you solve problems.

1. **Identify the problem.** Identify just what the problem or difficulty is that you are facing. Sometimes you face a difficult situation made up of several different problems. Each problem may require its own solution.

2. **Gather information.** Conduct research on any important issues related to the problem. Try to find the answers to questions like the following: What caused this problem? Who or what does it affect? When did it start?

3. **List and consider options.** Look at the problem and the answers to the questions you asked in Step 2. List and then think about all the possible ways in which the problem could be solved. These are your options—possible solutions to the problem.

4. **Examine advantages and disadvantages.** Consider the advantages and disadvantages of all the options that you have listed. Make sure that you consider the possible long-term effects of each possible solution. You should also determine what steps you will need to take to achieve each possible solution. Some suggestions may sound good at first but may turn out to be impractical or hard to achieve.

5. **Choose and implement a solution.** Select the best solution from your list and take the steps to achieve it.

6. **Evaluate the effectiveness of the solution.** When you have completed the steps needed to put your plan into action, evaluate its effectiveness. Is the problem solved? Were the results worth the effort required? Has the solution itself created any other problems?

## Practicing the Skill

1. Chapter 24, Section 2: East Africa's History and Culture, describes the challenges of religious and ethnic conflict occurring in the region. Imagine that you are an ambassador to Rwanda. Use the decision-making guidelines to help you come up with a plan to help resolve the problems there. Be prepared to defend your decision.

2. Identify a similar problem discussed in another chapter and apply the problem-solving process to come up with a solution.

# Becoming a Strategic Reader

*by Dr. Judith Irvin*

Everywhere you look, print is all around us. In fact, you would have a hard time stopping yourself from reading. In a normal day, you might read cereal boxes, movie posters, notes from friends, T-shirts, instructions for video games, song lyrics, catalogs, billboards, information on the Internet, magazines, the newspaper, and much, much more. Each form of print is read differently depending on your purpose for reading. You read a menu differently from poetry, and a motorcycle magazine is read differently than a letter from a friend. Good readers switch easily from one type of text to another. In fact, they probably do not even think about it, they just do it.

When you read, it is helpful to use a strategy to remember the most important ideas. You can use a strategy before you read to help connect information you already know to the new information you will encounter. Before you read, you can also predict what a text will be about by using a previewing strategy. During the reading you can use a strategy to help you focus on main ideas, and after reading you can use a strategy to help you organize what you learned so that you can remember it later. *Holt People, Places, and Change* was designed to help you more easily understand the ideas you read.  Important reading strategies employed in *Holt People, Places, and Change* include:

**A** Tools to help you **preview and predict** what the text will be about

**B** Ways to help you **use and analyze visual information**

**C** Ideas to help you **organize the information** you have learned

# A. Previewing and Predicting

*How can I figure out what the text is about before I even start reading a section?*

**Previewing** and **predicting** are good methods to help you understand the text. If you take the time to preview and predict before you read, the text will make more sense to you during your reading.

**1** Usually, your teacher will set the purpose for reading. After reading some new information, you may be asked to write a summary, take a test, or complete some other type of activity.

*"After reading about Spain and Portugal, you will work with a partner to present a history of the countries to a travel group..."*

### Previewing and Predicting

**step 1** Identify your purpose for reading. Ask yourself what you will do with this information once you have finished reading.

▼

**step 2** Ask yourself what is the main idea of the text and what are the key vocabulary words you need to know.

▼

**step 3** Use signal words to help identify the structure of the text.

▼

**step 4** Connect the information to what you already know.

**2** As you preview the text, use **graphic signals** such as headings, subheadings, and boldface type to help you determine what is important in the text. Each section of *Holt People, Places, and Change* opens by giving you important clues to help you preview the material.

Looking at the section's **main heading** and subheadings can give you an idea of what is to come.

**Read to Discover** questions give you clues as to the section's main ideas.

**Define** and **Locate** terms let you know the key vocabulary and places you will encounter in the section.

## Section 4 — Spain and Portugal

**Read to Discover**
1. What were some major events in the history of Spain and Portugal?
2. What are the cultures of Spain and Portugal like?
3. What are Spain and Portugal like today?

**Define**
Moors
dialect
cork

**Locate**
Lisbon
Madrid
Barcelona

**WHY IT MATTERS**
Some Basque separatists have used violence to try to gain their independence from Spain. Use CNNfyi.com or other current events sources to find examples of this problem. Record your findings in your journal.

*Paella, a popular dish in Spain*

**3** Other tools that can help you in previewing are **signal words**. These words prepare you to think in a certain way. For example, when you see words such as *similar to, same as,* or *different from,* you know that the text will probably compare and contrast two or more ideas. Signal words indicate how the ideas in the text relate to each other. Look at the list below for some of the most common signal words grouped by the type of text structures they include.

## SIGNAL WORDS

| Cause and Effect | Compare and Contrast | Description | Problem and Solution | Sequence or Chronological Order |
|---|---|---|---|---|
| because | different from | for instance | the question is | not long after |
| since | same as | for example | a solution | next |
| consequently | similar to | such as | one answer is | then |
| this led to...so | as opposed to | to illustrate | | initially |
| if...then | instead of | in addition | | before |
| nevertheless | although | most importantly | | after |
| accordingly | however | another | | finally |
| because of | compared with | furthermore | | preceding |
| as a result of | as well as | first, second ... | | following |
| in order to | either...or | | | on (date) |
| may be due to | but | | | over the years |
| for this reason | on the other hand | | | today |
| not only...but | unless | | | when |

**4** Learning something new requires that you connect it in some way with something you already know. This means you have to think before you read and while you read. You may want to use a chart like this one to remind yourself of the information already familiar to you and to come up with questions you want answered in your reading. The chart will also help you organize your ideas after you have finished reading.

| What I know | What I want to know | What I learned |
|---|---|---|
| | | |
| | | |
| | | |
| | | |
| | | |
| | | |

## B. Use and Analyze Visual Information

*How can all the pictures, maps, graphs, and time lines with the text help me be a stronger reader?*

**Using visual information** can help you understand and remember the information presented in *Holt People, Places, and Change*. Good readers make a picture in their mind when they read. The pictures, charts, graphs, and diagrams that occur throughout *Holt People, Places, and Change* are placed strategically to increase your understanding.

**1** You might ask yourself questions like these:

*Why did the writer include this image with the text? What details about this image are mentioned in the text?*

### Analyzing Visual Information

**step 1** As you preview the text, ask yourself how the visual information relates to the text.

▼

**step 2** Generate questions based on the visual information.

▼

**step 3** After reading the text, go back and review the visual information again.

▼

**step 4** Connect the information to what you already know.

**2** After you have read the text, see if you can answer your own questions.

→ Why are windmills important?

→ What technology do windmills use to pump water?

→ How might environment affect the use of windmills?

**2** Maps, graphs, and charts help you organize information about a place. You might ask questions like these:

*How does this map support what I have read in the text?*

*What does the information in this bar graph add to the text discussion?*

→ *What is the purpose of this map?*

→ *What special features does the map show?*

→ *What do the colors, lines, and symbols on the map represent?*

**Land Use and Resources**

→ *What information is the writer trying to present with this graph?*

→ *Why did the writer use a bar graph to organize this information?*

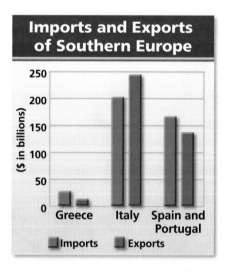

**Imports and Exports of Southern Europe**

**3** After reading the text, go back and review the visual information again.

**4** Connect the information to what you already know.

## C. Organize Information

*Once I learn new information, how do I keep it all straight so that I will remember it?*

To help you remember what you have read, you need to find a way of **organizing information**. Two good ways of doing this are by using graphic organizers and concept maps. **Graphic organizers** help you understand important relationships—such as cause and effect, compare/contrast, sequence of events, and problem/solution—within the text. **Concept maps** provide a useful tool to help you focus on the text's main ideas and organize supporting details.

## Identifying Relationships

Using graphic organizers will help you recall important ideas from the section and give you a study tool you can use to prepare for a quiz or test or to help with a writing assignment. Some of the most common types of graphic organizers are shown below.

### ▶ Cause and Effect

Events in history cause people to react in a certain way. Cause-and-effect patterns show the relationship between results and the ideas or events that made the results occur. You may want to represent cause-and-effect relationships as one cause leading to multiple effects,

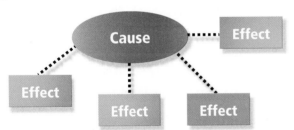

or as a chain of cause-and-effect relationships.

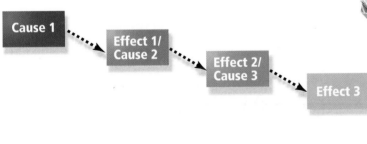

**Constructing Graphic Organizers**

**step 1** Preview the text, looking for signal words and the main idea.

▼

**step 2** Form a hypothesis as to which type of graphic organizer would work best to display the information presented.

▼

**step 3** Work individually or with your classmates to create a visual representation of what you read.

## ▶ Comparing and Contrasting

Graphic organizers are often useful when you are comparing or contrasting information. Compare-and-contrast diagrams point out similarities and differences between two concepts or ideas.

## ▶ Sequencing

Keeping track of dates and the order in which events took place is essential to understanding the history and geography of a place. Sequence or chronological-order diagrams show events or ideas in the order in which they happened.

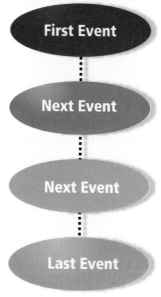

## ▶ Problem and Solution

Problem-solution patterns identify at least one problem, offer one or more solutions to the problem, and explain or predict outcomes of the solutions.

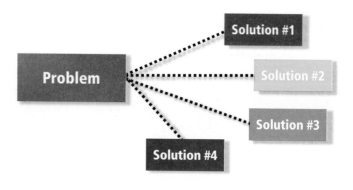

## Identifying Main Ideas and Supporting Details

One special type of graphic organizer is the concept map. A concept map allows you to zero in on the most important points of the text. The map is made up of lines, boxes, circles, and/or arrows. It can be as simple or as complex as you need it to be to accurately represent the text. Here are a few examples of concept maps you might use.

### Constructing Concept Maps

**step 1**  Preview the text, looking for what type of structure might be appropriate to display as a concept map.

▼

**step 2**  Taking note of the headings, boldface type, and text structure, sketch a concept map you think could best illustrate the text.

▼

**step 3**  Using boxes, lines, arrows, circles, or any shapes you like, display the ideas of the text in the concept map.

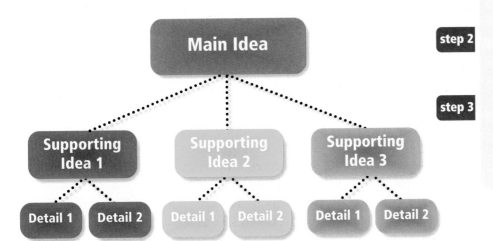

# Standardized Test-Taking Strategies

A number of times throughout your school career, you may be asked to take standardized tests. These tests are designed to demonstrate the content and skills you have learned. It is important to keep in mind that in most cases the best way to prepare for these tests is to pay close attention in class and take every opportunity to improve your general social studies, reading, writing, and mathematical skills.

## Tips for Taking the Test

1. Be sure that you are well rested.
2. Be on time, and be sure that you have the necessary materials.
3. Listen to the teacher's instructions.
4. Read directions and questions carefully.
5. **DON'T STRESS!** Just remember what you have learned in class, and you should do well.

**Practice the strategies at go.hrw.com**

## Tackling Social Studies

The social studies portions of many standardized tests are designed to test your knowledge of the content and skills that you have been studying in one or more of your social studies classes. Specific objectives for the test vary, but some of the most common include the following:

1. Demonstrate an understanding of issues and events in history.
2. Demonstrate an understanding of geographic influences on historical issues and events.
3. Demonstrate an understanding of economic and social influences on historical issues and events.
4. Demonstrate an understanding of political influences on historical issues and events.
5. Use critical thinking skills to analyze social studies information.

Standardized tests usually contain multiple-choice and, sometimes, open-ended questions. The multiple-choice items will often be based on maps, tables, charts, graphs, pictures, cartoons, and/or reading passages and documents.

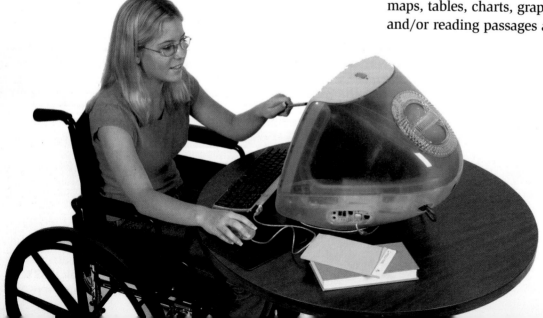

## Tips for Answering Multiple-Choice Questions

1. If there is a written or visual piece accompanying the multiple-choice question, pay careful attention to the title, author, and date.

2. Then read through or glance over the content of the written or visual piece accompanying the question to familiarize yourself with it.

3. Next, read the multiple-choice question first for its general intent. Then reread it carefully, looking for words that give clues or can limit possible answers to the question. For example, words such as *most* or *best* tell you that there may be several correct answers to a question, but you should look for the most appropriate answer.

4. Read through the answer choices. Always read all of the possible answer choices even if the first one seems like the correct answer. There may be a better choice farther down in the list.

5. Reread the accompanying information (if any is included) carefully to determine the answer to the question. Again, note the title, author, and date of primary-source selections. The answer will rarely be stated exactly as it appears in the primary source, so you will need to use your critical thinking skills to read between the lines.

6. Think of what you already know about the time in history or person involved and use that to help limit the answer choices.

7. Finally, reread the question and selected answer to be sure that you made the best choice and that you marked it correctly on the answer sheet.

## Strategies for Success

There are a variety of strategies you can prepare ahead of time to help you feel more confident about answering questions on social studies standardized tests. Here are a few suggestions:

1. Adopt an acronym—a word formed from the first letters of other words—that you will use for analyzing a document or visual piece that accompanies a question.

## Helpful Acronyms

For a document, use **SOAPS**, which stands for

**S** Subject
**O** Overview
**A** Audience
**P** Purpose
**S** Speaker/author

For a picture, cartoon, map, or other visual piece of information, use **OPTIC**, which stands for

**O** Occasion (or time)
**P** Parts (labels or details of the visual)
**T** Title
**I** Interrelations (how the different parts of the visual work together)
**C** Conclusion (what the visual means)

2. Form visual images of maps and try to draw them from memory. Standardized tests will most likely include maps showing many features, such as states, countries, continents, and oceans. Those maps may also show patterns in settlement and the size and distribution of cities. For example, in studying the United States, be able to see in your mind's eye such things as where the states and major cities are located. Know major physical features, such as the Mississippi River, the Appalachian and Rocky Mountains, the Great Plains, and the various regions of the United States, and be able to place them on a map. Such features may help you understand patterns in the distribution of population and the size of settlements.

3. When you have finished studying a geographic region or period in history, try to think of who or what might be important enough for a standardized test. You may want to keep your ideas in a notebook to refer to when it is almost time for the test.

4. Standardized tests will likely test your understanding of the political, economic, and social processes that

shape a region's history, culture, and geography. Questions may also ask you to understand the impact of geographic factors on major events. For example, some may ask about the effects of migration and immigration on various societies and population change. In addition, questions may test your understanding of the ways humans interact with their environment.

5. For the skills area of the tests, practice putting major events and personalities in order in your mind. Sequencing people and events by dates can become a game you play with a friend who also has to take the test. Always ask yourself "why" this event is important.

6. Follow the tips under "Ready for Reading" below when you encounter a reading passage in social studies, but remember that what you have learned about history can help you in answering reading-comprehension questions.

## Ready for Reading

The main goal of the reading sections of most standardized tests is to determine your understanding of different aspects of a piece of writing. Basically, if you can grasp the main idea and the writer's purpose and then pay attention to the details and vocabulary so that you are able to draw inferences and conclusions, you will do well on the test.

### Tips for Answering Multiple-Choice Questions

1. Read the passage as if you were not taking a test.

2. Look at the big picture. Ask yourself questions like, "What is the title?", "What do the illustrations or pictures tell me?", and "What is the writer's purpose?"

3. Read the questions. This will help you know what information to look for.

4. Reread the passage, underlining information related to the questions.

## Types of Multiple-Choice Questions

1. **Main Idea** This is the most important point of the passage. After reading the passage, locate and underline the main idea.

2. **Significant Details** You will often be asked to recall details from the passage. Read the question and underline the details as you read, but remember that the correct answers do not always match the wording of the passage precisely.

3. **Vocabulary** You will often need to define a word within the context of the passage. Read the answer choices and plug them into the sentence to see what fits best.

4. **Conclusion and Inference** There are often important ideas in the passage that the writer does not state directly. Sometimes you must consider multiple parts of the passage to answer the question. If answers refer to only one or two sentences or details in the passage, they are probably incorrect.

5. Go back to the questions and try to answer each one in your mind before looking at the answers.

6. Read all the answer choices and eliminate the ones that are obviously incorrect.

### Tips for Answering Short-Answer Questions

1. Read the passage in its entirety, paying close attention to the main events and characters. Jot down information you think is important.

2. If you cannot answer a question, skip it and come back later.

3. Words such as *compare, contrast, interpret, discuss,* and *summarize* appear often in short-answer questions. Be sure you have a complete understanding of each of these words.

4. To help support your answer, return to the passage and skim the parts you underlined.

5. Organize your thoughts on a separate sheet of paper. Write a general statement with which to begin. This will be your topic statement.

6. When writing your answer, be precise but brief. Be sure to refer to details in the passage in your answer.

## Targeting Writing

On many standardized tests, you will occasionally be asked to write an essay. In order to write a concise essay, you must learn to organize your thoughts before you begin writing the actual piece. This keeps you from straying too far from the essay's topic.

### Tips for Answering Composition Questions

1. Read the question carefully.

2. Decide what kind of essay you are being asked to write. Essays usually fall into one of the following types: persuasive, classificatory, compare/contrast, or "how to." To determine the type of essay, ask yourself questions like, "Am I trying to persuade my audience?", "Am I comparing or contrasting ideas?", or "Am I trying to show the reader how to do something?"

3. Pay attention to key words, such as *compare, contrast, describe, advantages, disadvantages, classify,* or *speculate.* They will give you clues as to the structure that your essay should follow.

4. Organize your thoughts on a sheet of paper. You will want to come up with a general topic sentence that expresses your main idea. Make sure this sentence addresses the question. You should then create an outline or some type of graphic organizer to help you organize the points that support your topic sentence.

5. Write your composition using complete sentences. Also, be sure to use correct grammar, spelling, punctuation, and sentence structure.

6. Be sure to proofread your essay once you have finished writing.

## Gearing Up for Math

On most standardized tests you will be asked to solve a variety of mathematical problems that draw on the skills and information you have learned in class. If math problems sometimes give you difficulty, have a look at the tips below to help you work through the problems.

### Tips for Solving Math Problems

1. Decide what is the goal of the question. Read or study the problem carefully and determine what information must be found.

2. Locate the factual information. Decide what information represents key facts—the ones you must have to solve the problem. You may also find facts you do not need to reach your solution. In some cases, you may determine that more information is needed to solve the problem. If so, ask yourself, "What assumptions can I make about this problem?" or "Do I need a formula to help solve this problem?"

3. Decide what strategies you might use to solve the problem, how you might use them, and what form your solution will be in. For example, will you need to create a graph or chart? Will you need to solve an equation? Will your answer be in words or numbers? By knowing what type of solution you should reach, you may be able to eliminate some of the choices.

4. Apply your strategy to solve the problem and compare your answer to the choices.

5. If the answer is still not clear, read the problem again. If you had to make calculations to reach your answer, use estimation to see if your answer makes sense.

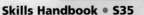

# UNIT 1

# Exploring Our World

Iceberg in sea ice, Antarctica

Carnival parade in Valletta, Malta

## A Physical Geographer in Mountain Environments

*Professor Francisco Pérez studies tropical mountain environments. He is interested in the natural processes, plants, and environments of mountains.* **WHAT DO YOU THINK?** *What faraway places would you like to study?*

Rosette plants, Ecuador

I became attracted to mountains when I was a child. While crossing the Atlantic Ocean in a ship, I saw snow-capped Teide Peak in the Canary Islands rising from the water. It was an amazing sight.

As a physical geographer, I am interested in the unique environments of high mountain areas. This includes geological history, climate, and soils. The unusual conditions of high mountain environments have influenced plant evolution. Plants and animals that live on separate mountains sometimes end up looking similar. This happens because they react to their environments in similar ways. For example, several types of tall, weird-looking plants called giant rosettes grow in the Andes, Hawaii, East Africa, and the Canary Islands. Giant rosettes look like the top of a pineapple at the end of a tall stem.

I have found other strange plants, such as rolling mosses. Mosses normally grow on rocks. However, if a moss plant falls to the ground, ice crystals on the soil surface lift the moss. This allows it to "roll" downhill while it continues to grow in a ball shape!

I like doing research in mountains. They are some of the least explored regions of our planet. Like most geographers, I cannot resist the attraction of strange landscapes in remote places.

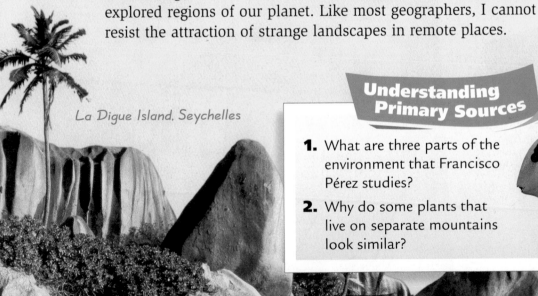
La Digue Island, Seychelles

## Understanding Primary Sources

**1.** What are three parts of the environment that Francisco Pérez studies?

**2.** Why do some plants that live on separate mountains look similar?

Sturgeonfish

# CHAPTER 1

# A Geographer's World

Chart of the
Mediterranean
and Europe, 1559

Hand-held compass

GPS (global
positioning
satellite)
receiver

# Section 1

## Developing a Geographic Eye

### Read to Discover

1. What role does perspective play in the study of geography?
2. What are some issues or topics that geographers study?
3. At what three levels can geographers view the world?

### Define

perspective
spatial perspective
geography
urban
rural

**WHY IT MATTERS**

What factors would you consider if you were moving to a new town or city? You would probably want to know about its geography. Use **CNN fyi.com** or other **current events** sources to investigate a place you might like to live. Record your findings in your journal.

*World map, 1598*

## Perspectives

People look at the world in different ways. Their experiences shape the way they understand the world. This personal understanding is called **perspective**. Your perspective is your point of view. A geographer's point of view looks at where something is and why it is there. This point of view is known as **spatial perspective**. Geographers apply this perspective when they study the arrangement of towns in a state. They might also use this perspective to examine the movement of cars and trucks on busy roads.

Geographers also work to understand how things are connected. Some connections are easy to see, like highways that link cities. Other connections are harder to see. For example, a dry winter in Colorado could mean that farms as far away as northern Mexico will not have enough water.

**Geography** is a science. It describes the physical and cultural features of Earth. Studying geography is important. Geographically informed people can see meaning in the arrangement of things on Earth. They know how people and places are related. Above all, they can apply a spatial perspective to real life. In other words, people familiar with geography can understand the world around them.

This fish-eye view of a large city shows highway patterns.

▼

✓ **READING CHECK:** *The World in Spatial Terms* What role does perspective play in the study of geography?

The movement of people is one issue that geographers study. For example, political and economic troubles led many Albanians to leave their country in 1991. Many packed onto freighters like this one for the trip. Geographers want to know how this movement affects the environment and other people.

**Interpreting the Visual Record** **How do you think Albania has been affected by so many people leaving the country?**

## Geographic Issues

Issues geographers study include Earth's processes and their impact on people. Geographers study the relationship between people and environment in different places. For example, geographers study tornadoes to find ways to reduce loss of life and property damage. They ask how people prepare for tornadoes. Do they prepare differently in different places? When a tornado strikes, how do people react?

Geographers also study how governments change and how those changes affect people. Czechoslovakia, for example, split into Slovakia and the Czech Republic in 1993. These types of political events affect geographic boundaries. People react differently to these changes. Some people are forced to move. Others welcome the change.

Other issues geographers study include religions, diet (or food), **urban** areas, and **rural** areas. Urban areas contain cities. Rural areas contain open land that is often used for farming.

✔ READING CHECK: ( *The Uses of Geography* ) What issues or topics do geographers study?

## Local, Regional, and Global Geographic Studies

With any topic, geographers must decide how large an area to study. They can focus their study at a local, regional, or global level.

**Local** Studying your community at the local, or close-up, level will help you learn geography. You know where homes and stores are located. You know how to find parks, ball fields, and other fun places. Over time, you see your community change. New buildings are constructed. People move in and out of your neighborhood. New stores open their doors, and others go out of business.

**Regional** Regional geographers organize the world into convenient parts for study. For example, this book separates the world into big areas like Africa and Europe. Regional studies cover larger areas than local studies. Some regional studies might look at connections like highways and rivers. Others might examine the regional customs.

**Global** Geographers also work to understand global issues and the connections between events. For example, many countries depend on oil from Southwest Asia. If those oil supplies are threatened, some countries might rush to secure oil from other areas. Oil all over the world could then become much more expensive.

The southwest is a region within the United States. One well-known place that characterizes the landscape of the southwest is the Grand Canyon. The Grand Canyon is shown in the photo at left and in the satellite image at right.

✓ **READING CHECK:** _The World in Spatial Terms_ What levels do geographers use to focus their study of an issue or topic?

**go.hrw.com**
**Homework Practice Online**
Keyword: SK3 HP1

## Section Review 1

**Define and explain:** perspective, spatial perspective, geography, urban, rural

### Reading for the Main Idea

1. _The Uses of Geography_ How can a spatial perspective be used to study the world?
2. _The Uses of Geography_ Why is it important to study geography?

### Critical Thinking

3. **Drawing Inferences and Conclusions** How do threatening weather patterns affect people, and why do geographers study these patterns?

4. **Drawing Inferences and Conclusions** Why is it important to view geography on a global level?

### Organizing What You Know

5. **Finding the Main Idea** Copy the following graphic organizer. Use it to examine the issues geographers study. Write a paragraph on one of these issues.

Issues geographers study

# Section 2  Themes and Essential Elements

## Read to Discover

1. What tools do geographers use to study the world?
2. What shapes Earth's features?
3. How do humans shape the world?
4. How does studying geography help us understand the world?

## Define

absolute location
relative location
subregions
diffusion
levees

*Tombs carved out of a mountain in Turkey*

### WHY IT MATTERS

Geographers often study the effect that new people have on a place. Use CNNfyi.com or other **current events** sources to find out how the arrival of new people has changed the United States or another country. Record your findings in your journal.

▲
The location of a place can be described in many ways.

**Interpreting the Visual Record** Looking at the photo of this hotel in Giza, Egypt, and at the map, how would you describe Giza's location?

## Themes

The study of geography has long been organized according to five important themes, or topics of study. One theme, *location*, deals with the exact or relative spot of something on Earth. *Place* includes the physical and human features of a location. *Human-environment interaction* covers the ways people and environments affect each other. *Movement* involves how people change locations and how goods are traded, as well as the effects of these movements. *Region* organizes Earth into geographic areas with one or more shared characteristics.

✓ **READING CHECK:** *The Uses of Geography* What are the five themes of geography?

## Six Essential Elements

Another way to look at geography is to study its essential elements, or most important parts. The six essential elements used to study geography are The World in Spatial Terms, Places and Regions, Physical Systems, Human Systems, Environment and Society, and The Uses of Geography. These six essential elements will be used throughout this textbook. They share many properties with the five themes of geography.

## Location
**Every place on Earth has a location. Location is defined by absolute and relative location.**

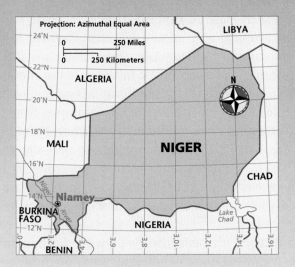

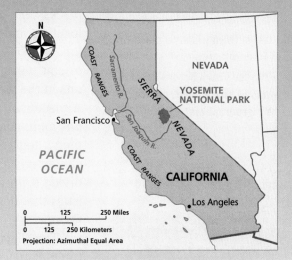

**Absolute Location:** the exact spot on Earth where something is found

**Example:** Niamey, the capital of Niger, is located at 13°31′ north latitude and 2°07′ east longitude.

**Relative Location:** the position of a place in relation to other places

**Example:** Yosemite National Park is north of Los Angeles, California, and east of San Francisco, California.

**You Be the Geographer**

1. Use an atlas to find the absolute location of your city or town.
2. Write a sentence describing the relative location of your home.

**The World in Spatial Terms** This element focuses on geography's spatial perspective. As you learned in Section 1, geographers apply spatial perspective when they look at the location of something and why it is there. The term *location* can be used in two ways. **Absolute location** defines an exact spot on Earth. For example, the address of the Smithsonian American Art Museum is an absolute location. The address is at 8th and G Streets, N.W., in Washington, D.C. City streets often form a grid. This system tells anyone looking for an address where to go. The grid formed by latitude and longitude lines also pinpoints absolute location. Suppose you asked a pilot to take you to 52° north latitude by 175° west longitude. You would land at a location on Alaska's Aleutian Islands.

**Relative location** describes the position of a place in relation to another place. Measurements of direction, distance, or time can define relative location. For example, the following sentences give relative location. "The hospital is one mile north of our school." "Canada's border is about an hour's drive from Great Falls, Montana."

A geographer must be able to use maps and other geographic tools and technologies to determine spatial perspective. A geographer must

Places can be described by what they do not have. This photo shows the result of a long period without rain.

also know how to organize and analyze information about people, places, and environments using geographic tools.

**Places and Regions** Our world has a vast number of unique places and regions. Places can be described both by their physical location and by their physical and human features. Physical features include coastlines and landforms. They can also include lakes, rivers, or soil types. For example, Colorado is flat in the east but mountainous in the west. This is an example of a landform description of place. A place can also be described by its climate. For example, Greenland has long, cold winters. Florida has mild winters and hot, humid summers. Regions are areas of Earth's surface with one or more shared characteristics. To study a region more closely, geographers often divide it into smaller areas called **subregions**. Many of the characteristics that describe places can also be used to describe regions or subregions.

The Places and Regions element also deals with the human features of places and regions. Geographers want to know how people have created regions based on Earth's features and how culture and other factors affect how we see places and regions on Earth.

**Physical Systems** Physical systems shape Earth's features. Geographers study earthquakes, mountains, rivers, volcanoes, weather patterns, and similar topics and how these physical systems have affected Earth's characteristics. For example, geographers might study how volcanic eruptions in the Hawaiian Islands spread lava, causing landforms to change. They might note that southern California's shoreline changes yearly, as winter and summer waves move beach sand.

Geographers also study how plants and animals relate to these nonliving physical systems. For example, deserts are places with cactus and other plants, as well as rattlesnakes and other reptiles, that can

People travel from place to place on miles of new roadway.
**Interpreting the Visual Record** **What other forms of human systems are studied by geographers?**

▼

Men in rural Egypt wear a long shirt called a *galabia*. This loose-fitting garment is ideal for people living in Egypt's hot desert climate. In addition, the galabia is made from cotton, an important agricultural product of Egypt.
**Interpreting the Visual Record** **How does the *galabia* show how people have adapted to their environment?**

▶

live in very dry conditions. Geographers also study how different types of plants, animals, and physical systems are distributed on Earth.

**Human Systems** People are central to geography. Our activities, movements, and settlements shape Earth's surface. Geographers study peoples' customs, history, languages, and religions. They study how people migrate, or move, and how ideas are communicated. When people move, they may go to live in other countries or move within a country. Geographers want to know how and why people move from place to place.

People move for many reasons. Some move to start a new job. Some move to attend special schools. Others might move to be closer to family. People move either when they are pushed out of a place or when they are pulled toward another place. In the Dust Bowl, for example, crop failures pushed people out of Oklahoma in the 1930s. Many were pulled to California by their belief that they would find work there. Geographers also want to know how ideas or behaviors move from one region to another. The movement of ideas occurs through communication. There are many ways to communicate. People visit with each other in person or on the phone. New technology allows people to communicate by e-mail. Ideas are also spread through films, magazines, newspapers, radio, and television. The movement of ideas or behaviors from one region to another is known as **diffusion**.

The things we produce and trade are also part of the study of human systems. Geographers study trading patterns and how countries depend on each other for certain goods. In addition, geographers look at the causes and results of conflicts between peoples. The study of governments we set up and the features of cities and other settlements we live in are also part of this study.

**Environment and Society** Geographers study how people and their surroundings affect each other. Their relationship can be examined in three ways. First, geographers study how humans depend on

A satellite dish brings different images and ideas to people in a remote area of Brazil.
**Interpreting the Visual Record How might resources have affected the use of technology here?**

This woman at a railway station in Russian Siberia sells some goods that were once unavailable in her country.
**Interpreting the Visual Record Which essential element is illustrated in this photo?**

Open-air markets like this one in Mali provide opportunities for farmers to sell their goods.

their physical environment to survive. Human life requires certain living and nonliving resources, such as freshwater and fertile soil for farming.

Geographers also study how humans change their behavior to be better suited to an environment. These changes or adaptations include the kinds of clothing, food, and shelter that people create. These changes help people live in harsh climates.

Finally, humans change the environment. For example, farmers who irrigate their fields can grow fruit in Arizona's dry climate. People in Louisiana have built **levees**, or large walls, to protect themselves when the Mississippi River floods.

**The Uses of Geography** Geography helps us understand the relationships among people, places, and the environment over time. Understanding how a relationship has developed can help in making plans for the future. For example, geographers can study how human use of the soil in a farming region has affected that region over time. Such knowledge can help them determine what changes have been made to the soil and whether any corrective measures need to be taken.

✓ **READING CHECK:** *The Uses of Geography* What are the six essential elements in studying geography?

# Section Review 2

**Define and explain:** absolute location, relative location, subregions, diffusion, levees

### Reading for the Main Idea

**1.** *The World in Spatial Terms* How do geographers study the world?

**2.** *Physical Systems* What shapes Earth's features? Give examples.

### Critical Thinking

**3. Finding the Main Idea** How do humans shape the world in which they live?

**4. Analyzing Information** What benefits can studying geography provide?

### Organizing What You Know

**5. Summarizing** Copy the following graphic organizer. Use it to identify and describe all aspects of each of the six essential elements.

| Element | Description |
| --- | --- |
|  |  |
|  |  |
|  |  |
|  |  |
|  |  |

# Section 3  The Branches of Geography

## Read to Discover

1. What is included in the study of human geography?
2. What is included in the study of physical geography?
3. What types of work do geographers do?

## Define

human geography
physical geography
cartography
meteorology
climatology

*Map of an ancient fortress*

### WHY IT MATTERS

Nearly every year, hurricanes hit the Atlantic or Gulf coasts of the United States. Predicting weather is one of the special fields of geography. Use CNNfyi.com or other **current events** sources to find out about hurricanes. Record your findings in your journal.

## Human Geography

The study of people, past or present, is the focus of **human geography**. People's location and distribution over Earth, their activities, and their differences are studied. For example, people living in different countries create different kinds of governments. Political geographers study those differences. Economic geographers study the exchange of goods and services across Earth. Cultural geography, population geography, and urban geography are some other examples of human geography. A professional geographer might specialize in any of these branches.

✓ **READING CHECK:** *Human Systems*  How is human geography defined?

A volunteer visits a poor area of Bangladesh. Geographers study economic conditions in regions to help them understand human geography.

## Physical Geography

The study of Earth's natural landscapes and physical systems, including the atmosphere, is the focus of **physical geography**. The world is full of different landforms such as deserts, mountains, and plains. Climates affect these landscapes. Knowledge of physical systems helps geographers understand how a landscape developed and how it might change.

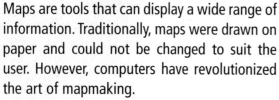

# CONNECTING TO *Technology*

*A mapmaker creates a digital map.*

Maps are tools that can display a wide range of information. Traditionally, maps were drawn on paper and could not be changed to suit the user. However, computers have revolutionized the art of mapmaking.

Today, mapmakers use computers to create and modify maps for different uses. They do this by using a geographic information system, or GIS. A GIS is a computer system that combines maps and satellite photographs with other kinds of spatial data—information about places on the planet. This information might include soil types, population figures, or voting patterns.

Using a GIS, mapmakers can create maps that show geographic features and relationships. For example, a map showing rainfall patterns in a particular region might be combined with data on soil types or human settlement to show areas of possible soil erosion.

The flexibility of a GIS allows people to seek answers to specific questions. Where should a new road be built to ease traffic congestion? How are changes in natural habitat affecting wildlife? These and many other questions can be answered with the help of computer mapping.

## Computer Mapping

### Understanding What You Read

1. How could a GIS help people change their environment?
2. What social, environmental, or economic consequences might future advances in GIS technology have?

Knowledge of physical and human geography will help you understand the world's different regions and peoples. In your study of the major world regions, you will see how physical and human geography connect to each other.

✓ **READING CHECK:** *Physical Systems* What is included in the study of physical geography?

## Working as a Geographer

Geography plays a role in almost every occupation. Wherever you live and work, you should know local geography. School board members know where children live. Taxi drivers are familiar with city streets. Grocery store managers know which foods sell well in certain areas.

They also know where they can obtain these products throughout the year. Local newspaper reporters are familiar with town meetings and local politicians. Reporters also know how faraway places can affect their communities. Doctors must know if their towns have poisonous snakes or plants. City managers know whether nearby rivers might flood. Emergency workers in mountain towns check snow depth so they can give avalanche warnings. Local weather forecasters watch for powerful storms and track their routes on special maps.

Some specially trained geographers practice in the field of **cartography**. Cartography is the art and science of mapmaking. Today, most mapmakers do their work on computers. Geographers also work as weather forecasters. The field of forecasting and reporting rainfall, temperature, and other atmospheric conditions is called **meteorology**. A related field is **climatology**. These geographers, known as climatologists, track Earth's larger atmospheric systems. Climatologists want to know how these systems change over long periods of time. They also study how people might be affected by changes in climate.

Governments and a variety of organizations hire geographers to study the environment. These geographers might explore such topics as pollution, endangered plants and animals, or rain forests. Some geographers who are interested in education become teachers and writers. They help people of all ages learn more about the world. Modern technology allows people all over the world to communicate instantly. Therefore, it is more important than ever to be familiar with the geographer's world.

▲

Experts examine snow to help forecast avalanches. They study the type of snow, weather conditions, and landforms. For example, wet snow avalanches can occur because of the formation of a particular type of ice crystal, called depth hoar, near the ground.

✓ **READING CHECK:** *The Uses of Geography* What types of work do geographers perform?

go.hrw.com **Homework Practice Online**
Keyword: SK3 HP1

## Section Review 3

**Define and explain:** human geography, physical geography, cartography, meteorology, climatology

### Reading for the Main Idea

1. *Human Systems* What topics are included in the study of human geography?

2. *The Uses of Geography* How do people who study the weather use geography?

### Critical Thinking

3. **Finding the Main Idea** Why is it important to study physical geography?

4. **Making Generalizations and Predictions** How might future discoveries in the field of geography affect societies, world economies, or the environment?

### Organizing What You Know

5. **Categorizing** Copy the following graphic organizer. Use it to list geographers' professions and their job responsibilities.

| Cartographer | | |
|---|---|---|
| —makes maps | | |
| —studies maps | | |

**A Geographer's World • 13**

# Reviewing What You Know

## Building Vocabulary

On a separate sheet of paper, write sentences to define each of the following words.

1. perspective
2. spatial perspective
3. geography
4. urban
5. rural
6. absolute location
7. relative location
8. levees
9. diffusion
10. subregions
11. human geography
12. physical geography
13. cartography
14. meteorology
15. climatology

## Reviewing the Main Ideas

1. (*The World in Spatial Terms*) What are three ways to view geography? Give an example of when each type could be used.

2. (*The World in Spatial Terms*) What kind of directions would you give to indicate a place's absolute location? Its relative location?

3. (*Human Systems*) What is diffusion, and why is it important?

4. (*Places and Regions*) Why do geographers create subregions?

5. (*The World in Spatial Terms*) Why is cartography important? What types of jobs do geographers do?

## Understanding Environment and Society

### Land Use

You are on a committee that will decide whether to close a park near your school. One proposed use for the land is a building where after-school activities could be held. However, the park is the habitat of an endangered bird. Write a report describing consequences of the park closing. Then organize information from your report to create a proposal on what decision should be made.

## Thinking Critically

1. **Analyzing Information** How can a geographer use spatial perspective to explain how things in our world are connected?

2. **Drawing Inferences and Conclusions** When and how do humans relate to the environment? Provide some examples of this relationship.

3. **Summarizing** How are patterns created by the movement of goods, ideas, and people?

4. **Finding the Main Idea** How are places and regions defined?

5. **Finding the Main Idea** How does studying geography help us understand the world?

**Map** ACTIVITY

On a separate sheet of paper, match the letters on the map with their correct labels.

Africa                Europe
Antarctica        North America
Asia                   South America
Australia

## Mental Mapping Skills ACTIVITY

To help you understand the relationships between places, create a seating chart of your classroom. Then draw a sketch of the floor plan of your school. Discuss why certain areas are located in particular parts of the campus.

## WRITING ACTIVITY

Write a letter persuading another student to enroll in a geography class. Include examples of professions that use geography and relate that information to the everyday life of a student. Be sure to use standard grammar, spelling, sentence structure, and punctuation.

## Alternative Assessment

## Portfolio ACTIVITY

**Learning About Your Local Geography**

**Individual Project** How do you define your community geographically? Is your community the area around your home or school? Write two or three sentences defining your community to share with the class.

☑ internet connect

**Internet Activity: go.hrw.com**
**KEYWORD: SK3 GT1**

Choose a topic to explore online:
• Learn to use online maps.
• Be a virtual geographer for a day.
• Compare regions around the world.

# CHAPTER 2

# Planet Earth

Erupting volcano

Earth as seen from space

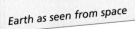

Fossilized shell

Galileo's telescope

Space observatory, Mauna Kea, Hawaii

# Section 1 — The Sun, Earth, and Moon

## Read to Discover

1. What objects make up the solar system?
2. What causes the seasons?
3. What are the four parts of the Earth system?

## Define

solar system
orbit
satellite
axis
rotation
revolution
Arctic Circle
Antarctic Circle
solstice
Tropic of Cancer
Tropic of Capricorn
equinoxes
atmosphere
ozone

### WHY IT MATTERS

In 2001 scientists labeled a rocky object beyond Pluto as the new largest minor planet. Use CNNfyi.com or other current events sources to discover more about this huge frozen rock, called 2001 KX76. Record your findings in your journal.

*Mechanical model of the solar system*

## The Solar System

The **solar system** consists of the Sun and the objects that move around it. The most important of those objects are the planets, their moons, and relatively small rocky bodies called asteroids. Our Sun is a star at the center of our solar system. Every object in the system travels around the Sun in an **orbit**, or path. These orbits are usually elliptical, or oval shaped.

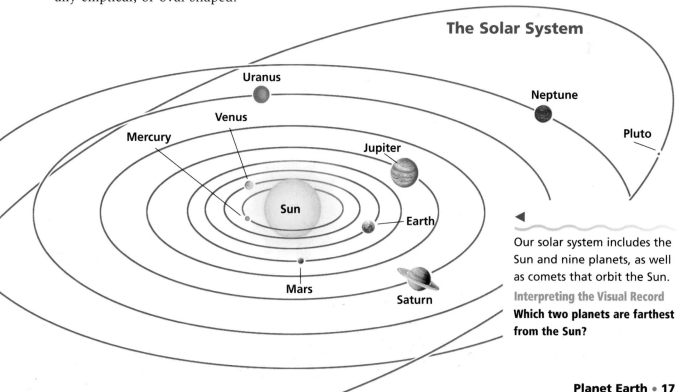

**The Solar System**

Uranus
Venus
Mercury
Neptune
Pluto
Jupiter
Sun
Earth
Mars
Saturn

Our solar system includes the Sun and nine planets, as well as comets that orbit the Sun.

**Interpreting the Visual Record**
**Which two planets are farthest from the Sun?**

Tides are higher than normal when the gravitational pull of the Moon and the Sun combine. These tides, called spring tides, occur twice a month. Tides are lower than normal during neap tides, when the Sun and the Moon are at right angles.

▼

The planet nearest the Sun is Mercury, followed by Venus, Earth, and Mars. Located beyond the orbit of Mars is a belt of asteroids. Beyond this asteroid belt are the planets Jupiter and Saturn. Even farther from the Sun are the planets Uranus, Neptune, and Pluto.

**The Moon**   Some of the planets in the solar system have more than one moon. Saturn, for example, has 18. Other planets have none. A moon is a **satellite**—a body that orbits a larger body. Earth has one moon, which is about one fourth the size of Earth. Our planet is also circled by artificial satellites that transmit signals for television, telephone, and computer communications. The Moon takes about 29½ days—roughly a month—to orbit Earth.

The Moon and Sun influence physical processes on Earth. This is because any two objects in space are affected by gravitational forces pulling them together. The gravitational effects of the Sun and the Moon cause tides in the oceans here on Earth.

**The Sun**   Compared to some other stars, our Sun is small. It is huge, however, when compared to Earth. Its diameter is about 100 times the diameter of our planet. The Sun appears larger to us than other stars. This is because it is much closer to us than other stars. The Sun is about 93 million miles (150 million km) from Earth. The next nearest star is about 25 trillion miles (40 trillion km) away.

Scientists are trying to learn if other planets in our solar system could support life. Mars seems to offer the best possibility. It is not clear, however, if life can, or ever did, exist on Mars.

✔ **READING CHECK:**   *Physical Systems*   What are the main objects that make up the solar system?

## Effects of the Moon and Sun on Tides

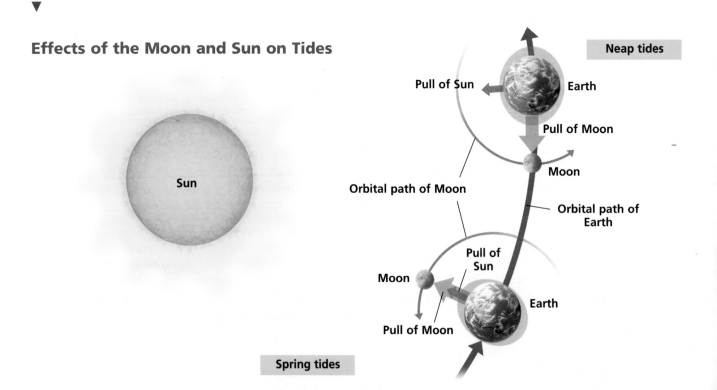

# Earth

Geographers are interested in how different places on Earth receive different amounts of energy from the Sun. Differences in solar energy help explain why the tropics are warm, why the Arctic region is cold, and why day is warmer than night. To understand these differences, geographers study Earth's rotation, revolution, and the tilt of its **axis**. The axis is an imaginary line that runs from the North Pole through Earth's center to the South Pole. Rotation, revolution, and tilt control the amount of solar energy reaching Earth.

**Rotation** One complete spin of Earth on its axis is called a **rotation**. Each rotation takes 24 hours, or one day. Earth turns on its axis, but to us it appears that the Sun is moving. The Sun seems to "rise" in the east and "set" in the west. Before scientists learned that Earth revolves around the Sun, people thought that the Sun revolved around Earth. They thought Earth was at the center of the heavens.

**Revolution** It takes a year for Earth to orbit the Sun, or to complete one **revolution**. More precisely, it takes 365¼ days. To allow for this fraction of a day and keep the calendar accurate, every fourth year becomes a leap year. An extra day—February 29—is added to the calendar.

**Tilt** The amount of the Sun's energy reaching different parts of Earth varies. This is because Earth's axis is not straight up and down. It is actually tilted, or slanted, at an angle of 23.5° from vertical to the plane of Earth's orbit. Because of Earth's tilt, the angle at which the Sun's rays strike the planet is constantly changing as Earth revolves around the Sun. For this reason, the point where the vertical rays of

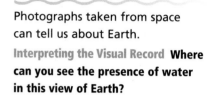

▲

Photographs taken from space can tell us about Earth.

**Interpreting the Visual Record** Where can you see the presence of water in this view of Earth?

**internet** connect

GO TO: go.hrw.com
KEYWORD: SK3 CH2
FOR: Web sites about planet Earth

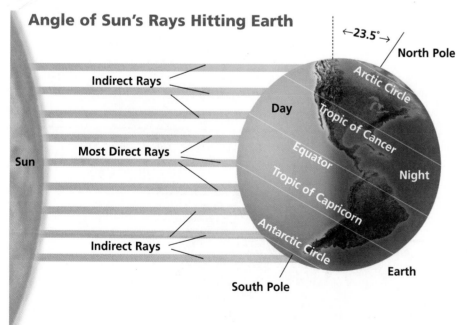

**Angle of Sun's Rays Hitting Earth**

←23.5°→

North Pole

Indirect Rays

Arctic Circle

Day

Tropic of Cancer

Sun

Most Direct Rays

Equator

Night

Tropic of Capricorn

Indirect Rays

Antarctic Circle

Earth

South Pole

◄

The tilt of Earth's axis and the position of the planet in its orbit determine where the Sun's rays will most directly strike the planet.

**Interpreting the Visual Record** Which areas of Earth receive only indirect rays from the Sun?

the Sun strike Earth shifts north and south of the equator. These vertical rays provide more energy than rays that strike at an angle.

✓ **READING CHECK:** ( *Physical Systems* ) How do rotation, revolution, and tilt affect solar energy reaching Earth?

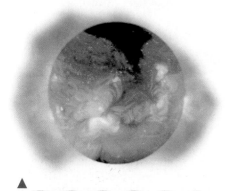

▲

The Sun's surface is always violently churning as heat flows outward from the interior.

# Solar Energy and Latitude

The angle at which the Sun's rays reach Earth affects temperature. In the tropics—areas in the low latitudes near the equator—the Sun's rays are nearly vertical throughout the year. In the polar regions—the areas near the North and South Poles—the Sun's rays are always at a low angle. As a result, the poles are generally the coldest places on Earth. The **Arctic Circle** is the line of latitude located 66.5° north of the equator. It circles the North Pole. The **Antarctic Circle** is the line of latitude located 66.5° south of the equator. It circles the South Pole.

As Earth revolves around the Sun, the tilt of the poles toward and away from the Sun causes the seasons to change.

Interpreting the Visual Record **At what point is the North Pole tilted toward the Sun?**

▼

# The Seasons

Each year is divided into periods of time called seasons. Each season is known for a certain type of weather, based on temperature and amount of precipitation. Winter, spring, summer, and fall are examples of seasons that are described by their average temperature. "Wet" and "dry" seasons are described by their precipitation. The seasons change as Earth orbits the Sun. As this happens, the amount of solar energy received in any given location changes.

## The Seasons

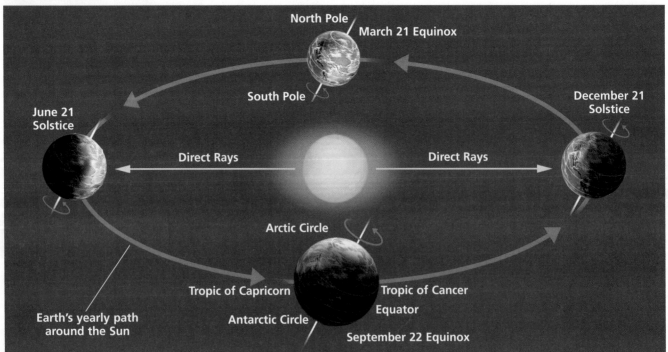

North Pole
March 21 Equinox
South Pole
December 21 Solstice
June 21 Solstice
Direct Rays
Direct Rays
Arctic Circle
Tropic of Capricorn
Tropic of Cancer
Equator
Earth's yearly path around the Sun
Antarctic Circle
September 22 Equinox

**Solstice** The day when the Sun's vertical rays are farthest from the equator is called a **solstice**. Solstices occur twice a year—about June 21 and about December 22. In the Northern Hemisphere the June solstice is known as the summer solstice. This is the longest day of the year and the beginning of summer. On this date the Sun's vertical rays strike Earth at the **Tropic of Cancer**. This is the line of latitude that is about 23.5° north of the equator. Six months later, about December 22, another solstice takes place. This is the winter solstice for the Northern Hemisphere. On this date the North Pole is pointed away from the Sun. The Northern Hemisphere experiences the shortest day of the year. On this date the Sun's rays strike Earth most directly at the **Tropic of Capricorn**. This line of latitude is about 23.5° south of the equator. In the Southern Hemisphere the seasons are reversed. June 21 is the winter solstice and December 22 is the summer solstice. The middle-latitude regions lie between the Tropic of Cancer and the Arctic Circle and between the Tropic of Capricorn and the Antarctic Circle.

**Equinox** Twice a year, halfway between summer and winter, Earth's poles are at right angles to the Sun. The Sun's rays strike the equator directly. On these days, called **equinoxes**, every place on Earth has 12 hours of day and 12 hours of night. Equinoxes mark the beginning of spring and fall. In the Northern Hemisphere the spring equinox occurs about March 21. The fall equinox occurs there about September 22. In the Southern Hemisphere the March equinox signals the beginning of fall, and the September equinox marks the beginning of spring.

Some regions on Earth, particularly in the tropics, have seasons tied to precipitation rather than temperature. Shifting wind patterns are one cause of seasonal change. For example, in January winds from the north bring dry air to India. By June the winds have shifted, coming from the southwest and bringing moisture from the Indian Ocean. These winds bring heavy rain to India. Some places in the United States also have seasons tied to moisture. East Coast states south of Virginia have a wet season in summer. These areas also have a hurricane season, lasting roughly from June to November. Some areas of the West Coast have a dry season in summer.

The seasons affect human activities. For example, in Minnesota, people shovel snow in winter to keep the walkways clear. Students waiting for a bus must wear warm clothes. The Sun rises late and sets early. As a result, people go to work and return home in darkness.

✓ **READING CHECK:** *Physical Systems* How do the seasons relate to the Sun's energy?

This map shows Earth's temperatures on January 28, 1997.

**Interpreting the Visual Record Which hemisphere is warmer in January?**

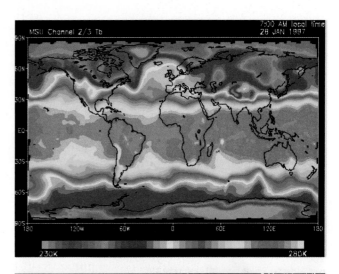

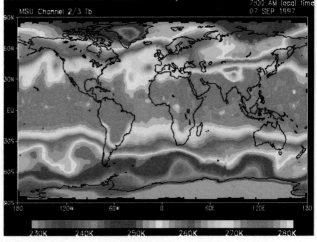

▲ This temperature map for September 7, 1997, shows summer in the Northern Hemisphere.

A **Atmosphere**  B **Biosphere**

L **Lithosphere**  H **Hydrosphere**

The interactions of the atmosphere, lithosphere, hydrosphere, and biosphere make up the Earth system.

**Interpreting the Visual Record** **Which items in this image are part of the hydrosphere?**

# The Earth System

Geographers need to be able to explain how and why places on Earth differ from each other. One way they do this is to study the interactions of forces and materials on the planet. Together, these forces and materials are known as the Earth system.

The Earth system has four parts: the **atmosphere**, the lithosphere, the hydrosphere, and the biosphere. The atmosphere is the layer of gases—the air—that surrounds Earth. These gases include nitrogen, oxygen, and carbon dioxide. The atmosphere also contains a form of oxygen called **ozone**. A layer of this gas helps protect Earth from harmful solar radiation. Another part of the Earth system is the lithosphere. The prefix *litho* means rock. The lithosphere is the solid, rocky outer layer of Earth, including the sea floor. The hydrosphere—*hydro* means water—consists of all of Earth's water, found in lakes, oceans, and glaciers. It also includes the moisture in the atmosphere. Finally, the biosphere—*bio* means life—is the part of the Earth system that includes all plant and animal life. It extends from high in the air to deep in the oceans.

By dividing Earth into these four spheres, geographers can better understand each part and how each affects the others. The different parts of the Earth system are constantly interacting in many ways. For example, a tree is part of the biosphere. However, to grow it needs to take in water, chemicals from the soil, and gases from the air.

✔ **READING CHECK:** ( *The World in Spatial Terms* ) What are the four parts of the Earth system?

go.hrw.com
**Homework Practice Online**
Keyword: SK3 HP2

**Define and explain:** solar system, orbit, satellite, axis, rotation, revolution, Arctic Circle, Antarctic Circle, solstice, Tropic of Cancer, Tropic of Capricorn, equinoxes, atmosphere, ozone .

**Reading for the Main Idea**

**1.** ( *Physical Systems* ) What are the major objects in the solar system?

**2.** ( *The World in Spatial Terms* ) What are the four parts of the Earth system?

**Critical Thinking**

**3. Summarizing** Which three things determine the amount of solar energy reaching places on Earth?

**4. Drawing Inferences and Conclusions** Why are the seasons reversed in the Northern and Southern Hemispheres?

**Organizing What You Know**

**5. Finding the Main Idea** Use this graphic organizer to explain solstice and equinox.

| Solstice | | Equinox |
|---|---|---|
| | ⇦⇨ | |

# Section 2  Water on Earth

## Read to Discover

1. Which processes make up the water cycle and how are they connected?
2. How is water distributed on Earth?
3. How does water affect people's lives?

## Define

water vapor
water cycle
evaporation
condensation

precipitation
tributary
groundwater

continental
shelf

### WHY IT MATTERS

Scientists study other parts of our solar system to find out if water exists or might have existed elsewhere. Use **CNNfyi.com** or other **current events** sources to learn more about space agencies and their searches to detect water. Record your findings in your journal.

*A limestone cavern*

## Characteristics of Water

Water has certain physical characteristics that influence Earth's geography. Water is the only substance on Earth that occurs naturally as a solid, a liquid, and a gas. We see water as a solid in snow and ice and as a liquid in lakes, oceans, and rivers. Water also occurs in the air as an invisible gas called **water vapor**.

Another characteristic of water is that it heats and cools slowly compared to land. Even on a very hot day, the ocean stays cool. A breeze blowing over the ocean brings cooler temperatures to shore. This keeps temperatures near the coast from getting as hot as they do farther inland. In winter the oceans cool more slowly than land. This generally keeps winters milder in coastal areas.

✓ **READING CHECK:** ( *Physical Systems* ) What are some important characteristics of water?

## The Water Cycle

The circulation of water from Earth's surface to the atmosphere and back is called the **water cycle**. The total amount of water on the planet does not change. Water, however, does change its form and its location.

Water rushes through the Stewart Mountain Dam in Arizona.

## The Water Cycle

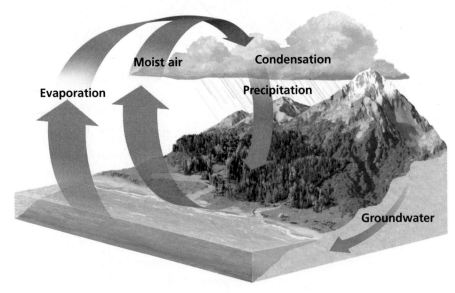

Moist air

Condensation

Evaporation

Precipitation

Groundwater

The circulation of water from one part of the hydrosphere to another depends on energy from the Sun. Water evaporates, condenses, and falls to Earth as precipitation.

Interpreting the Visual Record **How would a seasonal increase in the amount of the Sun's energy received by an area change the water cycle in that area?**

The Sun's energy drives the water cycle. **Evaporation** occurs when the Sun heats water on Earth's surface. The heated water evaporates, becoming water vapor and rising into the air. Energy from the Sun also causes winds to carry the water vapor to new locations. As the water vapor rises, it cools, causing **condensation**. This is the process by which water changes from a gas into tiny liquid droplets. These droplets join together to form clouds. If the droplets become heavy enough, **precipitation** occurs—that is, the water falls back to Earth. This water can be in the form of rain, hail, sleet, or snow. The entire cycle of evaporation, condensation, and precipitation repeats itself endlessly.

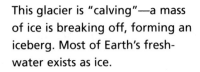
**READING CHECK:** ( *Physical Systems* ) What is the water cycle?

This glacier is "calving"—a mass of ice is breaking off, forming an iceberg. Most of Earth's freshwater exists as ice.

## Geographic Distribution of Water

The oceans contain about 97 percent of Earth's water. About another 2 percent is found in the ice sheets of Antarctica, the Arctic, Greenland, and mountain glaciers. Approximately 1 percent is found in lakes, streams, rivers, and under the ground.

Earth's freshwater resources are not evenly distributed. There are very dry places with no signs of water. Other places have many lakes and rivers. In the United States, for example, Minnesota is dotted with more than 11,000 lakes. Dry states such as Nevada have few natural lakes. In many dry places rivers have been dammed to create artificial lakes called reservoirs.

**Surface Water** Water sometimes collects at high elevations, where rivers begin their flow down toward the lowlands and coasts. The first and smallest streams that form from this runoff are called headwaters. When these headwaters meet and join, they form larger streams. In turn, these streams join with other streams to form rivers. Any smaller stream or river that flows into a larger stream or river is a **tributary**. For example, the Missouri River is an important tributary of the Mississippi River, into which it flows near St. Louis, Missouri.

Lakes are usually formed when rivers flow into basins and fill them with water. Most lakes are freshwater, but some are salty. For example, the Great Salt Lake in Utah receives water from the Bear, Jordan, and Weber Rivers but has no outlet. Because the air is dry here, the rate of evaporation is very high. When the lake water evaporates, it leaves behind salts and minerals, making the lake salty.

**Groundwater** Not all surface water immediately returns to the atmosphere through evaporation. Some water from rainfall, rivers, lakes, and melting snow seeps into the ground. This **groundwater** seeps down until all the spaces between soil and grains of rock are filled. In some places, groundwater bubbles out of the ground as a spring. Many towns in the United States get their water from wells—deep holes dug down to reach the groundwater. Motorized pumps allow people to draw water from very deep underground.

**Oceans** Most of Earth's water is found in the oceans. The Pacific, Atlantic, Indian, and Arctic Oceans connect with each other. This giant body of water covers some 71 percent of Earth's surface. These oceans also include smaller regions called seas and gulfs. The Gulf of Mexico and the Gulf of Alaska are two examples of smaller ocean areas.

Surrounding each continent is a zone of shallow ocean water. This gently sloping underwater land—called the **continental shelf**—is important to marine life. Although the oceans are huge, marine life is concentrated in these shallow areas. Deeper ocean water is home to fewer organisms. Overall, the oceans average about 12,000 feet (about 3,700 m) in depth. The deepest place is the Mariana Trench in the Pacific Ocean, at about 36,000 feet (about 11,000 m) deep.

✓ **READING CHECK:** *The World in Spatial Terms* How is water distributed on Earth?

## Groundwater

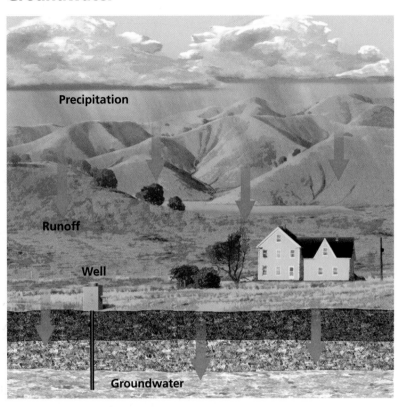

In some areas where rainfall is scarce, enough groundwater exists to support agriculture.

**Interpreting the Visual Record** **How do people gain access to groundwater?**

## The Continental Shelf

The continental shelf slopes gently away from the continents. The ocean floor drops steeply at the edge of the shelf.

## Water Issues

Water plays an important part in our survival. As a result, water issues frequently show up in the news. Thunderstorms, particularly when accompanied by hail or tornadoes, can damage buildings and ruin crops. Droughts also can be deadly. In the mountains, heavy snowfalls sometimes cause deadly snow slides called avalanches. Heavy fog can make driving or flying dangerous. Geographers are concerned with these issues. They work on ways to better prepare for natural hazards.

**Floods** Water can both support and threaten life. Heavy rains can cause floods, which are the world's deadliest natural hazard. Floods kill four out of every ten people who die from natural disasters, including hurricanes, earthquakes, tornadoes, and thunderstorms.

Some floods occur in dry places when strong thunderstorms drop a large amount of rain very quickly. The water races along on the hard, dry surface instead of soaking into the ground. This water can quickly gather in low places. Creekbeds that are normally dry can suddenly surge with rushing water. People and livestock are sometimes caught in these flash floods.

Floods also happen in low-lying places next to rivers and on coastlines. Too much rain or snowmelt entering a river can cause the water to overflow the banks. Powerful storms, particularly hurricanes, can sometimes cause ocean waters to surge into coastal areas. Look at a

This kelp forest is off the coast of southern California. The shallower parts of the oceans are home to many plants and animals.

Davenport, Iowa, suffered severe flooding in 1993. Many cities are located along rivers even though there is a danger of floods.

**Interpreting the Visual Record** Why are many cities located next to rivers?

map of the United States. You will see that most major cities are located either next to a river or along a coast. For this reason, floods can be a threat to lives and property.

**Flood Control** Dams are a means people use to control floods. The huge Hoover Dam on the Colorado River in the United States is one example. The Aswān Dam on the Nile River in Egypt and those on the Murray River in Australia are others. Dams help protect people from floods. They also store water for use during dry periods. However, dams prevent rivers from bringing soil nutrients to areas downstream. Sometimes farming is not as productive as it was before the dams were built.

**Clean Water** The availability of clean water is another issue affecting the world's people. Not every country is able to provide clean water for drinking and bathing. Pollution also threatens the health of the world's oceans—particularly in the shallower seabeds where many fish live and reproduce.

**Water Supply** Finding enough water to meet basic needs is a concern in regions that are naturally dry. The water supply is the amount of water available for use in a region. It limits the number of living things that can survive in a place. People in some countries have to struggle each day to find enough water.

✓ **READING CHECK:** *Environment and Society* What are some ways in which water affects people?

▲

The Atatürk Dam in Turkey is 604 feet (184 m) high.

**Interpreting the Visual Record** **How have people used dams to change their physical environment?**

## Section Review 2

**Define and explain:** water vapor, water cycle, evaporation, condensation, precipitation, tributary, groundwater, continental shelf

### Reading for the Main Idea

1. *Physical Systems* What are the steps in the water cycle?

2. *Environment and Society* What are some major issues related to water?

### Critical Thinking

3. **Analyzing Information** What are some important characteristics of water?

4. **Finding the Main Idea** Why is water supply a problem in some areas?

### Organizing What You Know

5. **Sequencing** Copy the following graphic organizer. Use it to explain the water cycle.

☐ ⇨ ☐ ⇨ ☐ ⇨ ☐ ⇨ ☐

**Read to Discover**

1. What are primary landforms?
2. What are secondary landforms?
3. How do humans interact with landforms?

**Define**

| | | | |
|---|---|---|---|
| landforms | core | subduction | alluvial fan |
| plain | mantle | earthquakes | floodplain |
| plateau | crust | fault | deltas |
| isthmus | magma | Pangaea | glaciers |
| peninsula | lava | weathering | |
| plate tectonics | continents | erosion | |

**WHY IT MATTERS**

Earth's surface has been the focus of scientific research for centuries. Use CNN fyi.com logo or other current events sources to explore how scientists use maps to study the surface of Earth and other planets. Record your findings in your journal.

*Mount Saint Helens, in southern Washington State*

## Landforms

**Landforms** are shapes on Earth's surface. One common landform is a **plain**—a nearly flat area. A **plateau** is an elevated flatland. An **isthmus** is a neck of land connecting two larger land areas. A **peninsula** is land bordered by water on three sides.

## Primary Landforms

The theory of **plate tectonics** helps explain how forces raise, lower, and roughen Earth's surface. According to this theory, Earth's surface is divided into several large plates, or pieces. There are also many smaller plates. The plates slowly move. Some plates are colliding. Some are moving apart. Others are sliding by each other. Landforms created by tectonic processes are called primary landforms. These include masses of rock raised by volcanic eruptions and deep ocean trenches. The energy that moves the tectonic plates comes from inside Earth. The inner, solid **core** of the planet is surrounded by a liquid layer called the **mantle**. The outer, solid layer of Earth is called the **crust**. Currents of heat from the core travel outward through the mantle. When the currents reach the upper mantle, rocks can melt to form **magma**.

Earth's thin crust floats on top of the liquid mantle.

**The Interior of Earth**

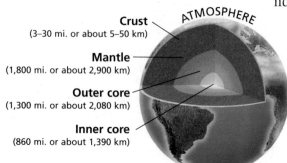

**Crust**
(3–30 mi. or about 5–50 km)

**Mantle**
(1,800 mi. or about 2,900 km)

**Outer core**
(1,300 mi. or about 2,080 km)

**Inner core**
(860 mi. or about 1,390 km)

ATMOSPHERE

## Plate Tectonics

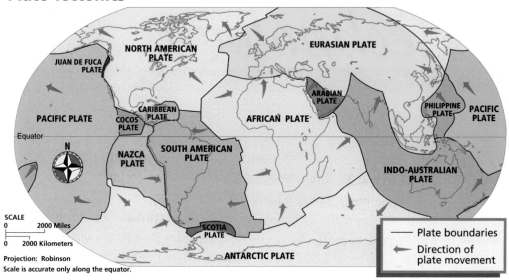

The plates that make up Earth's crust are moving, usually a few inches per year. This map shows the plates and the direction of their movement.

Magma sometimes breaks through the crust to form a volcano. After reaching Earth's surface, magma is called **lava**.

Plates cover Earth's entire surface, both the land and the ocean. In general, the plates under the oceans are made of dense rock. The plates on the **continents**—Earth's large landmasses—are made of lighter rock.

**Plates Colliding** When two plates collide, one plate can be pushed under another. When this occurs under the ocean, a very deep trench is sometimes created. This is happening near Japan, where the Pacific plate is slowly moving under the Eurasian and Philippine plates. Any time a heavier plate moves under a lighter one, trenches can form. This process is called **subduction**. **Earthquakes** are common in subduction zones. An earthquake is a sudden, violent movement along a fracture within Earth's crust. A series of shocks usually results from such a movement within the crust.

The borders of the Pacific plate move against neighboring plates. This causes volcanoes to erupt and earthquakes to strike in that area. The Pacific plate's edge has been called the Ring of Fire because it is rimmed by active volcanoes. Thousands of people have died and terrible destruction has resulted from the earthquakes and volcanoes there.

When a continental plate and an ocean plate collide, the lighter rocks of the continent do not sink. Instead, they crumple and form a mountain range. The Andes in South America were formed this way. When two continental plates collide, land is lifted, sometimes to great heights. The Himalayas, the world's highest mountain range, were created by the Indo-Australian plate pushing into the Eurasian plate.

### Subduction and Spreading

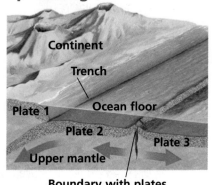

Where Plate 2 pushes under Plate 1, a deep trench forms. This process is called subduction. Where Plates 2 and 3 move apart, lava creates a mid-ocean ridge.

### Plates Colliding

Where two continental plates collide, Earth's crust is pushed upward, forming a mountain range.

# CONNECTING TO *Technology*

Since ancient times, people have tried to forecast earthquakes. A Chinese inventor even created a device to register earthquakes as early as A.D. 132.

The theory of plate tectonics gives modern-day scientists a better understanding of how and why earthquakes occur. Earthquake scientists, known as seismologists, have many tools to help them monitor movements in Earth's crust. They try to understand when and where earthquakes will occur.

The most common of these devices is the seismograph. It measures seismic waves—vibrations produced when two tectonic plates grind against each other. Scientists believe that an increase in seismic activity may signal a coming earthquake.

## forecasting earthquakes

*A scientist with a seismograph*

Other devices show shifts in Earth's crust. Tiltmeters measure the rise of tectonic plates along a fault line. Gravimeters record changes in gravitational strength caused by rising or falling land. Laser beams can detect lateral movements along a fault line. Satellites can note the movement of entire tectonic plates.

Scientists have yet to learn how to forecast earthquakes with accuracy. Nevertheless, their ongoing work may one day provide important breakthroughs in the science of earthquake forecasting.

**You Be the Geographer**
1. What social and economic consequences might earthquake forecasting have?
2. What technology has helped with earthquake forecasting?

**Plates Moving Apart** When two plates move away from each other, hot lava emerges from the gap that has been formed. The lava builds a mid-ocean ridge—a landform that is similar to an underwater mountain range. This process is currently occurring in the Atlantic Ocean where the Eurasian plate and the North American plate are moving away from each other.

**Plates Sliding** Tectonic plates can also slide past each other. Earthquakes occur from sudden adjustments in Earth's crust. In California the Pacific plate is sliding northwestward along the edge of the North American plate. This has created the San Andreas Fault zone. A **fault** is a fractured surface in Earth's crust where a mass of rocks is in motion.

Tectonic plates move slowly—just inches a year. If, however, we could look back 200 million years, we would see that the continents have moved a long way. From their understanding of plate tectonics, scientists proposed the theory of continental drift. This theory states that the continents were once united in a single super-continent. They then separated and moved to the positions they are in today. Scientists call this original landmass **Pangaea** (pan-GEE-uh).

## Continental Drift

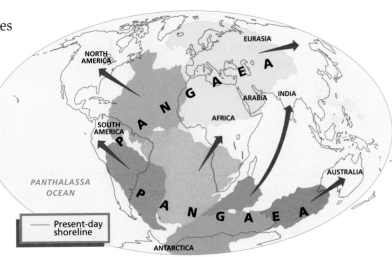

✔ **READING CHECK:** ( *Physical Systems* ) How are primary landforms formed?

About 200 million years ago it is believed there was only one conti-nent, Pangaea, and one ocean, Panthalassa. The continental plates slowly drifted into their present-day positions.

## Secondary Landforms

The forces of plate tectonics build up primary landforms. At the same time, water, wind, and ice constantly break down rocks and cause rocky material to move. The landforms that result when primary land-forms are broken down are called secondary landforms.

One process of breaking down and changing primary landforms into secondary landforms is called **weathering**. It is the process of breaking rocks into smaller pieces. Weathering occurs in several ways. Heat can cause rocks to crack. Water may get into cracks in rocks and freeze. This ice then expands with a force great enough to break the rock. Water can also work its way underground and slowly dissolve minerals such as limestone. This process sometimes creates caves. In

These steep peaks in Chile are part of the Andes.

**Interpreting the Visual Record How do these mountains show the effects of weathering and erosion?**

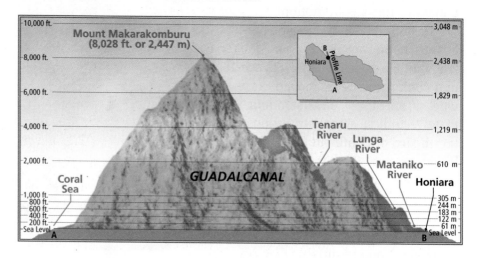

## ▶ Elevation Profile: Guadalcanal

Elevation is the height of the land above sea level. An elevation profile is a cross-section used to show the elevation of a specific area.

**Interpreting the Visual Record** What is the range of elevation for Guadalcanal?

some areas small plants called lichens attach to bare rock. Chemicals in the lichens gradually break down the stone. Some places in the world experience large swings in temperature. In the Arctic the ground freezes and thaws, which tends to lift stones to the surface in unusual patterns. Regardless of which weathering process is at work, rocks eventually break down into sediment. These smaller pieces of rock are called gravel, sand, silt, or clay, depending on particle size. Once weathering has taken place, water, ice, or wind can move the material and create new landforms.

✓ **READING CHECK:** *Physical Systems* What is one way in which secondary landforms are created?

## Erosion

Another process of changing primary landforms into secondary landforms is **erosion**. Erosion is the movement of rocky materials to another location. Moving water is the most common force that erodes and shapes the land.

River water, brown with sediment, enters the ocean.

▼

**Water** Flowing water carries sediment. This sediment forms different kinds of landforms depending on where it is deposited. For example, a river flowing from a mountain range onto a flat area, or plain, may deposit some of its sediment there. The sediment sometimes builds up into a fan-shaped form called an **alluvial fan**. A **floodplain** is created when rivers flood their banks and deposit sediment. A **delta** is formed when rivers carry some of their sediment all the way to the ocean. The sediment settles to the bottom where the river meets the ocean. The Nile and Mississippi Rivers have two of the world's largest deltas.

Waves in the ocean and in lakes also shape the land they touch. Waves can shape beaches into great dunes, such as on the shore of Long Island. The jagged coastline of Oregon also shows the erosive power of waves.

**Glaciers** In high mountain settings and in the coldest places on Earth are **glaciers**. These large, slow-moving rivers of ice have the power to move tons of rock.

Giant sheets of thick ice called continental glaciers cover Greenland and Antarctica. Earth has experienced several ice ages—periods of extreme cold. During the last ice age glaciers covered most of Canada and the northern United States. This ice age, which began about 2 million years ago and ended about 10,000 years ago, was broken up by warmer periods when the glaciers retreated. The Great Lakes were carved out by the movement of a continental glacier.

**Wind** Wind also shapes the land. Strong winds can lift soils into the air and carry them across great distances. On beaches and in deserts wind can deposit large amounts of sand to form dunes.

Blowing sand can wear down rock. The sand acts like sandpaper to polish jagged edges. An example of rocks worn down by blowing sand can be seen in Utah's Canyonlands National Park.

✓ **READING CHECK:** *Physical Systems* What forces cause erosion?

*Our Amazing Planet*

**W**aves 50 to 60 feet high, which the local people call Jaws, sometimes occur off the coast of Maui, Hawaii. They are caused by storms in the north Pacific and a high offshore ridge that focuses the waves' energy.

# People and Landforms

Geographers study how people adapt their lives to different landforms. Deltas and floodplains, for example, are usually fertile places to grow food. People also change landforms. Engineers build dams to control river flooding. They drill tunnels through mountains instead of making roads over mountaintops. People have used modern technology to build structures that are better able to survive disasters like floods and earthquakes.

✓ **READING CHECK:** *Environment and Society* What are some examples of humans adjusting to and changing landforms?

go.hrw.com **Homework Practice Online** Keyword: SK3 HP2

## Section Review 3

**Define and explain:** landforms, plain, plateau, isthmus, peninsula, plate tectonics, core, mantle, crust, magma, lava, continents, subduction, earthquakes, fault, Pangaea, weathering, erosion, alluvial fan, floodplain, deltas, glaciers

### Reading for the Main Idea

**1.** *Physical Systems* How are primary landforms created?

**2.** *Physical Systems* What forces cause weathering and erosion?

### Critical Thinking

**3. Summarizing** What is plate tectonics?

**4. Finding the Main Idea** How do people affect landforms? Give examples.

### Organizing What You Know

**5. Identifying Cause and Effect** Copy the following graphic organizer. Use it to describe the movement of plates and the movement's effects.

| movement | | resulting landforms and changes |
|---|---|---|
| | ⇨ | |
| | ⇨ | |
| | ⇨ | |

# Reviewing What You Know

## Building Vocabulary

On a separate sheet of paper, write sentences to define each of the following words.

1. solar system
2. orbit
3. solstice
4. equinoxes
5. atmosphere
6. water cycle
7. evaporation
8. condensation
9. precipitation
10. landforms
11. plate tectonics
12. continents
13. earthquakes
14. weathering
15. erosion

## Reviewing the Main Ideas

1. *Physical Systems*  In what ways do Earth's rotation, revolution, and tilt help determine how much of the Sun's energy reaches Earth?

2. *Physical Systems*  Explain how the Sun's energy drives the water cycle. Be sure to include a discussion of the three elements of the cycle.

3. *Physical Systems*  How does plate tectonics relate to the continents and their landforms?

4. *Physical Systems*  Describe how subduction zones are created.

5. *Physical Systems*  Describe the different ways secondary landforms are created.

## Understanding Environment and Society

### Water Use

The availability and purity of water are important for everyone. Research the water supply in your own city or community and prepare a presentation on it. You may want to think about the following:

- Where your city or community gets its drinking water,
- Drought or water shortages that have happened in the past,
- Actions your community takes to protect the water supply.

## Thinking Critically

1. **Drawing Inferences and Conclusions** How do the four parts of the Earth system help explain why places on Earth differ?

2. **Finding the Main Idea** Describe landforms that are shaped by water and wind.

3. **Drawing Inferences and Conclusions** Why do people continue to live in areas where floods are likely to occur?

4. **Identifying Cause and Effect** Describe the landforms that result (a) when two tectonic plates collide and (b) when two plates move away from each other.

5. **Summarizing** In what ways do people interact with landforms?

6. **Analyzing Information** How might mountains be primary and secondary landforms?

## Map ACTIVITY

On a separate sheet of paper, match the letters on the globe with their correct labels.

Tropic of Cancer

Tropic of Capricorn

equator

Arctic Circle

Antarctic Circle

North Pole

South Pole

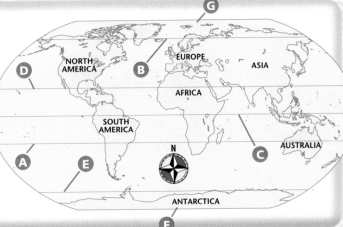

## Mental Mapping Skills ACTIVITY

On a separate sheet of paper, draw a freehand model of the solar system. Locate the following in relation to our Sun:

Earth

Jupiter

Mars

Mercury

Neptune

Pluto

Saturn

Uranus

Venus

## WRITING ACTIVITY

Considering the vastness of the solar system, as well as the interest in exploring it, write a job description for a space explorer. What kinds of qualifications would that person need to research space? Be sure to use standard grammar, spelling, sentence structure, and punctuation in your descriptions.

## Alternative Assessment

## Portfolio ACTIVITY

**Learning About Your Local Geography**

**Individual Project** Compare the latitude and longitude of your state's capital city with that of the capitals of three countries. How might the seasons be similar or different in each city?

### internet connect

Internet Activity: go.hrw.com
KEYWORD: SK3 GT2

Choose a topic to explore online:
- Learn more about Earth's seasons.
- Discover facts about Earth's water.
- Investigate earthquakes.

# Wind, Climate, and Natural Environments

Diver, coral, and fish, Fiji Islands

Tornado in Saskatoon, Canada

Igloo at night, Alaska Range

# Section 1 — Winds and Ocean Currents

## Read to Discover

1. How does the Sun's energy change Earth?
2. Why are wind and ocean currents important?

## Define

weather
climate
greenhouse effect
air pressure
front
currents

### WHY IT MATTERS

Changes in ocean temperatures create currents that affect Earth's landmasses. Use CNNfyi.com or other current events sources to find examples of the effects of changes in ocean temperatures, such as the La Niña weather pattern. Record your findings in your journal.

*Earth from space*

## The Sun's Energy

All planets in our solar system receive energy from the Sun. This energy has important effects. Among the most obvious effects we see on our planet are those on **weather** and **climate**. Weather is the condition of the atmosphere at a given place and time. Climate refers to the weather conditions in an area over a long period of time. How do you think the Sun's energy affects weather and climate?

**Energy Balance**  Although Earth keeps receiving energy from the Sun, it also loses energy. Energy that is lost goes into space. As a result, Earth—as a whole—loses as much energy as it gets. Thus, Earth's overall temperature stays about the same.

As you learned in Chapter 2, the Sun does not warm Earth evenly. The part of Earth in daylight takes in more energy than it loses. Temperatures rise. However, the rest of Earth is in darkness. That part of Earth loses more energy than it gets. Temperatures drop. In addition, when the direct rays of the Sun strike Earth at the Tropic of Cancer, it is summer in the Northern Hemisphere. Temperatures are warm. The Southern Hemisphere, on the other hand, is having winter. Temperatures are lower. The seasons reverse when the Sun's direct rays move above the Tropic of Capricorn. We can see that in any one place temperatures vary from day to day. From year to year, however, they usually stay about the same.

**Stored Energy**  Some of the heat energy that reaches Earth is stored. One place Earth stores heat is in the air. This keeps Earth's surface warmer than if there were no air around it. The process by which

Plants—like this fossil palm found in a coal bed—store the Sun's energy. When we burn coal—the product of long-dead plants—we release the energy the plants had stored.

internet connect

GO TO: go.hrw.com
KEYWORD: SK3 CH3
FOR: Web sites about wind, climates, and environments

## The Greenhouse Effect

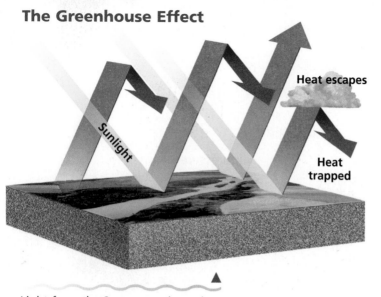

Light from the Sun passes through the atmosphere and heats Earth's surface. Most heat energy later escapes into space.

**You Be the Geographer What would happen if too much heat energy remained trapped in the atmosphere?**

This snow-covered waterfront town is located on Mackinac Island, Michigan.

Earth's atmosphere traps heat is called the **greenhouse effect**. In a greenhouse the Sun's energy passes through the glass and heats everything inside. The glass traps the heat, keeping the greenhouse warm.

Water and land store heat, too. As we learned in Chapter 2, water warms and cools slowly. This explains why in fall, long after temperatures have dropped, the ocean's water is only a little cooler than in summer. Land and buildings also store heat energy. For example, a brick building that has heated up all day stays warm after the Sun sets.

✔ **READING CHECK:** *Physical Systems* How does the Sun's energy affect Earth?

# Wind and Currents

Air and water both store heat. When they move from place to place, they keep different parts of the world from becoming too hot or too cold. By moving air and water, winds and ocean currents move heat energy between warmer and cooler places. Different parts of the world are kept from becoming too hot or too cold.

When the wind is blowing, air is moving from one place to another. Everyone has experienced these local winds. Global winds also exist. They move air and heat energy around Earth. Ocean currents, which are caused by wind, also move heat energy.

**Air Pressure** To understand why there are winds, we must understand **air pressure**. Air pressure is the weight of the air. Air is a mixture of gases. At sea level, a cubic foot of air weighs about 1.25 ounces (35 grams). We do not feel this weight because air pushes on us from all sides equally. The weight of air, however, changes with the weather. Cold air weighs more than warmer air. An instrument called a barometer measures air pressure.

When air warms, it gets lighter and rises. Colder air then moves in to replace the rising air. The result is wind. Wind travels from areas of high pressure to areas of low pressure. During the day land heats up faster than water. The air over the land heats up faster as well. Along the coast lower air pressure is located over land and higher air pressure is located over water. The air above land rises, and cool air flows in to shore to take its place. At night the land cools more quickly than the water. Air pressure over the land increases, and the wind changes direction.

Earth has several major areas where air pressure stays about the same throughout the year. Along the equator is an area of low air pressure. The pressure is low because the Sun is always warming this area.

▲

Wind shapes Earth and the life that thrives here. For example, this tree has grown in the direction blown by the area's prevailing winds.

**Interpreting the Visual Record How do you think wind shapes Earth's landscape?**

## Reading a Weather Map

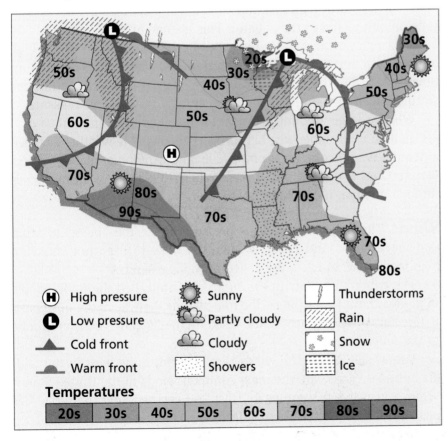

| H | High pressure | ☀ | Sunny | ⚡ | Thunderstorms |
| L | Low pressure | ☁ | Partly cloudy | ▨ | Rain |
| ▲ | Cold front | ☁ | Cloudy | ❄ | Snow |
| ◠ | Warm front | ⠿ | Showers | ⠿ | Ice |

**Temperatures**

| 20s | 30s | 40s | 50s | 60s | 70s | 80s | 90s |

◄

Weather maps show atmospheric conditions as they currently exist or as they are forecast for a particular time period. Most weather maps have legends that explain what the symbols on the map mean. This map shows a cold front sweeping through the central United States. A low-pressure system is at the center of a storm bringing rain and snow to the Midwest. Notice that temperatures behind the cold front are considerably cooler than those ahead of the front.

**You Be the Geographer What is the average temperature range for the southwestern states?**

# Pressure and Wind Systems

Winds between Earth's high- and low-pressure zones help regulate the globe's energy balance.

You Be the Geographer **What happens when warm westerlies come into contact with cold polar winds?**

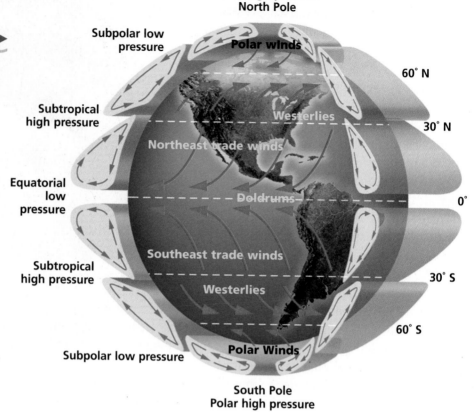

Polar high pressure
North Pole

Subpolar low pressure

Polar winds

60° N

Subtropical high pressure

Westerlies

30° N

Northeast trade winds

Equatorial low pressure

Doldrums

0°

Southeast trade winds

Subtropical high pressure

Westerlies

30° S

60° S

Subpolar low pressure

Polar Winds

South Pole
Polar high pressure

This ship uses wind to travel. As more wind catches the sails, the ship moves faster.

This warm air rises along the equator and moves north and south. Some of the warm air cools and sinks once it reaches about 30° latitude on either side of the equator. This change in temperature causes areas of high air pressure in the subtropics. The pressure is also high at the North and South Poles because the air is so cold. This cold air flows away from the Poles. Because the cold air is heavier, it lifts the warmer air in its path. The subpolar regions have low air pressure.

When a large amount of warm air meets a large amount of cold air, an area of unstable weather forms. This unstable weather is called a **front**. When cold air from Arctic and Antarctic regions meets warmer air, a polar front forms. When this type of front moves through an area, it can cause storms.

**Winds** The major areas of air pressure create the "belts" of wind that move air around Earth. Winds that blow in the same direction over large areas of Earth are called prevailing winds.

The winds that blow in the subtropics are called the trade winds. In the Northern Hemisphere, the trade winds blow from the northeast. Before ships had engines, sailors used trade winds to sail from Europe to the Americas.

The westerlies are the winds that blow from the west in the middle latitudes. These are the most common winds in the United States. When you watch a weather forecast you can see how the westerlies push storms across the country from west to east.

Few winds blow near the equator. This area is called the doldrums. Here, warm air rises rather than blowing east or west.

**Ocean Currents** Winds make ocean water move in the same general directions as the air above it moves. Warm ocean water from the tropics moves in giant streams, or **currents**, to colder areas. Cold water moves in streams from the polar areas to the tropics. This moves energy between different places. Warm air and warm ocean currents raise temperatures. On the other hand, cold winds and cold ocean currents lower temperatures.

The Gulf Stream is an ocean current. It moves warm water north along the east coast of the United States. The Gulf Stream then moves across the Atlantic Ocean toward western Europe. The warm air that moves with it keeps winters mild. As a result, areas such as Ireland have warmer winters than areas in Canada that are just as far north.

Ocean currents also bring heat energy into the Arctic Ocean. In the winter, warm currents create openings in the ice. These openings give arctic whales a place to breathe. They also give people a place to catch fish. Cold water also flows out of the Arctic Ocean into warmer waters of the Pacific and Atlantic Oceans. The cold water sinks below warmer water, causing mixing. This mixing brings food to sea life.

▲

Plants and animals adapt to their particular environments on Earth.

**Interpreting the Visual Record How do you think the bearded seal is able to live in Norway's cold environment?**

✔ **READING CHECK:** *Physical Systems* How do winds and currents create patterns on Earth's surface?

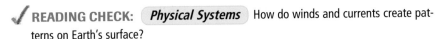

# Section Review 1

**Define and explain:** weather, climate, greenhouse effect, air pressure, front, currents

### Reading for the Main Idea

**1.** *Physical Systems* How does Earth's temperature stay balanced?

**2.** *Physical Systems* How does the greenhouse effect allow Earth to store the Sun's energy?

### Critical Thinking

**3. Drawing Inferences and Conclusions** How would weather in western Europe be different if there were no Gulf Stream?

**4. Analyzing Information** Why were the trade winds important to early sailors?

### Organizing What You Know

**5. Categorizing** Copy the following graphic organizer. Use it to show the names, locations, and directions of wind and air pressure belts.

| Name | Location | Direction |
|------|----------|-----------|
|      |          |           |
|      |          |           |
|      |          |           |
|      |          |           |

# CASE STUDY

## HURRICANE: TRACKING A NATURAL HAZARD

Hurricanes are large circulating storms that begin in tropical oceans. Hurricanes often move over land and into populated areas. When a hurricane approaches land, it brings strong winds, heavy rains, and large ocean waves.

The map below shows the path of Hurricane Fran in 1996. Notice how Fran moved to the west and became stronger until it reached land. It began as a tropical depression and became a powerful hurricane as it passed over warm ocean waters.

Scientists who study hurricanes try to predict where these storms will travel. They want to be able to warn people in the hurricane's path. Early warnings can help people be better prepared for the deadly winds and rain. It is a difficult job because hurricanes can change course suddenly. Hurricanes are one of the most dangerous natural hazards.

One way of determining a hurricane's strength is by measuring the atmospheric pressure inside it. The lower the pressure, the stronger the storm. Hurricanes are rated on a scale of one to five. Study Table 1 to see how wind speed and air pressure are used to help determine the strength of a hurricane.

Hurricane Mitch formed in October 1998. The National Weather Service (NWS) recorded Mitch's position and strength. They learned that Mitch's pressure was one of the lowest ever recorded. The NWS estimated that Mitch's maximum sustained surface winds reached 180 miles per hour.

### Table 1: Saffir-Simpson Scale

| HURRICANE TYPE | WIND SPEED MPH | AIR PRESSURE MB (INCHES) |
|---|---|---|
| Category 1 | 74–95 | more than 980 (28.94) |
| Category 2 | 96–110 | 965–979 (28.50–28.91) |
| Category 3 | 111–130 | 945–964 (27.91–28.47) |
| Category 4 | 131–155 | 920–944 (27.17–27.88) |
| Category 5 | more than 155 | less than 920 (27.17) |

**Source:** Florida State University, <http://www.met.fsu.edu/explores/tropical.html>

## Path of Hurricane Fran, 1996

SCALE
0    300    600 Miles
0    300    600 Kilometers
Projection: Miller Cylindrical

30 mph — Wind speed (in miles per hour)
1006 mb — Atmospheric pressure (in millibars)
○ Tropical depression
◉ Tropical storm
↪ Hurricane
— Fran's path

GULF OF MEXICO
PACIFIC OCEAN
CARIBBEAN SEA
ATLANTIC OCEAN

**Sept. 6** 989 mb 35 mph
**Sept. 5** 954 mb 100 mph
**Sept. 4** 956 mb 100 mph
**Sept. 3** 977 mb 75 mph
**Sept. 2** 976 mb 70 mph
**Sept. 1** 982 mb 65 mph
**Aug. 31** 984 mb 61 mph
**Aug. 30** 990 mb 65 mph
**Aug. 29** 984 mb 65 mph
**Aug. 28** 997 mb 52 mph
**Aug. 27** 1006 mb 30 mph
**Aug. 26** 1007 mb 30 mph
**Aug. 25** 1007 mb 30 mph
**Aug. 24** 1007 mb 30 mph

## Table 2: Hurricane Mitch, 1998 Position and Strength

| DATE | LATITUDE (DEGREES) | LONGITUDE (DEGREES) | WIND SPEED (MPH) | PRESSURE (MILLIBARS) | STORM TYPE |
|------|-----|------|-----|------|------|
| 10/22 | 12 N | 78 W | 30 | 1002 | Tropical depression |
| 10/24 | 15 N | 78 W | 90 | 980 | Category 2 |
| 10/26 | 16 N | 81 W | 130 | 923 | Category 4 |
| 10/27 | 17 N | 84 W | 150 | 910 | Category 5 |
| 10/31 | 15 N | 88 W | 40 | 1000 | Tropical storm |
| 11/01 | 15 N | 90 W | 30 | 1002 | Tropical depression |
| 11/03 | 20 N | 91 W | 40 | 997 | Tropical storm |
| 11/05 | 26 N | 83 W | 50 | 990 | Tropical storm |

**Source:** <http://www.met.fsu.edu/explores/tropical.html>

Hurricanes like Mitch cause very heavy rains in short periods of time. These heavy rains are particularly dangerous. The ground becomes saturated, and mud can flow almost like water. The flooding and mudslides caused by Mitch killed an estimated 10,000 people in four countries. Many people predicted that the region would not recover without help from other countries.

In the southeastern United States, many places have emergency preparedness units. The people assigned to these groups organize their communities. They provide food, shelter, and clothing for those who must evacuate their homes.

## You Be the Geographer

1. Trace a map of the Caribbean. Be sure to include latitude and longitude lines.

2. Use the data about Hurricane Mitch in Table 2 to plot its path. Make a key with symbols to show Mitch's strength at each location.

3. What happened to Mitch when it reached land?

▲

This satellite image shows the intensity of Hurricane Mitch. With advanced technology, hurricane tracking is helping to save lives.

# Section 2 Earth's Climate and Vegetation

## Read to Discover

1. What is included in the study of weather?
2. What are the major climate types, and what types of plants live in each?

## Define

rain shadow
monsoon
arid
steppe climate
hurricanes
typhoons
tundra climate
permafrost

### WHY IT MATTERS

Flooding often becomes a problem during severe weather. Use **CNN fyi.com** or other **current events** sources to find examples of the effects of flooding on nations around the world. Record your findings in your journal.

*A barometer*

Nature has many incredible sights. Lightning is one of the most spectacular occurrences. These flashes of light are produced by a discharge of atmospheric electricity.

▼

## Weather

As you have read, the condition of the atmosphere in a local area for a short period of time is called weather. Weather is a very general term. It can describe temperature, amount of sunlight, air pressure, wind, humidity, clouds, and moisture.

When warm and cool air masses come together, they form a front. Cold air lifts the warm air mass along the front. The air that is moved to higher elevations is cooled. If moisture is present in the lifted air, this cooling causes clouds to form. The moisture may fall to Earth as rain, snow, sleet, or hail. Moisture that falls in any form is called precipitation.

Another type of lifting occurs when warm, moist air is blown up against a mountain and forced to rise. The air cools as it is lifted, just as when air masses collide. Clouds form, and precipitation falls. The side of the mountain facing the wind— the windward side—often gets heavy rain. By the time the air reaches the other side of the mountain—the leeward side—it has lost most of its moisture. This can create a dry area called a **rain shadow**.

✓ **READING CHECK:** *Physical Systems* What is included in the study of weather?

## Landforms and Precipitation

Windward (wet)

Leeward (dry)

Snow

Warming dry air

Rain

Cooling moist air

Rain Shadow

Ocean

Inland

As moist air from the ocean moves up the windward side of a mountain, it cools. The water vapor in the air condenses and falls in the form of rain or snow. Descending, the drier air then moves down the leeward side of the mountain. This drier air brings very little precipitation to areas in the rain shadow.

# Low-Latitude Climates

If you charted the average weather in your community over a long period of time, you would be describing the climate for your area. Geographers have devised ways of describing climates based mainly on temperature, precipitation, and natural vegetation. In general, an area's climate is related to its latitude. In the low latitudes—the region close to the equator—there are two main types of climates: humid tropical and tropical savanna.

**Humid Tropical Climate** A humid tropical climate is warm and rainy all year. People living in this climate do not see a change from summer to winter. This is because the Sun heats the region throughout the year. The heat in the tropics causes a great deal of evaporation and almost daily rainstorms. One of the most complex vegetation systems in the world—the tropical rain forest—exists in this climate. The great rain forests of Brazil, Indonesia, and Central Africa are in the equatorial zone.

Some regions at higher latitudes have warm temperatures all year but have strong wet and dry seasons. Bangladesh and coastal India, for example, have an extreme wet season during the summer. Warm, moist air from the Indian Ocean reaches land. The air rises and cools, causing heavy rains. The rains continue until the wind changes direction in the fall. This seasonal shift of air flow and rainfall is known as a **monsoon**. A monsoon may be wet or dry. The monsoon system is particularly important in Asia.

The people of Tamil Nadu, India, adjust to the monsoon season.

Interpreting the Visual Record

**What problems might people face during the wet monsoon?**

**Tropical Savanna Climate** There is another type of tropical climate that has wet and dry seasons. However, this climate does not have the extreme shifts found in a monsoon climate. It is called a tropical savanna climate. The tropical savanna climate has a wet season soon after the warmest months. It has a dry season soon after the coolest months. Total rainfall, however, is fairly low. Vegetation in a tropical savanna climate is grass with scattered trees and shrubs.

✓ **READING CHECK:** *Physical Systems* Which climate regions are in the low latitudes?

# Dry Climates

Temperature and precipitation are the most important parts of climate. Some regions, for example, experience strong hot and cold seasons. Other regions have wet and dry seasons. Some places are wet or dry all year long. If an area is **arid** (dry) it receives little rain. Arid regions usually have few streams and plants.

**Desert Climate** Most of the world's deserts lie near the tropics. The high air pressure and settling air keep these desert climate regions dry most of the time. Other deserts are located in the interiors of continents and in the rain shadows of mountains. Few plants can survive in the driest deserts, so there are many barren, rocky, or sandy areas. Dry air and clear skies permit hot daytime temperatures and rapid cooling at night.

**Steppe Climate** Another dry climate—the **steppe climate**—is found between desert and wet climate regions. A steppe receives more rainfall than a desert climate. However, the total amount of precipitation is still low. Grasses are the most common plants, but trees can grow along creeks and rivers. Farmers can grow crops but usually need to irrigate. Steppe climates occur in Africa, Australia, Central Asia, eastern Europe, in the Great Plains of the United States and Canada, and in South America.

✓ **READING CHECK:** *The World in Spatial Terms* What are the dry climates?

In terms of loss of life, the worst natural disaster in U.S. history is still the hurricane that hit Galveston, Texas, on September 8, 1900. As many as 8,000 people died in Galveston.

Palo Duro Canyon State Park in Texas attracts thousands of visitors each year.

**Interpreting the Visual Record How can you tell that this canyon is located in a dry climate?**

# World Climate Regions

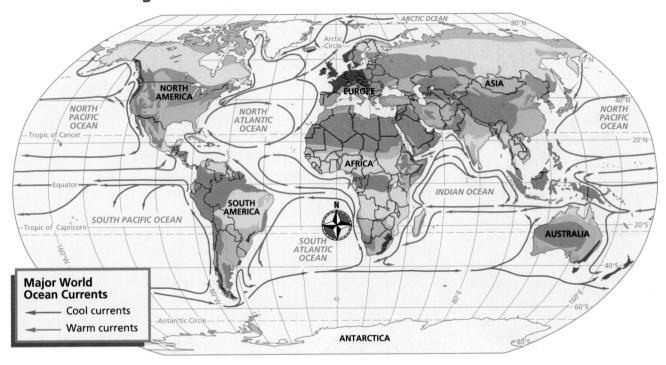

**Major World Ocean Currents**
← Cool currents
← Warm currents

| | Climate | | Geographic Distribution | Major Weather Patterns | Vegetation |
|---|---|---|---|---|---|
| **Low Latitudes** | HUMID TROPICAL | | along the equator | warm and rainy year-round, with rain totaling anywhere from 65 to more than 450 in. (165–1,143 cm) a year | tropical rain forest |
| | TROPICAL SAVANNA | | between the humid tropics and the deserts | warm all year; distinct rainy and dry seasons; at least 20 in. (51 cm) of rain during the summer | tropical grassland with scattered trees |
| **Dry** | DESERT | | centered along 30° latitude; some middle-latitude deserts are in the interior of large continents and along their western coasts | arid; less than 10 in. (25 cm) of rain a year; sunny and hot in the tropics and sunny with wide temperature ranges during the day in middle latitudes | a few drought-resistant plants |
| | STEPPE | | generally bordering deserts and interiors of large continents | semiarid; about 10–20 in. (25–51 cm) of precipitation a year; hot summers and cooler winters with wide temperature ranges during a day | grassland; few trees |
| **Middle Latitudes** | MEDITERRANEAN | | west coasts in middle latitudes | dry, sunny, warm summers and mild, wetter winters; rain averages 15–20 in. (38–51 cm) a year | scrub woodland and grassland |
| | HUMID SUBTROPICAL | | east coasts in the middle latitudes | hot, humid summers and mild, humid winters; rain year-round; coastal areas are in the paths of hurricanes and typhoons | mixed forest |
| | MARINE WEST COAST | | west coasts in the upper-middle latitudes | cloudy, mild summers and cool, rainy winters; strong ocean influence; rain averages 20–60 in. (51–152 cm) a year | temperate evergreen forest |
| | HUMID CONTINENTAL | | east coasts and interiors of upper-middle latitude continents | four distinct seasons; long, cold winters and short, warm summers; amounts of precipitation a year vary | mixed forest |
| **High Latitudes** | SUBARCTIC | | higher latitudes of the interior and east coasts of continents | extremes of temperature; long, cold winters and short, warm summers; little precipitation all year | northern evergreen forest |
| | TUNDRA | | high-latitude coasts | cold all year; very long, cold winters and very short, cool summers; little precipitation | moss, lichens, low shrubs; permafrost marshes |
| | ICE CAP | | polar regions | freezing cold; snow and ice year-round; little precipitation | no vegetation |
| | HIGHLAND | | high mountain regions | temperatures and amounts of precipitation vary greatly as elevation changes | forest to tundra vegetation, depending on elevation |

# Middle-Latitude Climates

The middle latitudes are the two broad zones between Earth's polar circles (66.5° north and south latitudes) and the tropics (23.5° north and south latitudes). Most of the climates in the middle latitudes have cool or cold winters and warm or hot summers. Climates with wet and dry seasons are also found. Middle-latitude climates may include rain shadow deserts.

**Mediterranean Climate** Several climates have clear wet and dry seasons. One of these, the Mediterranean climate, takes its name from the Mediterranean region. This climate has hot, dry summers followed by cooler, wet winters. Much of southern Europe and coastal North Africa have a Mediterranean climate. Parts of California, Australia, South Africa, and Chile do as well. Vegetation includes scrub woodlands and grasslands.

**Humid Subtropical Climate** The southeastern United States is an example of the humid subtropical climate. Warm, moist air from the ocean makes this region hot and humid in the summer. Winters are mild, but snow falls occasionally. People in a humid subtropical climate experience **hurricanes** and **typhoons**. These are tropical storms that bring violent winds, heavy rain, and high seas. The humid subtropical climate supports areas of mixed forests where deciduous and coniferous forests blend. Deciduous trees lose their leaves during the fall each year. Coniferous trees have needle-shaped leaves that remain green year-round.

**Marine West Coast Climate** Some coastal areas of North America and much of western Europe have a marine west coast climate. Westerly winds carry moisture from the ocean across the land, causing winter rainfall. Evergreen forests can grow in these regions because of regular rain.

The Mediterranean coast of France is part of the Riviera. The Riviera is located in a Mediterranean climate region.

**Interpreting the Visual Record**
**What features would make this area popular with tourists?**

The Mediterranean has a variety of vegetation. This Mediterranean scrub forest is in Corfu, Greece.

**Interpreting the Visual Record** **What kinds of vegetation do you see in this scrub forest?**

**Humid Continental Climate** Farther inland are regions with a humid continental climate. Winters in this region bring snowfall and cold temperatures, but there are some mild periods too. Summers are warm and sometimes hot. Most of the shifting weather in this climate region is the result of cold and warm air coming together along a polar front. Humid continental climates have four distinct seasons. Much of the midwestern and northeastern United States and southeastern Canada have a humid continental climate. This climate supports mixed forest vegetation.

✓ **READING CHECK:** *The World in Spatial Terms* What are the middle-latitude climates?

# High-Latitude Climates

Closer to the poles we find another set of climates. They are the high-latitude climates. They have cold temperatures and little precipitation.

**Subarctic Climate** The subarctic climate has long, cold winters, short summers, and little rain. In the inland areas of North America, Europe, and Asia, far from the moderating influence of oceans, subarctic climates experience extreme temperatures. However, summers in these regions can be warm. In the Southern Hemisphere there is no land in the subarctic climate zone. As a result, boreal (BOHR-ee-uhl) forests are found only in the Northern Hemisphere. Trees in boreal forests are coniferous and cover vast areas in North America, Europe, and northern Asia.

**Tundra Climate** Farther north lies the **tundra climate**. Temperatures are cold, and rainfall is low. Usually just hardy plants, including mosses, lichens, and shrubs, survive here. Tundra summers are so short and cool that a layer of soil stays frozen all year. This frozen layer is called **permafrost**. It prevents water from draining into the soil. As a result, many ponds and marshes appear in summer.

**Ice Cap Climate** The polar regions of Earth have an ice cap climate. This climate

Wildlife eat the summer vegetation in the Alaskan tundra.

*Interpreting the Visual Record* **Why is there snow on the mountain peaks during summer?**

The Amundsen-Scott South Pole Station is a research center in Antarctica.

**Interpreting the Visual Record** How does the design of this building show ways people have adapted to the ice cap climate?

is cold—the monthly average temperature is below freezing. Precipitation averages less than 10 inches (25 cm) annually. Animals adapted to the cold, like walruses, penguins, and whales, are found here. No vegetation grows in this climate.

✓ **READING CHECK:** **The World in Spatial Terms** How are tundra and ice cap climates different?

## Highland Climates

Mountains usually have several different climates in a small area. These climate types are known as highland climates. If you went from the base of a high mountain to the top, you might experience changes similar to going from the tropics to the Poles! The vegetation also changes with the elevation. It varies from thick forests or desert to tundra. Lower mountain elevations tend to be similar in temperature to the surrounding area. On the windward side, however, are zones of heavier rainfall or snowfall. As you go uphill, the temperatures drop. High mountains have a tundra zone and an icy summit.

✓ **READING CHECK:** **The World in Spatial Terms** What are highland climate regions?

go.hrw.com **Homework Practice Online**
Keyword: SK3 HP3

## Section Review 2

**Define and explain:** rain shadow, monsoon, arid, steppe climate, hurricanes, typhoons, tundra climate, permafrost

### Reading for the Main Idea

1. **Physical Systems** How is weather different from climate?

2. **The World in Spatial Terms** What are the major climate regions of the world?

### Critical Thinking

3. **Drawing Inferences and Conclusions** Why is it important to understand weather and climate patterns?

4. **Analyzing Information** How does latitude influence climate?

### Organizing What You Know

5. **Categorizing** Copy the following graphic organizer. Use it to describe Earth's climate types.

| Climate | Latitudes | Characteristics |
|---------|-----------|-----------------|
|         |           |                 |
|         |           |                 |
|         |           |                 |
|         |           |                 |
|         |           |                 |
|         |           |                 |
|         |           |                 |
|         |           |                 |

# Section 3  Natural Environments

## Read to Discover

1. How do environments affect life, and how do they change?
2. What substances make up the different layers of soil?

## Define

extinct
ecology
photosynthesis
food chain
nutrients

plant communities
ecosystem
plant succession
humus

**WHY IT MATTERS**

Plants and animals depend on their environment for survival. Use CNNfyi.com or other current events sources to find out how conservationists work to save animals whose environments are threatened. Record your findings in your journal.

*Acorns, the nut of an oak tree*

## Environmental Change

Geographers examine the distribution of plants and animals and the environments they occupy. They also study how people change natural environments. Changes in an environment affect the plants and animals that live in that environment. If environmental changes are extreme, some types of plants and animals may become **extinct**. This means they die out completely.

**Ecology and Plant Life** The study of the connections among different forms of life is called **ecology**. One process connecting life forms is **photosynthesis**—the process by which plants convert sunlight into chemical energy. Roots take in minerals, water, and gases from the soil. Leaves take in sunlight and carbon dioxide from the air. Plant cells take in these elements and combine them to produce special chemical compounds. Plants use some of these chemicals to live and grow.

Plant growth is the basis for all the food that animals eat. Some animals, like deer, eat only plants. When deer eat plants, they store some of the plant food energy in their bodies. Other animals, like wolves, eat deer and indirectly get the plant food the deer ate. The plants, deer, and wolves together make up a **food chain**. A food chain is a series of organisms in which energy is passed along.

▲

Plants use a particular environment's sunlight, water, gases, and minerals to survive.

# Food Web

Cougar
Sun
Eagles, Hawks
Human
Insect-eating Birds
Trees, Shrubs
Intestinal Parasite
Snakes
Rodents
Grass, Herbs
Spiders
Fish
Insects
Deer
Frogs
Mushrooms
Bacteria
Earthworms

Food chains rarely occur alone in nature. More common are food webs—interlocking networks of food chains. This food web includes tiny organisms, such as parasites and bacteria, as well as human beings and other large mammals.

**N**ot all predators are big. In Antarctica's dry areas a microscopic bacteria-eating worm that can survive years of being freeze-dried is at the top of the food chain.

**Limits for Life** Plants and animals cannot live everywhere. They are limited by environmental conditions. Any type of plant or animal tends to be most common in areas where it is best able to live, grow, and reproduce. A simple example shows why you do not find every kind of plant and animal in all regions on Earth. Trees do not survive in the tundra because it is too cold and there is not enough moisture. At the edge of the tundra, however, there are large boreal forests. Once in a while, wind carries tree seeds into the tundra. Some of the seeds sprout and grow. These young trees are generally small and weak. Eventually they die.

In this example life is limited by conditions of temperature and moisture. Other factors that can limit plant life include the amount of light, water, and soil **nutrients**. Nutrients are substances promoting growth. Some plant and animal life is limited by other plants and animals that compete for the same resources.

*There are more than 2,000 species of harmless mushrooms.*

## Soil Factory

The next time you see a fallen tree in the forest, do not think of it as a dead log. Think of it as a soil factory. As the tree decays and crumbles, it adds valuable nutrients to the forest soil. These nutrients enrich the soil. They also make it possible for new trees and plants to grow.

The fallen tree does not do its work alone, however. It is aided by many different living organisms that break down the wood and turn it into humus. Humus is a rich blend of organic material that mixes with the soil. A downed tree that lies on the forest floor is buzzing with the activity of hundreds of species of insects and plants that live and work inside it.

When a tree falls, insects, bacteria and other microorganisms invade the wood and start the process of decay. Insects like weevils, bark beetles, carpenter ants, and termites, among others, bore into the wood and break it down further. These insects, in turn, attract birds, spiders, lizards, and other predators who feed on insect life. Before long, the fallen tree is brimming with life. This happens even as the tree breaks apart on the forest floor.

Fallen trees provide as much as one third of the organic matter in forest soil. As forest ecologist Chris Maser notes, "Dead wood is no wasted resource. It is nature's reinvestment in biological capital."

### You Be the Geographer
1. How do fallen trees decompose?
2. How is fertile soil produced by downed trees?

**Plant Communities** Groups of plants that live in the same area are called **plant communities**. In harsh environments, such as tundra, plant communities tend to be simple. They may be made up of just a few different types of plants. Regions that receive more rainfall and have more moderate temperatures tend to have more complex plant communities. The greatest variety of plants and animals can be found in the rain forests of the tropics. This environment is warm and moist all year.

Each plant community has plants adapted to the environment of the region. Near the Arctic, for example, the shortage of sunlight limits plant growth. Some of the flowers that grow here turn to follow the Sun as it moves across the sky. Thus the flowers collect as much sunlight as they can. In other regions there are plants adapted to survive in poor soils or with limited moisture. Some large trees, for example, have deep roots that can reach water and soil nutrients far below the surface. Their spreading branches also collect large amounts of sunlight for photosynthesis.

Plants adapt to the sunlight, soil, and temperature of their region. They may also be suited to other plants found in their communities. For example, many ferns grow well in the shade found underneath trees. Some vines grow up tree trunks to reach sunlight.

All of the plants and animals in an area together with the nonliving parts of their environment—like climate and soil—form what is called an **ecosystem**. The size of an ecosystem varies, depending on how it is defined. A small pond, for example, can be considered an ecosystem. The entire Earth can also be considered an ecosystem.

Ecosystems can be affected by natural events like droughts, fires, floods, severe frosts, and windstorms. Human activities can also disturb ecosystems. This happens when land is cleared for development, new kinds of plants and animals are brought into an area, or pollution is released into air and water.

## Forest Succession After a Fire

Ⓐ Forest fire in progress

Ⓑ Early plant growth

Ⓒ Middle stage

Ⓓ Forest recovered

▲

Difficult conditions after a forest fire mean that the first plants to grow back must be very hardy.
You Be the Geographer **In this series of photos, which plants are the first to grow back?**

**Plant Succession** When natural or human forces disturb a plant community, the community may be replaced by a different group of plants suited to the new conditions. The gradual process by which one group of plants replaces another is called **plant succession**.

To better understand plant succession, imagine an area just after a forest fire. The first plants to return to the area need plenty of sunshine. These plants hold the soil in place. They also provide shade for the seeds of other plants. Gradually, seeds from small trees and shrubs grow under the protection of the first plants. These new plants grow taller and begin to take more and more of the sunlight. Many of the smaller plants die. Later, taller trees in the area replace the shorter trees and shrubs that grew at first.

It is important to remember that plant communities are not permanent. The conditions they experience change over time. Some changes affect a whole region. For example, a region's climate may gradually become colder, drier, warmer, or wetter. Additional changes may occur if new plants are introduced to the community.

✔ **READING CHECK:** *Physical Systems* How do environments affect life, and how do they change?

# Soils

In any discussion of plants, plant communities, or plant succession, it is important to know about the soils that support plant life. All soils are not the same. The type of soil in an area can contribute to the kinds of plants that can be grown there. It can also affect how well a plant grows. Plants need soil with minerals, water, and small air spaces if they are to survive and grow.

Soils contain decayed plant and animal matter, called **humus**. Soils rich in humus are fertile. This means they can support an abundance of plant life. Humus is formed by insects and bacteria that live in soil. They break down dead plants and animals and make the nutrients available to plant roots. Insects also make small air spaces as they move through soils. These air pockets contain moisture and gases that plant roots need for growth.

The processes that break down rocks to form soil take hundreds or even thousands of years. Over this long period of time soil tends to form layers. If you dig a deep hole, you can see these layers. Soils typically have three layers. The thickness of each layer depends on the conditions in a specific location. The top layer is called topsoil. It includes humus, insects, and plants. The layer beneath the surface soil is called the subsoil. Only the deep roots of some plants, mostly trees, reach the subsoil. Underneath this layer is broken rock that eventually breaks down into more soil. As the rock breaks down it adds minerals to the soil.

Soils can lose their fertility in several ways. Erosion by water or wind can sweep topsoil away. Nutrients can also be removed from soils by leaching. This occurs when rainfall dissolves nutrients in topsoil and washes them down into lower soil layers, out of reach of most plant roots.

✓ **READING CHECK:** *Physical Systems* What are the physical processes that produce fertile soil?

## Soil Layers

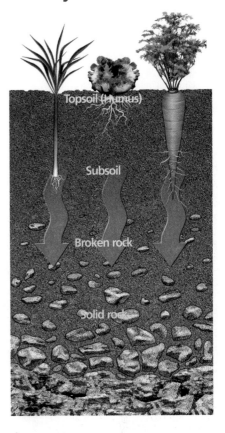

The three layers of soil are the topsoil, subsoil, and broken rock.
**Interpreting the Visual Record What do you think has created the cracks in the rocky layer below the broken rock?**

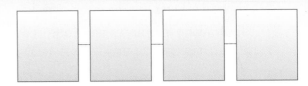

**Homework Practice Online**
Keyword: SK3 HP3

## Section Review 3

**Define and explain:** extinct, ecology, photosynthesis, food chain, nutrients, plant communities, ecosystem, plant succession, humus

### Reading for the Main Idea

1. *Physical Systems* Why cannot all plants and animals live everywhere? Provide an example to illustrate your answer.

2. *Physical Systems* What makes up soil, and what produces fertile soil?

### Critical Thinking

3. **Analyzing Information** What keeps tundra plant communities simple?

4. **Summarizing** How does plant succession occur?

### Organizing What You Know

5. **Sequencing** Copy the following graphic organizer. Use it to describe a food chain.

| | | | |
|---|---|---|---|
| | | | |

# Reviewing What You Know

## Building Vocabulary

On a separate sheet of paper, write sentences to define each of the following words.

1. weather
2. climate
3. greenhouse effect
4. air pressure
5. front
6. currents
7. rain shadow
8. monsoon
9. arid
10. permafrost
11. extinct
12. ecology
13. nutrients
14. ecosystem
15. humus

## Reviewing the Main Ideas

1. ( *The World in Spatial Terms* ) What are the major wind belts? Describe each.
2. ( *Physical Systems* ) How is the area around mountains affected by precipitation?
3. ( *The World in Spatial Terms* ) Into what main divisions can climate be grouped?
4. ( *Environment and Society* ) What do people do to change ecosystems?
5. ( *Physical Systems* ) What elements make up soil? How is fertile soil created?

## Understanding Environment and Society

### Tornadoes

Prepare an outline for a presentation on tornadoes. As you prepare your presentation from the outline, think about the following:

- How tornadoes are formed.
- How experts are able to forecast their occurrence more accurately.
- The safety precautions taken by people in tornado-prone areas.

## Thinking Critically

1. **Finding the Main Idea** How does Earth store the Sun's energy?
2. **Analyzing Information** What effect do wind patterns have on ocean currents?
3. **Drawing Inferences and Conclusions** Why is it important to study the weather?
4. **Drawing Inferences and Conclusions** Why is it important to understand the concept of latitude when learning about Earth's many climates?
5. **Drawing Inferences and Conclusions** Why is it important for scientists to study soils?

 **Map** ACTIVITY

On a separate sheet of paper, match the letters on the map with their correct labels.

The following natural disasters are experienced in the United States:

- **hurricanes on the East Coast**
- **hurricanes on the Gulf Coast**
- **forest fires on the West Coast**
- **tornadoes in Texas, Oklahoma, Kansas, Nebraska, and South Dakota**

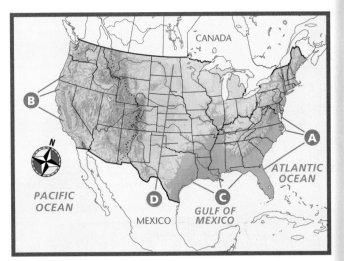

## Mental Mapping Skills ACTIVITY

Draw a freehand map of the globe. Draw lines to show the equator and low, middle, and high latitudes. Draw the continents in the appropriate areas.

## WRITING ACTIVITY

After studying different climate regions, decide in which of the regions you would like to live. Write a journal entry describing what your life would be like in this particular area. Be sure to use standard grammar, spelling, sentence structure, and punctuation in your story.

## Alternative Assessment

### Portfolio ACTIVITY

**Learning About Your Local Geography**

**Understanding Cause and Effect**

Research your local weather patterns. Create a graph that shows how recent weather conditions have affected humans, plants, and animals in your part of the state.

📁 **internet** connect

Internet Activity: **go.hrw.com**
KEYWORD: SK3 GT3

Choose a topic to explore online:
- Learn more about using weather maps.
- Follow El Niño, an ocean phenomenon that affects weather.
- Build a food web.

# Earth's Resources

Precious gems

Wind turbines

Valley in the
Andes of Ecuador

# Section 1  Soil and Forests

## Read to Discover

1. What physical processes produce fertile soil?
2. What processes threaten soil fertility?
3. Why are forests valuable resources, and how are they being protected?

## Define

renewable resources
crop rotation
terraces
desertification
deforestation
reforestation

### WHY IT MATTERS

Many people work to balance concerns about saving the rain forests with local economic needs. Use **CNN fyi.com** or other **current events** sources to learn more about these efforts. Record your findings in your journal.

*Corn, a major food crop*

## Soil

Soil is one of the most important **renewable resources** on Earth. Renewable resources are those that can be replaced by Earth's natural processes.

Soil types vary depending on geographic factors. As you learned in Chapter 3, soil contains rock particles and humus. It also contains water and gases. Because soil types vary, some are better able to support plant life than others.

**Soil Fertility** Soil conservation—protecting the soil's ability to nourish plants—is one challenge facing farmers. Plants must take up nutrients like calcium, nitrogen, phosphorus, and potassium in order to grow. These essential nutrients may become used up if fields are always planted with the same crops. Farmers can add these nutrients to soils in the form of fertilizers, sometimes called plant food. The first fertilizers used were manures. Later, chemical fertilizers were used to increase yields.

Some farmers choose not to use chemical fertilizers. Others cannot afford to use them. They rely on other ways to keep up the soil's ability to produce. One such method is **crop rotation**. This is a system of growing different crops on the same land over a period of years.

On this farm, fields are planted with corn and alfalfa. Alfalfa is a valued crop because it replaces nutrients in the soil.

▼

A row of poplar trees divides farmland near Aix-en-Provence, France.
**Interpreting the Visual Record** What effect will these trees have on erosion?

**A**bout 47,000 aspen trees in Utah share a root system and a set of genes. These trees are actually a single organism. These aspens cover 106 acres (43 hectares) and weigh at least 13 million pounds (5.9 million kg). Together they are probably the world's heaviest living thing.

**Salty Soil** Salt buildup is another threat to soil fertility. In dry climates farmers must irrigate their crops. They use well water or water brought by canals and ditches. Much of this water evaporates in the dry air. When the water evaporates, it leaves behind small amounts of salt. If too much salt builds up in the soil, crops cannot grow.

**Erosion** The problem of soil erosion is faced by farmers all over the world. Farmers have to work to keep soil from being washed away by rainfall. Soil can also be blown away by strong winds. To prevent soil loss, some farmers plant rows of trees to block the wind. Others who farm on steep hillsides build **terraces** into the slope. Terraces are horizontal ridges like stair steps. By slowing water movement the terraces stop the soil from being washed away. They also provide more space for farming.

**Loss of Farmland** The loss of farmland is a serious problem in many parts of the world. In some places farming has worn out the soil, and it can no longer grow crops. Livestock may then eat what few plants remain. Without plants to hold the soil in place, it may blow away. The long-term process of losing soil fertility and plant life is called **desertification**. Once this process begins, the desert can expand as people move on to better soils. They often repeat the destructive practices, damaging ever-larger areas.

Farmland is also lost when cities and suburbs expand into rural areas. Nearby farmers sell their land. The land is then used for housing or businesses, rather than for agriculture. This is happening in many poorer countries. It also happens in richer nations like the United States.

✔ **READING CHECK:**   *Environment and Society*   What physical processes help soil fertility, and what threatens it?

# Forests

Forests are renewable resources because new trees can be planted in a forest. If cared for properly, they will be available for future generations. Forests are important because they provide both people and wildlife with food and shelter. People depend on forests for a wide variety of products. Wood products include lumber, plywood, and shingles for building houses. Other wood-based manufactured products include cellophane, furniture, some plastics, and fibers such as rayon. Trees also supply fats, gums, medicines, nuts, oils, turpentine, waxes, and rubber. The forests are valuable not only for their products. People also use forests for recreational activities, such as camping and hiking.

**Deforestation** The destruction or loss of forest area is called **deforestation**. It is happening in the rain forests of Africa, Asia, and Central and South America. People clear the land and use it for farming, industry, and housing. Pollution also causes deforestation.

**Protecting Forests** Many countries, including the United States, are trying to balance their economic needs regarding forests with conservation efforts. Since the late 1800s Congress has passed laws to protect and manage forest and wilderness areas. In addition to protecting forests, people can also plant trees in places where forests have been cut down. This replanting is called **reforestation**. In some cases the newly planted trees can be "harvested" again in a few years.

▲
Villagers work on a reforestation project in Cameroon.

✓ **READING CHECK:** ( *Environment and Society* ) Why is preserving forests important, and how can people contribute to it?

Homework Practice Online
Keyword: SK3 HP4

## Section Review 1

**Define and explain:** renewable resources, crop rotation, terraces, desertification, deforestation, reforestation

### Reading for the Main Idea

1. ( *Environment and Society* ) What physical processes produce fertile soil?

2. ( *Environment and Society* ) What do forests provide, and how can they be protected?

### Critical Thinking

3. **Finding the Main Idea** Which two natural forces contribute to soil erosion? How can erosion be prevented?

4. **Drawing Inferences and Conclusions** Why is it important to manage forests?

### Organizing What You Know

5. **Categorizing** Copy the following graphic organizer. Use it to discuss whether or not rain forests should be protected.

| Reasons for . . . | Reasons against . . . |
|---|---|
|  |  |
|  |  |
|  |  |

# Section 2 Water and Air

## Read to Discover

1. Why is water an important resource?
2. What threatens our supplies of freshwater, and how can we protect these supplies?
3. What are some problems caused by air pollution?

## Define

semiarid
aqueducts
aquifers
desalinization
acid rain
global warming

*A water tank*

**WHY IT MATTERS**

Countries around the world have worked together to resolve problems regarding Earth's atmosphere. Use CNNfyi.com or other current events sources to learn about these efforts. Record your findings in your journal.

## Water

Dry regions are found in many parts of the world, including the western United States. There are also **semiarid** regions—regions that receive a small amount of rain. Semiarid places are usually too dry for farming. However, these areas may be suitable for grazing animals.

**Water Supply** Many areas of high mountains receive heavy snowfall in the winter. When that snow melts, it forms rivers that flow from the mountains to neighboring regions. People in dry regions use various means to bring the water where it is needed for agricultural and other uses. They build canals, reservoirs, and **aqueducts**—artificial channels for carrying water.

Some places have water deep underground in **aquifers**. These are water-bearing layers of rock, sand, or gravel. Some are quite large. For example, the Ogallala Aquifer stretches across the Great Plains from Texas to South Dakota. People drill wells to reach the water in the aquifer.

People in dry coastal areas have access to plenty of salt water. However, they typically do not have enough freshwater. In Southwest Asia this situation is common. To create a supply of

As people make their homes in dry areas, they add to the demand for water.

Canada

United States
San Bernardino

Mexico

62

freshwater, people in these places have built machines that take the salt out of seawater. This process, known as **desalinization**, is expensive and takes a lot of energy. However, in some places, it is necessary.

**Water Conservation** In recent decades people have developed new ways to save water. Many factories now recycle water. Farmers are able to irrigate their crops more efficiently. Cities build water treatment plants to purify water that might otherwise be wasted. Some people in dry climates are using desert plants instead of grass for landscaping. This means that they do not need to water as often.

It is important for people in all climates to conserve water. Wasting water in one location could mean that less water is available for use in other places.

**Water Quality** Industries and agriculture also affect the water supply. In many countries there are still places that cannot afford to build closed sewer systems. Some factories also operate without pollution controls because such controls would add a great deal of cost to operation.

Industrialized countries like the United States have water treatment plants and closed sewer systems. However, water can still be polluted when farmers use too much chemical fertilizer and pesticides. These chemicals can get into local streams. Waste from industries may also contain chemicals, metals, or oils that can pollute streams and rivers.

Rivers carry pollution to the oceans. The pollution can harm marine life such as fish and shellfish. Eating marine life from polluted waters can make people sick. So can drinking polluted water. Balancing industrial and agricultural needs with the need for clean water continues to be a challenge faced by many countries.

✓ READING CHECK: ( *Environment and Society* )  Why is water an important resource, and how does its availability affect people?

Pivoting sprinklers irrigate these circular cornfields in Kansas.
**Interpreting the Visual Record  Why might irrigation be necessary in these fields?**

Heavy smog clouds the Los Angeles skyline.

# Air

Air is essential to life. Plants and animals need the gases in the air to live and grow.

Human activities can pollute the air and threaten the health of life on the planet. Burning fuels for heating, for transportation, and to power factories releases chemicals into the air. Particularly in large cities, these chemicals build up in the air. The chemicals create a mixture called smog.

Some cities have special problems with air pollution. Denver, Los Angeles, and Mexico City, for example, are located in bowl-shaped valleys that can trap air pollution. This pollution sometimes builds up to levels that are dangerous to people's health.

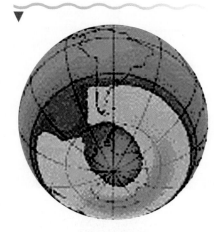

This satellite image of the Southern Hemisphere shows a thinning in the ozone layer in October 1979.

▼

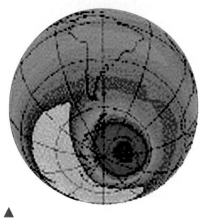

▲

By October 1992 the thinning area, shown in purple, had grown much larger.

**Acid Rain**  When air pollution combines with moisture in the air, it can form a mild acid. This can be similar in strength to vinegar. When it falls to the ground, this moisture is called **acid rain**. It can damage or kill trees. Acid rain can also kill fish.

Many countries have laws to limit pollution. However, pollution is an international problem. Winds can blow away air pollution, but the wind is only moving the pollution to another place. Pollution can pass from one country to another. It can even pass from one continent to another. Countries that limit their own pollution can still be affected by pollution from other countries.

**Pollution and Climate Change**  Smog and acid rain are short-term effects of air pollution. Air pollution may also have long-term effects by changing conditions in Earth's atmosphere. Certain kinds of pollution damage the ozone in the upper atmosphere. This ozone layer protects living things by absorbing harmful ultraviolet light from the Sun. Damage to Earth's ozone layer may cause health problems in people. For example, it could lead to an increase in skin cancer.

Another concern is **global warming**—a slow increase in Earth's average temperature. The Sun constantly warms Earth's surface. The gases and water vapor in the atmosphere trap some of this heat. This helps keep Earth warm. Without the atmosphere, this heat would return to space. Evidence suggests that pollution causes the atmosphere to trap more heat. Over time this would make Earth warmer.

Scientists agree that Earth's climate has warmed during the last century. However, they disagree about exactly why. Some scientists say that temperatures have warmed because of air pollution caused by human activities, particularly the burning of fossil fuels. Others think warmer temperatures have resulted from natural causes. Scientists also disagree about what has caused the thinning of the ozone layer.

✔ **READING CHECK:**   ( *Environment and Society* )   What are the different points of view about air pollution and climate change?

**Homework Practice Online**
Keyword: SK3 HP4

**Define and explain:**  semiarid, aqueducts, aquifers, desalinization, acid rain, global warming

**Reading for the Main Idea**

**1.** ( *Environment and Society* )  How have people changed the environment to increase the water supply in drier areas?

**2.** ( *Environment and Society* )  How do people cause water pollution?

**3.** ( *Environment and Society* )  What kinds of human activities have polluted the air?

**Critical Thinking**

**4. Drawing Inferences and Conclusions**  Why is desalinization rarely practiced?

**Organizing What You Know**

**5. Identifying Cause and Effect**  Use this graphic organizer to explain air pollution.

( Causes: )—( Air Pollution )—( Effects: )

# Section 3 — Minerals

**Read to Discover**

1. What are minerals?
2. What are the two types of minerals?

**Define**

nonrenewable resources

minerals

metallic minerals

nonmetallic minerals

**WHY IT MATTERS**

Most minerals are dug from deep in the ground by miners. Use CNN fyi.com or other current events sources to learn about life as a miner. Record your findings in your journal.

*Quartz crystals*

## Minerals

You have learned that renewable resources such as trees are always being produced. **Nonrenewable resources** are those that cannot be replaced by natural processes or are replaced very slowly.

Earth's crust is made up of substances called **minerals**. Minerals are an example of a nonrenewable resource. They provide us with many of the materials we need. More than 3,000 minerals have been identified, but fewer than 20 are common. Around 20 minerals make up most of Earth's crust. Minerals have four basic properties. First, they are inorganic. Inorganic substances are not made from living things or the remains of living things. Second, they occur naturally, rather than being manufactured like steel or brass. Third, minerals are solids in crystalline form, unlike petroleum or natural gas. Finally, minerals have a definite chemical composition or combination of elements. Although all minerals share these four properties, they can be very different from one another. Minerals are divided into two basic types: metallic and nonmetallic.

**Metallic Minerals** Metals, or **metallic minerals**, are shiny and can conduct heat and electricity. Metals are solids at normal room temperature. An exception is mercury, a metal that is liquid at room temperature.

Gold is one of the heaviest of all metals and is easily worked. For thousands of years people have highly valued gold. Precious metals are commonly made into jewelry and coins. Silver and platinum are other precious metals.

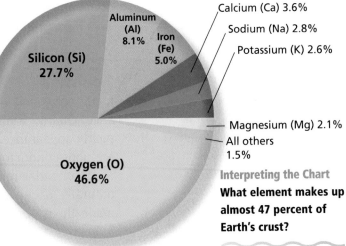

**The Most-Common Elements in Earth's Crust**

- Calcium (Ca) 3.6%
- Sodium (Na) 2.8%
- Potassium (K) 2.6%
- Aluminum (Al) 8.1%
- Iron (Fe) 5.0%
- Silicon (Si) 27.7%
- Oxygen (O) 46.6%
- Magnesium (Mg) 2.1%
- All others 1.5%

**Interpreting the Chart**

**What element makes up almost 47 percent of Earth's crust?**

# CONNECTING TO Art

*Art made from recycled products*

Many Americans now make a habit of recycling. They put their cans, bottles, and newspapers by the curb for pickup or take them to recycling centers. However, some people do their recycling in a different way. They use their junk to create art.

Much recycled art is folk art. These objects have a practical purpose but are made with creativity and a sense of style. The making of folk art objects from junk is common in the world's poorer countries, where resources are scarce.

Some examples of recycled folk art include dust pans made from license plates (Mexico), jugs made from old tires (Morocco), briefcases made from flattened tin cans (Senegal), and a toy helicopter made from plastic containers and film canisters (Haiti). As scientist Stephen J. Gould has written, "In our world of material wealth, where so many broken items are thrown away rather than mended . . . we forget that most of the world fixes everything and discards nothing."

Americans do have a tradition of making recycled art, however. The Amish make quilts from old scraps of cloth. Other folk artists build whimsical figures out of bottle caps and wire. Some modern artists create sculptures from "found objects" like machine parts, bicycle wheels, and old signs. Junk art can even be fashion. One movie costume designer went to the Academy Awards ceremony wearing a dress made of credit cards!

## JUNk ARt

## Understanding What You Read

1. How do some societies turn junk into art?
2. Where is much recycled folk art made?

---

Iron is the cheapest metal. Iron can be combined with certain other minerals to make steel. Aluminum is another common metal. This lightweight metal is used in such items as soft drink cans and airplanes. We handle copper every time we pick up a penny.

**Nonmetallic Minerals** Minerals that lack the characteristics of a metal are called **nonmetallic minerals**. These vary in their appearance. Quartz, a mineral often found in sand, looks glassy. Talc has a pearly appearance. Most nonmetallic minerals have a dull surface and are poor conductors of heat or electricity.

Diamonds are minerals made of pure carbon. They are the hardest naturally occurring substance. The brilliant look of diamonds has made them popular gems. Their hardness makes them valuable for industrial use. Other gemstones, like rubies, sapphires, and emeralds, are also nonmetallic minerals.

Gold is a metallic mineral.

# Mineral and Energy Resources in the United States

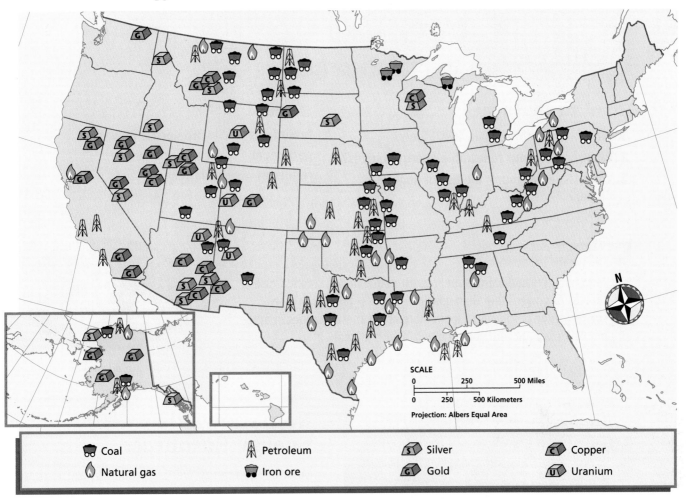

| | | | |
|---|---|---|---|
| Coal | Petroleum | Silver | Copper |
| Natural gas | Iron ore | Gold | Uranium |

Other mineral substances also have important uses. For example, people need salt to stay healthy. Sulfur is used in many ways, from making batteries to bleaching dried fruits. Graphite, another form of carbon, is used in making pencils.

✓ **READING CHECK:** *Physical Systems* What are the two types of minerals?

## Section Review 3

**Define and explain:** nonrenewable resources, minerals, metallic minerals, nonmetallic minerals

### Reading for the Main Idea

1. *Physical Systems* What is a nonrenewable resource?

2. *Environment and Society* Why are minerals important? What is the difference between a metallic mineral and a nonmetallic mineral?

### Critical Thinking

3. **Summarizing** How can minerals be used?

4. **Drawing Inferences and Conclusions** What makes gold such an important mineral?

### Organizing What You Know

5. **Contrasting** Copy the following graphic organizer. Use it to contrast types of minerals.

| Metallic minerals | Nonmetallic minerals |
|---|---|
| | |

# Section 4 — Energy Resources

## Read to Discover

1. What are the three main fossil fuels?
2. What are the four renewable energy sources?
3. What issues surround the use of nuclear power?

## Define

fossil fuels      hydroelectric power

petroleum      geothermal energy

refineries      solar energy

### WHY IT MATTERS

Automobile manufacturers are interested in building cars that use sources of power other than gasoline. Use CNNfyi.com or other current events sources to learn more about these changes in automobile design. Record your findings in your journal.

*An oil tanker*

A miner digs coal in a narrow tunnel.

## Nonrenewable Energy Resources

Most of the energy we use comes from the three main **fossil fuels**: coal, petroleum, and natural gas. Fossil fuels were formed from the remains of ancient plants and animals. These remains gradually decayed and were covered with sediment. Over long periods of time, pressure and heat changed these materials into fossil fuels. All fossil fuels are nonrenewable resources.

**Coal** Until the 1900s people mostly used wood and coal as sources of energy. Coal was used to make steel in giant furnaces and to run factories. However, the burning of coal polluted the air. The way coal is burned today has improved so that it releases less pollution. This new technology is more expensive, however. Some of the largest coal deposits are located in Australia, China, Russia, India, and the United States.

**Petroleum** Industrialized societies now use **petroleum**—an oily liquid—for a variety of purposes. When it is first pumped out of the ground, petroleum is called crude oil. It is then shipped or piped to **refineries**—factories where crude oil is processed, or refined. Petroleum is made into gasoline, diesel and jet fuels, and heating oil.

## Who Has the Oil?

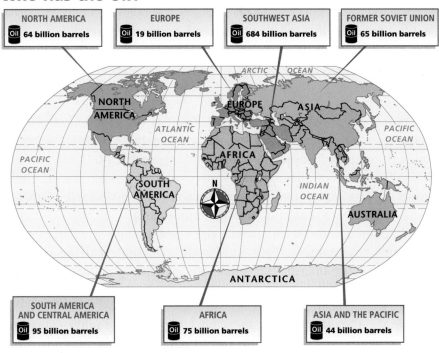

| NORTH AMERICA | EUROPE | SOUTHWEST ASIA | FORMER SOVIET UNION |
|---|---|---|---|
| Oil 64 billion barrels | Oil 19 billion barrels | Oil 684 billion barrels | Oil 65 billion barrels |

| SOUTH AMERICA AND CENTRAL AMERICA | AFRICA | ASIA AND THE PACIFIC |
|---|---|---|
| Oil 95 billion barrels | Oil 75 billion barrels | Oil 44 billion barrels |

**Source:** *BP Amoco Statistical Review of World Energy 2001*

◄ More than half of all known oil deposits are located in Southwest Asia. New deposits are still being found, but Southwest Asia will probably continue to hold the largest share.

Petroleum is not evenly distributed on Earth. Of the oil reserves that have been discovered, more than 65 percent are found in Southwest Asia. Most of that is in Saudi Arabia. North America has around 7 percent of the world's known oil, while South America has around 10 percent. Other regions have oil in small amounts.

**Natural Gas** The use of natural gas is growing rapidly. Natural gas is gas that comes from Earth's crust through natural openings or drilled wells. Large natural gas fields are found in Russia and Southwest Asia. Northern Canada also has large amounts of natural gas. However, the fields are located in the far north. Frozen seas and low temperatures make it difficult to pump and ship the gas safely.

Natural gas is the cleanest-burning fossil fuel. It produces much less air pollution than gasoline or diesel fuel. It is usually transported by pipeline, making it most useful for factories and electrical plants. It is also used for heating and cooking. Vehicles that run on natural gas have to carry the fuel in special, bulky containers. However, some large cities now have buses and taxis that use natural gas to help cut down on air pollution.

✓ **READING CHECK:** *Physical Systems* What physical processes produced fossil fuels?

The Alaska pipeline carries oil from north to south across Alaska.
**Interpreting the Visual Record** Why do you think this pipeline is above ground?

▼

**internet** connect

GO TO: go.hrw.com
KEYWORD: SK3 CH4
FOR: Web sites about
Earth's resources

# Renewable Energy Resources

People have also learned to use several renewable energy resources. They include waterpower, wind power, heat from within Earth, and the Sun's energy.

**Water** The most commonly used renewable energy source is **hydroelectric power**. Hydroelectric power is the production of electricity by waterpower. Dams harness the energy of falling water to power generators. These generators produce electricity. Dams produce about 9 percent of the electricity used in the United States. Other countries producing hydroelectric power include Brazil, Canada, China, Egypt, New Zealand, Norway, and Russia.

Although hydroelectric power does not pollute the air, it does affect the environment. Fish and wildlife habitats can be affected when reservoirs, or artificial lakes, are created by dams. Reservoirs may also cover farmland and forests.

**Wind** For thousands of years, wind has powered sailing ships and boats. People have also long used wind power to turn windmills. Such mills were used to pump water out of wells or to grind grain into flour. In some places windmills are still used for these purposes.

Today, wind has a new use. It can create electricity by turning a system of fan blades called a turbine. "Wind farms" with hundreds of wind turbines have been built in some windy places.

**Geothermal Energy** The heat of Earth's interior—**geothermal energy**—can also be used to generate electricity. This internal heat escapes through hot springs and steam vents on Earth's surface. This geothermal energy can be captured to power electric generators.

Wind turbines are just one source of electricity.

**Interpreting the Visual Record  How does this photo show human adaptation to the environment?**

**The Sun** The Sun's heat and light are known as **solar energy**. This energy can be used to heat water or homes. Special solar panels also absorb solar energy to make electricity. In the past, converting solar energy into electricity was expensive. New research, however, may make solar energy cheaper in the future.

✔ **READING CHECK:** *Physical Systems* What are four renewable energy sources?

Experimental cars like this one run on solar energy.

# Nuclear Energy

In the late 1930s scientists discovered nuclear energy. They learned that energy could be released by changes in the nucleus, or core, of atoms. Nuclear energy was first used to make powerful bombs. Scientists found out that nuclear energy can also be used to produce electricity. Lithuania, France, Belgium, Ukraine, and Sweden rely on nuclear energy for much of their power. This reduces their dependence on imported oil.

There are serious concerns about the use of nuclear power. Several nuclear power plants have had accidents. In 1986 an accident at a nuclear reactor in Chernobyl in Ukraine killed dozens of people. It also caused cancer in thousands more. Homes and farms in the area of the reactor had to be abandoned.

Nuclear energy produces waste that remains dangerous for thousands of years. People do not agree on how nuclear waste can be stored or transported safely. Because of this some countries are reducing their dependence on nuclear energy. Denmark and New Zealand avoid it altogether. The United States does not intend to expand its use of nuclear energy. As a result, scientists continue to search for other renewable energy sources.

✔ **READING CHECK:** *Environment and Society* What are the concerns associated with nuclear power?

---

## Section Review 4

go.hrw.com **Homework Practice Online** Keyword: SK3 HP4

**Define and explain:** fossil fuels, petroleum, refineries, hydroelectric power, geothermal energy, solar energy

### Reading for the Main Idea

1. *Physical Systems* What are the three main fossil fuels, and how were they formed?

2. *Physical Systems* What are the four most common renewable energy sources? Describe how each of these harnesses energy.

### Critical Thinking

3. **Finding the Main Idea** How do dams affect the environment?

4. **Analyzing Information** What are some of the problems associated with nuclear energy?

### Organizing What You Know

5. **Contrasting** Copy the following graphic organizer. Use it to contrast the characteristics of renewable and nonrenewable resources.

| Renewable resources | ↔ | Nonrenewable resources |
|---|---|---|
|  |  |  |

# Reviewing What You Know

## Building Vocabulary

On a separate sheet of paper, write sentences to define each of the following words.

1. renewable resources
2. desertification
3. deforestation
4. reforestation
5. aquifers
6. acid rain
7. nonrenewable resources
8. fossil fuels
9. hydroelectric power
10. solar energy

## Reviewing the Main Ideas

1. *Environment and Society*  Why is fertile soil important, and how is it created?
2. *Environment and Society*  What actions have people taken to increase their supply of water?
3. *Environment and Society*  What are minerals, and why are they important to us?
4. *Environment and Society*  For what are fossil fuels used?
5. *Environment and Society*  What are the four most common renewable energy sources, and how is each used?

## Understanding Environment and Society

### Chernobyl

On April 26, 1986, a nuclear reactor exploded in Chernobyl. Radiation caused serious problems in Ukraine and Belarus, as well as in Eastern and Western Europe. Create an outline for a presentation based on information about the following:

• Conditions of the environment then and now.
• Preventive measures taken to prevent future accidents.

## Thinking Critically

1. **Drawing Inferences and Conclusions** Why does the issue of use of rain forests cause such disagreement? What is happening to Earth's rain forests?

2. **Summarizing** What are the major causes of water and air pollution, and how does pollution affect life on this planet?

3. **Drawing Inferences and Conclusions** Why are minerals valued by society?

4. **Contrasting** How are metallic minerals different from nonmetallic minerals?

5. **Drawing Inferences and Conclusions** Why does the use of nuclear energy continue to be a debated topic?

## Map ACTIVITY

On a separate sheet of paper, match the letters on the map with their correct region. Then write the number of barrels of oil known to be located in each region.

**Africa**

**Europe**

**former Soviet Union**

**South and Central America**

**Southwest Asia**

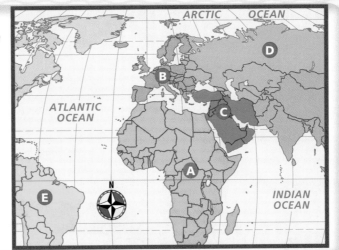

## Mental Mapping Skills ACTIVITY

On a separate sheet of paper, draw a freehand map of the United States. Label areas that have copper. Compare this map with a physical map of the United States. What, if any, physical features are located in the same regions as copper deposits?

## WRITING ACTIVITY

Write a short paper explaining which mineral is most important to you. Justify your selection with facts you have learned. Be sure to use standard grammar, spelling, sentence structure, and punctuation.

## Alternative Assessment

## Portfolio ACTIVITY

**Learning About Your Local Geography**

**Environmental Issues** Study your local environment. What issues of preservation and use are important to the people of your community? How does your government handle these issues?

---

**internet connect**

Internet Activity: **go.hrw.com**
KEYWORD: SK3 GT4

Choose a topic to explore Earth's resources:
- Trek through different kinds of forests.
- Investigate global warming.
- Make a recycling plan.

# CHAPTER 5

# The World's People

The Colosseum, Rome, Italy

1998 Olympic opening ceremony, Nagano, Japan

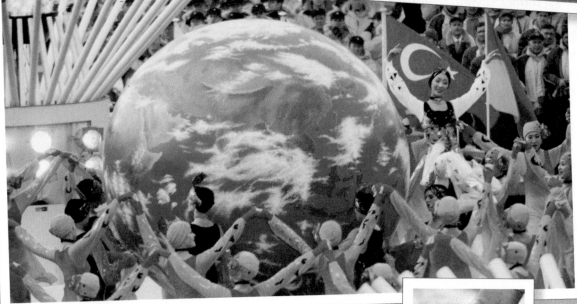

Easter Island, Chile

# Section 1 Culture

## Read to Discover

1. What is culture?
2. Why are cultural symbols important?
3. What influences how cultures develop?
4. How did agriculture affect the development of culture?

## Define

culture
culture region
culture traits
ethnic groups
multicultural
race

acculturation
symbol
domestication
subsistence agriculture
commercial agriculture
civilization

### WHY IT MATTERS

Throughout history, culture has both brought people together and created conflict among groups. Use CNNfyi.com or other current events sources to learn about cultural conflicts around the globe. Record your findings in your journal.

*Flags at the South Pole*

## Aspects of Culture

The people of the world's approximately 200 countries speak hundreds of different languages. They may dress in different ways and eat different foods. However, all societies share certain basic institutions, including a government, an educational system, an economic system, and religious institutions. These vary from society to society and are often based on that society's **culture**. Culture is a learned system of shared beliefs and ways of doing things that guides a person's daily behavior. Most people around the world have a national culture shared with people of their own country. They may also have religious practices, beliefs, and language in common with people from other countries. Sometimes a culture dominates a particular region. This is known as a **culture region**. In a culture region, people may share certain **culture traits**, or elements of culture, such as dress, food, or religious beliefs. West Africa is an example of a culture region. Culture can also be based on a person's job or age. People can belong to more than one culture and can choose which to emphasize.

**Race and Ethnic Groups** Cultural groups share beliefs and practices learned from parents, grandparents, and ancestors. These groups are sometimes called **ethnic groups**. An ethnic group's shared culture may include its religion, history, language, holiday traditions, and special foods.

When people from different cultures live in the same country, the country is described as **multicultural** or multiethnic. Many countries

Thousands of Czechs and Germans settled in Texas in the mid-1800s. Dancers from central Texas perform a traditional Czech dance.

▼

# World Religions

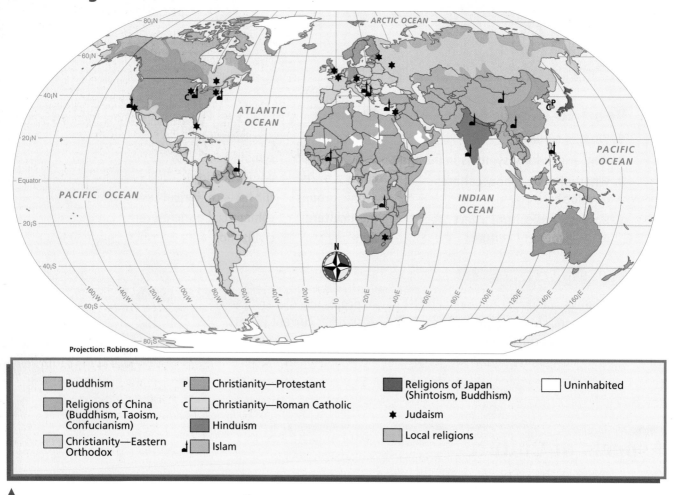

Projection: Robinson

| | | | |
|---|---|---|---|
| Buddhism | **P** Christianity—Protestant | Religions of Japan (Shintoism, Buddhism) | Uninhabited |
| Religions of China (Buddhism, Taoism, Confucianism) | **C** Christianity—Roman Catholic | ★ Judaism | |
| Christianity—Eastern Orthodox | Hinduism | Local religions | |
| | Islam | | |

▲
Religion is one aspect of culture.

A disc jockey sits at the control board of a Miami radio station that plays Cuban music.

are multicultural. In some countries, such as Belgium, different ethnic groups have cooperated to form a united country. In other cases, such as in French-speaking Quebec, Canada, ethnic groups have frequently been in conflict. Sometimes, people from one ethnic group are spread over two or more countries. For example, Germans live in different European countries: Germany, Austria, and Czechoslovakia. The Kurds, who are a people with no country of their own, live mostly in Syria, Iran, Iraq, and Turkey.

**Race** is based on inherited physical or biological traits. It is sometimes confused with ethnic group. For example, the Hispanic ethnic group in the United States includes people who look quite different from each other. However, they share a common Spanish or Latin American heritage. As you know, people vary in physical appearance. Some of these differences have developed in response to climate factors like cold and sunlight. Because people have moved from region to region throughout history, these differences are not clear-cut. Each culture defines race in its own way, emphasizing particular biological and ethnic characteristics. An example can be seen in Rwanda, a country in East Africa. In this country, the Hutu and the Tutsi have carried on a bitter civil war. Although both are East African, each one considers itself different from the other. Their definition of race involves height and facial features. Around the world, people tend to identify races based on obvious physical traits. However, these definitions of race are based primarily on attitudes, not actual biological differences.

**Cultural Change** Cultures change over time. Humans invent new ways of doing things and spread these new ways to others. The spread of one culture's ways or beliefs to another culture is called diffusion. Diffusion may occur when people move from one place to another. The English language was once confined to England and parts of Scotland. It is now one of the world's most widely spoken languages. English originally spread because people from England founded colonies in other regions. More recently, as communication among cultures has increased, English has spread through English-language films and television programs. English has also become an international language of science and technology.

People sometimes may borrow aspects of another culture as the result of long-term contact with another society. This process is called **acculturation**. For example, people in one culture may adopt the religion of another. As a result, they might change other cultural practices to conform to the new religion. For example, farmers who become Muslim may quit raising pigs because Islam forbids eating pork.

✓ **READING CHECK:** ( *Human Systems* ) What is the definition of culture?

Cultures mix in New York City's Chinatown.

**Interpreting the Visual Record** Why might immigrants to a new country settle in the same neighborhood?

internet connect

GO TO: go.hrw.com
KEYWORD: SK3 CH5
FOR: Web sites about the world's people

# Cultural Differences

A **symbol** is a sign that stands for something else. A symbol can be a word, a shape, a color, or a flag. People learn symbols from their culture. The sets of sounds of a language are symbols. These symbols have meaning for the people who speak that language. The same sound may mean something different to people who speak another language. The word *bad* means "evil" in English, "cool" to teenagers, and "bath" in German.

If you traveled to another country, you might notice immediately that people behave differently. For instance, they may speak a different language or wear different clothes. They might celebrate different holidays or salute a different flag. Symbols reflect the artistic, literary, and religious expressions of a society or culture. They also reflect that society's belief systems. Language, clothing, holidays, and flags are all symbols. Symbols help people communicate with each other and create a sense of belonging to a group.

✓ **READING CHECK:** ( *Human Systems* ) How do symbols reflect differences among societies and cultures?

Fans cheer for the U.S. Olympic soccer team.

**Interpreting the Visual Record** Why do you think symbols such as flags create strong emotions?

A couple prepares for a wedding ceremony in Kazakhstan.

**Interpreting the Visual Record** What aspects of these people's clothing indicate that they are dressed for a special event?

The layout of Marrakech, Morocco, is typical of many North African cities.

**Interpreting the Visual Record** How are the streets and houses of Marrakech different from those in your community?

Spain

Morocco

Marrakech

Algeria

# Development of a Culture

All people have the same basic needs for food, water, clothing, and shelter. People everywhere live in families and mark important family changes together. They usually have rituals or traditions that go with the birth of a baby, the wedding of a couple, or the death of a grandparent. All human societies need to deal with natural disasters. They must also deal with people who break the rules of behavior. However, people in different places meet these needs in unique ways. They eat different foods, build different kinds of houses, and form families in different ways. They have different rules of behavior. Two important factors that influence the way people meet basic needs are their history and environment.

**History** Culture is shaped by history. A region's people may have been conquered by the same outsiders. They may have adopted the same religion. They may have come from the same area and may share a common language. However, historical events may have affected some parts of a region but not others. For example, in North America French colonists brought their culture to Louisiana and Canada. However, they did not have a major influence on the Middle Atlantic region of the United States.

Cultures also shape history by influencing the way people respond to the same historical forces. Nigeria, India, and Australia were all colonized by the British. Today each nation still uses elements of the British legal system, but with important differences.

**Environment** The environment of a region can influence the development of culture. For example, in Egypt the Nile River is central to people's lives. The ancient Egyptians saw the fertile soils brought by the flooding of the Nile as the work of the gods. Beliefs in mountain spirits were important in many mountainous regions of the world. These areas include Tibet, Japan, and the Andes of South America.

Culture also determines how people use and shape their landscape. For example, city plans are cultural. Cities in Spain and its former colonies are organized around a central plaza, or square, with a church and a courthouse. On the other hand, Chinese cities are oriented to the four compass points. American cities often follow a rectangular grid plan. Many French city streets radiate out from a central core.

✓ **READING CHECK:** ( *Human Systems* ) What are some ways in which culture traits spread?

# Development of Agriculture

For most of human history people ate only wild plants and animals. When the food ran out in one place, they migrated, or moved to another place. Very few people still live this way today. Thousands of years ago, humans began to help their favorite wild plant foods to grow. They probably cleared the land around their campsites and dumped seeds or fruits in piles of refuse. Plants took root and grew. People may also have dug water holes to encourage wild cattle to come and drink. People began cultivating the largest plants and breeding the tamest animals. Gradually, the wild plants and animals changed. They became dependent on people. This process is called **domestication**. A domesticated species has changed its form and behavior so much that it depends on people to survive. Domestic sheep can no longer leap from rock to rock like their wild ancestors. However, the wool of domestic sheep is more useful to humans. It can be combed and twisted into yarn.

Domestication happened in many parts of the world. In Peru llamas and potatoes were domesticated. People in ancient Mexico and Central America domesticated corn, beans, squash, tomatoes, and hot peppers. None of these foods was grown in Europe, Asia, or Africa before the time of Christopher Columbus's voyages to the Americas. Meanwhile, Africans had domesticated sorghum and a kind of rice. Cattle, sheep, and goats were probably first raised in Southwest Asia. Wheat and rye were first domesticated in Central Asia. The horse was also domesticated there. These domesticated plants and animals were unknown in the Americas before the time of Columbus.

This ancient Egyptian wall painting shows domesticated cattle.

**Interpreting the Visual Record Can you name other kinds of domesticated animals?**

**Agriculture and Environment** Agriculture changed the landscape. To make room for growing food, people cut down forests. They also built fences, dug irrigation canals, and terraced hillsides. Governments were created to direct the labor needed for these large projects. Governments also defended against outsiders and helped people resolve problems. People could now grow enough food for a whole year. Therefore, they stopped migrating and built permanent settlements.

**Types of Agriculture** Some farmers grow just enough food to provide for themselves and their own families. This type of farming is called **subsistence agriculture**. In the wealthier countries of the world, a small number of farmers can produce food for everyone. Each farm is large and may grow only one product. This type of farming is called **commercial agriculture**. In this system companies rather than individuals or families may own the farms.

**Agriculture and Civilization** Agriculture enabled farmers to produce a surplus of food—more than they could eat themselves. A few people could make things like pottery jars instead of farming. They traded or sold their products for food. With more food a family could feed more children. As a result, populations began to grow. More people became involved in trading and manufacturing. Traders and craftspeople began to live in central market towns. Some towns grew into cities, where many people lived and carried out even more specialized tasks. For example, cities often supported priests and religious officials. They were responsible for organizing and carrying out religious ceremonies. When a culture becomes highly complex, we sometimes call it a **civilization**.

✓ **READING CHECK:** *Environment and Society* In what ways did agriculture affect culture?

*Our Amazing Planet*

Thousands of years ago, domesticated dogs came with humans across the Bering Strait into North America. A breed called the Carolina dog may be descended almost unchanged from those dogs. The reddish yellow, short-haired breed also appears to be closely related to Australian dingoes.

go.hrw.com **Homework Practice Online**
Keyword: SK3 HP5

# Section Review 1

**Define and explain:** culture, culture region, culture trait, ethnic groups, multicultural, race, acculturation, symbol, domestication, subsistence agriculture, commercial agriculture, civilization

## Reading for the Main Idea

**1.** *Human Systems* How can an individual belong to more than one cultural group?

**2.** *Human Systems* What institutions are basic to all societies?

## Critical Thinking

**3. Drawing Inferences and Conclusions** In what ways do history and environment influence or shape a culture? What examples can you find in the text that explain this relationship?

**4. Analyzing Information** What is the relationship between the development of agriculture and culture?

## Organizing What You Know

**5. Summarizing** Copy the following graphic organizer. Use it to describe culture by listing shared beliefs and practices.

Culture

# Section 2 — Population, Economy, and Government

## Read to Discover

1. Why does population density vary, and how has the world's population changed?
2. How do geographers describe and measure economies?
3. What are the different types of economic systems?
4. How do governments differ?

## Define

primary industries
secondary industries
tertiary industries
quaternary industries
gross national product
gross domestic product
developed countries
developing countries
free enterprise
factors of production
entrepreneurs
market economy
command economy
traditional economy
democracy
unlimited government
limited government

### WHY IT MATTERS

Human population has increased dramatically in the past 200 years. Use CNNfyi.com or other current events sources to find current projections for global or U.S. populations. Record your findings in your journal.

*Newborn baby*

## Calculating Population Density

The branch of geography that studies human populations is called demography. Geographers who study it are called demographers. They look at such things as population size, density, and age trends. Some countries are very crowded. Others are only thinly populated. Demographers measure population density by dividing a country's population by its area. The area is stated in either square miles or square kilometers. For example, the United States has 74 people for every square mile (29/sq km). Australia has just 6 people per square mile (2.3/sq km). Japan has 869 people per square mile (336/sq km), and Argentina has 35 people per square mile (14/sq km).

These densities include all of the land in a country. However, people may not be able to live on some land. Rugged mountains, deserts, frozen lands, and other similar places usually have very few people. Instead, people tend to live in areas where the land can be farmed. Major cities tend to be located in these same regions of dense population.

✓ **READING CHECK:** *Human Systems* What is population density?

## Differences in Population Density

Looking at this book's maps of world population densities allows us to make generalizations. Much of eastern and southern Asia is very

Shoppers crowd a street in Tokyo, Japan.

▼

densely populated. There are dense populations in Western Europe and in eastern areas of North America. There are also places with very low population densities. Canada, Australia, and Siberia have large areas where few people live. The same is true for the Sahara Desert. Parts of Asia, South America, and Africa also have low population densities.

Heavily populated areas attract large numbers of people for different reasons. Some places have been densely populated for thousands of years. Examples include the Nile River valley in Egypt and the Huang River valley in China. These places have fertile soil, a steady source of water, and a good growing climate. These factors allow people to farm successfully. People are also drawn to cities. The movement of people from farms to cities is called urbanization. In many countries people move to cities when they cannot find work in rural areas. In recent years this movement has helped create huge cities. Mexico City, Mexico; São Paulo, Brazil; and Lagos, Nigeria, are among these giant cities. Some European cities experienced similar rapid growth when they industrialized in the 1800s. During that period people left farms to come to the cities to work in factories.

✔ **READING CHECK:** ( *Human Systems* ) Why does population density vary?

**World Population Growth**

**Source:** U.S. Census

**Interpreting the Chart** **Approximately when did world population growth begin to increase significantly?**

▲

# Population Growth

Researchers estimate that about 10,000 years ago the world's entire human population was less than 10 million. The annual number of births was roughly the same as the annual number of deaths.

After people made the shift from hunting and gathering to farming, more food was available. People began to live longer and have more children. The world's population grew. About 2,000 years ago, the world had some 200 million people. By A.D. 1650 the world's population had grown to about 500 million. By 1850 there were some 1 billion people. Better health care and food supplies helped more babies survive into adulthood and have children. By 1930 there were 2 billion people on Earth. Just 45 years later that number had doubled to 4 billion. In 1999 Earth's population reached 6 billion. By the year 2025 the world's population could grow to about 9 billion.

Births add to a country's population. Deaths subtract from it. The number of births per 1,000 people in a year is called the birthrate. Similarly, the death rate is the annual number of deaths per 1,000 people. The birthrate minus the death rate equals the rate of natural increase. This number is expressed as a percentage. A country's population changes when people enter or leave the country.

✔ **READING CHECK:** ( *Human Systems* ) What is the rate of natural increase?

# Economic Activity

All of the activities that people do to earn a living are part of a system called the economy. This includes people going to work, making things, selling things, buying things, and trading services. Economics is the study of the production, distribution, and use of goods and services.

**Types of Economic Activities** Geographers divide economic activities into primary, secondary, tertiary, and quaternary industries. **Primary industries** are activities that directly involve natural resources or raw materials. These industries include farming, mining, and cutting trees.

The products of primary industries often have to go through several stages before people can use them. **Secondary industries** change the raw materials created by primary activities into finished products. For example, the sawmill that turns a tree into lumber is a secondary industry.

**Tertiary industries** handle goods that are ready to be sold to consumers. The stores that sell products are included in this group. The trucks and trains that move products to stores are part of this group. Banks, insurance companies, and government agencies are also considered tertiary industries.

The fourth part of the economy is known as **quaternary industries**. People in these industries have specialized skills. They work mostly with information instead of goods. Researchers, managers, and administrators fall into this category.

**Economic Indicators** A common means of measuring a country's economy is the **gross national product** (GNP). The GNP is the value of all goods and services that a country produces in one year. It includes goods and services made by factories owned by that country's citizens but located in foreign countries. Most geographers use **gross domestic product** (GDP) instead of GNP. GDP includes only those goods and services produced within a country. GDP divided by the country's population is called per capita GDP. This figure shows individual purchasing power and is useful for comparing levels of economic development.

Ⓐ **Primary industry:** A dairy farmer feeds his cows.

Ⓑ **Secondary industry:** Cheese is prepared in a factory.

Ⓒ **Tertiary industry:** A grocer is selling cheese to a consumer.

Ⓓ **Quaternary industry:** A technician inspects dairy products in a lab.

✓ **READING CHECK:** *Human Systems* What are primary, secondary, tertiary, and quaternary industries?

# Economic Development

Geographers use various measures including GNP, GDP, per capita GDP, life expectancy, and literacy to divide the world into two groups. Industrialized countries like the United States, Canada, Japan, and most European countries are wealthier. They are called **developed countries**. These countries have strong secondary, tertiary, and quaternary industries. They have good health care systems. Developed countries have good systems of education and a high literacy rate. The literacy rate is the percentage of people who can read and write. Most people in developed countries live in cities and have access to telecommunications systems—systems that allow long-distance communication. Geographers study the number of telephones, televisions, or computers in a country. They sometimes use these figures to estimate the country's level of technology.

**Developing countries** make up the second group. They are in different stages of moving toward development. About two thirds of the world's people live in developing countries. These countries are poorer. Their citizens often work in farming or other primary industries and earn low wages. Cities are often crowded with poorly educated people hoping to find work. They usually have little access to health care or telecommunications. Some developing countries have made economic progress in recent decades. South Korea and Mexico are good examples. These countries are experiencing strong growth in manufacturing and trade. However, some of the world's poorest countries are developing slowly or not at all.

✓ **READING CHECK:**   *Human Systems*   How do geographers distinguish between developed and developing countries?

## Comparing Developed and Developing Countries

| Country | Population | Rate of Natural Increase | Per Capita GDP | Life Expectancy | Literacy Rate | Telephone Lines |
|---------|-----------|--------------------------|----------------|-----------------|---------------|-----------------|
| United States | 281.4 million | 0.9% | $ 36,200 | 77 | 97% | 194 million |
| France | 59.5 million | 0.4% | $ 24,400 | 79 | 99% | 35 million |
| South Korea | 47.9 million | 0.9% | $ 16,100 | 75 | 98% | 24 million |
| Mexico | 101.8 million | 1.5% | $ 9,100 | 72 | 90% | 9.6 million |
| Poland | 38.6 million | −0.03% | $ 8,500 | 73 | 99% | 8 million |
| Brazil | 174.4 million | 0.9% | $ 6,500 | 63 | 83% | 17 million |
| Egypt | 69.5 million | 1.7% | $ 3,600 | 64 | 51% | 3.9 million |
| Myanmar | 42 million | 0.6% | $ 1,500 | 55 | 83% | 250,000 |
| Mali | 11 million | 3.0% | $ 850 | 47 | 31% | 23,000 |

**Sources:** Central Intelligence Agency, *The World Factbook 2001*

Interpreting the Visual Record **Which countries have the highest literacy rate?**

# Economic Systems

Countries organize their economies in different ways. Most developed countries organize the production and distribution of goods and services in a system called **free enterprise**. The United States operates under a free enterprise system. There are many benefits to this system. Companies are free to make whatever goods they wish. Employees can seek the highest wages for their work. People, rather than the government, control the **factors of production**. Factors of production are the things that determine what goods are produced in an economy. They include the natural resources that are available for making goods for sale. They also include the capital, or money, needed to pay for production and the labor needed to manufacture goods. The work of **entrepreneurs** (ahn-truh-pruh-NUHRS) makes up a fourth factor of production. Entrepreneurs are people who start businesses in a free enterprise system. Business owners in a free enterprise system sell their goods in a **market economy**. In such an economy, business owners and customers make decisions about what to make, sell, and buy.

In contrast, the governments of some countries control the factors of production. The government decides what, and how much, will be produced. It also sets the prices of goods to be sold. This is called a **command economy**. Some countries with a command economy are governed by an economic and political system called communism. Under communism, the government owns almost all the factors of production. Very few countries today are communist. Cuba is an example of a communist nation.

Finally, there are some societies around the world that operate within a **traditional economy**. A traditional economy is one that is based on custom and tradition. Economic activities are based on laws, rituals, religious beliefs, or habits developed by the society's ancestors. The Mbuti people of the Democratic Republic of the Congo practice a traditional economy, for example.

✓ **READING CHECK:** ( *Human Systems* ) What are the three types of economies?

◄

Large shopping malls, such as this one in New York City's Trump Tower, are common in countries that have market economies and a free enterprise system. Shoppers here can find a wide range of stores and goods concentrated in one area.

# World Governments

Just as countries use different economic systems, they also have different ways of organizing their governments. As you have read, some countries are communist—their governments control both the political and economic systems. Other countries are controlled by one ruler, such as a monarch or a dictator. For example, Saudi Arabia is ruled by a monarch. King Fahd bin Abd al-Aziz Al Saud is both the chief of state and the head of government.

In other countries, a relatively small group of people controls the government. Many countries—including the United States, New Zealand, and Germany—have democratic governments. In a **democracy**, voters elect leaders and rule by majority. Ideas about democratic government began in ancient Greece. The American and French Revolutions established the world's first modern democratic governments in the late 1700s. Today, most developed countries are democracies with free enterprise economies. However, some countries with democratic governments, such as Russia and India, struggle with economic issues.

How a government is organized determines whether it has limited or unlimited powers. **Unlimited governments**, such as the French monarchy before the French Revolution, have total control over their citizens. They also have no legal controls placed on their actions. In a **limited government**, government leaders are held accountable by citizens through their constitutions and the democratic process. These limitations help protect citizens from abuses of power. Today, many countries around the world, including the United States, have limited governments.

✓ **READING CHECK:** ( *Human Systems* ) What is the difference between limited and unlimited government?

---

## Section Review 2

**Define and explain:** primary industries, secondary industries, tertiary industries, quaternary industries, gross national product, gross domestic product, developed countries, developing countries, free enterprise, factors of production, entrepreneurs, market economy, command economy, traditional economy, democracy, unlimited governments, limited government

### Reading for the Main Idea

1. ( *Environment and Society* ) What geographic factors influence population density?

2. ( *Human Systems* ) What characteristics do developed countries share?

### Critical Thinking

3. **Finding the Main Idea** What are the different economic systems? Describe each.

4. **Drawing Inferences and Conclusions** How did democracy develop, and why did it help create limited government?

### Organizing What You Know

5. **Summarizing** Copy the following graphic organizer. Use it to study your local community and classify the businesses in your area.

| Primary Industries | Secondary Industries | Tertiary Industries | Quaternary Industries |
|---|---|---|---|
| • | • | • | • |
| • | • | • | • |

### Read to Discover

1. What problems are associated with high and low population growth rates?
2. What are two different views of population growth and resources?

### Define

scarcity
carrying capacity

**WHY IT MATTERS**

Some people believe that the world's limited resources cannot support a rapidly increasing human population. Use CNN**fyi**.com or other **current events** sources to find out what issues are raised by world population growth. Record your findings in your journal.

*Population sign for Anatone, Washington*

## Population Growth Rates

With the help of technology, humans can survive in a wide range of environments. People can build houses and wear clothing to survive in cold climates. Food can be grown in one place and shipped to another. For these reasons and others the human population has grown tremendously.

Population growth rates differ from place to place. Many developed countries have populations that are growing very slowly, holding steady, or even shrinking. However, the populations of most developing countries continue to grow rapidly.

*An Inuit family in northern Canada uses a snowmobile to pull a sled.*

**Growth Rate Issues** In general, a high population growth rate will hinder a country's economic development. Countries must provide jobs, education, and medical care for their citizens. A rapidly growing population can strain a country's resources and lead to **scarcity**—when demand is greater than supply. Many of the countries with the highest growth rates today are among the world's poorest.

However, a shortage of young people entering the workforce lowers a country's ability to produce goods. Young people are needed to replace older people who retire or die. Many countries with very low growth rates or shrinking overall populations must support a growing number of older people. These people may need more health care.

**Uneven Resource Distribution** Natural resources such as fresh water, minerals, and fertile land are not distributed evenly. A country's resources cannot always support its population. However, the country may be able to acquire needed resources by trading with other countries. In this system of economic interdependence, two countries can exchange resources or goods so that each gets what it needs. Japan, for example, has few energy resources but is a world leader in manufacturing. Japan sells manufactured goods to others, particularly the United States. Japan then uses the money to buy oil from Saudi Arabia.

The need for scarce resources usually leads countries to trade peacefully. However, it can also lead to military conflict. One country might try to take over a resource-rich area of a neighboring country. If we hope to avoid future wars over resources, the world's people must share resources more equally.

✓ **READING CHECK:** *Human Systems* How does scarcity of resources affect international trade and economic interdependence?

## World Population and Resources

Some people think Earth can easily support a much larger human population. They base this view partly on history. For example, new fertilizers and special seeds mean more food can be grown today than ever before. They also think that scientists will probably discover new energy resources. The Sun, for example, is a vast energy source. Today we can only use a fraction of its power, however. Another way to support more people would be to make better use of existing resources. For example, we can recycle materials and reduce the amount of waste we generate.

Many farmers in India still use traditional methods.

**Interpreting the Visual Record** What in this photo indicates a less developed agricultural society?

A buildup of salt has ruined this field in southern Iraq. This land is now useless for growing crops, thus contributing to the lack of land suitable for farming.

Other people hold the opposite opinion. They argue that the world is already showing signs of reaching its **carrying capacity**. Carrying capacity is the maximum number of a species that can be supported by an area's scarce resources. The amount of land available for farming is shrinking. Many areas are experiencing a shortage of fresh water. Oil, a nonrenewable resource, will eventually run out. Pollution is damaging the atmosphere and the oceans. The rich nations of the world are not always willing to share with poorer nations. In the future, these people think food and water supplies will run short in many countries. People without enough to eat will become ill more easily, leading to widespread disease. Such problems may lead a country to invade its neighbors to capture resources.

These are challenging issues that reach into all areas of life. They will become even more important in the future. A better understanding of geography will help you understand and deal with these issues.

✓ **READING CHECK:** ( *Environment and Society* ) What are two different views on population growth and resources?

go.hrw.com **Homework Practice Online** Keyword: SK3 HP5

## Section Review 3

**Define and explain:** scarcity, carrying capacity

### Reading for the Main Idea

1. ( *Human Systems* ) What problems are associated with rapid population growth?

2. ( *Human Systems* ) What are two viewpoints about future population growth?

### Critical Thinking

3. **Analyzing Information** How has technology helped the worldwide human population grow?

4. **Finding the Main Idea** How do countries deal with the uneven distribution of resources?

### Organizing What You Know

5. **Contrasting** Copy the following graphic organizer. Use it to discuss two arguments about population growth.

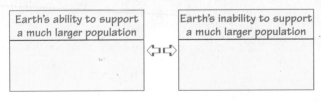

| Earth's ability to support a much larger population | | Earth's inability to support a much larger population |
|---|---|---|
| | ⟨⟩⟨⟩ | |

**The World's People** • 89

# Reviewing What You Know

## Building Vocabulary

On a separate sheet of paper, write sentences to define each of the following words.

1. culture
2. ethnic groups
3. multicultural
4. acculturation
5. symbol
6. domestication
7. subsistence agriculture
8. civilization
9. limited government
10. entrepreneurs
11. command economy
12. market economy
13. factors of production
14. free enterprise
15. carrying capacity

## Reviewing the Main Ideas

1. ( Human Systems )  What is culture, and why should people study it?
2. ( Environment and Society )  What is the difference between subsistence and commercial agriculture?
3. ( Human Systems )  What are some of the different ways countries organize governments?
4. ( Human Systems )  Why are telecommunications devices useful as economic indicators?
5. ( Environment and Society )  How do population growth rates affect resources?

## Understanding Environment and Society

### Domestication

Do you know how, when, and why people first domesticated dogs, cats, pigs, and hawks? What about oranges? Pick a domesticated plant or animal to research. As you prepare your presentation consider the following:

- Where the crop or animal was first domesticated.
- Differences between it and its wild ancestors.
- Humans spreading it to new areas.

## Thinking Critically

1. **Drawing Inferences and Conclusions** Why are ethnic groups sometimes confused with races?

2. **Making Generalizations and Predictions** Over the past 2,000 years, how many times has world population doubled? By when is it projected to double again? What might be the effect of this increase?

3. **Finding the Main Idea** What are the four basic divisions of industry? Give examples.

4. **Summarizing** What are the three economic systems, and what are the benefits of the U.S. free-enterprise system?

5. **Making Generalizations and Predictions** Do you think Earth has a carrying capacity for its human population? Why or why not?

6. **Summarizing** Explain unlimited and limited government. Give examples of each.

**Map** **ACTIVITY**

On a separate sheet of paper, match the letters on the map with their correct labels.

**Buddhism**

**Christianity—Eastern Orthodox**

**Christianity—Protestant**

**Christianity—Roman Catholic**

**Hinduism**

**Islam**

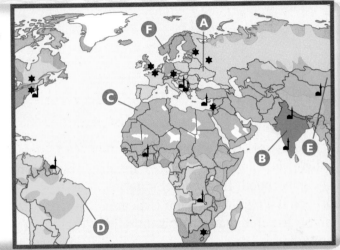

## Mental Mapping Skills **ACTIVITY**

Draw a map of the world and label Japan, Australia, the United Kingdom, and Argentina. Based on your knowledge of climates, population density, and resources, which of these countries probably depend on imported food? Which ones probably export food? Express this information on your map.

## WRITING

**ACTIVITY** Study the economy of your local community. Has the local economy grown or declined since 1985? Why? Predict how your local area could change economically during the next 10 years. Be sure to use standard grammar, spelling, sentence structure, and punctuation.

## Alternative Assessment

## Portfolio **ACTIVITY**

**Learning About Your Local Geography**

**Factors of Production** Recall the discussion of the factors of production. Create a model showing how these factors influence the economy of your community.

**☐ internet connect**

Internet Activity: go.hrw.com
KEYWORD: SK3 GT5

Choose a topic to explore online:
- Visit famous buildings and monuments around the world.
- Compare facts about life in different countries.
- Examine world population growth.

# FOCUS ON REGIONS

## What is a Region?

Think about where you live, where you go to school, and where you shop. These places are all part of your neighborhood. In geographic terms, your neighborhood is a region. A region is an area that has common features that make it different from surrounding areas.

What regions do you live in? You live on a continent, in a country, and in a state. These are all regions that can be mapped.

Regions can be divided into smaller regions called subregions. For example, Africa is a major world region. Africa's subregions include North Africa, West Africa, East Africa, central Africa, and southern Africa. Each subregion can be divided into even smaller subregions.

**Regional Characteristics** Regions can be based on physical, political, economic, or cultural characteristics. Physical regions are based on Earth's natural features, such as continents, landforms, and climates. Political regions are based on countries and their subregions, such as states, provinces, and cities. Economic regions are based on money-making activities such as agriculture or industries. Cultural regions are based on features such as language, religion, or ethnicity.

▲
East Africa is a subregion of Africa. It is an area of plateaus, rolling hills, and savanna grasslands.

# Major World Regions

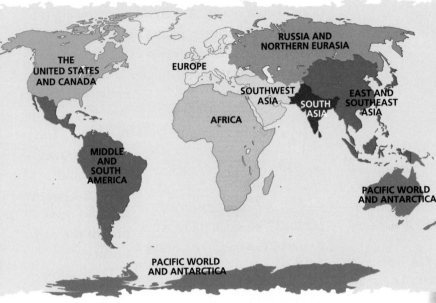

THE UNITED STATES AND CANADA

EUROPE

RUSSIA AND NORTHERN EURASIA

SOUTHWEST ASIA

AFRICA

SOUTH ASIA

EAST AND SOUTHEAST ASIA

MIDDLE AND SOUTH AMERICA

PACIFIC WORLD AND ANTARCTICA

PACIFIC WORLD AND ANTARCTICA

**Regional Boundaries** All regions have boundaries, or borders. Boundaries are where the features of one region meet the features of a different region. Some boundaries, such as coastlines or country borders, can be shown as lines on a map. Other regional boundaries are less clear.

Transition zones are areas where the features of one region change gradually to the features of a different region. For example, when a city's suburbs expand into rural areas, a transition zone forms. In the transition zone, it may be hard to find the boundary between rural and urban areas.

**Types of Regions** There are three basic types of regions. The first is a formal region. Formal regions are based on one or more common features. For example, Japan is a formal region. Its people share a common government, language, and culture.

The second type of region is a functional region. Functional regions are based on movement and activities that connect different places. For example, Paris, France, is a functional region. It is based on the goods, services, and people that move throughout the city. A shopping center or an airport might also be a functional region.

▲

The international border between Kenya and Tanzania is a clearly defined regional boundary.

The third type of region is a perceived region. Perceived regions are based on people's shared feelings and beliefs. For example, the neighborhood where you live may be a perceived region.

The three basic types of regions overlap to form complex world regions. In this textbook, the world is divided into nine major world regions (see map above). Each has general features that make it different from the other major world regions. These differences include physical, cultural, economic, historical, and political features.

## Understanding What You Read

**1.** Regions can be based on what types of characteristics?

**2.** What are the three basic types of regions?

# Building Skills for Life: Drawing Mental Maps

We create maps in our heads of all kinds of places—our homes, schools, communities, country, and the world. Some of these places we know well. Others we have only heard about. These images we carry in our heads are shaped by what we see and experience. They are also influenced by what we learn from news reports or other sources. Geographers call the maps that we carry around in our heads mental maps.

We use mental maps to organize spatial information about people and places. For example, our mental maps help us move from classroom to classroom at school or get to a friend's home. A mental map of the United States helps us list the states we would pass through driving from New York City to Miami.

We use our mental maps of places when we draw sketch maps. A sketch map showing the relationship between places and the relative size of places can be drawn using very simple shapes. For example, triangles and rectangles could be used to sketch a map of the world. This quickly drawn map would show the relative size and position of the continents.

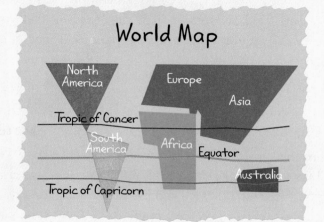

Think about some simple ways we could make our map of the world more detailed. Adding the equator, Tropic of Cancer, and Tropic of Capricorn would be one way. Look at a map of the world in your textbook's Atlas. Note that the bulge in the continent of Africa is north of the equator. Also note that all of Asia is north of the equator. Next note that the Indian subcontinent extends south from the Tropic of Cancer. About half of Australia is located north of the Tropic of Capricorn. As your knowledge of the world increases, your mental map will become even more detailed.

## THE SKILL

**1.** Look at the maps in your textbook's Atlas. Where does the prime meridian fall in relation to the continents?

**2.** On a separate sheet of paper, sketch a simple map of the world from memory. First draw the equator, Tropic of Cancer, Tropic of Capricorn, and prime meridian. Then sketch in the continents. You can use circles, rectangles, and triangles.

**3.** Draw a second map of the world from memory. This time, draw the international date line in the center of your map. Add the equator, Tropic of Cancer, and Tropic of Capricorn. Now sketch in the continents. What do you notice?

# HANDS on GEOGRAPHY

Mental maps are personal. They change as we learn more about the world and the places in it. For example, they can include details about places that are of interest only to you.

What is your mental map of your neighborhood like? Sketch your mental map of your neighborhood. Include the features that you think are important and that help you find your way around. These guidelines will help you get started.

1. Decide what your map will show. Choose boundaries so that you do not sketch more than you need to.

2. Determine how much space you will need for your map. Things that are the same size in reality should be about the same size on your map.

3. Decide on and note the orientation of your map. Most maps use a directional indicator. On most maps, north is at the top.

4. Label reference points so that others who look at your map can quickly and easily figure out what they are looking at. For example, a major street or your school might be a reference point.

5. Decide how much detail your map will show. The larger the area you want to represent, the less detail you will need.

6. Use circles, rectangles, and triangles if you do not know the exact shape of an area.

7. As you think of them, fill in more details, such as names of places or major land features.

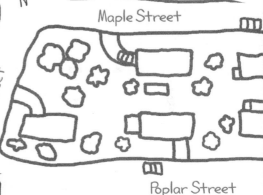

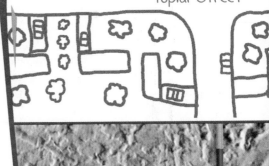

# Lab Report

1. What are the most important features on your map? Why did you include them?

2. Compare your sketch map to a published map of the area. How does it differ?

3. At the bottom, list three ways that you could make your sketch map more complete.

# UNIT 2

# Gaining a Historical Perspective

Young people working at one of York Archaeological Trust's site

Viking pot found at York

## An Archaeologist at Work

Leather boot found at York

*Dr. Ailsa Mainman is an archaeologist. She studies the remains and ruins of past cultures. She lives in York, in the northeastern part of England. She works for the York Archaeological Trust. Here she describes her work.* **WHAT DO YOU THINK?** *What part of Dr. Mainman's work would you enjoy the most?*

I chose archaeology because I loved history but I wanted to be in touch with real things, not just books. It still gives me a real thrill to hold something that was found in one of our digs. The object might be hundreds, sometimes thousands of years old. I like to think about what the people and their lives were like.

We have schoolchildren who come in the summer to help out on the digs, including some from the United States. They wash, sort, and draw these finds (valuable discoveries). Then the children try to work out what the objects are. Even broken bits of pot or bone have a lot to tell us about how people used to live.

Everyone thinks Vikings were just fierce warriors and raiders. They were, of course, but they were so much more. We have recreated the Viking city of Jorvik, which thrived in York beginning in A.D. 866. You can travel through the streets and houses and see the artisans and craftsmen. The Vikings were skilled at many crafts. They worked with gold, silver, iron, antler, bone, glass, and many other materials.

The Vikings were also tremendous shipbuilders. They explored and then settled in Iceland, Greenland, and Canada. Their trade routes linked them with Eastern Europe and even China!

Viking artifacts found at York

### Understanding Primary Sources

**1.** What has Dr. Mainman and others learned about the Vikings from the finds at their archaeological digs?

**2.** How does Dr. Mainman describe the Vikings?

Comb found at York

## Chapter 6
## 3,700,000 B.C–A.D. 476
# The Ancient World

**Gold funeral mask of Pharaoh Tutankhamen**

Greek vase showing potters at work

**Ancient Chinese art**

**c. 3200 B.C.**
**Politics**
Upper and Lower Egypt are united.

**c. 400,000 B.C.–100,000 B.C.**
**Global Events**
The first *Homo sapiens* appear.

**c. 800s B.C.–700s B.C.**
**Politics**
Sparta and Athens develop into powerful city-states.

| 2,500,000 B.C. | 500,000 B.C. | 8000 B.C. | 4000 B.C. | 1 B.C. | A.D. 500 |

**2,500,000 B.C.**
**Science and Technology**
The first stone tools appear.

**c. 8000 B.C.**
**Science and Technology**
Agricultural societies develop in Mesopotamia.

**c. Late 1000s B.C.**
**Politics**
The Zhou dynasty begins in China.

**A.D. 476**
**Global Events**
The Western Roman Empire falls.

**c. 2500 B.C.**
**Global Events**
The Harappan civilization appears in the Indus River valley.

*The Acropolis, Athens*

# Chapter 7
## A.D. 432–1800
# The World in Transition

Viking carving
of a lion's head

Crusaders at the gates of Jerusalem

**800**
**Politics**

Charlemagne is
crowned Emperor
of the Romans by
Pope Leo III.

**800–900s**
**Politics**

The Vikings invade
Western Europe.

**1347–1351**
**Global Events**

The Black Death
sweeps through
Europe.

**1492**
**Global Events**

Christopher
Columbus makes
his first voyage
to America.

**1517**
**Daily Life**

Martin Luther
posts his 95
theses.

Catherine the Great,
empress of Russia

| 1000 | 1200 | 1400 | 1600 | 1800 |
|------|------|------|------|------|

**1096**
**Global Events**

The first Crusade
begins.

**1271**
**Global Events**

Marco Polo
begins his trip
to China.

**c. 1450**
**Science and
Technology**

Johannes Gutenberg
invents the movable
type printing press.

**1762**
**Politics**

Catherine the
Great becomes
Empress of Russia.

**1632**
**Science and Technology**

Galileo proves that Earth
revolves around the Sun.

A Gutenberg Bible

Galileo Galilei

## UNIT 2

### Chapters 8 & 9
### 1550–Present
# The Modern World

Plate celebrating the coronation of
William III and Mary II

Women marching on Versailles during the French Revolution

**1594-95**
**The Arts**
William Shakespeare writes *Romeo and Juliet*.

**1688**
**Politics**
The Glorious Revolution occurs in England.

**1763**
**Global Events**
The Seven Years' War ends.

**1789**
**Politics**
The United States Constitution is ratified.

**1789**
**Politics**
The French Revolution begins.

| 1550 | 1650 | 1700 | 1750 | 1800 |
| --- | --- | --- | --- | --- |

**1558**
**Politics**
Elizabeth I becomes queen of England.

**1687**
**Science and Technology**
Isaac Newton publishes his most famous work, *Principia*.

**1737**
**Science and Technology**
Samuel F. B. Morse invents the telegraph.

**1776**
**Politics**
The American colonies declare independence from Great Britain.

**1769**
**Science and Technology**
James Watt builds the first steam engine.

Re-creation of Shakespeare's Globe Theatre

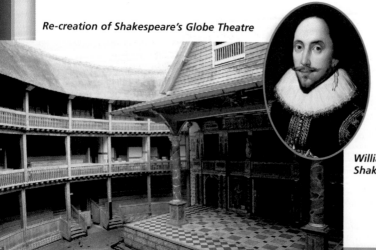

William
Shakespeare

Early steam locomotive

Glider flown by Wright brothers

Russian President Boris Yeltsin (center)

**1917**
**Global Events**
The United States enters World War I.

**1865**
**Daily Life**
Slavery is abolished in the United States at the end of the Civil War

**1917**
**Politics**
The Russian Revolution is fought.

**1945**
**Global Events**
World War II ends.

**1989**
**Global Events**
The Soviet Union collapses.

| 1850 | 1900 | 1950 | 2000 |
|------|------|------|------|

**1815**
**Global Events**
Napoleon is defeated at Waterloo.

**1903**
**Science and Technology**
The Wright brothers build the first working airplane.

**1929**
**Daily Life**
The Great Depression begins.

**1957**
**Science and Technology**
The first satellite in space, Sputnik, is launched.

**2001**
**Global Events**
Terrorists attack the World Trade Center in New York and the Pentagon in Washington, D.C.

World War I

September 11 interfaith memorial

# CHAPTER 6

# The Ancient World

This period lasted for thousands of years and saw the rise and fall of countless cultures. Even though these civilizations existed many years ago, you may find that you have something in common with students from that time.

*Statue of mythical Sumerian king Gilgamesh*

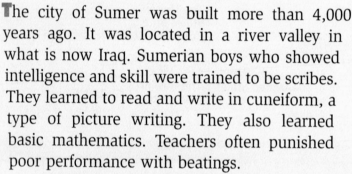

*Cuneiform table*

The city of Sumer was built more than 4,000 years ago. It was located in a river valley in what is now Iraq. Sumerian boys who showed intelligence and skill were trained to be scribes. They learned to read and write in cuneiform, a type of picture writing. They also learned basic mathematics. Teachers often punished poor performance with beatings.

Schoolboys who were late for class were also punished harshly. One Sumerian boy wrote about how afraid he was to explain his lateness to his teacher. Too scared to speak, he entered the room and bowed deeply to the teacher.

History does not record the outcome of the boy's tardiness.

*Sumerian mosaic, c. 2500*

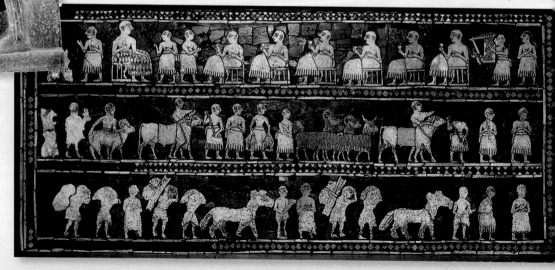

# Section 1 — The Birth of Civilization

## Read to Discover

1. What discoveries have scientists made about life in prehistoric times?
2. What are the four characteristics of civilization?
3. Where were the first civilizations located?

## Define

hominid
prehistory
nomads
land bridges
irrigation

division of labor
history

### WHY IT MATTERS

Scientists continue to uncover clues about how ancient people lived. Use CNNfyi.com or other current events sources to learn about recent discoveries. Record your findings in your journal.

*Hominid skeleton from about 3 million years ago*

## Prehistory

In the late 1970s in Tanzania, a country in East Africa, scientist Mary Leakey discovered parts of a skeleton dating back millions of years. She believed the bones were those of a **hominid**, an early human-like creature. Scientists use the remains of bodies and other objects they have found to make educated guesses about hominid life. For example, scientists can tell that hominids stood upright and used primitive tools made of stone.

The period during which hominids and even early humans lived is called **prehistory**. This means that no written records were made for historians to examine. The period of prehistory in which stone tools were used is called the Stone Age. It began about 2.5 million years ago and lasted for more than 2 million years.

Scientists carefully unearth objects in "digs" such as this one.

**Interpreting the Visual Record What kinds of objects might these scientists be looking for?**

This cave painting in Lascaux, France, was made before the invention of writing. People may have drawn on cave walls to express ideas.

▶

📘 **internet** connect

GO TO: go.hrw.com
KEYWORD: SK3 CH6
FOR: Web sites about the ancient world

In northeastern Europe, early humans used the bones of giant mammoths to build shelters similar to this museum model.

**Interpreting the Visual Record** Why did people use bones to build a shelter instead of materials such as wood or stone?

▼

**The First Humans** Early humans that looked like modern people probably appeared during the Stone Age between 100,000 and 400,000 years ago. These first humans, called *Homo sapiens*, may have first lived in Africa. They were **nomads** who moved from place to place in search of food. They lived on seeds, fruits, nuts, and other plants that they gathered. In time they also began to hunt small animals.

**Migration** Within the last 1.7 million years, Earth has gone through several periods of very cold weather. Together these periods are known as the Ice Age. During each period, large parts of Earth's surface were covered with ice. Sea levels dropped, leaving strips of dry land called **land bridges** between continents. One such land bridge connected the eastern part of Asia with what is now Alaska. Scientists think that early humans and animals migrated from Africa, into Asia, and across the land bridge onto the North American continent. Over time, humans spread to all parts of the world.

**Later Developments** In time *Homo sapiens* began to make more advanced tools. They were able to hunt larger animals with spears. They made clothes from animal skins. They also learned how to control fire and how to use it for warmth and cooking. Between 37,000 and 27,000 years ago, people began to create art to express their ideas. Carved ivory figures show that some groups had time for activities besides hunting and tool making. Beautiful paintings found on the walls of caves in France and Spain show graceful, elegant animals such as bison, bulls, and horses.

Later, between 10,000 and 5,500 years ago, people learned to make sharper tools by grinding and polishing stone. With better tools, people developed better methods of hunting. They made bows and arrows, which made hunting easier. They shaped fishhooks and harpoons from bones and antlers. People hollowed out logs to make canoes to fish in deep water and to cross rivers. Also around this time, people tamed the dog. Dogs helped people hunt. They may also have warned people if wild animals or strangers were approaching.

In the late Stone Age people learned to practice agriculture. We do not know why people made the change from gathering grains and other plants to growing them, but life changed drastically when they did. Instead of moving from place to place to hunt animals and gather food that grew wild, people began to stay in one place. They became farmers. People also domesticated animals such as cattle and sheep. That means people tamed animals that had been living wild.

**The Importance of Agriculture** Agriculture changed the ways in which people interacted with their environment. To grow food, people had to find ways to control and change their environment. They cleared forested areas to make room for fields. They invented **irrigation** systems, digging ditches and canals to move water from rivers to fields where crops grew.

Agriculture also changed the ways in which people interacted with each other. Because people who farmed stayed in one place, they began to live in larger groups and form societies. By about 9000 B.C., people began to live in permanent settlements and villages. Because farming made food more plentiful, populations increased. Small villages eventually grew into cities. In towns and cities, people shared new ideas and methods of doing things. Historians think that the first cities may have been founded more than 10,000 years ago. Jericho, the world's oldest known city, was founded at that time on the west bank of the Jordan River.

Our Amazing Planet

The dog was the first animal that humans tamed. Dogs and people have been companions for thousands of years. Some Stone Age people were even buried with their dogs.

Before people developed irrigation they depended on yearly floods of rivers such as the Nile to water fields.

# Emergence of Agriculture

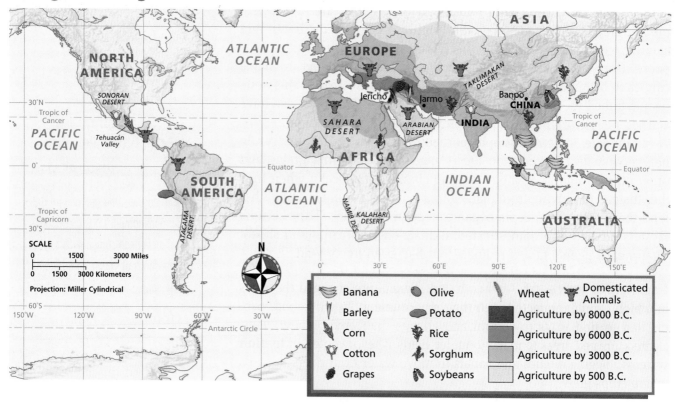

The practice of agriculture spread over a period of thousands of years.

**Interpreting the Map** Where was agriculture first developed?

People made stone and ivory tools during the Stone Age.

Because of the ways it changed people's lives, the development of agriculture was enormously important. In fact, learning how to grow food prepared the way for a new chapter in the story of human life—the story of civilization.

✓ **READING CHECK:** *Summarizing* How did agriculture change the ways in which people lived?

## The Beginnings of Civilization

Historians describe civilization as having four basic characteristics. First, a civilization is made up of people who live in an organized society, not simply as a loosely connected group. Second, people are able to produce more food than they need to survive. Third, they live in towns or cities with some form of government. And fourth, they practice **division of labor**. This means that each person performs a specific job.

**Agriculture and Civilization** How did the development of agriculture affect the growth of civilization? Before agriculture, people spent almost all of their time simply finding food. When people were able to grow their own food, they could produce more than they needed to survive. This meant that some people did not have to grow food at all. They had time to develop other skills, such as making pottery, cloth, and other goods. These people could trade the goods they produced and the services they offered for food or other needs.

**Trade** Once people began to trade, they had to deal with each other in more complex ways than before. Disagreements arose, creating a need for laws. Governments and priesthoods developed to fill that need. Governments made laws and saw that they were obeyed. Religion taught people what they should and should not do.

When people traded, they traveled to places where their goods were wanted and where they could get the things they wanted and needed. Some places where people exchanged goods grew into cities. In these cities, people traded not only goods but also ideas. Over time people built palaces, temples, and other public buildings in their cities.

**The Development of Writing** Trade, like business today, required people to keep records. Written languages may have developed from this need. The invention of written language began about 3,000 B.C. Farmers also needed a method to keep track of seasonal cycles. They had to know when it was time to plant new crops and when they could expect rain. Over time, they developed calendars.

Once they had writing and calendars, people began to keep written records of events. **History**, which is the written record of human civilization, had begun.

✓ **READING CHECK:** ( *Identifying Cause and Effect* ) How did trade lead to the development of writing?

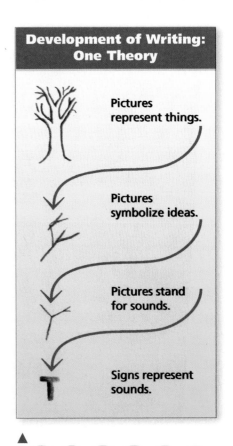

**Development of Writing: One Theory**

Pictures represent things.

Pictures symbolize ideas.

Pictures stand for sounds.

Signs represent sounds.

▲

The invention of the alphabet may have begun from pictures. This flowchart shows the possible development of the letter T.

## River Valley Civilizations

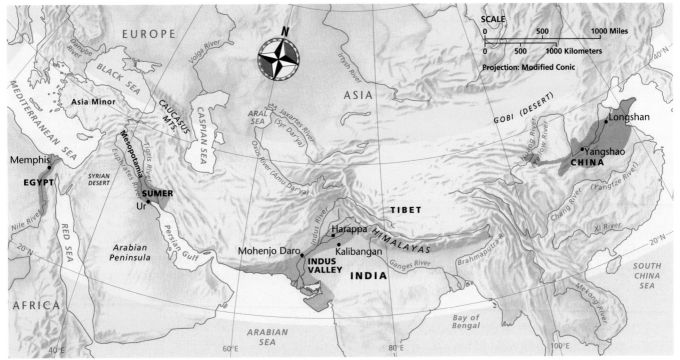

Scientists discovered the remains of mud-brick houses at Catalhüyük (chah-TUHL-hoo-YOOKH) in Turkey. This was one of the world's first cities.

# The First Civilizations

The world's first civilizations developed around four great river valleys. The earliest arose along the valley of the Tigris and Euphrates Rivers in Southwest Asia. Called Mesopotamia, this area was located in what is now Iraq. The ancient Egyptian civilization grew up around the valley of the Nile River. The first civilizations of India were centered on the Indus Valley. Early Chinese civilization began in the valley of the Huang, or Yellow River. (See the map on the previous page.)

These four great river valleys provided fertile soil for growing crops and rich water sources to irrigate crops. The people who lived in these valleys developed advanced civilizations. They learned how to make tools and weapons out of metal, first bronze and then iron. This was the end of the Stone Age. The civilizations that formed in each of these areas developed and declined for different reasons. All of them created written records of their cultures and societies. Thus, they mark the beginning of human history.

✓ READING CHECK: **Drawing Inferences** How did geography influence the beginnings of history?

Homework Practice Online
Keyword: SK3 HP6

## Section Review 1

**Define and explain:** hominid, prehistory, nomads, land bridges, irrigation, division of labor, history.

### Reading for the Main Idea

1. ( **Human Systems** ) Describe some important discoveries that scientists have made about life in prehistoric times.

2. ( **Human Systems** ) How did the division of labor lead to the development of trade?

3. ( **Environment and Society** ) Why were early civilizations located around river valleys?

### Critical Thinking

4. **Identifying Cause and Effect** How did the needs of early civilizations lead to the development of government and priesthoods?

### Organizing What You Know

5. **Summarizing** Copy the following graphic organizer. Use it to describe the traits of civilization.

What Is Civilization?

# Section 2 · The First Civilizations

## Read to Discover

1. How did physical geography shape the civilizations of the Fertile Crescent?
2. What was life like in ancient Egypt?
3. How did various peoples contribute to ancient Indian civilization?
4. What were some achievements of ancient China?

## Define

dynasty
pharaohs
hieroglyphics
subcontinent
dialects

## Locate

Fertile Crescent
Tigris River
Euphrates River
Nile Valley
Indus River
Huang River

### WHY IT MATTERS

Scientists continue to learn more about how ancient people lived and worked. Use CNN**fyi**.com or other current events sources to learn more about recent discoveries. Record your findings in your journal.

*Sumerian sheep's head sculpture*

## The Fertile Crescent

The Tigris, Euphrates, and Jordan Rivers are three of the main rivers in the Fertile Crescent.

## The Fertile Crescent

A strip of fertile land begins at the Isthmus of Suez and arcs through Southwest Asia to the Persian Gulf. This rich farmland region is known as the Fertile Crescent. By 8000 B.C., farmers in this region had begun to grow crops. In time they learned to work together to control flooding and to irrigate their fields. A new civilization developed as a result.

**The Land** The Tigris and the Euphrates (yoo-FRAY-teez) Rivers flow through the Fertile Crescent. These rivers start in what is now known as Turkey and flow southeast, joining before they reach the Persian Gulf. In the past, the Tigris and Euphrates Rivers frequently flooded. Ancient people built a system of canals and dikes to bring water to their fields and to return water to the rivers after floods. Several civilizations grew up in the Fertile Crescent. Each of them eventually declined and disappeared. Internal quarreling and poor leadership weakened them. No natural barriers protected them from invasion, and conquerors took over many of these kingdoms.

**The Sumerians** Historians believe that the Sumerians were the first civilization in the Fertile Crescent. They settled in the lower part of the Tigris-Euphrates valley, in an area called Sumer. There, they created what became known as the Sumerian civilization. Most Sumerians were farmers. After a time they were able to grow extra food. This allowed some people to become artisans and traders.

The Sumerians may have been the first people to use the wheel. Sumerian builders were the first to use the column, the vault, and the dome. The Sumerians also invented the world's first system of writing. Eventually, the Sumerians were conquered. Hundreds of years later, a new civilization, the Babylonians, grew up in the area.

**The Babylonians** In some ways the Babylonian and Sumerian civilizations were similar. The people were farmers, artisans, and traders. Like the Sumerians, the Babylonian merchants traded goods with distant parts of the Fertile Crescent and with Egypt and India.

Babylonian women had some legal and economic rights, including property rights. Women could be merchants, traders, or even scribes.

The greatest of the Babylonian kings was Hammurabi (ham-uh-RHAB-ee). In the 1790s B.C. he conquered most of the Tigris-Euphrates valley. Hammurabi was not only a powerful military leader but also an outstanding political leader. However, he is best remembered as a law-maker. He put together a group of several hundred laws governing all aspects of life. The collection is known as the Code of Hammurabi. Ideas from the Code are still found in laws today.

**The Persians** After the Babylonians, several other peoples settled in the Tigris-Euphrates valley. By about 550 B.C., the Persians had conquered Babylon and settled in what is now known as Iran. The kings of Persia waged many wars to add territory to their empire. Eventually, the empire expanded to include everything between India and southeastern Europe.

The Persians were more tolerant of local customs than some earlier conquerors had been. For example, they allowed local peoples to maintain their own religions. They also built a huge system of roads to hold the empire together. At one time, the Persian Royal Road was more than 1,500 miles (2,410 km) long. It allowed people of different cultures to exchange ideas, customs, and goods.

▲ As ruler, Hammurabi made great contributions to Babylonian society. He is best remembered for his code of laws.

The ruins of Persepolis reflect the former glory of the Persian Empire. King Darius I built Persepolis in about 500 B.C. as the capital of his empire.

## Persian Empire about 500 B.C.

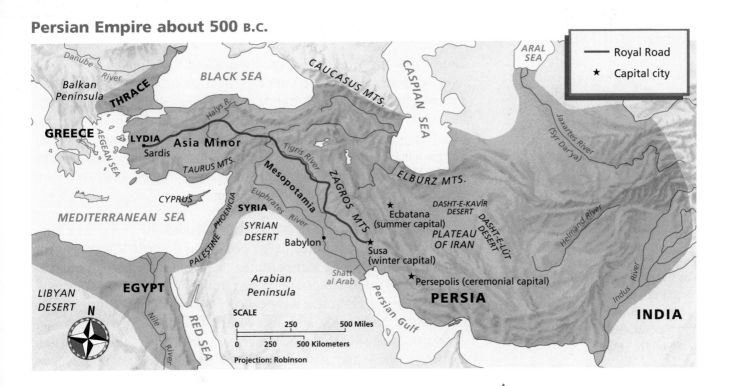

**Legend:**
— Royal Road
★ Capital city

At its height, the Persian Empire stretched from southeastern Europe to the Indus River in southwestern Asia.

**The Phoenicians** The Phoenician (fi-NEE-shuhn) civilization developed around 1200 B.C. It had its origins in what is now Israel, Lebanon, and Syria. The land to the east was not good for farming, so the Phoenicians turned to the sea. They may even have sailed as far as Britain and Western Africa. Phoenician traders set up colonies around the Mediterranean.

Their most important advance was the invention of the Phoenician alphabet. Earlier writing systems had thousands of symbols, but the Phoenician alphabet had just 22 letters. Other western cultures adopted and modified this alphabet for their own use.

**The Hebrews and Judaism** South of Phoenicia was a strip of land known as Canaan. Many peoples lived in this region at different times. Among them were the Hebrews, ancestors of the modern Jews. Early on, the Hebrews moved to Egypt, probably to escape drought and famine. Eventually the Egyptians made the Hebrews slaves. They remained enslaved for 400 years, until the 1200s or 1300s B.C.

At that time, a great Hebrew leader arose named Moses. Moses said the Hebrew god, Yahweh, had sent him to form a nation in Canaan. Moses led the Hebrews out of Egypt. They settled once again in Canaan, but only after they had wandered in the desert for many years. They were also forced to battle other peoples who had settled there. The Hebrews followed a new code of laws, the Ten Commandments. They are a key part of Judaism, and deal with the Hebrews' relationship to Yahweh. They also emphasize the importance of family and human life, as well as exercising self-control.

The Dead Sea Scrolls contain details about the history and principles of Judaism.

✓ **READING CHECK:** ( *Summarizing* ) What are some important contributions of ancient civilizations in the Fertile Crescent?

Hatshepsut (hat-SHEP-soot) declared herself pharaoh after the death of her husband. She dressed the part, and even wore the false beard reserved for kings.

Interpreting the Visual Record **Why do you think Hatshepsut dressed like a male pharaoh?**

## The Kingdom of Egypt around 1450 B.C.

Interpreting the Map **Into which body of water does the Nile River flow?**

# The Nile Valley

The Nile is the world's longest river, about 4,160 miles (6,693 km) long. It floods at the same time each year, and the waters spread fine soil over the river's banks. The Nile River flows south to north, which made it possible for early peoples to travel upland to the Mediterranean Sea. Deserts and seas afforded early civilizations natural protection from invaders. The Isthmus of Suez, a land bridge between Africa and Asia, provided trade routes between early Egyptian civilizations and their neighbors.

**Government and Society** Over hundreds of years, two kingdoms with distinct cultures developed along the Nile River in Egypt. Around 3200 B.C., King Menes united them and founded a **dynasty**, a family line of rulers that passes power from one generation to the next. In later years, these rulers were called **pharaohs**. They controlled the government completely and also served as judges, high priests, and generals of the armies. Egyptian society was divided into two classes. Priests, scribes, and government officials formed the upper class. Peasants and farmers formed the lower class. They had to grow food for the pharaoh. Some were also forced to serve in the military or work on building projects such as canals or the pyramids.

During the time of the pharaohs, Egypt's contact with other parts of the world grew either through conquest or trade. By about 1085 B.C., Egypt had expanded into what is now Syria, Israel, and Libya. The Egyptians traded with peoples throughout Southwest Asia and North Africa.

**Achievements** Egyptian architects and engineers were among the best in the ancient world. They built the pyramids, the Great Sphinx, and other monuments that still stand today. They developed a writing system that used pictures and symbols called **hieroglyphics**.

This mural shows Egyptian farmers processing grain.

Egyptians used a number system based on 10, and they understood both fractions and geometry. They had an accurate 365-day calendar, and they made important discoveries in medicine.

After Ramses the Great, who ruled in the 1200s B.C., Egypt had no great leaders. Attacks from foreign peoples, including the Phoenicians, the Persians, and the Greeks, weakened Egypt. By the 500s B.C., Egypt was no longer ruled by Egyptians.

✓ **READING CHECK:** ( *Analyzing* ) How was ancient Egypt protected from invaders?

# The Indus River Valley

East of the Fertile Crescent is the Indus River. It flows through what are India and Pakistan today. Several civilizations developed in the Indus River Valley.

**The Harappans** The first great civilization on the Indian **subcontinent** developed in the Indus River Valley around 2500 B.C. A subcontinent is a very large landmass that is smaller than a continent. These people are called Harappans, after one of their most important cities, Harappa. The civilization was located in what is known today as Pakistan, but it also extended into India.

Historians know very little about the Harappan people. They lived in large, well-planned cities with wide streets and a water system complete with public baths and brick sewers. Harappan civilization lasted a thousand years. Historians are not sure how it ended.

This baked-clay sculpture was made by the Harappan civilization.

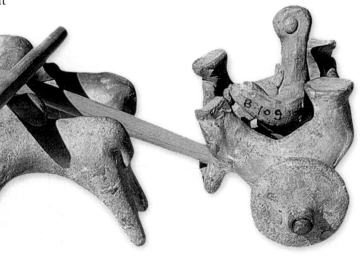

This Indian sculpture shows the Hindu god Vishnu.

**The Indo-Aryans** By about 1500 B.C. a new group of people had come into northern India. They were animal herders and skilled warriors who conquered all of northern India and mixed with the people already living there. Scholars call these people Indo-Aryans. Their looks and their culture were different from the people they conquered. They introduced many new ideas and a strict class system to India.

Most of what we know about the Indo-Aryans comes from the Vedas. These are the Indo-Aryans' great works of religious literature. For centuries people memorized the Vedas and retold them to their children. Later, the Indo-Aryans developed writing. Scholars wrote the Vedas down. This period of Indian history is sometimes called the Vedic Age. It lasted until about 1000 B.C.

The effect of Indo-Aryan culture is still felt in India today. Indian and Indo-Aryan religious beliefs and customs mixed as well, forming the beginnings of the Hindu religion. The Indo-Aryans' language, Sanskrit, became the basis for the main language of modern India.

**The Mauryans** In the early 500s B.C., 16 different kingdoms existed in northern India. By about 320 B.C. much of India was united under one able ruler, Candragupta Maurya. It became known as the Mauryan Empire. Candragupta made many advances. He established a system of efficient administrators to help govern the empire. He also set standards for doctors.

His grandson Aśoka extended the empire to include almost all of India, except for the southern tip. He tried to unite the many different peoples who came under his rule. Eventually he gave up war because of the pain and suffering it caused. Aśoka took up Buddhism and furthered its spread through India. He even sent missionaries to other countries in an effort to encourage the growth of Buddhism. Aśoka worked to improve living conditions in his empire. He dug wells and built rest houses along trade routes. He also planted trees along the roads to make travelers more comfortable. After his death the Mauryan Empire slowly lost strength. It collapsed about 140 years later.

**The Gupta** The Gupta Empire ruled India beginning around A.D. 320. By A.D. 400, the Gupta controlled the entire northern part of India. During this time, both Buddhism and Hinduism attracted many followers. Art, architecture, literature, mathematics, and medicine developed under the Guptas. People came from all over Asia to learn at Indian universities. However, in the late 400s, invaders from Central Asia attacked India. The Gupta Empire fell about 550.

## Indus River Valley

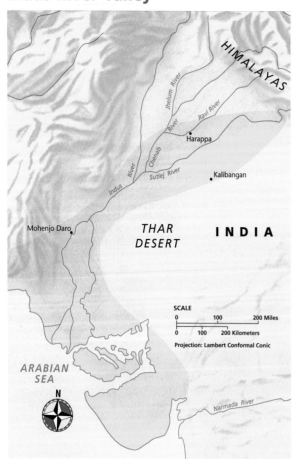

Indus River Valley

HIMALAYAS
Jhelum River
Ravi River
Chenab River
Harappa
Indus River
Sutlej River
Kalibangan
Mohenjo Daro
THAR DESERT
INDIA
ARABIAN SEA
Narmada River

SCALE
0        100        200 Miles
0    100    200 Kilometers
Projection: Lambert Conformal Conic

N

✔ **READING CHECK:** (*Summarizing*) What are the two main religions practiced in the Indus River valley?

## Early China, c. 10000 B.C.–c. 5000 B.C.

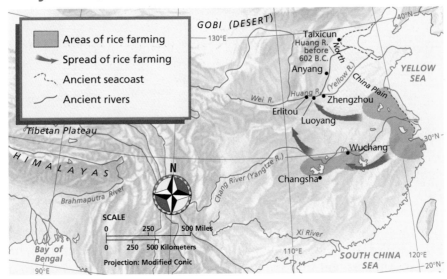

# The Huang River Valley

Ancient China was cut off from other civilizations by mountains and the Gobi Desert. Its isolation led to the development of a unique culture. The ancient northern Chinese people began forming dynasties in the Huang River Valley around 2000 B.C.

**The Shang** People have lived in the Huang Valley since prehistoric times. The first we know of were the Shang. The Shang people invaded the Huang Valley and established China's first dynasty. They brought irrigation and flood control to the Huang Valley.

The Shang developed a written language that could be used to write all the **dialects**—or different forms—of Chinese. Over more than 100 years, many different invaders attacked the Shang. In about 1050 B.C., the Zhou (JOH) overthrew the Shang and established their own dynasty.

**The Zhou** Under the Zhou and the two dynasties after it, China became a large and powerful state. Zhou rulers allowed each territory to have its own leader. These leaders fought each other as well as outside invaders. Philosophers tried to bring peace and harmony back into daily life. Some of their ideas have been carried into modern times.

**The Qin** The Qin (CHIN) dynasty lasted only 15 years, but it made many important changes in Chinese life. The Western name *China* comes from *Qin*. The Qin built huge walls to protect their borders. Later dynasties added to and connected these walls. Today, we call this structure the Great Wall of China.

In 206 B.C., the Qin people grew unhappy with their ruler. A commoner led a revolt and seized power. He established the Han dynasty. It ruled China for about 400 years.

These are life-size clay figures from the tomb of China's first emperor, Cheng, also called Shih Huang Ti. He unified China under Qin rule.

▼

In ancient China people who wanted to be government officials had to study hard in order to take civil service tests. Failing the test was considered a disgrace.

▶

▲

This device, developed around A.D. 132, warned of earthquakes. Ground tremors would cause metal balls to drop from the dragons' mouths to the frogs below.

**The Han** Han rulers expanded the empire until it was larger than the Roman Empire, and they extended the Great Wall. They introduced a civil service system to run the daily business of government. It was designed to be fair and to reward ability. People had to pass an exam in order to hold civil service jobs. Traders used the Silk Road, which stretched from China all the way to the Mediterranean region, to trade with Greece and Rome.

**Advances of the Huang Valley Civilizations** These people of ancient China figured out the precise length of a year and tracked the movement of the planets. They invented the sundial, the water clock, and a machine to measure earthquakes. Chinese doctors developed herbal medicines and learned how to set bones. By A.D. 105, the Chinese had invented paper, which would not be used in other parts of the world until 500 years later. They also invented a printing press. Use of printed books helped to establish a common culture across China.

✓ **READING CHECK:** *Main Idea* What were some of the achievements of the ancient Chinese?

# Section Review 2

**Define and explain:** dynasty, pharaohs, hieroglyphics, subcontinent, dialects

## Reading for the Main Idea

1. *Environment and Society* What made it possible for people in the Fertile Crescent to stop farming and become artisans and traders?

2. *Analyzing* What are some of the lasting contributions made by the peoples of the Fertile Crescent?

## Critical Thinking

3. **Making Generalizations** How did geography affect the ancient civilizations in this section?

4. **Human Systems** What caused many of the ancient civilizations to disappear?

## Organizing What You Know

5. **Time line** Copy the following time line onto a large piece of paper. Fill in as many events as you can.

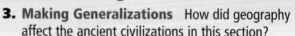

3000 B.C.    2000 B.C.    1000 B.C.    A.D. 1    A.D. 500

2500 B.C.    1500 B.C.    500 B.C.

# Section 3 Early Sub-Saharan Africa

## Read to Discover
1. How do historians study cultures that left no written records?
2. What were the kingdoms of Kush and Aksum like?
3. How did trade affect the growth of kingdoms in Sub-Saharan Africa?

## Define
oral history

## Locate
Nile River
Red Sea
Zimbabwe
Mauritania
Niger River
Timbuktu

### WHY IT MATTERS
Sub-Saharan Africa was a key player in ancient trade between cultures. Use CNNfyi.com or other current events sources to find out about international trade today. Record your findings in your journal.

Bronze statue from Benin

## Ancient Africa

Egypt was the first kingdom to develop in Africa, but it was not the only one. South of the vast desert called the Sahara, many different cultures developed. In time some of these groups established city-states, kingdoms, and even empires. It is sometimes difficult, however, for historians to study the earliest African civilizations.

**Language** One reason for this difficulty is the absence of written records. Spoken language developed in Sub-Saharan Africa long before writing did. Historians therefore must find other ways to study early cultures. One common method they use is the study of **oral history**, spoken information passed from one generation to the next. This information is often contained in stories or songs. Many of the stories tell about great kings and heroes from the past. In some parts of Africa these stories are still told today. Scholars today study these tales to learn about Africa's past.

The Lion Temple was built by the people of Kush, one of the largest kingdoms of Sub-Saharan Africa.

◄

Many houses built in Africa today are similar to those built in ancient times.
**Interpreting the Visual Record From what materials are traditional houses like this made?**

This gold plaque and tube show the influence of Egypt on Kushite art.

The modern languages of Africa can also provide clues about the continent's history. Historians have tried to figure out which African languages are related. This is often a clue that cultures have had contact with each other in the past. Some African languages are related to languages spoken in other parts of the world. Scholars have learned from this that early Africans had contact with people from distant lands. Other evidence suggests the same thing. Bananas, for example, have been popular in Africa for a long time, but the banana tree is not native to Africa. Early traders must have brought the plant from Asia.

**Life in Early Africa** Historians have been able to piece together a picture of life in ancient Sub-Saharan Africa. There is still, however, much that they do not know. Across most of the continent, life was centered around small villages. Most of the time, all of the people in a village were related to each other. This helped to tie the village together. Older members of a community were often its leaders. Everyone in the village respected and obeyed them. Women played many roles in early African societies. They were responsible for all farming. In addition, people in some societies traced their family lines through their mothers.

Life was very similar in many villages across Africa. Most people were involved in farming, herding, or fishing. Basic agricultural practices did not vary much from place to place. Most people in early Africa also had similar religious beliefs. They believed that spirits, including the spirits of their ancestors, were all around. They also believed in many gods who controlled nature and human activities.

✓ **READING CHECK:** ( *Summarizing* ) What do historians study to learn about ancient Africa?

# Kush and Aksum

Two great ancient kingdoms developed along the Nile south of Egypt. The first was Kush. It was eventually conquered by Aksum, its neighbor to the south.

**Kush** Kush was probably founded around 2000 B.C. In about 1500 B.C., however, it was conquered by Egypt. Egypt ruled Kush for about 500 years. The two countries were never completely unified, however, and Kush remained largely free from Egyptian control. In about 720 B.C., Kush invaded and conquered Egypt. The kings of Kush ruled Egypt for about 50 years. In the 600s B.C., invasions by groups from Southwest Asia weakened the kingdom. Kush survived, however, and became a powerful kingdom again.

The people of Kush were mostly traders. They traveled along the Nile to trade goods and ideas with Egypt. Because of this trade, Kush's culture was in many ways similar to Egypt's. Kush also lay along the trade routes between the Red Sea and the Nile. Caravans traveling between these two areas passed through Kush. This allowed the kingdom to become a rich trading center. The Kushites built huge pyramids and temples. They made beautiful pottery and jewelry. They also developed a written form of their language.

**Aksum** Another powerful kingdom arose to the southeast of Kush. This was Aksum. It lay in a hilly area called the Ethiopian Highlands. Like Kush, Aksum controlled trade routes between the Red Sea and the Nile. In addition, Aksum lay on trade routes between the Red Sea and central Africa. By the A.D. 100s, Aksum had grown into a major trading kingdom. Two hundred years later, it had also become a strong military power. In about A.D. 350 Aksum conquered Kush.

At the time of its conquest of Kush, Aksum was ruled by King 'Ēzānā. He was a strong leader who had control over other rulers in the area. While he was king, 'Ēzānā became a Christian. He made Christianity the official religion of Aksum. The form of Christianity that 'Ēzānā practiced included some local traditions, customs, and beliefs. This made it popular with other people throughout the region. Christianity slowly became a powerful influence in East Africa.

From the A.D. 300s to the 600s, Aksum continued to grow rich from trade. By this time it controlled nearly all the trade on the western shore of the Red Sea. By the late A.D. 500s, however, Aksum had begun to decline for several reasons. One reason may have been soil exhaustion. Farmers had been growing crops in this region for hundreds of years. Over time, it probably became more difficult for farmers to produce enough food to support the population.

Increased competition for trade also hurt Aksum. By the 700s the Persian Empire had become a powerful trading state. The Persians took over much of the trade along the Red Sea that Aksum had once controlled. Muslim traders from the north also took trade away from Aksum. Faced with these new trading empires, Aksum slowly lost most of its economic and political power.

✓ **READING CHECK:** *Contrasting* How was the form of Christianity practiced in Aksum different from the Christianity practiced elsewhere?

## Kush and Aksum

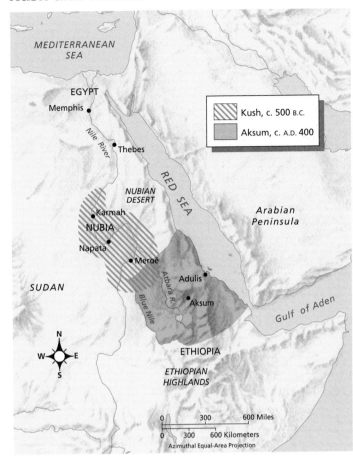

Kush, c. 500 B.C.

Aksum, c. A.D. 400

▲

Aksum conquered Kush by about A.D. 350.

**Interpreting the Map** On what river would goods from Kush be sent to Egypt?

▲

This coin pictures King 'Ēzānā, who made Aksum the first Christian kingdom in Africa.

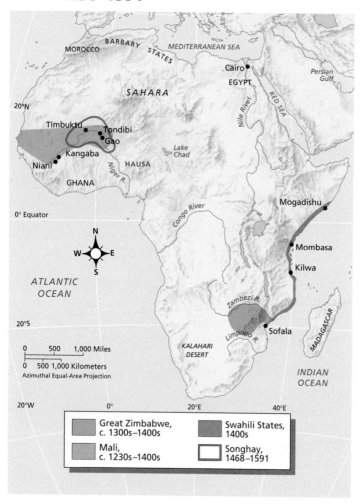

**Great Zimbabwe,**
c. 1300s–1400s

**Swahili States,**
1400s

**Mali,**
c. 1230s–1400s

**Songhay,**
1468–1591

# The Trading States

Kush and Aksum were the largest kingdoms in ancient Africa, but they were not the only ones. Like these two kingdoms, most of the civilizations of Sub-Saharan Africa were great traders. Across the continent, trade connected Africa with the rest of the ancient world.

**East Africa** Along the coast of East Africa, dozens of small city-states appeared. The earliest such city-states, like Mogadishu (moh-guh-DEE-shoo) and Mombasa, were located in the northern part of the region. Eventually city-states like these lined most of the eastern coast of Africa. They controlled trade in the Indian Ocean. They sold gold, ivory, hides, and tortoise shells to traders from around the world. They also sold slaves. In exchange, these traders brought weapons and porcelain to Africa.

Eventually a new culture arose out of this trade. A new language, called Swahili, developed. It was an African language but it also included many words from Arabic. For this reason, the city-states of East Africa are sometimes called the Swahili States.

**Zimbabwe** Later traders established settlements farther south. By A.D. 900, gold had been discovered in the interior of southeastern Africa. This gold was shipped to the coast on the Zambezi River. The discovery of gold increased trade along the Indian Ocean. Many peoples wanted to trade for it. African kingdoms fought to control the gold trade.

A group of people called the Shona gained control of the region in the 1200s. Their kingdom was centered around Great Zimbabwe, a huge stone city of more than 10,000 people. *Zimbabwe* is a Shona word that means "stone houses." From Great Zimbabwe, the Shona controlled the gold trade out of southeastern Africa. They also held great political power. Their kingdom lasted until the 1400s.

▲
Ruins of the Great Zimbabwe fortress near Masvingo, Zimbabwe

**West Africa** In West Africa, trade centered on the Atlantic Ocean. Many trading societies developed between the Atlantic and Lake Chad. The most powerful trading societies in these region were those who controlled trade routes across the Sahara. Traders from the north brought salt across the desert in exchange for gold from West Africa. Cities grew along these trade routes.

The first of the great West African trading kingdoms was Ghana. It grew up around a trading village in what is now Mauritania. Gold trade made the kings of Ghana rich and powerful. They built strong armies and conquered new lands. Eventually, however, Ghana began to decline. In about A.D. 1235, a neighboring people conquered Ghana. They set up a new empire called Mali.

Mali covered all of the area that had been Ghana. It also included new lands to the north and west. Mali reached the height of its power in the early 1300s under a ruler named Mansa Mūsā. He was a strong supporter of education and the arts. During his reign, the city of Timbuktu became an important center of learning and trade. People came from as far away as Egypt and Arabia to study at the university there. After Mansa Mūsā died, Mali began to grow weak. In 1468, rebels captured Timbuktu. They set up a new kingdom called Songhay.

Songhay was a powerful trading kingdom. It was centered on the city of Gao, a key trade city on the Niger River. By this time the Niger had become an important trade route. The kings of Songhay encouraged the growth of Islamic teachings at the university in Timbuktu. This helped Timbuktu remain an important cultural and trading center. Goods from Europe, India, and China were exchanged there. Timbuktu also remained a center of learning. Books sold for very high prices in the markets there. Songhay remained a powerful state until 1591. In that year it was conquered by Moroccan troops.

▲

Mansa Mūsā was a devout Muslim who encouraged the building of mosques, or Islamic centers for worship. This one, in Mali, was built in the 1300s.

✓ **READING CHECK:** *Identifying Cause and Effect* What led to the development of strong kingdoms in West Africa?

# Section Review 3

**Define and explain:** oral history

## Reading for the Main Idea

1. ( *Human Systems* ) What do scholars study to learn about early African civilizations?

2. ( *Places and Regions* ) What were the two most powerful kingdoms of Sub-Saharan Africa?

3. ( *Human Systems* ) What were some items traded by early African civilizations?

**go. hrw .com**
**Homework Practice Online**
Keyword: SK3 HP6

## Critical Thinking

4. **Drawing Inferences and Conclusions** Why were the most powerful kingdoms of Sub-Saharan Africa located on coasts or rivers?

## Organizing What You Know

5. **Comparing and Contrasting** Copy the following chart. Use it to name and describe the powerful trading kingdoms of Sub-Saharan Africa.

| State | Location in Africa | Features |
|-------|-------------------|----------|
|       |                   |          |
|       |                   |          |

## Read to Discover

1. How did ancient Greek civilization develop?
2. What events led to the birth and decline of the Roman Empire?
3. How did Christianity begin?

## Define

city-states
direct democracy
republic
aqueduct

## Locate

Aegean Sea
Greece
Crete
Athens
Italy
Rome
Adriatic Sea
Mediterranean Sea
Alps
Jerusalem

### WHY IT MATTERS

Both the Greek and Roman governments were based on the idea that people can govern themselves. Use CNN**fyi**.com or other current events sources to find out about how citizens of the United States and other countries take part in government.

Greek coins, c. 500s B.C.

## Aegean Civilization, c. 1450 B.C.-700 B.C.

# The Early Greeks

By 2000 B.C. civilizations were developing in the Nile River valley and the Fertile Crescent. At the same time another civilization was forming near the Balkan peninsula and the Aegean Sea. The people who settled this area later became known as the Greeks. From the Greeks came many of the ideas that formed the foundation for modern western civilization.

### Geography and Greek Civilization

Geography has much to do with the way the early Greeks lived. Greece is a rugged country that is made up of many peninsulas and islands separated by narrow waters. The land is covered with high mountains. They separated groups of people who lived in the valleys. These landforms contributed to the development of separate communities rather than one large and united kingdom. Because it was difficult to travel through the mountains, some Greeks preferred to travel by sea. Many became fighters, sailors, and traders.

# CONNECTING TO Art

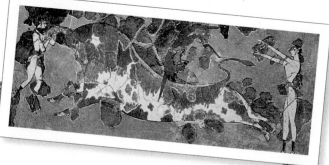

The Toreador fresco

**Frescoes** Today, on the island of Crete, visitors can see the ruins of the palace of King Minos. When the palace was first built around 1500 B.C., the walls were covered with beautiful, colorful paintings called frescoes. The paintings were damaged over the years, but some of them have been carefully restored so that people can tell how they first looked. Many of the paintings show scenes from nature. Some are of birds, fish, dolphins, and other animals.

The largest of these paintings is called the *Toreador Fresco*. A toreador is a bullfighter. It shows ancient Minoan athletes jumping over a bull. The bull jumper at the right is a woman.

**Understanding What You Read**

1. Why did the paintings have to be restored?
2. What do the paintings tell us about life on the island of Crete in ancient times?

**The Minoans** About 100 years ago on the island of Crete, scientists found the remains of the earliest Greek civilization. By 2000 B.C., the Minoan people had developed a great civilization. From the evidence scientists found, we know that the Minoans built cities and grand palaces that even had running water. We also know that they developed a system of writing and that Minoan artists carved beautiful statues from gold, ivory, and stone. Because Crete's soil was very poor, farming was not very productive. Many people became sailors and fishers. By 1400 B.C., the Minoan civilization began to decline. It was conquered by a group that lived on the Greek mainland, the Mycenaeans (my-suh-NEE-unhz).

**The Mycenaeans** The Mycenaeans controlled the Greek mainland from about 1600 B.C. to about 1200 B.C. They were a warlike people who lived in tribes. Each tribe had its own chief. The Mycenaean tribes built fort-like cities surrounded by stone walls. They carried out raids on other peoples throughout the eastern Mediterranean. Once they conquered the Minoans, they adopted many aspects of their civilization. For example, they used the Minoan system of writing. By 1200 B.C. earthquakes and wars had destroyed most of the Mycenaean cities. A later Greek poet named Homer wrote a long poem called the *Iliad*, which pulls together about 400 years of historical events, legends, and folk tales. It tells the story of the Trojan War. The Mycenaeans were the Greeks Homer wrote about in that story.

✓ **READING CHECK:** *Analyzing* How did the geography of the land affect the way the Minoans lived?

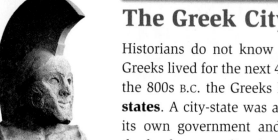

▶

Sparta's men were expected to serve in the military until they were 60 years old.

**Interpreting the Visual Record** **What does this bronze figure show about Spartan soldiers?**

# The Greek City-States

Historians do not know much about how the Greeks lived for the next 400 years. However, by the 800s B.C. the Greeks lived in separate **city-states**. A city-state was a city or town that had its own government and laws and controlled the land surrounding it. Each city-state had its own calendar, money, and system of weights and measures. Two of the largest city-states, Sparta and Athens, developed in different ways.

**Sparta** Spartans were very loyal to their city-state. It had a strong government that allowed little personal freedom. Sparta also had a powerful army. At the age of seven, boys left home to be trained as soldiers. When men grew older and left the army, they were expected to work for the public good. Girls received strict training at home. Both boys and girls were educated and encouraged to study music. However, Spartan culture left little time for the development of the arts, literature, philosophy, and science.

This photo shows part of a temple in honor of Athena, the Greek goddess of warfare and wisdom. It was built between about 421 B.C. and 415 B.C. Athens was named for Athena.

**Interpreting the Visual Record**

**What does this temple tell you about Athenian values?**

**Athens** The Athenians developed a form of government called **direct democracy**. In a direct democracy, citizens take part in making all decisions. Athenians also had courts where cases were decided by juries. Jurors were chosen by lot. The jury voted on each case by secret ballot. While the Athenians had much more freedom than the Spartans, Athenian women could not participate in government. Slavery was also permitted.

Athenians made great contributions to the arts, literature, philosophy, and science. Builders, artists, and sculptors created beautiful temples and other works. Athenian writers produced great works of literature. They were the first people to write drama, or plays. Scientists discovered new laws of mathematics and developed a system to classify animals and plants. The Greek physician Hippocrates is considered by many to be the father of medical science. Philosophers such as Socrates, Plato, and Aristotle studied questions of reality and human existence. Their thoughts formed the basis for many later ideas at the heart of Western culture. The 400s B.C. are known as the Golden Age of Athens.

▼

✓ **READING CHECK:**

| Comparing and Contrasting |

How did the Athenian way of life differ from the Spartan way of life?

# Alexander the Great

While Athens and other city-states fought, weakened, and declined, Macedonia, a kingdom to the north, gained strength. Macedonia's king, Philip II, took control of Greece and united it under his rule. When he was killed in 336 B.C., his son, who would become known as Alexander the Great, took his place. Alexander conquered much of the known world—including the Greek city-states—in a short period of time. He built cities that grew to be great centers of learning. Alexander admired the Greeks. Travel and trade along the routes that linked Alexander's empire to Asia spread Greek culture and ideas throughout the world. After Alexander died in 323 B.C., his empire was split into smaller kingdoms. In time, the Romans conquered Alexander's empire.

✓ **READING CHECK:** *Drawing Conclusions* How did Alexander help spread Greek culture throughout his empire?

Alexander's education prepared him to be a great leader. He got his military training from his father and his education from the great Greek philosopher Aristotle.

# The Early Romans

In about 750 B.C., while the city-states were growing in Greece, people called Latins were settling in villages along the Tiber River in Italy. In time, they united to form the city of Rome. During the late 600s B.C. they were conquered by a people called the Etruscans from the north. The Etruscans brought written language to Rome. Skilled and clever craftspeople, they built paved roads and sewers. Rome grew into a large and successful city. In time, the Greeks also settled in Italy. Their ideas and culture strongly influenced the Romans. Even the Roman religion was partly based on Greek beliefs.

**Geography and Roman Civilization** In some ways, the geography of Italy helped a great civilization to develop there. Italy is protected by the Alps to the north. The Mediterranean Sea to the west and the Adriatic Sea to the east of this boot-shaped peninsula made trade and travel easy. Not everything about Rome's location, however, was good. Geography also posed some problems. Passages through the Alps left Italy open to invasions. The peninsula's long coastlines left it open to attack from the sea.

✓ **READING CHECK:**

*Identifying Cause and Effect* How did the geography of Italy help the Roman civilization grow?

### Ancient Italy, c. 600 B.C.

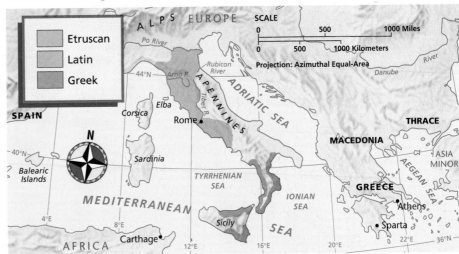

# The Roman Republic

In 509 B.C. a group of wealthy Romans overthrew the Etruscan king. They replaced the Etruscan rule with a **republic**. A republic is a government in which voters elect leaders to run the state. For the next 200 years, the Romans fought many wars. Their well-trained armies built bridges and roads. The republic grew as the Romans gained new territories. In time, however, controlling such a vast area became a problem for Rome's leaders.

**Julius Caesar** By 60 B.C. a popular public speaker named Julius Caesar began to win support among Rome's poor. Caesar soon became a powerful general who conquered more territory for the republic. He extended the rule of Rome to present-day France. He even marched into Egypt. He put Cleopatra, a daughter of the ruling family, on the throne as a Roman ally. Victorius, Caesar returned to Rome in 46 B.C. Two years later Roman officials made him ruler for life. However, there were some Roman leaders who feared Caesar's power. On March 15, 44 B.C. Caesar was assassinated.

✓ **READING CHECK:**  *Analyzing*  What events led to Caesar's rise to power?

Two of the men who killed Caesar were his friends.

**Interpreting the Visual Record Why do you think some Roman leaders feared Caesar?**

The Roman forum was the center of Rome's government.

# The Roman Empire

After Caesar's death, his grandnephew Octavian became the leader of the Roman world. The Romans called Octavian *Augustus*, which meant the "honored one." He became known as Augustus Caesar. Historians refer to Augustus as the first emperor of Rome. Augustus, however, never actually used the title of emperor.

Under Augustus, the Roman republic became a great empire. Augustus sent his armies out to conquer new lands. Soon the empire extended from Spain to Syria and from Egypt to the Sahara Desert. In the north, the empire reached all the way to the Rhine and Danube Rivers.

**Pax Romana** The reign of Augustus began a 200-year period called the Pax Romana, which means "Roman Peace." During this time Rome was a stable and peaceful empire. Laws became more fair. Widespread trade created a strong economy. In order to trade, people had to travel, so the Roman army built roads and bridges that helped unite the vast empire. The Roman army also helped keep the peace by defending Rome's borders against outside invaders.

✓ **READING CHECK:** ( *Summarizing* ) What was the Roman Empire like during the Pax Romana?

The Roman army built many great roads and bridges. If you travel in Europe today, you may use the same roads the Romans built some 2000 years ago.

## Trade in the Roman Empire A.D. 117

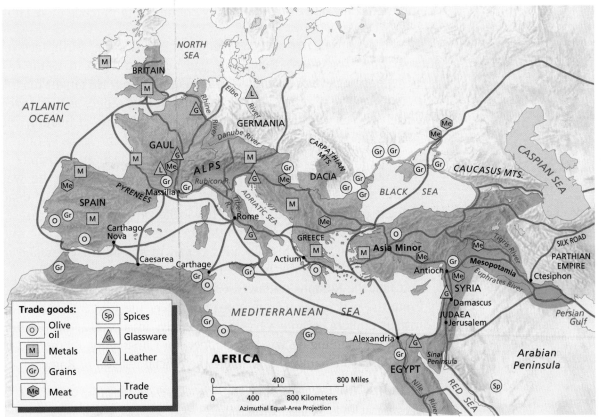

Trade goods:
- ⊙ Olive oil
- Ⓜ Metals
- Ⓖⱼ Grains
- Ⓜₑ Meat
- Ⓢₚ Spices
- △G Glassware
- △L Leather
- ▬▬ Trade route

Aqueducts were stone canals that carried water from mountains to the city.

# Rome's Achievements

The Romans made many important advances in science and engineering. They built temples, palaces, arenas, bridges, and roads. They figured out a way to transport water from one place to another by a system of aqueducts. An **aqueduct** is a sloped bridge-like structure that carries water. Skilled Roman architects designed buildings with domes and arches.

Some Romans were also very talented writers. The verses of ancient Roman poets such as Virgil, Horace, and Ovid are still read today. The biographer Plutarch wrote of the lives of famous Greeks and Romans. The Roman language, Latin, was used for many centuries. It became the basis for many modern languages including French, Spanish, Italian, Portuguese, and Romanian.

✓ **READING CHECK:** ( *Summarizing* ) What did Roman engineers contribute to their society?

# The Rise of Christianity

In A.D. 6, the land called Judea came under Roman control. Judea was the home of the Jews. Because the Jews wanted a separate state, they rebelled against Roman rule. After a series of uprisings, the Romans sacked the city of Jerusalem. They destroyed all but the western wall of the city. In A.D. 135, the Roman emperor Hadrian defeated the Jews and banned them from the city of Jerusalem. The Jews continued to build communities outside of the city. They continued to practice their faith.

**The Teachings of Jesus** Judea was also the birthplace of Christianity. It was here that Jesus had begun to teach in about A.D. 27. His teachings were grounded in Jewish tradition. He taught his followers to believe in only one true God and to love others as they loved themselves. He was said to have performed miracles of healing. He defended the poor. People came from all over to hear Jesus speak. In time, the Romans began to fear that Jesus would lead an uprising.

Eventually, the Romans arrested Jesus. Soon afterward, he was nailed to a cross. His followers believed that Jesus rose from the dead and lived on Earth for 40 days. They believed that he then rose to heaven. Jesus' followers accepted that he was the Messiah, or the savior of the Jews. Soon, his disciples began to spread this message to other people. Christianity had begun to take root.

At first the Romans outlawed Christianity, but their efforts failed to prevent the new religion from spreading. Over the next 300 years, the Christian church became very large. Finally, in A.D. 312, the Roman emperor Constantine declared his support for Christianity. By the end of the century, Christianity had become the official religion of Rome.

✓ **READING CHECK:** ( *Identifying Cause and Effect* ) What are some of the events that led to the death of Jesus?

This modern stained glass window shows Jesus surrounded by children. According to the Gospel of Matthew, Jesus said that people should change to become more like children.

**Interpreting the Visual Record** **What do you think Jesus meant by this?**

# The Decline of the Roman Empire

In the early A.D. 200s, Rome faced troubled times. Ambitious generals frequently decided to seize power for themselves. Some of them even assassinated emperors and took their places. Over time, the army lost its loyalty to Rome. Soldiers became more interested in becoming wealthy than in defending the empire. Dishonest leaders fought for power. Their neglect of the empire made it possible for invaders to threaten the borders. Invasions were costly and drained the empire of its resources. Inside the empire, civil wars had begun. Daily life became more difficult as taxes and the cost of goods rose higher.

**A Split in the Empire** By A.D. 284 the Roman Empire could no longer be ruled well by one person. The emperor Diocletian selected a co-emperor to help rule. About 20 years later, the emperor Constantine, who had accepted Christianity, took over the eastern part of the empire. Constantine was a strong ruler. The empire in the east fared much better than the crumbling and weakened empire in the west.

**The Fall of Rome** As the years passed, invasions from the north continued. Groups such as the Vandals, Visigoths, and Huns set up tribal kingdoms within the empire. In 476, the last emperor of Rome was overthrown by invaders. This marked the end of the empire in the west. The empire of the east was able to fight off invaders. This part of the empire became known as the Byzantine Empire. It lasted until 1453 when it fell to the Ottoman Turks.

**✓ READING CHECK:** ( *Finding the Main Idea* ) How did weak leadership lead to the fall of Rome?

go.hrw.com **Homework Practice Online** Keyword: SK3 HP6

## Section Review 4

**Define and explain:** city-states, direct democracy, republic, aqueduct

### Reading for the Main Idea

1. ( *Environment and Society* ) How did the geography of Greece lead to the development of its city-states?

2. ( *Human Systems* ) What events under the rule of Augustus helped the Roman Republic become the Roman Empire?

3. ( *Human Systems* ) How did the problems in Judea lead to the rise of Christianity?

### Critical Thinking

4. **Comparing and Contrasting** How did the direct democracy of the Athenians differ from government in the United States today?

### Organizing What You Know

5. Copy the following graphic organizer. Use it to compare the governments, people, and geography of ancient Greece and ancient Rome.

|  | Ancient Greece | Ancient Rome |
|---|---|---|
| Government |  |  |
| Early People |  |  |
| Geography |  |  |

# Reviewing What You Know

## Building Vocabulary

On a separate sheet of paper, write sentences to define each of the following words.

1. hominid
2. prehistory
3. nomads
4. land bridges
5. irrigation
6. civilization
7. division of labor
8. history
9. dynasty
10. pharaohs
11. hieroglyphics
12. city-states
13. direct democracy
14. republic
15. aqueduct

## Reviewing the Main Ideas

1. **Human Systems** What are the four characteristics of civilization?

2. **Environment and Society** How did the development of agriculture lead to the growth of villages and towns?

3. **Environment and Society** How did the land protect Egypt from invaders?

4. **Environment and Society** Why did the city-states in ancient Greece develop differently from each other?

5. **Human Systems** What were some of the ancient Romans' achievements?

## Understanding History and Society

**The Road to Civilization**
People of the early civilizations lived very differently from the first humans. Make a flow chart that shows the development of civilization from nomadic hunters and gatherers to city dwellers. As you prepare your presentation about human development, consider the following:
- How people made better tools.
- How agriculture changed society.
- How trade affected the way people lived.

## Thinking Critically

1. **Drawing Conclusions** Why is the ability to make and use tools an important step in human development?

2. **Drawing Inferences** Why are the developments of a calendar, a system of counting, and a system of writing so important to a civilization?

3. **Predicting** How do you think civilization might change in the future?

4. **Comparing and Contrasting** How were the cultures of the ancient Greeks and the ancient Romans similar? How were they different?

5. **Identifying Cause and Effect** Give at least two reasons why civilizations decline.

### Map ACTIVITY

On a separate sheet of paper, match the letters on the map with their correct labels.

Macedon          Asia Minor
Ionian Sea       Athens
Aegean Sea       Crete
Knossos

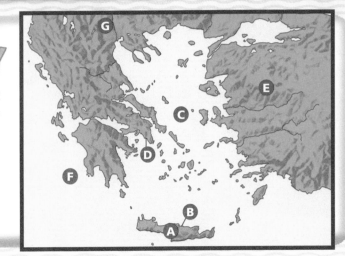

### Mental Mapping Skills ACTIVITY

On a separate sheet of paper, draw a freehand map of the Fertile Crescent. Make a key for the map and label the following:

Tigris River          Jordan River
Euphrates River

### WRITING ACTIVITY

The *Iliad*, a long poem by the ancient Greek poet Homer, tells the story of a great war. Write a short poem that tells the story of another event from ancient history. Your poem does not have to rhyme.

## Alternative Assessment

### Portfolio ACTIVITY

**Learning About Your Local History**

**Early Settlers** Research how your town or city was founded. On poster board, create a display that shows who the first people were to settle in your town.

**internet connect**

Internet Activity: go.hrw.com
KEYWORD: SK3 GT6

Choose a topic to explore about the ancient world:
- List different divisions of labor in early civilization.
- Report on Minoan civilization.
- Create a newspaper article about ancient Athens.

# CHAPTER 7

# The World in Transition

The next 2000 years in human history were a time of great change. In this chapter you will read about the growth of new empires, the development of new political systems, and the search for new ideas.

During the Middle Ages about 1,000 years ago, society was separated into distinct classes. Certain young women of the time who were born into noble families had to undergo training on how to behave.

Young girls from the families of lesser nobles often went to live in the households of higher-ranking noblewomen. There they would be trained in the skills and responsibilities that were expected of women in their rank.

Generally a young noblewoman was taught to sew, to weave, to cook, to play musical instruments, and to sing. She also learned the social conduct that was proper for women of the nobility. In some cases girls and young women were also instructed in the skills of household supervision.

*Young noblewoman from the Middle Ages*

*Knight with female admirers*

*Papal palace in Avignon, France*

# Section 1 — Empires in Asia

## Read to Discover

1. How did the growth of Islam influence Asian history?
2. What dynasties helped to shape Chinese history?
3. What were some key events in Japan's history?

## Define

caliph
mosques
shah
daimyo
shogun
samurai

## Locate

Arabian Peninsula
Mecca
Medina
Constantinople
China
Mongolia
Japan

### WHY IT MATTERS

Asia is a continent of many different peoples and many different cultures. Use CNNfyi.com or other current events sources to find out about Asian cultures today. Record your findings in your journal.

*A page from the Qur'an*

## The Birth of Islam

By the year 600, the western Roman Empire had fallen apart. In Southwest Asia, however, a new empire was growing. It was based on a new religion called Islam. Muhammad, the founder of Islam, lived from about 570 to 632. He was born in Mecca, a city in the western part of the Arabian Peninsula. When Muhammad was about 40, he announced that he had been visited by an angel who told him to spread the word of God. The word *God* in Arabic is *Allah*. At first Muhammad was opposed by the leaders of Mecca. He left the city and traveled north to the city now called Medina. There Muhammad quickly gained many followers. People who follow the teachings of Islam are called Muslims. In 630 Muhammad and an army of his followers took control of Mecca. More people began to follow his teaching, and Islam began to spread through Southwest Asia.

**The Teachings of Islam** Muslims believe that Allah's message to Muhammad is contained in the Qur'an, Islam's holy book. It contains rules and instructions on how to lead a good life. Among other things, these rules require all Muslims to pray five times every day and to give money to the poor. The Qur'an also instructs Muslims to live humble lives, be tolerant, and avoid pork and alcoholic beverages.

The Kaaba in the Great Mosque at Mecca—one of Islam's holiest sites. Millions of Muslims visit it every year.

▼

This piece of art shows a Muslim doctor treating a patient.

**Interpreting the Visual Record** What is the doctor in this image doing?

**internet** connect

GO TO: go.hrw.com
KEYWORD: SK3 CH7
FOR: Web sites about the world in transition

The Safavids built this mosque in Persia. Many mosques are decorated with geometric designs.

**The Spread of Islam** By Muhammad's death in 632, his followers controlled most of the Arabian Peninsula. Soon after he died, however, his followers broke into two groups. They could not agree who should be **caliph**, or leader. The two groups eventually became known as the Sunni and the Shia.

This division did not slow the growth of Islam. Within about 100 years of Muhammad's death, Muslim armies had conquered the Arabian Peninsula, North Africa, Spain, and Persia. Many of the people who lived in these areas converted to Islam.

**Muslim Civilization** The Muslim Empire grew rich from trade with other parts of the world. Goods from Muslim lands were in demand across Europe, Africa, India, and China. Centers of learning like Córdoba and Toledo in Spain attracted scholars from around the world. Muslim doctors were skilled with surgery and medicines. Geographers drew beautiful maps, and mathematicians created the number system we use today. Throughout the Islamic world, architects built beautiful places of worship called **mosques**.

✓ **READING CHECK:** *Summarizing* What were some achievements of the Islamic Empire?

# Islamic Empires

During the 1300s a group of Muslim warriors captured most of what is now Turkey. They were called the Ottoman Turks. In 1453 they took the Christian city of Constantinople and made it their capital. The Ottoman Empire continued to grow in the 1500s under the leadership of Süleyman. Under his rule, the Ottomans ruled much of eastern Europe, western Asia, and northern Africa. Although it slowly lost power, the empire lasted until 1922.

Another Muslim kingdom, the Safavid Empire, included much of what is now Iran. It was founded about 1500 when a Shia Muslim ruler conquered Persia. He took the title **shah**, an ancient Persian word for king. The Safavids built their wealth on trade. Their capital, Esfahan, was one of the world's most beautiful cities. The Safavid Empire collapsed by 1736.

A third Muslim empire, the Mughal Empire, was founded in northern India in the 1500s. Its first leader was a Mongol leader called Babur the Tiger. One of the most famous Mughal rulers was Shah Jahan, who built the famous Taj Mahal in the mid-1600s. Soon after his reign, however, the Mughal Empire began to crumble. In the 1700s, the British began to take over Mughal lands.

✓ **READING CHECK:** *Finding the Main Idea* What were three major Islamic empires?

# Empires in East Asia

Around the same time that Islamic leaders were building empires in western Asia, powerful rulers were doing the same farther east. Beginning in about 500, great empires began to develop in China, Mongolia, and Japan.

**China** When the Han dynasty collapsed in 220, China broke up into several small kingdoms. The political system broke apart, and Chinese society was in disorder for many years. Finally the Sui dynasty reunited China in the late 500s. They ruled China for only a short time but achieved a great deal. Their greatest accomplishment was the Grand Canal, which linked north and south China. It is the oldest and longest canal system in the world.

The T'ang dynasty followed the Sui. They ruled China for about 300 years. The T'ang were powerful military leaders who saved China from invading Turks. Under the T'ang, China grew larger and more powerful. It became the world's most advanced country. Great works of art and literature were produced during this period.

When the T'ang dynasty collapsed, the Sung came to power. They were great inventors. During their rule, the Chinese developed gunpowder and movable type, which allowed them to mass produce books. They were also experts in irrigating farmlands.

**The Mongol Empire** An army of Mongols under Genghis Khan invaded China from the north in the early 1200s. They swept into China from what is now called Mongolia. They were skilled warriors who fought on horseback. Under Genghis Khan, the Mongols captured the city now called Beijing.

Two grandsons of Genghis Khan added to the Mongol Empire. One, named Batu, led an army into Europe around 1240. His army was called the Golden Horde. They reached as far as Vienna before they were turned back. The other grandson, Kublai Khan, completed the conquest of China and founded the Yuan dynasty. Kublai Khan was a wise and powerful ruler. He improved communications by creating a system of fast-moving couriers, or messengers on horseback. During his reign, contact between China and Europe increased. Kublai Khan even allowed Italian trader Marco Polo to become his special representative within the empire. When Kublai Khan died in 1294, he was followed by weak rulers. The Chinese rebelled. The Yuan dynasty fell in 1368.

✓ **READING CHECK:** ( *Analyzing Information* ) What were some achievements of the Mongol Empire?

The Mongols were known as skilled warriors. They fought mostly from horseback.

The Grand Canal, the great project of the Sui dynasty, was actually completed by the Mongols in the 1200s. The canal, which has been extended since the 1950s, is still used today.

Samurai warriors wore elaborate suits of armor.

**Japan** Until the early 300s Japan had no central government. At that time, however, the first Japanese emperor came to power. The first emperor was a member of the Yamato clan. Since the 300s, every Japanese emperor has been a member of this same imperial family. For many years, Japan's government was very much like China's. Beginning in the 800s, however, a new system began to develop. Although the emperor remained the head of government, real power was held by local lords called **daimyo**. The most powerful daimyo was sometimes given the title **shogun**. The daimyo and the shogun were protected by hired warriors called **samurai**. Under this system Japan had no strong central government. Local wars were common.

This changed in 1603 when the Tokugawa shogunate, or dynasty, came to power. Tokugawa leaders built a strong central government by limiting the power of other daimyo. Because they feared that Europeans would threaten their society, the Tokugawa did not allow European traders into Japan. Japanese people were not allowed to travel outside the country.

In 1853 American warships under Commodore Matthew Perry arrived in Japan. Perry had been sent by President Millard Fillmore to trade with Japan. The shogun agreed to begin trading the next year. Soon Japan opened its ports to European countries as well.

In 1868 a group of samurai overthrew the last shogun. They restored political power to the emperor. This political revolution is called the Meiji Restoration. *Meiji* means "enlightened rule." After this revolution, Japan entered a new modern age. Japan's old class system was abandoned. A new constitution passed in 1899 gave more Japanese a say in the government. The economy also began to modernize. By 1900 Japan had become the first industrialized Asian country.

✓ **READING CHECK:** ( *Summarizing* ) What was the Meiji Restoration?

Homework Practice Online
Keyword: SK3 HP7

# Section Review 1

**Define and explain:** caliph, mosques, shah, daimyo, shogun, samurai

## Reading for the Main Idea

**1.** ( *Human Systems* ) How did Islam spread through Southwest Asia?

**2.** ( *Human Systems* ) How did the Sung dynasty improve life in China?

**3.** ( *Human Systems* ) What was the government of Japan like after 800?

## Critical Thinking

**4. Identifying Points of View** How do you think Japanese leaders and American traders viewed Japan differently?

## Organizing What You Know

**5. Categorizing** Copy the following graphic organizer. Use it to describe the major dynasties of China.

| Dynasty | Achievements |
|---------|--------------|
| Sui | |
| T'ang | |
| Sung | |
| Yuan | |

## Read to Discover

1. What were the Middle Ages?
2. What was society like during the Middle Ages?
3. How did the Middle Ages come to an end?

## Define

feudalism
nobles
fief
vassals
knight
chivalry

manors
serfs
clergy
cathedrals
Crusades

middle class
vernacular

## Locate

France
England
Normandy
Norway
Denmark
Sweden

Jerusalem
Spain

### WHY IT MATTERS

The desire to control Jerusalem, which led to the Crusades, is still a cause of conflict. Use CNNfyi.com or other current events sources to learn what is happening in Jerusalem today. Record your findings in your journal.

*A medieval knight*

## The Rise of the Middle Ages

In the year A.D. 476, the last of the western Roman emperors was defeated by invading Germanic tribes. These invaders from the north brought new ideas and traditions that gradually developed into new ways of life for people in Europe. Historians see the years between the last of the Roman emperors and the beginnings of the modern world in about 1500 as a period of change. Because it falls between the ancient and modern worlds, this time in history is called the Middle Ages or the medieval period. *Medieval* comes from the Latin for "middle age."

The time from the 400s to around 1000 is known as the Early Middle Ages. As this period began, the Roman system of laws and government had broken down. Western Europe was in a state of disorder. It was divided into many kingdoms ruled by kings who had little authority. For example, Britain was largely controlled by two Germanic tribes, the Angles and the Saxons. These groups had established several independent kingdoms.

Nobles in the Middle Ages built their own castles for protection.

Charlemagne (742-814) united most of the Christian lands in western Europe. He built libraries and supported the collection and copying of Roman books. His rule became a model for later kings in medieval Europe.

**Interpreting the Visual Record**
**What qualities made Charlemagne a good king?**

**internet** connect

GO TO: go.hrw.com
KEYWORD: SK3 CH7
FOR: Web sites about the world in transition

Between A.D. 600 and 1000, many people invaded western Europe.
**Interpreting the Map** **What group of invaders were most active in the Mediterranean area?**

**The Franks** The Franks were one of the Germanic tribes that moved into western Europe. In the 490s, Clovis, the king of the Frankish tribes, became a Christian and gained the support of the church. He conquered other Frankish tribes and won control of the territory of Gaul. Today this area is called France after the Franks. In 732 a Frankish army under King Charles Martel held off an army of Spanish Moors who had invaded his kingdom. This conflict is called the Battle of Tours. This defeat drove the Muslim Moors back into Spain, creating a border between the Christian and Muslim worlds.

The greatest Frankish king, Charlemagne (SHAR–luh–mayn), ruled from 768 to 814. A strong, smart leader, Charlemagne established schools and encouraged people to learn to read and write. His greatest accomplishment was to unite most of western Europe under his rule. Charlemagne's empire included most of the old Roman Empire plus some new additional territory. It later became known as the Holy Roman Empire because the pope declared Charlemagne "Emperor of the Romans."

After Charlemagne died, his grandsons weakened the empire by dividing it among themselves. Muslims invaded from the south. Slavs invaded from the east. From the north came the dreaded Vikings.

**The Vikings** During the 800s and 900s the Vikings were feared throughout western Europe. They came from what are now the countries of Denmark, Norway, and Sweden. The Vikings were not only farmers but also skilled sailors and fierce warriors who raided towns along the coasts of Europe. Eventually these invaders settled in England, Ireland, and other parts of Europe. A large Viking settlement in northwestern France gave that region its name. It is called Normandy, from the French word for "Northmen." The Vikings there came to be known as the Normans.

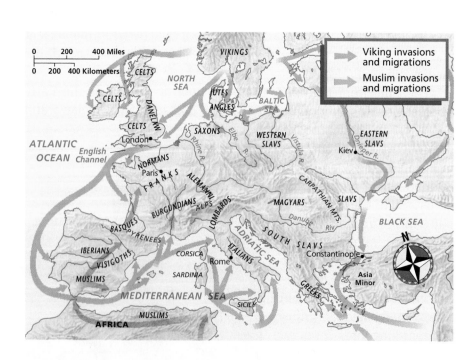

# Life in the Middle Ages

**Feudalism** Within 100 years of Charlemagne's death, the organized central government he had put in place was gone. By the 900s most of Europe was governed by local leaders under a system known as **feudalism**. It was a way of organizing and governing people based on land and service. In most feudal societies, the king, who owned all the land in his kingdom, granted some lands to **nobles**—people who were born into wealthy, powerful families. The grant of land was called a **fief**. Nobles had complete power over their land—power to collect taxes, enforce laws, and maintain armies. In return for land, they became **vassals** of the king. This means that they promised to serve the king, especially in battle. A noble could, in turn, grant fiefs to lesser nobles. In so doing, that noble would become a lord, and the lesser nobles would become his vassals. A vassal owed service—especially military service—to his lord.

This stained-glass window shows a lord and his vassals.

*Interpreting the Visual Record*
**What details in the picture show that the lord is more powerful than the vassals?**

Feudalism was a very complex system. Its rules varied from kingdom to kingdom. Feudal relationships in France, for example, were not the same as those in Germany. The relationships between kings and nobles in England were very different from those in either France or Germany. In addition, the nature of feudal relationships were constantly changing. Laws that governed a king's or a vassal's behavior one year might not apply just a few years later. It was sometimes very difficult, even during the Middle Ages, for people to keep track of their feudal obligations.

Nevertheless, powerful lords were the ruling class in Europe for more than 400 years. Some lords were so powerful that the king remained on the throne only with their support. Over time it became the custom that the owner of a fief would pass his land on to his son. By about 1100 the custom was that the eldest son inherited his father's land. Women had few rights when it came to owning property. If a woman who owned land married, her husband gained control of her land.

**Knights** The most common type of nobleman was the **knight**, or warrior, who received land from a lord in return for military service. Knights lived by a code of behavior called **chivalry**. This code said that a knight had to be brave, fight fairly, be loyal, and keep his word. He had to treat defeated enemies with respect and be polite to women. In battle, a knight wore heavy metal armor and a metal helmet. He carried a sword, a shield, a lance, and other weapons. Knights had plenty of opportunities to fight. In addition to large-scale wars that occurred during the Middle Ages, frequent smaller battles took place between lords who tried to seize each other's lands.

To become a knight, a boy usually had to come from a noble family. Boys began their training at the age of seven.

*Interpreting the Visual Record* **How do the knights in this picture look, and how do you think they feel?**

This picture, made during the 1400s, shows peasants at work during a harvest.

**Interpreting the Visual Record** What do you think farming was like in the Middle Ages?

**The Manorial System** Trade declined after the end of the Roman Empire. Most people took up farming for a living. The large farm estates which some nobles developed were called **manors**. Such manors included large houses, farmed lands, wooded land, pastures, fields, and villages. The lord of a manor ruled over peasants called **serfs** who lived on his land. Serfs were poor and had no rights. They had to work the lord's land and give him part of their crops. They could not leave the manor without the lord's permission. A manor was usually self-sufficient. Almost everything people needed, including food and clothing, was produced right there.

**The Church** One of the largest and wealthiest landowners during the Middle Ages was the Catholic Church. Headed by the pope, the church was enormously powerful, with its own laws and courts.

Officials of the church were known as the **clergy**. Beneath the pope were bishops and priests. Other members of the clergy were monks, who lived in monasteries, and nuns, who lived in convents. While most ordinary people could not read or write, many members of the clergy were educated. In monasteries, monks prayed, studied, and copied ancient books.

Eventually, huge churches, called **cathedrals**, were built. Cathedrals cost a great deal of money and were beautifully decorated. Some of the most common decorations were elaborate stained-glass windows.

**The Crusades** In the late 1000s, the pope asked the lords of Europe to join in a great war against the Turks, who had gained control of Palestine, which the Christians called the Holy Land. This war turned into a long series of battles called the **Crusades**. The First Crusade lasted from 1095 to 1099. Crusaders captured Jerusalem and killed many of the Muslims and Jews who lived there. However, over the next 100 years, the Turks won back the land they had lost. Three more major Crusades were launched. Although the Holy Land was not recaptured, the Crusades led to important changes in Europe.

✓ **READING CHECK:** ( *Summarizing* ) How did feudalism make the nobles and their vassals depend on each other?

Knights in the Middle Ages often fought from horseback.

# The High Middle Ages

The Crusades brought about major economic and political changes in Europe. The period following the Crusades to about 1300 is known as the High Middle Ages.

**Stronger Nations** Many lords sold their lands to raise money in order to join the Crusades. Without land, they had no power. In addition, many lords died in the Crusades. With fewer powerful lords, kings grew stronger. By the end of the Middle Ages, England, France, and Spain had become powerful nations. Strong central governments and the decline of the nobility's power helped to bring about the end of feudalism in Europe.

In 1066 William, Duke of Normandy in northwestern France, claimed the English throne. He landed in England, defeated the Anglo-Saxon army, and was crowned King William I of England. He became known as William the Conqueror. William built a strong central government in England. When William's great-grandson John took the throne, however, he pushed the nobles too far by raising taxes. In 1215 a group of nobles forced King John to sign Magna Carta, one of the most important documents in European history.

Magna Carta stated that the king could not collect new taxes without the consent of the Great Council, a body of nobles and church leaders. The king could not take property without paying for it. Any person accused of a crime had the right to a trial by jury. The most important provision of Magna Carta was that the law, not the king, is the supreme power in England. The king had to obey the law. The Great Council was the forerunner of England's Parliament, which governs Great Britain today.

People exchanged goods at trade fairs in the Middle Ages.

**The Growth of Trade** The Crusades increased Europeans' demand for Asian dyes, medicines, silks, and spices. People also began buying lemons, apricots, melons, rice, and sugar from Asia. In exchange, Europeans traded timber, leather, wine, glassware, and woolen cloth.

Increased trade led to the growth of manufacturing and banking. A **middle class** of merchants and craftsmen arose between the nobility and the peasants. The late medieval economy formed the basis for our modern economic system.

A lecturer teaches at a university during the Middle Ages. Medieval universities taught religion, the liberal arts, medicine, and law.

**The Growth of Cities** As Europe's economy got stronger, cities grew. Centers for trade and industry, cities attracted merchants and craftsmen as well as peasants, who hoped to find opportunities for better lives and more freedom. Both the manorial system and the feudal system began to fall apart.

During the Middle Ages, cities were crowded and dirty. When disease struck, it spread rapidly. In 1347 a deadly disease called the Black Death swept through Europe. Even this disastrous plague, however, had some positive effects. With the decrease in population came a shortage of labor. This meant that people could begin to demand higher wages for their work.

**Education and Literature** Most people could not read or write. As cities grew and trade increased, so did the demand and need for education. Between the late 1000s and the late 1200s, four important universities developed in England, France, and Italy. By the end of the 1400s, many more universities had opened throughout Europe.

Most people during the Middle Ages did not speak, read, or write Latin, the language of the Church. They spoke **vernacular** languages—everyday speech that varied from place to place. Writers such as Dante Alighieri in Italy and Geoffrey Chaucer in England began writing literature in vernacular languages. Dante is best known for *The Divine Comedy.* Chaucer's most famous work is *The Canterbury Tales.*

**The End of the Middle Ages** The decline of feudalism and the manorial system, the growh of stronger central governments, the growth of cities, and a renewed interest in education and trade brought an end to the Middle Ages. In addition, stronger kings challenged the power of the Catholic church. By the end of the 1400s, a new age had begun.

✓ **READING CHECK:** *Finding the Main Idea* Why did kings become more powerful after the Crusades?

Between 1347 and 1351 the Black Death killed about one third of Europe's entire population.

# Section Review 2

**Define and explain:** feudalism, nobles, fief, vassals, knight, chivalry, manors, serfs, clergy, cathedrals, Crusades, middle class, vernacular

## Reading for the Main Idea

**1.** *Human Systems* Why is the time between the A.D. 400s and about 1500 called the Middle Ages?

**2.** *Human Systems* What was life like in the Middle Ages?

**3.** *Human Systems* What led to the end of the Middle Ages?

Homework Practice Online

Keyword: SK3 HP7

## Critical Thinking

**4. Evaluating** Why is Magna Carta considered one of the most important documents in European history?

## Organizing What You Know

**5. Analyzing** Copy the following graphic organizer. Use the right-hand column to describe briefly each person's responsibility.

| Person | Responsibility |
|--------|----------------|
| noble  |                |
| vassal |                |

# Section 3 — The Renaissance and Reformation

## Read to Discover

1. What were the main interests of Renaissance scholars?
2. How did people's lives change during the Renaissance?
3. What changes took place during the Reformation and Counter-Reformation?

## Define

Renaissance
humanists
Reformation
Protestants
Counter-Reformation

## Locate

Rome
Florence

**WHY IT MATTERS**

Works of Renaissance art have remained popular for hundreds of years. Use **CNNfyi.com** or other **current events** sources to learn about Renaissance paintings displayed in museums around the world today. Record your findings in your journal.

*Leonardo da Vinci's sketch of a flying machine*

## New Interests and New Ideas

The Crusades and trade in distant lands caused great changes in Europe. During their travels, traders and Crusaders discovered scholars who had studied and preserved Greek and Roman learning. While trading in Southwest Asia and Africa, people learned about achievements in science and medicine. Such discoveries encouraged more curiosity. During the 1300s, this new creative spirit developed and sparked a movement known as the **Renaissance** (re-nuh-SAHNS). This term comes from the French word for "rebirth." The Renaissance brought fresh interest in exploring the achievements of the ancient world, its ideas, and its art.

**Beginning of the Renaissance** The Renaissance started in Italy. Italian cities such as Florence and Venice had become rich through industry and trade. Among the population was a powerful middle class. Many members of this class were wealthy and well-educated. They had many interests beside their work. Many studied ancient history, the arts, and education. They used their fortunes to support painters, sculptors, and architects, and to encourage learning. Scholars revived the learning of ancient Greece and Rome. Enthusiasm for art and literature increased. Over time the ideas of the Renaissance spread from Italy into other parts of Europe.

**The Humanities** As a result of increased interest in ancient Greece and Rome, scholars encouraged the study of subjects that had been taught in ancient Greek and Roman schools. These subjects, including history, poetry, and grammar, are called the humanities.

▲

The powerful Medici family ruled Florence for most of the Renaissance. Banker Cosimo de' Medici, seen here, was a great supporter of the arts.

Isabella d'Este was a very intelligent and powerful member of a wealthy Italian noble family. She was educated in languages and poetry. She supported the arts and hired noted architects to design parts of her palace.

**Humanists**, the people who studied these subjects, were practical. They wanted to learn more about the world and how things worked. Reading ancient texts helped them recover knowledge that had been forgotten or even lost. They believed that people should support the arts. They also thought that education was the only way to become a well-rounded person. People were urged to focus on what they could achieve in this life.

✓ **READING CHECK:** *Cause and Effect* How did the Renaissance begin?

## The Creative Spirit

During the Renaissance, interest in painting, sculpture, architecture, and writing was renewed. Inspired by Greek and Roman works, artists produced some of the world's greatest masterpieces for private buyers as well as for churches and other public places.

**Art** Leonardo da Vinci and Michelangelo truly represented the Renaissance. Leonardo achieved the Renaissance ideal of excelling in many things. He was not only a painter but also an architect, engineer, sculptor, and scientist. He sketched plants and animals. He made detailed drawings of a flying machine and a submarine. He used mathematics to organize space in his paintings and knowledge about the human body to make figures more realistic. Michelangelo was not only a brilliant sculptor, but also an accomplished painter, musician, poet, and architect.

Northern European merchants carried Italian paintings home, and painters went from northern Europe to study with Italian masters. In time, Renaissance ideas spread into northern and western Europe.

This painting by Pieter Brueghel shows children's games in the 1500s. Many Renaissance painters chose to focus their attention on daily life.
**Interpreting the Visual Record** **What activities do you see that children still do today?**

## The Printing Press

During the Middle Ages books were written and copied by hand. It took a long time and great expense to produce a book. A German inventor, Johannes Gutenberg, developed a printing press in the 1400s. It could print much faster than a human could write. Gutenberg used his printing press to print copies of the Bible. This began the era of the printed book, which had a huge impact on the world of learning. Books printed on the printing press helped to spread the ideas of the Renaissance, and later of the Reformation.

**Understanding What You Read**

1. How was the printing press an improvement over the old ways of making books?
2. Why do you think the printing press helped to spread ideas?

**Writing** Writers of the time expressed the attitudes of the Renaissance. Popular literature was written in the vernacular, the people's language, instead of in Latin. Dutch writer Desiderius Erasmus criticized ignorance and superstition is his work *In Praise of Folly*. In *Gargantua*, French writer François Rabelais promoted the study of the arts and sciences. Spanish writer Miguel de Cervantes wrote *Don Quixote* in which he mocked the ideals of the Middle Ages. Italian writers such as Machiavelli and Baldassare Castiglione wrote handbooks of proper behavior for rulers and nobles.

Of all Renaissance writers, William Shakespeare is probably the most widely known. He was talented at turning popular stories into great drama. His plays and poetry show a great understanding of human nature. He used the popular English language of his time to skillfully express the thoughts and human feelings of his characters. Many of Shakespeare's subjects and ideas are still important to people today.

✓ **READING CHECK:** *Summarizing* What was the Renaissance attitude?

William Shakespeare wrote such famous plays as *Romeo and Juliet, Hamlet,* and *Macbeth.*

During the Renaissance, more people learned to read and write. This painting shows a couple working together in their banking business.

**Interpreting the Visual Record** What does this painting suggest about the changing role of women during the Renaissance?

The city of Florence was the center of the early Renaissance. The large domed building is the Duomo, the cathedral of Florence

# The Renaissance and Daily Life

The Renaissance was not only a time of learning, art, and invention. It was also a time of change in people's daily lives. As the manorial system of the Middle Ages fell apart, many peasants left the manors on which they had lived. Because there were fewer people to work the land, many of these peasants could now demand wages for their labor. For the first time, they had money to spend. As Europe's population began to increase again after the Black Death, however, prices rose very quickly. Only wealthy people could afford many goods.

Although they now had some money, most peasants were still poor. Some migrated to cities in search of work. Instead of raising their food, they bought it in shops. In the 1500s traders brought to Europe new vegetables such as beans, lettuce, melons, spinach, and tomatoes. Traders also brought new luxury items such as coffee and tea. As the idea of the printing press caught on in Europe, books became more common. More and more people learned how to read. Gradually a new way of life developed, and the quality of life slowly began to change.

✔ **READING CHECK:** *Comparing and Contrasting* In what ways did life in Europe change during the Renaissance?

# The Reformation

As humanism became more popular, people began to question their religious beliefs. Northern humanists thought the Roman Catholic Church had become too powerful and too worldly. They thought that it was too rich and owned too much land and that it had lost the true message of Jesus. Some people began to question the pope's authority. The humanists' claims sparked a movement that split the church in western Europe during the 1500s. This movement is called the **Reformation**.

**Martin Luther** A German monk named Martin Luther disagreed with the Catholic Church about how people should act. The Church taught that the way to heaven lay in attending church, giving money to the church, and doing good deeds. Luther said that the way to heaven was simply to have faith in God. He argued that the Bible was the only authority for Christians. The printing press helped Luther's ideas spread. He gained followers who became known as **Protestants** because they protested against the Catholic Church's teachings and practices. Luther eventually broke with the Church and founded the Lutheran Church.

▲
Martin Luther believed that God viewed all people of faith equally.

**John Calvin** Another important thinker of the Reformation was John Calvin. Many of his ideas are similar to those of Martin Luther. Like Luther, Calvin taught that the Bible was the most important element of Christianity. Priests and other clergy were not necessary. Unlike Luther, however, Calvin believed that God had already decided who was going to go to heaven, even before these people were born. He encouraged his followers to dedicate themselves completely to God and to live lives of self-restraint.

Calvin's teachings were very popular, particularly in Switzerland. In 1536 he and his followers took over the city of Geneva. There they passed laws requiring that everyone live according to Calvinist teachings.

**Henry VIII of England** Henry brought major religious change to England. At first he was a great defender of the Roman Catholic Church, but this changed after a conflict with the pope. Henry wanted a son to inherit his throne, but his wife could not have more children after their daughter was born. Henry asked the pope for permission to divorce her, but the pope refused. Henry then claimed that the pope did not have authority over the powerful English monarchy. He broke away from the Roman Catholic Church and had laws passed that created the Church of England. The new Church granted Henry VIII a divorce.

▲
Renaissance painter Hans Holbein the Younger created this famous portrait of King Henry VIII.

**The Counter-Reformation** In response to the rise of Protestantism, the Catholic Church attempted to reform itself. This movement is called the **Counter-Reformation**. Church leaders began to focus more on spiritual matters and on making Church teachings easier for people to understand. They also attempted to stop the spread of Protestantism. Since about 1478, Spanish leaders had put on trial and severely punished people who questioned Catholic teachings. Leaders of what was called the Spanish Inquisition saw their fierce methods as a way to protect the Catholic Church from its enemies. During the Counter-Reformation, the pope brought the Spanish Inquisition to Rome.

**Results of Religious Struggle** Terrible religious wars broke out in France, Germany, the Netherlands, and Switzerland after the Reformation. By the time these wars ended, important social and political changes had occurred in Europe. Many different churches arose in Europe.

A stronger interest in education arose. Catholics saw education as a tool to strengthen people's belief in the teachings of the Church. Protestants believed that people could find their own way to Christian faith by studying the Bible. Although both Catholics and Protestants placed importance on literacy, the ability to read, education did not make people more tolerant. Both Catholic and Protestant leaders opposed views that differed from their own.

As Protestantism became more popular, the Catholic Church lost some of its power. It was no longer the only church in Europe. As a result, it lost some of the tremendous political power it had held there. As the power of the Church and the pope decreased, the power of monarchs and national governments increased.

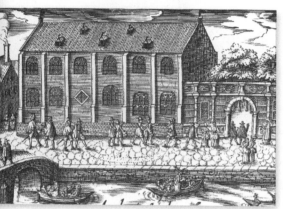

Many schools, including the Dutch University of Leiden shown here, were established during the Reformation.

**Interpreting the Visual Record** What goal of the Renaissance humanists was shared by both Catholics and Protestants?

✓ **READING CHECK:** ( *Identifying Cause and Effect* ) How did the religious conflicts of the 1500s change life in Europe?

---

## Section Review 3

**Define and explain:** Renaissance, humanists, Reformation, Protestants, Counter-Reformation

### Reading for the Main Idea

1. ( *Human Systems* ) What brought about the Renaissance?

2. ( *Human Systems* ) What were some important changes in daily life during the Renaissance?

3. ( *Human Systems* ) After the Reformation and Counter-Reformation, how was life in Europe different?

go.hrw.com **Homework Practice Online**
Keyword: SK3 HP7

### Critical Thinking

4. **Drawing Inferences** Why did national governments gain strength as the power of the Catholic Church declined?

### Organizing What You Know

5. **Categorizing** Copy and complete the following graphic organizer with the achievements of some key people of the Renaissance and the Reformation.

| Person | Achievement |
|--------|-------------|
|        |             |
|        |             |

# Section 4 Exploration and Conquest

## Read to Discover

1. What was the Scientific Revolution?
2. What started the Age of Exploration?
3. How was the English monarchy different from others in Europe?
4. What was the relationship between England and its American colonies?

## Define

Scientific Revolution
Age of Exploration
colony
mercantilism
absolute authority
limited monarchy
limited monarchy
Parliament
Puritan
constitution
Restoration

## Locate

India
China
Spain
Portugal
Mexico
Bahamas
France
Russia
Austria
England

### WHY IT MATTERS

Countries often try to increase their power through conquest. Use CNNfyi.com or other **current events** sources to find examples of conquest going on today. Record your findings in your journal.

*Galileo's telescope*

## The Scientific Revolution

You have read that Renaissance humanists encouraged learning, curiosity, and discovery. The spirit of the Renaissance paved the way for a development during the 1500s and 1600s known as the **Scientific Revolution**. During this period, Europeans began looking at the world in a different way. Using new instruments such as the microscope and the telescope, they made more accurate observations than were possible before. They set up scientific experiments and used mathematics to learn about the natural world.

This scientific approach produced new knowledge in the fields of astronomy, physics, and biology. For example, in 1609 Galileo Galilei built a telescope and observed the sky. He eventually proved that an earlier scientist, Copernicus, had been correct in saying that the planets circle the sun. Earlier, people had believed that the planets moved around the Earth. In 1687 Sir Isaac Newton explained the law of gravity. In the 1620s William Harvey discovered the circulation of blood.

Other discoveries and advances such as better ships, improved maps, compasses and other sailing equipment allowed explorers to venture farther over the seas than before. These discoveries paved the way for the Age of Exploration.

✓ **READING CHECK:** *Identifying Cause and Effect* What brought about the Scientific Revolution?

The model pictured below is of an English explorer's ship. Although they appear tiny and fragile by today's standards, ships like this carried European explorers to new lands around the world.

▼

This map shows the routes taken by Portuguese, Spanish, French, English, and Dutch explorers. They sailed both east and west to discover new lands.

Interpreting the Map **Find Magellan's course on the map. Describe the route he found from the Atlantic Ocean to the Pacific Ocean.**

▶

The Dutch artist Jan Vermeer, who painted during the 1600s, often showed his subjects in the midst of work activities. Vermeer's *The Astronomer* shows research and work connected to mapmaking.

▼

## European Explorations, 1492–1535

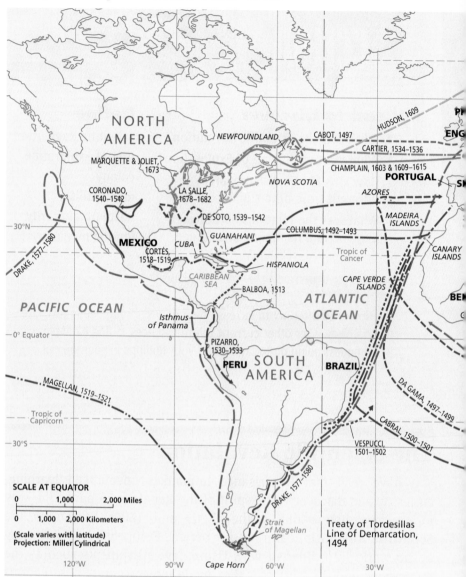

NORTH AMERICA

NEWFOUNDLAND

CABOT, 1497

HUDSON, 1609

CARTIER, 1534–1536

ENG

MARQUETTE & JOLIET, 1673

CHAMPLAIN, 1603 & 1609–1615

NOVA SCOTIA

PORTUGAL

CORONADO, 1540–1542

LA SALLE 1678–1682

AZORES

S

DE SOTO, 1539–1542

MADEIRA ISLANDS

30°N

COLUMBUS, 1492–1493

Tropic of Cancer

CANARY ISLANDS

MEXICO

CUBA

GUANAHANI

DRAKE, 1577–1580

CORTÉS, 1518–1519

HISPANIOLA

CAPE VERDE ISLANDS

BE

CARIBBEAN SEA

BALBOA, 1513

ATLANTIC OCEAN

PACIFIC OCEAN

Isthmus of Panama

0° Equator

PIZARRO, 1530–1533

DA GAMA, 1497–1499

PERU

SOUTH AMERICA

BRAZIL

MAGELLAN, 1519–1521

CABRAL, 1500–1501

Tropic of Capricorn

VESPUCCI, 1501–1502

30°S

DRAKE, 1577–1580

**SCALE AT EQUATOR**

0    1,000    2,000 Miles

0    1,000    2,000 Kilometers

(Scale varies with latitude)
Projection: Miller Cylindrical

Strait of Magellan

Treaty of Tordesillas Line of Demarcation, 1494

120°W        90°W        Cape Horn    60°W        30°W

## The Age of Exploration

Europeans were eager to find new and shorter sea routes so that they could trade with India and China for spices, silks, and jewels. The combination of curiosity, technology, and the demand for new and highly valued products launched a period known as the **Age of Exploration**.

A member of the Portuguese royal family named Prince Henry encouraged Portugal to become a leader in exploration. He wanted to find a route to the rich spice trade of India. Portuguese explorers did eventually succeed in finding a way. They reached India by sailing around Africa.

Hoping to find another route to India, Spain sponsored the voyage of the Italian navigator Christopher Columbus. He hoped to find a direct route to India by sailing westward across the Atlantic Ocean. In

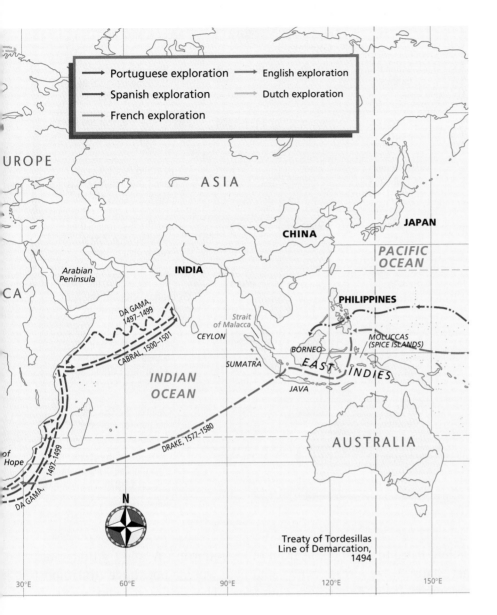

**Map Legend:**
→ Portuguese exploration  → English exploration
→ Spanish exploration  → Dutch exploration
→ French exploration

ASIA

CHINA

JAPAN

INDIA

PACIFIC OCEAN

Arabian Peninsula

PHILIPPINES

DA GAMA, 1497–1499

Strait of Malacca

CEYLON

CABRAL, 1500–1501

MOLUCCAS (SPICE ISLANDS)

BORNEO

SUMATRA

EAST INDIES

INDIAN OCEAN

JAVA

DRAKE, 1577–1580

AUSTRALIA

of Hope

1497–1499

DA GAMA,

N

Treaty of Tordesillas Line of Demarcation, 1494

30°E  60°E  90°E  120°E  150°E

EUROPE

CA

▲

Sailors of the 1500s had many new tools such as this astrolabe to hold a course and measure their progress. A sailor would sight a star along the bar of the astrolabe.
By lining the bar with markings on the disk, he could figure out the latitude of the ship's position.

1492 Columbus reached an island in what is now called the Bahamas. Because he had no idea that the Americas lay between Europe and Asia, Columbus believed he had reached the east coast of India.

Later Spanish explorers who knew of the Americas were motivated more by the promise of conquest and riches than by curiosity and the opening of trade routes. The chart on the following page provides an overview of the major explorers from the late 1400s through the 1500s, their voyages, and their accomplishments.

**Conquest and Colonization** Over time the Spanish, French, English, Dutch, and others established American colonies. A **colony** is a territory controlled by people from a foreign land. As they expanded overseas, Europeans developed an economic theory called **mercantilism**. This theory said that a government should do everything it could to increase its wealth. One way it could do so was by

## European Explorers

| NAME | SPONSORING COUNTRY | DATE | ACCOMPLISHMENT |
|------|------|------|------|
| Christopher Columbus | Spain | 1492–1504 | Discovered islands in the Americas, claimed them for Spain |
| Amerigo Vespucci | Spain, Portugal | 1497–1504 | Reached America, realized it was not part of Asia |
| Vasco Núñez de Balboa | Spain | 1513 | Reached Pacific Ocean, proved that the Americas were not part of Asia |
| Ferdinand Magellan | Spain | 1519 | Made the first round-the-world voyage, first to reach Asia by water |
| Hernán Cortés | Spain | 1519 | Conquered Aztec civilization, brought smallpox to Central America |
| Francisco Pizarro | Spain | 1530 | Conquered Inca empire, claimed the land from present-day Ecuador to Chile for Spain |
| Jacques Cartier | France | 1535 | Claimed the Quebec region for France |
| Sir Francis Drake | England | 1577–1580 | Sailed around the World, claimed the California coast for England |

European explorers sailed in search of goods like gold and cinnamon. In addition, some found new foods, like tomatoes, to bring back to Europe.

selling more than it bought from other countries. A country that could get natural resources from colonies would not have to import resources from competing countries. The desire to win overseas sources of materials helped fuel the race for colonies. The Age of Exploration changed both Europe and the lands it colonized. Colonized lands did benefit from these changes. However, in general, Europe gained the most. During this time, goods, plants, animals, and even diseases were exchanged between Europe and the Americas.

**The Slave Trade** A tragic result of exploration and colonization was the spread of slavery. During the 1500s Europeans began to use enslaved Africans to work in their colonies overseas. In exchange for slaves, European merchants shipped cotton goods, weapons, and liquor to Africa. These slaves were sent across the Atlantic to the Americas, where they were traded for goods such as sugar and cotton. These goods were then sent to Europe in exchange for manufactured products to be sold in the Americas. Conditions aboard the slave ships were horrific, and slaves were treated brutally. Many died crossing the Atlantic.

✓ **READING CHECK:** *Identifying Cause and Effect* What were two results of European exploration?

# Monarchies in Europe

Wealth flowed into European nations from their colonies. At the same time the Church's power over rulers and governments lost strength. The power of monarchs increased. In France, Russia, and Central Europe, monarchs ruled with **absolute authority**, meaning they alone had the power to make all the decisions about governing their nation. This situation would not change much until the 1700s.

France was ruled by a royal family called the Bourbons. Its most powerful member was Louis XIV, who ruled France from 1643 to 1715. Like many European monarchs, Louis believed that he had been chosen by God to rule. He had absolute control of the government and made all important decisions himself. Under Louis, France became a very powerful nation. In Russia, the Romanov dynasty came to power in the early 1600s. The most powerful of the Romanov czars was Peter the Great, who took the throne in 1682. He wanted to make Russia more like countries in Western Europe. Like Louis XIV, Peter the Great was an absolute monarch who strengthened his country. In Central Europe, two great families competed for power. The Habsburgs ruled the Austrian Empire, while the Hohenzollerns controlled Prussia to the north.

England's situation was different. When King John signed Magna Carta during the Middle Ages, he set a change in motion for England's government. England became a **limited monarchy**. This meant that the powers of the king were limited by law. By the 1500s, **Parliament**, an assembly made up of nobles, clergy, and common people, had gained the power to pass laws and make sure they were upheld.

**English Civil War** English monarchs such as Henry VIII and Elizabeth I had to work with or around Parliament to achieve their political goals. Later English monarchs fought with Parliament for power. Some even went to war over this issue. The struggle between king and Parliament reached its peak in the mid-1600s. Armies of Parliament supporters under Oliver Cromwell defeated King Charles I, ended the monarchy, and proclaimed England a commonwealth, a nation in which the people held most of the authority.

A special court tried Charles I for crimes against the people. Oliver Cromwell, a **Puritan**, took control of England. Puritans were a group of Protestants who thought that the Church of England was too much like the Catholic Church. The Puritans were a powerful group in Parliament at the time, and Cromwell was their leader.

Empress Maria Theresa of Austria was a member of the Habsburg family.

Oliver Cromwell led the Puritan forces that overthrew the English monarchy. He ruled England from 1653 to 1658.

▶

The death warrant of Charles I was signed and sealed by members of Parliament. Parliament chose to behead King Charles I in public.

**Interpreting the Visual Record**

**Why might Parliament have decided to have Charles I beheaded where everyone could see?**

Charles II, shown here as a boy, became king following the fall of Cromwell's commonwealth in 1660.

▼

**Cromwell's Commonwealth** Cromwell controlled England for about five years. He used harsh methods to create a government that represented the people. Twice he tried to establish a **constitution**, a document that outlined the country's basic laws, but his policies were unpopular. Discontent became widespread. In 1660, two years after Cromwell died, Parliament invited the son of Charles I to rule England. Thus the English monarchy was restored under Charles II. This period of English history was called the **Restoration**.

**Last Change in Government** Cheering crowds greeted Charles II when he reached London. One observer recalled that great celebrations were held in the streets, which were decorated with flowers and tapestries. People hoped that the Restoration would bring peace and progress to England.

Although England had a king again, the Civil War and Cromwell's commonwealth had made lasting changes in the government. Parliament strictly limited the king's power.

**The Glorious Revolution** When Charles II died, his brother became King James II. James's belief in absolute rule angered Parliament. They demanded that he give up the throne and invited his daughter, Mary, and her Dutch husband, William of Orange, to replace him. This transfer of power, which was accomplished without bloodshed, was called the Glorious Revolution. The day before William and Mary took the throne in 1689, they had to agree to a document called the Declaration of Rights. It stated that Parliament would choose who ruled the country. It also said that the ruler could not make laws, impose taxes, or maintain an army without Parliament's approval. By 1700 Parliament had replaced the monarchy as the major source of political power in England.

✓ **READING CHECK:** *Drawing Inferences* How did the English Civil War and events that followed affect the English government?

# English Colonial Expansion

During the 1600s, English explorers began claiming and conquering lands overseas. In 1607 the British established Jamestown in what is now the state of Virginia. Jamestown was the first permanent English settlement in North America. In 1620, settlers founded Plymouth in what is now Massachusetts.

**Mercantilism and the British Colonies** The British government, with its policy of mercantilism, thought that the colonies should exist only for the benefit of England. Parliament passed laws that required colonists to sell certain products only to Britain, even if another country would pay a higher price. Other trade laws imposed taxes on sugar and other goods that the colonies bought from non-British colonies.

**Resistance in the Colonies** The American colonists saw these trade laws as a threat to their liberties. They found many ways to break the laws. For example, they avoided paying taxes whenever and however they could. Parliament, however, continued to impose new taxes. With each new tax, colonial resistance increased. Relations between England and the colonies grew steadily worse. The stage was set for revolution.

✓ **READING CHECK:** *Finding the Main Idea* How did England regard the American colonies?

The settlers at Jamestown settled close by the James River.
Interpreting the Visual Record
**Why do you think the colonists built their settlement in the manner shown here?**

Colonial Williamsburg Foundation

---

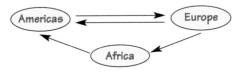

**Define and explain:** Scientific Revolution, Age of Exploration, colony, mercantilism, absolute authority, limited monarchy, Parliament, Puritan, constitution, Restoration

## Reading for the Main Idea

**1.** *Human Systems* How did the Scientific Revolution aid European exploration?

**2.** *Places and Regions* What prompted Europeans to explore and colonize land overseas?

**3.** *Human Systems* How was England different from other monarchies in Europe?

## Critical Thinking

**4. Drawing Inferences** How did England's treatment of the American colonies set the stage for revolution?

## Organizing What You Know

**5. Summarizing** Copy the following graphic organizer. Use it to show how the slave trade worked between Europe, Africa, and the Americas. Alongside each arrow, list the items that were traded along that route.

# Reviewing What You Know

## Building Vocabulary

On a separate sheet of paper, write sentences to define each of the following words.

1. mosques
2. shah
3. samurai
4. feudalism
5. vassals

6. chivalry
7. serfs
8. clergy
9. Renaissance
10. humanists

11. Reformation
12. Scientific Revolution
13. colony
14. mercantilism
15. constitution

## Reviewing the Main Ideas

1. (Human Systems) What were some achievements of the Islamic Empire?

2. (Human Systems) What was humanism?

3. (Human Systems) What were the results of the Reformation and Counter-Reformation?

4. (Environment and Society) How did the Scientific Revolution pave the way for European exploration?

5. (Human Systems) What was mercantilism?

## Understanding History and Society

### The Feudal System

Throughout Europe in the Middle Ages, the feudal system was the most important political structure. Create a chart to explain the relationships among kings, lords, vassals, and knights. Consider the following:

- Who granted lands and who received the grants.
- How a person became a knight.
- What a king or lord expected from his vassals.

## Thinking Critically

1. **Analyzing** Under what kind of social conditions did people of the early Chinese and Mongol Empires produce their achievements?

2. **Identifying Cause and Effect** Why did the growth of cities and trade during the High Middle Ages increase the need for education?

3. **Contrasting** How did political power in Europe change after the Counter-Reformation?

4. **Supporting a Point of View** How did mercantilism both help and harm Great Britain as a colonial power?

5. **Identifying Cause and Effect** How did the English Civil War change the politics in Great Britain?

## Map ACTIVITY

On a separate sheet of paper, match the letters on the map with their correct labels.

**Spain**          **Mexico**
**Portugal**       **Europe**
**South America**
**North America**

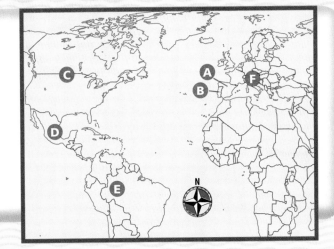

## Mental Mapping Skills ACTIVITY

On a separate sheet of paper, draw a freehand map of the world. On your map, sketch and label each of the following explorers' routes:

**Columbus**          **Drake**
**Magellan**

## WRITING ACTIVITY

Imagine that you are a peasant during the Middle Ages. Write a short dialogue in which you talk with another person about your lives on a manor. In your dialogue, discuss both positive and negative aspects of that life. Be sure to use standard grammar, spelling, sentence structure, and punctuation.

## Alternative Assessment

## Portfolio ACTIVITY

### Learning About Your Local History

**Local Artists and Writers** The Renaissance produced many great artists and writers. Conduct research on the Internet or in your local library to find out about artists and writers in your state or region. Write a brief report on one of these artists or writers.

**🔲 internet connect**

Internet Activity: **go.hrw.com**
KEYWORD: **SK3 GT7**

Choose a topic to explore about the world in transition:
- Write a report on daily life in the Middle Ages.
- Create a biography of a Renaissance artist or writer.
- Learn more about an explorer described in this chapter.

# CHAPTER 8

# The Birth of the Modern World

*The basis for the democratic and modern world we live in today dates back to the 1700s and 1800s. When you read this chapter, you might just wish you had been part of this stirring time of upheaval and great accomplishment.*

From the mid-1760s through the mid-1770s, British policies and actions toward the 13 colonies in North America became intolerable. Many colonists called Patriots believed that independence from Great Britain was necessary to guarantee their freedom and right to a government of, for, and by the people.

When the American Revolution started in April 1775, patriots of all ages joined the fight for independence. Many young boys between the ages of 14 and 16 enlisted in the American army. Other boys, some as young as six, served as drummers for the troops, like the one pictured on this page. Their job was to signal commands, which sometimes put them in the midst of battle.

The American navy had its share of young sailors as well. Small boys served as deckhands or "powder monkeys." They carried ammunition to the gunners during battle.

*Drummer boy from the American Revolution*

Harbor at Charleston, South Carolina       Colonial Williamsburg Foundation

*Revolutionary War cannon*

# Section 1 · The Enlightenment

## Read to Discover

1. What was the Enlightenment?
2. What ideas about government did Enlightenment thinkers suggest?
3. How did the Enlightenment lead to changes in society?

## Define

Enlightenment
reason
secularism
individualism

popular sovereignty
social contract

### WHY IT MATTERS

Our American government and way of life are largely based on the ideas of the Enlightenment. Use CNN **fyi**.com or other **current events** sources to find out how these ideas continue to cause changes today all around the world. Record your findings in your journal.

*Monticello, home of American Enlightenment thinker, Thomas Jefferson*

## The Birth of a New Age

You have read about how greatly European society changed during the Middle Ages, the Renaissance, the Reformation, and the Scientific Revolution. You have also learned how advances in science and technology paved the way for exploration and expansion overseas. As time went on, many changes in the world continued to take place, especially in people's thinking about their relationship with their nation's government.

From the mid 1600s through the 1700s, most European countries were ruled by monarchs. These rulers increasingly wanted absolute control over their governments and their subjects. Many, although not all, literary people, scientists, and philosophers, or thinkers, in these countries saw the need for change. They believed it was necessary to combat the political and social injustices people suffered every day. These critics claimed that the monarchs and nobility took too much from the common people and gave back too little. They wanted a new social order that was fairer for all people. These ideas were published in books, pamphlets, plays, and newspapers. Historians call this era of new ideas the **Enlightenment**.

✓ **READING CHECK:**   *Identifying Cause and Effect*   What about the political and social order of European nations caused many people to want change?

▲
John Locke (1632-1704) was an important English philosopher. He is considered the founder of the Enlightenment in England.

Mary Wollstonecraft was a British writer of the Enlightenment. She argued that women should have the same rights as men, including the right to an equal education.

# Enlightenment Thinking

The Enlightenment is also called the Age of Reason. At this time, scientists began to use **reason**, or logical thinking, to discover the laws of nature. They believed that the laws of nature governed the universe and all its creatures. Some also thought there was a natural law that governed society and human behavior. They tried to use their powers of reasoning to discover this natural law. By following natural law, they hoped to solve society's problems and improve people's lives.

While religion was important to some thinkers, other thinkers played down its importance. Playing down the importance of religion became known as **secularism**. The ideas of secularism and **individualism**—a belief in the political and economic independence of individuals—would later influence some ideas about the separation of church and state in government. These ideas led to more rights for all people, individual freedoms, and government by the people.

**The Enlightenment in England** The English philosopher John Locke believed that natural law gave individuals the right to govern themselves. Locke wrote that freedom was people's natural state. He thought individuals possessed natural rights to life, liberty, and property. Locke also claimed people should have equality under the law.

Much of Locke's writing focused on government. Locke argued that government should be based on an agreement between the people and their leaders. According to Locke, people give their rulers the power to rule. If the ruler does not work for the public good, the people have the right to change the government. Locke's writings greatly influenced other thinkers of the Enlightenment. They also influenced the Americans who shaped and wrote the Declaration of Independence and the Constitution.

**The Enlightenment in France** In France, the thinkers of the Enlightenment believed that science and reason could work together to improve people's lives. They spoke out strongly for individual rights, such as freedom of speech and freedom of worship.

🔲 internet connect

GO TO: go.hrw.com
KEYWORD: SK3 CH8

FOR: Web sites about the birth of the modern world

The Encyclopedia, published by Enlightenment philosophers, became the most famous publication of the period.

**Voltaire** The French writer Voltaire was a leading voice of the Enlightenment. As a young man, Voltaire became a famous poet and playwright. He used his wit to criticize the French monarchy, the nobility, and the religious controls of the church. His criticisms got him into trouble. He eventually went to England after being imprisoned twice.

In England, Voltaire was delighted by the freedom of speech he found. In defense of this freedom, he wrote, "I may disapprove of what you say, but I will defend to the death your right to say it."

Voltaire also studied the writings of John Locke. When Voltaire returned to France, he published many essays and tales. These writings explored Enlightenment ideas, such as justice, good government, and human rights.

**Rousseau** Jean-Jacques Rousseau (roo-SOH) was another French thinker of the Enlightenment. He believed that people could only preserve their freedom if they chose their own government, and that good government must be controlled by the people. This belief is called **popular sovereignty**.

Rousseau's most famous book, *The Social Contract*, published in 1762, expressed his views. "Man was born free, and everywhere he is in chains," Rousseau wrote. He meant that people in society lose the freedom they have in nature. Like Locke, Rousseau believed that government should be based on an agreement made by the people. He called this agreement the **social contract**.

**The Encyclopedia** *The Encyclopedia* was the most famous publication of the Enlightenment. It brought together the writings of Voltaire, Rousseau, and other philosophers. The articles in *The Encyclopedia* covered science, religion, government, and the arts. Many articles criticized the French government and the Catholic church. Some philosophers went to jail for writing these articles. Nevertheless, the *Encyclopedia* helped spread Enlightenment ideas.

✓ **READING CHECK:**  ( *Summarizing* )  What did the thinkers of the Enlightenment believe?

In 1717, when Voltaire was 23, he spent eleven months in prison for making fun of the government. During that time, he wrote his first play. Its success made him the greatest playwright in France.

▲
Jean-Jacques Rousseau

◄
In France, writers and artists gathered each week at meetings like the one shown in this painting. Their purpose was to discuss the new ideas of the Enlightenment.

**Interpreting the Visual Record**
**How might the group pictured here encourage the free sharing of ideas?**

The philosopher Baron de Montesquieu (MOHN-tes-kyoo) thought governments should be divided into three branches. His ideas helped the writers of the U.S. Constitution form our government.

# The Enlightenment and Society

When the philosophers began to publish their ideas, there was little freedom of expression in Europe. Most countries were ruled by absolute monarchs. Few people dared to criticize the court or the nobility. Most nations had official religions, and there was little toleration of other faiths.

As time passed, Enlightenment ideas about freedom, equality, and government became more influential. Eventually, they inspired the American and French revolutions. In that way, the Enlightenment led to more freedom for individuals and to government by the people.

go.
hrw
.com

Homework
Practice
Online

Keyword: SK3 HP8

## Section Review 1

**Define and explain** Enlightenment, reason, secularism, individualism, popular sovereignty, social contract

### Reading for the Main Idea

**1.** ( *Human Systems* ) Why was the Enlightenment also called the Age of Reason?

**2.** ( *Human Systems* ) What important ideas about government came from Enlightenment thinkers?

### Critical Thinking

**3. Drawing Conclusions** Why might the French nobility and the church dislike *The Encyclopedia*?

**4. Analyzing** In what ways did John Locke and other philosophers of the Enlightenment help pave the way for democracy in the United States?

### Organizing What You Know

**5. Categorizing** Copy the following graphic organizer. Use details from the chapter to fill it in. Then write a title for the chart.

| Writer | Country | Important Ideas |
|--------|---------|-----------------|
| Locke | | |
| Voltaire | | |
| Rousseau | | |

# Section 2 — The Age of Revolution

## Read to Discover

1. What started the American Revolution and what were its results?
2. How did the French Revolution change France?
3. How did Europe change during and after the Napoléonic Era?

## Define

Patriots
Loyalists
alliance
oppression

Reign of Terror
balance of power
reactionaries

WHY IT MATTERS

The revolutions of the 1700s in the United States and France gave many new rights and freedoms to ordinary citizens. Use CNNfyi.com or other current events sources to find examples of recent revolutions that have occurred in countries around the world.

American teapot with anti-Stamp Act slogan

Colonial Williamsburg Foundation

## The American Revolution

Enlightenment philosophers' ideas about freedom, equality, and government were not confined to Europe in the 1700s. By the 1750s, the British had established 13 colonies along the Atlantic Coast in North America. These British colonists had developed a new way of life and a new relationship with their home country. The colonists held their own elections and made their own laws. However, the colonists were still British subjects, and they had no representation in the British Parliament.

**The Growing Conflict** While the British had colonies along the Atlantic Coast in North America, the French colonies—New France— lay to the north and west. As British colonists pushed westward into French-controlled territory, tensions mounted.

France and Great Britain had long been enemies in Europe. In 1754, their conflict spilled over into North America, sparking the French and Indian War. In Europe this war was called the Seven Years' War. It began in 1756 and ended in 1763. As the victor in this war, the British gained control of most of North America.

To help pay for the war, the British taxed goods that their colonists in North America needed. Many colonists thought these new taxes were unfair, since they had no representatives in Parliament to express their views. Americans resisted the new taxes by refusing to buy British goods.

The Stamp Act required Americans to purchase stamps like this one and to place them on many types of public documents.

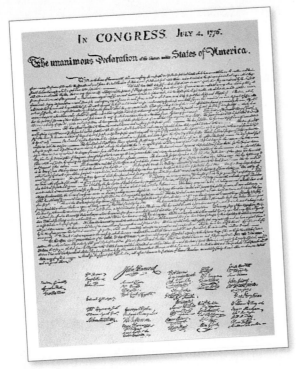

The Declaration of Independence declared the American colonies free from British control. It was adopted on July 4, 1776—now celebrated as Independence Day.

As their unhappiness increased, the colonies united against the British. In 1774, 12 colonies sent representatives to the First Continental Congress. The Congress pledged to stop trade with Britain until the colonies had representation in Parliament.

Some American colonists believed the best way to guarantee their rights was to break away from British rule. Colonists called **Patriots** wanted independence. They made up one third of the population. Another third, the **Loyalists**, wanted to remain loyal to Great Britain. The rest of the colonists were undecided.

**The Declaration of Independence** In 1776 the Continental Congress adopted the Declaration of Independence. Thomas Jefferson was the Declaration's main author. The Declaration clearly showed the influence of Enlightenment thinkers, especially Locke and Rousseau. The Declaration stated that that "all men are created equal" and have the right to "life, liberty, and the pursuit of happiness." The ideal of individual liberty was only applied in a limited way. Women and slaves were not included. Nevertheless, the Declaration was still a great step forward toward equality and justice.

Locke's and Rousseau's ideas about popular sovereignty were clearly seen in the Declaration. It stated that all powers of government come from the people. It said that no government can exist without the consent of its citizens and that government is created to protect individual rights. In addition, it stated that if a government fails to protect these rights, the people may change it and set up a new government.

**War and Peace** By the time the Declaration of Independence was written, the colonies were already at war with Great Britain. At first, the British seemed unbeatable. Then in late 1777, France formed an **alliance** with the Americans. An alliance is an agreement formed to help both sides. By helping the Americans, France hoped to weaken the British Empire.

In 1781 the American forces—commanded by George Washington—and their French allies defeated the main British army in Virginia. The Americans had won the Revolutionary War. The final peace terms were settled in the Treaty of Paris in 1783. The British recognized the independence of the United States. All land east of the Mississippi now belonged to the new country.

The first battle of the American Revolution was fought in Lexington, Massachusetts, on April 19, 1775.

✓ **READING CHECK:** _Finding the Main Idea_ How did the ideas of the Enlightenment influence the American Revolution?

# Effects of American Independence

In 1777 the Americans adopted a plan of government called the Articles of Confederation. The Articles set up a central government, but it was purposely weak. Many Americans did not trust that a central government would always protect the individual rights and liberties they had fought for in the Revolution. Thus Congress could not levy taxes or coin money. It could not regulate trade. Within 10 years, however, it became clear that a weak central government was not helping the country to work as a whole.

In May 1787 delegates from all the states met at a convention in Philadelphia to revise the Articles. The delegates soon realized that making changes in the Articles would not be enough. They decided instead to write a new constitution.

After choosing George Washington to preside over the convention, the delegates went to work. They wanted a strong central government. They also wanted some powers kept for the states. As a result, the new Constitution they wrote set up a federal system of government. This is a system of government in which power is divided between a central government and individual states. The central government was given several important powers. It could declare war, raise armies, and make treaties. It could coin money and regulate trade with foreign countries. The states and the people kept all other powers. The Constitution was approved in 1789. The federal government had three branches. Each branch acted as a check on the power of the others. The executive branch enforced the laws. The legislative branch made the laws. The judicial branch interpreted the laws.

The American Revolution and the writing of the U.S. Constitution were major events in world history. Enlightenment ideas were finally put into practice. The success of the American democracy also encouraged people around the world. They realized they could fight for political freedoms, too.

Of course, American democracy in 1789 was not perfect. Women had few rights, and slaves had no rights at all. Still, the world now had a democratic country that inspired the loyalty of most of its citizens.

✓ **READING CHECK:** *Comparing and Contrasting* How was the new Constitution different from the old Articles of Confederation?

## The United States in 1783

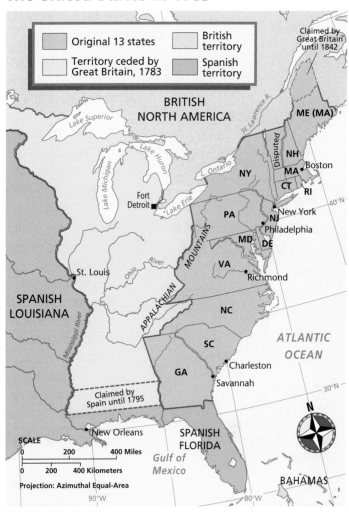

The Treaty of Paris doubled the size of the United States.

**Interpreting the Map** **What nation controlled the region to the south of the United States? To the north? To the west?**

George Washington (1732–1799) led the American troops to victory in the Revolution and was elected the first president of the United States.

# The French Revolution

For over 100 years France had been the largest and most powerful nation in Europe. For all of this time, a monarch with absolute power had ruled France. Yet within months of the beginning of the French Revolution in 1789, the king lost all power.

**Growing Discontent** As the United States won its independence, the French people struggled against **oppression**. Oppression is the cruel and unjust use of power against others. By the 1770s discontent with the nobility was widespread. Food shortages and rising prices led to widespread hunger. To make matter worse, the nobles, who owned most of the land, raised rents. Taxes were also raised on the peasants and middle classes while the nobles and the clergy paid no taxes. Some French people took to the streets, rioting against high prices and taxes.

At the same time, the French monarchy was losing authority and respect. Due to the king's expensive habits and spending on foreign wars, France was in deep debt. To pay the debts, King Louis XVI tried to tax the nobles and the clergy. When they refused to pay the taxes, France faced financial collapse.

The French peasants and middle classes had different complaints against the king. They did, however, share certain Enlightenment ideas. For example, they spoke of liberty and equality as their natural rights. These ideas united them against the king and nobles.

The nobles of France seemed to care little for the suffering of ordinary people. When Marie-Antoinette, the wife of King Louis XVI, was told that many peasants had no bread to eat, she is said to have replied, "Let them eat cake."

## The Outbreak of Revolution

In 1789 a group representing the majority of the people declared itself to be the National Assembly. It was determined to change the existing government. This action marked the beginning of the French Revolution.

When Louis XVI moved troops into Paris and Versailles, there was fear that the soldiers would drive out the National Assembly by force. In Paris, the people took action. Angry city dwellers destroyed the Bastille prison, which they called a symbol of royal oppression. The violence spread as peasants attacked manor houses and monasteries throughout France.

On July 14, 1789, a crowd destroyed the Bastille, freeing its prisoners. Bastille Day marked the spread of the Revolution and is celebrated in France every July 14.

The National Assembly quickly took away the privileges of the clergy and nobles. Feudalism was ended and peasants were freed from their old duties. The National Assembly also adopted the *Declaration of the Rights of Man and Citizen*. This document stated that men are born equal and remain equal under the law. It guaranteed basic rights and also defined the principles of the French Revolution—liberty, equality, and fraternity.

## The End of the Monarchy

In 1791 the National Assembly completed a constitution for France. This constitution allowed for the king to be the head of the government, but limited his authority. The constitution divided the government into three branches—executive, legislative, and judicial. Louis XVI pretended to agree to this new government. In secret, he tried to overthrow it. When he and his family tried to escape France in 1791, they were arrested and sent back to Paris.

## The French Republic

In 1792 a new group of people, the National Convention, gathered and declared France a republic. The National Convention also put Louis XVI on trial as an enemy of the state. Urged on by a lawyer named Maximilien Robespierre, the members found the king guilty. In 1793, the king was sent to the guillotine, a machine that dropped a huge blade to cut off a person's head.

Robespierre was the leader of a political group known as the Jacobins. Many of the Jacobins wanted to bring about sweeping reforms that would benefit all classes of French society. As the French Revolution went on, the Jacobins gained more and more power. By the time Louis XVI was executed, Robespierre was probably the most powerful man in France. He and his allies controlled the actions of the National Convention.

This poster summarizes the main goals of the French Revolution: liberty, equality, and fraternity. Fraternity means "brotherhood."

The frequent use of the guillotine shocked people in France, Europe, and the United States. As a result, the French Revolution lost many supporters.

A group called the Jacobins controlled the National Convention. Robespierre was a powerful leader of the Jacobins.

Under Robespierre, the National Convention looked for other enemies. Anyone who had supported the king or criticized the revolution was a suspect. Thousands of people—nobles and peasants alike—died at the guillotine. This period, called the **Reign of Terror**, ended in 1794 when Robespierre himself was put to death. Despite the terror, the revolutionaries did achieve some goals. They replaced the monarchy with a republic. They also gave peasants and workers new political rights. They opened new schools and supported the idea of universal elementary education. They established wage and price controls in an effort to stop inflation. They abolished slavery in France's colonies. They encouraged religious tolerance.

Between 1795 and 1799, a government called the Directory tried to govern France. A new two-house legislature was created to make laws. This legislature also elected five officials called directors to run the government. The people selected to be directors, however, could not agree on many issues. They were corrupt and quarreled about many issues. They quickly became unpopular with the French people. In addition, by 1799 enemy armies were again threatening France. Food shortages were causing panic in the cities. Many French people concluded their country needed one strong leader to restore law and order.

✔ **READING CHECK:** ( *Summarizing* ) Why did many French peasants and poor workers support the Revolution?

## The Napoléonic Era

In 1799 a young general named Napoléon Bonaparte overthrew the Directory and took control of the French government. Most people in France accepted Napoléon. In turn he supported the changes brought about by the Revolution. In 1804 France was declared an empire, and Napoléon was crowned emperor.

**Napoléon as Emperor** In France Napoléon used his unlimited power to restore order. He organized French law into one system—the Napoléonic Code. He set up the Bank of France to run the country's finances. Influenced by the Enlightenment, he built schools and universities.

A brilliant general, Napoléon won many land battles in Europe. By 1809 he ruled the Netherlands and Spain. He forced Austria and Prussia to be France's allies. He abolished the Holy Roman Empire. He also unified the northern Italian states into the Kingdom of Italy, under his control. Within five years of becoming emperor, Napoléon had reorganized and dominated Europe. Because of the important role that he played, the wars that France fought from 1796 until 1815 are called the Napoléonic Wars.

Napoléon had a way of getting the public's attention. He was very popular with the French people.

Napoléon also made changes in the lands he controlled. He put the Napoléonic Code into effect in the countries he conquered and abolished feudalism and serfdom. He also introduced new military techniques throughout Europe. Without intending to, the French increased feelings of loyalty and patriotism among the people Napoléon had conquered. In some places this increased opposition to French rule. Over time, the armies of Napoléon's enemies grew stronger.

In 1812 Napoléon invaded Russia with more than 500,000 soldiers. The invasion was a disaster. The cold Russian winter, hunger, and disease claimed the lives of most of the French soldiers. Napoléon finally ordered his soldiers to retreat.

**Napoléon's Defeat** The monarchs of Europe took advantage of Napoléon's weakened state. Prussia, Austria, and Great Britain joined together to invade France. These allies captured Paris in 1814. Napoléon gave up the throne and went into exile on the island of Elba, near Italy. Louis XVIII, the brother of the executed king, was made the new king of France.

The following year Napoléon made a short-lived attempt to retake his empire. This period is known as the Hundred Days. Between March and June of 1815, Napoléon regained control of France. The king fled into exile. Soon, however, Napoléon's enemies sent armies against him. The other European nations defeated him at Waterloo in Belgium. Napoléon was sent to St. Helena, a small island in the South Atlantic. He lived there under guard and died in 1821. In 1840 the British allowed the French to bring Napoléon's remains back to Paris, where they lie to this day.

**Europe After Napoléon** During the years of Napoléon's rule, France had become bigger and stronger than the other countries in Europe. After Napoléon's defeat, delegates from all over Europe met at the Congress of Vienna. Their goal was to bring back the **balance of power** in Europe. Having a balance of power is a way to keep peace by making sure no one nation or group of nations becomes too powerful.

Napoléon had not always upheld the ideals of the French Revolution, but he did extend their influence throughout Europe. This led other governments to fear that rebellions against monarchy might spread. Having defeated Napoléon, the major European powers wanted to restore order, keep the peace, and suppress the ideas of the revolution.

This painting captures the glory of Napoléon as a military leader.

| Governments of France, 1774-1814 | |
|---|---|
| 1774 | Louis XVI becomes king. |
| 1789 | Third Estate, as the National Assembly, assumes power. |
| 1791 | Legislative Assembly, with Louis XVI as constitutional monarch, begins rule. |
| 1799 | Napoléon establishes himself as First Consul. |
| 1804 | Napoléon is crowned emperor. |
| 1814 | Napoléon is defeated and the monarchy is restored. |

After being ruled as a republic and then an empire, France became a monarchy once again in 1814.

Many delegates to the Congress of Vienna were **reactionaries**. Reactionaries not only oppose change. They would like to actually undo certain changes. In this case they wanted to return to an earlier political system. These delegates were not comfortable with the ideals of the French Revolution, such as liberty and equality. They worried that these ideals would overturn the monarchies in their own countries.

One of the most influential leaders at the Congress of Vienna was Prince Metternich of Austria. To protect his absolute power in Austria, Metternich suppressed ideas such as freedom of speech and of the press. He encouraged other leaders to censor newspapers and to spy on individuals they suspected of revolutionary activity.

The Congress of Vienna redrew the map of Europe. Lands that Napoléon had conquered were taken away from France. In the end, France's boundaries were returned to where they had been in 1790. Small countries around France were combined into bigger, stronger ones. This was done to prevent France from ever again threatening the peace of Europe. France also had to pay other countries for the damages it had caused. Ruling families were returned to their thrones in Spain, Portugal, and parts of Italy. Switzerland alone kept its constitutional government but had to promise to remain neutral in European wars.

The Congress of Vienna also led to an alliance between Great Britain, Russia, Prussia, and Austria. The governments of these countries agreed to work together to keep order in Europe. For 30 years the alliance successfully prevented new revolutions in Europe.

Many of Europe's royal families came to Vienna during the winter of 1814–15. They attended balls while diplomats and rulers discussed the situation of Europe after Napoléon.

✔ **READING CHECK:** *Drawing Conclusions* Why did the other countries of Europe want to defeat Napoléon?

go.
hrw
.com

**Homework Practice Online**

Keyword: SK3 HP8

# Section Review 2

**Define and explain** Patriots, Loyalists, alliance, oppression, Reign of Terror, balance of power, reactionaries

## Reading for the Main Idea

**1.** (*Human Systems*) Why did the 13 American colonies rebel against Great Britain?

**2.** (*Human Systems*) What were the causes and effects of the French Revolution?

**3.** (*Human Systems*) How did Napoléon change France and the rest of Europe?

## Critical Thinking

**4. Supporting a Point of View** Many people argue that the United States was not really created until 1789. Why do you think this is so? Explain your answer.

## Organizing What You Know

**5. Identifying Time Order** Copy the following time line. Use it to list some important events of both the American Revolution and the French Revolution.

| 1775 | 1780 | 1785 | 1790 | 1795 | 1800 |
|------|------|------|------|------|------|

# Section 3 — The Industrial Revolution

## Read to Discover

1. How did the Industrial Revolution begin?
2. What developments in transportation and communications helped spread industrial development?
3. What features of business affected life in the Industrial Age?

## Define

Industrial Revolution
factors of production
capital
factories
capitalism
mass production

### WHY IT MATTERS

The high standards of living that most Americans enjoy today were made possible by the Industrial Revolution. Use CNNfyi.com or other current events sources to find out more about industry and industrialized nations.

*An early steam locomotive*

## The Origins of the Industrial Revolution

In the early 1700s inventors began putting the ideas of the Scientific Revolution to work by creating many new machines. Advances in industry, business, transportation, and communications changed people's lives around the world in almost every way. This period, which lasted through the 1700s and 1800s, was called the **Industrial Revolution**.

**New Needs in Agriculture** The first stages of the Industrial Revolution took place in agricultural communities in Great Britain. Ways of dividing, managing, and using the land had changed greatly since the Middle Ages. People had begun to think about land in new ways. Wealthy farmers began to buy more land to increase the size of their farms. Small farmers, unable to compete with these large operations, sometimes lost their land. At the same time, Europe's population continued to grow, which meant that the demand for food grew as well. Farmers recognized the need to improve farming methods and increase production.

One such farmer was Jethro Tull. He invented a new farm machine, called a seed drill, for planting seeds in straight rows. More inventors soon followed with other new farm machines. The machinery made farms more productive, and farmers were able to grow more food with fewer workers. As a result, many farm workers lost their jobs. Many of these people moved to cities to look for other kinds of work.

▲

This painting shows the original McCormick reaper, used to cut grain. It was invented by Cyrus H. McCormick in 1831.

**Factors of Production** The Industrial Revolution began in Great Britain because the country had the right **factors of production**. These are items necessary for industry to grow. They include land, natural resources, workers, and **capital**. Capital refers to the money and tools needed to make a product.

Great Britain had rich deposits of coal and iron ore. It also had many rivers to provide water power for **factories** and transportation. Money was available, since many British people had grown wealthy during the 1700s. They were willing to invest their money in new businesses. The British government allowed people to start businesses and protected their property. Labor was available since many ex-farm workers needed jobs.

✓ **READING CHECK:** ( *Summarizing* ) What factors of production helped Great Britain to develop early industries?

Our Amazing Planet

One early water-powered machine in an English mill was said to spin more than 300 million yards of silk thread every day!

# The Growth of Industry

As mentioned earlier, agricultural needs led to new machines and methods for farming. People in other industries began to wonder how machines could help them as well. For example, before the early 1700s, British people had spun thread and woven their own cloth at home on simple spinning wheels and looms. It was a slow process, and the demand for cloth was always greater than the supply.

**The Textile Industry** To speed up cloth making in the early 1700s, English inventors built new types of spinning machines and looms. In 1769 Richard Arkwright invented a water-powered spinning machine. He eventually set up his spinning machines in mills and hired workers to run them. Workers earned a fixed rate of pay for a set number of hours of work. Arkwright brought his workers and machinery together in a large building called a factory. Arkwright's arrangement with his workers was the beginning of the factory system.

In 1785 Edmund Cartwright built a water-powered loom. It could weave cloth much faster than could a hand loom. In fact, one worker with a powered loom could produce as much cloth as several people with traditional ones. Each new invention that improved the spinning and weaving process led to more inventions and improvements.

This painting shows one artist's view of a factory. By 1800, textiles made in English factories were shipped all over the world.

The factory system soon spread to other industries. Machines were invented to make shoes, clothing, furniture, and other goods. Machines were also used for printing, papermaking, lumber and food processing, and for making other machines. More and more British people went to work in factories and mills.

**The Steam Engine** Early machines in factories were driven by water power. This system, however, had drawbacks. It meant that a factory had to be located on a stream or river, preferably next to a waterfall or dam. In many cases these streams and rivers were far from raw materials and overland transportation routes. The water flow in rivers can change from season to season, and sometimes rivers run dry. People recognized that a lighter, movable, and more dependable power source was needed. Many inventors thought using steam power to run machines was the answer.

Steam engines boil water and use the steam to do work. Early steam engines were not efficient though. In 1769 James Watt, a Scottish inventor, built a modern steam engine that did work well. With Watt's invention, steam power largely replaced water power. This meant that factories could be built anywhere.

The factory system changed the lives of workers. In the past, workers had taken years to learn their trades. In a factory, however, a worker could learn to run a machine in just a day or two. Factory owners hired unskilled workers—often young men, women, and children—and paid them as little as possible. As a result, the older skilled workers were often out of work.

New industries needed much steel for machinery. The Bessemer converter, invented in the 1850s, was a cheaper, better way to make steel.

✓ **READING CHECK:** *Cause and Effect* How was the textile industry created in Great Britain?

# The Spread of the Industrial Revolution

Great Britain quickly became the world's leading industrial power. British laws encouraged people to use capital to set up factories. Great Britain's stable government was good for industry too.

The rest of Europe did not develop industry as quickly. For one thing, the French Revolution and Napoléon's wars had disrupted Europe's economies. That made it difficult to put the factors of production to work. Many countries also lacked the resources needed to industrialize.

These steamboats from the 1850s carried people and goods on the Mississippi River.

The Industrial Revolution did spread quickly to the United States though. The United States had a stable government, rich natural resources, and a growing labor force. Americans were quick to adapt British inventions and methods to their own industries.

**Transportation** Since the Middle Ages, horse-drawn wagons had been the main form of transportation in Europe. Factory owners needed better transportation to get raw materials and send goods to market. To move goods faster, stone-topped roads were built in Europe and the United States. Canals were dug to link rivers. The steam engine was also put to work in transportation. In 1808 American inventor Robert Fulton built the first steamboat. Within a few decades, steamships were crossing the Atlantic.

Steam also powered the first railroads. An English engineer, George Stephenson, perfected a steam locomotive that ran on rails. By the 1830s, railways were being built across Great Britain, mainland Europe, and the United States.

**Communication** Even before 1800, scientists had known that electricity and magnetism were related. American inventor Samuel F. B. Morse put this knowledge to practical use. Morse sent an electrical current through a wire. The current made a machine at the other end click. Morse also invented a code of clicking dots and dashes to send messages this way.

Morse's inventions—the telegraph and the Morse code—brought about a major change in communications. Telegraph wires soon stretched across continents and under oceans. Suddenly information and ideas could travel at the speed of electricity.

The telegraph revolutionized communications in the 1850s. This device is a telegraph receiver.

## Life in the Industrial Age

The 1800s are sometimes called the Industrial Age. This was an age of new inventions. It was a time when businesses found new ways to produce and distribute goods. The owners of factories in the Industrial Age often became very wealthy. Low factory wages, however, meant many workers faced poverty.

**The Rise of Capitalism** In the late 1800s European and American individuals owned and operated factories. This economic system is called **capitalism**. In a capitalist system, individuals or companies, not the government, control the factors of production.

The early capitalists wanted to make as much profit as possible from their factories. They divided each manufacturing process into a series of steps. Each worker performed just one of the steps, over and over again. This division of labor meant workers could produce more goods in less time.

Factory owners used machines to make the parts for their products. These parts were identical and interchangeable. To speed up production, the parts were carried to the workers in the factory. Each worker added one part, and the product moved on to the next worker. This method of production is called an assembly line.

**Mass Production** The division of labor, interchangeable parts, and the assembly line made mass production possible. **Mass production** is a system of producing large numbers of identical items. Mass production lowered the cost of clothing, furniture, and other goods. It allowed more people to buy manufactured products and to enjoy a higher standard of living.

In the early 1900s, Henry Ford used an assembly line to build cars.

*Interpreting the Visual Record* **How do you think the assembly line might have made work easier for these people?**

✔ **READING CHECK:** *Finding the Main Idea* What is capitalism and how did it affect the Industrial Revolution?

---

# Section Review 3

go.hrw.com **Homework Practice Online** Keyword: SK3 HP8

**Define and explain** Industrial Revolution, factors of production, capital, factories, capitalism, mass production

## Reading for the Main Idea

1. *Environmental and Society* Where did the Industrial Revolution begin and why?

2. *Human Systems* What advances in transportation and communications helped to spread the Industrial Revolution?

3. *Human Systems* How did capitalism and mass production affect people's standard of living in the late 1800s?

## Critical Thinking

4. **Drawing Conclusions** Why do you think the steam engine was such an important invention of the Industrial Revolution?

## Organizing What You Know

5. **Categorizing** Copy the following graphic organizer. Use it to describe some important inventions of the Industrial Revolution.

| Invention | Inventor | Importance |
|---|---|---|
| seed drill | | |
| spinning machine | | |
| water-powered loom | | |
| steam engine | | |
| steam locomotive | | |
| telegraph | | |

# Section 4 Expansion and Reform

## Read to Discover

1. How did life in Europe and America change after 1850?
2. What led to reforms in the later 1800s?
3. How did nationalism change the map of Europe in the mid-1800s?

## Define

working class
literacy
emigrate
suburbs

reform
suffragettes
nationalism

### WHY IT MATTERS

By the later 1800s, new ideas and technology began to improve city life. Use CNN fyi.com or other current events sources to find out about solutions to today's urban problems.

*Thomas Edison's electric light bulb*

## The Rise of the Middle Class

The Industrial Revolution changed how people in Europe and America worked and lived. Industries and cities grew, and new inventions made life easier.

During the later 1800s many people became better educated. Some became wealthy. This group included bankers, doctors, lawyers, professors, engineers, factory owners, and merchants. Also in this group were the managers who helped keep industries running. Together these people and their families were known as the middle class. Membership in the middle class was based upon economic standing rather than upon birth.

The ideas of the middle class influenced many areas of life in Western Europe and in the United States. Over time, the middle class's wealth, social position, lifestyle, and political power grew. Government leaders began turning to some middle-class individuals for advice, particularly about business and industry.

Many middle-class families had enough money that women did not need to work outside the home. They cleaned, cooked, and took care of the children, often with hired help. In the mid-1800s, however, many middle-class women started to express a desire for roles outside the home.

Doctors were one of the groups who made up the middle class of the late 1800s. Medical advances made during this period made their jobs safer and more efficient.

▼

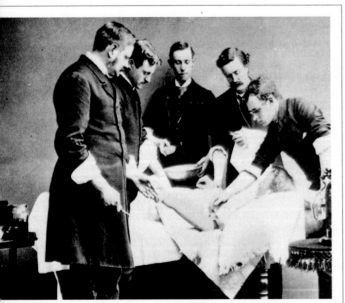

For some women, doing something outside the home meant independence. It was also a way to earn a living. During the late 1800s more jobs opened up to women. They became nurses, secretaries, telephone operators, and teachers.

✓ **READING CHECK:** *Finding the Main Idea* What role did the middle class play in the society of the late 1800s?

After 1870, more and more women went to high school. For the first time they began to study the same subjects as men did.

# The Growth of Society

The middle class was not the only group of people to enjoy the benefits of the Industrial Age. By the 1870s life was improving in some ways for both the middle class and the **working class,** people who worked in factories and mines.

**Technology and Communication** In the 1870s a tremendous new power source was developed. That power source was electricity. This led to a new wave of inventions in Western Europe and the United States. The electric generator produced the power needed to run all kinds of machines and engines. Thomas Edison's electric light bulb created a new way of lighting rooms, streets, and cities. Alexander Graham Bell's telephone made it possible to transmit the human voice over long distance.

In the late 1800s the first successful gasoline-driven automobile was built. In 1908 American inventor Henry Ford produced the Model T. This was the first automobile to become popular with American buyers.

Scientists of the 1800s used microscopes like this one to study cells.

**Other Advances** Advances in science and medicine also transformed people's lives. Scientists discovered more about the connection between food and health. This new knowledge, plus new information about diseases, made it possible for people to live healthier, longer lives.

Scientists of this time also made great advances in the fields of chemistry and physics. For example, they formed new theories about the structure of the atom and organized all known elements into the periodic table. It was also at this time that X-rays were discovered and first used in medicine. Scientists like Max Planck and Albert Einstein developed new ideas that changed the study of physics. Their ideas were the basis for the work of many later experiments.

Several new fields of study, together called the social sciences, gained popularity during this period. Scholars saw these fields as a way to study people as members of society. The social sciences include such fields as economics, politics, anthropology, and psychology. The study of history also changed. Historians searched for evidence of the past in documents, diaries, letters, and other written sources. As a result, new views of history began to emerge from their research.

As greater numbers of people learned to read, newspapers competed for their attention. They published eye-catching stories and cartoons.

**Public Education** After 1870, governments in Europe and the United States required all children to attend school. The spread of education had many benefits. As **literacy**—the ability to read—became widespread, more books and magazines were published. Newspapers that carried stories from all over the world also became very popular. By reading them, citizens became more informed about their governments.

**Arts and Entertainment** City dwellers of the late 1800s found themselves with more time and money for entertainment. Theaters opened to meet a demand for concerts, plays, and vaudeville shows. Art collections were made available to the public by displaying them in museums. Free public libraries opened in many cities. Sports became more organized, and cities began to sponsor teams with official rules and national competitions. Many cities began to construct public parks. These parks allowed people who lived in the cities to enjoy outdoor activities. By the end of the 1800s many of these parks had begun to include playgrounds for children.

**A Growing Population** One of the greatest changes of the later 1800s was the rapid growth of cities in the United States. Faced with crowded, dirty cities and seeking new opportunities, many Europeans chose to emigrate to the United States. To **emigrate** means to leave one country to live in another. The United States was not the only destination for these emigrants. Many also chose to seek new lives in South America, Africa, Australia, and New Zealand.

Between 1870 and 1900 more than 10 million people left Europe for the United States. These newcomers hoped to find economic opportunities. Some sought political and religious freedom as well.

This is a painting of a croquet game in a public park. It reflects the increased participation in free-time activities during the late 1800s. **Interpreting the Visual Record** **What does this painting suggest about sports in the later 1800s?**

# CONNECTING TO Art

## A New Art Period

Works of art not only show the values of an artist but also the values of the society in which the artist lives. The American and French Revolutions, for example, changed society deeply. Many artists were inspired to paint stirring scenes from history and nature. These artists were called *romantics*. Their scenes showed life to be more exciting and satisfying than it normally is.

By the mid-1800s, however, many artists had rejected romanticism. These artists instead wanted to portray life as it really was. A style called *realism* developed. The realists painted ordinary living conditions and familiar settings. They tried to re-create what they saw around them, accurately and honestly.

Honore Daumier was a French realist. He painted *The Washerwoman* during the Industrial Revolution in France, a time when many city workers were struggling to survive. The subject in the painting is one of these workers.

**Understanding What You Read**
1. How was realism different from romanticism?
2. What types of subjects and scenes might a realist paint?

---

**City Improvements** Faced with rapidly growing populations and changes in society, many cities needed civic improvements. Local governments began to provide water and sewer service to city dwellers. Many streets were also paved. In 1829 London organized a police force. Many other cities soon had police forces, too.

Cities around the world grew rapidly in the 1800s. By the early 1900s, more people lived in cities than in the country. Many cities—including New York, London, Paris, and Berlin—had populations of more than 1 million.

Cities also created public transportation systems. Horse-drawn streetcars and buses were used mainly within cities. Trains, however, could take people far outside a city. As a result, some people began to move outside cities to areas called **suburbs**. These people usually took trains into cities each morning and returned to their homes in the suburbs at night.

✓ READING CHECK: _Summarizing_ What were some advances of the later 1800s?

### Our Amazing Planet

Between 1865 and 1900 most American cities doubled or tripled in size. Much of this growth was due to immigration. Many immigrants to the United States moved to New York City. By 1900 the city's population was nearly five times larger than it had been in 1850.

# Political and Social Reform

In addition to great advances in technology, communications, science, and medicine, the mid-1800s and early 1900s saw many political and social reforms. To **reform** something is to remove its faults. Around the world, citizens worked to improve their governments and societies.

**Great Britain** In Great Britain reformers passed laws that allowed male factory workers in cities to vote. Laws were also passed to improve conditions in factories, and slavery was abolished. New laws were passed to provide health insurance, unemployment insurance, and money for the elderly.

Beginning in the late 1800s, many women in Great Britain became **suffragettes**. These women campaigned for their right to vote. They were led by outspoken women like Emmeline Pankhurst. British women gained this right in 1928.

**France** A revolution in France in 1848 forced the king from the throne. A new government called the Second Republic was established. It guaranteed free speech and gave the vote to all men. In 1875, a new French constitution established the Third Republic. This constitution lasted for nearly 70 years.

**United States** The issue of slavery divided the United States in the mid-1800s. In late 1860 and early 1861 several southern states broke from the Union to form the Confederate States of America. The Civil War followed and raged until 1865 when the Confederacy surrendered. Congress then amended the Constitution to abolish slavery and grant citizenship to former slaves. The vote was given to all men, regardless of race or color.

Many reforms were the results of efforts by women such as Elizabeth Cady Stanton and Lucretia Mott. As early as 1848 they had campaigned for the abolition of slavery, equality for women, and the right to vote. In the 1890s and early 1900s, the movement for women's right to vote grew stronger. The Nineteenth Amendment to the Constitution, ratified in 1920, finally gave women this right.

✓ **READING CHECK:** *Comparing and Contrasting* How were reforms in Great Britain, France, and the United States in the mid-1800s and early 1900s similar?

Emmeline Pankhurst (1858–1928) led many demonstrations and marches on behalf of the women's suffrage movement in Great Britain.

RÉPUBLIQUE FRANÇAISE.
Combat du peuple parisien dans les journées des 22, 23 et 24 Février 1848.

In 1848, French citizens overthrew the king and set up the Second Republic.

# Nationalism in Europe

**Nationalism** is the love of one's country more than the love of one's native region or state. In the 1800s, nationalism led to the unification of Italy and of Germany. It was also a driving force for change in Russia.

In the early 1800s the Congress of Vienna had divided Italy into several states, some of which were ruled by Austria. In the 1850s and 1860s, a nationalist named Giuseppe Garibaldi led a movement to unify these states. He and his army defeated the Austrians and their French allies and drove them out of Italy. Largely because of his efforts, most of present-day Italy had been unified by 1861. In that year Victor Emmanuel II was made the king of Italy.

Germany in the mid-1800s was a patchwork of 39 independent states. The largest was Prussia, ruled by William I. In 1862 he appointed Otto von Bismarck one of his advisers. Both men wanted to make Germany into a powerful unified country. Bismarck convinced the other German states to join in this effort and to declare war first on Austria, Prussia's chief rival, and then on France. After the war, the German states were joined together into the German Empire. William I became the first kaiser, or emperor.

In the 1800s Russia had more territory and people than any other country in Europe. Its economy, however, was not as developed as those of other countries. People from Russia's many ethnic groups felt very little unity with each other. In the 1850s Czar Alexander II tried to introduce major reforms. He freed all the serfs in Russia and introduced political changes. Later czars, however, tried to undo these reforms. Censorship and discrimination against minorities became widespread. This repression created an explosive situation in Russia. In 1905, a group of revolutionaries tried to overthrow the czar but failed.

▲
Otto von Bismarck (1815–1898) was known for his strong will and determination.

✓ **READING CHECK:** ( *Drawing Inferences* ) How did nationalism help reshape nations?

go.hrw.com **Homework Practice Online** Keyword: SK3 HP8

## Section Review 4

**Define and explain** working class, literacy, emigrate, suburbs, reform, suffragettes, nationalism

### Reading for the Main Idea

1. ( *Human Systems* ) What allowed people's lives to improve during the last half of the 1800s?

2. ( *Human Systems* ) How did reforms of the later 1800s and early 1900s affect people's lives?

3. ( *Human Systems* ) How did nationalism lead to the unification of Italy and Germany in the mid-1800s?

### Critical Thinking

4. **Analyzing** What effect did immigration of the later 1800s have on the United States?

### Organizing What You Know

5. **Categorizing** Copy the following chart. List the home country of each leader. Then give details about his accomplishments.

| Leader | Country | Accomplishments |
|---|---|---|
| Giuseppe Garibaldi | | |
| Otto von Bismarck | | |
| Czar Alexander II | | |

# Reviewing What You Know

## Building Vocabulary

On a separate sheet of paper, write sentences to define each of the following.

1. Enlightenment
2. reason
3. individualism
4. popular sovereignty
5. Patriots

6. alliance
7. oppression
8. factors of production
9. capital
10. capitalism

11. mass production
12. literacy
13. emigrate
14. reform
15. nationalism

## Reviewing the Main Ideas

1. **Human Systems** What did Enlightenment thinkers hope to discover?

2. **Human Systems** What led to the defeat of the British in the American Revolution?

3. **Environment and Society** What conditions in Great Britain gave rise to the Industrial Revolution?

4. **Environment and Society** How did education change greatly in Europe and the United States during the later 1800s and what were the benefits?

5. **Human Systems** What were the effects of nationalism on European nations in the late 1800s?

## Understanding History and Society

### Plans for Reform

Imagine you are the mayor of a large European city in the mid-1800s. Using a chart, make a presentation that lists and describes the reforms and changes you think should be made in your city. Consider the following:

- Health and safety issues.
- Communication and transportation needs.
- Education needs.

## Thinking Critically

1. **Analyzing** How did Enlightenment ideas influence American democracy?

2. **Drawing Conclusions** Why did revolutions break out in America and France in the late 1700s?

3. **Analyzing** How did Napoléon Bonaparte change France and the rest of Europe in the early 1800s?

4. **Supporting a Point of View** Which three advances in the later 1800s do you think changed people's lives the most? Explain your answer.

5. **Evaluating** Why was the middle class so important to the Industrial Revolution?

**Map ACTIVITY** On a separate sheet of paper, match the letters on the map with their correct labels.

Maine
New Hampshire
Massachusetts
Connecticut
New York

Pennsylvania
Maryland
Virginia
North Carolina
Georgia

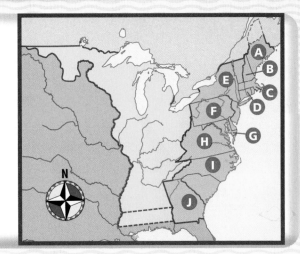

## Mental Mapping Skills ACTIVITY

On a separate sheet of paper, draw a freehand map of Europe in the late 1800s. Make a key for your map and label the following:

Great Britain
France
Germany

Italy
Russia
Austria

### WRITING ACTIVITY

Imagine you are a news reporter in France in 1789, just as the French Revolution is breaking out. Write a news story about why the French people are in revolt and what they hope to achieve. Be sure to use standard grammar, spelling, sentence structure, and punctuation.

## Alternative Assessment

### Portfolio ACTIVITY

**Learning About Your Local History**

**Industries in Your Town** Research one or two of the main industries of your town, region, or state. Create a chart to explain when, where, why, and how the industry or industries were developed.

**internet connect**

Internet Activity: go.hrw.com
KEYWORD: SK3 GT8

Choose a topic to explore about the birth of the modern world:
- Explore the ideas of the Enlightenment.
- Investigate the causes of the French Revolution.
- Understand capitalism.

# CHAPTER 9

# The Modern World

The 1900s were filled with change. Great wars, economic depressions, horrible injustices, and tremendous technological advances have all taken place. You will find out how it all happened in this chapter.

One of the events that affected the world in the 1900s was the Great Depression. In the early 1930s millions of workers throughout the world could not find jobs and people had no money to buy goods.

During the Great Depression, young people faced special problems. In some cases, parents expected children to work when the parents themselves could not. Children were often a burden in poor families. For many youngsters, running away seems the only solution. At one point, almost 250,000 teenaged "hoboes" were roaming the United States. Many of these young people searched for any kind of work or odd job that they could find.

*Poster from the Great Depression*

*Depression-era farmhouse*

*Migrant child*

# Section 1 — World War I

## Read to Discover

1. What were the causes of World War I?
2. How did science and technology make this war different from earlier wars?
3. How was the world changed because of World War I?

## Define

militarism
U-boats
armistice

## Locate

England
France
Germany
Russia
Austria-Hungary
Ottoman Empire
Serbia
Sarajevo

### WHY IT MATTERS

World War I started in the Balkans—a region that is still the scene of much conflict. Use CNN**fyi**.com or other current events sources to learn what is happening in this region today. Record your findings in your journal.

*German poster from World War I*

## Beginning of World War I

By the early 1900s, countries across Europe were competing for power. They built up strong armies to protect themselves and their interests. Powerful nations feared each other. Tensions were high. The stage was set for war.

The spirit of nationalism was still strong in Europe in the early 1900s. Nationalism is a fierce pride in one's country. Many European countries wanted more power and more land. They built strong armies and threatened to use force to get what they wanted. The use of strong armies and the threat of force to gain power is called **militarism**.

Europe's leaders did not trust one another. To protect their nations against strong enemies, they formed alliances. An alliance is an agreement between countries. If a country is attacked, its allies—the members of the alliance—help it fight.

By 1907 Europe was divided into two opposing sides. Germany, Austria-Hungary, and Italy had formed one alliance. England, France, and Russia had formed another.

The attention of both alliances was soon drawn to the Balkans, a region in southeastern Europe. In 1878 Serbia, part of this region, had become an independent country. Serbian nationalists now wanted control of Bosnia and Herzogovina, which belonged to Austria-Hungary.

On June 28, 1914, a Serbian nationalist shot and killed the heir to the Austro-Hungarian throne, Archduke Francis Ferdinand. As a result, Austria-Hungary declared war on Serbia. Russia supported Serbia; Germany supported Austria-Hungary. With Russia and its allies on one side and Germany and its allies on the other, conflict quickly spread.

This drawing of the killing of Archduke Francis Ferdinand in Sarajevo was published in French newspapers.

**internet connect**

GO TO: go.hrw.com
KEYWORD: SK3 CH9
FOR: Web sites about the
modern world

In August 1914 Germany declared war on Russia. Russia was allied with France, so Germany declared war on France, too. England declared war on Germany. Japan also declared war on Germany. England, France, Russia, and Japan became known as the Allied Powers. The alliance of Germany, Austria-Hungary, the Ottoman Empire, and Bulgaria was called the Central Powers. Later in the war, Italy left the Central Powers and joined the Allied Powers. Eventually, the Allied Powers included 32 countries.

✔ **READING CHECK:** _Identifying Cause and Effect_ How did militarism and alliances help set the stage for war in Europe?

## A New Kind of War

New weapons played a major role in World War I. Germany introduced submarines, which were called **U-boats**. This name is short for "underwater boats." Germany also introduced poison gas, which was later used by both sides and caused great loss of life. Other new weapons included large, long-range cannons and the machine gun. Machine guns could kill hundreds of people in a few minutes.

World War I was also the first war to use the airplane. At first airplanes were used mainly to observe enemy troops. Later, machine guns were placed on airplanes, so they could fire on troops and shoot at each other in the sky. England also introduced the tank during the war. This huge, heavy vehicle could not be easily stopped. With machine guns mounted on them, tanks could kill large numbers of soldiers.

The Allied Powers and the Central Powers divided Europe into two opposing sides.

▼

### Europe at the Beginning of World War I

Cutaway view of a German U-Boat

## U-Boats

A U-boat had two hulls, or walls. Between the hulls was an open space. When the U-boat took water into this space, the extra weight made the boat sink below the surface of the ocean. When water was pumped out of the space, the boat became lighter, and the U-boat rose.

When the U-boat was under water, the men on the boat could look at the surface through a tube called a periscope. U-boats could also fire torpedoes while underwater. This allowed them to make devastating surprise attacks on enemy ships.

### Understanding What You Read

1. How did a U-boat submerge and surface?
2. Why were U-boats such a threat to the Allies' ships?

**The Early Years of the War** Early in the war, Germany attacked France. The German army almost reached Paris, the French capital. However, Russia attacked Germany and Austria-Hungary, forcing Germany's attention east. At sea, England used its powerful navy to stop supplies from reaching Germany by ship. Germany used its deadly U-boats to sink ships carrying supplies to Great Britain.

At first, both sides thought they would win a quick victory. They were wrong. Armies dug in for a long and costly fight. World War I would go on for four years.

**The United States and World War I** At first, the United States stayed out of World War I. In 1917, however, Germany tried to persuade Mexico to join the Central Powers. The Germans promised to help Mexico retake Arizona, New Mexico, and Texas from the United States after the war. This angered many Americans.

At the same time, German U-boats were attacking American ships carrying supplies to the Allies. Many ships were sunk and many Americans died.

The United States had another motivation for joining the war. The major Allied countries had moved toward democracy, but the Central Powers had not. President Woodrow Wilson told Congress that "the world must be made safe for democracy." On April 6, 1917, the United States declared war on Germany.

American soldiers march through Paris during World War I.

✓ **READING CHECK:** ( *Summarizing* ) Why did the United States enter World War I?

## Military Losses in World War I

### Allied Powers

Russia
British Empire
France
Italy
United States
Romania
Serbia
Belgium

Wounded
Dead

### Central Powers

Germany
Austria-Hungary
Turkey
Bulgaria

0  1  2  3  4  5

Casualties (in Millions)
Source : *Encyclopedia of Military History*

**Interpreting the Graph** Which of the Allied Powers had the highest number of total casualties? Which of the Central Powers had the highest casualties?

# The War Ends

During World War I, Russian citizens held protests and demonstrations because they did not have enough food and because so many Russians were dying in the war. The Russian army joined the people in their protests. In March 1917 the czar, or king, was overthrown and put in prison.

A new government was set up. Political groups called soviets, or councils, were also formed. The most powerful soviet leader was Vladimir Lenin. He offered the Russian people peace, food, and land. Lenin's ideas were part of an economic and political system known as communism. On November 7, 1917, Lenin's followers took control of Russia.

Lenin's government signed a peace treaty with the Central Powers, and Russia withdrew from the war. In 1918 Lenin's followers established a communist party. Some Russians wanted the czar to return, and Civil War broke out. The Communists won. In 1922 they renamed their country the Union of Soviet Socialist Republics, or the Soviet Union.

With Russia out of the war, the tide began to turn in favor of Germany. The German army advanced on Paris. However, when the United States entered the war, the German army was pushed back to its own border. Germany's allies began to surrender. At last, Germany itself surrendered. An **armistice** was signed. An armistice is an agreement to stop fighting.

The fighting stopped on November 11, 1918. More than 8.5 million soldiers had been killed, and 21 million more wounded. Millions who did not fight died from starvation, disease, and bombs.

**Making Peace** In January 1919 the Allied nations met near Paris to decide what would happen now that the war was over. This meeting came to be known as the Paris Peace Conference.

President Wilson wanted fair peace terms to end the war. He felt that harsh terms might lead to future wars. His ideas were called the Fourteen Points. These ideas called for no secret treaties, freedom of the seas for everyone, and the establishment of an association of nations to promote peace and international cooperation. That association, the League of Nations, was formed later but the United States never joined.

Other Allied leaders wanted to punish Germany. They felt that Germany had started the war and should pay for it. They believed that the way to prevent future wars was to make sure that Germany could never become powerful again.

The agreement these leaders finally reached became known as the Treaty of Versailles. Germany was forced to admit it had started the war and to pay money to the Allies. Germany also lost territory. The treaty stated that Germany could not make tanks, military planes, large weapons, or submarines. The United States never agreed to the Treaty of Versailles. It eventually signed a separate peace treaty with Germany.

▲
Allied Leaders at the Paris Peace Conference. President Woodrow Wilson is at the far right.

**A New Europe** World War I changed the map of Europe. France and Belgium gained territory that had belonged to Germany. Austria, and Hungary became separate countries. Poland and Czechoslovakia gained their independence. Bosnia and Herzegovina, Croatia, Montenegro, Serbia, and Slovenia were united as Yugoslavia. Finland, Estonia, Latvia, and Lithuania, all of which had been part of Russia, also became independent nations. Bulgaria and the Ottoman Empire likewise lost territory.

✔ **READING CHECK:** ( *Comparing and Contrasting* ) How did the peace terms Woodrow Wilson wanted compare to those in the Treaty of Versailles?

# A New World

After World War I, the world was very different. New ideas, new art, new music, and new kinds of books reflected the feeling that the world no longer made sense. Some writers called the people who had been through the war "the lost generation." Composers wrote music that sounded different from the music people were used to hearing. Many people thought it didn't sound pretty. Artists like Pablo Picasso and Salvador Dali created paintings that looked more like scenes from dreams than from the real world. People were tired of war. They wanted to have fun, and not worry so much about what might happen tomorrow. Jazz music, which gave musicians more freedom, became popular. Women wanted more freedom. They began to wear their hair and their skirts short. In the United States, women demanded and won the right to vote.

✔ **READING CHECK:** ( *Drawing Inferences* ) Why were there so many new ideas and new kinds of art after World War I?

▲ Women vote in the United States, c. 1920.

---

go. hrw .com **Homework Practice Online**
Keyword: SK3 HP9

## Section Review 1

**Define and explain:** militarism, U-boats, armistice

### Reading for the Main Idea

1. ( *Human Systems* ) What was Europe like just before World War I?

2. ( *Human Systems* ) What role did science and technology play in the war?

3. ( *Human Systems* ) How did World War I change the world?

### Critical Thinking

4. **Drawing Inferences and Conclusions** How might World War I have been different if there had not been alliances in Europe?

### Organizing What You Know

5. **Categorizing** Copy the following chart. Use it to list the members of each alliance.

| Allied Powers | Central Powers |
| --- | --- |
|  |  |
|  |  |
|  |  |

# Section 2 The Great Depression and the Rise of Dictators

## Read to Discover

1. What led to the Great Depression?
2. What is a dictatorship?
3. How did the Great Depression help dictators come to power in Europe?

## Define

stock market
bankrupt
Great Depression
New Deal
dictator
fascism
communism
police state
collective farms

Dorothea Lange's photograph Migrant Mother

During the stock market crash, people rushed to get money out of banks.

## The Great Depression

During the 1920s industrialized countries such as the United States and Great Britain experienced great economic growth. However, less than 10 years later, many of these countries struggled with high rates of unemployment and poverty.

**Causes of the Depression** During World War I, much farmland in Europe was destroyed. Farmers all over the world planted more crops to sell food to European countries. Many American farmers borrowed money to buy farm machinery and more land. When the war ended, there was less demand for food in Europe. Prices went down. Farmers could not pay back the money they had borrowed. Many lost their land.

During the 1920s, the **stock market** did very well. The stock market is an organization through which shares of stock in companies are bought and sold. People who buy stock are buying shares in a company. If people sell their stock when the price per share has risen above the original price, they make a profit.

In the 1920s, stock prices rose very high and many people invested their money in the stock market. People thought stock prices would stay high, so they borrowed money to buy more stocks. Unfortunately, stock prices fell. Low stock prices made people rush to sell their shares before they lost any more money. So many people all selling stock at once drove prices down even more quickly. Finally the stock market crashed, or hit bottom, on October 29, 1929.

People who had borrowed to buy stocks suddenly had to pay back the money. They rushed to the banks to take money out. But the banks did not have enough money to give everyone their savings all at once. In a very short time, banks, factories, farms, and people went **bankrupt**. This meant they had no more money.

This is a breadline in New York City, during the Great Depression. People who could not find jobs stood in these lines to receive free food from the government.

This was the beginning of the **Great Depression**. All over the world, prices and wages fell, banks closed, business slowed or stopped, and people could not find jobs. Many people were poor. Many did not even have enough money to buy food. Some people sold apples on street corners to make a little money.

Governments around the world tried to lessen the effects of the Great Depression. Some limited the number of imports they allowed into their countries. They thought this would encourage citizens to buy products made by businesses in their own countries. This plan did not work. In fact, the loss of foreign markets for their products drove many countries even further into debt.

**The New Deal** In 1932 Franklin D. Roosevelt became president of the United States. He created a program to help end the Great Depression. This program was called the **New Deal**. The federal government gave money to each state to help people. The government also created jobs. It hired people to construct buildings and roads and work on other projects.

Laws were passed to regulate banks and stock exchanges better. In 1938, Congress passed the Fair Labor Standards Act. It established the lowest amount of money a worker could be paid to keep a healthy standard of living. Many people today refer to it as the minimum wage law. Congress also guaranteed workers the right to form unions so they could demand better pay and better working conditions. The Social Security Act, passed in 1935, created benefits for people who were unemployed or elderly.

Under the New Deal, the United States became deeply involved in the well-being of its citizens. For the first time, the government created large-scale social programs to better the lives of American citizens. The New Deal did not, however, completely end the Great Depression in the United States. Government programs helped the economy grow somewhat, but they were not enough to solve the economic crisis completely. The Great Depression would not end in the United States until World War II.

The Great Depression affected the entire world. By 1932, more than 30 million people throughout the world could not find jobs.

✓ **READING CHECK:** *Identifying Cause and Effect* How did the Great Depression start?

# The Rise of Dictators in Europe

As the Great Depression continued in Europe, life got harder. Many people became unhappy with their governments, which were not able to help them. In some countries, people were willing to give up democracy to have strong leaders who promised them more money and better lives. It was easy for dictators to take control of these governments. A **dictator** is an absolute, or total, ruler. A government ruled by a dictator is called a dictatorship. Powerful dictators seized control of Italy and Germany.

**Italy Becomes a Dictatorship** Benito Mussolini told the Italians that he had the answers to their problems. Mussolini called his ideas **fascism** and started the Fascist Party. Fascism was a political movement that put the needs of the nation above the needs of the individual. The nation's leader was supposed to represent the will of the nation. The leader had total control over the people and the economy.

When he became dictator of Italy, Benito Mussolini took the title *il Duce* (il DOO-chay), Italian for "the leader."

Fascist nations became strong through militarism. Their leaders feared communism for a good reason. **Communism** promised a society in which property would be shared by everyone. Mussolini promised that he would not let communists take over Italy. He also promised he would bring Italy out of the Great Depression and return Italy to the glory of the Roman Empire.

In 1924, the Fascist Party won Italy's national election. Mussolini took control of the government and became a dictator. He turned Italy into a police state. A **police state** is a country in which the government has total control over people and uses secret police to find and punish people who rebel or protest.

**Germany** After World War I many Germans felt that their government had betrayed them by signing the Treaty of Versailles. Many also blamed the German government for the unemployment and inflation brought by the Great Depression. Several groups attempted to overthrow and replace the old government. Eventually a new party called the Nazi Party gained power. It too was a fascist party. Adolf Hitler was its leader.

Hitler promised to break the treaty of Versailles. He said he would restore Germany's economy, rebuild Germany's military power, and take back territory that Germany had lost after the war. Hitler told the Germans that they were superior to other people. Many Germans eagerly listened to Hitler's message. They thought he would restore Germany to its former power.

Hitler was a very powerful speaker. He often twisted the truth in his speeches. He claimed that the bigger a lie was, the more likely people would be to believe it.

The Nazis quickly gained power in Germany. In 1933 Hitler took control of the German government. He made himself dictator and used the title *der Führer* (FYOOR-ur), which is German for "the leader." He turned Germany into a police state. Newspapers and political parties that opposed the Nazis were outlawed. Groups of people that Hitler claimed were inferior, especially Jews, lost their civil liberties.

Hitler began to secretly rebuild Germany's army and navy. He was going to make Germany a mighty nation again. He called his rule the Third Reich. *Reich* is the German word for *empire*. In 1936 Hitler formed a partnership with Mussolini called the Rome-Berlin Axis.

**The Soviet Union** Russia had suffered terribly during World War I. Lenin's Communist government had promised an ideal society in which people would share things and live well. However, most Russians remained poor.

After Lenin died, Joseph Stalin gained control of the Communist Party. Stalin's government took land from farmers and forced farmers to work on large **collective farms** owned and controlled by the central government. Stalin also tried to industrialize the Soviet Union. However, for ordinary Russians food and manufactured goods remained scarce.

Religious worship was forbidden. Artists were even told what kind of pictures to make. Secret police spied on people. If people did not obey Stalin's policies they were arrested and put in jail or killed. Scholars think that by 1939 more than 5 million people had been arrested, deported, sent to forced labor camps, or killed.

For many years, many Soviet people thought Joseph Stalin was a great hero. Later, people became more aware of his responsibility for the deaths of millions of Russians for "crimes against the state."

✓ **READING CHECK:** *Analyzing* How did Hitler use the Treaty of Versailles to help him gain power in Germany?

## Section Review 2

Homework Practice Online
Keyword: SK3 HP9

**Define and explain:** stock market, bankrupt, Great Depression, New Deal, dictator, fascism, communism, police state, collective farms

### Reading for the Main Idea

1. ( *Human Systems* ) What happened during the Great Depression?

2. ( *Human Systems* ) What is life like in a dictatorship?

3. ( *Human Systems* ) How did European dictators take advantage of the Great Depression to gain power?

### Critical Thinking

4. **Making Inferences and Conclusions** How were Woodrow Wilson's concerns about the Treaty of Versailles proven correct by the rise of Adolf Hitler?

### Organizing What You Know

5. **Identifying Cause and Effect** Copy the following graphic organizer. Fill it in to summarize what happened in the Great Depression.

| Cause | Effect |
|---|---|
| Europe needs food during the war. | |
| The war ends and crop prices fall. | |
| Stock prices rise very high. | |
| People rush to sell their stocks. | |
| People rush to take money out of the banks. | |

# Section 3 Nationalist Movements in Africa and Asia

## Read to Discover

1. How did World War I increase feelings of nationalism in Africa and Asia?
2. When and how did African colonies become independent?
3. How did the communists come to power in China?

## Define

boycotted
apartheid

## Locate

Ghana
South Africa
India
Pakistan
Japan
China
Iran
Turkey

### WHY IT MATTERS

Many countries in Africa and Asia are still working to strengthen their economies and governments. Use CNNfyi.com or other current events sources to find out how these countries participate in world affairs today. Record your findings in your journal.

A political campaign button from South Africa

## Beginnings of Nationalism in Africa and Asia

Until the years following World War I, nearly all of Africa and many parts of Asia were controlled by European countries. As European colonies these places gained access to better health care, more effective farming methods, and improved roads and railroads. The people who lived in these colonies, however, had few rights. They played little part in running their countries, and their cultures were usually not nurtured or respected.

Around the end of World War I, the people in these colonies began to express resentment over this European control. They developed more pride in their own cultures and national identities. These feelings of nationalism led to a demand for self-rule. By the 1930s many colonies in Africa and Asia were calling for independence.

Indian citizens protest against British rule in India.

**Interpreting the Visual Record Why do you think they are protesting?**

✓ **READING CHECK:** *Summarizing* Why did many colonies in Africa and Asia want to become independent?

# African Nationalism

The growth of nationalism in Africa was in part caused by World War I. However, most countries did not actually become independent until after World War II. African soldiers who had fought in British and French armies during the war had been exposed to new ideas. They probably learned about European political systems from their fellow soldiers. When they returned home, they brought some new ideas with them. Some began to protest against racism and political oppression.

These protests were linked to a worldwide movement called Pan-Africanism. It was begun in England, the United States, and the West Indies by people who wanted cultural unity and equality for everyone of African heritage. Members of the Pan-African movement wanted two things. First, they wanted to end European control of Africa. They also wanted Africa to become a unified homeland for all people of African descent. Despite these efforts, however, it took many years for most African colonies to gain independence. In some countries the people were able to achieve their goals peacefully. In others, however, the fight for independence became violent.

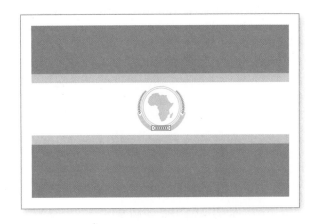

The Organization of African Unity (OAU), whose flag is seen here, grew out of the Pan-African movement. It was formed in 1963. More than 50 countries belong to this organization today.

**British Colonies** The first British African colony to gain independence was the Gold Coast. Protestors staged demonstrations and **boycotted**, or refused to buy, British goods. Finally in 1957 the British agreed to let the people of the Gold Coast choose their own government. The people voted for independence. The Gold Coast became the independent nation of Ghana. Other British colonies followed this example. The colonies that became Kenya, Malawi, Nigeria, and Zambia all won their independence by 1970. Zimbabwe became independent in 1980.

**Other Colonies** By 1962 France had granted independence to nearly all of its African colonies. Other European countries were not as quick to give up their colonies. Belgium gave up any claim to its Congo colony—which later became the Democratic Republic of the Congo—after violence broke out in 1959. Portugal also refused to free its colonies until after bloody civil wars. Angola, the last Portuguese colony in Africa, won its independence in 1975.

Kwame Nkrumah (at left) led the struggle to win independence for Ghana. He became the country's first leader.

In 1986 Nigerian Wole Soyinka became the first African writer to win the Nobel Prize in literature.

▼

**South Africa** The Independent Union of South Africa was created in 1910. However, from the beginning, its government had been controlled by the descendents of British and Dutch settlers. White South Africans enforced a policy of **apartheid**. This was a system of laws that denied black South Africans any political rights. Many South Africans—both black and white—protested apartheid laws. Some protests turned violent, and others were violently put down. Many people were killed. Black leaders like Nelson Mandela were thrown into prison. Other countries around the world also disapproved of apartheid policies. Some of these countries refused to trade or have any dealings with South Africa.

Things changed in the 1990s. South Africa banned apartheid. Nelson Mandela was freed from prison and was elected president in 1994. Mandela and his government worked to establish a new government based on equality for everyone.

✔ **READING CHECK:** *Contrasting* How was South Africa different from other African countries?

# Life in Independent Africa

Independence did not solve all of the problems of the former African colonies. In addition, new challenges faced the newly independent countries. At the same time, however, people around the world developed a new interest in Africa and its cultures.

**Challenges** Many political leaders of the new African countries were inexperienced. If they were unable to improve conditions in their countries, military leaders sometimes took control. Many African countries were run by military dictatorships through the late 1900s. Civil wars broke out between ethnic groups in some countries. Thousands of people died. Many countries also fell into debt. Crops failed due to droughts and the overuse of land, and millions more people died. Outbreaks of diseases like malaria and AIDS have also killed many Africans.

**Cultural Revival** As the demand for independence in Africa grew, people around the world developed an interest in African culture. Authors like Nigeria's Wole Soyinka and Chinua Achebe won awards for their stories about African life. African music and art became more popular around the world. Also, African directors made movies that were appreciated in many countries.

✔ **READING CHECK:** *Summarizing* How did life in Africa change after independence?

Nelson Mandela called on the people of South Africa to "heal the wounds of the past."

**Interpreting the Visual Record What do you think the phrase "heal the wounds of the past" means?**

▼

# Nationalism in Asia

Africa was not the only region in which people wanted to break free of European control. A spirit of nationalism similar to the one that affected Africa swept through Asia in the mid-1900s.

**India** Great Britain had promised India more self-government in return for troops and money during World War I. People in both countries, however, were divided on the question of Indian independence. Some wanted India to remain part of the British Empire. Others wanted the country to be completely free from European influence. An Indian lawyer named Mohandas Gandhi led nonviolent protests against British control. Largely due to Gandhi's courageous and inspiring leadership, India won its independence in 1947.

Within India, however, Muslims and Hindus did not get along. When the British withdrew in 1947, they created two new countries. India was mainly Hindu. Pakistan was mostly Muslim. In 1948 Gandhi was assassinated by a Hindu who thought the leader was too kind to Muslims. Jawaharlal Nehru became the first prime minister of independent India. His daughter, Indira Gandhi, became prime minister in 1966.

**Japan** By the early 1900s Japan had emerged as a world power. It was quickly becoming a major industrial power as well. When the Great Depression began in 1929, however, many Japanese felt that the country should turn away from Western ideas. They wanted the country to return to its own traditions. The country became less democratic and more militaristic. After it was defeated in World War II, Japan went through difficult times politically and economically. In time the Japanese rebuilt their economy. Since the 1950s, Japan has become a modern, technologically advanced, and democratic nation. It has strong ties to other countries in Asia and the West.

**China** A new dynasty, the Qing, rose to power in China in the 1600s. Under the Qing, trade between China and the West increased. Over time, other countries came to dominate the Chinese economy and government. By 1900 China was completely under foreign control. That year a group of Chinese tried to force all foreigners out of China but were defeated in the Boxer Rebellion.

By 1912 nationalist feelings had begun to grow among Chinese who resented foreign control. The Nationalist Party, led by Sun Yat-sen, wanted China to become more industrial and democratic. The Nationalists overthrew the last Qing emperor and took control of China in 1912. When Sun died, the military leader Chiang Kai-shek took over the Nationalist Party. He set up a one-party government in China and became a military dictator.

Mohandas Gandhi led India's independence movement.

When Chiang Kai-shek took over the Nationalist Party, powerful warlords still ruled most of the country through their personal armies. Under Chiang, the Nationalist army broke the power of the warlords and unified China.

**Interpreting the Visual Record** What does this photograph suggest about Chiang Kai-shek?

Mao Zedong wanted to modernize China. He and his followers destroyed thousands of books and works of art that reflected China's history.

In 1921 a group broke away from the Nationalist Party to form the Chinese Communist Party. They demanded fair treatment for peasants and workers. In the early 1930s Chiang's forces drove the communists into northwestern China. Chased by Nationalist troops, many died on the 6,000-mile trip, known as the Long March.

On this trip, a man named Mao Zedong established himself as the leader of the communists. Mao and his followers encouraged the peasants and workers to support a revolution. In 1949, Communists led by Mao took over China and established the People's Republic of China. Mao soon became a dictator and instituted sweeping changes in China. The Nationalists, opposed to communism, fled to the island of Taiwan.

**Other Asian Countries** Other countries in Asia also sought independence after World War I. In 1921 Reza Khan, a Persian army officer, seized control of the Persian government. He took the title *shah*, the ancient Persian word for king, and changed his country's name to Iran. Reza Shah Pahlavi did much to modernize Iran, but he ruled the country as a dictator.

Turkey was occupied by Greek troops after World War I. In 1922, Turkish nationalists led by Mustafa Kemal drove the Greeks out of their country. Kemal changed his name to Kemal Atatürk and established the Republic of Turkey. Atatürk modernized Turkey, improving education and giving women the right to vote.

✓ **READING CHECK:** ( *Summarizing* ) What was the Long March?

# Section Review 3

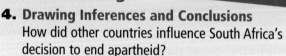 Homework Practice Online
Keyword: SK3 HP9

**Define and explain:** boycotted, apartheid

## Reading for the Main Idea

1. ( *Human Systems* ) How did World War I lead to the growth of nationalism in Africa?

2. ( *Human Systems* ) What led to the creation of Pakistan as an independent country?

3. ( *Human Systems* ) What were the goals of the Chinese Communist Party?

## Critical Thinking

4. **Drawing Inferences and Conclusions** How did other countries influence South Africa's decision to end apartheid?

## Organizing What You Know

5. **Identifying Cause and Effect** Copy the following graphic organizer. Use it describe the process that led to the growth of nationalism and independence for African colonies.

□ ⇨ □ ⇨ □

# Section 4 — World War II

## Read to Discover

1. What were the causes of World War II?
2. What was the Holocaust?
3. How did World War II end?

## Define

aggression
anti-Semitism
genocide
Holocaust

## Locate

Japan
Italy
Germany
Hawaii
Ethiopia

Poland
Sicily
Pearl Harbor
Normandy

## WHY IT MATTERS

Acts of aggression still happen. Use CNN**fyi**.com or other **current events** sources to find examples of aggression in today's world. Record your findings in your journal.

*National Iwo Jima Memorial Monument*

## Threats to World Peace

During the 1930s, Japan, Italy, and Germany committed acts of aggression against other countries. **Aggression** is warlike action, such as an invasion or an attack. At first, little was done to stop them. Eventually, their actions led to a full-scale war that involved much of the world.

In 1931, Japanese forces took control of Manchuria, a part of China. The League of Nations protested, but took no military action to stop Japan. Continuing its aggressive actions, Japan succeeded in controlling about one fourth of China by 1939. At about the same time, Italy invaded Ethiopia, a country in East Africa. Many countries protested, but they did not want to go to war again. Like Japan, Italy saw that the rest of the world would not try hard to stop its aggression.

Pablo Picasso painted *Guernica* after the Spanish town of the same name was bombed.

**Interpreting the Visual Record** What human feelings about war does Picasso express?

▼

Women cry as they give the Nazi salute to German troops in Sudentenland.

**Interpreting the Visual Record** Why do you think these women are showing strong feelings?

▼

**Spanish Civil War** In 1936, civil war broke out in Spain. On one side were fascists led by General Francisco Franco. Both Italy and Germany sent troops and supplies to help Franco's forces. On the other side were Loyalists, people loyal to the elected Spanish government. The Soviet Union sent aid to the Loyalists. Volunteers from France, Great Britain, and the United States also fought on their side, but their help was not enough. In 1939, the fascists defeated the Loyalists.

Franco set up a dictatorship. He ended free elections and most civil rights. By the end of the 1930s, it was clear that fascism was growing in Europe.

**Hitler's Aggressions** In the late 1930s many Germans lived in Austria, Czechoslovakia, and Poland. Hitler wanted to unite these countries to bring all Germans together. In 1938 German soldiers marched into Austria, and Hitler declared Austria to be part of the Third Reich. Great Britain and France protested but did not attack Germany. Later that year Hitler took over the Sudentenland, a region of western Czechoslovakia. Other European countries were worried, but they still did not want a war. Hitler soon conquered the rest of Czechoslovakia.

Eventually Britain and France realized they could not ignore Hitler. They asked the Soviet Union to be their ally in a war against Germany. However, Soviet leader Joseph Stalin had made a secret plan with Hitler. They decided that their countries would never attack each other. This deal was called the German-Soviet nonaggression pact.

In September 1939 Hitler invaded Poland. Two days later, Great Britain and France declared war on Germany. World War II had begun. On one side were Germany, Italy, and Japan. They called themselves the Axis Powers, or the Axis. Great Britain, France, and other countries that fought against the Axis called themselves the Allies.

✓ **READING CHECK:** ( *Drawing Inferences* ) How might British and French leaders have prevented World War II?

Joseph Stalin (second from right) made an agreement that the Soviet Union and Germany would not attack each other.

▶

Carrying whatever belongings they can, people in northern France try to escape from attacks.

# War

At the beginning of the war, the Germans won many victories. Poland fell in one month. In 1940 Germany conquered Denmark, Norway, the Netherlands, Belgium, and Luxembourg. In June 1940 Germany invaded and quickly defeated France. In less than one year, Hitler had gained control of almost all of western Europe. Next he sent German planes to bomb Great Britain. The British fought back with their own air force. This struggle became known as the Battle of Britain.

In June 1941, Hitler turned on his ally and invaded the Soviet Union. As winter set in, however, the Germans found themselves vulnerable to Soviet attacks. Without enough supplies, Hitler's troops were defeated by a combination of the freezing Russian winter and the Soviet Red Army. For the first time in the war, German soldiers were forced to retreat.

**The United States** Many people in the United States did not want their country to go to war. The United States sent supplies, food, and weapons to the British but did not actually enter the war until 1941. In that year Japan was taking control of Southeast Asia and the Pacific. Seeing the United States as a possible enemy, Japanese military leaders attempted to destroy the U.S. naval fleet in the Pacific. On December 7, 1941, Japan launched a surprise air attack on the naval base at Pearl Harbor, Hawaii. The attack sank or damaged U.S. battleships and killed more than 2,300 American soldiers. The next day President Franklin D. Roosevelt announced that the United States was at war with Japan. Great Britain also declared war on Japan. Three days later, Germany and Italy—both allies of Japan—declared war on the United States. In response, Congress declared war on both countries.

Newspapers around the country ran headlines similar to this one after the Japanese attack on Pearl Harbor.
**Interpreting the Visual Record How do you think Americans felt when they saw headlines like this one?**

✓ READING CHECK:    *Evaluating*    How were Hitler's invasion of the Soviet Union and Japan's attack on Pearl Harbor turning points in the war?

## The Holocaust

Hitler believed that Germans were a superior people, and planned to destroy or enslave people whom he believed were inferior. Hitler hated many peoples, but he particularly hated the Jews. Hatred of Jews is called **anti-Semitism**. The Nazis rounded up Europe's Jews and imprisoned them in concentration camps.

**Death Camps** In 1941, Hitler ordered the destruction of Europe's entire Jewish population. The Nazis built death camps in Poland to carry out this plan. People who could work were forced into slave labor. Those who could not work were sent to gas chambers where they were killed. Some Jews were shot in large groups. Thousands of other people died from conditions in the camps. The dead were buried in mass graves or burned in large ovens.

By the time the Nazi government fell, its leaders and followers had murdered an estimated 6 million European Jews. The Nazi **genocide**, the planned killing of a race of people, is called the **Holocaust**. Millions of non-Jews were also killed.

**Resisting the Nazis** Some Jews tried to fight back. Others hid. Most, however, were unable to escape. Many Europeans ignored what was happening to the Jews, but some tried to save people from the Holocaust. The Danes helped about 7,000 Jews escape to Sweden. In Poland and Czechoslovakia, the German businessman Oskar Schindler saved many Jews by employing them in his factories.

✓ **READING CHECK:**  *Summarizing*  What were Nazi concentration camps like?

## The End of the War

In 1942 the Germans tried to capture the Soviet city of Stalingrad. The battle lasted six months, but the Soviet defenders held out. The Germans were never able to take the city. This was a major blow to the Germans, who never fully recovered from this defeat. At the same time, American and British forces defeated the Germans in Africa. The war began to turn in favor of the Allies. That same year in the Pacific Japan lost several important battles. Led by the United States, Allied forces—including troops from Australia and New Zealand—began a campaign to regain some of the Pacific islands Japan had taken. Slowly, the Allies pushed the Japanese forces back across the Pacific Ocean.

In the summer of 1943 the Allies captured the island of Sicily in Italy. Italians forced Mussolini to resign, and Italy's new leader dissolved the Fascist Party. In September, Italy agreed to stop fighting the Allies.

**Victory in Europe** On June 6, 1944, Allied forces landed on the beaches of Normandy in northern France. This was the D-Day invasion. The invasion was a success. In August, Allied troops entered Paris. By September they were at Germany's western border. With the

Anne Frank (1930-1945) was a Jewish teenager. During the Holocaust her family hid in an attic for two years to escape the Nazis. Anne kept a diary in which she wrote her thoughts and feelings.

Peace Memorial Park marks the spot where the first atomic bomb was dropped August 6, 1945, in Hiroshima, Japan.

Soviets attacking Germany from the east, the Nazis' defenses fell apart. On April 30 Hitler killed himself, and within a week, Germany surrendered.

**Victory over Japan** Fighting continued in the Pacific. The Allies bombed Japan, but the Japanese would not surrender. Finally President Harry Truman decided to use the atomic bomb against Japan. On August 6, 1945, the most powerful weapon the world had ever seen was dropped on the city of Hiroshima. The bomb reduced the city to ashes and destroyed the surrounding area. About 130,000 people were killed and many more were injured. Countless more people died later. On August 9 another atomic bomb was dropped on the Japanese city of Nagasaki. Five days later Japan surrendered.

**A New Age** World War II resulted in more destruction than any other war in history. More than 50 million people were killed, and millions more were wounded. Unlike in most earlier wars, many of the people killed were civilians. Civilians are people who are not in the military. Millions were killed in the Holocaust. Thousands were killed by bombs dropped on cities in Europe and Japan. Thousands more died in prison camps in Japan and the Soviet Union. In time, people began to question how such cruel acts against human life and human rights were allowed to happen and how they could be prevented in the future.

The American use of the atomic bomb began the atomic age. With it came many questions and fears. How would this new weapon be used? What effect would it have on future wars? After World War II, world leaders would struggle with these questions.

**READING CHECK:** *Analyzing* How was World War II unlike any war that came before it?

## Losses of the Major Wartime Powers in World War II, 1939 - 1945

| Country | Military losses | Civilian losses |
| --- | --- | --- |
| Soviet Union | 10,000,000 | 10,000,000 |
| China | 2,500,000 | 7,400,000 |
| Great Britain | 300,000 | 50,000 |
| United States | 274,000 | 0 |
| France | 250,000 | 350,000 |
| Germany | 4,500,000 | 2,000,000 |
| Japan | 2,000,000 | 350,000 |
| Italy | 400,000 | 100,000 |

Oxford Companion to World War II, 1995

**Interpreting the Graph** What three countries had the highest civilian losses? What do you think caused these losses?

Homework Practice Online

Keyword: SK3 HP9

# Section Review 4

**Define and explain:** aggression, anti-Semitism, genocide, Holocaust

## Reading for the Main Idea

1. ( *Human Systems* ) What events led to World War II?
2. ( *Human Systems* ) What happened during the Holocaust?
3. ( *Human Systems* ) What were the results of World War II?

## Critical Thinking

4. **Cause and Effect** How did the rise of fascism in Europe lead to World War II?

## Organizing What You Know

5. **Drawing Inferences and Conclusions** Copy the following graphic organizer. Fill it in, telling why each event was important in the war.

| Event | Why Important? |
| --- | --- |
| Hitler invades Poland. | |
| Hitler gains control of western Europe. | |
| Germany invades the Soviet Union. | |
| Japan attacks Pearl Harbor. | |
| The Allies invade Europe on D-Day. | |
| The United States drops the atomic bomb on Japan. | |

**Read to Discover**

1. What was the Cold War?
2. Where in the world has conflict arisen since World War II?
3. What are some important events that happened at the end of the 1900s?

**Define**

bloc
arms race
partition
globalization

**Locate**

Israel       Vietnam
China        Cuba
Korea

**WHY IT MATTERS**

Created in 1945, the United Nations continues to promote international cooperation and peace. Use CNN fyi.com or other current events sources to find examples of UN action to stop violence. Record your findings in your journal.

*compact discs*

## The Cold War

Although the Soviet Union and the United States were allies in World War II, the alliance fell apart after the war. The former allies clashed over ideas about freedom, government, and economics. Because this struggle did not turn into a shooting or "hot" war, it is known as the Cold War.

**A Struggle of Ideas** The struggle that started the Cold War was between two ideas—communism and capitalism. Communism is an economic system in which a central authority controls the government and the economy. Capitalism is a system in which businesses are privately owned. During the Cold War, the Soviet government functioned as a dictatorship which controlled the economy. However, the United States and other democratic nations practiced some form of capitalism.

In June 1948 the Soviets set up a blockade along the East German border to prevent supplies from getting into West Berlin. The people of West Berlin faced starvation. The United States and Great Britain organized an airlift to supply West Berlin. Food and supplies were flown in daily to the people.

**Europe Divided** After World War II Joseph Stalin, leader of the Soviet Union, brought most countries in Eastern Europe under communist control. The Soviet Union and those communist-controlled countries were known as the Eastern bloc. A **bloc** is a group of nations united under a common idea or for a common purpose. The United States and the democracies in Western Europe were known as the Western bloc. While Western countries experienced periods of great economic growth, industries in most communist countries did not develop. People in these countries suffered from shortages of goods, food, and money.

**Two Germanies** After World War II the Allies divided Germany into four zones to keep it from becoming powerful again. Britain, France, the United States, and the Soviet Union each controlled a zone. Germany could no longer have an army, and the Nazi Party was outlawed. By 1948, the Western Allies were ready to unite their zones, but the Soviets did not want Germany united as a democratic nation. The next year the American, British, and French zones became the Federal Republic of Germany, or West Germany. The Soviets established the German Democratic Republic, or East Germany. The city of Berlin, although part of East Germany, was divided into East and West Berlin, with West Berlin under Allied control. The Berlin Wall, which became a famous symbol of the Cold War, separated the two parts of the city.

**The Soviet Union After Stalin** Joseph Stalin, who had led the Soviet Union through World War II, died in 1953. The next Soviet leader was Nikita Khrushchev. He criticized Stalin's policies and reduced the government's control over the economy.

During the 1950s and 1960s some Eastern bloc nations tried to break free of communism. In East Germany, Czechoslovakia, and Hungary, for example, people rebelled against Soviet control, but the Soviets crushed these revolts.

▲

The Berlin Wall did not stop people from trying to reach West Berlin. More than 130 people died trying to escape over the heavily guarded wall.

**Interpreting the Visual Record** Why do you think people risked death to escape communism?

In this picture U.S. President Harry Truman signs the North Atlantic Pact, which created NATO. Shown above is the NATO emblem.

**Interpreting the Visual Record** How would you explain the NATO emblem?

**The United Nations** World leaders did not want the Cold War to turn "hot." Although the League of Nations had failed to prevent World War II, people still wanted an international organization that could settle problems peacefully. In April, 1945, the United Nations (UN) was created. Its purpose was to solve economic and social problems as well as to promote international cooperation and maintain peace. Representatives of 50 countries formed the original United Nations. Today there are nearly 200 member nations. The six official languages of the United Nations are Arabic, Chinese, English, French, Russian, and Spanish. The headquarters of the United Nations are in New York City. It also has offices in Geneva, Switzerland, and Vienna, Austria.

**New Alliances** Fearing war but hoping to preserve peace, nations around the world formed new alliances. In 1949, 12 Western nations, including the United States, created the North Atlantic Treaty Organization (NATO). In 1954 the Southeast Asia Treaty Organization (SEATO) was created in an attempt to halt the spread of communism in Southeast Asia. Many Eastern bloc countries, including the Soviet Union, signed the Warsaw Pact in 1955. The Warsaw Pact countries had more total troops than the NATO members. This difference in the number of troops encouraged the Western powers to rely on nuclear weapons to establish a balance of power.

**The End of the Cold War** Throughout the Cold War, the Soviet Union and the United States had been a waging an **arms race**. The countries competed to create more advanced weapons and to have more nuclear missiles than each other. The arms race was expensive and took its toll on the already shaky Soviet economy.

In 1985, Mikhail Gorbachev became head of the Soviet Union. He reduced government control of the economy and increased individual liberties, such as freedom of speech and the press. He also improved relations with the United States.

These reforms in the Soviet Union encouraged democratic movements in Eastern bloc countries. In 1989, Poland and Czechoslovakia threw off communist rule. In November, the Berlin Wall came down. In October 1990, East and West Germany became one democratic nation. Soviet republics also began to seek freedom and independence. By the end of 1991, the Soviet Union no longer existed. The Cold War was over. The arms race could stop.

Mikhail Gorbachev, with his wife, Raisa. In 1990, Gorbachev won the Nobel Peace Prize for his reform work in the Soviet Union.

In October 1990 young people in Berlin wave German flags to celebrate the reunification of Germany.

The breakup of the Soviet Union created several independent countries. Russia was the largest of these new nations. Its new leader was Boris Yeltsin. Under Yeltsin, Russia moved toward democracy. Yeltsin also improved Russia's relations with the West. In 2000, Vladimir Putin became leader of Russia. Under Putin, relations with the United States improved further.

Some tension arose, however, between Russia and the former Soviet republics. For example, Russia and the Ukraine clashed over military issues in the 1990s.

✓ **READING CHECK:** ( *Evaluating* ) How did the end of the Soviet Union affect the world?

Israel's Knesset, or parliament, meets here. The Knesset is the supreme power in Israel.

## Other World Conflicts

Since the end of World War II, many conflicts have shaken the world. Some have been resolved, while others continue to threaten world peace. The lessons of two world wars and the threat of mass destruction that would result from a nuclear war has kept these conflicts contained. World War III has not occurred, and the hope of people everywhere is that it never will.

**Southwest Asia** After World War I Britain said it would help create a Jewish homeland in Palestine, a region of Southwest Asia. Many Arab nations, however, wanted an Arab state in Palestine. In 1947 the UN voted to **partition**, or divide, Palestine, creating both a Jewish state and an Arab state. While the Arabs rejected this plan, Jewish leaders in Palestine accepted it. In May 1948, Israel was established as a Jewish state.

The establishment of Israel enraged many Palestinian Arabs and Arab nations. Attacked by neighboring Arab countries, Israel fought back. By early 1949 a cease-fire was reached. Israel survived, but Palestinian Arabs had no homeland. In 1967, tensions between Israel and its Arab neighbors exploded into war again. In what became known as the Six-Day War, Israel captured territory from Egypt, Syria, and Jordan. After the Six-Day War, the Palestine Liberation Organization (PLO), led by Yasir Arafat, launched many attacks on Israel.

The many attempts to bring peace to the Middle East have failed. The Israelis and the Arabs do not trust each other. Both sides make demands that the other side will not meet. When one side commits acts of violence, the other side strikes back. The failure to achieve peace in the Middle East continues to be one of the most disturbing issues facing the world.

At the end of the Korean War, the two sides set up a neutral area, called the demilitarized zone, or DMZ. It is a buffer zone, and no military forces from either side may enter the area.

**Korea** At the end of World War II the Soviet Union controlled northern Korea. U.S. troops controlled southern Korea. A Communist government took power, and in 1950, North Korea invaded South Korea. The United Nations sent troops to stop the invasion. The Korean War lasted until 1953, when a cease-fire was signed. Korea remains divided.

**Cuba** In 1959 Fidel Castro established a Communist government in Cuba. In 1961 President John F. Kennedy approved an invasion of Cuba by anti-Castro forces. The invasion failed, and Castro turned to the Soviet Union for support. The Soviet Union, which by this time possessed nuclear weapons, sent nuclear missiles to Cuba. Kennedy demanded that the missiles be withdrawn, but Khruschev refused. NATO and Warsaw Pact military forces prepared for combat. For several days the Cuban missile crisis held the world on the brink of nuclear war. Finally, the Soviet Union agreed to remove its missiles, and the United States promised it would not invade Cuba.

**Vietnam** Vietnam had been a colony of France for more than 60 years. In 1945 Ho Chi Minh, a Communist leader, declared Vietnam independent. In 1954 Vietnam became divided. North Vietnam was communist. South Vietnam was not. In the late 1950s, when North Vietnam invaded South Vietnam, the United States sent troops to South Vietnam to fight the communists. Many Americans were unhappy that the country had become involved in this war, and American troops pulled out of Vietnam in 1973. South Vietnam surrendered in 1975. Nearly 1.7 million Vietnamese and about 58,000 Americans lost their lives in the Vietnam War. In 1976 Vietnam was united under a Communist government.

**Northern Ireland** When the Republic of Ireland gained independence from Great Britain in 1922, the territory of Northern Ireland remained part of Britain. The Protestant majority in Northern Ireland controlled both the government and the economy. This caused resentment among Northern Irish Catholics. During the late 1960s Catholic protests began to turn violent. The British have tried to resolve the conflict both through political means and military force. While the situation has improved, a permanent peaceful solution has not yet been found.

**The Breakup of Yugoslavia** Yugoslavia was created after World War I by uniting several formerly independent countries. These included Bosnia, Croatia, Slovenia, and Serbia. After the fall of communism in Eastern Europe, Eastern Orthodox Serbs tried to dominate parts of Yugoslavia where people were mainly Roman Catholic or Muslim. Fighting broke out between Serbia and Croatia, which was mainly Roman Catholic. Yugoslavia was once again divided into several countries in the early 1990s, but this did not end the violence. In 1992 Bosnian Serbs began a campaign of terror and murder intended to drive the Muslims out of Bosnia. Finally, NATO bombed Serbian targets in 1995, and the fighting stopped. Several Serb leaders were tried as war criminals.

**The War on Terrorism** On September 11, 2001, terrorists attacked the World Trade Center in New York City and the Pentagon in Washington, D.C. Following these attacks, the United States asked for support of nations around the world. Many nations, including Russia, China, Cuba, Pakistan, and Saudi Arabia, supported the United States in what President George W. Bush called a "war on terrorism." That show of support indicated that nations of the world might be beginning to leave behind some of the struggles of the last century.

✔ **READING CHECK:** ( *Evaluating* ) What has prevented conflicts in different parts of the world from becoming world wars?

▲

After the Vietnam War more than a million people fled Vietnam by boat.

**Interpreting the Visual Record** **What kinds of conditions might make people willing to leave their homes?**

◄

Mostar, the unofficial capital of Bosnia and Herzegovina, was bombed heavily in the 1990s.

After the terrorist attacks, members of New York City's fire and police departments risked their lives to help people.

**Interpreting the Visual Record** What qualities can a terrible disaster bring out in people?

▲

The launch of the *Sputnik* satellite, shown above, began a space race between the U.S. and the Soviet Union to see who would reach the moon first.

# Progress and Problems

During the late 1900s enormous advances of all kinds occurred in science, medicine, space travel, communication, and technologies. Also during this period, however, problems developed that must be addressed in the new century.

**Space** On October 4, 1957, the Soviet Union launched *Sputnik*, the world's first space satellite. The space age had begun. In 1961 Soviet Yury Gagarin became the first person to travel into space. In 1969 Neil Armstrong, an American, became the first person to walk on the moon. Beginning in the late 1990s, the United States, Russia, and 14 other nations worked together to build an International Space Station (ISS) The first crew members reached the ISS late in 2000. Researchers in space have conducted many useful experiments in geography, engineering, medicine, and other fields of study.

**Genetics** Genes are small units in the body that determine all our physical characteristics. Knowledge of genetics is leading to new cures for diseases. It has also given scientists the ability to clone, or make an identical copy, of an animal. In 1997, for example, scientists cloned a sheep. Although cloning has raised some ethical debates that have not been resolved, it is still a remarkable scientific advance.

**The Computer Age** The first modern computer, called ENIAC, was built in 1946. It was so large that it filled an entire room. By the end of the 1950s, however, the manufacturing of computers was a growing industry. Over time, computers became smaller and faster. Now many people around the world use computers every day at home, at work, and at school. They are important parts of many products, from cars to medical equipment to rockets. New technologies like the Internet and the World Wide Web have made computers even more useful. Today computers can send messages around the world in just a few seconds.

# Europe:
## Climate

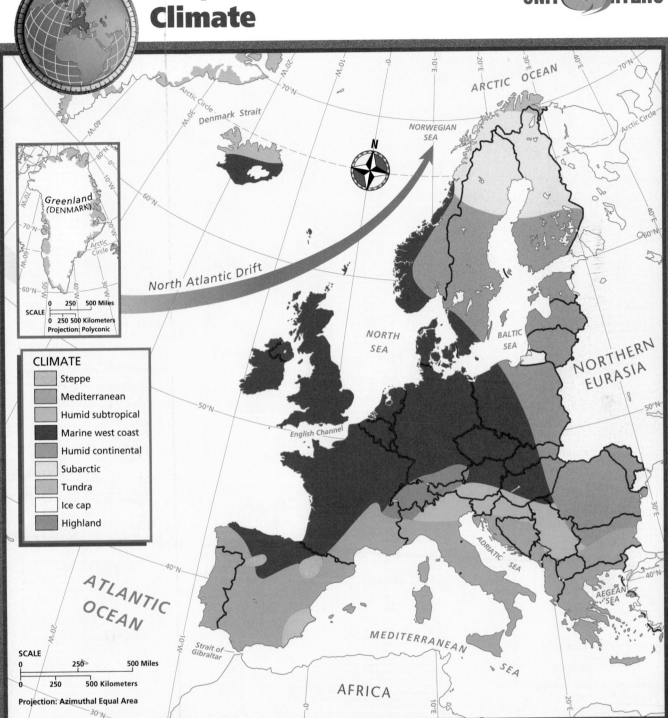

**CLIMATE**

- Steppe
- Mediterranean
- Humid subtropical
- Marine west coast
- Humid continental
- Subarctic
- Tundra
- Ice cap
- Highland

Greenland
(DENMARK)

SCALE
0    250    500 Miles
0  250 500 Kilometers
Projection: Polyconic

Arctic Circle

Denmark Strait

North Atlantic Drift

ARCTIC OCEAN

NORWEGIAN SEA

N

NORTH SEA

BALTIC SEA

NORTHERN EURASIA

ATLANTIC OCEAN

English Channel

ADRIATIC SEA

AEGEAN SEA

Strait of Gibraltar

MEDITERRANEAN SEA

AFRICA

SCALE
0         250         500 Miles
0         250         500 Kilometers
Projection: Azimuthal Equal Area

**1.** (Physical Systems) Which climate type takes its name from a sea in the region?

**2.** (Places and Regions) Which two independent countries have climate types that are not found in any other European country? Which climate types do these two countries have?

## Critical Thinking

**3. Comparing** Compare this map to the **physical** and **population maps**. Which physical feature in central Europe has a highland climate and relatively few people? This physical feature is in which countries?

**Europe • 223**

POPULATION DENSITY

| Persons per sq. mile | Persons per sq km |
|---|---|
| 520 | 200 |
| 260 | 100 |
| 130 | 50 |
| 25 | 10 |
| 3 | 1 |
| 0 | 0 |

● Metropolitan areas with more than 2 million inhabitants

○ Metropolitan areas with 1 million to 2 million inhabitants

Projection: Azimuthal Equal Area

SCALE
0   250   500 Miles
0   250 500 Kilometers
Projection: Polyconic

**1.** *Places and Regions* Examine the **climate map**. Why are northern Norway, Sweden, and Finland so thinly populated?

**2.** *Places and Regions* Compare this map to the **political map**. Which countries have between 25 and 130 persons per square mile in all areas?

## Critical Thinking

**3. Analyzing Information** Use the map to create a chart, graph, database, or model of population centers in Europe.

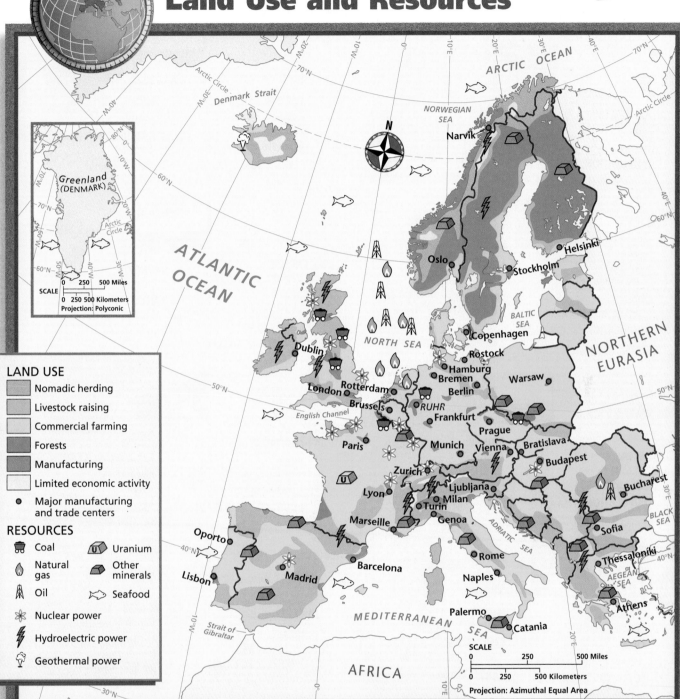

**LAND USE**

- Nomadic herding
- Livestock raising
- Commercial farming
- Forests
- Manufacturing
- Limited economic activity
- ● Major manufacturing and trade centers

**RESOURCES**

- Coal
- Uranium
- Natural gas
- Other minerals
- Oil
- Seafood
- Nuclear power
- Hydroelectric power
- Geothermal power

1. **Places and Regions** What is the only country in the region that uses geothermal power?

2. **Places and Regions** Which country in the region mines uranium?

3. **Places and Regions** In which body of water is oil and gas production concentrated?

## Critical Thinking

4. **Analyzing Information** Use the map on this page to create a chart, graph, database, or model of economic activities in Europe.

# Fast FACTS
## Europe

### ALBANIA

**CAPITAL:** Tiranë

**AREA:**
11,100 sq. mi. (28,748 sq km)

**POPULATION:** 3,510,484

**MONEY:** lek (ALL)

**LANGUAGES:**
Albanian, Greek

**CARS:** data not available

### BULGARIA

**CAPITAL:** Sofia

**AREA:**
42,822 sq. mi.
(110,910 sq km)

**POPULATION:** 7,707,495

**MONEY:**
lev (BGL)

**LANGUAGES:**
Bulgarian

**CARS:** 1,650,000

### ANDORRA

**CAPITAL:**
Andorra la Vella

**AREA:**
181 sq. mi. (468 sq km)

**POPULATION:** 67,627

**MONEY:**
euro (€), 1-01-2002

**LANGUAGES:**
Catalan (official), French
Castilian

**CARS:** 35,358

### CROATIA

**CAPITAL:**
Zagreb

**AREA:**
21,831 sq. mi.
(56,542 sq km)

**POPULATION:** 4,334,142

**MONEY:**
Croatian kuna (HRK)

**LANGUAGES:**
Croatian

**CARS:** 698,000

### AUSTRIA

**CAPITAL:** Vienna

**AREA:**
32,378 sq. mi.
(83,858 sq km)

**POPULATION:** 8,150,835

**MONEY:**
euro (€),
1-01-2002

**LANGUAGES:** German

**CARS:** 3,780,000

### CZECH REPUBLIC

**CAPITAL:** Prague

**AREA:**
30,450 sq. mi.
(78,866 sq km)

**POPULATION:** 10,264,212

**MONEY:**
Czech koruna (CZK)

**LANGUAGES:**
Czech

**CARS:** 4,410,000

### BELGIUM

**CAPITAL:**
Brussels

**AREA:**
11,780 sq. mi. (30,510 sq km)

**POPULATION:** 10,258,762

**MONEY:**
euro (€), 1-01-2002

**LANGUAGES:**
Dutch, French, German

**CARS:** 4,420,000

### DENMARK

**CAPITAL:**
Copenhagen

**AREA:**
16,639 sq. mi.
(43,094 sq km)

**POPULATION:** 5,352,815

**MONEY:**
Danish krone (DKK)

**LANGUAGES:**
Danish, Faroese, Greenlandic
(an Inuit dialect), German

**CARS:** 1,790,000

### BOSNIA AND HERZEGOVINA

**CAPITAL:**
Sarajevo

**AREA:**
19,741 sq. mi. (51,129 sq km)

**POPULATION:** 3,922,205

**MONEY:**
marka (BAM)

**LANGUAGES:**
Croatian, Serbian, Bosnian

**CARS:** data not available

### ESTONIA

**CAPITAL:**
Tallinn

**AREA:**
17,462 sq. mi.
(45,226 sq km)

**POPULATION:** 1,423,316

**MONEY:**
Estonian kroon (EEK)

**LANGUAGES:**
Estonian (official), Russian,
Ukrainian, English, Finnish

**CARS:** 338,000

Countries not drawn to scale.

## FINLAND

**CAPITAL:** Helsinki

**AREA:**
130,127 sq. mi.
(337,030 sq km)

**POPULATION:** 5,175,783

**MONEY:**
euro (€), 1-01-2002

**LANGUAGES:** Finnish, Swedish

**CARS:** 1,940,000

## FRANCE

**CAPITAL:** Paris

**AREA:**
211,208 sq. mi.
(547,030 sq km)

**POPULATION:** 59,551,227

**MONEY:**
euro (€), 1-01-2002

**LANGUAGES:** French

**CARS:** 25,500,000

## GERMANY

**CAPITAL:** Berlin

**AREA:**
137,846 sq. mi.
(357,021 sq km)

**POPULATION:** 83,029,536

**MONEY:**
euro (€), deutsche mark
(DM)

**LANGUAGES:** German

**CARS:** 41,330,000

## GREECE

**CAPITAL:**
Athens

**AREA:**
50,942 sq. mi.
(131,940 sq km)

**POPULATION:** 10,623,835

**MONEY:**
euro (€), 1-01-2002

**LANGUAGES:**
Greek (official), English,
French

**CARS:** 2,340,000

## HUNGARY

**CAPITAL:** Budapest

**AREA:**
35,919 sq. mi.
(93,030 sq km)

**POPULATION:** 10,106,017

**MONEY:**
forint (HUF)

**LANGUAGES:**
Hungarian

**CARS:** 2,280,000

## ICELAND

**CAPITAL:** Reykjavik

**AREA:**
39,768 sq. mi.
(103,000 sq km)

**POPULATION:** 277,906

**MONEY:**
Icelandic krona (ISK)

**LANGUAGES:**
Icelandic

**CARS:** 132,468

## IRELAND

**CAPITAL:**
Dublin

**AREA:**
27,135 sq. mi. (70,280 sq km)

**POPULATION:** 3,840,838

**MONEY:**
euro (€), 1-01-2002

**LANGUAGES:**
English, Irish (Gaelic)

**CARS:** 1,060,000

## ITALY

**CAPITAL:**
Rome

**AREA:**
116,305 sq. mi.
(301,230 sq km)

**POPULATION:** 57,679,825

**MONEY:**
euro (€), 1-01-2002

**LANGUAGES:**
Italian, German, French,
Slovene

**CARS:** 31,000,000

## LATVIA

**CAPITAL:** Riga

**AREA:**
24,938 sq. mi.
(64,589 sq km)

**POPULATION:** 2,385,231

**MONEY:** Latvian lat (LVL)

**LANGUAGES:**
Lettish (official), Lithuanian,
Russian

**CARS:** 252,000

## LIECHTENSTEIN

**CAPITAL:** Vaduz

**AREA:**
62 sq. mi. (160 sq km)

**POPULATION:**
32,528

**MONEY:**
Swiss franc (CHF)

**LANGUAGES:** German

**CARS:** data not available

**Sources:** Central Intelligence Agency, *The World Factbook 2001; The World Almanac and Book of Facts 2001;* population figures are 2001 estimates.

## LITHUANIA

**CAPITAL:** Vilnius

**AREA:**
25,174 sq. mi.
(65,200 sq km)

**POPULATION:**
3,610,535

**MONEY:**
litas (LTL)

**LANGUAGES:**
Lithuanian (official), Polish,
Russian

**CARS:** 653,000

## MONACO

**CAPITAL:**
Monaco

**AREA:**
0.75 sq. mi. (1.95 sq km)

**POPULATION:**
31,842

**MONEY:**
euro (€), 1-01-2002

**LANGUAGES:**
French (official), English,
Italian, Monegasque

**CARS:** 17,000

## LUXEMBOURG

**CAPITAL:**
Luxembourg

**AREA:**
998 sq. mi. (2,586 sq km)

**POPULATION:**
429,080

**MONEY:** euro (€),
Luxembourg franc (LuxF)

**LANGUAGES:**
Luxembourgish, German,
French

**CARS:** 231,666

## NETHERLANDS

**CAPITAL:** Amsterdam

**AREA:**
16,033 sq. mi.
(41,526 sq km)

**POPULATION:** 15,981,472

**MONEY:**
euro (€), 1-01-2002

**LANGUAGES:** Dutch

**CARS:** 5,810,000

## MACEDONIA

**CAPITAL:** Skopje

**AREA:**
9,781 sq. mi.
(25,333 sq km)

**POPULATION:** 2,046,209

**MONEY:**
Macedonian denar (MKD)

**LANGUAGES:**
Macedonian, Albanian,
Turkish, Serbo-Croatian

**CARS:** 263,000

## NORWAY

**CAPITAL:** Oslo

**AREA:**
125,181 sq. mi.
(324,220 sq km)

**POPULATION:** 4,503,440

**MONEY:**
Norwegian
krone (NOK)

**LANGUAGES:** Norwegian

**CARS:** 1,760,000

## MALTA

**CAPITAL:**
Valletta

**AREA:**
122 sq. mi. (316 sq km)

**POPULATION:**
394,583

**MONEY:**
Maltese lira (MTL)

**LANGUAGES:**
Maltese (official), English
(official)

**CARS:** 122,100

## POLAND

**CAPITAL:** Warsaw

**AREA:**
120,728 sq. mi.
(312,685 sq km)

**POPULATION:** 38,633,912

**MONEY:**
zloty (PLN)

**LANGUAGES:**
Polish

**CARS:** 7,520,000

## MOLDOVA

**CAPITAL:** Chişinău

**AREA:**
13,067 sq. mi.
(33,843 sq km)

**POPULATION:** 4,431,570

**MONEY:**
Moldovan leu (MDL)

**LANGUAGES:**
Moldovan (official), Russian,
Gagauz

**CARS:** 169,000

## PORTUGAL

**CAPITAL:** Lisbon

**AREA:**
35,672 sq. mi.
(92,391 sq km)

**POPULATION:** 10,066,253

**MONEY:**
euro (€), 1-01-2002

**LANGUAGES:** Portuguese

**CARS:** 2,950,000

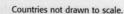
Countries not drawn to scale.

## ROMANIA

**CAPITAL:**
Bucharest

**AREA:**
91,699 sq. mi.
(237,500 sq km)

**POPULATION:** 22,364,022

**MONEY:**
leu (ROL)

**LANGUAGES:**
Romanian, Hungarian, German

**CARS:** 2,390,000

## SAN MARINO

**CAPITAL:**
San Marino

**AREA:**
23.6 sq. mi. (61.2 sq km)

**POPULATION:** 27,336

**MONEY:**
euro (€), 1-01-2002

**LANGUAGES:**
Italian

**CARS:** 24,825

## SLOVAKIA

**CAPITAL:**
Bratislava

**AREA:**
18,859 sq. mi.
(48,845 sq km)

**POPULATION:** 5,414,937

**MONEY:**
Slovak koruna (SKK)

**LANGUAGES:**
Slovak (official), Hungarian

**CARS:** 994,000

## SLOVENIA

**CAPITAL:**
Ljubljana

**AREA:**
7,820 sq. mi.
(20,253 sq km)

**POPULATION:** 1,930,132

**MONEY:**
tolar (SIT)

**LANGUAGES:**
Slovenian, Serbo-Croatian

**CARS:** 657,000

## SPAIN

**CAPITAL:**
Madrid

**AREA:**
194,896 sq. mi.
(504,782 sq km)

**POPULATION:** 40,037,995

**MONEY:**
euro (€), peseta (Pta)

**LANGUAGES:**
Castilian Spanish, Catalan, Galician

**CARS:** 15,300,000

## SWEDEN

**CAPITAL:** Stockholm

**AREA:**
173,731 sq. mi.
(449,964 sq km)

**POPULATION:** 8,875,053

**MONEY:**
Swedish krona (SEK)

**LANGUAGES:** Swedish

**CARS:** 3,700,000

## SWITZERLAND

**CAPITAL:**
Bern

**AREA:**
15,942 sq. mi.
(41,290 sq km)

**POPULATION:** 7,283,274

**MONEY:**
Swiss franc (CHF)

**LANGUAGES:**
German, French, Italian

**CARS:** 3,320,000

## UNITED KINGDOM

**CAPITAL:** London

**AREA:**
94,525 sq. mi.
(244,820 sq km)

**POPULATION:** 59,647,790

**MONEY:** British pound (GBP)

**LANGUAGES:**
English, Welsh, Scottish form of Gaelic

**CARS:** 25,590,000

## VATICAN CITY

**CAPITAL:** Vatican City

**AREA:**
0.17 sq. mi. (0.44 sq km)

**POPULATION:** 890

**MONEY:**
euro (€), 1-01-2002

**LANGUAGES:** Italian, Latin

**CARS:** data not available

## YUGOSLAVIA

**CAPITAL:** Belgrade

**AREA:** 39,517 sq. mi.
(102,350 sq km)

**POPULATION:** 10,677,290

**MONEY:** New Yugoslav dinar (YUM)

**LANGUAGES:**
Serbian, Albanian

**CARS:** 1,000,000

**☑ internet** connect

**COUNTRY STATISTICS**
**GO TO:** go.hrw.com
**KEYWORD:** SK3 FactsU3
**FOR:** more facts about Europe

**Sources:** Central Intelligence Agency, *The World Factbook 2001; The World Almanac and Book of Facts 2001;* population figures are 2001 estimates.

Europe **229**

# CHAPTER 10

## Southern Europe

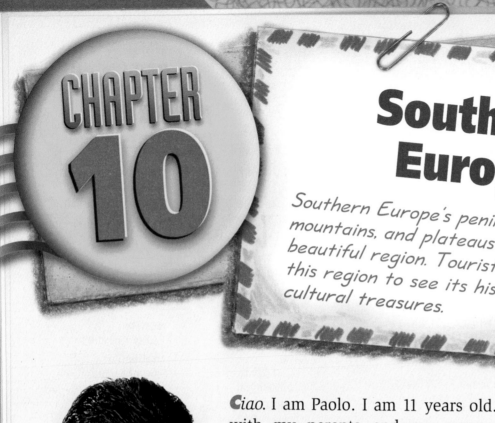

*Southern Europe's peninsulas, islands, mountains, and plateaus form a beautiful region. Tourists enjoy visiting this region to see its historical and cultural treasures.*

*Ciao.* I am Paolo. I am 11 years old. I live in an apartment with my parents and my *nonna,* which is Italian for "grandma." Nonna is teaching me how to cook while she makes dinner for the family. I have no brothers or sisters, but on Sundays my aunts and uncles and three cousins all come for a big lunch. After lunch, the cousins play outside on the playground swings.

In the mornings, I walk to school with my mother before she goes to her job as a professor. My school is not too strict. We study English, Italian, and religion. After school I practice with my team at the swim club.

My favorite holiday is Christmas. On Christmas Eve we go to my other grandmother's house for a special dinner. We have smoked salmon, then grilled trout and spaghetti with mussels. Then there are special Christmas sweets: Pandoro—a cake sprinkled with sugar, and Torrone—a candy log with chocolate and nuts.

**Abito a Roma, la capitale dell'Italia.**

▲
Translation: I live in Rome, the capital of Italy.

# Section 1  Physical Geography

## Read to Discover

1. What are the major landforms and rivers of southern Europe?
2. What are the major climate types and resources of this region?

## Define

mainland
sirocco

## Locate

Mediterranean Sea
Strait of Gibraltar

Iberian Peninsula
Cantabrian Mountains
Pyrenees Mountains
Alps
Apennines
Aegean Sea
Peloponnesus

Ebro River
Douro River
Tagus River
Guadalquivir River
Po River
Tiber River

### WHY IT MATTERS

Southern Europe's location on peninsulas encouraged its cultures to become great seafarers. Use CNN fyi.com or other current events sources to find examples of trade on the region's oceans today. Record your findings in your journal.

Cave painting from 12,000 B.C.

## Southern Europe: Physical-Political

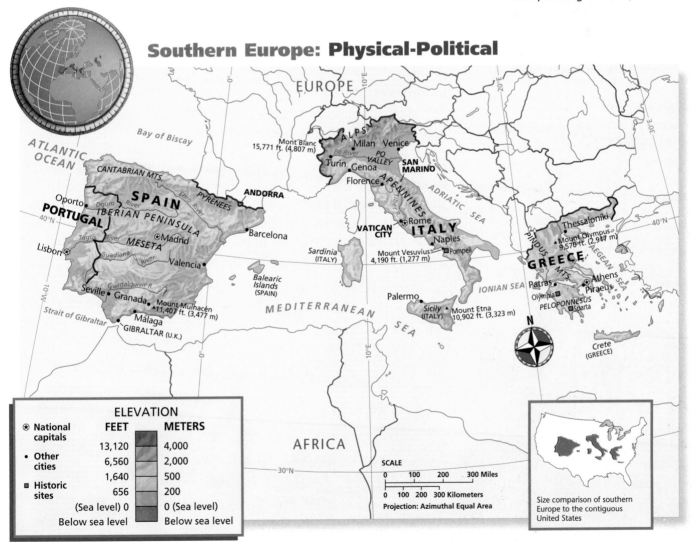

### ELEVATION

| | FEET | METERS |
|---|---|---|
| ⊛ National capitals | 13,120 | 4,000 |
| • Other cities | 6,560 | 2,000 |
| | 1,640 | 500 |
| ▪ Historic sites | 656 | 200 |
| | (Sea level) 0 | 0 (Sea level) |
| | Below sea level | Below sea level |

SCALE
0    100    200    300 Miles
0  100  200  300 Kilometers
Projection: Azimuthal Equal Area

Size comparison of southern Europe to the contiguous United States

# Physical Features

Southern Europe is also known as Mediterranean Europe because most of its countries are on the sea's shores. The Mediterranean Sea stretches some 2,300 miles (3,700 km) from east to west. *Mediterranean* means "middle of the land" in Latin. In ancient times, the Mediterranean was considered the center of the Western world, since it is surrounded by Europe, Africa, and Asia. The narrow Strait of Gibraltar (juh-BRAWL-tuhr) links the Mediterranean to the Atlantic Ocean.

**The Land** Southern Europe is made up of three peninsulas. Portugal and Spain occupy one, Italy occupies another, and Greece is located on a third peninsula. Portugal and Spain are on the Iberian (eye-BIR-ee-uhn) Peninsula. Much of the peninsula is a high, rocky plateau. The Cantabrian (kan-TAY-bree-uhn) and the Pyrenees (PIR-uh-neez) Mountains form the plateau's northern edge. Italy's peninsula includes the southern Alps. A lower mountain range, the Apennines (A-puh-nynz), runs like a spine down the country's back. Islands in the central and western Mediterranean include Italy's Sicily and Sardinia (sahr-DI-nee-uh), as well as Spain's Balearic (ba-lee-AR-ik) Islands.

Greece's **mainland**, or the country's main landmass, extends into the Aegean (ee-JEE-uhn) Sea in many jagged little peninsulas. The largest one is the Peloponnesus (pe-luh-puh-NEE-suhs). Greece is mountainous and includes more than 2,000 islands. The largest island is Crete (KREET).

On all three peninsulas, coastal lowlands and river valleys provide excellent areas for growing crops and building cities. Soils on the region's uplands are thin and stony. They are also easily eroded. In this area of young mountains, earthquakes are common. They are particularly common in Greece and Italy.

**The Rivers** Several east-west rivers cut through the Iberian Peninsula. The Ebro River drains into the Mediterranean. The Douro, Tagus, and Guadalquivir (gwah-thahl-kee-VEER) Rivers, however, flow to the Atlantic Ocean. The Po (POH) is Italy's largest river. It creates a fertile agricultural region in northern Italy. Farther south, along the banks of the much smaller Tiber River, is the city of Rome.

✓ **READING CHECK:** *Physical Systems* What physical processes cause problems in parts of southern Europe?

## Imports and Exports of Southern Europe

Source: Central Intelligence Agency, *The World Factbook, 2001*

**Interpreting the Graph** Which country has the fewest imports and exports?

Greece, a land of mountains and sea, is home to the ancient city of Lindos on the island of Rhodes.

# Climate and Resources

Much of southern Europe enjoys a warm, sunny climate. Most of the rain falls during the mild winter. Rainfall sometimes causes floods and mudslides due to erosion from overgrazing and deforestation. A hot, dry wind from North Africa called a **sirocco** (suh-RAH-koh) picks up some moisture over the Mediterranean Sea. It blows over Italy during spring and summer. The Po Valley is humid. Northern Italy's Alps have a highland climate. In Spain, semiarid climates are found in pockets. Northern Spain is cool and humid.

Southern Europeans have often looked to the sea for trade. Important Mediterranean ports include Barcelona, Genoa, Naples, Piraeus (py-REE-uhs)—the port of Athens—and Valencia. Lisbon, the capital of Portugal, is an important Atlantic port. The Atlantic Ocean supports Portugal's fishing industry. Although the Mediterranean suffers from pollution, it has a wealth of seafood.

The region's resources vary. Northern Spain has iron ore mines. Greece mines bauxite, chromium, lead, and zinc. Italy and Greece quarry marble. Falling water generates hydroelectricity throughout the region's uplands. Otherwise, resources are scarce.

The region's sunny climate and natural beauty have long attracted visitors. Millions of people explore castles, museums, ruins, and other cultural sites each year. Spain's beaches help make that country one of Europe's top tourist destinations.

▲ Workers prepare to separate a giant block of marble from a wall in a quarry in Carrara, Italy.

✓ **READING CHECK:** ( *Places and Regions* ) What climate types and natural resources are found in the region?

---

## Section Review 1

go.hrw.com **Homework Practice Online**
Keyword: SK3 HP10

**Define and explain:** mainland, sirocco

**Working with Sketch Maps** On a map of southern Europe that you draw or that your teacher provides, label Greece, Italy, Spain, and Portugal. Also label the Mediterranean Sea and the Strait of Gibraltar.

### Reading for the Main Idea

1. ( *Places and Regions* ) Why is southern Europe known as Mediterranean Europe?

2. ( *Places and Regions* ) What countries occupy the region's three main peninsulas?

3. ( *Environment and Society* ) Why might people settle in river valleys and in coastal Southern Europe?

### Critical Thinking

4. **Drawing Inferences and Conclusions** In what ways could the region's physical geography aid the development of trade?

### Organizing What You Know

5. **Summarizing** Copy the following graphic organizer. Use it to list the region's physical features, climates, and resources.

| | Physical Features | Climate | Resources |
|---|---|---|---|
| Spain and Portugal | | | |
| Italy | | | |
| Greece | | | |

# Section 2 Greece

## Read to Discover

1. What were some of the achievements of the ancient Greeks?
2. What are two features of Greek culture?
3. What is Greece like today?

## Define

city-states
mosaics

## Locate

Athens
Thessaloníki

### WHY IT MATTERS

The Olympic Games first started in Greece. Today we continue the tradition and hold both Summer and Winter Games. Use **CNN fyi.com** or other **current events** sources to find out more about the modern Olympic Games. Record your findings in your journal.

*Ancient coin of Alexander the Great*

## History

The Greek islands took an early lead in the development of trade and shipping between Asia, Africa, and Europe. By about 2000 B.C. large towns and a complex civilization existed on Crete.

**Ancient Greece** About 800 B.C. Greek civilization arose on the mainland. The mountainous landscape there favored small, independent **city-states**. Each Greek city-state, or *polis,* was made up of a city and the land around it. Each had its own gods, laws, and form of government. The government of the city-state of Athens was the first known democracy. Democracy is the form of government in which all citizens take part. Greek philosophers, artists, architects, and writers made important contributions to Western civilization. For example, the Greeks are credited with inventing theater. Students still study ancient Greek literature and plays.

Eventually, Greece was conquered by King Philip. Philip ruled Macedonia, an area north of Greece. About 330 B.C. Philip's son, Alexander the Great, conquered Asia Minor, Egypt, Persia, and part of India. His empire combined Greek culture with influences from Asia and Africa. In the 140s B.C. Greece and Macedonia were conquered by the Roman Empire.

The Greeks believed that the Temple of Delphi—shown below—was the center of the world.

**Interpreting the Visual Record Why do you think remains of this temple have lasted for so many years?**

▼

**The Byzantine Empire** About A.D. 400 the Roman Empire was divided into two parts. The western half was ruled from Rome. It soon fell to Germanic peoples the Romans called barbarians. Barbarian means both *illiterate* and *wanderer*. The eastern half of the Roman Empire was known as the Byzantine Empire. It was ruled from Constantinople. Constantinople was located on the shore of the Bosporus in what is now Turkey. This city—today known as Istanbul—served as a gathering place for people from Europe and Asia. The Byzantine Empire carried on the traditions of the Roman Empire for another 1,000 years. Gradually, an eastern form of Christianity developed. It was influenced by Greek language and culture. It became known as Eastern Orthodox Christianity. It is the leading form of Christianity in Greece, parts of eastern Europe, and Russia.

▲

The Acropolis in Athens was built in the 400s B.C. The word *acropolis* is Greek for "city at the top."

**Interpreting the Visual Record** Why would it be important to build a city on a hill?

**Turkish Rule** In 1453 Constantinople was conquered by the Ottoman Turks, a people from Central Asia. Greece and most of the rest of the region came under the rule of the Ottoman Empire. It remained part of this empire for nearly 400 years. In 1821 the Greeks revolted against the Turks, and in the early 1830s Greece became independent.

**Government** In World War II Greece was occupied by Germany. After the war Greek communists and those who wanted a king and constitution fought a civil war. When the communists lost, the military took control. Finally, in the 1970s the Greek people voted to make their country a republic. They adopted a new constitution that created a government with a president and a prime minister.

✓ **READING CHECK:** ( *Human Systems* ) What were some of the achievements of ancient Greece?

# Culture

Turkish influences on Greek art, food, and music can still be seen. However, Turkey and Greece disagree over control of the islands and shipping lanes of the Aegean Sea.

**Religion** Some 98 percent of Greeks are Eastern Orthodox Christians, commonly known as Greek Orthodox. Easter is a major holiday and cause for much celebration. The traditional Easter meal is eaten on Sunday—roasted lamb, various vegetables, Easter bread, and many desserts. Because the Greek Orthodox Church has its own calendar, Christmas and Easter are usually celebrated one to two weeks later than in the West.

▲

The people of Karpathos and their religious leaders are participating in an Easter celebration.

# CONNECTING TO Math

Greek postage stamp of the Pythagorean Theorem

## Greek Math and Science

Greek civilization made many contributions to world culture. We still admire Greek art and literature. Greek scholars also paved the way for modern mathematics and science.

More than 2,000 years ago Thales (THAY-leez), a philosopher, began the use of deduction in mathematical proofs. Pythagoras (puh-THAG-uh-ruhs) worked out an equation to calculate the dimensions of a right triangle. The equation became known as the Pythagorean Theorem. By 300 B.C. Euclid (YOO-kluhd) had stated the basic principles of geometry in his book *Elements*. Soon after, Archimedes (ahr-kuh-MEED-eez) calculated the value of *pi*. This value is used to measure circles and spheres. He also explained how and why the lever, a basic tool, works.

Aristarchus (ar-uh-STAHR-kuhs), an astronomer, worked out a model of the solar system. His model placed the Sun at the center of the universe. Eratosthenes (er-uh-TAHS-thuh-neez) estimated the circumference of Earth with great accuracy.

Two important figures in the life sciences were Hippocrates (hip-AHK-ruh-teez) and Aristotle (AR-uh-staht-uhl). Hippocrates was a doctor who treated medicine as a science. He understood that diseases have natural causes. Aristotle gathered information on a wide variety of plants and animals. He helped establish the importance of observation and classification in the study of nature. In many ways, the Greeks began the process of separating scientific fact from superstition.

### Understanding What You Read

1. How did Greeks further the study of mathematics?
2. What were some of the Greeks' scientific achievements?

---

This Greek vase shows a warrior holding a shield. Kleophrades is thought to have made this vase, which dates to 500 B.C.

This mosaic of a dog bears the inscription "Good Hunting."

**The Arts** The ancient Greeks produced beautiful buildings, sculpture, poetry, plays, pottery, and gold jewelry. They also made **mosaics** (moh-ZAY-iks)—pictures created from tiny pieces of colored stone—that were copied throughout Europe. The folk music of Greece shares many features with the music of Turkey and Southwest Asia. In 1963 the Greek writer George Seferis won the Nobel Prize in literature.

✔ **READING CHECK:** *Human Systems* Why is there a Turkish influence in Greek culture?

# Greece Today

When people think of Greece now, they often recall the past. For example, many have seen pictures of the Parthenon, a temple built in the 400s B.C. in Athens. It is one of the world's most photographed buildings.

**Economy** Greece today lags behind other European nations in economic growth. More people work in agriculture than in any other industry. However, only about 19 percent of the land can be farmed because of the mountains. For this reason old methods of farming are used rather than modern equipment. Farmers raise cotton, tobacco, vegetables, wheat, lemons, olives, and raisins.

Service and manufacturing industries are growing in Greece. However, the lack of natural resources limits industry. Tourism and shipping are key to the Greek economy.

**Cities** About 20 percent of the Greek labor force works in agriculture. About 40 percent of Greeks live in rural areas. In the past few years, people have begun to move to the cities to find better jobs.

Athens, in central Greece, is the capital and by far the largest city. About one third of Greece's population lives in the area in and around Athens. Athens and its seaport, Piraeus, have attracted both people and industries. Most of the country's economic growth is centered there. However, the city suffers from air pollution, which causes health problems. Air pollution also damages historical sites, such as the Parthenon. Greece's second-largest city is Thessaloníki. It is the major seaport for northern Greece.

✓ **READING CHECK:** *Environment and Society* How does scarcity of natural resources affect Greece's economy?

### Greece

| COUNTRY | POPULATION/ GROWTH RATE | LIFE EXPECTANCY | LITERACY RATE | PER CAPITA GDP |
|---|---|---|---|---|
| Greece | 10,623,835 0.2% | 76, male 81, female | 95% | $17,200 |
| United States | 281,421,906 0.9% | 74, male 80, female | 97% | $36,200 |

**Sources:** Central Intelligence Agency, *The World Factbook 2001;* U.S. Census Bureau

**Interpreting the Chart** **Why might life expectancy be higher in Greece than in the United States?**

**Homework Practice Online**

Keyword: SK3 HP10

## Section Review 2

**Define and explain:** city-states, mosaics

**Working with Sketch Maps** On the map you created in Section 1, label Athens and Thessaloníki. What physical features do these cities have in common? What economic activities might they share?

### Reading for the Main Idea

1. *Human Systems* What groups influenced Greek culture?

2. *Human Systems* For what art forms is Greece famous?

### Critical Thinking

3. **Drawing Inferences and Conclusions** How did the physical geography of this region influence the growth of major cities?

4. **Finding the Main Idea** On what does Greece rely to keep its economy strong?

### Organizing What You Know

5. **Sequencing** Create a time line that documents the history of ancient Greece from 2000 B.C. to A.D. 1453.

2000 B.C.        A.D. 1453

# Section 3 Italy

## Read to Discover

1. What was the early history of Italy like?
2. How has Italy added to world culture?
3. What is Italy like today?

## Define

pope
Renaissance
coalition
  governments

## Locate

Rome
Genoa
Naples
Milan
Turin
Florence

### WHY IT MATTERS

Leonardo da Vinci and Galileo are just two famous Italians who have made significant contributions to science and art. Use CNN**fyi**.com or other **current events** sources to find examples of recent Italian scientists and artists. Record your findings in your journal.

*Artifact from a warrior's armor, 400s B.C.*

The Appian Way was a road from Rome to Brindisi. It was started in 312 B.C. by the emperor Claudius.

**Interpreting the Visual Record How do you think this road has withstood more than 2,000 years of use?**

## History

About 750 B.C. a tribe known as the Latins established the city of Rome on the Tiber River. Over time, these Romans conquered the rest of Italy. They then began to expand their rule to lands outside Italy.

**Roman Empire** At its height about A.D. 100, the Roman Empire stretched westward to what is now Spain and Portugal and northward to England and Germany. The Balkans, Turkey, parts of Southwest Asia, and coastal North Africa were all part of the empire. Roman laws, roads, engineering, and the Latin language could be found throughout this huge area. The Roman army kept order, and people could travel safely throughout the empire. Trade prospered.

The Romans made advances in engineering, including roads and aqueducts—canals that transported water. They also learned how to build domes and arches. Romans also produced great works of art and literature.

About A.D. 200, however, the Roman Empire began to weaken. The western part, with its capital in Rome, fell in A.D. 476. The eastern part, the Byzantine Empire, lasted until 1453.

Roman influences in the world can still be seen today. Latin developed into the modern languages of French, Italian, Portuguese, Romanian, and Spanish. Many English words have Latin origins as well. Roman laws and political ideas have influenced the governments and legal systems of many modern countries.

◀

The Colosseum is a giant amphitheater. It was built in Rome between A.D. 70 and 80 and could seat 50,000 people.

**Interpreting the Visual Record**
**For what events do you think the Colosseum was used? What type of modern buildings look like this?**

Christianity began in the Roman province of Judaea (modern Israel and the West Bank). It then spread through the Roman Empire. Some early Christians were persecuted for refusing to worship the traditional Roman gods. However, in the early A.D. 300s the Roman emperor, Constantine, adopted Christianity. It quickly became the main religion of the empire. The **pope**—the bishop of Rome—is the head of the Roman Catholic Church.

**The Renaissance** Beginning in the 1300s a new era of learning began in Italy. It was known as the **Renaissance** (re-nuh-SAHNS). In French this word means "rebirth." During the Renaissance, Italians rediscovered the work of ancient Roman and Greek writers. Scholars applied reason and experimented to advance the sciences. Artists pioneered new techniques. Leonardo da Vinci, painter of the *Mona Lisa*, was also a sculptor, engineer, architect, and scientist. Another Italian, Galileo Galilei, perfected the telescope and experimented with gravity.

Christopher Columbus opened up the Americas to European colonization. Although Spain paid for his voyages, Columbus was an Italian from the city of Genoa. The name *America* comes from another Italian explorer, Amerigo Vespucci.

**Government** Italy was divided into many small states until the late 1800s. Today Italy's central government is a democracy with an elected parliament. Italy has had many changes in leadership in recent years. This has happened because no political party has won a majority of votes in Italian elections. As a result, political parties must form **coalition governments**. A coalition government is one in which several parties join together to run the country. Unfortunately, these coalitions usually do not last long.

▲
Leonardo da Vinci painted the *Mona Lisa* about 1503–06.

**Interpreting the Visual Record** **Why do you think Leonardo's painting became famous?**

✔ **READING CHECK:** ( *Human Systems* ) How is the Italian government different from that of the United States?

This view of the Pantheon in Rome shows the oculus—the opening at the top. The Pantheon was built as a temple to all Roman gods.

**Interpreting the Visual Record** Why did the Romans need to design buildings that let in light?

▼

In Rome people attend mass in St. Peter's Square, Vatican City. Vatican City is an independent state within Rome.

**Interpreting the Visual Record** How does a plaza, or open area, help create a sense of community?

▼

# Culture

People from other places have influenced Italian culture. During the Renaissance, many Jews who had been expelled from Spain moved to Italian cities. Jews often had to live in segregated areas called ghettoes. Today immigrants have arrived from former Italian colonies in Africa. Others have come from the eastern Mediterranean and the Balkans.

**Religion and Food** Some 98 percent of Italians belong to the Roman Catholic Church. The leadership of the church is still based in the Vatican in Rome. Christmas and Easter are major holidays in Italy. Italians also celebrate All Souls' Day on November 2 by cleaning and decorating their relatives' graves.

Italians enjoy a range of regional foods. Recipes are influenced by the history and crops of each area. In the south, Italians eat a Mediterranean diet of olives, bread, and fish. Dishes are flavored with lemons from Greece and spices from Africa. Tomatoes, originally from the Americas, have become an important part of the diet. Some Italian foods, such as pizza, are popular in the United States. Modern pizza originated in Naples. Northern Italians eat more rice, butter, cheeses, and mushrooms than southern Italians.

**The Arts** The ancient Romans created beautiful glassware and jewelry as well as marble and bronze sculptures. During the Renaissance, Italy again became a center for art, particularly painting and sculpture. Italian artists discovered ways to make their paintings more lifelike. They did this by creating the illusion of three dimensions. Italian writers like Francesco Petrarch and Giovanni Boccaccio wrote some of the most important literature of the Renaissance. More recently, Italian composers have written great operas. Today, Italian designers, actors, and filmmakers are celebrated worldwide.

✔ **READING CHECK:** ( *Human Systems* ) What are some examples of Italian culture?

# Italy Today

Italy is slightly smaller than Florida and Georgia combined, with a population of about 57 million. A shared language, the Roman Catholic Church, and strong family ties continue to bind Italians together.

**Economy** After its defeat in World War II, Italy rebuilt its industries in the north. Rich soil and plenty of water make the north Italy's "breadbasket," or wheat growing area. Italy's most valuable crop is grapes. Although grapes are grown throughout the country, northern Italy produces the best crops. These grapes help make Italy the world's largest producer of wine. Tourists are also important to Italy's economy. They visit northern and central Italy to see ancient ruins and Renaissance art. Southern Italy remains poorer with lower crop yields. Industrialization there also lags behind the north. Tourist resorts, however, are growing in the south and promise to help the economy.

**Cities** The northern cities of Milan, Turin, and Genoa are important industrial centers. Their location near the center of Europe helps companies sell products to foreign customers. Also in the north are two popular tourist sites. One is Venice, which is famous for its romantic canals and beautiful buildings. The other is Florence, a center of art and culture. Rome, the capital, is located in central Italy. Naples, the largest city in southern Italy, is a major manufacturing center and port.

✓ **READING CHECK:** *Environment and Society* What geographic factors influence Italy's economy?

## Italy

| COUNTRY | POPULATION/ GROWTH RATE | LIFE EXPECTANCY | LITERACY RATE | PER CAPITA GDP |
|---------|-------------------------|-----------------|---------------|----------------|
| Italy | 57,679,825 .07% | 76, male 83, female | 98% | $22,100 |
| United States | 281,421,906 0.9% | 74, male 80, female | 97% | $36,200 |

**Sources:** Central Intelligence Agency, *The World Factbook 2001;* U.S. Census Bureau

*Interpreting the Chart* **What is the difference in the growth rate of Italy and the United States?**

# Section Review 3

go. hrw .com **Homework Practice Online**
Keyword: SK3 HP10

**Define and explain:** pope, Renaissance, coalition governments

**Working with Sketch Maps** On the map you created in Section 2, label Florence, Genoa, Milan, Naples, Rome, and Turin. Why are they important?

## Reading for the Main Idea

1. *Human Systems* What were some of the important contributions of the Romans?

2. *Human Systems* What are some art forms for which Italy is well known?

## Critical Thinking

3. **Finding the Main Idea** Which of Italy's physical features encourage trade? Which geographical features make trading difficult?

4. **Analyzing Information** Why is the northern part of Italy known as the country's "breadbasket"?

## Organizing What You Know

5. **Finding the Main Idea** Copy the following graphic organizer. Use it to describe the movement of goods and ideas to and from Italy during the early days of trade and exploration.

| | ⇨ | Italy | ⇨ | |
|---|---|-------|---|---|

# Section 4 | Spain and Portugal

## Read to Discover

1. What were some major events in the history of Spain and Portugal?
2. What are the cultures of Spain and Portugal like?
3. What are Spain and Portugal like today?

## Define

Moors
dialect
cork

## Locate

Lisbon
Madrid
Barcelona

### WHY IT MATTERS

Some Basque separatists have used violence to try to gain their independence from Spain. Use CNN fyi.com or other **current events** sources to find examples of this problem. Record your findings in your journal.

*Paella, a popular dish in Spain*

## History

Beautiful paintings of bison and other animals are found in caves in northern Spain. Some of the best known are at Altamira and were created as early as 16,000 B.C. Some cave paintings are much older. These paintings give us exciting clues about the early people who lived here.

**Ancient Times**  Spain has been important to Mediterranean trade for several thousand years. First, the Greeks and then the Phoenicians, or Carthaginians, built towns on Spain's southern and eastern coasts. Then, about 200 B.C. Iberia became a part of the Roman Empire and adopted the Latin language.

These windmills in Consuegra, Spain, provided water for the people of the region.

**Interpreting the Visual Record  How do you think windmills pump water?**

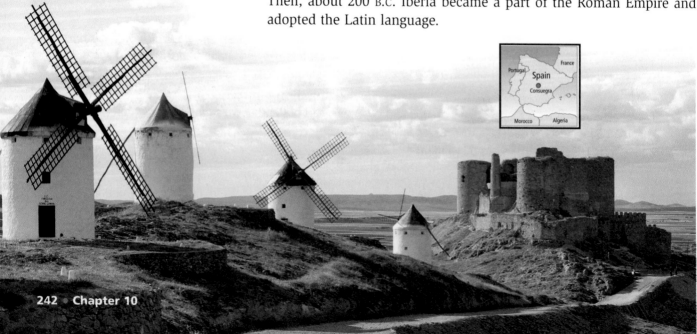

The Muslim North Africans, or **Moors**, conquered most of the Iberian Peninsula in the A.D. 700s. Graceful Moorish buildings, with their lacy patterns and archways, are still found in Spanish and Portuguese cities. This is particularly true in the old Moorish city of Granada in southern Spain.

**Great Empires** From the 1000s to the 1400s Christian rulers fought to take back the peninsula. In 1492 King Ferdinand and Queen Isabella conquered the kingdom of Granada, the last Moorish outpost in Spain. That same year, they sponsored the voyage of Christopher Columbus to the Americas. Spain soon established a large empire in the Americas.

The Portuguese also sent out explorers. Some of them sailed around Africa to India. Others crossed the Atlantic and claimed Brazil. In the 1490s the Roman Catholic pope drew a line to divide the world between Spain and Portugal. Western lands, except for Brazil, were given to Spain, and eastern lands to Portugal.

With gold and agricultural products from their American colonies, and spices and silks from Asia, Spain and Portugal grew rich. In 1588 Philip II, king of Spain and Portugal, sent a huge armada, or fleet, to invade England. The Spanish were defeated, and Spain's power began to decline. However, most Spanish colonies in the Americas did not win independence until the early 1800s.

**Government** In the 1930s the king of Spain lost power. Spain became a workers' republic. The new government tried to reduce the role of the church and to give the nobles' lands to farmers. However, conservative military leaders under General Francisco Franco resisted. A civil war was fought from 1936 to 1939 between those who supported Franco and those who wanted a democratic form of government. Franco's forces won the war and ruled Spain until 1975. Today Spain is a democracy, with a national assembly and prime minister. The king also plays a modest role as head of state.

Portugal, like Spain, was long ruled by a monarch. In the early 1900s the monarchy was overthrown. Portugal became a democracy. However, the army later overthrew the government, and a dictator took control. A revolution in the 1970s overthrew the dictatorship. For a few years disagreements between the new political parties brought violence. Portugal is now a democracy with a president and prime minister.

✓ **READING CHECK:** ( *Human Systems* ) How did Spain and Portugal move from unlimited to limited governments?

The interior of the Great Mosque in Córdoba, Spain, shows the lasting beauty of Moorish architecture. A cathedral was built within the mosque after Christians took back the city.

**Interpreting the Visual Record  Why do you think arches are important in certain building designs?**

**O**ne of the world's most endangered wild cats is the Iberian lynx. About 50 survive in a preserve on the Atlantic coast of Spain.

## Spain and Portugal

| Country | Population/ Growth Rate | Life Expectancy | Literacy Rate | Per Capita GDP |
|---|---|---|---|---|
| Portugal | 10,066,253 0.2% | 72, male 80, female | 87% | $15,800 |
| Spain | 40,037,995 0.1% | 75, male 83, female | 97% | $18,000 |
| United States | 281,421,906 0.9% | 74, male 80, female | 97% | $36,200 |

**Sources:** Central Intelligence Agency, *The World Factbook 2001;* U.S. Census Bureau

**Interpreting the Chart How do the growth rates of these countries compare?**

# Culture

The most widely understood Spanish **dialect** (DY-uh-lekt), or variation of a language, is Castilian. This is the form spoken in central Spain. Spanish and Portuguese are not the only languages spoken on the Iberian Peninsula, however. Catalan is spoken in northeastern Spain (Catalonia). Basque is spoken by an ethnic group living in the Pyrenees.

Spain faces a problem of unrest among the Basque people. The government has given the Basque area limited self-rule. However, a small group of Basque separatists continue to use violence to protest Spanish control.

**Food and Festivals** Spanish and Portuguese foods are typical of the Mediterranean region. Many recipes use olives and olive oil, lemons, wheat, wine, and fish. Foods the explorers brought back from the Americas—such as tomatoes and peppers—are also important.

Both Spain and Portugal remain strongly Roman Catholic. The two countries celebrate major Christian holidays like Christmas and Easter. As in Italy, each village has a patron saint whose special day is the occasion for a fiesta, or festival. A bull fight, or *corrida*, may take place during the festival.

**The Arts** Spanish and Portuguese art reflects the many peoples who have lived in the region. The decoration of Spanish porcelain recalls Islamic art from North Africa. The sad melodies of the Portuguese fado singers and the intense beat of Spanish flamenco dancing also show African influences. In the 1900s the Spanish painter Pablo Picasso boldly experimented with shape and perspective. He became one of the most famous artists of modern times.

✓ **READING CHECK:** **Human Systems** How has the mixture of different ethnic groups created some conflict in Spanish society?

Flamenco dancers perform at a fair in Málaga, Spain.

# Spain and Portugal Today

Like Greece and Italy, both Spain and Portugal belong to the European Union (EU). The EU allows free trade, travel, and exchange of workers among its members. The economies of Spain and Portugal have been growing rapidly. However, they remain poorer than the leading EU countries.

Agricultural products of Spain and Portugal include wine, fruit, olives, olive oil, and **cork**. Cork is the bark stripped from a certain type of oak tree. Spain exports oranges from the east, beef from the north, and lamb from ranches on the Meseta. Portugal also makes and exports clothing and timber products. Spain makes cars and trucks, and most of its industry is located in the north. Tourism is also an important part of the Spanish economy. This is particularly true along Spain's coasts and on the Balearic Islands.

Portugal's capital and largest city is Lisbon. It is located on the Atlantic coast at the mouth of the Tagus River. Madrid, Spain's capital and largest city, is located inland on the Meseta. Spain's second-largest city is the Mediterranean port of Barcelona.

Porto, Portugal, combines modern industry with the historical sea trade.

▲ A worker uses an ax to strip the bark from a cork oak.

✔ **READING CHECK:** *Places and Regions* What are Spain and Portugal like today?

**Define and explain:** Moors, dialect, cork

**Working with Sketch Maps** On the map that you created in Section 3, label Lisbon, Madrid, and Barcelona. How are Lisbon and Barcelona different from Madrid?

**Reading for the Main Idea**

1. ( *Human Systems* ) How do the performing arts of this region reflect different cultures?

2. ( *Human Systems* ) How have Spain and Portugal worked to improve their economies?

**Homework Practice Online**
Keyword: SK3 HP10

**Critical Thinking**

3. **Analyzing Information** Which groups influenced the culture of Spain and Portugal?

4. **Summarizing** How was the government of Spain organized during the 1900s?

**Organizing What You Know**

5. **Sequencing** Copy the following graphic organizer. Use it to list important events in the history of Spain and Portugal from the 700s to the 1600s.

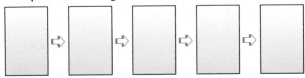

# Reviewing What You Know

## Building Vocabulary

On a separate sheet of paper, write sentences to define each of the following words.

1. mainland
2. sirocco
3. city-states
4. mosaics
5. pope
6. Renaissance
7. coalition governments
8. Moors
9. dialect
10. cork

## Reviewing the Main Ideas

1. ( *Places and Regions* ) What are the important physical features of southern Europe?

2. ( *Environment and Society* ) Why has southern Europe been a major tourist attraction for centuries?

3. ( *Human Systems* ) What are the major economic differences between northern and southern Italy?

4. ( *Human Systems* ) What is the main religion in Italy? Where is the leadership of this religion based?

5. ( *Human Systems* ) How did both Spain and Portugal become wealthy during the 1400s and 1500s?

## Understanding Environment and Society

### The Arts

Environment influences a culture's art. For example, grapes might be featured in a mosaic. Create a presentation about the influence of the environment on the arts. Write a description of each piece and explain how it might have been influenced by the artist's environment.

## Thinking Critically

1. **Drawing Influences and Conclusions** In what ways do you think the geography of southern Europe made trade and exploration possible?

2. **Summarizing** What parts of Greek culture have been most strongly influenced by Turkish customs? Why is this the case?

3. **Drawing Inferences and Conclusions** Recall what you have learned about the Roman Empire. What about the Italian peninsula made it a good location for a Mediterranean empire?

4. **Drawing Inferences and Conclusions** How are agricultural products of southern Europe used in food?

5. **Finding the Main Idea** Why do many tourists continue to visit historical cities in southern Europe?

## Map ACTIVITY

On a separate sheet of paper, match the letters on the map with their correct labels.

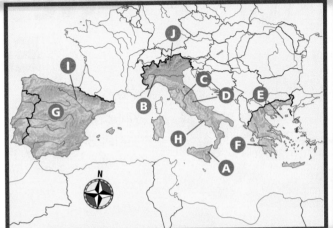

| | |
|---|---|
| Alps | Po River |
| Apennines | Tiber River |
| Aegean Sea | Naples |
| Peloponnesus | Sicily |
| Ebro River | Meseta |

## Mental Mapping Skills ACTIVITY

On a separate sheet of paper, draw a freehand map of southern Europe. Make a key for your map and label the following:

| | |
|---|---|
| Athens | Portugal |
| Greece | Rome |
| Italy | Spain |
| Mediterranean Sea | Strait of Gibraltar |

## WRITING ACTIVITY

Find a recording of Portuguese fado music. Then write a review that explains what the lyrics of the songs reveal about Portuguese culture. Be sure to use standard grammar, spelling, sentence structure, and punctuation in your review.

## Alternative Assessment

## Portfolio ACTIVITY

### Learning About Your Local Geography

**Individual Project** The cultures of southern European influence the United States in many ways. Investigate southern European influences in your community. List some of those influences in a chart.

🖅 **internet** connect

Internet Activity: go.hrw.com
KEYWORD: SK3 GT10

Choose a topic to explore southern Europe:
- Explore the islands and peninsulas on the Mediterranean coast.
- Take an online tour of ancient Greece.
- Learn the story of pizza.

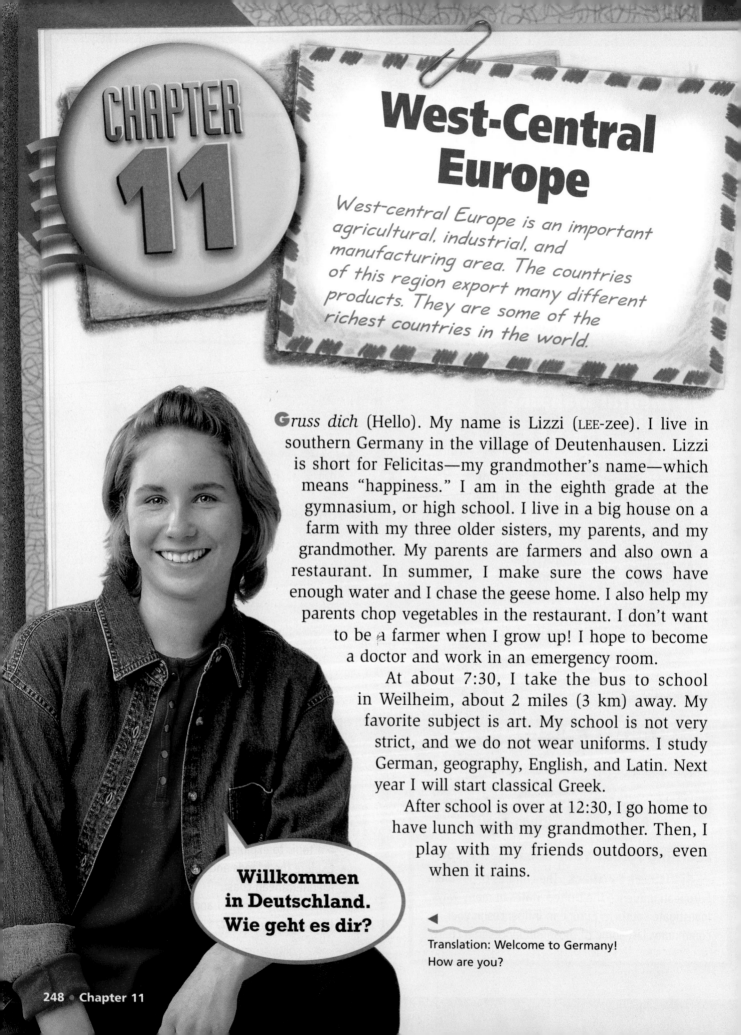

# CHAPTER 11

# West-Central Europe

West-central Europe is an important agricultural, industrial, and manufacturing area. The countries of this region export many different products. They are some of the richest countries in the world.

*Gruss dich* (Hello). My name is Lizzi (LEE-zee). I live in southern Germany in the village of Deutenhausen. Lizzi is short for Felicitas—my grandmother's name—which means "happiness." I am in the eighth grade at the gymnasium, or high school. I live in a big house on a farm with my three older sisters, my parents, and my grandmother. My parents are farmers and also own a restaurant. In summer, I make sure the cows have enough water and I chase the geese home. I also help my parents chop vegetables in the restaurant. I don't want to be a farmer when I grow up! I hope to become a doctor and work in an emergency room.

At about 7:30, I take the bus to school in Weilheim, about 2 miles (3 km) away. My favorite subject is art. My school is not very strict, and we do not wear uniforms. I study German, geography, English, and Latin. Next year I will start classical Greek.

After school is over at 12:30, I go home to have lunch with my grandmother. Then, I play with my friends outdoors, even when it rains.

**Willkommen in Deutschland. Wie geht es dir?**

◄

Translation: Welcome to Germany! How are you?

# Section 1 — Physical Geography

## Read to Discover

1. Where are the area's major landform regions?
2. What role do rivers, canals, and harbors play in the region?
3. What are west-central Europe's major resources?

## Define

navigable
loess

## Locate

Northern European Plain
Pyrenees
Alps
Seine River
Rhine River
Danube River
North Sea
Mediterranean Sea
English Channel
Bay of Biscay

### WHY IT MATTERS

Nuclear power is important in west-central Europe. However, nuclear reactors can pose problems for the environment. Use CNNfyi.com or other current events sources to find out more about alternative sources of power. Record your findings in your journal.

*Neuschwanstein Castle, Germany*

## West-Central Europe: Physical-Political

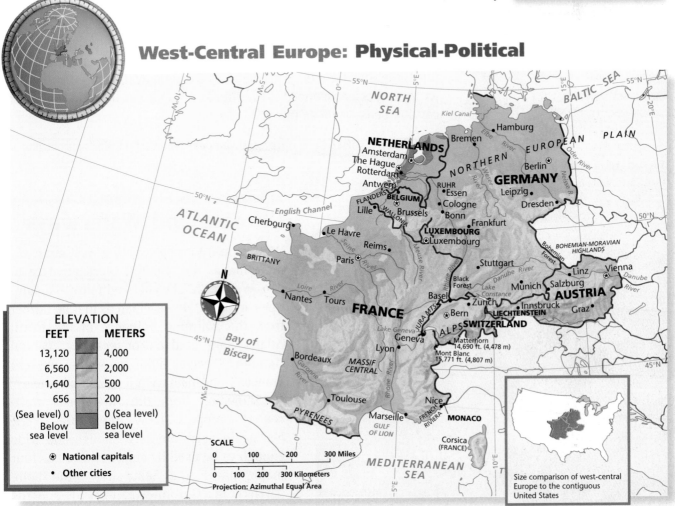

**ELEVATION**

| FEET | | METERS |
|---|---|---|
| 13,120 | | 4,000 |
| 6,560 | | 2,000 |
| 1,640 | | 500 |
| 656 | | 200 |
| (Sea level) 0 | | 0 (Sea level) |
| Below sea level | | Below sea level |

⊛ National capitals
• Other cities

SCALE
0   100   200   300 Miles
0   100   200   300 Kilometers
Projection: Azimuthal Equal Area

Size comparison of west-central Europe to the contiguous United States

The Rhine River has been an important transportation route since Roman times.

**Interpreting the Visual Record** How might the Rhine influence the location of German industry?

The Alps have many large glaciers, lakes, and valleys.

# Physical Features

West-central Europe includes France, Germany, Belgium, the Netherlands, Luxembourg, Switzerland, and Austria. Belgium, the Netherlands, and Luxembourg are called the Benelux countries. The word Benelux is a combination of the first letters of each country's name. They are also sometimes called the Low Countries. Large areas of Switzerland and Austria lie in the Alps mountain range. For this reason, they are called the Alpine countries.

**Lowlands** The main landform regions of west-central Europe are arranged like a fan. The outer edge of the fan is the Northern European Plain. Brittany, a peninsula jutting from northern France, rises slightly above the plain. In Belgium and the Netherlands, the Northern European Plain dips below sea level.

**Uplands** Toward the middle of the fan a wide band of uplands begins at the Pyrenees (PIR-uh-neez) Mountains. Another important uplands region is the Massif Central (ma-SEEF sahn-TRAHL) in France. Most of the southern two thirds of Germany is hilly. The Schwarzwald (SHFAHRTS-vahlt), or Black Forest, occupies the southwestern corner of Germany's uplands region.

**Mountains** At the center of the fan are the Alps, Europe's highest mountain range. Many peaks in the Alps reach heights of more than 14,000 feet (4,267 m). The highest peak, France's Mont Blanc (mawn BLAHN), reaches to 15,771 feet (4,807 m). Because of their high elevations, the Alps have large glaciers and frequent avalanches. During the Ice Age, glaciers scooped great chunks of rock out of the mountains, carving peaks such as the Matterhorn.

✓ **READING CHECK:** *Places and Regions* What are the area's major landforms?

# Climate and Waterways

West-central Europe's marine west coast climate makes the region a pleasant place to live. Winters can be cold and rainy, but summers are mild. However, areas that lie farther from the warming influence of the North Atlantic are colder. For example, central Germany receives more snow than western France. The Alps have a highland climate.

Snowmelt from the Alps feeds west-central Europe's many **navigable** rivers. Navigable rivers are deep enough and wide enough to be used by ships. France has four major rivers: the Seine (SEN), the Loire (LWAHR), the Garonne (gah-RAWN), and the

Rhone (ROHN). Germany has five major rivers: the Rhine (RYN), the Danube (DAN-yoob), the Elbe (EL-buh), the Oder (OH-duhr), and the Weser (VAY-zuhr). These rivers and the region's many canals are important for trade and travel. Many large harbor cities are located where rivers flow into the North Sea, Mediterranean Sea, English Channel, or Bay of Biscay. The region's heavily indented coastline has hundreds of excellent harbors.

✓ **READING CHECK:** *Environment and Society* What economic role do rivers, canals, and harbors play in west-central Europe?

## Resources

Most of the forests that once covered west-central Europe were cut down centuries ago. The fields that remained are now some of the most productive in the world. Germany's plains are rich in **loess** (LES)—fine, wind-blown soil deposits. Germany and France produce grapes for some of the world's finest wines. Switzerland's Alpine pastures support dairy cattle.

▲ The Grindelwald Valley in Switzerland has excellent pastures.

The distribution of west-central Europe's mineral resources is uneven. Germany and France have deposits of iron ore but must import oil. Energy resources are generally in short supply in the region. However, there are deposits of coal in Germany and natural gas in the Netherlands. Nuclear power helps fill the need for energy, particularly in France and Belgium. Alpine rivers provide hydroelectric power in Switzerland and Austria. Natural beauty is perhaps the Alpine countries' most valuable natural resource, attracting millions of tourists every year.

**BUILD on WHAT You Know**

**D**o you remember what you learned about hydroelectric power? See Chapter 4 to review.

✓ **READING CHECK:** *Environment and Society* What geographic factors contribute to the economy of the region?

go.hrw.com **Homework Practice Online** Keyword: SK3 HP11

## Section Review 1

**Define and explain:** navigable, loess

**Working with Sketch Maps** On a map of west-central Europe that you draw or that your teacher provides, label the following: the Northern European Plain, Alps, North Sea, Mediterranean Sea, English Channel, and Bay of Biscay.

### Reading for the Main Idea

1. *Places and Regions* What are the landform regions of west-central Europe?

2. *Places and Regions* What type of climate dominates this region?

### Critical Thinking

3. **Making Generalizations and Predictions** What might be the advantages of having many good harbors and navigable rivers?

4. **Drawing Inferences and Conclusions** How do you think an uneven distribution of resources has affected this region?

### Organizing What You Know

5. **Categorizing** Copy the following graphic organizer. Use it to describe the major rivers of west-central Europe. Add rows as needed.

| River | Country/Countries | Flows into. . . |
|-------|-------------------|-----------------|
|       |                   |                 |
|       |                   |                 |
|       |                   |                 |

## Read to Discover

1. Which foreign groups affected the historical development of France?
2. What are the main features of French culture?
3. What products does France export?

### WHY IT MATTERS

France is a key member of NATO, the North Atlantic Treaty Organization. Use CNNfyi.com or other current events sources to find out more about NATO. Record your findings in your journal.

## Define

medieval
NATO
impressionism

## Locate

Brittany
Normandy
Paris
Marseille
Nice

*French croissants*

In this illustration messengers inform Charlemagne of a recent military victory.

# History

France has been occupied by people from many other parts of Europe. In ancient times, France was part of a region known as Gaul. Thousands of years ago, people moved from eastern Europe into Gaul. These people spoke Celtic languages related to modern Welsh and Gaelic. Breton is a Celtic language still spoken in the region of Brittany.

**Early History** About 600 B.C. the Greeks set up colonies on Gaul's southern coast. Several centuries later, the Romans conquered Gaul. They introduced Roman law and government to the area. The Romans also established a Latin-based language that developed into French.

Roman rule lasted until the A.D. 400s. A group of Germanic people known as the Franks then conquered much of Gaul. It is from these people that France takes its name. Charlemagne was the Franks' greatest ruler. He dreamed of building a Christian empire that would be as great as the old Roman Empire. In honor of this, the pope crowned Charlemagne Emperor of the Romans in

A.D. 800. During his rule, Charlemagne did much to strengthen government and improve education and the arts in Europe.

The Franks divided Charlemagne's empire after his death. Invading groups attacked from many directions. The Norsemen, or Normans, were one of these groups. They came from northern Europe. The area of western France where the Normans settled is known today as Normandy.

The period from the collapse of the Roman Empire to about 1500 is called the Middle Ages, or **medieval** period. The word medieval comes from the Latin words *medium*, meaning "middle," and *aevum*, meaning "age." During much of this period kings in Europe were not very powerful. They depended on cooperation from nobles, some of whom were almost as powerful as kings.

In 1066 a noble, the duke of Normandy, conquered England, becoming its king. As a result, the kings of England also ruled part of France. In the 1300s the king of England tried to claim the throne of France. This led to the Hundred Years' War, which lasted from 1337 to 1453. Eventually, French armies drove the English out of France. The French kings then slowly increased their power over the French nobles.

During the Middle Ages the Roman Catholic Church created a sense of unity among many Europeans. Many tall, impressive cathedrals were built during this time. Perhaps the most famous is the Cathedral of Notre Dame in Paris. It took almost 200 years to build.

French and English knights clash in this depiction of the Hundred Years' War.

**Revolution and Napoléon's Empire** From the 1500s to the 1700s France built a global empire. The French established colonies in the Americas, Asia, and Africa. During this period most French people lived in poverty and had few rights. In 1789 the French Revolution began. The French overthrew their king and established an elected government. About 10 years later a brilliant general named Napoléon Bonaparte took power. As he gained control, he took the title of emperor. Eventually, Napoléon conquered most of Europe. Napoléon built new roads throughout France, reformed the French educational system, and established the metric system of measurement. In 1815 an alliance including Austria, Great Britain, Prussia, and Russia finally defeated Napoléon. The French king regained the throne.

**World Wars** During World War I (1914–18) the German army controlled parts of northern and eastern France. In the early years of World War II, Germany defeated France and occupied the northern and western parts of the country. In 1944, Allied armies including U.S., British, and Canadian soldiers landed in Normandy and drove the Germans out. However, after two wars in 30 years France was devastated. Cities, factories, bridges, railroad lines, and train stations had been destroyed. The North Atlantic Treaty Organization, or **NATO**, was formed in 1949 with France as a founding member. This military alliance was created to defend Western Europe against future attacks.

Napoléon Bonaparte became the ruler of France and conquered most of Europe.

The euro replaced the currencies of most of the individual EU countries.
**Interpreting the Visual Record** **What are the advantages of a shared currency?**

Many French cheeses, such as Brie, Camembert, and Roquefort, are named after the places where they are made.

Workers harvest grapes at a vineyard in the Rhone Valley near Lyon.
**Interpreting the Visual Record** **Has modern technology changed the grape-growing process?**

**Government** In the 1950s and 1960s most French colonies in Asia and Africa achieved independence. However, France still controls several small territories around the world. Today, France is a republic with a parliament and an elected president. France is also a founding member of the European Union (EU). France is gradually replacing its currency, the franc, with the EU currency, the euro.

✓ **READING CHECK:** ( *Human Systems* ) Which foreign groups have affected France's historical development?

# Culture

About 90 percent of French people are Roman Catholic, and 3 percent practice Islam. Almost all French citizens speak French. However, small populations of Bretons in the northwest and Basques in the southwest speak other languages. In Provence-Alpes-Côte d'Azur and Languedoc-Roussillon in the south and on the island of Corsica, some people speak regional dialects along with French. Immigrants from former colonies in Africa, the Caribbean, and Southeast Asia also influence French culture through their own styles of food, clothing, music, and art.

**Customs** In southern France people eat Mediterranean foods like wheat, olives and olive oil, cheeses, and garlic. In the north food is more likely to be prepared with butter, herbs, and mushrooms. Wine is produced in many French regions, and France produces more than 400 different cheeses. French people celebrate many festivals, including Bastille Day on July 14. On this date in 1789 a mob stormed the Bastille, a royal prison in Paris. The French recognize this event as the beginning of the French Revolution.

**The Arts and Literature** France has a respected tradition of poetry, philosophy, music, and the visual arts. In the late 1800s and early 1900s France was the center of an artistic movement called **impressionism**. Impressionist artists tried to capture the rippling of light rather than an exact, realistic image. Famous impressionists include Monet, Renoir, and Degas. French painters, like Cézanne and Matisse, influenced styles of modern painting. Today, France is a world leader in the arts and film industry.

| France | | | | |
|---|---|---|---|---|
| COUNTRY | POPULATION/ GROWTH RATE | LIFE EXPECTANCY | LITERACY RATE | PER CAPITA GDP |
| France | 59,551,227 0.4% | 75, male 83, female | 99% | $24,400 |
| United States | 281,421,906 0.9% | 74, male 80, female | 97% | $36,200 |

**Sources:** Central Intelligence Agency, *The World Factbook 2001*; U.S. Census Bureau

**Interpreting the Chart** How do France's life expectancy and literacy rate compare to those of the United States?

✔ **READING CHECK:** *Human Systems* How did French art affect the world?

## France Today

France is a major agricultural and industrial country. Its resources, labor force, and location in the heart of Europe have helped spur economic growth. France exports wheat, olives, wine, and cheeses as well as other dairy products. French factories produce cars, airplanes, shoes, clothing, machinery, and chemicals. France's largest city is Paris, which has nearly 10 million people in its metropolitan area. Other major cities include Marseille, Nice, Lyon, and Lille. France's major cities are linked by high-speed trains and excellent highways.

✔ **READING CHECK:** *Human Systems* What are some products that France exports?

go. hrw .com **Homework Practice Online** Keyword: SK3 HP11

**Section Review 2**

**Define and explain:** medieval, NATO, impressionism

**Working with Sketch Maps** On the map you created in Section 1, label Brittany, Normandy, Paris, Marseille, and Nice.

**Reading for the Main Idea**

1. *Human Systems* What were the main periods of French history?

2. *Human Systems* What are the main features of French culture?

**Critical Thinking**

3. **Finding the Main Idea** What were some long-lasting achievements of Charlemagne and Napoléon?

4. **Summarizing** What is the French economy like?

**Organizing What You Know**

5. **Identifying Cause and Effect** Copy the following graphic organizer. Use it to list the causes and effects of the Hundred Years' War.

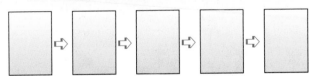

# Section 3

## Germany

### Read to Discover

1. What effects have wars had on Germany?
2. What are Germany's major contributions to world culture?
3. How did the division of Germany affect its economy?

### Define

Reformation
Holocaust
chancellor

### Locate

Berlin
Bonn
Essen
Frankfurt
Munich
Hamburg
Cologne

**WHY IT MATTERS**

The Berlin Wall had fallen by 1990, and East and West Germany were reunited as a single nation. What have been the effects of reunification? Use CNNfyi.com or other current events sources to find out more about Germany. Record your findings in your journal.

*A VW Turbo beetle*

This medieval castle overlooks a German town.

**Interpreting the Visual Record** **What geographic features made this a good place to build a fortress?**

## History

Many Germans are descendants of tribes that migrated from northern Europe in ancient times. The Romans conquered the western and southern fringes of the region. They called this land Germania, from the name of one of the tribes that lived there.

**The Holy Roman Empire** When the Roman Empire collapsed, the Franks became the most important tribe in Germany. The lands ruled by the Frankish king Charlemagne in the early 800s included most of what is now Germany. Charlemagne's empire was known as the Holy Roman Empire.

**Reformation and Unification** During the 1500s Germany was the center of the **Reformation**—a movement to reform Christianity. The reformers were called Protestants. Protestants rejected many practices of the Roman Catholic Church. At the time, Germany was made up of many small states. Each state was ruled by a prince who answered to the Holy Roman emperor. Many of the princes became Protestants. This angered the Holy Roman emperor, who was Catholic. He sent armies against the princes. Although the princes won the right to choose the religion of their states, conflict continued. This conflict eventually led to the Thirty Years' War (1618–48). This war was costly. Many towns were destroyed and nearly one third of the population died. Germany remained divided for more than 200 years. In the late 1800s Prussia, the strongest state, united Germany.

**World Wars** In 1914 national rivalries and a conflict in the Balkans led to World War I. Austria, Germany, and the Ottoman Empire, later joined by Bulgaria, fought against Britain, France, and Russia, later joined by Italy and the United States. By 1918 Germany and its allies were defeated.

During the 1920s Austrian war veteran Adolf Hitler led a new political party in Germany called the Nazis. The Nazis took power in 1933. In the late 1930s Germany invaded Austria, Czechoslovakia, and finally Poland, beginning World War II. By 1942 Germany and Italy had conquered most of Europe. The Nazis forced many people from the occupied countries into concentration camps to be enslaved or killed. About 6 million Jews and millions of other people were murdered in a mass killing called the **Holocaust**.

To defeat Germany, several countries formed an alliance. These Allies included Britain, the Soviet Union, the United States, and many others. The Allies defeated Germany in 1945. Germany and its capital, Berlin, were divided into Soviet, French, British, and U.S. occupation zones. Britain, France, and the United States later combined their zones to create a democratic West Germany with its capital at Bonn. In its zone, the Soviet Union set up the Communist country of East Germany with an unlimited totalitarian government. Its capital became East Berlin; however, West Berlin became part of West Germany. In 1961 the East German government built the Berlin Wall across the city to stop East Germans from escaping to the West.

**Reunification and Modern Government** West Germany's roads, cities, railroads, and industries were rebuilt after the war with U.S. financial aid. East Germany was also rebuilt, but it was not as prosperous as West Germany. Unlike the West German government, the East German government allowed people very little freedom. Also, its command economy—managed by the government—was less productive than the free enterprise, market system of West Germany. In the late 1980s East Germans and people throughout Eastern Europe demanded democratic reform. In 1989 the Berlin Wall was torn down. In 1990 East and West Germany reunited. Germany's capital again became Berlin. Today, all Germans enjoy democratic rights. A parliament elects the president and prime minister, or **chancellor**. Germany is a member of the EU and NATO.

✓ **READING CHECK:** ( *Human Systems* ) How were the economies of East and West Germany organized following World War II?

▲

German youth salute Adolf Hitler in Nürnberg in 1938.

▲

For nearly 30 years the Berlin Wall separated East and West Berlin. Many people in West Berlin protested by painting graffiti on the wall.

**Interpreting the Visual Record** Why would the government make the wall solid instead of a barrier that would allow people visual access?

# Culture

About 34 percent of Germans are Roman Catholic, and 38 percent are Protestant. Most other Germans have no religious association. Many of these people are from eastern Germany, where the communist government suppressed religion from 1945 to 1990.

**Diversity**  About 90 percent of Germany's inhabitants are ethnic Germans. However, significant numbers of Turks, Poles, and Italians have come to Germany to live and work. These "guest workers" do not have German citizenship. Germany has also taken in thousands of refugees from Eastern Europe during the last 50 years.

**Customs**  Traditional German food emphasizes the products of the forests, farms, and seacoasts. Each region produces its own varieties of sausage, cheese, wine, and beer. German celebrations include Oktoberfest; *Sangerfast,* a singing festival; and *Fastnacht,* a religious celebration. The major German festival season is Christmas. The Germans began the custom of bringing an evergreen tree indoors at Christmas and decorating it with candles.

**The Arts and Literature**  Germany has a great tradition of literature, music, and the arts. The first European to print books using movable metal type was a German, Johannes Gutenberg. In the 1700s and 1800s, Germany led Europe in the development of classical music. World-famous German composers include Johann Sebastian Bach and Ludwig van Beethoven. The operas of Richard Wagner revived the folktales of ancient Germany.

✓ READING CHECK:  ( *Human Systems* )  What technology and other contributions have Germans made to world culture?

Crowds gather in a German town for a Christmas market. Christmas markets have been popular in Germany for more than 400 years. From the beginning of Advent until Christmas, booths are set up on the market place in most cities. Here people can buy trees, decorations, and gifts.

**Interpreting the Visual Record** **What does this photo suggest about the importance of Christmas in Germany?**

# Germany Today

Germany has a population of 83 million, more people than any other European country. Germany also has Europe's largest economy. Nearly one fourth of all goods and services produced by the EU come from Germany.

**Economy** Ample resources, labor, and capital have made Germany one of the world's leading industrial countries. The nation exports a wide variety of products. You may be familiar with German automakers like Volkswagen, Mercedes-Benz, and BMW. The German government provides education, medical care, and pensions for its citizens, but Germans pay high taxes. Unemployment is high. Many immigrants work at low-wage jobs. These "guest workers" are not German citizens and cannot receive many government benefits. Since reunification, Germany has struggled to modernize the industries, housing, and other facilities of the former East Germany.

**Cities** Germany's capital city, Berlin, is a large city with wide boulevards and many parks. Berlin was isolated and economically restricted during the decades after World War II. However, Germans are now rebuilding their new capital to its former splendor.

Near the Rhine River and the coal fields of Western Germany is a huge cluster of cities, including Essen and Düsseldorf. They form Germany's largest industrial district, the Ruhr. Frankfurt is a city known for banking and finance. Munich is a manufacturing center. Other important cities include Hamburg, Bremen, Cologne, and Stuttgart.

✓ **READING CHECK:**  ( *Human Systems* )  How did the division of Germany affect its economy?

### Germany

| COUNTRY | POPULATION/ GROWTH RATE | LIFE EXPECTANCY | LITERACY RATE | PER CAPITA GDP |
|---|---|---|---|---|
| Germany | 83,029,536 0.3% | 74, male 81, female | 99% | $23,400 |
| United States | 281,421,906 0.9% | 74, male 80, female | 97% | $36,200 |

**Sources:** Central Intelligence Agency, *The World Factbook 2001*; U.S. Census Bureau

**Interpreting the Chart** What might the literacy rate of Germany suggest about its culture?

---

## Section Review 3

Homework Practice Online
Keyword: SK3 HP11

**Define and explain:** Reformation, Holocaust, chancellor

**Working with Sketch Maps** On the map you created in Section 2, label Berlin, Bonn, Essen, Frankfurt, Munich, Hamburg, and Cologne.

### Reading for the Main Idea

1. ( *Human Systems* ) How did wars affect the development of Germany in the 1900s?

2. ( *Human Systems* ) What are some notable features of the German economy?

### Critical Thinking

3. **Drawing Inferences and Conclusions** How has Germany's history influenced the religious makeup of the population?

4. **Summarizing** What have been some results of the unification of Germany in 1990?

### Organizing What You Know

5. **Sequencing** Create a time line listing key events in the history of Germany from 1000 B.C. to 1990.

1000 B.C.                                          A.D. 1990

# The Benelux Countries

## Read to Discover

1. How were the Benelux countries influenced by larger countries?
2. What is this region's culture like?
3. What are the Benelux countries like today?

## Define

cosmopolitan

## Locate

Flanders    Antwerp
Wallonia    Brussels
Amsterdam

### WHY IT MATTERS

The Benelux countries are key members of the European Union (EU). Use  or other **current events** sources to find out more about the membership, functions, and goals of the EU. Record your findings in your journal.

*Dutch wooden shoes*

The Dutch city of Rotterdam is one of the world's busiest ports.

**Interpreting the Visual Record** Why might this city be an important transportation center?

## History

Celtic and Germanic tribes once lived in this region, as in most of west-central Europe. They were conquered by the Romans. After the fall of the Roman Empire and the conquests of Charlemagne, the region was ruled alternately by French rulers and by the Holy Roman emperor.

In 1555 the Holy Roman emperor presented the Low Countries to his son, King Philip II of Spain. In the 1570s the Protestants of the Netherlands won their freedom from Spanish rule. Soon after, the Netherlands became a great naval and colonial power. Belgium had been ruled at times by France and the Netherlands. However, by 1830 Belgium had broken away to become an independent kingdom.

Both world wars scarred this region. Many of the major battles of World War I were fought in Belgium. Then in World War II Germany occupied the Low Countries. In 1949 Belgium, the Netherlands, and Luxembourg were founding members of NATO. Later they joined the EU. Today, each of the three countries is ruled by a parliament and a monarch. The monarchs' duties are mostly ceremonial. The Netherlands controls several Caribbean islands. However, its former colonies in Asia and South America are now independent.

✓ **READING CHECK:** *Human Systems* How are the governments of the Benelux countries organized?

# CONNECTING TO *Technology*

## Dutch Polders

Much of the Netherlands lies below sea level and was once covered with water. For at least 2,000 years, the Dutch have been holding back the sea. First they lived on raised earthen mounds. Later they built walls or dikes to keep the water out. After building dikes, the Dutch installed windmills to pump the water out of reclaimed areas, called polders.

Using this system, the Dutch have reclaimed large amounts of land. Cities like Amsterdam and Rotterdam sit on reclaimed land. The dike and polder system has become highly sophisticated. Electric pumps have largely replaced windmills, and dikes now extend along much of the country's coastline. However, this system is difficult to maintain. It requires frequent and expensive repairs. Creating polders has

*A polder in the Netherlands*

also produced sinking lowlands and other environmental damage. As a result, the Dutch are considering changes to the system. These changes might include restoring some of the polders to wetlands and lakes.

**Understanding What You Read**
1. What are polders?
2. How did the Dutch use technology to live on land previously under water?

## Culture

The people of Luxembourg and Belgium are mostly Roman Catholic. The Netherlands is more evenly divided among Catholic, Protestant, and those who have no religious ties. Dutch is the language of the Netherlands. Flemish is a language related to Dutch that is spoken in Flanders, the northern part of Belgium. Belgium's coast and southern interior are called Wallonia. People in Wallonia speak mostly French and are called Walloons. In the past, cultural differences between Flemish and Walloons have produced conflict in Belgium. Today street signs and other notices are often printed in both Flemish and French. The Benelux countries are also home to immigrants from Asia and Africa.

These children in Brussels, Belgium, are wearing traditional clothing.

## Benelux Countries

| COUNTRY | POPULATION/ GROWTH RATE | LIFE EXPECTANCY | LITERACY RATE | PER CAPITA GDP |
|---|---|---|---|---|
| Belgium | 10,258,762 0.2% | 75, male 81, female | 98% | $25,300 |
| Luxembourg | 442,972 1.3% | 74, male 81, female | 100% | $36,400 |
| Netherlands | 15,807,641 0.5% | 75, male 81, female | 99% | $24,400 |
| United States | 281,421,906 0.9% | 74, male 80, female | 97% | $36,200 |

**Sources:** Central Intelligence Agency, *The World Factbook 2001;* U.S. Census Bureau

**Interpreting the Chart** Which country's per capita GDP is closest to that of the United States?

The region's foods include dairy products, fish, and sausage. The Dutch spice trade led to dishes flavored with spices from Southeast Asia. The Belgians claim they invented french fries, which they eat with mayonnaise.

The Netherlands and Belgium have been world leaders in fine art. In the 1400s and 1500s, Flemish artists painted realistic portraits and landscapes. Dutch painters like Rembrandt and Jan Vermeer experimented with different qualities of light. In the 1800s Dutch painter Vincent van Gogh portrayed southern France with bold brush strokes and bright colors.

✔ **READING CHECK:** ( *Human Systems* ) What is the relationship between cultures in Belgium?

# The Benelux Countries Today

The Netherlands is famous for its flowers, particularly tulips. Belgium and the Netherlands export cheeses, chocolate, and cocoa. Amsterdam and Antwerp, Belgium, are major diamond-cutting centers. The Netherlands also imports and refines oil. Luxembourg earns much of its income from services such as banking. The region also produces steel, chemicals, and machines. Its **cosmopolitan** cities are centers of international business and government. A cosmopolitan city is one that has many foreign influences. Brussels, Belgium, is the headquarters for many international organizations such as the EU and NATO.

✔ **READING CHECK:** ( *Places and Regions* ) What are the Benelux countries like today?

go. hrw .com **Homework Practice Online**
**Keyword: SK3 HP11**

## Section Review 4

**Define and explain:** cosmopolitan

**Working with Sketch Maps** On the map you created in Section 3, label Flanders, Wallonia, Amsterdam, Antwerp, and Brussels.

### Reading for the Main Idea

1. ( *Human Systems* ) What are the main cultural features of the Benelux countries?

2. ( *Human Systems* ) In what ways do the people of the Benelux countries differ?

### Critical Thinking

3. **Drawing Inferences and Conclusions** Why might the economies of the Benelux countries be dependent on international trade?

4. **Analyzing Information** Why have groups in Belgium been in conflict?

### Organizing What You Know

5. **Comparing** Copy the following graphic organizer. Use it to compare the Benelux countries' industries.

| Belgium | Luxembourg | Netherlands |
|---|---|---|
| | | |

# Section 5 — The Alpine Countries

## Read to Discover

1. What are some of the major events in the history of the Alpine countries?
2. What are some cultural features of this region?
3. How are the economies of Switzerland and Austria similar?

## Define

cantons
nationalism

## Locate

Geneva    Zurich
Salzburg  Basel
Vienna    Bern

### WHY IT MATTERS

When people think of chocolate they often think of Switzerland, one of the world's leading producers of chocolate. Use **CNNfyi.com** or other **current events** sources to find out more about chocolate. Record your findings in your journal.

*Swiss cuckoo clock*

## History

Austria and Switzerland share a history of Celtic occupation, Roman and Germanic invasions, and rule by the Holy Roman Empire.

**Switzerland** Swiss **cantons**, or districts, gradually broke away from the Holy Roman Empire, and in the 1600s Switzerland became independent. Today Switzerland is a confederation of 26 cantons. Each controls its own internal affairs, and the national government handles defense and international relations. Switzerland's location in the high Alps has allowed it to remain somewhat separate from the rest of Europe. It has remained neutral in the European wars of the last two centuries. Switzerland has not joined the United Nations, EU, or NATO. Because of this neutrality, the Swiss city of Geneva is home to many international organizations.

**Austria** During the Middle Ages, Austria was a border region of Germany. This region was the home of the Habsburgs, a powerful family of German nobles. From the 1400s onward the Holy Roman emperor was always a Habsburg. At the height of their power the Habsburgs ruled Spain and the Netherlands, as well as large areas of Germany, eastern Europe, and Italy. This empire included different

The International Red Cross has offices in almost every country in the world.

**Interpreting the Visual Record What symbol of the Red Cross is displayed on this building?**

263

The Danube River passes through Vienna, the capital of Austria.

**Interpreting the Visual Record** How does this river influence movement and trade?

Austrians wearing carved wooden masks celebrate the return of spring and milder weather.

ethnic groups, each with its own language, government, and system of laws. The empire was united only in its allegiance to the emperor and in its defense of the Roman Catholic religion.

With the conquests of Napoléon after 1800, the Holy Roman Empire was formally eliminated. It was replaced with the Austrian Empire, which was also under Habsburg control. When Napoléon was defeated, the Austrian Empire became the dominant power in central Europe.

Through the 1800s the diverse peoples of the empire began to develop **nationalism**, or a demand for self-rule. In 1867 the Austrians agreed to share political power with the Hungarians. The Austrian Empire became the Austro-Hungarian Empire. After World War I the empire was dissolved. Austria and Hungary became separate countries. Shortly before World War II the Germans took over Austria and made it part of Germany. After the war, the Allies occupied Austria. Today Austria is an independent member of the EU.

✓ **READING CHECK:** *Human Systems* What were the major events in the history of the Alpine countries?

## Culture

About 46 percent of the population in Switzerland is Roman Catholic, and 40 percent is Protestant. Austria's population is mainly Roman Catholic. Only about 5 percent of its people are Protestant, while 17 percent follow Islam or other religions.

**Languages and Diversity** About 64 percent of Swiss speak German, 19 percent speak French, and 8 percent speak Italian. Small groups in the southeast speak a language called Romansh. Other European languages are also spoken in Switzerland. Austria is almost entirely German-speaking, but contains small minorities of Slovenes and Croatians.

**Customs** Christmas is a major festival in both countries. People make special cakes and cookies at this time. In rural parts of Switzerland people take cattle up to the high mountains in late spring and return in the fall. Their return is celebrated by decorating homes and cows' horns with flowers. A special feast is also prepared.

The Alpine region is particularly well known for its music. In the 1700s Mozart wrote symphonies and operas in the Austrian city of Salzburg. Every year a music festival is held there in his honor. Austria's capital, Vienna, is also known as a center of music and fine art.

✓ **READING CHECK:** *Human Systems* What role have the arts played in this region?

## The Alpine Countries

| COUNTRY | POPULATION/ GROWTH RATE | LIFE EXPECTANCY | LITERACY RATE | PER CAPITA GDP |
|---|---|---|---|---|
| Austria | 8,150,835 0.2% | 75, male 81, female | 98% | $25,500 |
| Switzerland | 7,283,274 0.3% | 77, male 83, female | 99% | $28,600 |
| United States | 281,421,906 0.9% | 74, male 80, female | 97% | $36,200 |

**Sources:** Central Intelligence Agency, *The World Factbook 2001;* U.S. Census Bureau

**Interpreting the Chart** **How do the populations of the Alpine countries compare with that of the United States?**

# The Alpine Countries Today

Switzerland and Austria both produce dairy products, including many kinds of cheese. Switzerland is also famous for the manufacturing of watches, optical instruments, and other machinery. Swiss chemists discovered how to make chocolate bars. Switzerland is a major producer of chocolate, although it must import the cocoa beans.

Switzerland and Austria are linked to the rest of Europe by excellent highways, trains, and airports. Several long tunnels allow trains and cars to pass through mountains in the Swiss Alps. Both countries attract many tourists with their mountain scenery, lakes, and ski slopes.

Located on the Danube, Vienna is Austria's commercial and industrial center. Switzerland's two largest cities are both in the German-speaking north. Zurich is a banking center, while Basel is the starting point for travel down the Rhine to the North Sea. Switzerland's capital is Bern, and Geneva is located in the west.

✓ **READING CHECK:** *Human Systems* How are the economies of Switzerland and Austria similar?

**go. hrw .com** **Homework Practice Online** Keyword: SK3 HP11

## Section Review 5

**Define and explain:** cantons, nationalism

**Working with Sketch Maps** On the map you created in Section 4, label Geneva, Salzburg, Vienna, Zurich, Basel, and Bern.

### Reading for the Main Idea

1. *Human Systems* What were the main events in the history of the Alpine countries?

2. *Human Systems* What are some notable aspects of Swiss and Austrian culture?

### Critical Thinking

3. **Drawing Inferences and Conclusions** How might geography have been a factor in Switzerland's historical neutrality?

4. **Drawing Inferences and Conclusions** How have foreign invasions of Austria shaped its history?

### Organizing What You Know

5. **Comparing/Contrasting** Use this graphic organizer to compare and contrast the culture, language, economies, and history of Switzerland and Austria.

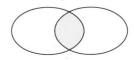

# Reviewing What You Know

## Building Vocabulary

On a separate sheet of paper, write sentences to define each of the following words.

1. navigable
2. loess
3. medieval
4. impressionism
5. Reformation
6. Holocaust
7. chancellor
8. cosmopolitan
9. cantons
10. nationalism

## Reviewing the Main Ideas

1. ( *Places and Regions* ) What is the climate of west-central Europe like?
2. ( *Human Systems* ) What were the effects of religious conflicts on Germany?
3. ( *Places and Regions* ) What energy resources are available to the countries of this region?
4. ( *Human Systems* ) Name five artists from west-central Europe who have made notable contributions to culture.
5. ( *Human Systems* ) What international organizations have created ties between countries of west-central Europe since World War II?

## Understanding Environment and Society

### Cleaning up Pollution

Create a presentation on East German industries' pollution of the environment. Include a chart, graph, database, model, or map showing patterns of pollutants, as well as the German government's clean-up effort. Consider the following:
• Pollution in the former East Germany.
• Pollution today.
• Costs of stricter environmental laws.
Write a five-question quiz, with answers about your presentation to challenge fellow students.

## Thinking Critically

1. **Drawing Inferences and Conclusions** What geographic features have encouraged travel and trade in west-central Europe? What geographic features have hindered travel and trade?

2. **Finding the Main Idea** How have the people of Switzerland altered their environment?

3. **Analyzing Information** What landform regions give France natural borders? Which French borders do not coincide with physical features?

4. **Drawing Inferences and Conclusions** Why might Brussels, Belgium, be called the capital of Europe?

5. **Comparing** What demographic factors are shared by all countries of west-central Europe today? How do they reflect levels of economic development?

### Map ACTIVITY

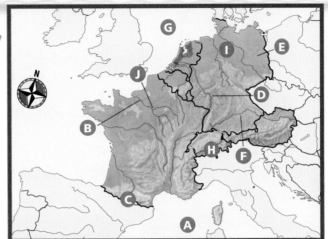

On a separate sheet of paper, match the letters on the map with their correct labels.

| | |
|---|---|
| Northern European Plain | Danube River |
| Pyrenees | North Sea |
| Alps | Mediterranean Sea |
| Seine River | Paris |
| Rhine River | Berlin |

### Mental Mapping Skills ACTIVITY

On a separate sheet of paper, draw a freehand map of west-central Europe. Make a key for your map and label the following:

| | |
|---|---|
| Austria | Luxembourg |
| Belgium | the Netherlands |
| France | North Sea |
| Germany | Switzerland |

### WRITING ACTIVITY

Imagine you are taking a boat tour down the Rhine River. You will travel from Basel, Switzerland, to Rotterdam, the Netherlands. Keep a journal describing the places you see and the stops you make. Be sure to use standard grammar, spelling, sentence structure, and punctuation.

## Alternative Assessment

### Portfolio ACTIVITY

**Learning About Your Local Geography**
**Agricultural Products** Some countries in west-central Europe are major exporters of agricultural products. Research the agricultural products of your state. Draw a map that shows important products and areas they are produced.

▣ **internet** connect

Internet Activity: **go.hrw.com**
KEYWORD: **SK3 GT11**

Choose a topic to explore about west-central Europe:
- Tour the land and rivers of Europe.
- Travel back in time to the Middle Ages.
- Visit Belgian and Dutch schools.

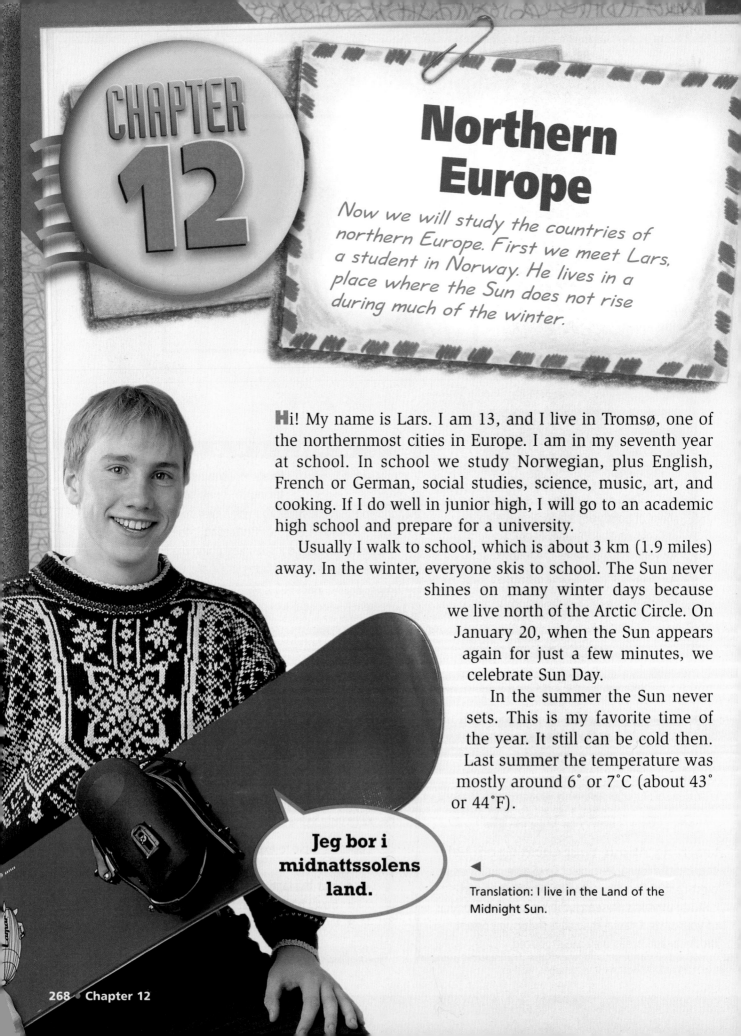

# CHAPTER 12

# Northern Europe

*Now we will study the countries of northern Europe. First we meet Lars, a student in Norway. He lives in a place where the Sun does not rise during much of the winter.*

Hi! My name is Lars. I am 13, and I live in Tromsø, one of the northernmost cities in Europe. I am in my seventh year at school. In school we study Norwegian, plus English, French or German, social studies, science, music, art, and cooking. If I do well in junior high, I will go to an academic high school and prepare for a university.

Usually I walk to school, which is about 3 km (1.9 miles) away. In the winter, everyone skis to school. The Sun never shines on many winter days because we live north of the Arctic Circle. On January 20, when the Sun appears again for just a few minutes, we celebrate Sun Day.

In the summer the Sun never sets. This is my favorite time of the year. It still can be cold then. Last summer the temperature was mostly around 6° or 7°C (about 43° or 44°F).

**Jeg bor i midnattssolens land.**

◀

Translation: I live in the Land of the Midnight Sun.

# Section 1 — Physical Geography

## Read to Discover

1. What are the region's major physical features?
2. What are the region's most important natural resources?
3. What climates are found in northern Europe?

## Define

fjords      lochs      North Atlantic Drift

## Locate

British Isles
English Channel
North Sea
Great Britain

Ireland
Iceland
Greenland
Scandinavian
    Peninsula

Jutland Peninsula
Kjølen Mountains
Northwest Highlands
Shannon River
Baltic Sea

### WHY IT MATTERS

An important physical feature of Northern Europe is the North Sea. Use CNNfyi.com or other current events sources to learn more about America's dependence on oil. Record your findings in your journal.

*A Viking ship post*

## Northern Europe: Physical-Political

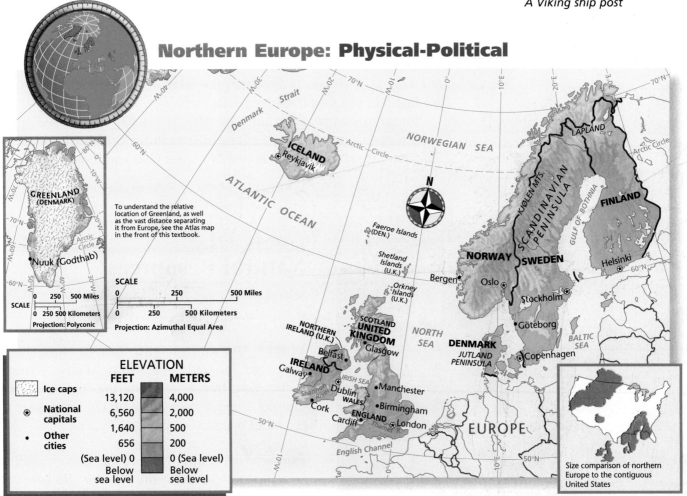

To understand the relative location of Greenland, as well as the vast distance separating it from Europe, see the Atlas map in the front of this textbook.

GREENLAND (DENMARK)

Nuuk (Godthab)

SCALE
0   250   500 Miles
0  250 500 Kilometers
Projection: Polyconic

SCALE
0        250        500 Miles
0        250        500 Kilometers
Projection: Azimuthal Equal Area

**ELEVATION**

| | FEET | METERS |
|---|---|---|
| Ice caps | | |
| National capitals | 13,120 | 4,000 |
| | 6,560 | 2,000 |
| Other cities | 1,640 | 500 |
| | 656 | 200 |
| | (Sea level) 0 | 0 (Sea level) |
| | Below sea level | Below sea level |

Size comparison of northern Europe to the contiguous United States

**S**cotland's Loch Ness contains more fresh water than all the lakes in England and Wales combined. It is deeper, on average, than the nearby North Sea.

# Physical Features

Northern Europe includes several large islands and peninsulas. The British Isles lie across the English Channel and North Sea from the rest of Europe. They include the islands of Great Britain and Ireland and are divided between the United Kingdom and the Republic of Ireland. This region also includes the islands of Iceland and Greenland. Greenland is the world's largest island.

To the east are the Scandinavian and Jutland Peninsulas. Denmark occupies the Jutland Peninsula and nearby islands. The Scandinavian Peninsula is divided between Norway and Sweden. Finland lies farther east. These countries plus Iceland make up Scandinavia.

**Landforms** The rolling hills of Ireland, the highlands of Great Britain, and the Kjølen (CHUH-luhn) Mountains of Scandinavia are part of Europe's Northwest Highlands region. This is a region of very old, eroded hills and low mountains.

Southeastern Great Britain and southern Scandinavia are lowland regions. Much of Iceland is mountainous and volcanic. More than 10 percent of it is covered by glaciers. Greenland is mostly covered by a thick ice cap.

**Coasts** Northern Europe has long, jagged coastlines. The coastline of Norway includes many **fjords** (fee-AWRDS). Fjords are narrow, deep inlets of the sea set between high, rocky cliffs. Ice-age glaciers carved the fjords out of coastal mountains.

**Lakes and Rivers** Melting ice-age glaciers left behind thousands of lakes in the region. In Scotland, the lakes are called **lochs**. Lochs are found in valleys carved by glaciers long ago.

Northern Europe does not have long rivers like the Mississippi River in the United States. The longest river in the British Isles is the Shannon River in Ireland. It is just 240 miles (390 km) long.

✓ **READING CHECK:** *Places and Regions* What are the physical features of the region?

Fjords like this one shelter many harbors in Norway.

**Interpreting the Visual Record**
**How are fjords created?**

▼

# Natural Resources

Northern Europe has many resources. They include water, forests, and energy sources.

**Water** The ice-free North Sea is especially important for trade and fishing. Parts of the Baltic Sea freeze over during the winter months. Special ships break up the ice to keep sea lanes open to Sweden and Finland.

**Forests and Soil** Most of Europe's original forests were cleared centuries ago. However,

Sweden and Finland still have large, coniferous forests that produce timber. The region's farmers grow many kinds of cool-climate crops.

**Energy** Beneath the North Sea are rich oil and natural gas reserves. Nearly all of the oil reserves are controlled by the nearby United Kingdom and Norway. However, these reserves cannot satisfy all of the region's needs. Most countries import oil and natural gas from southwest Asia, Africa, and Russia. Some, such as Iceland, use geothermal and hydroelectric power.

✓ **READING CHECK:** ( *Environment and Society* ) In what way has technology allowed people in the region to keep the North Sea open during the winter?

# Climate

Despite its northern location, much of the region has a marine west coast climate. Westerly winds blow over a warm ocean current called the **North Atlantic Drift**. These winds bring mild temperatures and rain to the British Isles and coastal areas. Atlantic storms often bring even more rain. Snow and frosts may occur in winter.

Central Sweden and southern Finland have a humid continental climate. This area has four true seasons. Far to the north are subarctic and tundra climates. In the forested subarctic regions, winters are long and cold with short days. Long days fill the short summers. In the tundra region it is cold all year. Only small plants such as grass and moss grow there.

✓ **READING CHECK:** ( *Places and Regions* ) What are the region's climates?

**D**o you remember what you learned about ocean currents? See Chapter 3 to review.

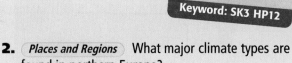

Homework Practice Online
Keyword: SK3 HP12

**Define and explain:** fjords, lochs, North Atlantic Drift

**Working with Sketch Maps** On an outline map that you draw or that your teacher provides, label the following: British Isles, English Channel, North Sea, Great Britain, Ireland, Iceland, Greenland, Scandinavian Peninsula, Jutland Peninsula, Kjølen Mountains, Northwest Highlands, Shannon River, and Baltic Sea. In the margin, write a short caption explaining how the North Atlantic Drift affects the region's climates.

**Reading for the Main Idea**

1. ( *Places and Regions* ) Which parts of northern Europe are highland regions? Which parts are lowland regions?

2. ( *Places and Regions* ) What major climate types are found in northern Europe?

**Critical Thinking**

3. **Finding the Main Idea** How has ice shaped the region's physical geography?

4. **Making Generalizations and Predictions** Think about what you have learned about global warming. How might warmer temperatures affect the climates and people of northern Europe?

**Organizing What You Know**

5. **Summarizing** Copy the following graphic organizer. Use it to describe the region's important natural resources.

| Water | Forests and soil | Energy |
|---|---|---|
|  |  |  |

# Section 2  The United Kingdom

## Read to Discover

1. What are some important events in the history of the United Kingdom?
2. What are the people and culture of the country like?
3. What is the United Kingdom like today?

## Define

textiles
constitutional
 monarchy
glen

## Locate

England
Scotland
Wales
Northern Ireland
Irish Sea
London

Birmingham
Manchester
Glasgow
Cardiff
Belfast

### WHY IT MATTERS

The United States has been heavily influenced by the British people. Use CNNfyi.com or other current events sources to find out about present-day ties between the United States and Great Britain. Record your findings in your journal.

*British crown*

▲ Early peoples of the British Isles built Stonehenge in stages from about 3100 B.C. to about 1800 B.C.

## History

Most of the British are descended from people who came to the British Isles long ago. The Celts (KELTS) are thought by some scholars to have come to the islands around 450 B.C. Mountain areas of Wales, Scotland, and Ireland have remained mostly Celtic.

Later, from the A.D. 400s to 1000s, new groups of people came. The Angles and Saxons came from northern Germany and Denmark. The Vikings came from Scandinavia. Last to arrive in Britain were the Normans from northern France. They conquered England in 1066. English as spoken today reflects these migrations. It combines elements from the Anglo-Saxon and Norman French languages.

**A Global Power** England became a world power in the late 1500s. Surrounded by water, the country developed a powerful navy that protected trade routes. In the 1600s the English began establishing colonies around the world. By the early 1800s they had also united England, Scotland, Wales, and Ireland into one kingdom. From London the United Kingdom built a vast British Empire. By 1900 the empire covered nearly one fourth of the world's land area.

▶ This beautiful Anglo-Saxon shoulder clasp from about A.D. 630 held together pieces of clothing.

The United Kingdom also became an economic power in the 1700s and 1800s. It was the cradle of the Industrial Revolution, which began in the last half of the 1700s. Large supplies of coal and iron and a large labor force helped industries grow. The country also developed a good transportation network of rivers, canals, and railroads. Three of the early industries were **textiles**, or cloth products, shipbuilding, iron, and later steel. Coal powered these industries. Birmingham, Manchester, and other cities grew up near Britain's coal fields.

**Decline of Empire** World wars and economic competition from other countries weakened the United Kingdom in the 1900s. All but parts of northern Ireland became independent in 1921. By the 1970s most British colonies also had gained independence. Most now make up the British Commonwealth of Nations. Members of the Commonwealth meet to discuss economic, scientific, and business matters.

The United Kingdom still plays an important role in world affairs. It is a leading member of the United Nations (UN), the European Union (EU), and the North Atlantic Treaty Organization (NATO).

**The Government** The United Kingdom's form of government is called a **constitutional monarchy**. That is, it has a monarch—a king or queen—but a parliament makes the country's laws. The monarch is the head of state but has largely ceremonial duties. Parliament chooses a prime minister to lead the national government.

In recent years the national government has given people in Scotland and Wales more control over local affairs. Some people think Scotland might one day seek independence.

✓ **READING CHECK:** *Human Systems* How are former British colonies linked today?

▲

Queen Elizabeth I (1533–1603) ruled England as it became a world power in the late 1500s.

The British government is seated in London, the capital. The Tower Bridge over the River Thames [TEMZ] is one of the city's many famous historical sites.

**Interpreting the Visual Record**
**Why do you think London became a large city?**

▼

Millions of Americans watched the Beatles, a British rock band, perform on television in 1964. The Beatles and other British bands became popular around the world.

**Interpreting the Visual Record** How do you think television helps shape world cultures today?

# Culture

Nearly 60 million people live in the United Kingdom today. English is the official language. Some people in Wales and Scotland also speak the Celtic languages of Welsh and Gaelic [GAY-lik]. The Church of England is the country's official church. However, many Britons belong to other Protestant churches or are Roman Catholic.

**Food and Festivals** Living close to the sea, the British often eat fish. One popular meal is fish and chips—fried fish and potatoes. However, British food also includes different meats, oat porridge and cakes, and potatoes in many forms.

The British celebrate many religious holidays, such as Christmas. Other holidays include the Queen's official birthday celebration in June. In July many Protestants in Northern Ireland celebrate a battle in 1690 in which Protestants defeated Catholic forces. In recent years the day's parades have sometimes sparked protests and violence between Protestants and Catholics.

**Art and Literature** British literature, art, and music have been popular around the world. Perhaps the most famous British writer is William Shakespeare. He died in 1616, but his poetry and plays, such as *Romeo and Juliet*, remain popular. In the 1960s the Beatles helped make Britain a major center for modern popular music. More recently, British performers from Elton John to the Spice Girls have attracted many fans.

✓ **READING CHECK:** *Human Systems* What aspects of British culture have spread around the world?

## The United Kingdom

| COUNTRY | POPULATION/ GROWTH RATE | LIFE EXPECTANCY | LITERACY RATE | PER CAPITA GDP |
|---------|------------------------|-----------------|---------------|----------------|
| United Kingdom | 59,647,790 0.2% | 75, male 81, female | 99% | $22,800 |
| United States | 281,421,906 0.9% | 74, male 80, female | 97% | $36,200 |

**Sources:** Central Intelligence Agency, *The World Factbook 2001;* U.S. Census Bureau

**Interpreting the Chart** How does the literacy rate in the United Kingdom compare with that of the United States?

# The United Kingdom Today

Nearly 90 percent of Britons today live in urban areas. London, the capital of England, is the largest city. It is located in southeastern England. London is also the capital of the whole United Kingdom.

More than 7 million people live in London. The city is a world center for trade, industry, and services, particularly banking and insurance. London also has one of the world's busiest airports. Many tourists visit London to see its famous historical sites, theaters, and shops. Other important cities include Glasgow, Scotland; Cardiff, Wales; and Belfast, Northern Ireland.

**The Economy** Old British industries like mining and manufacturing declined after World War II. Today, however, the economy is stronger. North Sea reserves have made the country a major producer of oil and natural gas. Birmingham, Glasgow, and other cities are attracting new industries. One area of Scotland is called Silicon Glen. This is because it has many computer and electronics businesses. **Glen** is a Scottish term for a valley. Today many British work in service industries, including banking, insurance, education, and tourism.

**Agriculture** Britain's modern farms produce about 60 percent of the country's food. Still, only about 1 percent of the labor force works in agriculture. Important products include grains, potatoes, vegetables, and meat.

**Northern Ireland** One of the toughest problems facing the country has been violence in Northern Ireland. Sometimes Northern Ireland is called Ulster. The Protestant majority and the Roman Catholic minority there have bitterly fought each other. Violence on both sides has resulted in many deaths.

Many Catholics believe they have not been treated fairly by the Protestant majority. Therefore, many want Northern Ireland to join the mostly Roman Catholic Republic of Ireland. Protestants fear becoming a minority on the island. They want to remain part of the United Kingdom. Many people hope that recent agreements made by political leaders will lead to a lasting peace. In 1999, for example, Protestant and Roman Catholic parties agreed to share power in a new government. However, there have been problems putting that agreement into effect.

✓ **READING CHECK:** ( *Human Systems* ) What has been the cause of conflict in Northern Ireland?

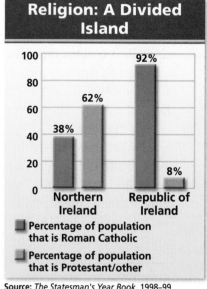

**Religion: A Divided Island**

Source: *The Statesman's Year Book, 1998–99.*

**Interpreting the Graph** How does the number of Roman Catholics in the Republic of Ireland differ from that of Northern Ireland?

---

# Section Review 2

**go.hrw.com**
**Homework Practice Online**
Keyword: SK3 HP12

**Define and explain:** textiles, constitutional monarchy, glen

**Working with Sketch Maps** On the map you created in Section 1, label the United Kingdom, England, Scotland, Wales, Northern Ireland, Irish Sea, London, Birmingham, Manchester, Glasgow, Cardiff, and Belfast.

### Reading for the Main Idea

**1.** ( *Human Systems* ) What peoples came to the British Isles after the Celts? When did they come?

**2.** ( *Places and Regions* ) What was the British Empire?

### Critical Thinking

**3. Contrasting** How is the British government different from the U.S. government?

**4. Drawing Inferences and Conclusions** Why do you think Protestants in Northern Ireland want to remain part of the United Kingdom?

### Organizing What You Know

**5. Sequencing** Create a timeline that lists important events in the period.

*800 B.C.*            A.D. 2000

# CASE STUDY

## MAPPING THE SPREAD OF CHOLERA

Medical geographers want to discover why a disease occurs in a particular place. Does a disease occur in a certain type of environment? Is there a pattern to the way a disease spreads? Mapping is one tool medical geographers use to answer these questions. They first used maps in this way to fight cholera.

Cholera has existed in India for hundreds of years. It did not appear in Europe, however, until the 1800s. At that time better transportation systems helped spread cholera around the world. For example, in 1817 India experienced an unusually bad outbreak of the disease. India was then part of the British Empire. British soldiers and ships carried cholera to new places. By 1832 the disease had spread to the British Isles and to North America.

No one knew what caused cholera. In fact, no one knew about bacteria or how they caused disease. What was known was that sick people suffered from diarrhea and vomiting. They often died quickly. In just 10 days in 1854, more than 500 people in one London neighborhood died from cholera. Dr. John Snow thought he knew why.

Dr. Snow believed that people got cholera from dirty water. To test his theory, he mapped the location of some of London's public water pumps. (Houses at that time did not have running water.) Then he marked the location of each cholera death on his map. He found most of the deaths were scattered around the water pump on Broad Street. He persuaded officials to remove the pump's handle. After the pump was shut down, there were few new cases of cholera. Not everyone, however, believed Dr. Snow's evidence.

This illustration shows London's Regent Street in about 1850. An outbreak of cholera in this neighborhood killed hundreds of people in 1854.

# Cholera Deaths in London, 1854

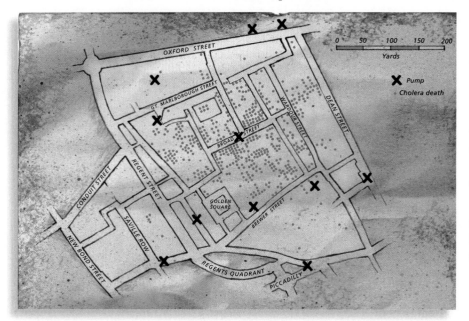

Dr. Snow plotted cholera deaths for the first 10 days of September 1854 on a map of the neighborhood. Dr. Snow believed that people were getting impure water from the Broad Street pump. A check of the pump showed that a leaking sewer had contaminated the pump's water.

**Interpreting the Map** What does the map tell you about the relationship between deaths and the Broad Street pump?

Bacteria was discovered in the 1880s. Yet many people still believed that bad air from river mud or swamps spread diseases like cholera. It took another epidemic to convince everyone that dirty water made people sick.

In 1892 an outbreak of cholera in the German port city of Hamburg ended the debate. Once again, the locations of people who became sick were mapped. This mapping was the key to proving that water could spread cholera.

At the time, a street separated Hamburg and another town, Altona. Both towns got their water from the Elbe River. There was, however, an important difference in the two towns' water supplies. Altona had a system for cleaning its water. Hamburg did not. People living on the Hamburg side of the street got sick. Those on the Altona side of the street did not. The air on both sides of the street was the same. Therefore, no one could argue that bad air caused the outbreak. Hamburg then moved quickly to install a system to clean its water.

## Understanding What You Read

1. Why did Dr. Snow make a map of a neighborhood's cholera deaths and the location of its water pumps?

2. Why was it important that people on the Hamburg side of the street got sick but people on the Altona side did not?

Dr. John Snow, 1813–1858, was one of the first medical geographers.

## Read to Discover

1. What are the key events in Ireland's history?
2. What are the people and culture of Ireland like?
3. What kinds of economic changes has Ireland experienced in recent years?

## Define

famine
bog
peat

## Locate

Dublin
Cork
Galway

### WHY IT MATTERS

Millions of Americans trace their heritage to Ireland. Use **CNNfyi.com** or other **current events** sources to learn about Ireland and its people today. Record your findings in your journal.

*An Irish harp*

# History

The Irish are descendants of the Celts. Irish Gaelic, a Celtic language, and English are the official languages. Most people in Ireland speak English. Gaelic is spoken mostly in rural western areas.

**English Conquest** England conquered Ireland in the A.D. 1100s. By the late 1600s most of the Irish had become farmers on land owned by the British. This created problems between the two peoples. Religious differences added to these problems. Most British were Protestant, while most Irish were Roman Catholic. Then, in the 1840s, millions of Irish left for the United States and other countries because of a poor economy and a potato **famine**. A famine is a great shortage of food.

**Independence** The Irish rebelled against British rule. In 1916, for example, Irish rebels attacked British troops in the Easter Rising.

Stone fences divide the green fields of western Ireland, the Emerald Isle.

**Interpreting the Visual Record** **What kind of climate would you expect to find in a country with rich, green fields such as these?**

At the end of 1921, most of Ireland gained independence. Some counties in northern Ireland remained part of the United Kingdom. Ties between the Republic of Ireland and the British Empire were cut in 1949.

**Government** Ireland has an elected president and parliament. The president has mostly ceremonial duties. Irish voters in 1990 elected a woman as president for the first time.

The parliament makes the country's laws. The Irish parliament chooses a prime minister to lead the government.

✓ **READING CHECK:** *Human Systems* What are some important events in Ireland's history?

# Culture

Centuries of English rule have left their mark on Irish culture. For example, today nearly everyone in Ireland speaks English. Irish writers, such as George Bernard Shaw and James Joyce, have been among the world's great English-language writers.

A number of groups promote traditional Irish culture in the country today. The Gaelic League, for example, encourages the use of Irish Gaelic. Gaelic and English are taught in schools and used in official documents. Another group promotes Irish sports, such as hurling. Hurling is an outdoor game similar to field hockey and lacrosse.

Elements of Irish culture have also become popular outside the country. For example, traditional Irish folk dancing and music have attracted many fans. Music has long been important in Ireland. In fact, the Irish harp is a national symbol. Many musicians popular today are from Ireland, including members of the rock band U2.

More than 90 percent of the Irish today are Roman Catholic. St. Patrick's Day on March 17 is a national holiday. St. Patrick is believed to have brought Christianity to Ireland in the 400s.

✓ **READING CHECK:** *Human Systems* What is Irish culture like today?

▲
Many Irish enjoy a meal of lamb chops with mustard sauce, soda bread, carrots, and mashed potatoes.

# Ireland Today

Ireland used to be one of Europe's poorest countries. Today it is a modern, thriving country with a strong economy and growing cities.

| COUNTRY | POPULATION/ GROWTH RATE | LIFE EXPECTANCY | LITERACY RATE | PER CAPITA GDP |
|---------|------------------------|-----------------|---------------|----------------|
| Ireland | 3,840,838 1.1% | 74, male 80, female | 98% | $21,600 |
| United States | 281,421,906 0.9% | 74, male 80, female | 97% | $36,200 |

**Sources:** Central Intelligence Agency, *The World Factbook 2001;* U.S. Census Bureau

**Interpreting the Chart** **How does life expectancy in Ireland compare with that of the United States?**

**Economy** Until recently, Ireland was mostly an agricultural country. This was true even though much of the country is either rocky or boggy. A **bog** is soft ground that is soaked with water. For centuries, **peat** dug from bogs has been used for fuel. Peat is made up of dead plants, usually mosses.

Today Ireland is an industrial country. Irish workers produce processed foods, textiles, chemicals, machinery, crystal, and computers. Finance, tourism, and other service industries are also important.

How did this change come about? Ireland's low taxes, well-educated workers, and membership in the European Union have attracted many foreign companies. Those foreign companies include many from the United States. These companies see Ireland as a door to millions of customers throughout the EU. In fact, goods from their Irish factories are exported to markets in the rest of Europe and countries in other regions.

**Cities** Many factories have been built around Dublin. Dublin is Ireland's capital and largest city. It is a center for education, banking, and shipping. Nearly 1 million people live there. Housing prices rapidly increased in the 1990s as people moved there for work.

Other cities lie mainly along the coast. These cities include the seaports of Cork and Galway. They have old castles, churches, and other historical sites that are popular among tourists.

✔ READING CHECK: (Human Systems) What important economic changes have occurred in Ireland and why?

Homework Practice Online Keyword: SK3 HP12

# Section Review 3

**Define and explain:** famine, bog, peat

**Working with Sketch Maps** On the map you created in Section 2, label Ireland, Dublin, Cork, and Galway. In the margin explain the importance of Dublin to the Republic of Ireland.

## Reading for the Main Idea

**1.** (Human Systems) What were two of the reasons many Irish moved to the United States and other countries in the 1800s?

**2.** (Human Systems) What are some important reasons why the economy in Ireland has grown so much in recent years?

## Critical Thinking

**3.** **Drawing Inferences and Conclusions** Why do you think the Irish fought against British rule?

**4.** **Drawing Inferences and Conclusions** Why do you suppose housing prices rapidly increased in Dublin in the 1990s?

## Organizing What You Know

**5.** **Comparing/Contrasting** Copy the following graphic organizer. Use it to compare and contrast the history, culture, and governments of the Republic of Ireland and the United Kingdom.

| Ireland | United Kingdom |
|---------|----------------|
| Conquered by England in the 1100s | Created vast world empire |

# Section 4

## Scandinavia

### Read to Discover

1. What are the people and culture of Scandinavia like?
2. What are some important features of each of the region's countries, plus Greenland, and Lapland?

### Define

neutral
uninhabitable
geysers

### Locate

Oslo
Bergen
Stockholm
Göteborg
Copenhagen
Nuuk (Godthab)

Reykjavik
Gulf of Bothnia
Gulf of Finland
Helsinki
Lapland

Smoked salmon, a popular food in Scandinavia

### WHY IT MATTERS

Much of the fish Americans eat comes from the nations of Scandinavia. Use CNNfyi.com or other current events sources to learn more about the economic importance of these nations. Record your findings in your journal.

## People and Culture

Scandinavia once was home to fierce, warlike Vikings. Today the countries of Norway, Sweden, Denmark, Iceland, and Finland are peaceful and prosperous.

The people of the region enjoy high standards of living. They have good health care and long life spans. Each government provides expensive social programs and services. These programs are paid for by high taxes.

The people and cultures in the countries of Scandinavia are similar in many ways. For example, the region's national languages, except for Finnish, are closely related. In addition, most people in Scandinavia are Lutheran Protestant. All of the Scandinavian countries have democratic governments.

✓ **READING CHECK:**
*Human Systems* How are the people and cultures of Scandinavia similar?

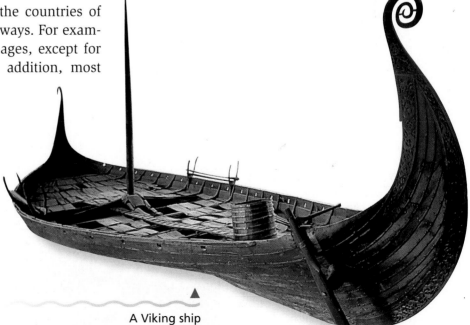

A Viking ship

## Scandinavia

| Country | Population/ Growth Rate | Life Expectancy | Literacy Rate | Per Capita GDP |
|---------|-------------------------|-----------------|---------------|----------------|
| Denmark | 5,352,815 0.3% | 74, male 80, female | 100% | $25,500 |
| Finland | 5,175,783 0.2% | 74, male 81, female | 100% | $22,900 |
| Iceland | 277,906 0.5% | 77, male 82, female | 100% | $24,800 |
| Norway | 4,503,440 0.5% | 76, male 82, female | 100% | $27,700 |
| Sweden | 8,875,053 .02% | 77, male 83, female | 99% | $22,200 |
| United States | 281,421,906 0.9% | 74, male 80, female | 97% | $36,200 |

**Sources:** Central Intelligence Agency, *The World Factbook 2001;* U.S. Census Bureau

**Interpreting the Chart** **What is noteworthy about life expectancy in Iceland, Norway, and Sweden?**

# Norway

Norway is a long, narrow, and rugged country along the western coast of the Scandinavian Peninsula. Norway once was united with Denmark and then Sweden. In 1905 Norway became independent. Today Norway is a constitutional monarchy with an elected parliament.

About 75 percent of the people live in urban areas. The largest cities are the capital, Oslo, and Bergen on the Atlantic coast. Oslo is a modern city. It lies at the end of a wide fjord on the southern coast. The city is Norway's leading seaport, as well as its industrial and cultural center.

Norway has valuable resources, especially oil and natural gas. However, Norway's North Sea oil fields are expected to run dry over the next century. A long coastline and location on the North Sea have helped make Norway a major fishing and shipping country. Fjords shelter Norway's harbors and its fishing and shipping fleets.

# Sweden

Sweden is Scandinavia's largest and most populous country. It is located between Norway and Finland. Most Swedes live in cities and towns. The largest cities are Stockholm, which is Sweden's capital, and Göteborg. Stockholm is located on the Baltic Sea coast. It is a beautiful city of islands and forests. Göteborg is a major seaport.

Like Norway, Sweden is a constitutional monarchy. The country has been at peace since the early 1800s. Sweden remained **neutral** during World Wars I and II. A neutral country is one that chooses not to take sides in an international conflict.

Sweden's main sources of wealth are forestry, farming, mining, and manufacturing. Wood, iron ore, automobiles, and wireless telephones are exports. Hydroelectricity is important.

Riddarholmen—Knight's Island—is one of several islands on which the original city of Stockholm was built.

**Interpreting the Visual Record** **Why might a group of islands be a good place to build a city?**

# CONNECTING TO Art

*A stave church in Norway*

# Stave Churches

In Norway you will find some beautiful wooden churches built during the Middle Ages. They are known as stave churches because of their corner posts, or staves. The staves provide the building's basic structure. Today stave churches are a reminder of the days when Viking and Christian beliefs began to merge in Norway.

As many as 800 stave churches were built in Norway during the 1000s and 1100s. Christianity was then beginning to spread throughout the country. It was replacing the old religious beliefs of the Viking people. Still, Viking culture is clearly seen in stave buildings.

Except for a stone foundation, stave churches are made entirely of wood. Workers used methods developed by Viking boat builders. For example, wood on Viking boats was coated with tar to keep it from rotting. Church builders did the same with the wood for their churches. They also decorated the churches with carvings of dragons and other creatures. The stave church at Urnes even has a small Viking ship decorated with nine candles.

When the plague, or Black Death, arrived in Norway about 1350, many communities were abandoned. Many stave churches fell apart. Others were replaced by larger stone buildings. Today only 28 of the original buildings remain. They have been preserved for their beauty and as reminders of an earlier culture.

**Understanding What You Read**
1. What are staves?
2. How did stave churches reflect new belief systems in Norway?

# Denmark

Denmark is the smallest and most densely populated of the region's countries. Most of Denmark lies on the Jutland Peninsula. About 500 islands make up the rest of the country.

Denmark is also a constitutional monarchy. The capital and largest city is Copenhagen. It lies on an island between the Jutland Peninsula and Sweden. Some 1.4 million people—about 25 percent of Denmark's population—live there.

About 60 percent of Denmark's land is used for farming. Farm products, especially meat and dairy products, are important exports. Denmark also has a modern industrial economy. Industries include food processing, machinery, furniture, and electronics.

Greenland's capital lies on the island's southwestern shore.

*Interpreting the Visual Record*

**Why do most people in Greenland live along the coast?**

**The Great Geysir in southwestern Iceland can spout water nearly 200 feet (61 m) into the air. Some geysers shoot steam and boiling water to a height of more than 1,600 feet (nearly 500 m)!**

# Greenland

The huge island of Greenland is part of North America, but it is a territory of Denmark. Greenland's 56,000 people have their own government. They call their island Kalaallit Nunaat. The capital is Nuuk, also called Godthab. Most of the island's people are Inuit (Eskimo). Fishing is the main economic activity. Some Inuit still hunt seals and small whales.

The island's icy interior is **uninhabitable**. An uninhabitable area is one that cannot support human settlement. Greenland's people live mostly along the southwestern coast in the tundra climate regions.

# Iceland

Between Greenland and Scandinavia is the country of Iceland. This Atlantic island belonged to Denmark until 1944. Today it is an independent country. It has an elected president and parliament.

Unlike Greenland, Iceland is populated mostly by northern Europeans. The capital and largest city is Reykjavik (RAYK-yuh-veek). Nearly 40 percent of the country's people live there.

Icelanders make good use of their country's natural resources. For example, about 70 percent of the country's exports are fish. These fish come from the rich waters around the island. In addition, hot water from Iceland's **geysers** heats homes and greenhouses. The word *geyser* is an Icelandic term for hot springs that shoot hot water and steam into the air. Volcanic activity forces heated underground water to rise from the geyser.

# Finland

Finland is the easternmost of the region's countries. It lies mostly between two arms of the Baltic Sea: the Gulf of Bothnia and the Gulf of Finland. The capital and largest city is Helsinki, which is located on the southern coast.

The original Finnish settlers probably came from northern Asia. Finnish belongs to a language family that includes Estonian and Hungarian. About 6 percent of Finns speak Swedish. Finland was part of Sweden from the 1100s to 1809. It then became part of Russia. Finland gained independence at the end of World War I.

As in the other countries of the region, trade is important to Finland. The country is a major producer of paper and other forest products as well as wireless telephones. Metal products, shipbuilding, and electronics are also important industries. Finland imports energy and many of the raw materials needed in manufacturing.

## Lapland

Across northern Finland, Sweden, and Norway is a culture region known as Lapland. This region is populated by the Lapps, or Sami, as they call themselves.

The Sami are probably descended from hunters who moved to the region from northern Asia. The languages they speak are related to Finnish. The Sami have tried to keep their culture and traditions, such as reindeer herding. Many now earn a living from tourism.

▲

Young Sami couples here are dressed in traditional clothes for the Easter reindeer races in northern Norway.

**Interpreting the Visual Record** What climates would you find in the lands of the Sami?

✓ **READING CHECK:** ( *Human Systems* ) Around what activities are the economies of the countries and territories discussed in this section organized?

**Define and explain:** neutral, uninhabitable, geysers

**Working with Sketch Maps** On the map you created in Section 3, label the countries of Scandinavia, Oslo, Bergen, Stockholm, Göteborg, Copenhagen, Nuuk (Godthab), Reykjavik, Gulf of Bothnia, Gulf of Finland, Helsinki, and Lapland. In the margin describe the people of the Lapland region.

### Reading for the Main Idea

1. ( *Human Systems* ) What are two of the cultural similarities among the peoples of Scandinavia?

2. ( *Environment and Society* ) In what ways have Icelanders adapted to their natural environment?

3. ( *Human Systems* ) How have the history and culture of Finland been different from that of other countries in Scandinavia?

### Critical Thinking

4. **Making Generalizations and Predictions** How do you think the location of Greenland and the culture of its people will affect the island's future relationship with Denmark?

### Organizing What You Know

5. **Summarizing** Copy the following graphic organizer. Label the center of the organizer "Scandinavia." In the ovals, write one characteristic of each country and region discussed in this section. Then do the same for the other countries, as well as for Greenland and Lapland.

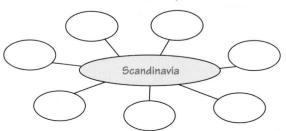

Scandinavia

# Reviewing What You Know

## Building Vocabulary

On a separate sheet of paper, write sentences to define each of the following words.

1. fjords
2. lochs
3. North Atlantic Drift
4. constitutional monarchy
5. famine
6. bog
7. peat
8. neutral
9. uninhabitable
10. geysers

## Reviewing the Main Ideas

1. ( *Places and Regions* ) What islands make up the British Isles? What bodies of water surround the British Isles?

2. ( *Places and Regions* ) What are the four main climates in northern Europe?

3. ( *Places and Regions* ) What large North Atlantic island is a territory of Denmark?

4. ( *Human Systems* ) What happened to the British Empire?

5. ( *Human Systems* ) What are the two major religions in Northern Ireland? What do these religions have to do with violence in Northern Ireland?

## Understanding Environment and Society

### Resource Use

Prepare a presentation, along with a map, graph, chart, model, or database, on the distribution of oil and natural gas in the North Sea. You may want to think about the following:

- How oil and natural gas are recovered there.
- How countries divided up the North Sea's oil and natural gas.

Write a five-question quiz, with answers, about your presentation to challenge fellow students.

## Thinking Critically

1. **Drawing Inferences and Conclusions** Why do you think British literature, art, and music have been popular around the world?

2. **Drawing Inferences and Conclusions** Why do you think industrial cities like Birmingham and Manchester in Great Britain grew up near coal deposits?

3. **Drawing Inferences and Conclusions** Why do you think most Irish speak English rather than Gaelic?

4. **Making Generalizations and Predictions** How do you think Scandinavians have adapted to life in these very cold environments?

5. **Finding the Main Idea** Why are climates in the British Isles milder than in much of Scandinavia?

## Map ACTIVITY

On a separate sheet of paper, match the letters on the map with their correct labels.

| | |
|---|---|
| London | Oslo |
| Manchester | Stockholm |
| Belfast | Copenhagen |
| Dublin | Reykjavik |
| Cork | Helsinki |

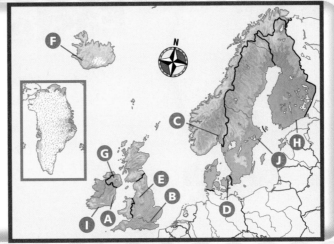

## Mental Mapping Skills ACTIVITY

On a separate sheet of paper, draw a freehand map of northern Europe. Make a key for your map and label the following:

| | |
|---|---|
| Baltic Sea | Ireland |
| Denmark | Norway |
| Finland | Scandinavian |
| Great Britain | Peninsula |
| Iceland | Sweden |

## WRITING ACTIVITY

Use print resources to find out more about the Vikings and how they lived in their cold climate. Write a short story set in a Viking village or on a Viking voyage. Describe daily life in the village or on the voyage. Include a bibliography showing references you used. Be sure to use standard grammar, spelling, sentence structure, and punctuation.

## Alternative Assessment

## Portfolio ACTIVITY

**Learning About Your Local Geography**

**Research Project** Northern Europe's social programs are supported by taxes. Research the taxes that people in your area must pay. Interview residents, asking their feelings about taxes.

🔗 **internet** connect

Internet Activity: **go.hrw.com**
KEYWORD: SK3 GT12

Choose a topic to explore northern Europe:
- Explore the islands and fjords on the Scandinavian coast.
- Visit historic palaces in the United Kingdom.
- Investigate the history of skiing.

# CHAPTER 13

# Eastern Europe

*In this chapter you will learn about countries that share common physical features but have developed very different cultures. First, however, we meet Marta, a Hungarian student.*

Hello! My name is Marta, and I am from Kecskemét (KECH-ke-mayt), Hungary. My mother is a secretary, and my father is an agricultural engineer. I am in my last year of high school.

Our apartment has no living or dining room, just a kitchen, a tiny balcony, a bathroom, a hallway, and two bedrooms. In the morning, we eat in my parents' room, where we also study and talk during the day.

Our lives changed very much in 1991 when the Soviet Union collapsed. Before this, we had to study Russian in school. Also, my family is Catholic, but we had to have church services in secret. My parents would have risked losing their jobs if anyone found out. Now everyone goes to church freely. My favorite sports in school are basketball, swimming, and fencing. On Friday night we have parties organized by the school. Sometimes we go to the movies. In the summer, I used to work picking cherries. Now I work in a factory processing chickens.

**Üdvözöljük Magyarországon!**

Translation: Welcome to Hungary!

# Section 1 Physical Geography

## Read to Discover

1. What are the major physical features of Eastern Europe?
2. What climates and natural resources does this region have?

## Define

oil shale
lignite
amber

## Locate

Baltic Sea
Adriatic Sea
Black Sea
Danube River

Dinaric Alps
Balkan Mountains
Carpathian
  Mountains

### WHY IT MATTERS

The Danube and its tributaries are important transportation links in Eastern Europe. The rivers also help spread pollution. Use CNNfyi.com or other current events sources to find examples of pollution problems facing the region's rivers. Record your findings in your journal.

*Amber*

## Eastern Europe: Physical-Political

**ELEVATION**

| FEET | METERS |
| --- | --- |
| 13,120 | 4,000 |
| 6,560 | 2,000 |
| 1,640 | 500 |
| 656 | 200 |
| (Sea level) 0 | 0 (Sea level) |
| Below sea level | Below sea level |

⊛ National capitals
• Other cities

SCALE

0    200    400 Miles
0    200    400 Kilometers

Projection: Azimuthal Equal Area

Size comparison of Eastern Europe to the contiguous United States

## Our Amazing Planet

**A**mber is golden, fossilized tree sap. The beaches along the eastern coast of the Baltic Sea are the world's largest and most famous source of amber. Baltic amber is approximately 40 million years old.

This aerial view of the Danube Delta shows Romania's rich farmland.

# Physical Features

Eastern Europe stretches southward from the often cold, stormy shores of the Baltic Sea. In the south are the warmer and sunnier beaches along the Adriatic and Black Seas. We can divide the countries of this region into three groups. Poland, the Czech Republic, Slovakia, and Hungary are in the geographical heart of Europe. The Baltic countries are Estonia, Latvia, and Lithuania. Yugoslavia, Bosnia and Herzegovina, Croatia, Slovenia, Macedonia, Romania, Moldova, Bulgaria, and Albania are the Balkan countries.

**Landforms** Eastern Europe is a region of mountains and plains. The plains of Poland and the Baltic countries are part of the huge Northern European Plain. The Danube River flows through the Great Hungarian Plain, also called the Great Alföld.

The Alps extend from central Europe southeastward into the Balkan Peninsula. Where they run parallel to the Adriatic coast, the mountains are called the Dinaric (duh-NAR-ik) Alps. As the range continues eastward across the peninsula its name changes to the Balkan Mountains. The Carpathian (kahr-PAY-thee-uhn) Mountains stretch from the Czech Republic across southern Poland and Slovakia and into Ukraine. There they curve south and west into Romania. In Romania they are known as the Transylvanian Alps.

**Rivers** Eastern Europe's most important river for trade and transportation is the Danube. The Danube stretches for 1,771 miles (2,850 km) across nine countries. It begins in Germany's Alps and flows eastward to the Black Sea. Some 300 tributaries flow into the Danube. The river carries and then drops so much silt that its Black Sea delta grows by 80 to 100 feet (24 to 30 m) every year. The river also carries a heavy load of industrial pollution.

✓ **READING CHECK:** ( *Places and Regions* ) What are the main physical features in Eastern Europe?

# Climate and Resources

The eastern half of the region has long, snowy winters and short, rainy summers. Farther south and west, winters are milder and summers become drier. A warm, sunny climate has drawn visitors to the Adriatic coast for centuries.

Eastern Europe's mineral and energy resources include coal, natural gas, oil, iron, lead, silver, sulfur, and zinc. The region's varied resources support many industries. Some areas of the Balkan region and Hungary are major producers of bauxite. Romania has oil. Estonia has deposits of **oil shale**, or layered rock that yields oil when heated. Estonia uses this oil to generate electricity, which is exported to other Baltic countries and Russia. Slovakia and Slovenia mine a soft form of coal called **lignite**. Nevertheless, many countries must import their energy because demand is greater than supply.

For thousands of years, people have traded **amber**, or fossilized tree sap. Amber is found along the Baltic seacoast. Salt mining, which began in Poland in the 1200s, continues in central Poland today.

During the years of Communist rule industrial production was considered more important than the environment. The region suffered serious environmental damage. Air, soil, and water pollution, deforestation, and the destruction of natural resources were widespread. Many Eastern European countries have begun the long and expensive task of cleaning up their environment.

✓ **READING CHECK:** *Environment and Society* What factors affect the location of economic activities in the region?

**B**o you remember what you learned about climate types? See Chapter 3 to review.

---

**Homework Practice Online**
Keyword: SK3 HP13

# Section Review 1

**Define and explain:** oil shale, lignite, amber

**Working with Sketch Maps** On a map of Eastern Europe that you draw or that your teacher provides, label the following: Baltic Sea, Adriatic Sea, Black Sea, Danube River, Dinaric Alps, Balkan Mountains, and Carpathian Mountains.

## Reading for the Main Idea

1. *Places and Regions* On which three major seas do the countries of Eastern Europe have coasts?

2. *Environment and Society* What types of mineral and energy resources are available in this region? How does this influence individual economies?

## Critical Thinking

3. **Making Generalizations and Predictions** Would this region be suitable for agriculture? Why?

4. **Identifying Cause and Effect** How did Communist rule contribute to the pollution problems of this region?

## Organizing What You Know

5. **Summarizing** Copy the following graphic organizer. Use it to summarize the physical features, climate, and resources of the heartland, the Baltics, and the Balkans. Then write and answer one question about the region's geography based on the chart.

| Region | Physical features | Climate | Resources |
|--------|-------------------|---------|-----------|
|        |                   |         |           |
|        |                   |         |           |
|        |                   |         |           |

# Section 2 The Countries of Northeastern Europe

## Read to Discover

1. What peoples contributed to the early history of northeastern Europe?
2. How was northeastern Europe's culture influenced by other cultures?
3. How has the political organization of this region changed since World War II?

## Define

Indo-European

## Locate

| | | |
|---|---|---|
| Estonia | Lithuania | Warsaw |
| Poland | Latvia | Vistula River |
| Czech Republic | Prague | Bratislava |
| Slovakia | Tallinn | Budapest |
| Hungary | Riga | |

### WHY IT MATTERS

Jerzy Giedroye, a Polish editor living in France, helped keep the free exchange of ideas alive in Eastern Europe during Communist rule. Use CNNfyi.com or other current events sources to discover the efforts of people like Giedroye. Record your findings in your journal.

Musical score by Hungarian Béla Bartók

---

## History

Migrants and warring armies have swept across Eastern Europe over the centuries. Each group of people brought its own language, religion, and customs. Together these groups contributed to the mosaic of cultures we see in Eastern Europe today.

The Teutonic knights, a German order of soldier monks, brought Christianity and feudalism to northeastern Europe. They built this castle at Malbork, Poland, in the 1200s.

**Early History** Among the region's early peoples were the Balts. The Balts lived on the eastern coast of the Baltic Sea. They spoke **Indo-European** languages. The Indo-European language family includes many languages spoken in Europe. These include Germanic, Baltic, and Slavic languages. More than 3,500 years ago, hunters from the Ural Mountains moved into what is now Estonia. They spoke a very different, non-Indo-European language. The language they spoke provided the early roots of today's Estonian and Finnish languages. Beginning around A.D. 400, a warrior people called the Huns invaded the region from Asia. Later, the Slavs came to the region from the plains north of the Black Sea.

In the 800s the Magyars moved into the Great Hungarian Plain. They spoke a language related to Turkish. In the 1200s the Mongols rode out of Central Asia into Hungary. At the same time German settlers pushed eastward, colonizing Poland and Bohemia—the western region of the present-day Czech Republic.

**Emerging Nations** Since the Middle Ages, Austria, Russia, Sweden, and the German state of Prussia have all ruled parts of Eastern Europe. After World War I ended in 1918, a new map of Eastern Europe was drawn. The peace treaty created two new countries: Yugoslavia and Czechoslovakia. Czechoslovakia included the old regions of Bohemia, Moravia, and Slovakia. At about the same time, Poland, Lithuania, Latvia, and Estonia also became independent countries.

✓ **READING CHECK:** ( **Human Systems** ) What peoples contributed to the region's early history?

Hungarian dancers perform in traditional dress.
**Interpreting the Visual Record**
**How does this Hungarian costume compare to those you have seen from other countries?**

▼

# Culture

The culture and festivals of this region show the influence of the many peoples who contributed to its history. As in Scandinavia, Latvians celebrate a midsummer festival. The festival marks the summer solstice, the year's longest day. Poles celebrate major Roman Catholic festivals. Many of these have become symbols of the Polish nation. The annual pilgrimage, or journey, to the shrine of the Black Madonna of Częstochowa (chen-stuh-KOH-vuh) is an example.

**Traditional Foods** The food of the region reflects German, Russian, and Scandinavian influences. As in northern Europe, potatoes and sausages are important in the diets of Poland and the Baltic countries. Although the region has only limited access to the sea, the fish of lakes and rivers are often the center of a meal. These fish often include trout and carp. Many foods are preserved to last through the long winter. These include pickles, fruits in syrup, dried or smoked hams and sausages, and cured fish.

**The Arts, Literature, and Science**
Northeastern Europe has made major contributions to the arts, literature, and sciences. For example, Frédéric Chopin (1810–1849) was a famous Polish pianist and composer. Marie Curie (1867–1934), one of the first female physicists, was also born in Poland. The writer Franz Kafka (1883–1924) was born to Jewish parents in Prague (PRAHG), the

## Northeastern Europe

| COUNTRY | POPULATION/ GROWTH RATE | LIFE EXPECTANCY | LITERACY RATE | PER CAPITA GDP |
|---------|------------------------|-----------------|---------------|----------------|
| Czech Republic | 10,264,212 −0.1% | 71, male 78, female | 100% | $12,900 |
| Estonia | 1,423,316 −0.6% | 64, male 76, female | 100% | $10,000 |
| Hungary | 10,106,017 −0.3% | 67, male 76, female | 99% | $11,200 |
| Latvia | 2,385,231 −0.8% | 63, male 75, female | 100% | $7,200 |
| Lithuania | 3,610,535 −0.3% | 63, male 76, female | 98% | $7,300 |
| Poland | 38,633,912 −0.03% | 69, male 78, female | 99% | $8,500 |
| Slovakia | 5,414,937 0.1% | 70, male 78, female | not available | $10,200 |
| United States | 281,421,906 0.9% | 74, male 80, female | 97% | $36,200 |

**Sources:** Central Intelligence Agency, *The World Factbook 2001;* U.S. Census Bureau

**Interpreting the Chart** **Based on the data in the table, which two countries have the lowest levels of economic development?**

This suspension bridge spans the Western Dvina River in Riga, the capital of Latvia.

present-day capital of the Czech Republic. Astronomer Nicolaus Copernicus (1473–1543) was born in Toruń (TAWR-oon), a city in north-central Poland. He set forth the theory that the Sun—not Earth—is the center of the universe.

✓ **READING CHECK:** *Human Systems* How is the region's culture a reflection of its past and location?

## Northeastern Europe Today

Estonia, Latvia, and Lithuania lie on the flat plain by the eastern Baltic Sea. Once part of the Russian Empire, the Baltic countries gained their independence after World War I ended in 1918. However, they were taken over by the Soviet Union in 1940 and placed under Communist rule. The Soviet Union collapsed in 1991. Since then, the countries of northeastern Europe have been moving from communism to capitalism and democracy.

**Estonia** A long history of Russian control is reflected in Estonia today. Nearly 30 percent of Estonia's population is ethnic Russian. Russia remains one of Estonia's most important trading partners. However, Estonia is also building economic ties to other countries, particularly Finland. Ethnic Estonians have close cultural ties to Finland. In fact, the Estonian language is related to Finnish. Also, most people in both countries are Lutherans. Ferries link the Estonian capital of Tallinn (TA-luhn) with Helsinki, Finland's capital.

# CONNECTING TO *Literature*

*Toy robot*

*While he wrote many books, Czech writer Karel Capek is probably best known for his play* R.U.R. *This play added the word* robot *to the English language. The Czech word* robota *means "drudgery" or forced labor. The term is given to the artificial workers that Rossum's Universal Robots factory make to free humans from drudgery. Eventually, the Robots develop feelings and revolt. The play is science fiction. Here, Harry Domin, the factory's manager, explains the origin of the Robots to visitor Helena Glory.*

## ROBOT ROBOTA

Domin: "Well, any one who has looked into human anatomy will have seen at once that man is too complicated, and that a good engineer could make him more simply. So young Rossum began to overhaul anatomy and tried to see what could be left out or simplified. . . . [He] said to himself: 'A man is something that feels happy, plays the piano, likes going for a walk, and in fact, wants to do a whole lot of things that are really unnecessary. . . .

But a working machine must not play the piano, must not feel happy, must not do a whole lot of other things. A gasoline motor must not have tassels or ornaments, Miss Glory. And to manufacture artificial workers is the same thing as to manufacture gasoline motors. The process must be of the simplest, and the product of the best from a practical point of view. . . .

Young Rossum . . . rejected everything that did not contribute directly to the progress of work—everything that makes man more expensive. In fact, he rejected man and made the Robot. My dear Miss Glory, the Robots are not people. Mechanically they are more perfect than we are, they have an enormously developed intelligence, but they have no soul."

### Analyzing Primary Sources

1. Why does Rossum design the Robots without human qualities?
2. How has Karel Capel's play influenced other cultures?

**Latvia** Latvia is the second largest of the Baltic countries. Its population has the highest percentage of ethnic minorities. Some 57 percent of the population is Latvian. About 30 percent of the people are Russian. The capital, Riga (REE-guh), has more than 1 million people. It is the largest urban area in the three Baltic countries. Like Estonia, Latvia also has experienced strong Scandinavian and Russian influences. As well as having been part of the Russian Empire, part of the country once was ruled by Sweden. Another tie between Latvia, Estonia, and the Scandinavian countries is religion. Traditionally most people in these countries are Lutheran. In addition, Sweden and Finland are important trading partners of Latvia today.

This Polish teenager wears traditional dress during a local festival.

**Lithuania** Lithuania is the largest and southernmost Baltic country. Its capital is Vilnius (VIL-nee-uhs). Lithuania's population has the smallest percentage of ethnic minorities. More than 80 percent of the population is Lithuanian. Nearly 9 percent is Russian, while 7 percent is Polish. Lithuania has ancient ties to Poland. For more than 200 years, until 1795, they were one country. Roman Catholicism is the main religion in both Lithuania and Poland today. As in the other Baltic countries, agriculture and production of basic consumer goods are important parts of Lithuania's economy.

**Poland** Poland is northeastern Europe's largest and most populous country. The total population of Poland is about the same as that of Spain. The country was divided among its neighbors in the 1700s. Poland regained its independence shortly after World War I. After World War II the Soviet Union established a Communist government to rule the country.

In 1989 the Communists finally allowed free elections. Many businesses now are owned by people in the private sector rather than by the government. The country has also strengthened its ties with Western countries. In 1999 Poland, the Czech Republic, and Hungary joined the North Atlantic Treaty Organization (NATO).

Warsaw, the capital, has long been the cultural, political, and historical center of Polish life. More than 2 million people live in the urban area. The city lies on the Vistula River in central Poland. This location has made Warsaw the center of the national transportation and communications networks as well.

**The Former Czechoslovakia** Czechoslovakia became an independent country after World War I. Until that time, its lands had been part of the Austro-Hungarian Empire. Then shortly before World War II, it fell under German rule. After the war the Communists, with the support of the Soviet Union, gained control of the government. As in Poland, the Communists lost power in 1989. In 1993 Czechoslovakia peacefully split into two countries. The western part became the Czech Republic. The eastern part became Slovakia. This peaceful split helped the Czechs and Slovaks avoid the ethnic problems that have troubled other countries in the region.

**The Czech Republic** The Czech Republic experienced economic growth in the early 1990s. Most of the country's businesses are completely or in part privately owned. However, some Czechs worry that the government remains too involved in the economy. As in Poland, a variety of political parties compete in free elections. Czech lands have coal and other important

Prague's Charles Bridge is lined with historical statues.

**Interpreting the Visual Record** How does this bridge compare to other bridges you have seen?

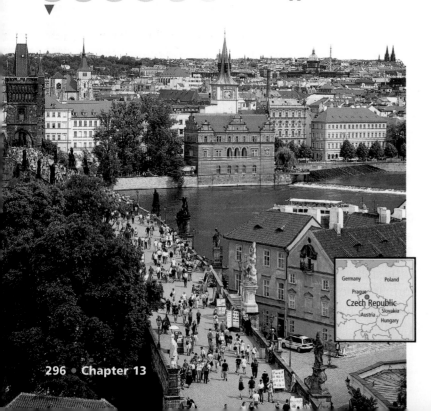

mineral resources that are used in industry. Much of the country's industry is located in and around Prague, the capital. The city is located on the Vltava River. More than 1.2 million people live there. Prague has beautiful medieval buildings. It also has one of Europe's oldest universities.

**Slovakia** Slovakia is more rugged and rural, with incomes lower than in the Czech Republic. The move toward a freer political system has been slow. However, progress has been made. Bratislava (BRAH-tyee-slah-vah), the capital, is located on the Danube River. The city is the country's most important industrial area and cultural center. Many rural Slovaks move to Bratislava looking for better-paying jobs. Most of the country's population is Slovak. However, ethnic Hungarians account for more than 10 percent of Slovakia's population.

**Hungary** Hungary separated from the Austro-Hungarian Empire at the end of World War I. Following World War II, a Communist government came to power. A revolt against the government was put down by the Soviet Union in 1956. The Communists ruled until 1989.

Today the country has close ties with the rest of Europe. In fact, most of Hungary's trade is with members of the European Union. During the Communist era, the government experimented with giving some businesses the freedom to act on their own. For example, it allowed local farm managers to make key business decisions. These managers kept farming methods modern, chose their crops, and marketed their products. Today, farm products from Hungary's fertile plains are important exports. Much of the country's manufacturing is located in and around the capital, Budapest (BOO-duh-pest). Budapest is Hungary's largest city. Nearly 20 percent of the population lives there.

The Danube River flows through Budapest, Hungary.

**Interpreting the Visual Record** Why might Hungary's capital have grown up along a river?

✔ **READING CHECK:** ( *Human Systems* ) How have the governments and economies of the region been affected by recent history?

# Section Review 2

**Homework Practice Online**
Keyword: SK3 HP13

**Define and explain:** Indo-European

**Working with Sketch Maps** On the map you drew in Section 1, label the countries of the region, Prague, Tallinn, Riga, Warsaw, Vistula River, Bratislava, and Budapest.

### Reading for the Main Idea

1. ( *Human Systems* ) How did invasions and migrations help shape the region?

2. ( *Places and Regions* ) What has the region contributed to the arts?

### Critical Thinking

3. **Drawing Inferences and Conclusions** How did the Soviet Union influence the region?

4. **Summarizing** What social changes have taken place here since the early 1990s?

### Organizing What You Know

5. **Sequencing** Copy the following graphic organizer. Use it to show the history of the Baltics since 1900.

1900        1945        1999

# Section 3 — The Countries of Southeastern Europe

## Read to Discover

1. How did Southeastern Europe's early history help shape its modern societies?
2. How does culture both link and divide the region?
3. How has the region's past contributed to current conflicts?

## Define

Roma

## Locate

| | | |
|---|---|---|
| Bulgaria | Albania | Zagreb |
| Romania | Yugoslavia | Ljubljana |
| Croatia | Kosovo | Skopje |
| Slovenia | Montenegro | Bucharest |
| Serbia | Macedonia | Moldova |
| Bosnia and | Belgrade | Chişinău |
| Herzegovina | Podgorica | Sofia |
| | Sarajevo | Tiranë |

### WHY IT MATTERS

Bosnia and the other republics of the former Yugoslovia have experienced ethnic violence since independence. Use CNNfyi.com or other **current events** sources to check on current conditions in the region. Record your findings in your journal.

*Dolls in traditional Croatian dress*

These ancient ruins in southern Albania date to the 500s B.C.

**Interpreting the Visual Record** What cultural influence does this building show?

## History

Along with neighboring Greece, this was the first region of Europe to adopt agriculture. From here farming moved up the Danube River valley into central and western Europe. Early farmers and metalworkers in the south may have spoken languages related to Albanian. Albanian is an Indo-European language.

**Early History** Around 750–600 B.C. the ancient Greeks founded colonies on the Black Sea coast. The area they settled is now Bulgaria and Romania. Later, the Romans conquered most of the area from the Adriatic Sea to the Danube River and across into Romania. When the Roman Empire divided into west and east, much of the Balkans and Greece became part of the Eastern Roman Empire. This eastern region eventually became known as the Byzantine Empire. Under Byzantine rule, many people of the Balkans became Orthodox Christians.

**Kingdoms and Empires** Many of today's southeastern European countries first appear as kingdoms between A.D. 800 and 1400. The Ottoman Turks conquered the region and ruled until the 1800s. The Ottomans, who were Muslims, tolerated other religious faiths. However, many peoples, such as the Bosnians and Albanians, converted to Islam. As the Ottoman Empire began to weaken in the late 1800s, the Austro-Hungarians took control of Croatia and Slovenia. They imposed Roman Catholicism.

**Slav Nationalism** The Russians, meanwhile, were fighting the Turks for control of the Black Sea. The Russians encouraged Slavs in the Balkans to revolt against the Turks. The Russians appealed to Slavic nationalism— to the Slav's sense of loyalty to their country. The Serbs did revolt in 1815 and became self-governing in 1817. By 1878 Bulgaria and Romania were also self-governing.

The Austro-Hungarians responded to Slavic nationalism by occupying additional territories. Those territories included the regions of Bosnia and Herzegovina. To stop the Serbs from expanding to the Adriatic coast, European powers made Albania an independent kingdom.

In August 1914 a Serb nationalist shot and killed the heir to the Austro-Hungarian throne. Austria declared war on Serbia. Russia came to Serbia's defense. These actions sparked World War I. All of Europe's great powers became involved. The United States entered the war in 1917.

**Creation of Yugoslavia** At the end of World War I Austria-Hungary was broken apart. Austria was reduced to a small territory. Hungary became a separate country but lost its eastern province to Romania. Romania also gained additional lands from Russia. Albania remained independent. The peace settlement created Yugoslavia. *Yugoslavia* means "land of the southern Slavs." Yugoslavia brought the region's Serbs, Bosnians, Croatians, Macedonians, Montenegrins, and Slovenes together into one country. Each ethnic group had its own republic within Yugoslavia. Some Bosnians and other people in Serbia were Muslims. Most Serbs were Orthodox Christians, and the Slovenes and Croats were Roman Catholics. These ethnic and religious differences created problems that eventually led to civil war in the 1990s.

✔ **READING CHECK:** ( *Human Systems* ) How is southeastern Europe's religious and ethnic makeup a reflection of its past?

This bridge at Mostar, Bosnia, was built during the 1600s. This photograph was taken in 1982.

This photograph shows Mostar after civil war in the 1990s.
**Interpreting the Visual Record** What differences can you find in the two photos?

Ethnic Albanians worship at a mosque in Pristina, Serbia.

# Culture

The Balkans are the most diverse region of Europe in terms of language, ethnicity, and religion. It is the largest European region to have once been ruled by a Muslim power. It has also been a zone of conflict between eastern and western Christianity. The three main Indo-European language branches—Romance (from Latin), Germanic, and Slavic—are all found here, as well as other branches like Albanian. Non-Indo-European languages like Hungarian and Turkish are also spoken here.

Balkan diets combine the foods of the Hungarians and the Slavs with those of the Mediterranean Greeks, Turks, and Italians. In Greek and Turkish cuisines, yogurt and soft cheeses are an important part of most meals, as are fresh fruits, nuts, and vegetables. Roast goat or lamb are the favorite meats for a celebration.

In the Balkans Bosnian and ethnic Albanian Muslims celebrate the feasts of Islam. Christian holidays—Christmas and Easter—are celebrated on one day by Catholics and on another by Orthodox Christians. Holidays in memory of ancient battles and modern liberation days are sources of conflict between ethnic groups.

✓ **READING CHECK:** *Places and Regions* Why is religion an important issue in southeastern Europe?

**Our Amazing Planet**

The Danube Delta, on the Romanian coast of the Black Sea, is part of a unique ecosystem. Most of the Romanian caviar-producing sturgeon are caught in these waters. Caviar is made from the salted eggs from three types of sturgeon fish. Caviar is considered a delicacy and can cost as much as $50 per ounce.

# Southeastern Europe Today

Like other southeastern European countries, Yugoslavia was occupied by Germany in World War II. A Communist government under Josip Broz Tito took over after the war. Tito's strong central government prevented ethnic conflict. After Tito died in 1980, Yugoslavia's Communist government held the republics together. Then in 1991 the republics of Slovenia, Croatia, Bosnia and Herzegovina, and Macedonia began to break away. Years of bloody civil war followed. Today the region struggles with the violence and with rebuilding economies left weak by years of Communist-government control.

**Yugoslavia** The republics of Serbia and Montenegro remain united and have kept the name of Yugoslavia. Belgrade is the capital of both Serbia and Yugoslavia. It is located on the Danube River. The capital of Montenegro is Podgorica (PAWD-gawr-eet-sah). The Serbian government supported ethnic Serbs fighting in civil wars in Croatia and in Bosnia and Herzegovina in the early 1990s. Tensions between ethnic groups also have been a problem within Serbia. About 65 percent of the people in Serbia and Montenegro are Orthodox Christians. In the southern Serbian province of Kosovo, the majority of people are ethnic Albanian and Muslim. Many of the Albanians want independence. Conflict between Serbs and Albanians led to civil war in the late 1990s. In 1999 the United States, other Western countries, and Russia sent troops to keep the peace.

**Bosnia and Herzegovina** Bosnia and Herzegovina generally are referred to as Bosnia. Some 40 percent of Bosnians are Muslims, but large numbers of Roman Catholic Croats and Orthodox Christian Serbs also live there. Following independence, a bloody civil war broke out between these groups as they struggled for control of territory. During the fighting the once beautiful capital of Sarajevo (sar-uh-YAY-voh) was heavily damaged.

**Croatia** Croatia's capital is Zagreb (ZAH-greb). Most of the people of Croatia are Roman Catholic. In the early 1990s, Serbs made up about 12 percent of the population. In 1991 the ethnic Serbs living in Croatia claimed part of the country for Serbia. This resulted in heavy fighting. By the end of 1995 an agreement was reached and a sense of stability returned to the country. Many Serbs left the country.

These Muslim refugees are walking to Travnik, Bosnia, with the assistance of UN troops from Britain in the 1990s.

**Interpreting the Visual Record** What effect might the movement of refugees have on a region?

**Slovenia** Slovenia is a former Austrian territory. It looks to Western European countries for much of its trade. Most people in Slovenia are Roman Catholic, and few ethnic minorities live there. Partly because of the small number of ethnic minorities, little fighting occurred after Slovenia declared independence from Yugoslavia. The major center of industry is Ljubljana (lee-oo-blee-AH-nuh), the country's capital.

Slovenia's capital, Ljubljana, lies on the Sava River.

## Ethnic Groups in Macedonia

**67%**
**23%**
**4%**
**2%**
**2%**

- Macedonians
- Albanians
- Turks
- Roma
- Serbs
- Other

**Source:** Central Intelligence Agency, *The World Factbook 2001*

In 2001 ethnic Albanian rebels launched months of fighting in hopes of gaining more rights for Macedonia's Albanian minority.

**Interpreting the Chart** **What percentage of Macedonia's people are Albanian?**

**Macedonia** When Macedonia declared its independence from Yugoslavia, Greece immediately objected to the country's new name. Macedonia is also the name of a province in northern Greece that has historical ties to the republic. Greece feared that Macedonia might try to take over the province.

Greece responded by refusing to trade with Macedonia until the mid-1990s. This slowed Macedonia's movement from the command— or government-controlled—economy it had under Communist rule to a market economy in which consumers help to determine what is to be produced by buying or not buying certain goods and services. Despite its rocky start, in recent years Macedonia has made progress in establishing free markets.

**Romania** A Communist government took power in Romania at the end of World War II. Then in 1989 the Communist government was overthrown during bloody fighting. Change, however, has been slow. Bucharest, the capital, is the biggest industrial center. Today more people work in agriculture than in any other part of the economy. Nearly 90 percent of the country's population is ethnic Romanian. **Roma**, or Gypsies as they were once known, make up almost 2 percent of the population. They are descended from people who may have lived in northern India and began migrating centuries ago. Most of the rest of Romania's population are ethnic Hungarian.

**Moldova** Throughout history control of Moldova has shifted many times. It has been dominated by Turks, Polish princes, Austria, Hungary, Russia, and Romania. Not surprisingly, the country's population reflects this diverse past. Moldova declared its independence in

Turkish Roma girls

1991 from the Soviet Union. However, the country suffers from difficult economic and political problems. About 40 percent of the country's labor force works in agriculture. Chişinău (kee-shee-NOW), the major industrial center of the country, is also Moldova's capital.

**Bulgaria** Mountainous Bulgaria has progressed slowly since the fall of communism. However, a market economy is growing gradually, and the people have more freedoms. Most industries are located near Sofia (SOH-fee-uh), the capital and largest city. About 9 percent of Bulgaria's people are ethnic Turks.

**Albania** Albania is one of Europe's poorest countries. The capital, Tiranë (ti-RAH-nuh), has a population of about 270,000. About 70 percent of Albanians are Muslim. Albania's Communist government feuded with the Communist governments in the Soviet Union and, later, in China. As a result, Albania became isolated. Since the fall of its harsh Communist government in the 1990s, the country has tried to move toward both democracy and a free market system.

✓ **READING CHECK:** ( *Human Systems* ) What problems does the region face, and how are they reflections of its Communist past?

## Southeastern Europe

| COUNTRY | POPULATION/ GROWTH RATE | LIFE EXPECTANCY | LITERACY RATE | PER CAPITA GDP |
|---|---|---|---|---|
| Albania | 3,510,484 0.9% | 69, male 75, female | 93% | $3,000 |
| Bosnia and Herzegovina | 3,922,205 1.4% | 69, male 74, female | not available | $1,700 |
| Bulgaria | 7,707,495 −1.1% | 68, male 75, female | 98% | $6,200 |
| Croatia | 4,334,142 1.5% | 70, male 78, female | 97% | $5,800 |
| Macedonia | 2,046,209 0.4% | 72, male 76, female | not available | $4,400 |
| Moldova | 4,431,570 0.05% | 60, male 69, female | 96% | $2,500 |
| Romania | 22,364,022 −0.2% | 66, male 74, female | 97% | $5,900 |
| Yugoslavia (Serbia and Montenegro) | 10,677,290 −0.3% | 70, male 76, female | 93% | $2,300 |
| United States | 281,421,906 0.9% | 74, male 80, female | 97% | $36,200 |

**Sources:** Central Intelligence Agency, *The World Factbook 2001;* U.S. Census Bureau

**Interpreting the Chart** **Based on the table, which southeastern European country has the highest level of economic development?**

# Section Review 3

**Define and explain:** Roma

**Working with Sketch Maps** On the map you drew in Section 2, label the region's countries and their capitals. They are listed at the beginning of the section. In a box in the margin, identify the countries that once made up Yugoslavia.

### Reading for the Main Idea

1. ( *Human Systems* ) How has the region's history influenced its religious and ethnic makeup?

2. ( *Human Systems* ) What events and factors have contributed to problems in Bosnia and other countries in the region since independence?

### Critical Thinking

3. **Summarizing** How was Yugoslavia created?

4. **Analyzing Information** How are the region's governments and economies changing?

### Organizing What You Know

5. **Categorizing** Copy the following graphic organizer. Use it to identify languages, foods, and celebrations in the region.

*Homework Practice Online* Keyword: SK3 HP13

# CHAPTER 13

# Reviewing What You Know

## Building Vocabulary

On a separate sheet of paper, write sentences to define each of the following words.

1. oil shale
2. lignite
3. amber
4. Indo-European
5. Roma

## Reviewing the Main Ideas

1. **( Places and Regions )** What are the major landforms of Eastern Europe?

2. **( Human Systems )** What groups influenced the culture of Eastern Europe? How can these influences be seen in modern society?

3. **( Environment and Society )** What were some environmental effects of Communist economic policies in Eastern Europe?

4. **( Human Systems )** What political and economic systems were most common in Eastern Europe before the 1990s? How and why have these systems changed?

5. **( Human Systems )** List the countries that broke away from Yugoslavia in the early 1990s. What are the greatest sources of tension in these countries?

## Understanding Environment and Society

### Economic Geography

During the Communist era, the Council for Economic Assistance, or COMECON, played an important role in planning the economies of countries in the region. Create a presentation comparing the practices of this organization to the practices now in place in the region. Consider the following:

- How COMECON organized the distribution of goods and services.
- How countries in the region now organize distribution.

## Thinking Critically

1. **Drawing Inferences and Conclusions** How has Eastern Europe's location influenced the diets of the region's people?

2. **Analyzing Information** What is Eastern Europe's most important river for transportation and trade? How can you tell that the river is important to economic development?

3. **Identifying Cause and Effect** What geographic factors help make Warsaw the transportation and communication center of

Poland? Imagine that Warsaw is located along the Baltic coast of Poland or near the German border. How might Warsaw have developed differently?

4. **Comparing/Contrasting** Compare and contrast the breakups of Yugoslavia and Czechoslovakia.

5. **Summarizing** How has political change affected the economies of Eastern European countries?

**Map** ACTIVITY

On a separate sheet of paper, match the letters on the map with their correct labels.

| | |
|---|---|
| **Baltic Sea** | **Balkan** |
| **Adriatic Sea** | **Mountains** |
| **Black Sea** | **Carpathian** |
| **Danube River** | **Mountains** |
| **Dinaric Alps** | |

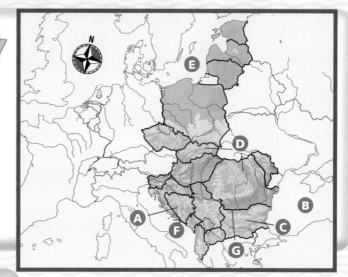

## Mental Mapping Skills ACTIVITY

Using the chapter map or a globe as a guide, draw a freehand map of Eastern Europe and label the following:

| | |
|---|---|
| **Bosnia and** | **Hungary** |
| **Herzegovina** | **Macedonia** |
| **Croatia** | **Poland** |
| **Czech Republic** | **Yugoslavia** |
| **Estonia** | |

### WRITING

ACTIVITY Imagine that you are a teenager living in Romania and want to write a family memoir of life in Romania. Include accounts of life for your grandparents under strict Soviet rule and life for your parents during the Soviet Union's breakup. Also describe your life in free Romania. Be sure to use standard grammar, spelling, sentence structure, and punctuation.

## Alternative Assessment

### Portfolio ACTIVITY

**Learning About Your Local Geography**

**Cooperative Project** Ask international agencies or search the Internet for help in contacting a boy or girl in Eastern Europe. As a group, write a letter to the teen, telling about your daily lives.

**🔗 internet** connect

**Internet Activity: go.hrw.com**
**KEYWORD: SK3 GT13**

Choose a topic to explore Eastern Europe:
- Investigate the conflicts in the Balkans.
- Take a virtual tour of Eastern Europe.
- Learn about Baltic amber.

## The European Union

**What if . . . ?** Imagine you are traveling from Texas to Minnesota. You have to go through a border checkpoint in Oklahoma to prove your Texas identity. The guard charges a tax on the cookies you are bringing to a friend in Minnesota. Buying gas presents more problems. You try to pay with Texas dollars, but the attendant just looks at you. You discover that they speak "Kansonian" in Kansas and use Kansas coins. All this would make traveling from one place to another much more difficult.

**The European Union** Fortunately, that was just an imaginary situation. However, it is similar

The Eurostar train carries passengers from London to Paris. These two cities are only about 200 miles (322 km) apart. However, they have different cultures and ways of life.

to what might happen while traveling across Europe. European countries have different languages, currencies, laws, and cultures. For example, someone from France has different customs than someone from Ireland.

However, many Europeans also share common interests. For example, they are interested in peace in the region. They also have a common interest in Europe's economic success.

A shared belief in economic and political cooperation has resulted in the creation of the European Union (EU). The EU has 15 countries that are members. They are: Austria, Belgium, Denmark, Finland, France, Germany, Great Britain, Greece, Ireland, Italy, Luxembourg, the Netherlands, Portugal, Spain, and Sweden.

### The Beginnings of a Unified Europe

Proposals for an economically integrated Europe first came about in the 1950s. After World War II, the countries of Europe had many economic problems. A plan was made to unify the coal and steel production of some countries. In 1957 France, Germany, Italy, Belgium, the Netherlands, and Luxembourg formed the European Economic Community (EEC). The name was later shortened to simply the European Community (EC). The goal of the EC was to combine each country's economy into a single market. Having one market would make trading among them easier. Eventually, more countries became interested in joining the EC. In 1973 Britain, Denmark, and Ireland joined. In the 1980s Greece, Portugal, and Spain joined.

The European Union (EU)

The 15 EU countries produce a wide range of exports and are one of the world's richest markets.

The flag of the EU features 12 gold stars on a blue background. The EU's currency, the euro, replaced the currencies of most EU countries.

In the early 1990s, a meeting was held in Maastricht, the Netherlands, to discuss the future of the EC. This resulted in the Maastricht Treaty. The treaty officially changed the EC's name from the European Community to the European Union (EU).

**The Future** Some people believe the EU is laying the foundation for a greater sense of European identity. A European Court of Justice has been set up to enforce EU rules. According to some experts, this is helping to build common European beliefs, responsibilities, and rights.

When the European Union was first established, each country had its own form of money. For example, France used the franc. Italy used the lira. Portugal used the escudo. On January 1, 2002, the euro became a common form of money for most EU countries. With the exception of Denmark, Sweden, and the United Kingdom, the euro replaced the currencies of member countries.

Another goal of the EU is to extend membership to other countries.

The EU has resulted in many important changes in Europe. Cooperation between member countries has increased. Trade has also increased. EU members have adopted a common currency and common economic laws. The EU is creating a more unified Europe. Some people even believe that the EU might someday lead to a "United States of Europe."

## Understanding What You Read

**1.** What was the first step toward European economic unity?

**2.** What is the euro? How will it affect the other currencies of the EU countries?

# Building Skills for Life: Analyzing Settlement Patterns

▲
This illustration shows a German medieval city in the 1400s.

There are many different kinds of human settlements. Some people live in villages where they farm and raise animals. Others live in small towns or cities and work in factories or offices. Geographers analyze these settlement patterns. They are interested in how settlements affect people's lives.

All settlements are unique. Even neighboring villages are different. One village might have better soil than its neighbors. Another village might be closer to a main road or highway. Geographers are interested in the unique qualities of human settlements.

Geographers also study different types of settlements. For example, many European settlements could be considered medieval cities. Medieval cities are about 500–1,500 years old. They usually have walls around them and buildings made of stone and wood. Medieval cities also have tall churches and narrow, winding streets.

Analyzing settlement patterns is important. It helps us learn about people and environments. For example, the architecture of a city might give us clues about the culture, history, and technology of the people who live there.

You can ask questions about individual villages, towns, and cities to learn about settlement patterns. What kinds of activities are going on? How are the streets arranged? What kinds of transportation do people use? You can also ask questions about groups of settlements. How are they connected? Do they trade with each other? Are some settlements bigger or older than others? Why is this so?

## PRACTICING THE SKILL

1. How do you think a city, a town, and a village are different from each other? Write down your own definition of each word on a piece of paper. Then look them up in a dictionary and write down the dictionary's definition. Were your definitions different?

2. Analyze the settlement where you live. How old is it? How many people live there? What kinds of jobs do people have? How is it connected to other settlements? How is it unique?

3. Besides medieval cities, what other types of cities can you think of? Make a list of three other possible types.

# HANDS on

One type of settlement is called a planned city. A planned city is carefully designed before it is built. Each part fits into an overall plan. For example, the size and arrangement of streets and buildings might be planned.

There are many planned cities in the world. Some examples are Brasília, Brazil; Chandigarh, India; and Washington, D.C. Many other cities have certain parts that are planned, such as individual neighborhoods. These neighborhoods are sometimes called planned communities.

Suppose you were asked to plan a city. How would you do it? On a separate sheet of paper, create your own planned city. These guidelines will help you get started.

**1.** First, decide what the physical environment will be like. Is the city on the coast, on a river, or somewhere else? Are there hills, lakes, or other physical features in the area?

**2.** Decide what to include in your city. Most cities have a downtown, different neighborhoods, and roads or highways that connect areas together. Many cities also have parks, museums, and an airport.

**3.** Plan the arrangement of your city. Where will the roads and highways go? Will the airport be close to downtown? Try to arrange the different parts of your city so that they fit together logically.

**4.** Draw a map of your planned city. Be sure to include a title, scale, and orientation.

▲ Some people think the city plan for Brasília looks like a bird, a bow and arrow, or an airplane. **Interpreting the Visual Record What do you notice about the arrangement of Brasília's streets?**

## Lab Report

**1.** How was your plan influenced by the physical environment you chose?

**2.** How do you think planned cities are different from cities that are not planned?

**3.** What problems might people have when they try to plan an entire city?

# UNIT 4

## Russia and Northern Eurasia

**CHAPTER 14**
*Russia*

**CHAPTER 15**
*Ukraine, Belarus, and the Caucasus*

**CHAPTER 16**
*Central Asia*

*Dancers in Russian national dress*

St. Basil's Cathedral, Moscow, Russia

Church overlooking the Black Sea, Ukraine

## Journalists in Russia

*Journalists Gary Matoso and Lisa Dickey traveled more than 5,000 miles across Russia. They wrote this account of their visit with Buyanto Tsydypov. He is a Buryat farmer who lives in the Lake Baikal area. The Buryats are one of Russia's many minority ethnic groups.* **WHAT DO YOU THINK?** *If you visited a Buryat family, what would you like to see or ask?*

"You came to us like thunder out of the clear blue sky," said our host. The surprise of our visit did not, however, keep him from greeting us warmly.

Buyanto brought us to a special place of prayer. High on a hillside, a yellow wooden frame holds a row of tall, narrow sticks. On the end of each stick, Buddhist prayer cloths flutter in the biting autumn wind.

In times of trouble and thanks, Buryats come to tie their prayer cloths—called *khimorin*—to the sticks and make their offerings to the gods. Buyanto builds a small fire. He unfolds an aqua-blue *khimorin* to show the drawings.

"All around are the Buddhist gods," he says, "and at the bottom we have written our names and the names of others we are praying for."

He fans the flames slowly with the cloth, purifying it with sacred smoke. After a time he moves to the top of the hill where he ties the *khimorin* to one of the sticks.

*Buryat people, Lake Baikal area, Russia*

### Understanding Primary Sources

**1.** How do you know that Buyanto Tsydypov was surprised to meet the two American journalists?

**2.** What is a *khimorin*?

*Brown bear*

# Russia and Northern Eurasia

## Elevation Profile

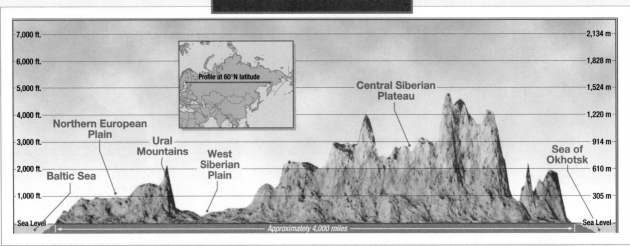

7,000 ft. — 2,134 m
6,000 ft. — 1,828 m
5,000 ft. — 1,524 m
4,000 ft. — 1,220 m
3,000 ft. — 914 m
2,000 ft. — 610 m
1,000 ft. — 305 m
Sea Level — Sea Level

Profile at 60°N latitude

Northern European Plain
Ural Mountains
West Siberian Plain
Central Siberian Plateau
Baltic Sea
Sea of Okhotsk

Approximately 4,000 miles

## The United States and Russia and Northern Eurasia
## Comparing Sizes

## GEOSTATS:

### Russia

World's largest country in area: 6,659,328 sq. mi. (17,075,200 sq km)

World's sixth-largest population: 145,470,197 (July 2001 estimate)

World's largest lake: Caspian Sea—143,244 sq. mi. (371,002 sq km)

World's deepest lake: Lake Baikal—5,715 ft. (1,742 m)

Largest number of time zones: 11

Highest mountain in Europe: Mount Elbrus—18,510 ft. (5,642 m)

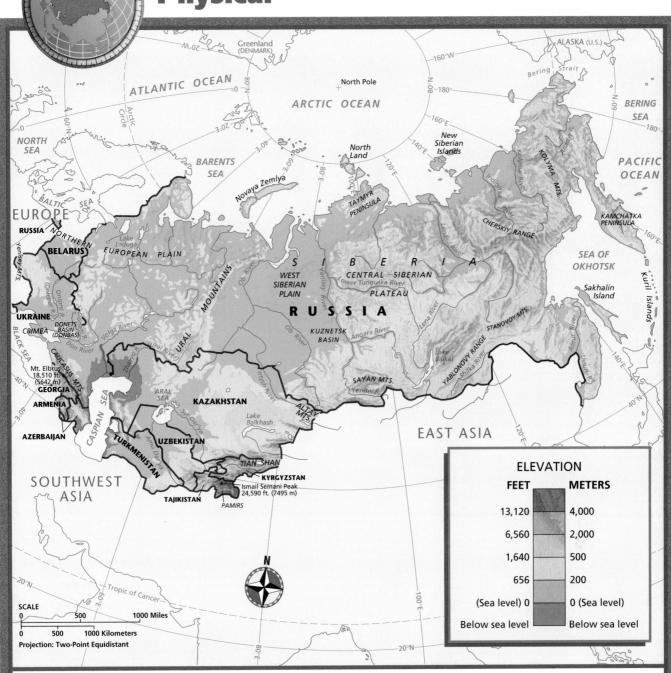

ELEVATION

| FEET | METERS |
|---|---|
| 13,120 | 4,000 |
| 6,560 | 2,000 |
| 1,640 | 500 |
| 656 | 200 |
| (Sea level) 0 | 0 (Sea level) |
| Below sea level | Below sea level |

SCALE
0   500   1000 Miles
0   500   1000 Kilometers
Projection: Two-Point Equidistant

**1.** ( *Places and Regions* )  In what general direction do the great rivers of Siberia flow?

**2.** ( *Places and Regions* )  Which countries have areas that are below sea level?

## Critical Thinking

**3. Drawing Inferences and Conclusions**  Russia has often been invaded by other countries. Which part of Russia might be easy to invade? Why do you think this area would be a good invasion route?

**4. Comparing**  Northern Russia appears to have many good harbors. Compare this map to the **climate map** of the region. Why have few harbors been developed on Russia's north coast?

Greenland (DENMARK)

ALASKA (U.S.)

ATLANTIC OCEAN

North Pole

ARCTIC OCEAN

BERING SEA

NORTH SEA

BARENTS SEA

PACIFIC OCEAN

BALTIC SEA

EUROPE

RUSSIA

⊛ St. Petersburg

Minsk ⊛
BELARUS

SEA OF OKHOTSK

Chernobyl •
• ⊛ Kiev
• Moscow

• Nizhniy Novgorod

UKRAINE • Kharkiv

R U S S I A

• Samara

• Yekaterinburg

BLACK SEA

• Novosibirsk

GEORGIA
• T'bilisi
Astana ⊛

• Vladivostok

ARMENIA
Yerevan ⊛
Baku ⊛

KAZAKHSTAN

EAST ASIA

AZERBAIJAN

CASPIAN SEA

TURKMENISTAN

UZBEKISTAN

Bishkek ⊛ • Almaty

Ashgabat ⊛

Tashkent ⊛

KYRGYZSTAN

SOUTHWEST ASIA

⊛ TAJIKISTAN
Dushanbe •

N

Tropic of Cancer

SCALE
0          500          1000 Miles

0     500    1000 Kilometers
Projection: Two-Point Equidistant

**Legend:**
- Boundaries
- ⊛ National capitals
- • Other cities

---

**1.** *Places and Regions* Compare this map to the **physical map** of the region. Do any physical features define a border between Russia and the countries of Europe?

## Critical Thinking

**2. Analyzing Information** About how far apart are Russia and the Alaskan mainland? the Russian mainland and the North Pole?

**3. Analyzing Information** Which borders separating the countries south and southeast of Russia appear to follow natural features?

**4. Drawing Inferences and Conclusions** Compare this map to the **physical** and **climate maps** of the region. Why do you think the boundary between Kazakhstan and northwestern Uzbekistan is two straight lines?

**CLIMATE**

- Desert
- Steppe
- Mediterranean
- Humid subtropical
- Humid continental
- Subarctic
- Tundra
- Highland

SCALE
0    500    1000 Miles
0    500    1000 Kilometers
Projection: Two-Point Equidistant

1. (Places and Regions) Compare this map to the **political map**. Which is the only country that has a humid subtropical climate?

2. (Physical Systems) Which climate types stretch across Russia from Europe to the Pacific?

3. (Places and Regions) Compare this map to the **political map**. Which country has only a humid continental climate?

## Critical Thinking

4. **Drawing Inferences and Conclusions** Compare this map to the **land use and resources map**. Why do you think nomadic herding is common east of the Caspian Sea?

5. **Comparing** Compare this to the **political map**. In which countries would you expect to find the highest mountains? Why?

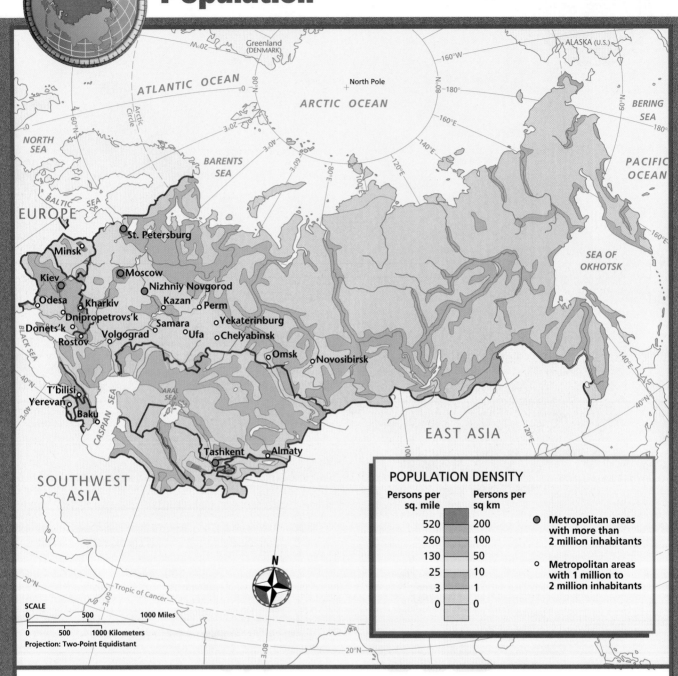

**POPULATION DENSITY**

| Persons per sq. mile | Persons per sq km | |
|---|---|---|
| 520 | 200 | |
| 260 | 100 | |
| 130 | 50 | |
| 25 | 10 | |
| 3 | 1 | |
| 0 | 0 | |

● Metropolitan areas with more than 2 million inhabitants

○ Metropolitan areas with 1 million to 2 million inhabitants

SCALE
0          500          1000 Miles
0     500     1000 Kilometers
Projection: Two-Point Equidistant

**1.** ( *Places and Regions* ) Which countries have a large area with more than 260 people per square mile and cities of more than 2 million people?

**2.** ( *Places and Regions* ) Which country has areas in the north where no one lives?

## Critical Thinking

**3. Making Generalizations and Predictions** What can you assume about landforms and farming in western Russia just by looking at the **population map**? Check the **physical** and **land use and resources maps** to be sure.

**4. Analyzing Information** Use the map on this page to create a chart, graph, database, or model of population centers in Russia and northern Eurasia.

# Russia and Northern Eurasia:
# Land Use and Resources

LAND USE
- Nomadic herding
- Livestock raising
- Commercial farming
- Subsistence farming
- Forests
- Manufacturing
- Limited economic activity
- Major manufacturing and trade centers

RESOURCES
- Coal
- Natural gas
- Oil
- Nuclear power
- Hydroelectric power
- Gold
- Silver
- Diamonds
- Other minerals
- Seafood

SCALE
0    500    1000 Miles
0  500   1000 Kilometers
Projection: Two-Point Equidistant

1. **(Places and Regions)** Where are most oil reserves in the region located?

2. **(Places and Regions)** Where are most gold mines in the region located?

3. **(Places and Regions)** Which country has diamonds? Which countries in the region have silver deposits?

## Critical Thinking

4. **Comparing** Compare this to the **physical map**. Which waterways might be used to transport mineral resources mined near Irkutsk to manufacturing and trade centers?

5. **Analyzing Information** Use the map on this page to create a chart, graph, database, or model of economic activities in the region.

# Russia and Northern Eurasia

## ARMENIA

**CAPITAL:**
Yerevan

**AREA:**
11,506 sq. mi. (29,800 sq km)

**POPULATION:**
3,336,100

**MONEY:**
dram (AMD)

**LANGUAGES:**
Armenian, Russian

**UNEMPLOYMENT:**
20 percent

## BELARUS

**CAPITAL:**
Minsk

**AREA:**
80,154 sq. mi. (207,600 sq km)

**POPULATION:**
10,350,194

**MONEY:**
Belarusian rubel (BYB/BYR)

**LANGUAGES:**
Byelorussian, Russian

**UNEMPLOYMENT:**
2.1 percent (and many underemployed workers)

## AZERBAIJAN

**CAPITAL:**
Baku

**AREA:**
33,436 sq. mi. (86,600 sq km)

**POPULATION:**
7,771,092

**MONEY:**
manat (AZM)

**LANGUAGES:**
Azeri, Russian, Armenian

**UNEMPLOYMENT:**
20 percent

## GEORGIA

**CAPITAL:**
T'bilisi

**AREA:**
26,911 sq. mi. (69,700 sq km)

**POPULATION:**
4,989,285

**MONEY:**
lari (GEL)

**LANGUAGES:**
Georgian (official), Russian, Armenian, Azeri

**UNEMPLOYMENT:**
14.9 percent

## KAZAKHSTAN

**CAPITAL:**
Astana

**AREA:**
1,049,150 sq. mi. (2,717,300 sq km)

**POPULATION:**
16,731,303

**MONEY:**
tenge (KZT)

**LANGUAGES:**
Kazakh, Russian

**UNEMPLOYMENT:**
13.7 percent

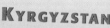

## KYRGYZSTAN

**CAPITAL:**
Bishkek

**AREA:**
76,641 sq. mi. (198,500 sq km)

**POPULATION:**
4,753,003

**MONEY:**
Kyrgyzstani som (KGS)

**LANGUAGES:**
Kirghiz, Russian

**UNEMPLOYMENT:**
6 percent

Geese flock to this pasture in Ukraine

Countries not drawn to scale.

*Mosque in Uzbekistan*

# UKRAINE

**CAPITAL:** Kiev

**AREA:** 233,089 sq. mi. (603,700 sq km)

**POPULATION:** 48,760,474

**MONEY:** hryvna

**LANGUAGES:** Ukranian, Russian, Romanian, Polish, Hungarian

**UNEMPLOYMENT:** 4.3 percent officially registered (and many unregistered or underemployed)

# RUSSIA

**CAPITAL:** Moscow

**AREA:** 6,592,735 sq. mi. (17,075,200 sq km)

**POPULATION:** 145,470,197

**MONEY:** Russian ruble (RUR)

**LANGUAGES:** Russian

**UNEMPLOYMENT:** 10.5 percent (and many underemployed workers)

# UZBEKISTAN

**CAPITAL:** Tashkent

**AREA:** 172,741 sq. mi. (447,400 sq km)

**POPULATION:** 25,155,064

**MONEY:** Uzbekistani sum (UZS)

**LANGUAGES:** Uzbek, Russian, Tajik

**UNEMPLOYMENT:** 10 percent (and many underemployed)

# TAJIKISTAN

**CAPITAL:** Dushanbe

**AREA:** 55,251 sq. mi. (143,100 sq km)

**POPULATION:** 6,578,681

**MONEY:** somoni (SM)

**LANGUAGES:** Tajik (official), Russian

**UNEMPLOYMENT:** 5.7 percent (and many underemployed workers)

**internet** connect

**COUNTRY STATISTICS**

**GO TO:** go.hrw.com

**KEYWORD:** SK3 FACTSU4

**FOR:** more facts about Russia and northern Eurasia

# TURKMENISTAN

**CAPITAL:** Ashgabat

**AREA:** 188,455 sq. mi. (488,100 sq km)

**POPULATION:** 4,603,244

**MONEY:** Turkmen manat (TMM)

**LANGUAGES:** Turkmen, Uzbek, Russian

**UNEMPLOYMENT:** data not available

**Sources:** Central Intelligence Agency, *The World Factbook 2001; The World Almanac and Book of Facts 2001;* pop. figures are 2001 estimates.

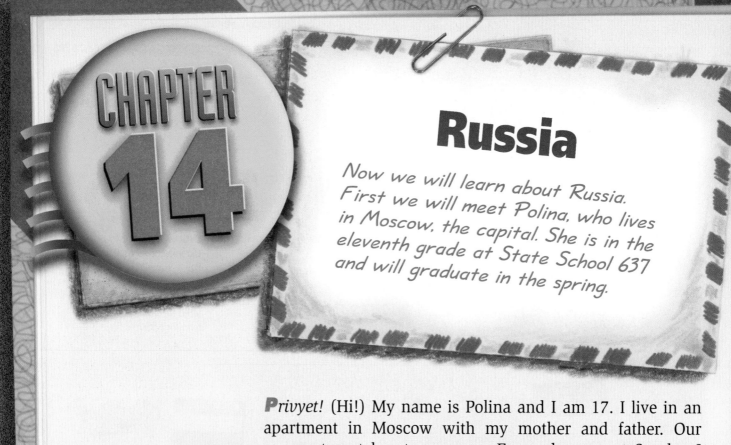

# Russia

Now we will learn about Russia. First we will meet Polina, who lives in Moscow, the capital. She is in the eleventh grade at State School 637 and will graduate in the spring.

*P*rivyet! (Hi!) My name is Polina and I am 17. I live in an apartment in Moscow with my mother and father. Our apartment has two rooms. Every day except Sunday I wake up at 7:00 A.M., have some bread and cheese with tea, and take the subway to school. At the end of eighth grade, we had to choose whether to study science or humanities. I chose humanities. My favorite subjects are history, literature, and English—my history teacher is great!

We have about five or six classes with a 15-minute break between each one. During the breaks, I often eat a snack like *pirozhki*, a small meat pie, at the school snack bar. I go home at 2:00 P.M. for lunch (meat, potatoes, and a salad of cooked vegetables and mayonnaise) and a nap. When I wake up, I go out with my friends to a park. Sometimes my parents and I join my uncle, aunt, and grandmother for Sunday dinner. My uncle makes my favorite dishes, like meat salad with mayonnaise. I love ice cream, too!

Привет!
Я живу в Москве.

Translation: Hi! I live in Moscow.

# Section 1  Physical Geography

## Read to Discover

1. What are the physical features of Russia?
2. What climates and vegetation are found in Russia?
3. What natural resources does Russia have?

## Define

taiga
steppe

## Locate

Arctic Ocean
Caucasus Mountains
Caspian Sea
Ural Mountains
West Siberian Plain
Central Siberian Plateau
Kamchatka Peninsula
Kuril Islands
Volga River
Baltic Sea

### WHY IT MATTERS

Like many nations, Russia is concerned about environmental issues. Use CNNfyi.com and other current events sources to investigate environmental concerns there. Record your findings in your journal.

*A Siberian sable*

## Russia: Physical-Political

North Pole

ARCTIC OCEAN

NORTH SEA

BARENTS SEA

Murmansk

Novaya Zemlya

BALTIC SEA

Kaliningrad
RUSSIA

St. Petersburg (Leningrad)

Lake Ladoga

NORTHERN EUROPEAN PLAIN

Moscow

Nizhniy Novgorod (Gorky)

Kazan'

Yekaterinburg (Sverdlovsk)

Chelyabinsk

Magnitogorsk

Volgograd (Stalingrad)

Astrakhan

Mt. Elbrus 18,510 ft. (5642 m)

CAUCASUS MTS.

BLACK SEA

CASPIAN SEA

Dnepr R. (Dnieper R.)

Don R.

Volga River

URAL MOUNTAINS

Ob River

WEST SIBERIAN PLAIN

RUSSIA

Yenisey R.

KUZNETSK BASIN

Trans-Siberian Railroad

Novosibirsk

Yenisey R.

S  I  B  E  R  I  A

CENTRAL SIBERIAN PLATEAU

Lena River

Baikal-Amur Mainline

Lake Baikal

Amur R.

Ussuri R.

Khabarovsk

Vladivostok

BERING SEA

Bering Strait

PACIFIC OCEAN

KAMCHATKA PENINSULA

SEA OF OKHOTSK

Sakhalin Island

Kuril Islands

SEA OF JAPAN

Arctic Circle

### ELEVATION

| FEET | | METERS |
|---|---|---|
| ⊛ National capital | | |
| • Other cities | | |
| 13,120 | | 4,000 |
| 6,560 | | 2,000 |
| 1,640 | | 500 |
| 656 | | 200 |
| (Sea level) 0 | | 0 (Sea level) |
| Below sea level | | Below sea level |

SCALE
0     500     1000 Miles
0     500     1000 Kilometers
Projection: Two-Point Equidistant

N

Size comparison of Russia to the contiguous United States

internet connect

GO TO: go.hrw.com
KEYWORD: SK3 CH14
FOR: Web sites about Russia

# Physical Features

Russia was by far the largest republic of what was called the Union of Soviet Socialist Republics, or the Soviet Union. Russia is the largest country in the world. It stretches 6,000 miles (9,654 km), from Eastern Europe to the Bering Sea and Pacific Ocean.

**The Land** Much of western, or European, Russia is part of the Northern European Plain. This is the country's heartland, where most Russians live. To the north are the Barents Sea and the Arctic Ocean. Far to the south are the Caucasus (KAW-kuh-suhs) Mountains. There Europe's highest peak, Mount Elbrus, rises to 18,510 feet (5,642 m). The Caucasus Mountains stretch from the Black Sea to the Caspian (KAS-pee-uhn) Sea. The Caspian is the largest inland body of water in the world.

East of the Northern European Plain is a long range of eroded low mountains and hills. These are called the Ural (YOOHR-uhl) Mountains. The Urals divide Europe from Asia. They stretch from the Arctic coast in the north to Kazakhstan in the south. The highest peak in the Urals rises to just 6,214 feet (1,894 m).

East of the Urals lies a vast region known as Siberia. Much of Siberia is divided between the West Siberian Plain and the Central Siberian Plateau. The West Siberian Plain is a large, flat area with many marshes. The Central Siberian Plateau lies to the east. It is a land of elevated plains and valleys.

A series of high mountain ranges runs through southern and eastern Siberia. The Kamchatka (kuhm-CHAHT-kuh) Peninsula, Sakhalin (sah-kah-LEEN) Island, and the Kuril (KYOOHR-eel) Islands surround the Sea of Okhotsk (uh-KAWTSK). These are in the Russian Far East. The rugged Kamchatka Peninsula and the Kurils have active volcanoes. Earthquakes and volcanic eruptions are common. The Kurils separate the Sea of Okhotsk from the Pacific Ocean.

**Rivers** Some of the world's longest rivers flow through Russia. These include the Volga (VAHL-guh) and Don Rivers in European Russia. The Ob (AWB), Yenisey (yi-ni-SAY), Lena (LEE-nuh), and Amur (ah-MOOHR) Rivers are located in Siberia and the Russian Far East. The Amur forms part of Russia's border with China.

The Volga is Europe's longest river. Its course and length make it an important transportation route. It flows southward for 2,293 miles (3,689 km) across the Northern European Plain to the Caspian Sea. Barges can travel by canal from the Volga to the Don River. The Don empties into the Black Sea. Canals also connect the Volga to rivers that drain into the Baltic Sea far to the northwest.

In Siberia, the Ob, Yenisey, and Lena Rivers all flow thousands of miles northward. Eventually, they reach Russia's Arctic coast. These and other Siberian rivers that drain into the Arctic Ocean freeze in winter. In spring, these rivers thaw first in the south. Downstream in

A train chugs through the cold Siberian countryside.

**Interpreting the Visual Record** What does this photograph tell you about the physical features and climate of Siberia?

Our Amazing Planet

The coldest temperature ever recorded outside of Antarctica in the last 100 years was noted on February 6, 1933, in eastern Siberia: −90° F (−68°C).

the north, however, the rivers remain frozen much longer. As a result, ice jams there block water from the melting ice and snow. This causes annual floods in areas along the rivers.

✓ **READING CHECK:** *Places and Regions* What are the major physical features of Russia?

# Climate and Vegetation

Nearly all of Russia is located at high northern latitudes. The country has tundra, subarctic, humid continental, and steppe climates. Because there are no high mountain barriers, cold Arctic winds sweep across much of the country in winter. Winters are long and cold. Ice blocks most seaports until spring. However, the winters are surprisingly dry in much of Russia. This is because the interior is far from ocean moisture.

Winters are particularly severe throughout Siberia. Temperatures often drop below –40°F (–40°C). Although they are short, Siberian summers can be hot. Temperatures can rise to 100°F (38°C).

Vegetation varies with climates from north to south. Very cold temperatures and permafrost in the far north keep trees from taking root. Mosses, wildflowers, and other tundra vegetation grow there.

The vast **taiga** (TY-guh), a forest of mostly evergreen trees, grows south of the tundra. The trees there include spruce, fir, and pine. In European Russia and in the Far East are deciduous forests. Many temperate forests in European Russia have been cleared for farms and cities.

Wide grasslands known as the **steppe** (STEP) stretch from Ukraine across southern Russia to Kazakhstan. Much of the steppe is used for growing crops and grazing livestock.

✓ **READING CHECK:** *Physical Systems* How does Russia's location affect its climate?

**B**UILD on **WHAT** You Know

**D**o you remember what you learned about tundra climates? See Chapter 3 to review.

Camels graze on open land in southern Siberia near Mongolia.

Russia

China

India

A blast furnace is used to process nickel in Siberia. Nickel is just one of Russia's many natural resources.

# Resources

Russia has enormous energy, mineral, and forest resources. However, those resources have been poorly managed. For example, much of the forest west of the Urals has been cut down. Now wood products must be brought long distances from Siberia. Still, the taiga provides a vast supply of trees for wood and paper pulp.

Russia has long been a major oil producer. However, many of its oil deposits are far from cities, markets, and ports. Coal is also plentiful. More than a dozen metals are available in large quantities. Russia also is a major diamond producer. Many valuable mineral deposits in remote Siberia have not yet been mined.

✓ **READING CHECK:** *Places and Regions* How might the location of its oil deposits prevent Russia from taking full advantage of this resource?

## Section Review 1

**Define and explain:** taiga, steppe

**Working with Sketch Maps** On a map of Russia that you sketch or that your teacher provides, label the following: Arctic Ocean, Caucasus Mountains, Caspian Sea, Ural Mountains, West Siberian Plain, Central Siberian Plateau, Kamchatka Peninsula, Kuril Islands, Volga River, and Baltic Sea.

### Reading for the Main Idea

**1.** *Places and Regions* What low mountain range in central Russia divides Europe from Asia?

**2.** *Places and Regions* How is the Volga River linked to the Baltic and Black Seas?

go. hrw .com **Homework Practice Online** Keyword: SK3 HP14

**3.** *Environment and Society* What are winters like in much of Russia? How might they affect people?

### Critical Thinking

**4. Making Generalizations and Predictions** How might Russia's natural resources make the country more prosperous?

### Organizing What You Know

**5. Categorizing** Copy the following graphic organizer. Use it to list the climates, vegetation, and resources of Russia.

| Climates | Vegetation | Resources |
|----------|------------|-----------|
|          |            |           |
|          |            |           |

# Section 2 History and Culture

## Read to Discover

1. What was Russia's early history like?
2. How did the Russian Empire grow and then fall?
3. What was the Soviet Union?
4. What is Russia like today?

## Define

czar
abdicated
allies
superpowers
Cold War
consumer goods

## Locate

Moscow

Russian caviar, blini (pancakes), and smoked salmon

### WHY IT MATTERS

Russia is well known for its ballet companies. Use CNN**fyi**.com or other current events sources to discover more about Russia's culture and its international recognition in the field of dance and other arts. Record your findings in your journal.

## Early Russia

The roots of the Russian nation lie deep in the grassy plains of the steppe. For thousands of years, people moved across the steppe bringing new languages, religions, and ways of life.

**Early Migrations** Slavic peoples have lived in Russia for thousands of years. In the A.D. 800s, Viking traders from Scandinavia helped shape the first Russian state among the Slavs. These Vikings called themselves Rus (ROOS). The word *Russia* comes from their name. The state they created was centered on Kiev. Today Kiev is the capital of Ukraine.

In the following centuries, missionaries from southeastern Europe brought Orthodox Christianity and a form of the Greek alphabet to Russia. Today the Russian language is written in this Cyrillic alphabet.

**Mongols** After about 200 years, Kiev's power began to decline. In the 1200s, Mongol invaders called Tatars swept out of Central Asia across the steppe. The Mongols conquered Kiev and added much of the region to their vast empire.

The Mongols demanded taxes but ruled the region through local leaders. Over time, these local leaders established various states. The strongest of these was Muscovy, north of Kiev. Its chief city was Moscow.

✓ **READING CHECK:** *Human Systems* What was the effect of Viking traders on Russia?

▲
This painting from the mid-1400s shows a battle between soldiers of two early Russian states.

## History of Russian Expansion

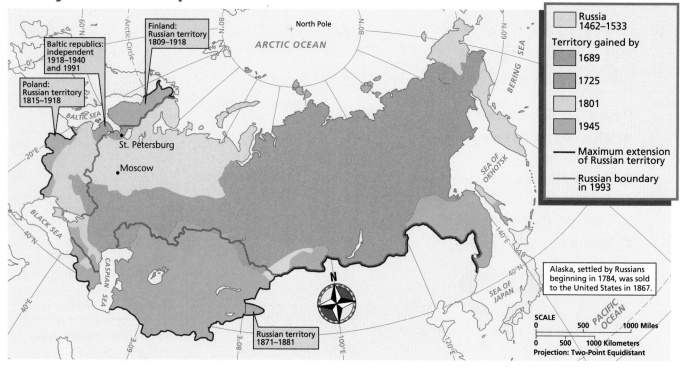

The colors in this map show land taken by the Russian Empire and the Soviet Union over time.

**Interpreting the Map** When was the period of Russia's greatest expansion?

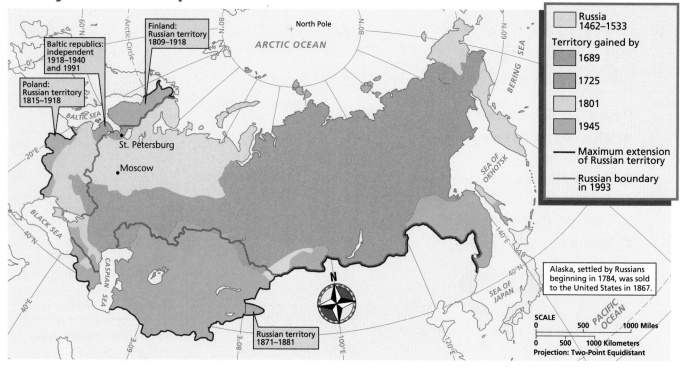

Ivan the Terrible became grand prince of Moscow in 1533. He was just three years old. He ruled Russia from 1547 to his death in 1584.

# The Russian Empire

In the 1400s Muscovy won control over parts of Russia from the Mongols. In 1547 Muscovy's ruler, Ivan IV—known as Ivan the Terrible—crowned himself **czar** (ZAHR) of all Russia. The word *czar* comes from the Latin word *Caesar* and means "emperor."

**Expansion** Over more than 300 years, czars like Peter the Great (1672–1725) expanded the Russian empire. By the early 1700s the empire stretched from the Baltic to the Pacific.

Russian fur traders crossed the Bering Strait in the 1700s and 1800s. They established colonies along the North American west coast. Those colonies stretched from coastal Alaska to California. Russia sold Alaska to the United States in 1867. Around the same time, Russia expanded into Central Asia.

**Decline** The Russian Empire's power began to decline in the late 1800s. Industry grew slowly, so Russia remained largely agricultural. Most people were poor farmers. Far fewer were the rich, factory workers, or craftspeople. Food shortages, economic problems, and defeat in war further weakened the empire in the early 1900s.

In 1917, during World War I, the czar **abdicated**, or gave up his throne. Later in 1917 the Bolshevik Party, led by Vladimir Lenin, overthrew the government. This event is known as the Russian Revolution.

✔ **READING CHECK:** *Human Systems* What conflict brought a change of government to Russia?

# The Soviet Union

The Bolsheviks, or Communists, established the Soviet Union in 1922. Most of the various territories of the Russian Empire became republics within the Soviet Union.

Under Lenin and his successor, Joseph Stalin, the Communists took over all industries and farms. Religious practices were discouraged. The Communists outlawed all other political parties. Many opponents were imprisoned, forced to leave the country, or even killed.

The Soviet leaders established a command economy, in which industries were controlled by the government. At first these industries grew dramatically. However, over time the lack of competition made them inefficient and wasteful. The quality of many products was poor. Government-run farms failed to produce enough food to feed the population. By the late 1950s the Soviet Union had to import large amounts of grain.

**Cold War** The Soviet Union in the 1950s was still recovering from World War II. The country had been a major battleground in the war. The United States and the Soviet Union had been **allies**, or friends, in the fight against Germany. After the war the two **superpowers**, or powerful countries, became rivals. This bitter rivalry became known as the **Cold War**. The Cold War lasted from the 1940s to the early 1990s. The Soviet Union and the United States built huge military forces, including nuclear weapons. The two countries never formally went to war with each other. However, they supported allies in small wars around the world.

**Collapse of the Soviet Union** The costs of the Cold War eventually became too much for the Soviet Union. The Soviet government spent more and more money on military goods. **Consumer goods** became expensive and in short supply. Consumer goods are products used at home and in everyday life. The last Soviet leader, Mikhail Gorbachev, tried to bring about changes to help the economy. He also promoted a policy allowing more open discussion of the country's problems. However, the various Soviet republics pushed for independence. Finally, in 1991 the Soviet Union collapsed. The huge country split into 15 republics.

In late 1991 Russia and most of the other former Soviet republics formed the Commonwealth of Independent States, or CIS. The CIS does not have a strong central government. Instead, it provides a way for the former Soviet republics to address shared problems.

✓ **READING CHECK:**
*Human Systems* What was the Cold War, and how did it eventually cause the Soviet Union's collapse?

Tourists can visit the czar's Summer Palace in St. Petersburg.
**Interpreting the Visual Record How do you think the rich lifestyle of the czars helped the Bolsheviks gain support?**

A man lights candles in front of portraits of the last czar, Nicholas II, and his wife. Russians are divided over what kind of government their country should have today.
**Interpreting the Visual Record Why do you think some Russians might wish to have a czar again?**

# CONNECTING TO *Literature*

*The former Soviet Union was composed of many republics, which are now independent countries. Nina Gabrielyan's* The Lilac Dressing Gown *is told from the point of view of an Armenian girl living in Moscow before the Soviet breakup.*

Aunt Rimma. . . came to visit and gave me a pink caramel which I, naturally, popped straight in my mouth. "Don't swallow it," Aunt Rimma says in an odd sort of voice. "You're not supposed to swallow it, only chew it." "Why," I ask, puzzled by her solemn tone. "It's chewing gum," she says with pride in her eyes. "Chewing gum?" I don't know what she means. "American chewing gum," Aunt Rimma explains. "Mentor's sister sent it to us from America." "Oh, from America? Is that where the capitalists are? What is she doing there?" "She's living there," says Aunt Rimma, condescending to my foolishness.

But I am not as foolish as I used to be. I know that Armenians live in Armenia. Our country is very big and includes many republics: Armenia, Georgia, Azerbaijan, Tajikistan, Uzbekistan, Ukraine, Belorussia [Belarus], the Caucasus and Transcaucasia. All this together is the Soviet Union. Americans . . . live in America. Clearly, Mentor's sister cannot possibly be American. . . . Rimma goes on boasting: "Oh! the underwear they have there! . . . And the children's clothes!"

I begin to feel a bit envious. . . . Nobody in our house has anyone living in America, but Aunt Rimma does. My envy becomes unbearable. So I decide to slay our boastful neighbor on the spot: "Well we have cockroaches! This big! Lots and lots of them!'"

## Analyzing Primary Sources

1. How does the Armenian girl's frame of reference affect her view of the United States?
2. What does Aunt Rimma seem to think the United States is like?

## Russia Today

Russia has been making a transition from communism to democracy and a free market economy since 1991. Change has been slow, and the country faces difficult challenges.

**People and Religion** More than 146 million people live in Russia today. More than 80 percent are ethnic Russians. The largest of Russia's many minority groups are Ukrainians and Tatars. These Tatars are the descendants of the early Mongol invaders of Russia.

In the past, the government encouraged ethnic Russians to settle in areas of Russia far from Moscow. They were encouraged to move to places where other ethnic groups were in the majority. Today, many non-Russian peoples in those areas resent the domination of ethnic Russians. Some non-Russians want independence from Moscow. At times this has led to violence and even war, as in Chechnya in southern Russia.

Since 1991 a greater degree of religious expression has been allowed in Russia. Russian Orthodox Christianity is becoming popular again. Cathedrals have been repaired, and their onion-shaped domes have been covered in gold leaf and brilliant colors. Muslims around the Caspian Sea and the southern Urals are reviving Islamic practices.

**Food and Festivals** Bread is an important part of the Russian diet. It is eaten with every meal. It may be a rich, dark bread made from rye and wheat flour or a firm white bread. As in other northern countries, the growing season is short and winter is long. Therefore, the diet includes many canned and preserved foods, such as sausages, smoked fish, cheese, and vegetable and fruit preserves.

Black caviar, one of the world's most expensive delicacies, comes from Russia. The fish eggs that make up black caviar come from sturgeon. Sturgeon are fish found in the Caspian Sea.

The anniversary of the 1917 Russian Revolution was an important holiday during the Soviet era. Today the Orthodox Christian holidays of Christmas and Easter are again becoming popular in Russia. Special holiday foods include milk puddings and cheesecakes.

**The Arts and Sciences** Russia has given the world great works of art, literature, and music. For example, you might know *The Nutcracker,* a ballet danced to music composed by Peter Tchaikovsky (1840–93). It is a popular production in many countries.

### Russia

| COUNTRY | POPULATION/ GROWTH RATE | LIFE EXPECTANCY | LITERACY RATE | PER CAPITA GDP |
|---|---|---|---|---|
| Russia | 145,470,197 −0.4% | 62, male 73, female | 98% | $7,700 |
| United States | 281,421,906 0.9% | 74, male 80, female | 97% | $36,200 |

**Sources:** Central Intelligence Agency, *The World Factbook 2001;* U.S. Census Bureau

**Interpreting the Chart How many times greater is the U.S. population than the Russian population?**

Ballet dancers perform Peter Tchaikovsky's *Swan Lake* at the Mariinsky Theater in St. Petersburg.

Many Russian writers are known for how they capture the emotions of characters in their works. Some writers, such as Aleksandr Solzhenitsyn (1918– ), have written about Russia under communism.

Russian scientists also have made important contributions to their professions. For example, in 1957 the Soviet Union launched *Sputnik*. It was the first artificial satellite in space. Today U.S. and Russian engineers are working together on space projects. These include building a large space station and planning for a mission to Mars.

**Government** Like the U.S. government, the Russian Federation is governed by an elected president and a legislature called the Federal Assembly. The Federal Assembly includes representatives of regions and republics within the Federation. Non-Russians are numerous or in the majority in many of those regions and republics.

The government faces tough challenges. One is improving the country's struggling economy. Many government-owned companies have been sold to the private sector. However, financial problems and corruption have made people cautious about investing in those companies.

Corruption is a serious problem. A few people have used their connections with powerful government officials to become rich. In addition, many Russians avoid paying taxes. This means the government has less money for salaries and services. Agreement on solutions to these problems has been hard.

## Republics of the Russian Federation

| | |
|---|---|
| Adygea | Karachay-Cherkessia |
| Alania | Karelia |
| Bashkortostan | Khakassia |
| Buryatia | Komi |
| Chechnya | Mari El |
| Chuvashia | Mordvinia |
| Dagestan | Sakha |
| Gorno-Altay | Tatarstan |
| Ingushetia | Tuva |
| Kabardino-Balkaria | Udmurtia |
| Kalmykia | |

✓ **READING CHECK:** *Human Systems* What are the people and culture of Russia like today?

# Section Review 2

**Homework Practice Online**
Keyword: SK3 HP14

**Define and explain:** czar, abdicated, allies, superpowers, Cold War, consumer goods

**Working with Sketch Maps** On the map you created in Section 1, label Moscow. In the margin, explain the role Kiev played in Russia's early history.

## Reading for the Main Idea

1. *Places and Regions* How did Russia get its name?

2. *Human Systems* What was the Bolshevik Party?

3. *Places and Regions* What are some of the challenges that Russia faces today?

## Critical Thinking

4. **Comparing** Compare the factors that led to the decline of the Russian Empire and the Soviet Union. List the factors for each.

## Organizing What You Know

5. **Summarizing** Copy the following graphic organizer. Use it to identify important features of Russia's ethnic population, religion, food, and arts and sciences.

Russian people and culture

# Section 3  The Russian Heartland

## Read to Discover

1. Why is European Russia considered the country's heartland?
2. What are the characteristics of the four regions of European Russia?

## Define

light industry
heavy industry
smelters

## Locate

St. Petersburg
Nizhniy Novgorod
Astrakhan
Yekaterinburg
Chelyabinsk
Magnitogorsk

### WHY IT MATTERS

Following the fall of Communism, some Russian cities' landscapes began to change. In the larger cities like Moscow there are newer buildings and more restaurants. Use **CNNfyi.com** or other **current events** sources to find information about Moscow and other large Russian cities. Record your findings in your journal.

*Jeweled box made by Peter Carl Fabergé*

## The Heartland

The European section of Russia is the country's heartland. The Russian nation expanded outward from there. It is home to the bulk of the Russian population. The national capital and large industrial cities are also located there.

The plains of European Russia make up the country's most productive farming region. Farmers focus mainly on growing grains and raising livestock. Small gardens near cities provide fresh fruits and vegetables for summer markets.

The Russian heartland can be divided into four major regions. These four are the Moscow region, the St. Petersburg region, the Volga region, and the Urals region.

✓ **READING CHECK:** *Places and Regions* Why is European Russia the country's heartland?

## The Moscow Region

Moscow is Russia's capital and largest city. More than 9 million people live there. In addition to being Russia's political center, Moscow is the country's center for transportation and communication. Roads, railroads, and air routes link the capital to all points in Russia.

At Moscow's heart is the Kremlin. The Kremlin's red brick walls and towers were built in the late 1400s. The government offices, beautiful palaces, and gold-domed churches within its walls are popular tourist attractions.

Twenty towers, like the one in the lower left, are spaced along the Kremlin's walls.

**Interpreting the Visual Record What was the advantage of locating government buildings and palaces within the walls of one central location?**

Vendors sell religious art and other crafts at a sidewalk market in Moscow.

**Interpreting the Visual Record** What do the items in this market suggest about the status of religion in Russia since the communist era?

Moscow is part of a huge industrial area. This area also includes the city of Nizhniy Novgorod, called Gorky during the communist era. About one third of Russia's population lives in this region.

The Soviet government encouraged the development of **light industry**, rather than **heavy industry**, around Moscow. Light industry focuses on the production of lightweight goods, such as clothing. Heavy industry usually involves manufacturing based on metals. It causes more pollution than light industry. The region also has advanced-technology and electronics industries.

## The St. Petersburg Region

Northwest of Moscow is St. Petersburg, Russia's second-largest city and a major Baltic seaport. More than 5 million people live there. St. Petersburg was Russia's capital and home to the czars for more than 200 years. This changed in 1918. Palaces and other grand buildings constructed under the czars are tourist attractions today. St. Petersburg was known as Leningrad during the communist era. Much of the city was heavily damaged during World War II.

The surrounding area has few natural resources. Still, St. Petersburg's harbor, canals, and rail connections make the city a major center for trade. Important universities and research institutions are located there. The region also has important industries.

✔ **READING CHECK:** *Human Systems*
Why are Moscow and St. Petersburg such large cities?

The Mariinsky Theater of Opera and Ballet is one of St. Petersburg's most beautiful buildings. It was called the Kirov during the communist era.

# The Volga Region

The Volga region stretches along the middle part of the Volga River. The Volga is often more like a chain of lakes. It is a major shipping route for goods produced in the region. Hydroelectric power plants and nearby deposits of coal and oil are important sources of energy.

During World War II, many factories were moved to the Volga region. This was done to keep them safe from German invaders. Today the region is famous for its factories that produce goods such as motor vehicles, chemicals, and food products. Russian caviar comes from a fishery based at the old city of Astrakhan on the Caspian Sea.

# The Urals Region

Mining has long been important in the Ural Mountains region. Nearly every important mineral except oil has been discovered there. Copper and iron **smelters** are still important. Smelters are factories that process copper, iron, and other metal ores.

Many large cities in the Urals started as commercial centers for mining districts. The Soviet government also moved factories to the region during World War II. Important cities include Yekaterinburg (yi-kah-ti-reem-BOOHRK) (formerly Sverdlovsk), Chelyabinsk (chel-YAH-buhnsk), and Magnitogorsk (muhg-nee-tuh-GAWRSK). Now these cities manufacture machinery and metal goods.

✓ **READING CHECK:** *Places and Regions* What industries are important in the Volga and Urals regions?

▲

A fisher gathers sturgeon in a small shipboard pool in the Volga region. The eggs for making caviar are taken from the female sturgeon. Then the fish is released back into the water.

# Section Review 3

go. hrw .com **Homework Practice Online**
Keyword: SK3 HP14

**Define and explain:** light industry, heavy industry, smelters

**Working with Sketch Maps** On the map you created in Section 2, label St. Petersburg, Nizhniy Novgorod, Astrakhan, Yekaterinburg, Chelyabinsk, and Magnitogorsk. In the margin of your map, write a short caption explaining the significance of Moscow and St. Petersburg.

## Reading for the Main Idea

1. *Places and Regions* Why might so many people settle in Russia's heartland?

2. *Places and Regions* Where did the Soviet government move factories during World War II?

## Critical Thinking

3. **Drawing Inferences and Conclusions** Why do you think the Soviet government encouraged the development of light industry around Moscow?

4. **Finding the Main Idea** What role has the region's physical geography played in the development of European Russia's economy?

## Organizing What You Know

5. **Contrasting** Use this graphic organizer to identify European Russia's four regions. Write one feature that makes each region different from the other three.

European Russia

# Section 4

## Siberia

### Read to Discover

1. What is the human geography of Siberia like?
2. What are the economic features of the region?
3. How has Lake Baikal been threatened by pollution?

### Define

habitation fog

### Locate

Siberia
Trans-Siberian Railroad
Baikal-Amur Mainline
Kuznetsk Basin
Ob River
Yenisey River
Novosibirsk
Lake Baikal

### WHY IT MATTERS

It takes more than a week by train to cross Russia. The Trans-Siberian Railroad and the Baikal-Amur Mainline let travelers see more of the country. Use CNN fyi.com or other current events sources to learn more about these rail systems. Record your findings in your journal.

*Russian* matryoshka *nesting doll*

## A Sleeping Land

East of European Russia, across the Ural Mountains, is Siberia. Siberia is enormous. It covers more than 5 million square miles (12.95 million sq. km) of northern Asia. It extends all the way to the Pacific Ocean. That is nearly 1.5 times the area of the United States! To the north of Siberia is the Arctic Ocean. To the south are the Central Asian countries, Mongolia, and China.

Many people think of Siberia as simply a vast, frozen wasteland. In fact, in the Tatar language, *Siberia* means "Sleeping Land." In many ways, this image is accurate. Siberian winters are long, dark, and severe. Often there is little snow, but the land is frozen for months. During winter, **habitation fog** hangs over cities. A habitation fog is a fog caused by fumes and smoke from cities. During the cold Siberian winter, this fog is trapped over cities.

Siberia has lured Russian adventurers for more than 400 years. It continues to do so today. This vast region has a great wealth of natural resources. Developing those resources may be a key to transforming Russia into an economic success.

Reindeer graze around a winter camp in northern Siberia.

**Interpreting the Visual Record** What climate does this area appear to have, tundra or subarctic?

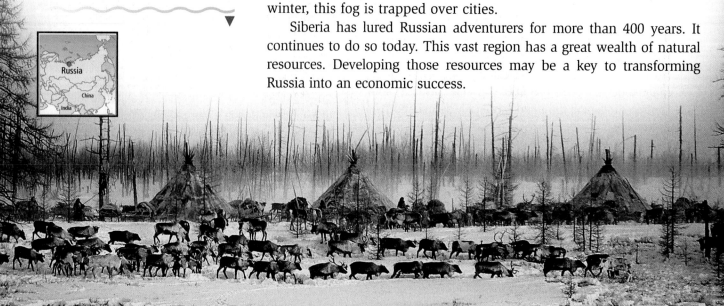

**People** Siberia is sparsely populated. In fact, large areas have no human population at all. Most of the people live in cities in western and southern parts of the region.

Ethnic Russians make up most of the population. However, minority groups have lived there since long before Russians began to expand into Siberia.

**Settlements** Russian settlement in Siberia generally follows the route of the Trans-Siberian Railroad. Construction of this railway started in 1891. When it was completed, it linked Moscow and Vladivostok, a port on the Sea of Japan.

Russia's Trans-Siberian Railroad is the longest single rail line in the world. It is more than 5,700 miles (9,171 km) long. For many Siberian towns, the railroad provides the only transportation link to the outside world. Another important railway is the Baikal-Amur Mainline (BAM), which crosses many mountain ranges and rivers in eastern Siberia.

✔ **READING CHECK:** *Places and Regions* Where is Russian settlement located in Siberia, and why do you think this is the case?

The Omsk (AWMSK) Cathedral in Omsk, Siberia, provides an example of Russian architecture. Omsk was founded in the early 1700s.

# Siberia's Economy

The Soviet government built the Baikal-Amur Mainline so that raw materials from Siberia could be easily transported to other places. Abundant natural resources form the foundation of Siberia's economy. They are also important to the development of Russia's struggling economy. Siberia's natural resources include timber, mineral ores, diamonds, and coal, oil, and natural gas deposits.

Although Siberia has rich natural resources, it contains a small percentage of Russia's industry. The harsh climate and difficult terrain have discouraged settlement. Many people would rather live in European Russia, even though wages may be higher in Siberia.

Lumbering and mining are the most important Siberian industries. Large coal deposits are mined in the Kuznetsk Basin, or the Kuzbas. The Kuzbas is located in southwestern Siberia between the Ob and Yenisey Rivers. It is one of Siberia's most important industrial regions.

Siberia's largest city, Novosibirsk, is located near the Kuznetsk Basin. The city's name means "New Siberia." About 1.5 million people live there. It is located about halfway between Moscow and Vladivostok on the Trans-Siberian Railroad. Novosibirsk is Siberia's manufacturing and transportation center.

✔ **READING CHECK:** *Environment and Society* How do Siberia's natural resources influence the economies of Siberia and Russia?

A worker repairs an oil rig in Siberia.

**Interpreting the Visual Record** **How is this worker protected from the cold Siberian climate?**

The scenery around Lake Baikal is breathtaking. The lake is seven times as deep as the Grand Canyon.

**Interpreting the Visual Record**
**How would pollution affect this lake and the plants and animals that live there?**

Lake Baikal covers less area than do three of the Great Lakes: Superior, Huron, and Michigan. Still, Baikal is so deep that it contains about one fifth of all the world's freshwater!

# Lake Baikal

Some people have worried that economic development in Siberia threatens the region's natural environment. One focus of concern has been Lake Baikal (by-KAHL), the "Jewel of Siberia."

Baikal is located north of Mongolia. It is the world's deepest lake. In fact, it holds as much water as all of North America's Great Lakes. The scenic lake and its surrounding area are home to many kinds of plants and animals. Some, such as the world's only freshwater seal, are endangered.

For decades people have worried about pollution from a nearby paper factory and other development. They feared that pollution threatened the species that live in and around the lake. In recent years scientists and others have proposed plans that allow some economic development while protecting the environment.

✓ **READING CHECK:** *Environment and Society* How has human activity affected Lake Baikal?

Homework Practice Online
Keyword: SK3 HP14

Section Review 4

**Define and explain:** habitation fog

**Working with Sketch Maps** On the map you created in Section 3, label Siberia, Trans-Siberian Railroad, Baikal-Amur Mainline, Kuznetsk Basin, Ob River, Yenisey River, Novosibirsk, and Lake Baikal.

**Reading for the Main Idea**

1. *Places and Regions* What are the boundaries of Siberia?

2. *Human Systems* Where do most people in Siberia live? Why?

3. *Places and Regions* Why does this huge region with many natural resources have little industry?

**Critical Thinking**

4. **Making Generalizations and Predictions** Do you think Russians should be more concerned about rapid economic development or protecting the environment? Why?

**Organizing What You Know**

5. **Categorizing** Use this organizer to list the region's resources and industries that use them.

| Natural Resources | ⇨ | Major Industries |
| --- | --- | --- |

# Section 5  The Russian Far East

## Read to Discover

1. How does the Russian Far East's climate affect agriculture in the region?
2. What are the major resources and cities of the region?
3. What island regions are part of the Russian Far East?

## Define

icebreakers

## Locate

Sea of Okhotsk
Sea of Japan
Amur River
Khabarovsk
Vladivostok
Sakhalin Island

*A Russian figurine*

### WHY IT MATTERS

Because of conflict over the Kuril Islands, Russia and Japan did not sign a peace agreement to end World War II. Use CNN fyi.com or other **current events** sources to find information on this controversy and other political concerns. Record your findings in your journal.

## Agriculture

Off the eastern coast of Siberia are the Sea of Okhotsk and the Sea of Japan. Their coastal areas and islands make up a region known as the Russian Far East.

The Russian Far East has a less severe climate than the rest of Siberia. Summer weather is mild enough for some successful farming. Farms produce many goods, including wheat, sugar beets, sunflowers, meat, and dairy products. However, the region cannot produce enough food for itself. As a result, food must also be imported.

Fishing and hunting are important in the region. There are many kinds of animals, including deer, seals, rare Siberian tigers, and sables. Sable fur is used to make expensive clothing.

✓ **READING CHECK:** *Environment and Society* How does scarcity of food affect the Russian Far East?

◀

The Siberian tiger is endangered. The few remaining of these large cats roam parts of the Russian Far East. They are also found in northern China and on the Korean Peninsula.

# Economy

Like the rest of Siberia, the Russian Far East has a wealth of natural resources. These resources have supported the growth of industrial cities and ports in the region.

**Resources**  Much of the Russian Far East remains forested. The region's minerals are only beginning to be developed. Lumbering, machine manufacturing, woodworking, and metalworking are the major industries there.

The region also has important energy resources, including coal and oil. Another resource is geothermal energy. This resource is available because of the region's tectonic activity. Two active volcanic mountain ranges run the length of the Kamchatka Peninsula. Russia's first geothermal electric-power station was built on this peninsula.

**Cities**  Industry and the Trans-Siberian Railroad aided the growth of cities in the Russian Far East. Two of those cities are Khabarovsk (kuh-BAHR-uhfsk) and Vladivostok (vla-duh-vuh-STAHK).

More than 600,000 people live in Khabarovsk, which was founded in 1858. It is located where the Trans-Siberian Railroad crosses the Amur River. This location makes Khabarovsk ideal for processing forest and mineral resources from the region.

Vladivostok is slightly larger than Khabarovsk. *Vladivostok* means "Lord of the East" in Russian. The city was established in 1860 on the coast of the Sea of Japan. Today it lies at the eastern end of the Trans-Siberian Railroad.

Vladivostok is a major naval base and the home port for a large fishing fleet. **Icebreakers** must keep the city's harbor open in winter. An icebreaker is a ship that can break up the ice of frozen waterways. This allows other ships to pass through them.

**B**UILD on **WHAT** You Know

**D**o you remember what you learned about plate tectonics? See Chapter 2 to review.

Historical monuments and old architecture compete for attention in Vladivostok. ▼

The Soviet Union considered Vladivostok very important for defense. The city was therefore closed to foreign contacts until the early 1990s. Today it is an important link with China, Japan, the United States, and the rest of the Pacific region.

✓ **READING CHECK:** *Environment and Society* How do the natural resources of the Russian Far East affect its economy?

# Islands

The Russian Far East includes two island areas. Sakhalin is a large island that lies off the eastern coast of Siberia. To the south is the Japanese island of Hokkaido. The Kuril Islands are much smaller. They stretch in an arc from Hokkaido to the Kamchatka Peninsula.

Sakhalin has oil and mineral resources. The waters around the Kurils are important for commercial fishing.

Russia and Japan have argued over who owns these islands since the 1850s. At times they have been divided between Japan and Russia or the Soviet Union. The Soviet Union took control of the islands after World War II. Japan still claims rights to the southernmost islands.

Like other Pacific regions, Sakhalin and the Kurils sometimes experience earthquakes and volcanic eruptions. An earthquake in 1995 caused severe damage on Sakhalin Island, killing nearly 2,000 people.

✓ **READING CHECK:** *Environment and Society* How does the environment of the Kuril Islands and Sakhalin affect people?

▲

An old volcano created Crater Bay in the Kuril Islands. The great beauty of the islands is matched by the terrible power of earthquakes and volcanic eruptions in the area.

**Interpreting the Visual Record** **What do you think happened to the volcano that formed Crater Bay?**

**Define and explain:** icebreakers

**Working with Sketch Maps** On the map you created in Section 4, label the Sea of Okhotsk, the Sea of Japan, the Amur River, Khabarovsk, Vladivostok, and Sakhalin Island. In the margin, explain which countries dispute possession of Sakhalin Island and the Kuril Islands.

**Reading for the Main Idea**

1. *Places and Regions* How does the climate of the Russian Far East compare to the climate throughout the rest of Siberia?

2. *Places and Regions* What are the region's major crops and energy resources?

go.hrw.com **Homework Practice Online** Keyword: SK3 HP14

**Critical Thinking**

3. **Drawing Inferences and Conclusions** In what ways do you think Vladivostok is "Lord of the East" in Russia today?

4. **Drawing Inferences and Conclusions** Why do you think Sakhalin and the Kuril Islands have been the subject of dispute between Russia and Japan?

**Organizing What You Know**

5. **Finding the Main Idea** Copy the following graphic organizer. Use it to explain how the location of each city has played a role in its development.

| Khabarovsk | Vladivostok |
|---|---|
|  |  |

# Reviewing What You Know

## Building Vocabulary

On a separate sheet of paper, write sentences to define each of the following words.

1. taiga
2. steppe
3. czar
4. abdicated
5. allies
6. superpower
7. Cold War
8. consumer goods
9. light industry
10. heavy industry
11. smelters
12. habitation fog
13. icebreakers

## Reviewing the Main Ideas

1. *Places and Regions* What are the major physical features of Russia? Where in Siberia are large coal deposits?

2. *Places and Regions* What landform separates Europe from Asia?

3. *Human Systems* How is Russia's government organized, and how does it compare with that of the United States?

4. *Places and Regions* What four major regions make up European Russia?

5. *Places and Regions* Where were Russian factories relocated during World War II and why?

## Understanding Environment and Society

### Resource Use

The grasslands of the steppe are one of Russia's most valuable agricultural resources. Create a presentation on farming in the steppe. You may want to consider the following:

• The crops that are grown in the Russian steppe.
• The kinds of livestock raised in the region.
• How the climate limits agriculture in the steppe.

## Thinking Critically

1. **Finding the Main Idea** In what ways might Siberia be important to making Russia an economic success?

2. **Contrasting** What kind of economic system did the Soviet Union have, and how did it differ from that of the United States?

3. **Drawing Inferences and Conclusions** Why is transportation an issue for Russia? What have Russians done to ease transportation between European Russia and the Russian Far East?

4. **Analyzing Information** How does Vladivostok's location make it an important link between Russia and the Pacific world?

5. **Identifying Cause and Effect** What problems existed in the Russian Empire and the Soviet Union in the 1900s, and what was their effect?

### Map ACTIVITY

On a separate sheet of paper, match the letters on the map with their correct labels.

Arctic Ocean

Caucasus Mountains

Caspian Sea

West Siberian Plain

Central Siberian Plateau

Kamchatka Peninsula

Volga River

Moscow

St. Petersburg

Vladivostok

### Mental Mapping Skills ACTIVITY

On a separate sheet of paper, draw a freehand map of Russia and label the following:

Baltic Sea

Kuril Islands

Lake Baikal

Sakhalin Island

Siberia

Ural Mountains

### WRITING ACTIVITY

Imagine that you are a tour guide on a trip by train from St. Petersburg to Vladivostok. Use the chapter map or a classroom globe to write a one-page description of some of the places people would see along the train's route. How far would you travel? Be sure to use standard grammar, spelling, sentence structure, and punctuation.

## Alternative Assessment

### Portfolio ACTIVITY

**Learning About Your Local Geography**

**Youth Organizations** The Baikal-Amur Mainline (BAM) was built partly by youth organizations. Make a list of some projects of youth organizations in your community.

**internet connect**

Internet Activity: **go.hrw.com**
KEYWORD: SK3 GT14

Choose a topic to explore about Russia:
- Take a trip on the Trans-Siberian Railroad.
- Examine the breakup of the Soviet Union.
- View the cultural treasures of Russia.

# CHAPTER 15

# Ukraine, Belarus, and the Caucasus

*This region consists of plains in the north and mountains in the south. Both of these physical features made this area important to ancient invaders. Before you learn the history of this region, you should meet Ana.*

Hi! I am a senior in high school in the city of T'bilisi, Georgia. I live with my parents and my younger sister. I go to school from 9:00 A.M. to 2:00 P.M. and study foreign languages—English and Spanish. I hope to be a journalist. In school the teachers decide which classes everyone must take.

After school I do my homework as fast as possible and then get together with my friends. I come home in the early evening and listen to music, read, or watch television.

We also have great food. My favorite dish is baked chicken with nuts. If you came to Georgia, I would take you to the mountains, to the seaside, and to some hot springs. We might also go to a festival where you could see Georgians in the country's national dress. Women wear a long red or purple robe with a white head scarf. Men wear a black suit or robe with gold embroidery.

Привіт! Я Анна.

Translation: Hi! I am Ana.

# Section 1 Physical Geography

## Read to Discover

1. What are the region's major physical features?
2. What climate types and natural resources are found in the region?

## Define

nature reserves

## Locate

Black Sea
Caucasus Mountains

Caspian Sea
Pripyat Marshes
Carpathian Mountains
Crimean Peninsula
Sea of Azov

Mount Elbrus
Dnieper River
Donets Basin

## WHY IT MATTERS

Ukraine is trying to create a nature reserve to protect its natural environment. Use CNNfyi.com or other current events sources to find information about how other countries are trying to protect their environments. Record your findings in your journal.

*A gold pig from Kiev*

## Ukraine, Belarus, and the Caucasus: Physical-Political

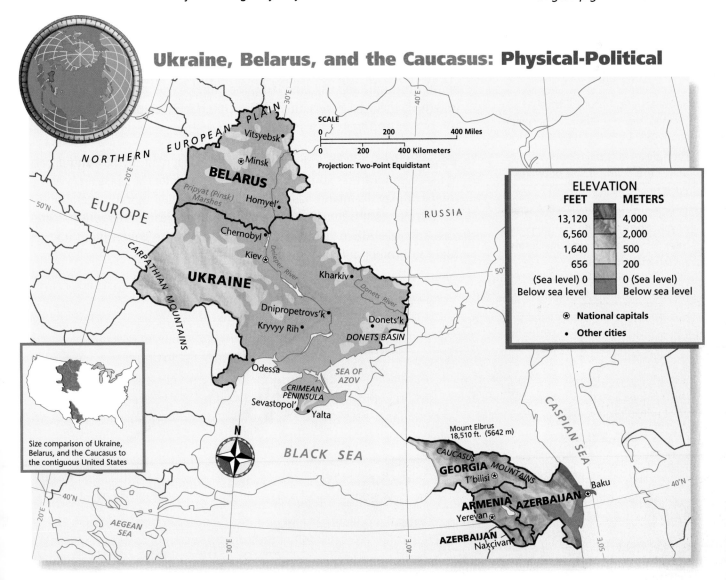

NORTHERN EUROPEAN PLAIN

NORTHERN EUROPE

Vitsyebsk•

⊛ Minsk

**BELARUS**

Pripyat (Pinsk) Marshes

Homyel'•

Chernobyl•

Kiev ⊛

CARPATHIAN MOUNTAINS

Dnieper River

**UKRAINE**

Kharkiv•

Donets River

Dnipropetrovs'k•

Donets'k•

Kryvyy Rih•

**DONETS BASIN**

Odessa•

SEA OF AZOV

CRIMEAN PENINSULA

Sevastopol'•

•Yalta

RUSSIA

BLACK SEA

Mount Elbrus
18,510 ft. (5642 m)

CAUCASUS MOUNTAINS

CASPIAN SEA

**GEORGIA**
T'bilisi ⊛

Baku•

**ARMENIA** **AZERBAIJAN**
Yerevan ⊛

**AZERBAIJAN**
Naxçivan•

AEGEAN SEA

### SCALE

0        200        400 Miles

0    200    400 Kilometers

Projection: Two-Point Equidistant

### ELEVATION

| FEET | METERS |
|---|---|
| 13,120 | 4,000 |
| 6,560 | 2,000 |
| 1,640 | 500 |
| 656 | 200 |
| (Sea level) 0 | 0 (Sea level) |
| Below sea level | Below sea level |

⊛ National capitals
• Other cities

Size comparison of Ukraine, Belarus, and the Caucasus to the contiguous United States

☑ internet connect

GO TO: go.hrw.com
KEYWORD: SK3 CH15
FOR: Web sites about
Ukraine, Belarus, and the
Caucasus

# Physical Features

The countries of Ukraine (yoo-KRAYN) and Belarus (byay-luh-ROOS) border western Russia. Belarus is landlocked. Ukraine lies on the Black Sea. Georgia, Armenia (ahr-MEE-nee-uh), and Azerbaijan (a-zuhr-by-JAHN) lie in a rugged region called the Caucasus (KAW-kuh-suhs). It is named for the area's Caucasus Mountains. The Caucasus region is located between the Black Sea and the Caspian Sea.

**Landforms** Most of Ukraine and Belarus lie in a region of plains. The Northern European Plain sweeps across northern Belarus. The Pripyat (PRI-pyuht) Marshes, also called the Pinsk Marshes, are found in the south. The Carpathian Mountains run through part of western Ukraine. The Crimean (kry-MEE-uhn) Peninsula lies in southern Ukraine. The southern Crimean is very rugged and has high mountains. It separates the Black Sea from the Sea of Azov (uh-ZAWF).

In the north along the Caucasus's border with Russia is a wide mountain range. The region's and Europe's highest peak, Mount Elbrus (el-BROOS), is located here. As you can see on the chapter map, the land drops below sea level along the shore of the Caspian Sea. South of the Caucasus is a rugged, mountainous plateau. Earthquakes often occur in this region.

**Rivers** One of Europe's major rivers, the Dnieper (NEE-puhr), flows south through Belarus and Ukraine. Ships can travel much of its length. Dams and reservoirs on the Dnieper River provide hydroelectric power and water for irrigation.

**Vegetation** Mixed forests were once widespread in the central part of the region. Farther south, the forests opened onto the grasslands of the steppe. Today, farmland has replaced much of the original vegetation.

Ukraine is trying to preserve its natural environments and has created several **nature reserves**. These are areas the government has set aside to protect animals, plants, soil, and water.

✔ READING CHECK: ( *Places and Regions* ) What are the region's major physical features?

Snow-capped Mount Elbrus is located along the border between Georgia and Russia. The surrounding Caucasus Mountains lie along the dividing line between Europe and Asia.

**Interpreting the Visual Record** What physical processes do you think may have formed the mountains in this region of earthquakes?

Russia
● Mt. Elbrus
Georgia
Turkey

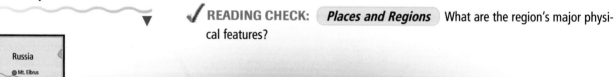

# Climate

**D**o you remember what you learned about steppe climates? See Chapter 3 to review.

Like much of western Russia, the northern two thirds of Ukraine and Belarus have a humid continental climate. Winters are cold. Summers are warm but short. Southern Ukraine has a steppe climate. Unlike the rest of the country, the Crimean Peninsula has a Mediterranean climate. There are several different climates in the Caucasus. Georgia's coast has a mild climate similar to the Carolinas in the United States. Azerbaijan contains mainly a steppe climate. Because it is so mountainous, Armenia's climate changes with elevation.

✓ **READING CHECK:** ( *Places and Regions* ) What climate types are found in this area?

# Resources

Rich farmlands are Ukraine's greatest natural resource. Farming is also important in Belarus. Lowland areas of the Caucasus have rich soil and good conditions for farming.

The Donets (duh-NYETS) Basin in southeastern Ukraine is a rich coal-mining area. Kryvyy Rih (kri-VI RIK) is the site of a huge open-pit iron-ore mine. The region's most important mineral resources are Azerbaijan's large and valuable oil and gas deposits. These are found under the shallow Caspian Sea. Copper, manganese, iron, and other metals are also present in the Caucasus.

✓ **READING CHECK:** ( *Environment and Society* ) How have this region's natural resources affected economic development?

**go.hrw.com** **Homework Practice Online**
Keyword: SK3 HP15

## Section Review 1

**Define and explain:** nature reserves

**Working with Sketch Maps** On a map of Europe that you draw or that your teacher provides, label the following: Black Sea, Caucasus Mountains, Caspian Sea, Pripyat Marshes, Carpathian Mountains, Crimean Peninsula, Sea of Azov, Mount Elbrus, Dnieper River, and Donets Basin. Where in the region is a major coal-mining area?

### Reading for the Main Idea

1. ( *Places and Regions* ) What three seas are found in this region?

2. ( *Places and Regions* ) What creates variation in Armenia's climate?

### Critical Thinking

3. **Drawing Inferences and Conclusions** Why has so much farming developed in Ukraine, Belarus, and the Caucasus?

4. **Drawing Inferences and Conclusions** How do you think heavy mining in this region could create pollution?

### Organizing What You Know

5. **Categorizing** Copy the following graphic organizer. Use it to describe the region's physical features, climates, and resources.

| | Physical features | Climate | Resources |
|---|---|---|---|
| Belarus | | | |
| Caucasus | | | |
| Ukraine | | | |

# Section 2 Ukraine and Belarus

## Read to Discover

1. Which groups have influenced the history of Ukraine and Belarus?
2. What are some important economic features and environmental concerns of Ukraine?
3. How has the economy of Belarus developed?

## Define

serfs
Cossacks
soviet

## Locate

Ukraine
Belarus
Kiev
Chernobyl
Minsk

### WHY IT MATTERS

Energy created by nuclear power plants is important to the United States, Ukraine, and Belarus. Go to CNN **fyi**.com or other **current events** sources to find information about nuclear energy. Record your findings in your journal.

*A hand-painted Ukrainian egg*

## гео·гра·фия

▲

These are the syllables for the Russian word for geography, written in the Cyrillic alphabet.

# History and Government

About 600 B.C. the Greeks established trading colonies along the coast of the Black Sea. Much later—during the A.D. 400s—the Slavs began to move into what is now Ukraine and Belarus. Today, most people in this region speak closely related Slavic languages.

**Vikings and Christians** In the 800s Vikings took the city of Kiev. Located on the Dnieper River, it became the capital of the Vikings' trading empire. Today, this old city is Ukraine's capital. In the 900s the Byzantine, or Greek Orthodox, Church sent missionaries to teach the Ukrainians and Belorussians about Christianity. These missionaries introduced the Cyrillic alphabet.

St. Sophia Cathedral in Kiev was built in the 1000s. It was one of the earliest Orthodox cathedrals in this area. Religious images decorate the dome's interior.

◀

**Mongols and Cossacks** A grandson of Genghis Khan led the Mongol horsemen that conquered Ukraine in the 1200s. They destroyed most of the towns and cities there, including Kiev.

Later, northern Ukraine and Belarus came under the control of Lithuanians and Poles. Under foreign rule, Ukrainian and Belorussian **serfs** suffered. Serfs were people who were bound to the land and worked for a lord. In return, the lords provided the serfs with military protection and other services. Some Russian and Ukrainian serfs left the farms and formed bands of nomadic horsemen. Known as **Cossacks**, they lived on the Ukrainian frontier.

**The Russian Empire** North and east of Belarus, a new state arose around Moscow. This Russian kingdom of Muscovy won independence from the Mongols in the late 1400s. The new state set out to expand its borders. By the 1800s all of modern Belarus and Ukraine were under Moscow's rule. Now the Cossacks served the armies of the Russian czar. However, conditions did not improve for the Ukrainian and Belorussian serfs and peasants.

**Soviet Republics** The Russian Revolution ended the rule of the czars in 1917. Ukraine and Belarus became republics of the Soviet Union in 1922. Although each had its own governing **soviet**, or council, Communist leaders in Moscow made all major decisions.

Ukraine was especially important as the Soviet Union's richest farming region. On the other hand, Belarus became a major industrial center. It produced heavy machinery for the Soviet Union. While Ukraine and Belarus were part of the Soviet Union, the Ukrainian and Belorussian languages were discouraged. Practicing a religion was also discouraged.

After World War II economic development continued in Ukraine and Belarus. Factories and power plants were built with little concern for the safety of nearby residents.

This watercolor on rice paper depicts Kublai Khan. He was the founder of the vast Mongol empire in the 1200s. The Mongols conquered large areas of Asia and Europe, including Ukraine.

Kiev remained an important cultural and industrial center during the Soviet era. Parts of the city were destroyed during World War II and had to be rebuilt. Today tree-lined streets greet shoppers in the central city.

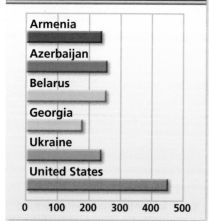

Near the end of World War II, Soviet, American, and British leaders met at Livadia Palace in Yalta, Ukraine. There they planned the defeat and occupation of Germany.

**End of Soviet Rule** When the Soviet Union collapsed in 1991, Belarus and Ukraine declared independence. Each now has a president and a prime minister. Both countries still have economic problems. Ukraine has also had disagreements with Russia over control of the Crimean Peninsula and the Black Sea naval fleet.

✓ **READING CHECK:** ( *Human Systems* ) Which groups have influenced the history of Ukraine and Belarus?

## Patients per Doctor

|  | |
|---|---|
| Armenia | |
| Azerbaijan | |
| Belarus | |
| Georgia | |
| Ukraine | |
| United States | |

0   100   200   300   400   500

Source: *The World Book Encyclopedia of People and Places*

**Interpreting the Graph** In what country is the number of patients per doctor greatest?

# Ukraine

Ethnic Ukrainians make up about 75 percent of Ukraine's population. The largest minority group in the country is Russian. There are other ties between Ukraine and Russia. For example, the Ukrainian and Russian languages are closely related. In addition, both countries use the Cyrillic alphabet.

**Economy** Ukraine has a good climate for growing crops and some of the world's richest soil. As a result, agriculture is important to its economy. Ukraine is the world's largest producer of sugar beets. Ukraine's food-processing industry makes sugar from the sugar beets. Farmers also grow fruits, potatoes, vegetables, and wheat. Grain is made into flour for baked goods and pasta. Livestock is also raised. Ukraine is one of the world's top steel producers. Ukrainian factories make automobiles, railroad cars, ships, and trucks.

# CONNECTING TO Science

*A combine used during July harvest*

## Wheat: From Field to Consumer

Wheat is one of Ukraine's most important farm products. The illustration below shows how wheat is processed for use by consumers.

• The head of the wheat plant contains the wheat kernels, wrapped in husks. The kernel includes the bran or seed coat, the endosperm, and the germ from which new wheat plants grow.

• Whole wheat flour contains all the parts of the kernel. White flour is produced by grinding only the endosperm. Vitamins are added to some white flour to replace vitamins found in the bran and germ.

• People use wheat to make breads, pastas, and breakfast foods. Wheat by-products are used in many other foods.

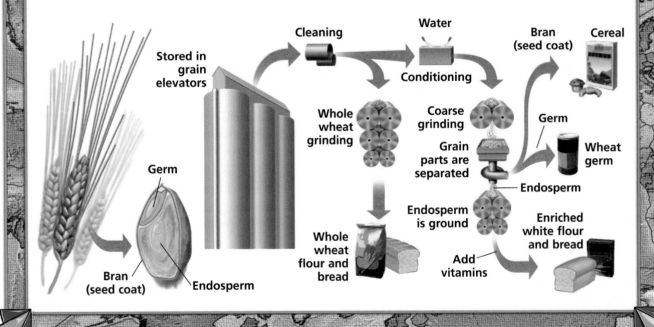

**Environment** During the Soviet period, Ukraine experienced rapid industrial growth. There were few pollution controls, however. In 1986 at the town of Chernobyl, the world's worst nuclear-reactor disaster occurred. Radiation spread across Ukraine and parts of northern Europe. People near the accident died. Others are still suffering from cancer. Many Ukrainians now want to reduce their country's dependence on nuclear power. This has been hard because the country has not developed enough alternative sources of power.

✓ **READING CHECK:** *Environment and Society* How has the scarcity of alternative sources of power affected Ukraine?

| COUNTRY | POPULATION/ GROWTH RATE | LIFE EXPECTANCY | LITERACY RATE | PER CAPITA GDP |
|---------|-------------------------|-----------------|---------------|----------------|
| **Belarus and Ukraine** | | | | |
| Belarus | 10,350,194 −0.2% | 62, male 75, female | 98% | $7,500 |
| Ukraine | 48,760,474 −0.9% | 61, male 72, female | 98% | $3,850 |
| United States | 281,421,906 0.9% | 73, male 80, female | 97% | $36,200 |

**Sources:** Central Intelligence Agency, *The World Factbook 2001;* U.S. Census Bureau

**Interpreting the Chart** **How does life expectancy in the region compare to that of the United States? Why do you think this is the case?**

# Belarus

The people of Belarus are known as Belorussians, which means "white Russians." Ethnically they are closely related to Russians. Their language is also very similar to Russian.

**Culture** Ethnic Belorussians make up about 75 percent of the country's population. Russians are the second-largest ethnic group. Both Belorussian and Russian are official languages. Belorussian also uses the Cyrillic alphabet. Minsk, the capital of Belarus, is the administrative center of the Commonwealth of Independent States.

**Economy** Belarus has faced many difficulties. Fighting in World War II destroyed most of the agriculture and industry in the country. Belarus also received the worst of the radiation fallout from the Chernobyl nuclear disaster, which contaminated the country's farm products and water. Many people developed health problems as a result. Another problem has been slow economic progress since the collapse of the Soviet Union. Belarus has resisted economic changes made by other former Soviet republics.

There are various resources in Belarus, however. The country has a large reserve of potash, which is used for fertilizer. Belarus leads the world in the production of peat, a source of fuel found in the damp marshes. Mining and manufacturing are important to the economy. Flax, one of the country's main crops, is grown for fiber and seed. Cattle and pigs are also raised. Nearly one third of Belarus is covered by forests that produce wood and paper products.

✓ **READING CHECK:** ( *Human Systems* ) How has the economy of Belarus developed?

go. hrw .com **Homework Practice Online**

**Keyword: SK3 HP15**

## Section Review 2

**Define and explain:** serfs, Cossacks, soviet

**Working with Sketch Maps** On your map from Section 1, label Ukraine, Belarus, Kiev, Chernobyl, and Minsk.

### Reading for the Main Idea

**1.** ( *Human Systems* ) What contributions were made by early groups that settled in this region?

**2.** ( *Human Systems* ) What ethnic groups and languages are found in this region today?

### Critical Thinking

**3. Finding the Main Idea** How did the end of Soviet rule affect Ukraine and Belarus?

**4. Summarizing** How has the nuclear disaster at Chernobyl affected the region?

### Organizing What You Know

**5. Sequencing** Copy the time line below. Use it to trace the region's history from the A.D. 900s to today.

A.D. 900                           Today

# Section 3

## The Caucasus

### Read to Discover

1. What groups influenced the early history and culture of the Caucasus?
2. What is the economy of Georgia like?
3. What is Armenia like today?
4. What is Azerbaijan like today?

### Define
homogeneous
agrarian

### Locate
Georgia
Armenia
Azerbaijan

**WHY IT MATTERS**

Each of the countries in this section has been involved in a war since the collapse of the Soviet Union in 1991. Use CNNfyi.com or other current events sources to find information about the reasons for this unrest. Record your findings in your journal.

*Cover of* The Knight in Panther's Skin

## History

In the 500s B.C. the Caucasus region was controlled by the Persian Empire. Later it was brought under the influence of the Byzantine Empire and was introduced to Christianity. About A.D. 650, Muslim invaders cut the region off from Christian Europe. By the late 1400s other Muslims, the Ottoman Turks, ruled a vast empire to the south and west. Much of Armenia eventually came under the rule of that empire.

**Modern Era** During the 1800s Russia took over eastern Armenia, much of Azerbaijan, and Georgia. The Ottoman Turks continued to rule western Armenia. Many Armenians spread throughout the Ottoman Empire. However, they were not treated well. Their desire for more independence led to the massacre of thousands of Armenians. Hundreds of thousands died while being forced to leave Turkey during World War I. Some fled to Russian Armenia.

After the war Armenia, Azerbaijan, and Georgia were briefly independent. By 1922 they had become part of the Soviet Union. They again became independent when the Soviet Union collapsed in 1991.

This wall painting is one of many at the ancient Erebuni Citadel in Yerevan, Armenia's capital. The fortress was probably built in the 800s B.C. by one of Armenia's earliest peoples, the Urartians.

▼

**Government** Each country has an elected parliament, president, and prime minister. In the early 1990s there was civil war in Georgia. Armenia and Azerbaijan were also involved in a war during this time. Ethnic minorities in each country want independence. Disagreements about oil and gas rights may cause more regional conflicts in the future.

✓ **READING CHECK:** ( *Human Systems* ) How has conflict among cultures been a problem in this region?

▲

This Georgian family's breakfast includes local specialties such as *khachapuri*—bread made with goat cheese.

**Interpreting the Visual Record**

**What other agricultural products do you see on the table?**

# Georgia

Georgia is a small country located between the high Caucasus Mountains and the Black Sea. It has a population of about 5 million. About 70 percent of the people are ethnic Georgians. The official language, Georgian, has its own alphabet. This alphabet was used as early as A.D. 400.

As in all the former Soviet republics, independence and economic reforms have been difficult. Georgia has also suffered from civil war. By the late 1990s the conflicts were fewer but not resolved.

Georgia has little good farmland. Tea and citrus fruits are the major crops. Vineyards are an important part of Georgian agriculture. Fish, livestock, and poultry contribute to the economy. Tourism on the Black Sea has also helped the economy. Because its only energy resource is hydropower, Georgia imports most of its energy supplies.

✓ **READING CHECK:** ( *Human Systems* ) In what way has scarcity of energy resources affected Georgia's economy?

# Armenia

Armenia is a little smaller than Maryland. It lies just east of Turkey. It has fewer than 4 million people and is not as diverse as other countries

The Orthodox Christian Agartsya Monastery was built in Armenia in the 1200s.

**Interpreting the Visual Record**

**Why do you think this building's exterior is so well preserved?**

▶

in the Caucasus. Almost all the people are Armenian, belong to the Armenian Orthodox Church, and speak Armenian.

Armenia's progress toward economic reform has not been easy. In 1988 a massive earthquake destroyed nearly one third of its industry. Armenia's industry today is varied. It includes mining and the production of carpets, clothing, and footwear.

Agriculture accounts for about 40 percent of Armenia's gross domestic product. High-quality grapes and fruits are important. Beef and dairy cattle and sheep are raised on mountain pastures.

✓ **READING CHECK:** *Environment and Society*
How did the 1998 earthquake affect the people of Armenia?

## The Caucasus

| COUNTRY | POPULATION/ GROWTH RATE | LIFE EXPECTANCY | LITERACY RATE | PER CAPITA GDP |
|---|---|---|---|---|
| Armenia | 3,336,100 −0.2% | 62, male 71, female | 99% | $3,000 |
| Azerbaijan | 7,771,092 0.3% | 59, male 68, female | 97% | $3,000 |
| Georgia | 4,989,285 −0.6% | 61, male 68, female | 99% | $4,600 |
| United States | 281,421,906 0.9% | 74, male 80, female | 97% | $36,200 |

**Sources:** Central Intelligence Agency, *The World Factbook 2001;* U.S. Census Bureau

**Interpreting the Chart** Which countries have the lowest per capita GDP in the region? Why might this be the case?

# Azerbaijan

Azerbaijan has nearly 8 million people. Its population is becoming ethnically more **homogeneous**, or the same. The Azeri, who speak a Turkic language, make up about 90 percent of the population.

Azerbaijan has few industries except for oil production. It is mostly an **agrarian** society. An agrarian society is organized around farming. The country's main resources are cotton, natural gas, and oil. Baku, the national capital, is the center of a large oil-refining industry. Oil is the most important part of Azerbaijan's economy. Fishing is also important because of the sturgeon of the Caspian Sea.

✓ **READING CHECK:** *Human Systems* What are some cultural traits of the people of Azerbaijan?

**Homework Practice Online**
Keyword: SK3 HP15

**Define and explain:** homogeneous, agrarian

**Working with Sketch Maps** On the map you created for Section 2, label Georgia, Armenia, and Azerbaijan. How has the location of this region helped and hindered its growth?

## Reading for the Main Idea

**1.** *Human Systems* Which groups influenced the early history of the Caucasus?

**2.** *Human Systems* Which country controlled the Caucasus during most of the 1900s?

## Critical Thinking

**3. Analyzing Information** Why has economic reform been difficult in Armenia?

**4. Finding the Main Idea** How is Azerbaijan's economy organized?

## Organizing What You Know

**5. Comparing/Contrasting** Copy the following graphic organizer. Use it to show the similarities and differences among the countries of the Caucasus region.

# Reviewing What You Know

## Building Vocabulary

On a separate sheet of paper, write sentences to define each of the following words.

1. nature reserves
2. serfs
3. Cossacks
4. soviet
5. homogeneous
6. agrarian

## Reviewing the Main Ideas

1. **( Human Systems )** Which industries have traditionally been very important to the economies of the countries covered in this chapter?

2. **( Human Systems )** What is the relative location of Kiev? Which group of people founded Kiev?

3. **( Human Systems )** What peoples were apparently the first to settle in Belarus and Ukraine?

4. **( Environment and Society )** How did industrialization under Soviet rule affect these regions?

5. **( Environment and Society )** What effect did the earthquake in 1988 have on Armenia's economy?

## Understanding Environment and Society

### Resource Use

Prepare a chart and presentation on oil and natural gas production in the Caucasus. In preparing your presentation, consider the following:

- When and where oil and natural gas were discovered.
- The importance of oil and natural gas production to the former Soviet Union.
- How oil is transported from there to international markets today.

When you have finished your chart and presentation, write a five-question quiz, with answers, about your chart to challenge fellow students.

## Thinking Critically

1. **Drawing Inferences and Conclusions** How might ethnic diversity affect relations among countries?

2. **Analyzing Information** How did the location of Ukraine and Belarus contribute to their devastation during World War II?

3. **Analyzing Information** Of the countries covered in this chapter, which do you think was the most important to the former Soviet Union? Why do you think this was so?

4. **Summarizing** Why did the countries of the Caucasus develop so differently from Russia, Ukraine, and Belarus?

5. **Finding the Main Idea** Why are the economies of each of the Caucasus countries so different from one another?

### Map ACTIVITY

On a separate sheet of paper, match the letters on the map with their correct labels.

Caucasus Mountains    Crimean Peninsula

Pripyat Marshes    Mount Elbrus

Carpathian Mountains    Donets Basin

Chernobyl

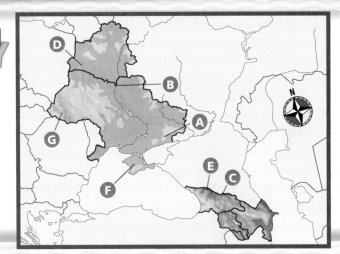

### Mental Mapping Skills ACTIVITY

On a separate sheet of paper, draw a freehand map of Ukraine, Belarus, and the Caucasus. Include Russia and Turkey for location reference. Make a map key and label the following:

| | |
|---|---|
| Armenia | Dnieper River |
| Azerbaijan | Georgia |
| Belarus | Russia |
| Black Sea | Turkey |
| Caspian Sea | Ukraine |

### WRITING ACTIVITY

Choose one of the countries covered in this chapter to research. Write a report about your chosen country's struggle to establish stability since 1991. Include information about the country's government and economic reforms. Describe the social, political, and economic problems the country has faced. Be sure to use standard grammar, sentence structure, spelling, and punctuation.

## Alternative Assessment

### Portfolio ACTIVITY

**Learning About Your Local Geography**

**Cooperative Project** What is an important crop in your region of the United States? Work with a partner to create an illustrated flowchart that shows how this crop is made ready for consumers.

### internet connect

Internet Activity: **go.hrw.com**
KEYWORD: SK3 GT15

Choose a topic to explore about Ukraine, Belarus, and the Caucasus.
- Trek through the Caucasus Mountains.
- Design Ukrainian Easter eggs.
- Investigate the Chernobyl disaster.

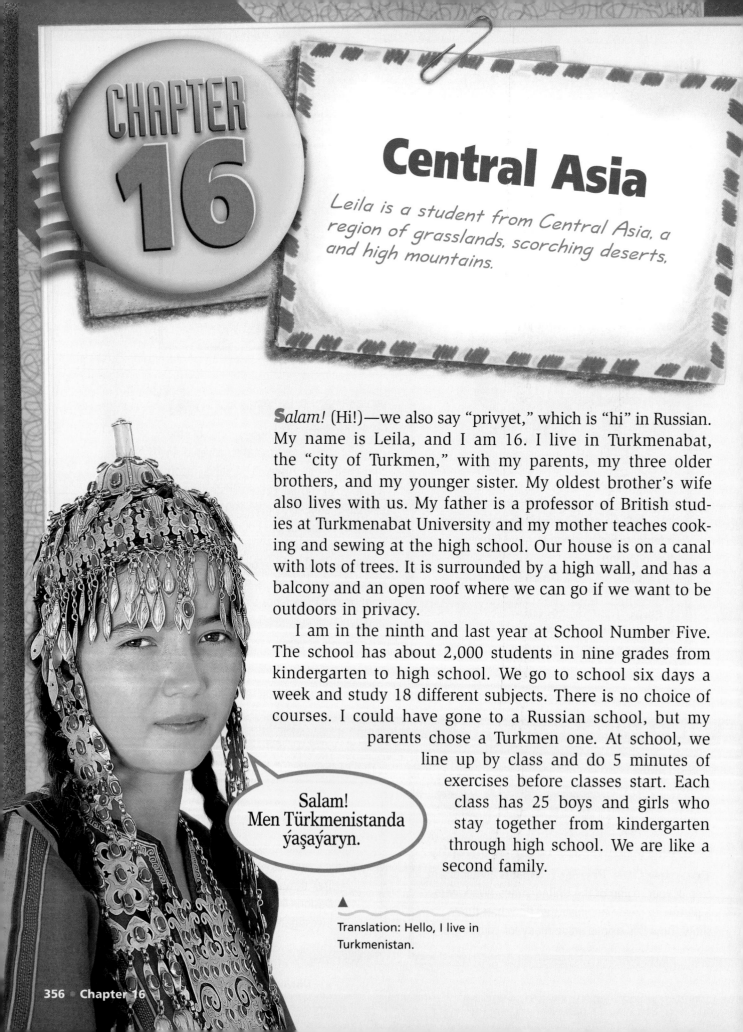

# CHAPTER 16

# Central Asia

*Leila is a student from Central Asia, a region of grasslands, scorching deserts, and high mountains.*

*S*alam! (Hi!)—we also say "privyet," which is "hi" in Russian. My name is Leila, and I am 16. I live in Turkmenabat, the "city of Turkmen," with my parents, my three older brothers, and my younger sister. My oldest brother's wife also lives with us. My father is a professor of British studies at Turkmenabat University and my mother teaches cooking and sewing at the high school. Our house is on a canal with lots of trees. It is surrounded by a high wall, and has a balcony and an open roof where we can go if we want to be outdoors in privacy.

I am in the ninth and last year at School Number Five. The school has about 2,000 students in nine grades from kindergarten to high school. We go to school six days a week and study 18 different subjects. There is no choice of courses. I could have gone to a Russian school, but my parents chose a Turkmen one. At school, we line up by class and do 5 minutes of exercises before classes start. Each class has 25 boys and girls who stay together from kindergarten through high school. We are like a second family.

Salam!
Men Türkmenistanda
ýaşaýaryn.

▲
Translation: Hello, I live in Turkmenistan.

# Section 1 Physical Geography

## Read to Discover

1. What are the main landforms and climates of Central Asia?
2. What resources are important to Central Asia?

## Define

landlocked
oasis

## Locate

Pamirs
Tian Shan
Aral Sea
Kara-Kum

Kyzyl Kum
Syr Dar'ya
Amu Dar'ya
Fergana Valley

### WHY IT MATTERS

The countries of Uzbekistan, Kazakhstan, and Turkmenistan have large oil and natural gas reserves. Use CNN fyi.com or other current events sources to find examples of efforts to develop these resources. Record your findings in your journal.

A Bactrian camel and rider

## Central Asia: Physical-Political

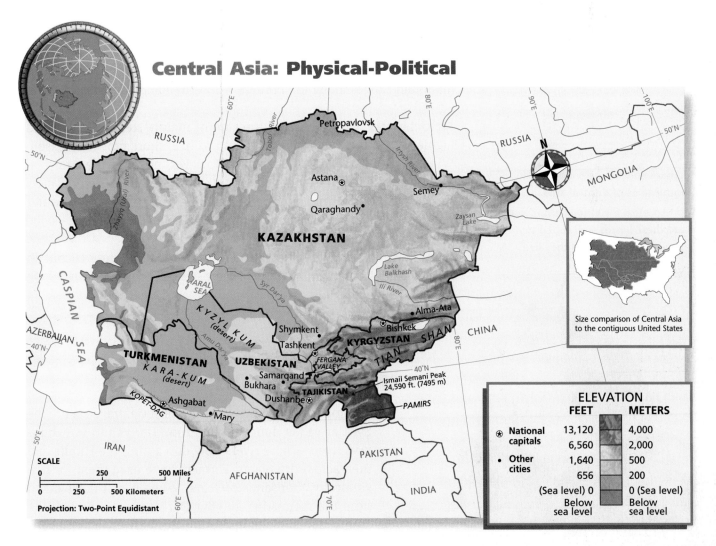

Size comparison of Central Asia to the contiguous United States

| ELEVATION | | |
|---|---|---|
| | FEET | METERS |
| ⊛ National capitals | 13,120 | 4,000 |
| | 6,560 | 2,000 |
| • Other cities | 1,640 | 500 |
| | 656 | 200 |
| | (Sea level) 0 | 0 (Sea level) |
| | Below sea level | Below sea level |

SCALE
0    250    500 Miles
0    250    500 Kilometers
Projection: Two-Point Equidistant

Mountain climbers make camp before attempting to scale a peak in the Pamirs.

## Our Amazing Planet

**W**ith temperatures above 122°F (50°C), it is not surprising that the creatures that live in the Kara-Kum are a tough group. Over a thousand species live there, including cobras, scorpions, tarantulas, and monitor lizards. These lizards can grow to more than 5 feet (1.5m) long.

Lynxes can still be found in the mountains of Central Asia.
**Interpreting the Visual Record How are these lynxes well suited to the environment in which they live?**

# Landforms and Climate

This huge, **landlocked** region is to the east of the Caspian Sea. Landlocked means the region does not border an ocean. The region lies north of the Pamirs (puh-MIRZ) and Tian Shan (TYEN SHAHN) mountain ranges.

**Diverse Landforms** As the name suggests, Central Asia lies in the middle of the largest continent. Plains and low plateaus cover much of this area. Around the Caspian Sea the land is as low as 95 feet (29 m) below sea level. However, the region includes high mountain ranges along the borders with China and Afghanistan.

**Arid Lands** Central Asia is a region of mainly steppe, desert, and highland climates. Summers are hot, with a short growing season. Winters are cold. Rainfall is sparse. However, north of the Aral (AR-uhl) Sea rainfall is heavy enough for steppe vegetation. Here farmers can grow crops using rain, rather than irrigation, as their water source. South and east of the Aral Sea lie two deserts. One is the Kara-Kum (kahr-uh-KOOM) in Turkmenistan. The other is the Kyzyl Kum (ki-ZIL KOOM) in Uzbekistan and Kazakhstan. Both deserts contain several **oasis** settlements where a spring or well provides water.

✔ **READING CHECK:** *Places and Regions* What are the landforms and climates of Central Asia?

# Resources

The main water sources in southern Central Asia are the Syr Dar'ya (sir duhr-YAH) and Amu Dar'ya (uh-MOO duhr-YAH) rivers. These rivers flow down from the Pamirs and then across dry plains. Farmers have used them for irrigation for thousands of years. When it first flows down from the mountains, the Syr Dar'ya passes through the

Fergana Valley. This large valley is divided among Uzbekistan, Kyrgyzstan, and Tajikistan. As the river flows toward the Aral Sea, irrigated fields line its banks.

During the Soviet period, the region's population grew rapidly. Also, the Soviets encouraged farmers to grow cotton. This crop grows well in Central Asia's sunny climate. However, growing cotton uses a lot of water. Increased use of water has caused the Aral Sea to shrink.

**A Dying Sea** Today, almost no water from the Syr Dar'ya or Amu Dar'ya reaches the Aral Sea. The rivers' waters are used up by human activity. The effect on the Aral Sea has been devastating. It has lost more than 60 percent of its water since 1960. Its level has dropped 50 feet (15 m) and is still dropping. Towns that were once fishing ports are now dozens of miles from the shore. Winds sweep the dry seafloor, blowing dust, salt, and pesticides hundreds of miles.

**Mineral Resources** The Central Asian countries' best economic opportunity is in their fossil fuels. Uzbekistan, Kazakhstan, and Turkmenistan all have huge oil and natural gas reserves. However, transporting the oil and gas to other countries is a problem. Economic and political turmoil in some surrounding countries has made it difficult to build pipelines.

Several Central Asian countries are also rich in other minerals. They have deposits of gold, copper, uranium, zinc, and lead. Kazakhstan has vast amounts of coal. Rivers in Kyrgyzstan and Tajikistan could be used to create hydroelectric power.

■ **internet** connect

GO TO: go.hrw.com
KEYWORD: SK3 CH16

FOR: Web sites about Central Asia

This boat sits rusting on what was once part of the Aral Sea. The sea's once thriving fishing industry has been destroyed.

✓ **READING CHECK:** *Environment and Society* How has human activity affected the Aral Sea?

---

# Section Review 1

**go.hrw.com**

**Homework Practice Online**

Keyword: SK3 HP16

**Define and explain:** landlocked, oasis

**Working with Sketch Maps** On a map of Central Asia that you draw or that your teacher provides, label the following: Pamirs, Tian Shan, Aral Sea, Kara-Kum, Kyzyl Kum, Syr Dar'ya, Amu Dar'ya, and Fergana Valley.

## Reading for the Main Idea

**1.** *Environment and Society* What has caused the drying up of the Aral Sea?

**2.** *Places and Regions* What mineral resources does Central Asia have?

## Critical Thinking

**3. Analyzing Information** Why did the Soviets encourage Central Asian farmers to grow cotton?

**4. Finding the Main Idea** What factors make it hard for the Central Asian countries to export oil and gas?

## Organizing What You Know

**5. Sequencing** Copy the following graphic organizer. Use it to describe the courses of the Syr Dar'ya and Amu Dar'ya, including human activities that use water.

| Melting snows in the Pamirs | ⇨ | | ⇨ | Aral Sea |

# Section 2 History and Culture

## Read to Discover

1. How did trade and invasions affect the history of Central Asia?
2. What are political and economic conditions like in Central Asia today?

## Define

nomads
caravans

### WHY IT MATTERS

Even though the Soviet Union has collapsed, traces of its influence remain in Central Asia, particularly in government. Use CNNfyi.com or other current events sources to find examples of political events in these countries. Record your findings in your journal.

*An ancient Kyrgyz stone figure*

## History

For centuries, Central Asians have made a living by raising horses, cattle, sheep, and goats. Many of these herders lived as **nomads**, people who often move from place to place. Other people became farmers around rivers and oases.

**Trade** At one time, the best land route between China and the eastern Mediterranean ran through Central Asia. Merchants traveled in large groups, called **caravans**, for protection. The goods they carried included silk and spices. As a result, this route came to be called the Silk Road. Cities along the road became centers of wealth and culture.

Central Asia's situation changed after Europeans discovered they could sail to East Asia through the Indian Ocean. As a result, trade through Central Asia declined. The region became isolated and poor.

Bukhara, in Uzbekistan, was once a powerful and wealthy trading center of Central Asia.

**Interpreting the Visual Record**

**What architectural features can you see that distinguish Bukhara as an Islamic city?**

▼

*Silk processing in modern Uzbekistan*

## The Silk Road

The Silk Road stretched 5,000 miles (8,000 km) across Central Asia from China to the Mediterranean Sea. Along this route passed merchants, armies, and diplomats. These people forged links between East and West.

The facts of the Silk Road are still wrapped in mystery. Chinese trade and military expeditions probably began moving into Central Asia in the 100s B.C. Chinese trade goods soon were making their way to eastern Mediterranean ports.

Over the next several centuries, trade in silk, spices, jewels, and other luxury goods increased. Great caravans of camels and oxcarts traveled the Silk Road in both directions. They crossed the harsh deserts and mountains of Central Asia. Cities like Samarqand and Bukhara grew rich from the trade. In the process, ideas and technology also moved between Europe and Asia.

Travel along the Silk Road was hazardous. Bandits often robbed the caravans. Some travelers lost their way in the desert and died. In addition, religious and political turmoil occasionally disrupted travel.

### Understanding What You Read
1. What was the Silk Road?
2. Why was the Silk Road important?

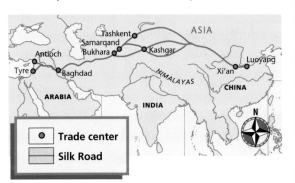

**Invasions and the Soviet Era** About A.D. 500, Turkic-speaking nomads from northern Asia spread through Central Asia. In the 700s Arab armies took over much of the region, bringing Islam. In the 1200s the armies of Mongol leaders conquered Central Asia. Later, another Turkic people, the Uzbeks, took over parts of the region. In the 1800s the Russian Empire conquered Central Asia.

After the Russian Revolution, the Soviet government set up five republics in Central Asia. The Soviets encouraged ethnic Russians to move to this area and made the nomads settle on collective ranches or farms. Religion was discouraged. Russian became the language of government and business. The government set up schools and hospitals. Women were allowed to work outside the home.

✓ **READING CHECK:** ( *Human Systems* ) What type of government system did the five republics set up by the Soviet Union have?

**D**o you remember what you learned about acculturation? See Chapter 5 to review.

A Kyrgyz teacher conducts class.

**Interpreting the Visual Record**

**How is this class similar to yours?**

# Central Asia Today

The five republics became independent countries when the Soviet Union broke up in 1991. All have strong economic ties to Russia. Ethnic Russians still live in every country in the region. However, all five countries are switching from the Cyrillic alphabet to the Latin alphabet. The Cyrillic alphabet had been imposed on them by the Soviet Union. The Latin alphabet is used in most Western European languages, including English, and in Turkey.

**Government** All of these new countries have declared themselves to be democracies. However, they are not very free or democratic. Each is ruled by a strong central government that limits opposition and criticism.

**Economy** Some of the Central Asian countries have oil and gas reserves that may someday make them rich. For now, though, all are suffering economic hardship. Causes of the hardships include outdated equipment, lack of funds, and poor transportation links.

Farming is important in the Central Asian economies. Crops include cotton, wheat, barley, fruits, vegetables, almonds, tobacco, and rice. Central Asians raise cattle, sheep, horses, goats, and camels. They also raise silkworms to make silk thread.

Industry in Central Asia includes food processing, wool textiles, mining, and oil drilling. Oil-rich Turkmenistan and Kazakhstan also process oil into other products. Kazakhstan and Uzbekistan make heavy equipment such as tractors.

✓ **READING CHECK:** *Human Systems* How do political freedoms in the region compare to those of the United States?

go.
hrw
.com

Homework
Practice
Online

Keyword: SK3 HP16

# Section Review 2

**Define and explain:** nomads, caravans

**Working with Sketch Maps** On the map you created in Section 1, draw and label the five Central Asian countries.

**Reading for the Main Idea**

**1.** *Environment and Society* How have the people of Central Asia made a living over the centuries?

**2.** *Human Systems* What are four groups that invaded Central Asia?

**3.** *Human Systems* How did Soviet rule change Central Asia?

**Critical Thinking**

**4. Drawing Inferences and Conclusions** What does the switch to the Latin alphabet suggest about the Central Asian countries?

**Organizing What You Know**

**5. Categorizing** Copy the following graphic organizer. Use it to categorize economic activities in Central Asia. Place the following items in the chart: making cloth, growing crops, mining metals, making food products, raising livestock, making chemicals from oil, drilling for oil, and manufacturing tractors.

| Primary industries | Secondary industries |
|---|---|
|  |  |
|  |  |

# Section 3 The Countries of Central Asia

## Read to Discover

1. What are some important aspects of culture in Kazakhstan?
2. How does Kyrgyz culture reflect nomadic traditions?
3. Why have politics in Tajikistan in recent years been marked by violence?
4. What are two important art forms in Turkmenistan?
5. How is Uzbekistan's population significant?

## Define

yurt
mosques

## Locate

Tashkent
Samarqand

*A warrior's armor from Kazakhstan*

### WHY IT MATTERS

Since the collapse of the Soviet Union, religious freedom is more common in Central Asia. Use CNN fyi.com or other **current events** sources to find examples of religious and ethnic differences in the countries of Central Asia. Record your findings in your journal.

## Kazakhstan

Of the Central Asian nations, Kazakhstan was the first to be conquered by Russia. Russian influence remains strong there. About one third of Kazakhstan's people are ethnic Russians. Kazakh and Russian are both official languages. Many ethnic Kazakhs grow up speaking Russian at home and have to learn Kazakh in school.

Kazakhstanis celebrate the New Year twice—on January 1 and again on Nauruz, the start of the Persian calendar's year. Nauruz falls on the spring equinox.

Food in Central Asia combines influences from Southwest Asia and China. Rice, yogurt, and grilled meat are common ingredients. One Kazakh specialty is smoked horsemeat sausage with cold noodles.

✓ **READING CHECK:** *Human Systems* How has Kazakhstan been influenced by Russia?

A woman in Uzbekistan grills meat on skewers.

▼

## Kyrgyzstan

Kyrgyzstan has many mountains, and the people live mostly in valleys. People in the southern part of the country generally share cultural ties with Uzbekistan. People in northern areas are more linked to nomadic cultures and to Kazakhstan.

## Ethnic Makeup of Kazakhstan and Uzbekistan

**Kazakhstan**

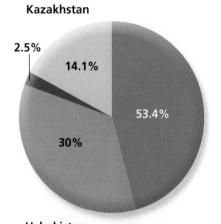

2.5%
14.1%
53.4%
30%

**Uzbekistan**

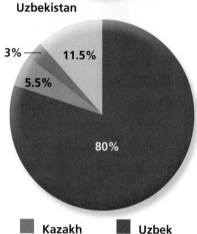

3%
11.5%
5.5%
80%

■ Kazakh    ■ Uzbek
■ Russian   ■ Other

**Source:** Central Intelligence Agency, *The World Factbook 2001*

**Interpreting the Chart** How does the number of Russians in Kazakhstan compare to that in Uzbekistan?

Turkoman women display carpets. Central Asian carpets are famous for their imaginative patterns, bright colors, and expert artistry.

**Interpreting the Visual Record** Why were carpets suited to the nomadic way of life?

▶

The word *kyrgyz* means "forty clans." Clan membership is still important in Krygyz social, political, and economic life. Many Kyrgyz men wear black and white felt hats that show their clan status.

Nomadic traditions are still important to many Kyrgyz. The **yurt** is a movable round house of wool felt mats over a wood frame. Today the yurt is a symbol of the nomadic heritage. Even people who live in cities may put up yurts for weddings and funerals.

✓ **READING CHECK:** ( *Human Systems* ) In what ways do the Kyrgyz continue traditions of their past?

## Tajikistan

In the mid-1990s Tajikistan experienced a civil war. The Soviet-style government fought against a mixed group of reformers, some of whom demanded democracy. Others called for government by Islamic law. A peace agreement was signed in 1996, but tensions remain high.

The other major Central Asian languages are related to Turkish. However, the Tajik language is related to Persian. Tajiks consider the great literature written in Persian to be part of their cultural heritage.

✓ **READING CHECK:** ( *Human Systems* ) What has happened in politics in recent years in Tajikistan?

## Turkmenistan

The major first language of Turkmenistan is Turkmen. In 1993 Turkmenistan adopted English, rather than Russian, as its second official language. However, some schools teach in Russian, Uzbek, or Kazakh.

Islam has experienced a revival in Central Asia since the breakup of the Soviet Union. Many new **mosques**, or Islamic houses of worship, are being built and old ones are being restored. Donations from other Islamic countries, such as Saudi Arabia and Iran, have helped

these efforts. The government of Turkmenistan supports this revival and has ordered schools to teach Islamic principles. However, like the other states in the region, Turkmenistan's government views Islam with some caution. It does not want Islam to become a political movement.

Historically, the nomadic life required that all possessions be portable. Decorative carpets were the essential furniture of a nomad's home. They are still perhaps the most famous artistic craft of Turkmenistan. Like others in Central Asia, the people of Turkmenistan also have an ancient tradition of poetry.

✔ **READING CHECK:** *Human Systems* What are two forms of art in Turkmenistan, and how do they reflect its cultural traditions?

## Central Asia

| COUNTRY | POPULATION/ GROWTH RATE | LIFE EXPECTANCY | LITERACY RATE | PER CAPITA GDP |
|---|---|---|---|---|
| Kazakhstan | 16,731,303 .03% | 58, male 69, female | 98% | $5,000 |
| Kyrgyzstan | 4,753,003 1.4% | 59, male 68, female | 97% | $2,700 |
| Tajikistan | 6,578,681 2.1% | 61, male 67, female | 98% | $1,140 |
| Turkmenistan | 4,603,244 1.9% | 57, male 65, female | 98% | $4,300 |
| Uzbekistan | 25,155,064 1.6% | 60, male 68, female | 99% | $2,400 |
| United States | 281,421,906 0.9% | 74, male 80, female | 97% | $36,200 |

**Sources:** Central Intelligence Agency, *The World Factbook 2001;* U.S. Census Bureau

**Interpreting the Chart** Which country has the lowest per capita GDP in the region?

## Uzbekistan

Uzbekistan has the largest population of the Central Asian countries—about 24 million people. Uzbek is the official language. People are required to study Uzbek to be eligible for citizenship.

Tashkent and Samarqand are ancient Silk Road cities in Uzbekistan. They are famous for their mosques and Islamic monuments. Uzbeks are also known for their art of embroidering fabric with gold.

✔ **READING CHECK:** *Human Systems* What is one of an Uzbekistan citizen's responsibilities?

go.hrw.com **Homework Practice Online** Keyword: SK3 HP16

### Define and explain: yurt, mosques

### Working with Sketch Maps
On the map you created in Section 2, label Tashkent and Samarqand.

### Reading for the Main Idea

1. **Places and Regions** In which Central Asian nation is the influence of Russia strongest? Why is this true?

2. **Human Systems** What were the two sides in Tajikistan's civil war fighting for?

3. **Human Systems** What is the role of Islam in the region today?

### Critical Thinking

4. **Finding the Main Idea** What are two customs or artistic crafts of modern Central Asia that are connected to the nomadic lifestyle?

### Organizing What You Know

5. **Contrasting** Copy the following graphic organizer. Use it to describe the conditions in Central Asia during the Soviet era and today.

| | Soviet era | Today |
|---|---|---|
| Type of government | | |
| Official language | | |
| Alphabet | | |
| Government attitude toward Islam | | |

# CASE STUDY

## KAZAKHS: PASTORAL NOMADS OF CENTRAL ASIA

Nomads are people who move around from place to place during the year. Nomads usually move when the seasons change so that they will have enough food to eat. Herding, hunting, gathering, and fishing are all ways that different nomadic groups get their food.

Nomads that herd animals are called pastoral nomads. Their way of life depends on the seasonal movement of their herds. Pastoral nomads may herd cattle, horses, sheep, goats, yaks, reindeer, camels, or other animals. Instead of keeping their animals inside fenced pastures, pastoral nomads let them graze on open fields. However, they must make sure the animals do not overgraze and damage the pastureland. To do this, they keep their animals moving throughout the year. Some pastoral nomads live in steppe or desert environments. These nomads often have to move their animals very long distances between winter and summer pastures.

The Kazakhs of Central Asia are an example of a pastoral nomadic group. They have herded horses, sheep, goats, and cattle for hundreds of years. Because they move so much, the Kazakhs do not have permanent homes. They bring their homes with them when they travel to new places.

A Kazakh nomad keeps a watchful eye over a herd of horses.

▼

Yurts are carefully stitched together by hand. When it is time to move to new pastures, they are carried from place to place on horseback or on small wagons.

The Kazakhs live in tent-like structures called yurts. Yurts are circular structures made of bent poles covered with thick felt. Yurts can be easily taken apart and moved. They are perfect homes for the Kazakhs' nomadic lifestyle.

During the year, a Kazakh family may move its herds of sheep, horses, and cattle as far as 500 miles (805 km). For one Kazakh family, each year is divided into four different parts. The family spends the first part of the year in winter grazing areas. Then, in early spring, they move to areas with fresh grass shoots. When these spring grasses are gone, the family moves their animals to summer pastures. In the fall, the animals are kept for six weeks in autumn pastures. Finally, the herds are taken back to their winter pastures. Each year, the cycle is repeated.

The nomadic lifestyle of the Kazakhs has changed, however. In the early 1800s people from Russia and eastern Europe began to move into the region. These people were farmers. They started planting crops in areas that the Kazakhs used for pasture. This made it more difficult for the Kazakhs to move their animals during the year. Later, when Kazakhstan was part of the Soviet Union, government officials encouraged the Kazakhs to settle in villages and cities. Many Kazakhs still move their animals during the year. However, tending crops has also become an important way to get food.

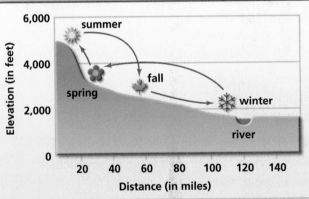

During the year, a Kazakh family may move its herds to several different pasture areas as the seasons change.

**Interpreting the Graph** Why do you think animals are moved to higher elevations during the summer and to lower elevations during the winter?

## Understanding What You Read

**1.** Why do some pastoral nomads have to travel such great distances?

**2.** How has the nomadic lifestyle of the Kazakhs changed during the last 100 years?

# Reviewing What You Know

## Building Vocabulary

On a separate sheet of paper, write sentences to define each of the following words.

1. landlocked
2. oasis
3. nomads
4. caravans
5. yurt
6. mosques

## Reviewing the Main Ideas

1. ( *Places and Regions* )  What types of climates are most common in Central Asia?

2. ( *Environment and Society* )  What problems have resulted from the shrinking of the Aral Sea?

3. ( *Human Systems* )  How did Soviet rule change Central Asians' way of life?

4. ( *Human Systems* )  What kinds of ties do the Central Asian countries have to Russia today?

5. ( *Places and Regions* )  What are the various languages spoken in Central Asia?

## Understanding Environment and Society

### Aral Sea in Danger

The rapid disappearance of the Aral Sea is a serious concern in Central Asia. Research and create a presentation on the Aral Sea. You may want to think about the following:

• Actions that could be taken to preserve the Aral Sea.
• What could be done to help slow the dropping of the sea's water level.
• Possible consequences if the level of the Aral Sea continues to drop.

Include a bibliography of the sources you used.

## Thinking Critically

1. **Summarizing** How have politics influenced language and the alphabet used in Central Asia?

2. **Finding the Main Idea** How do the artistic crafts of Central Asia reflect the nomadic lifestyle?

3. **Analyzing Information** Why did the Soviets encourage cotton farming in the region? What were the environmental consequences?

4. **Finding the Main Idea** What obstacles are making it hard for the Central Asian countries to export their oil?

5. **Summarizing** What are some reasons the Central Asian countries have experienced slow economic growth since independence? How are they trying to improve the situation?

### Map ACTIVITY

On a separate sheet of paper, match the letters on the map with their correct labels.

| | |
|---|---|
| Caspian Sea | Kara-Kum |
| Pamirs | Kyzyl Kum |
| Tian Shan | Tashkent |
| Aral Sea | Samarqand |

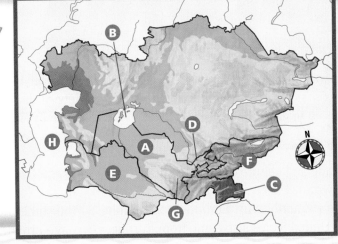

### Mental Mapping Skills ACTIVITY

On a separate sheet of paper, draw a freehand map of Central Asia. Make a key for your map and label the following:

| | |
|---|---|
| Amu Dar'ya | Syr Dar'ya |
| Aral Sea | Tajikistan |
| Kazakhstan | Turkmenistan |
| Kyrgyzstan | Uzbekistan |

### WRITING ACTIVITY

Imagine that you are a caravan trader traveling along the Silk Road during the 1200s. Write a journal entry describing your journey from the Mediterranean Sea through Central Asia. Be sure to use standard grammar, spelling, sentence structure, and punctuation.

## Alternative Assessment

### Portfolio ACTIVITY

**Learning About Your Local Geography**

**History** The Mongol conqueror Genghis Khan is a hero to many Central Asians. Use biographies or interviews with residents to find out about a person who is special to your area. Report your findings.

**☑ internet connect**

Internet Activity: **go.hrw.com**
KEYWORD: **SK3 GT16**

Choose a topic to explore about Central Asia:
- Study the climate of Central Asia.
- Travel along the historic Silk Road.
- Learn about nomads and caravans.

## Facing the Past and Present

Patterns of trade and culture can change quickly in our modern world. For example, the United States used to trade primarily with Europe. Most immigrants to the United States also came from Europe. Today, the American connection to Europe has faded. The United States now trades more with Japan and other Pacific Rim countries than with Europe. New ideas, new technology, and immigrants to the United States come from all around the world.

**Central Asia** Since the breakup of the Soviet Union, similar changes have taken place in Central Asia. In the past, Central Asia had many ties to the Soviet Union. For example, the economies of the two regions were linked. Central Asia exported cotton and oil to Russia and to countries in Eastern Europe. In exchange, Central Asia received a variety of manufactured goods. The Soviet Union also heavily influenced the culture of Central Asia. Many Central Asians learned to speak Russian.

**Looking South** Today, Central Asia's links to the former Soviet Union have weakened. At the same time, its ancient ties to Southwest Asia have grown stronger. The Silk Road once linked Central Asian cities to Southwest Asian ports on the Mediterranean. Now the peoples of Central Asia are looking southward once again. New links are forming between Central Asia and Turkey. Many people in Central Asia are traditionally Turkic in culture and language. Turkey's business leaders are working to expand their industries in Central Asia. Also, regular air travel from Turkey to cities in Central Asia is now possible as well.

Religion also links both Central Asia and Southwest Asia. Islam was first introduced into Central Asia in the A.D. 700s. It eventually became the region's dominant religion. However, Islam declined during the Soviet era. Missionaries from Arab countries and Iran are now working to strengthen this connection. Iran is also spending millions of dollars to build roads and rail lines to Central Asia.

◄ These children are learning about Islam in Dushanbe, Tajikistan. Although the former Communist government discouraged the practice of religion, today Islam flourishes in the independent Central Asian republics.

# Language Groups of Southwest and Central Asia

This map shows the major language groups that link peoples throughout Southwest and Central Asia. Very often, however, the links between peoples are overshadowed by differences in culture and history.

**DOMINANT LANGUAGES**

| | | | |
|---|---|---|---|
| Turkic | | Greek | |
| Iranic | | Other | |
| Semitic | | Sparsely populated | |

Central Asia and Southwest Asia share a similar climate, environment, and way of life. Both regions are dry, and water conservation and irrigation are important. Many people in both regions grow cotton and herd animals. In addition, both Central Asia and Southwest Asia are dealing with changes caused by the growing influence of Western culture. Some people are worried that compact discs, videotapes, and satellite television from the West threaten traditional beliefs and ways of life. Shared fears of cultural loss may bring Central Asia and Southwest Asia closer together.

**Defining the Region** As the world changes, geographers must reexamine this and other regions of the world. Will geographers decide to include the countries of Central Asia in the region of Southwest Asia? Will Russia regain control of Central Asia? The geographers are watching and waiting.

Many people in Central and Southwest Asia grow cotton, such as here in Uzbekistan.

## Understanding What You Read

1. What ties did Central Asia have to the Soviet Union in the past?
2. Why are ties between Central Asia and Southwest Asia growing today?

# Building Skills for Life: Addressing Environmental Problems

▲
An oil spill in northwestern Russia caused serious environmental damage in 1995.

**Interpreting the Visual Record**
**Can you see how these people are cleaning up the oil spill?**

The natural environment is the world around us. It includes the air, animals, land, plants, and water. Many people today are concerned about the environment. They are called environmentalists. Environmentalists are worried that human activities are damaging the environment. Environmental problems include air, land, and water pollution, global warming, deforestation, plant and animal extinction, and soil erosion.

People all over the world are working to solve these environmental problems. The governments of many countries are trying to work together to protect the environment. International organizations like the United Nations are also addressing environmental issues.

## THE SKILL

1. **Gather Information.** Create a plan to present to the city council for solving a local environmental problem. Select a problem and research it using databases or other reference materials. How does it affect people's lives and your community's culture or economy?

2. **List and Consider Options.** After reviewing the information, list and consider options for solving this environmental problem.

3. **Consider Advantages and Disadvantages.** Now consider the advantages and disadvantages of taking each option. Ask yourself questions like, "How will solving this environmental problem affect business in the area?" Record your answers.

4. **Choose, Implement, and Evaluate a Solution.** After considering the advantages and disadvantages, you should create your plan. Be sure to make your proposal clear. You will need to explain the reasoning behind the choices you made in your plan.

# HANDS on GEOGRAPHY

The countries of the former Soviet Union face some of the worst environmental problems in the world. For more than 50 years, the region's environment was polluted with nuclear waste and toxic chemicals. Today, environmental problems in this region include air, land, and water pollution.

One place that was seriously polluted was the Russian city of Chelyabinsk. Some people have called Chelyabinsk the most polluted place on Earth. The passage below describes some of the environmental problems in Chelyabinsk. Read the passage and then answer the Lab Report questions.

Chelyabinsk was one of the former Soviet Union's main military production centers. A factory near Chelyabinsk produced nuclear weapons. Over the years, nuclear waste from this factory polluted a very large area. A huge amount of nuclear waste was dumped into the Techa River. Many people in the region used this river as their main source of water. They also ate fish from the river.

In the 1950s many deaths and health problems resulted from pollution in the Techa River. Because it was so polluted, the Soviet government evacuated 22 villages along the river. In 1957 a nuclear accident in the region released twice as much radiation as the Chernobyl accident in 1986. However, the accident near Chelyabinsk was kept secret. About 10,000 people were evacuated. The severe environmental problems in the Chelyabinsk region led to dramatic increases in birth defects and cancer rates.

The village of Mitlino was evacuated after a nuclear accident in 1957.

## Lab Report

1. How did environmental problems near Chelyabinsk affect people who lived in the region?

2. What might be done to address environmental problems in the Chelyabinsk region?

3. How can a geographical perspective help to solve these problems?

# Southwest Asia

## CHAPTER 17
### The Arabian Peninsula, Iraq, Iran, and Afghanistan

## CHAPTER 18
### The Eastern Mediterranean

Western Wall and Dome of the Rock, Jerusalem, Israel

Bottle trees, Yemen

## An Exchange Student in Turkey

*Sara Lewis was an American exchange student in Turkey. Here she describes how teenagers live in Istanbul, Turkey's largest city, and the month-long fast of Ramadan.* **WHAT DO YOU THINK?** *What would it be like to live in a place where you can see the remains of thousands of years of history?*

The people of Istanbul are very traditional and family-oriented, but today's Turk also has European-style tastes. Turkish teens go dancing and hang out in coffeehouses. All around them, though, are reminders of the past. There are many monuments left over from Greek, Roman, Byzantine, and Ottoman times.

Islam plays a big part in daily life. Five times every day I can hear the people being called to prayer. For more than a month, my host parents fasted during Ramadan. They didn't eat or drink anything while the sun was up. My host sister and I fasted for one day. By the time the sun went down we were starving! I'm glad we weren't expected to continue the fast. Then we shopped for new clothes. It is the custom to wear new clothes to the feast at the end of Ramadan. The fresh clothes seem to stand for the cleanliness one achieves during the month of fasting.

Family preparing food for the end of Ramadan

Jewish girls, Zefat, Israel

## Understanding Primary Sources

**1.** What do modern Turkish teenagers do for fun?

**2.** How is Ramadan observed in Turkey?

Sooty falcon

# Southwest Asia

## Elevation Profile

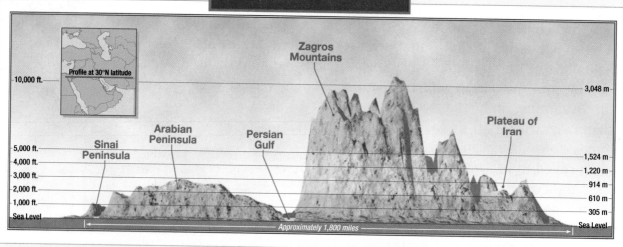

Profile at 30°N latitude

Zagros Mountains

Plateau of Iran

Arabian Peninsula

Sinai Peninsula

Persian Gulf

10,000 ft. — 3,048 m

5,000 ft. — 1,524 m
4,000 ft. — 1,220 m
3,000 ft. — 914 m
2,000 ft. — 610 m
1,000 ft. — 305 m
Sea Level — Sea Level

Approximately 1,800 miles

## The United States and Southwest Asia: Comparing Sizes

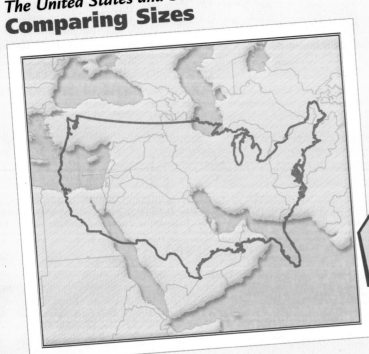

## GEOSTATS:

- World's lowest point on land: the Dead Sea, in Israel and Jordan—1,312 feet (400 m) below sea level

- World's leading exporter of oil: Saudi Arabia

- Approximate amount of proven oil reserves in Saudi Arabia: 261 billion barrels

- Estimated number of barrels of oil that pass through the Strait of Hormuz every day: 15.4 million

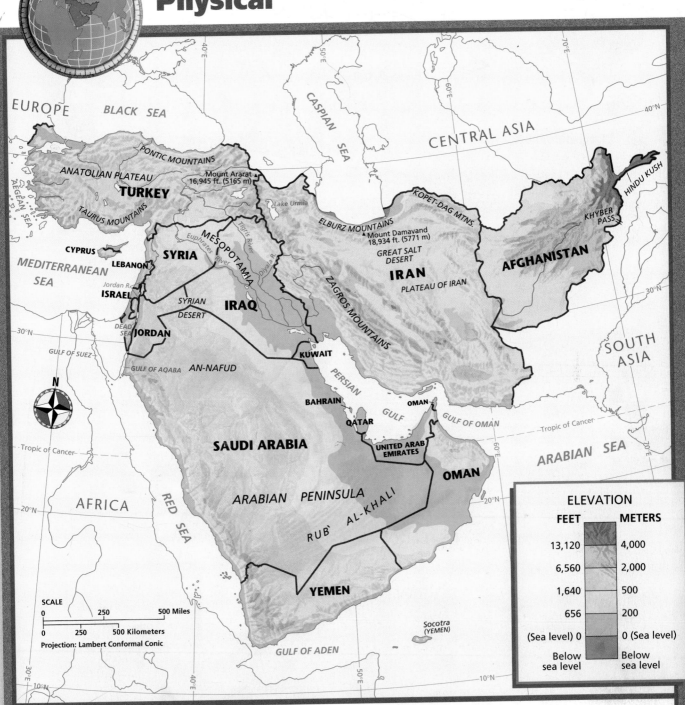

EUROPE BLACK SEA

CASPIAN SEA

CENTRAL ASIA

40°N

PONTIC MOUNTAINS

ANATOLIAN PLATEAU

Mount Ararat
16,945 ft. (5165 m)

**TURKEY**

Lake Urmia

KOPET-DAG MTNS.

HINDU KUSH

TAURUS MOUNTAINS

ELBURZ MOUNTAINS

KHYBER PASS

AEGEAN SEA

CYPRUS

LEBANON

Euphrates River

MESOPOTAMIA

Tigris River

Diyala R.

Mount Damavand
18,934 ft. (5771 m)

GREAT SALT DESERT

**AFGHANISTAN**

MEDITERRANEAN SEA

**SYRIA**

**IRAN**

PLATEAU OF IRAN

30°N

**ISRAEL**

Jordan R.

SYRIAN DESERT

**IRAQ**

ZAGROS MOUNTAINS

SOUTH ASIA

DEAD SEA

**JORDAN**

GULF OF SUEZ

GULF OF AQABA

AN-NAFUD

**KUWAIT**

N

PERSIAN

**BAHRAIN**

**QATAR**

GULF

OMAN

GULF OF OMAN

Tropic of Cancer

Tropic of Cancer

**SAUDI ARABIA**

**UNITED ARAB EMIRATES**

ARABIAN SEA

AFRICA

RED SEA

ARABIAN   PENINSULA

AL-KHALI

**OMAN**

20°N

20°N

RUB` AL-KHALI

SCALE

0        250        500 Miles

0        250        500 Kilometers

Projection: Lambert Conformal Conic

**YEMEN**

Socotra
(YEMEN)

GULF OF ADEN

30°N

10°N

10°N

### ELEVATION

| FEET | | METERS |
|---|---|---|
| 13,120 | | 4,000 |
| 6,560 | | 2,000 |
| 1,640 | | 500 |
| 656 | | 200 |
| (Sea level) 0 | | 0 (Sea level) |
| Below sea level | | Below sea level |

1. *Environment and Society*  What landforms might make north-south travel difficult in Iran?

2. *Places and Regions*  Where are the region's highest mountains? What are these mountains called?

3. *Places and Regions*  Which country is partly in Europe and partly in Asia?

## Critical Thinking

4. **Analyzing Information**  How might one travel overland from Syria to Oman? Why?

5. **Comparing**  Compare this map to the **population map**. What physical features contribute to Iraq's relatively high population density?

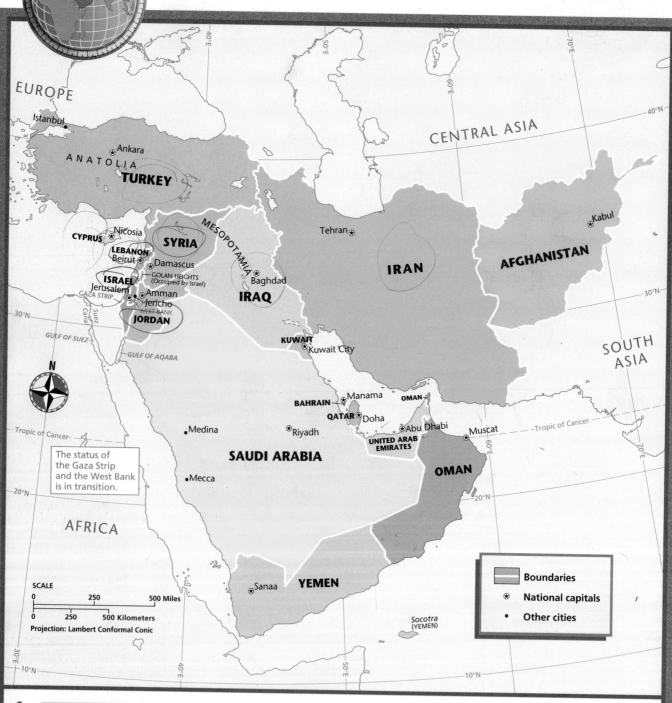

The status of the Gaza Strip and the West Bank is in transition.

SCALE

| 0 | 250 | 500 Miles |

| 0 | 250 | 500 Kilometers |

Projection: Lambert Conformal Conic

Boundaries
⊛ National capitals
• Other cities

**1.** *Places and Regions* What are the region's two largest countries? the region's smallest?

## Critical Thinking

**2. Comparing** Examine the **climate map**. Why do you think so many of the boundaries in this region are straight lines? Why might some maps show Saudi Arabia's southern border as a dotted line?

**3. Drawing Inferences and Conclusions** Which countries lie along the Persian Gulf and the Gulf of Oman? Why might conflicts occur among these countries?

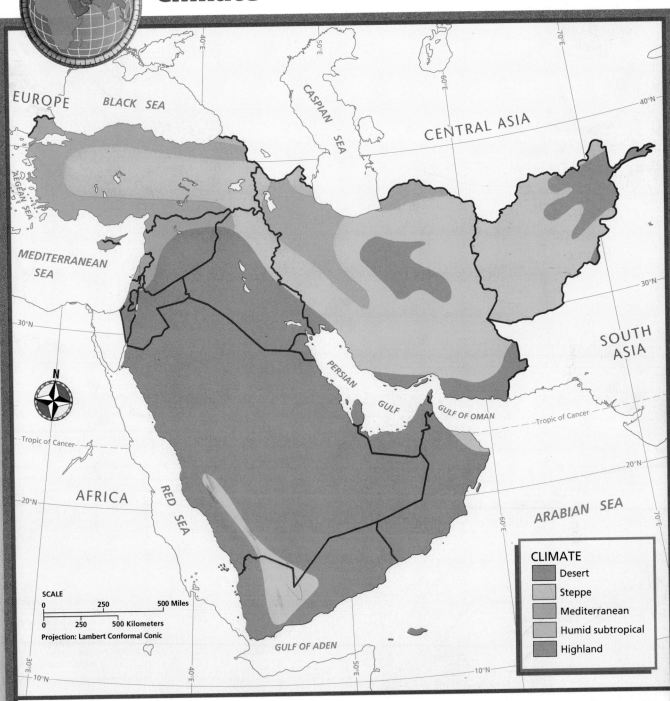

CLIMATE
- Desert
- Steppe
- Mediterranean
- Humid subtropical
- Highland

SCALE
0    250    500 Miles
0    250    500 Kilometers
Projection: Lambert Conformal Conic

1. *Places and Regions* Which countries have desert climates?

2. *Places and Regions* Which two countries have only a Mediterranean climate?

## Critical Thinking

3. **Comparing** Compare this map to the **population map**. How might climate influence the region's population patterns?

4. **Analyzing Information** Compare this map to the **physical** and **land use and resources maps**. Why is commercial farming possible in central Iraq?

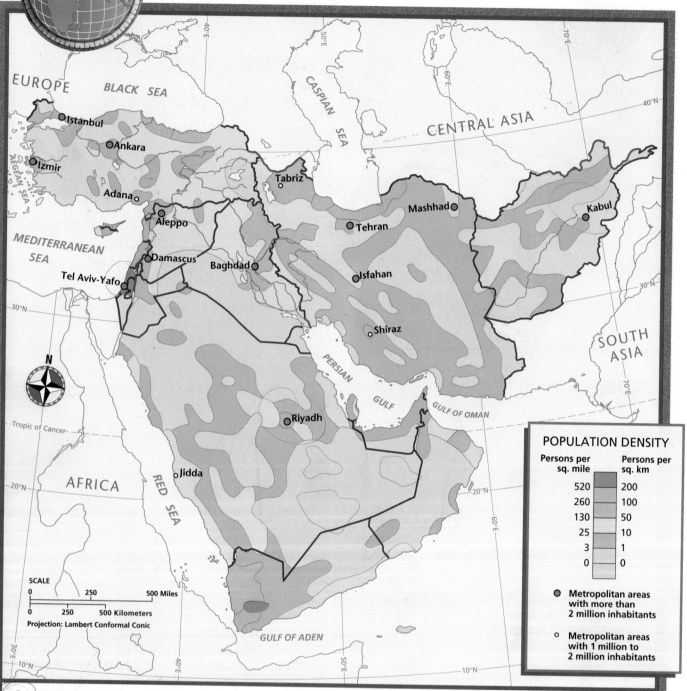

EUROPE

BLACK SEA

Istanbul
Ankara
Izmir
AEGEAN SEA
Adana
Aleppo
MEDITERRANEAN SEA
Damascus
Tel Aviv-Yafo
Baghdad
Tabriz
Tehran
Mashhad
Kabul
Isfahan
Shiraz
Riyadh

CASPIAN SEA

CENTRAL ASIA

SOUTH ASIA

PERSIAN GULF
GULF OF OMAN

Tropic of Cancer

AFRICA
RED SEA
Jidda

GULF OF ADEN

N

SCALE
0     250     500 Miles
0     250     500 Kilometers
Projection: Lambert Conformal Conic

**POPULATION DENSITY**

| Persons per sq. mile | | Persons per sq. km |
|---|---|---|
| 520 | | 200 |
| 260 | | 100 |
| 130 | | 50 |
| 25 | | 10 |
| 3 | | 1 |
| 0 | | 0 |

● Metropolitan areas with more than 2 million inhabitants

○ Metropolitan areas with 1 million to 2 million inhabitants

**1.** *Places and Regions* Which countries have only one city of more than 2 million people?

**2.** *Places and Regions* Compare this map to the **physical map** of the region. Which desert area has almost no residents?

**3.** *Places and Regions* Which country has an area of high population density but no big cities?

## Critical Thinking

**4. Analyzing Information** Use this map to create a chart, graph, database, or model of population centers in Southwest Asia.

**5. Analyzing Information** Look at Istanbul's location. Why is it good for a large city?

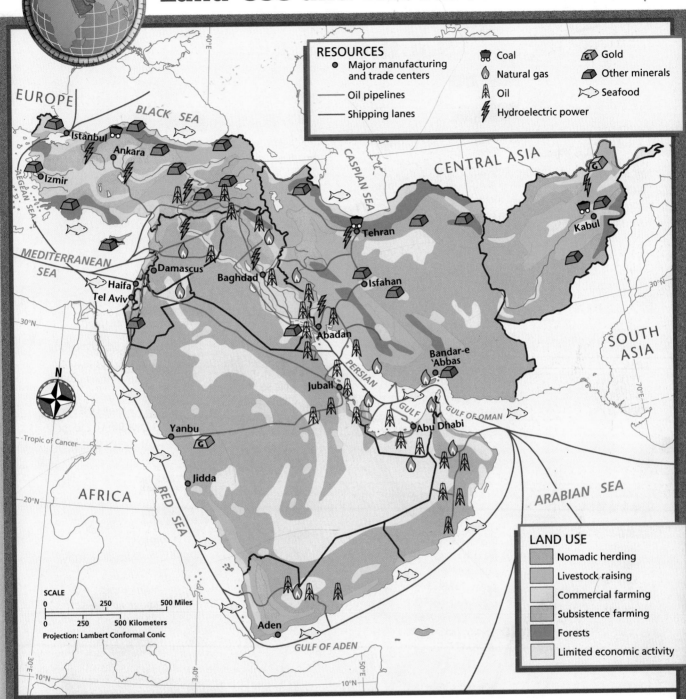

**RESOURCES**
- Major manufacturing and trade centers
- Oil pipelines
- Shipping lanes
- Coal
- Natural gas
- Oil
- Hydroelectric power
- Gold
- Other minerals
- Seafood

**LAND USE**
- Nomadic herding
- Livestock raising
- Commercial farming
- Subsistence farming
- Forests
- Limited economic activity

SCALE
0    250    500 Miles
0    250    500 Kilometers
Projection: Lambert Conformal Conic

1. **Human Systems** By what route would an oil tanker travel from Abadan to Mediterranean ports?

2. **Places and Regions** What two energy resources are often found together in the region?

3. **Places and Regions** Which countries have gold? Which countries have deposits of coal?

## Critical Thinking

4. **Analyzing Information** Use this map to create a chart, graph, database, or model of economic activities in Southwest Asia.

5. **Drawing Inferences and Conclusions** Why might vegetables be costly in Kuwait?

# Southwest Asia

## AFGHANISTAN

**CAPITAL:**
Kabul

**AREA:**
250,000 sq. mi.
(647,500 sq km)

**POPULATION:**
26,813,057

**MONEY:**
afghani (AFA)

**LANGUAGES:**
Pashtu, Afghan Persian
(Dari), Turkic languages

**TELEPHONE LINES:**
29,000 (1996)

## IRAQ

**CAPITAL:**
Baghdad

**AREA:**
168,753 sq. mi.
(437,072 sq km)

**POPULATION:** 23,331,985

**MONEY:**
Iraqi dinar (IQD)

**LANGUAGES:**
Arabic, Kurdish

**TELEPHONE LINES:**
675,000 (1997)

## BAHRAIN

**CAPITAL:**
Manama

**AREA:**
239 sq. mi.
(620 sq km)

**POPULATION:**
645,361

**MONEY:**
Bahraini dinar (BHD)

**LANGUAGES:**
Arabic, English, Farsi, Urdu

**TELEPHONE LINES:**
152,000 (1997)

## ISRAEL

**CAPITAL:**
Jerusalem

**AREA:**
8,019 sq. mi.
(20,770 sq km)

**POPULATION:**
5,938,093

**MONEY:**
new Israeli shekel (ILS)

**LANGUAGES:**
Hebrew (official), Arabic,
English

**TELEPHONE LINES:**
2,800,000 (1999)

## CYPRUS

**CAPITAL:**
Nicosia

**AREA:**
3,571 sq. mi. (9,250 sq km)

**POPULATION:**
762,887

**MONEY:**
Cypriot pound (£C), Turkish
lira (TRL)

**LANGUAGES:**
Greek, Turkish, English

**TELEPHONE LINES:**
Greek Cypriot area: 405,000
(1998); Turkish Cypriot area:
83,162 (1998)

## JORDAN

**CAPITAL:**
Amman

**AREA:**
35,637 sq. mi.
(92,300 sq km)

**POPULATION:**
5,153,378

**MONEY:**
Jordanian dinar (JOD)

**LANGUAGES:**
Arabic, English

**TELEPHONE LINES:**
403,000 (1997)

## IRAN

**CAPITAL:**
Tehran

**AREA:**
636,293 sq. mi.
(1,648,000 sq km)

**POPULATION:**
66,128,965

**MONEY:**
Iranian rial (IRR)

**LANGUAGES:**
Persian, Turkic, Kurdish

**TELEPHONE LINES:**
6,313,000 (1997)

## KUWAIT

**CAPITAL:**
Kuwait City

**AREA:**
6,880 sq. mi.
(17,820 sq km)

**POPULATION:**
2,041,961

**MONEY:**
Kuwaiti dinar (KWD)

**LANGUAGES:**
Arabic, English

**TELEPHONE LINES:**
412,000

Countries not drawn to scale.

## LEBANON

**CAPITAL:**
Beirut

**AREA:**
4,015 sq. mi.
(10,400 sq km)

**POPULATION:** 3,627,774

**MONEY:**
Lebanese pound (LBP)

**LANGUAGES:**
Arabic (official), French

**TELEPHONE LINES:**
700,000 (1999)

## SYRIA

**CAPITAL:**
Damascus

**AREA:**
71,498 sq. mi.
(185,180 sq km)

**POPULATION:** 16,728,808

**MONEY:**
Syrian pound (SYP)

**LANGUAGES:**
Arabic (official), Kurdish

**TELEPHONE LINES:**
1,313,000 (1997)

## OMAN

**CAPITAL:**
Muscat

**AREA:**
82,031 sq. mi.
(212,460 sq km)

**POPULATION:** 2,662,198

**MONEY:**
Omani rial (OMR)

**LANGUAGES:**
Arabic (official), English

**TELEPHONE LINES:**
201,000 (1997)

## TURKEY

**CAPITAL:** Ankara

**AREA:**
301,382 sq. mi.
(780,580 sq km)

**POPULATION:**
66,493,970

**MONEY:**
Turkish lira (TRL)

**LANGUAGES:** Turkish (official),
Kurdish

**TELEPHONE LINES:**
19,500,000 (1999)

## QATAR

**CAPITAL:**
Doha

**AREA:**
4,416 sq. mi.
(11,437 sq km)

**POPULATION:**
769,152

**MONEY:**
Qatari rial (QAR)

**LANGUAGES:**
Arabic (official), English

**TELEPHONE LINES:**
142,000 (1997)

## UNITED ARAB EMIRATES

**CAPITAL:** Abu Dhabi

**AREA:**
32,000 sq. mi.
(82,880 sq km)

**POPULATION:** 2,407,460

**MONEY:**
Emirati dirham (AED)

**LANGUAGES:**
Arabic (official), Persian

**TELEPHONE LINES:** 915,223
(1998)

## SAUDI ARABIA

**CAPITAL:**
Riyadh

**AREA:**
756,981 sq. mi.
(1,960,582 sq km)

**POPULATION:**
22,757,092

**MONEY:**
Saudi riyal (SAR)

**LANGUAGES:**
Arabic

**TELEPHONE LINES:**
3,100,000

## YEMEN
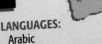

**CAPITAL:**
Sanaa

**AREA:**
203,849 sq. mi.
(527,970 sq km)

**POPULATION:**
18,078,035

**MONEY:**
Yemeni rial (YRI)

**LANGUAGES:**
Arabic

**TELEPHONE LINES:**
291,359 (1999)

**📁 internet connect**

**COUNTRY STATISTICS**
GO TO: go.hrw.com
KEYWORD: SK3 FactsU5
FOR: more facts about
Southwest Asia

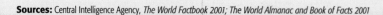

**Sources:** Central Intelligence Agency, *The World Factbook 2001; The World Almanac and Book of Facts 2001*

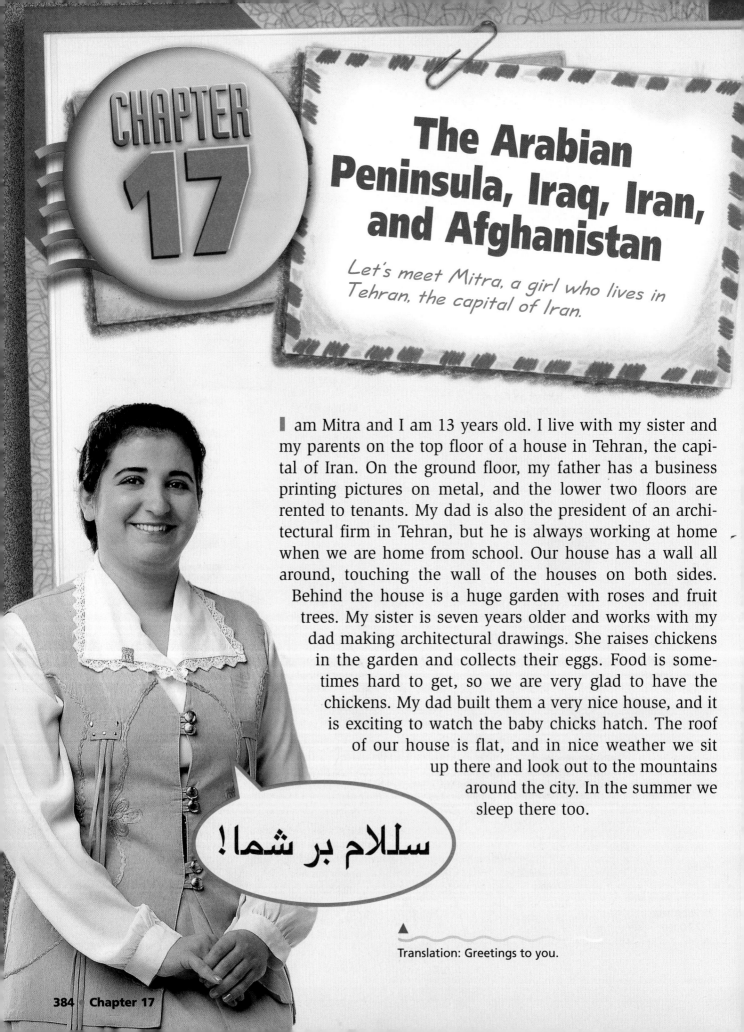

# CHAPTER 17

# The Arabian Peninsula, Iraq, Iran, and Afghanistan

*Let's meet Mitra, a girl who lives in Tehran, the capital of Iran.*

I am Mitra and I am 13 years old. I live with my sister and my parents on the top floor of a house in Tehran, the capital of Iran. On the ground floor, my father has a business printing pictures on metal, and the lower two floors are rented to tenants. My dad is also the president of an architectural firm in Tehran, but he is always working at home when we are home from school. Our house has a wall all around, touching the wall of the houses on both sides. Behind the house is a huge garden with roses and fruit trees. My sister is seven years older and works with my dad making architectural drawings. She raises chickens in the garden and collects their eggs. Food is sometimes hard to get, so we are very glad to have the chickens. My dad built them a very nice house, and it is exciting to watch the baby chicks hatch. The roof of our house is flat, and in nice weather we sit up there and look out to the mountains around the city. In the summer we sleep there too.

سلام بر شما!

Translation: Greetings to you.

# Section 1 Physical Geography

## Read to Discover

1. What are the major physical features of the region?
2. What climates are found in this region?
3. What are the region's important resources?

## Define

exotic rivers
wadis
fossil water

## Locate

Persian Gulf
Arabian Peninsula
Red Sea
Arabian Sea
Tigris River

Euphrates River
Elburz Mountains
Zagros Mountains
Hindu Kush
Rub' al-Khali

### WHY IT MATTERS

This region holds about half of the world's known reserves of oil, or petroleum. Use **CNN fyi.com** or other **current events** sources to find out how and why oil is so important in the world today. Record your findings in your journal.

*Golden lion from Iran*

## The Arabian Peninsula, Iraq, Iran, and Afghanistan: Physical-Political

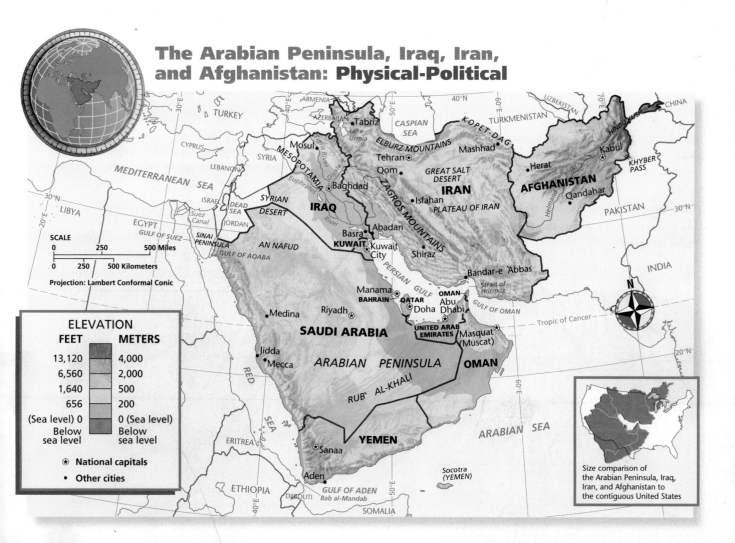

**ELEVATION**

| FEET | METERS |
|------|--------|
| 13,120 | 4,000 |
| 6,560 | 2,000 |
| 1,640 | 500 |
| 656 | 200 |
| (Sea level) 0 | 0 (Sea level) |
| Below sea level | Below sea level |

⊛ National capitals
• Other cities

SCALE
0     250     500 Miles
0   250   500 Kilometers
Projection: Lambert Conformal Conic

Size comparison of the Arabian Peninsula, Iraq, Iran, and Afghanistan to the contiguous United States

⊡ **internet** connect

**GO TO: go.hrw.com**
**KEYWORD: SK3 CH17**
**FOR: Web sites about the Arabian Peninsula, Iraq, Iran, and Afghanistan**

**BUILD on WHAT You Know**

**D**o you remember what you learned about desert climates? See Chapter 3 to review.

Cold nighttime temperatures and extremely hot days help break rock into sand in Saudi Arabia's Rub' al-Khali, or "empty quarter."

**Interpreting the Visual Record** How do you think wind affects these sand dunes?

# Physical Features

The 10 countries of this region are laid out like a semicircle, with the Persian Gulf in the center. They are Saudi Arabia, Kuwait (koo-WAYT), Bahrain (bah-RAYN), Qatar (KAH-tuhr), the United Arab Emirates (E-muh-ruhts), Oman (oh-MAHN), Yemen (YE-muhn), Iraq (i-RAHK), Iran (i-RAN), and Afghanistan (af-GA-nuh-stan).

This area can be divided into three landform regions. The Arabian Peninsula is a large rectangular area. The Red Sea, Gulf of Aden, Arabian Sea, and Persian Gulf border the peninsula. North of the Arabian Peninsula is the plain of the Tigris (TY-gruhs) and Euphrates (yooh-FRAY-teez) Rivers. In ancient times, this area was called Mesopotamia (me-suh-puh-TAY-mee-uh), or the "land between the rivers." East of this plain is a region of mountains and plateaus. It stretches through Iran and Afghanistan.

The surface of the Arabian Peninsula rises gradually as one moves westward from the Persian Gulf. The highest point is in the southwest, in the mountains of Yemen.

North of the Arabian Peninsula is a low, flat plain. It runs from the Persian Gulf into northern Iraq. The Tigris and Euphrates Rivers flow across this plain. They are what are known as **exotic rivers**. Exotic rivers begin in humid regions and then flow through dry areas.

East of this low plain the land climbs sharply. Most of Iran is a plateau bordered by mountains. The Elburz (el-BOOHRZ) Mountains and Kopet-Dag range lie in the north. The Zagros (ZA-gruhs) Mountains lie in the southwest. Afghanistan includes many mountain ranges, such as the towering Hindu Kush range.

✓ **READING CHECK:** ⟨ **Places and Regions** ⟩ What are the major physical features of this area?

# Climate

Most of Southwest Asia has a desert climate. A nearly constant high-pressure system in the atmosphere causes this climate. Some areas—mostly high plateaus and the region's edges—do get winter rains or snow. These areas generally have steppe climates. Some mountain peaks receive more than 50 inches (130 cm) of rain per year.

The desert can be both very hot and very cold. In summer, afternoon temperatures can reach 129°F (54°C). During the night, however, the temperature may drop quickly. Temperatures sometimes dip below freezing during winter nights.

The Rub' al-Khali (ROOB ahl-KAH-lee), or "empty quarter," of southern Saudi Arabia is the largest sand desert in the world. In northern Saudi Arabia is the An Nafud (ahn nah-FOOD), another desert.

✓ **READING CHECK:** ( *Places and Regions* ) What are the climates of this region?

Beneath the Red Sea lie many valuable resources, such as oil, sulfur, and metal deposits.

# Resources

Water is an important resource everywhere, but in this region it is crucial. Many desert regions are visited only by nomads and their animal herds. In many places, springs or wells provide water. Nomads sometimes get water by digging shallow wells into dry streambeds called **wadis**. Wells built with modern technology can reach water deep underground. The groundwater in these wells is often **fossil water**. Fossil water is water that is not being replaced by rainfall. Wells that pump fossil water will eventually run dry.

Other than water, oil is the region's most important mineral resource. Most of the oilfields are located near the shores of the Persian Gulf. The countries of the region are not rich in resources other than oil. Iran is an exception, with deposits of many metals.

✓ **READING CHECK:** ( *Places and Regions* ) What are the region's important resources?

---

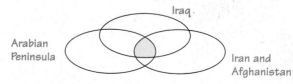
**Homework Practice Online**
Keyword: SK3 HP17

**Define and explain:** exotic rivers, wadis, fossil water

**Working with Sketch Maps** On a map of the Arabian Peninsula, Iraq, Iran, and Afghanistan that you draw or that your teacher provides, label the following: Persian Gulf, Arabian Peninsula, Red Sea, Arabian Sea, Tigris River, Euphrates River, Elburz Mountains, Zagros Mountains, Hindu Kush, and Rub' al-Khali.

### Reading for the Main Idea

**1.** ( *Places and Regions* ) Why do you think Mesopotamia was important in ancient times?

**2.** ( *Places and Regions* ) What is the region's climate?

### Critical Thinking

**3. Drawing Inferences and Conclusions** Why do you think the Persian Gulf is important to international trade?

**4. Drawing Inferences and Conclusions** What settlement pattern might you find in this region?

### Organizing What You Know

**5. Summarizing** Copy the following graphic organizer. Use it to list as many details of landforms, resources, and climate as you can. Place them in the correct part of the diagram.

Iraq

Arabian Peninsula

Iran and Afghanistan

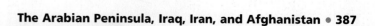

# Section 2 The Arabian Peninsula

## Read to Discover

1. What are Saudi Arabia's history, government, and people like?
2. What kinds of government and economy do the other countries of the Arabian Peninsula have?

## Define
Muslims
caliph
Sunni
Shia
Qur'an
OPEC

## Locate
Mecca
Riyadh

### WHY IT MATTERS

Saudi Arabia has long been an important U.S. ally in this region. Use CNNfyi.com or other current events sources to learn about current relations between the United States and Saudi Arabia. Record your findings in your journal.

*Spicy Arabian food*

## Saudi Arabia

Saudi Arabia is by far the largest country of the Arabian Peninsula. Although the kingdom of Saudi Arabia was not created until the 1930s, the region has long been an important cultural center.

**Islam** The history of the Arabian Peninsula is closely linked to Islam. This religion was founded by Muhammad, a merchant from the Arabian town of Mecca. Around A.D. 610 he had a vision that he had been named a prophet by Allah, or God. Arab armies and merchants carried Muhammad's teachings to new areas. Islam spread quickly across North Africa, much of Asia, and parts of Europe. Followers of Islam are called **Muslims**. Islam provides a set of rules to guide human behavior.

The Islamic world was originally ruled by a religious and political leader called a **caliph**. Gradually this area broke up into several empires. There are also religious divisions within Islam. Followers of the largest branch of Islam are called **Sunni**. Followers of the second-largest branch of Islam are called **Shia**. In the late 600s

Non-Muslims are not allowed to enter Mecca, Islam's holiest city.

these two groups disagreed over who should lead the Islamic world. There are many smaller groups within Islam as well.

Islamic culture helps to unite Muslims around the world. For example, all Muslims learn Arabic to read the **Qur'an**, the holy book of Islam. Muslims are also expected to visit the holy city of Mecca at least once. These practices and many others help make Muslims part of one community.

## Government and Economy
In the 1920s a local ruler from the Saud family of central Arabia conquered his neighbors and in 1932 created the kingdom of Saudi Arabia. Members of the Saud family have ruled the country ever since. Riyadh, a city near the center of the country, became the capital.

Saudi Arabia is a monarchy with no written constitution or elected legislature. Most government officials are relatives of the king. The king may ask members of his family, Islamic scholars, and tribal leaders for advice on important decisions.

In recent years, Saudi Arabia and the United States have established a close relationship. Both countries have strategic military and economic interests in the region. Saudi Arabia purchases U.S. weapons, such as fighter planes. In 1990, when Iraq invaded Kuwait, the Saudi government allowed U.S. military forces to operate from Saudi Arabia.

Oil and related industries are the most important part of the Saudi economy. Saudi Arabia has the world's largest reserves of oil. It is also the world's leading exporter of oil. Saudi Arabia is a leader of the Organization of Petroleum Exporting Countries, or **OPEC**. The members of OPEC try to influence the price of oil on world markets.

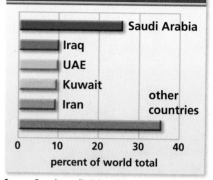

### Estimated Oil Reserves, 1999

Saudi Arabia
Iraq
UAE
Kuwait
Iran
other countries

0   10   20   30   40
percent of world total

Source: *Encyclopaedia Britannica*

**Interpreting the Graph** Which nation in the region has the largest oil reserves?

Opened in 1986, this causeway links Saudi Arabia to Bahrain.

**Interpreting the Visual Record** How important do you think modern transportation systems are to a country's economy?

Fossil water has been used to convert desert land northwest of Riyadh into circular fields.

**Interpreting the Visual Record** Why do you think these fields are circular?

A *sabchat* is a thick, slushy deposit of sand, silt, mud, and salt found in coastal Saudi Arabia. A *sabchat* can trap people and animals who do not see it in time.

Oil was discovered in Saudi Arabia in the 1930s. Before this time farming and herding had been the main economic activities. Crops included barley, dates, fruits, millet, vegetables, and wheat. Nomads kept herds of sheep, goats, horses, and camels.

Like other oil-rich states in the region, Saudi Arabia has tried to increase its food production. Because freshwater is scarce, desalination plants are used to remove the salt from seawater. This water is then used in farming. Income from oil allows the Saudi government to pay for this expensive process. Even so, Saudi Arabia imports much of its food.

**People and Customs** Nearly all Saudis are ethnic Arabs and speak Arabic. About 85 percent are Sunni. The rest are Shia. Most Saudis now live in cities, and a sizable middle class has developed. The Saudi government provides free health care and education to its citizens.

More than 5 million foreigners live and work in Saudi Arabia. Most come from Turkey, Egypt, Jordan, Yemen, and countries in southern and eastern Asia. Many Americans and Europeans work in the country's oil industry.

Saudi laws and customs limit women's freedoms. For example, a woman rarely appears in public without her husband or a male relative. Women are also not allowed to drive cars. In 1999, women made up just 5 percent of Saudi Arabia's workforce.

Islamic practices are an important part of Saudi Arabia's culture. Muslims pray five times each day. Friday is their holy day. Because Islam encourages modesty, Saudi clothing keeps arms and legs covered. Men traditionally wear a loose, ankle-length shirt. They often wear a cotton headdress held in place with a cord. These are practical in the desert, giving protection from sun, wind, and dust. Saudi women usually wear a black cloak and veil when they are in public.

Two major celebrations mark the Islamic calendar. Each year, some 2 million Muslims travel to Mecca to worship. The journey ends with 'Id al-Adha, the Festival of Sacrifice. The year's second celebration is 'Id al-Fitr, a feast ending the month of Ramadan. During Ramadan, Muslims do not eat or drink anything between dawn and sunset.

**READING CHECK:** *Human Systems* What is significant about Saudi Arabia's history, government, and people?

# Other Countries of the Arabian Peninsula

Six small coastal countries share the Arabian Peninsula with Saudi Arabia. All are heavily dependent on oil. All but Yemen are monarchies, and each is overwhelmingly Islamic. Oil is a major part of each country's economy. However, possession of differing amounts of oil has made some countries much richer than others.

# CONNECTING TO Math

## Muslim Contributions to Mathematics

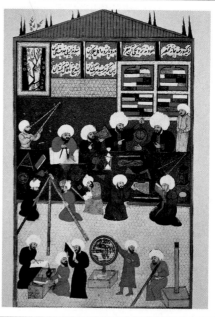

*Muslim astronomers in the 1500s*

During the period of Western history called the Dark Ages, European art, literature, and science declined. However, during this same period Islamic civilization, stretching from Spain to the borders of China, was flowering. Muslim scholars made important advances in art, literature, medicine, and mathematics.

The system of numerals we call Arabic, including the use of the zero, was first created in India. However, it was Muslim thinkers who introduced that system to Europe. They also developed algebra, geometry, and trigonometry. In fact, words like *algebra* and *algorithm* are translations of Arabic words.

Other Muslims advanced the study of astronomy and physics. Arab geographers calculated distances between cities, longitudes and latitudes, and the direction from one city to another. Muslims developed the first solution for cubic equations. They also defined ratios and used mathematics to explain the rainbow.

### Understanding What You Read
1. Where did the Arabic system of numerals originate, and how did it get to Europe?
2. How did Muslim scholars contribute to our knowledge of geography?

**Kuwait** The country of Kuwait was established in the mid-1700s. Trade and fishing were once the main economic activities there. Oil, which was discovered in the 1930s, has made Kuwait very rich. The Iraqi invasion of 1990 caused massive destruction.

As in Saudi Arabia, a royal family dominates politics in Kuwait. In 1992, however, Kuwait held elections for a legislature. Less than 15 percent of Kuwait's population were given the right to vote. These people were all men from well-established families.

**Bahrain and Qatar** Bahrain is a group of small islands in the western Persian Gulf. It is a constitutional monarchy that is headed by a ruling royal family and a legislature. These islands have been a center of trade since ancient times. In 1986 a 15.5 mile (25 km) bridge was completed that connects Bahrain to Saudi Arabia, making movement between the two countries easier.

## The Arabian Peninsula

| Country | Population/ Growth Rate | Life Expectancy | Literacy Rate | Per Capita GDP |
|---|---|---|---|---|
| Bahrain | 645,361 (228,424 noncitizens) 1.7% | 71, male 76, female | 85% | $15,900 |
| Kuwait | 2,041,961 (1,519,913 noncitizens) 3.4% | 75, male 77, female | 79% | $15,000 |
| Oman | 2,622,198 3.4% | 70, male 74, female | 80% | $7,700 |
| Qatar | 769,152 3.2% | 70, male 75, female | 79% | $20,300 |
| Saudi Arabia | 22,757,092 (5,360,526 noncitizens) 3.3% | 66, male 70, female | 63% | $10,500 |
| United Arab Emirates | 2,407,460 (1,576,472 noncitizens) 1.6% | 72, male 77, female | 79% | $22,800 |
| Yemen | 18,078,035 3.4% | 58, male 62, female | 38% | $820 |
| United States | 281,421,906 0.9% | 74, male 80, female | 97% | $36,200 |

**Sources:** Central Intelligence Agency, *The World Factbook 2001;* U.S. Census Bureau

**Interpreting the Chart** **Which country has the lowest standard of living?**

Oil was discovered in Bahrain in the 1930s, creating wealth for the country. However, by the 1990s this oil was starting to run out, and banking and tourism are now becoming important to the economy. Bahrain also refines crude oil imported from nearby Saudi Arabia.

Qatar occupies a small peninsula in the Persian Gulf. Like Bahrain, Qatar is ruled by a powerful monarch. In the 1990s, Qatar's ruler announced a plan to make the country more democratic. He also ended censorship of Qatari newspapers and television.

Qatar has sizable oil reserves and even larger reserves of natural gas—some of the largest in the world.

**The United Arab Emirates** The United Arab Emirates, or UAE, consists of seven tiny kingdoms. They are ruled by emirs. This country also has great reserves of oil and natural gas. Profits from these resources have created a modern, comfortable lifestyle for the people of the UAE. The government has also worked to build up other industries.

Like Saudi Arabia and many of the small Persian Gulf countries, the UAE depends on foreign workers. In the UAE, foreign workers outnumber citizens.

**Oman** Oman is located just outside the mouth of the Persian Gulf. The country is slightly smaller than Kansas. In ancient times, Oman was a major center of trade for merchants traveling the Indian Ocean. Today, Oman's economy is heavily dependent on oil. However, Oman does not have the oil wealth of Kuwait or the UAE. Therefore, the government, ruled by the Al Bu Sa'id family, is attempting to create new industries.

◀

Kindergarten students in the United Arab Emirates kneel to pray.
**Interpreting the Visual Record** **For what cultural reason do you think these girls and boys are seated in separate rows?**

**Yemen** Yemen is located on the southern corner of the Arabian Peninsula. It borders the Red Sea and the Gulf of Aden. Yemen was formed in 1990 by the joining of North Yemen and South Yemen. The country has an elected government and several political parties. However, political corruption and internal conflicts have threatened this young democracy.

In ancient times, farmers in this area used very advanced methods of irrigation and farming. Yemen was famous for its coffee. Today, Yemen is the poorest country on the Arabian Peninsula. Oil was not discovered there until the 1980s. It now generates a major part of the national income.

✓ **READING CHECK:** *Human Systems* How are the governments and economies of the countries of the Arabian Peninsula organized?

An important part of Yemen's culture is its distinctive architecture, which features tall buildings and carved wooden windows.
►

**Homework Practice Online**
Keyword: SK3 HP17

# Section Review 2

**Define and explain:** Muslims, caliph, Sunni, Shia, Qur'an, OPEC

**Working with Sketch Maps** On the map you created in Section 1, label Mecca and Riyadh. Why is Riyadh's location more suitable than Mecca's to be the capital city of Saudi Arabia?

## Reading for the Main Idea

**1.** *Places and Regions* What kind of government does Saudi Arabia have?

**2.** *Environment and Society* What role does oil play in the economies of small countries on the Arabian Peninsula?

## Critical Thinking

**3. Drawing Inferences and Conclusions** How might trips to Mecca help create a sense of community among Muslims?

**4. Drawing Inferences and Conclusions** Why would a country like Saudi Arabia or the United Arab Emirates bring in large numbers of foreign workers?

## Organizing What You Know

**5. Comparing** Copy the following graphic organizer. Use it to list these countries' locations, governments, and economies. Place them in the appropriate part of the chart.

|  | Location | Government | Economy |
|---|---|---|---|
| Saudi Arabia |  |  |  |
| Kuwait |  |  |  |
| Bahrain |  |  |  |
| Qatar |  |  |  |
| UAE |  |  |  |
| Oman |  |  |  |
| Yemen |  |  |  |

# CASE STUDY

## SAUDI ARABIA: HOW OIL HAS CHANGED A COUNTRY

At the beginning of the 1900s, Saudi Arabia was a poor country. Most people followed traditional ways of life and lived by herding animals, farming, or fishing. There were few good roads or transportation systems, and health care was poor.

## Major Oil Fields in Saudi Arabia

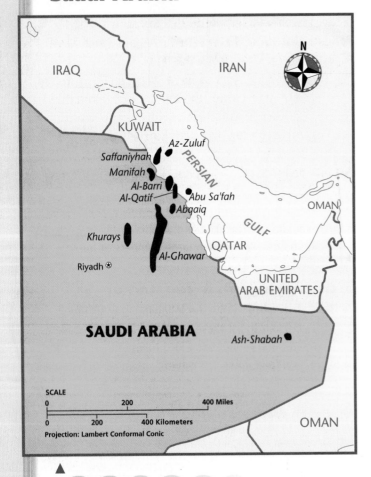

▲
Saudi Arabia's huge oil fields contain about one quarter of the world's known oil reserves.

Then, in the mid-1930s, oil was discovered in Saudi Arabia. Soon, even larger oil reserves were found. Eventually it was learned that Saudi Arabia had the largest oil reserves in the world. Most of the country's oil reserves are located in eastern Saudi Arabia along the Persian Gulf coast. The Al-Ghawar oil field, discovered in 1948, is the largest in the world. In addition to this field, Saudi Arabia has at least nine other major oil fields. The discovery of these huge oil reserves changed Saudi Arabia's economy and society.

Rising income from oil exports gave Saudi Arabia's government more and more money to invest. New airports, apartments, communications systems, oil pipelines, and roads were built. In 1960 Saudi Arabia had about 1,000 miles (1,600 km) of roads. By 1997 it had about 91,000 miles (145,600 km). Saudi Arabia's cities grew as people left small villages. These changes helped modernize Saudi Arabia's economy.

Saudi society was also affected. The standard of living rose, and people had more money to spend on goods. Foreign companies began to open stores and restaurants in Saudi Arabia. New schools were built throughout the country, and education became available to all citizens. The literacy rate increased from about 3 percent to about 63 percent. Thousands of Saudis traveled to other countries, and many new universities were opened. Health care also improved.

As Saudi Arabia's economy grew, many foreign workers came to the country to work. In the early 2000s foreign workers made up about 25 percent of Saudi Arabia's population. These workers included people from Yemen, Egypt, Palestine, Syria, Iraq, South Korea, and the Philippines. Americans and Europeans also went to Saudi Arabia to work in the oil industry.

The development of the oil industry greatly increased Saudi Arabia's importance in the world. In 1960 Saudi Arabia was a founding member of

◄

Oil is refined in eastern Saudi Arabia. Then it is pumped into ships and exported to countries around the world.

the Organization of Petroleum Exporting Countries (OPEC). Members of OPEC try to influence the price of oil on the world market. Saudi Arabia's huge oil reserves make it one of OPEC's most powerful member countries.

The Saudi government has also bought military equipment from the United States and other countries. This military strength has increased Saudi Arabia's importance in the Persian Gulf region. Since 1991, Saudi Arabia has given large sums to countries that sided with it against Iraq in the Persian Gulf War. Egypt, Turkey, and Syria have especially benefited from this aid.

Today, Saudi Arabia is a wealthy country. This wealth has come almost entirely from the sale of oil. Saudi Arabia is currently the world's leading oil exporter. Oil provides about 90 percent of the government's export earnings. Saudi Arabia exports oil to Japan, the United States, South Korea, and many other countries.

◄

Since the mid-1960s Saudi Arabia has expanded its transportation network. A modern road system now connects many parts of the country.

## Understanding What You Read

1. What was Saudi Arabia like before oil was discovered there?

2. How has oil changed Saudi Arabia's economy and society?

**Read to Discover**

1. What were the key events in Iraq's history?
2. What are Iraq's government and economy like?
3. What is the makeup of Iraq's population?

**Define**

embargo

**Locate**

Baghdad

*A Sumerian clay tablet*

### WHY IT MATTERS

The United States has used both economic and military action against Iraq in the 1990s and early 2000s. Use CNNfyi.com or other current events sources to learn about U.S. relations with Iraq today. Record your findings in your journal.

▲ Murals and posters of Saddam Hussein can be found throughout Baghdad, Iraq's capital.

## History

The history of Mesopotamia, an ancient region in Iraq, stretches back to some of the world's first civilizations. The Sumerian, Babylonian, and Assyrian cultures arose in this area. The Persians conquered Mesopotamia in the 500s B.C. Alexander the Great made it part of his empire in 331 B.C.

In the A.D. 600s the Arabs conquered Mesopotamia. The people of the area gradually converted to Islam. The city of Baghdad became one of the world's greatest centers of trade and culture. However, it was destroyed by the Mongols in 1258.

In the 1500s Mesopotamia became part of the Ottoman Empire. During World War I it was taken over by the British. In 1932 the British set up the kingdom of Iraq and placed a pro-British ruler in power. In the 1950s a group of Iraqi army officers overthrew this government. After several more changes in government, the Ba'ath Party took power in 1968.

A Ba'ath leader named Saddam Hussein slowly gained more power. In the late 1970s he became president of Iraq and leader of the armed forces.

In 1980 Iraq invaded Iran. Saddam Hussein hoped to take advantage of the confusion following the Iranian Revolution. The Iranians fought back, however, and the Iran-Iraq War dragged on until 1988. Hundreds of thousands of people were killed on both sides. Each side tried to attack the other's oil tankers and refineries. Both countries' economies were damaged.

In 1990, Iraq invaded the small, oil-rich country of Kuwait. Saddam Hussein used an old claim that Kuwait was part of Iraq to justify this invasion. Many Western leaders believed that Iraq should not be allowed to conquer its neighbors. They were also concerned that Iraq would control such a large share of the world's oil. Also, Iraq had missiles, poison gas, and perhaps nuclear weapons. An alliance of countries, led by the United States and Great Britain, sent troops, tanks, and planes to Saudi Arabia. In the Persian Gulf War of 1991 this alliance forced the Iraqis out of Kuwait.

### Iraq

| COUNTRY | POPULATION/ GROWTH RATE | LIFE EXPECTANCY | LITERACY RATE | PER CAPITA GDP |
|---------|-------------------------|-----------------|---------------|----------------|
| Iraq | 23,332,985 2.8% | 66, male 68, female | 58% | $2,500 |
| United States | 281,421,906 0.9% | 74, male 80, female | 97% | $36,200 |

**Sources:** Central Intelligence Agency, *The World Factbook 2001;* U.S. Census Bureau

✔ **READING CHECK:** *Human Systems* What are some key events in Iraq's history?

**Interpreting the Chart What percentage of the Iraqi population is literate?**

## Government and Economy

The government of Iraq is still firmly controlled by the Ba'ath Party and Saddam Hussein. The Iraqi leader has built up a large army and a secret police force. He has also placed his relatives in many important government positions.

Iraq has the world's second-largest known oil reserves, but its economy has suffered recently. Before the war with Iran, Iraq was the world's second-largest oil exporter. That war and the Persian Gulf War damaged Iraq's oil industry. Furthermore, the United Nations placed an **embargo**, or limit on trade, on Iraq. Today, Iraq exports much less oil than it did in the 1980s.

Other industries include construction, mining, and manufacturing. Many factories produce weapons for Iraq's army. More than 3 million people live in Baghdad, and most of Iraq's industries are there.

Irrigation from the Tigris and Euphrates Rivers supports Iraq's farming sector. Chief crops include barley, dates and other fruit, cotton, rice, vegetables, and wheat.

✔ **READING CHECK:** *Human Systems* How is Iraq's government organized, and what is its economy like?

**Our Amazing Planet**

**D**ust storms occur throughout Iraq and can rise to several thousand feet above the ground. These storms often happen during the summer. Five or six usually strike central Iraq in July, the worst month.

Many Iraqis shop for food in local markets.

The Ma'dan, sometimes called the Marsh Arabs, are a minority group in Iraq. They live in Iraq's southern marshes.

# People

Nearly all Iraqis are Muslim. More than 75 percent of the population are Arabs. Some 15 to 20 percent are Kurds, and the rest belong to small minority groups. Many Kurds living in Iraq's northern mountains have resisted control by the Baghdad government. After the Gulf War, Shia Arabs living in southern Iraq also rebelled against Saddam Hussein. The Iraqi government has used military force to crush these uprisings.

✓ **READING CHECK:** *Human Systems* What is the makeup of Iraq's population?

go.hrw.com
**Homework Practice Online**
Keyword: SK3 HP17

## Section Review 3

**Define and explain:** embargo

**Working with Sketch Maps** On the map you created in Section 2, label Baghdad. Where would you expect most of Iraq's population to be concentrated? Why?

### Reading for the Main Idea

1. *Human Systems* What are some different groups that have controlled Mesopotamia?

2. *Human Systems* What is Iraq's government like?

### Critical Thinking

3. **Finding the Main Idea** Why did several countries force Iraqi troops out of Kuwait?

4. **Analyzing Information** How have recent wars affected Iraq's economy?

### Organizing What You Know

5. **Sequencing** Create a time line tracing the history of the area now known as Iraq. List events from the Arab conquest to 1991.

A.D. 600s            1991

# Section 4   Iran and Afghanistan

## Read to Discover

1. What were some important events in Iran's history?
2. What are Iran's government and people like?
3. What problems does Afghanistan face today?

## Define

shah

theocracy

## Locate

Tehran

Khyber Pass

Kabul

### WHY IT MATTERS

The nation of Afghanistan has been involved in many conflicts in recent history. Use CNN**fyi**.com or other current events sources to learn about the situation in Afghanistan today. Record your findings in your journal.

*A Persian manuscript*

## Iran

Iran is a large country with a large population, rich history, and valuable natural resources. A revolution in 1979 made Islam the guiding force in Iran's government.

**History** The Persian Empire, established in the 500s B.C., was centered in what is now Iran. It was the greatest empire of its time and was an important center of learning. In the 300s B.C. Alexander the Great conquered the Persian Empire. In the A.D. 600s Arabs invaded the region and established Islam. Persian cultural and scientific contributions became elements of Islamic civilization. Later, different peoples ruled the region, including the Mongols and the Safavids.

In the dry climates of Iran and Afghanistan, some farmers still use an ancient method of irrigating crops. Runoff from mountains is moved through underground tunnels, called *qanats* (kuh-NAHTS), to fields below the mountains.

▼

### *Qanat* Irrigation System

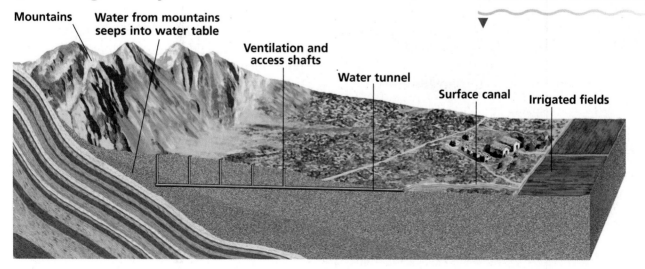

Mountains

Water from mountains seeps into water table

Ventilation and access shafts

Water tunnel

Surface canal

Irrigated fields

In 1921 an Iranian military officer took power and encouraged reform. He claimed the old Persian title of **shah**, or king. In 1941 the Shah's son took control. He was an ally of the United States and Britain and tried to modernize Iran. His programs were unpopular, however, and in 1979 he was overthrown.

Iran's new government set up an Islamic republic. Soon afterward, relations with the United States broke down. A mob of students attacked the U.S. Embassy in Iran's capital, Tehran, in November 1979. They took Americans hostage with the approval of Iran's government. More than 50 Americans were held by force for a year. The Iranian Revolution itself was soon followed by a long, destructive war with Iraq beginning in 1980.

**Government and Economy** Iran is a **theocracy**—a government ruled by religious leaders. The country has an elected president and legislature. An expert on Islamic law is the supreme leader, however.

Iran's government has supported many hard-line policies. For example, the country's government has called for the destruction of the state of Israel. Iran has also supported terrorist groups in other countries. However, in the late 1990s signs indicated that Iran was trying to make democratic reforms.

Iran has the fifth-largest oil reserves in the world. Oil is its main industry. Iran is a member of OPEC. Iran's other industries include construction, food processing, and the production of beautiful woven carpets. About one third of Iran's workforce is employed in agriculture.

During Iran's New Year celebrations grass is used to symbolize spring and life.

**People and Customs** Iran has a population of about 65 million—one of the largest in Southwest Asia. It is also quite diverse. Ethnic Persians make up a slight majority. Other groups include ethnic Azerbaijanis, Kurds, Arabs, and Turkomans. Persian is the official language. Almost all Iranians speak Persian, although some speak it as a second language. The region's other languages include several Kurdish dialects, some Turkic languages, and Arabic.

The Shia branch of Islam is Iran's official religion. About 90 percent of Iranians are Shia. About 10 percent of Iran's residents are Sunni Muslim. The rest are Christian, Jewish, or practice other religions.

In addition to the Islamic holy days, Iranians celebrate Nauruz—the Persian New Year. They also recognize the anniversary of the Iranian Revolution on February 11. Iranian food features rice, bread, vegetables, fruits, and lamb. Strong tea is a popular drink among many Iranians.

✓ READING CHECK:  *Human Systems*  What are Iran's government and people like?

# Afghanistan

Afghanistan is a landlocked country of high mountains and fertile valleys. Merchants, warriors, and missionaries have long used the Khyber (KY-buhr) Pass to reach India. This narrow passage through the Hindu Kush lies between Afghanistan and Pakistan.

**History and People** In 1979 the Soviet Union sent troops into Afghanistan to help the communist government there in a civil war. This led to a long war between Soviet troops and Afghan rebels. The Soviets left in 1989, and an alliance of Afghan groups took power. Turmoil continued, and in the mid-1990s a radical Muslim group known as the Taliban arose. Its leaders took over most of the country, including the capital, Kabul. The Taliban ruled Afghanistan strictly. For example, they forced women to wear veils and to stop working outside the home.

In 2001 Taliban officials came into conflict with the United States. Investigation of terrorist attacks on September 11 on Washington, D.C., and New York City led to terrorist Osama bin Laden and his al Qaeda network, based in Afghanistan. U.S. and British forces then attacked Taliban and al Qaeda targets and toppled the Taliban government.

The long period of war has damaged Afghanistan's industry, trade, and transportation systems. Farming and herding are the most important economic activities now.

Afghans belong to many different ethnic groups. The most numerous are the Pashtun, Tajik, Hazara, and Uzbek. Almost all Afghans are Muslims, and about 84 percent are Sunni.

✔ **READING CHECK:** ( *Human Systems* ) What are some of the challenges Afghanistan faces today?

## Iran and Afghanistan

| COUNTRY | POPULATION/ GROWTH RATE | LIFE EXPECTANCY | LITERACY RATE | PER CAPITA GDP |
|---|---|---|---|---|
| Afghanistan | 26,813,057 3.5% | 47, male 45, female | 32% (1999) | $800 |
| Iran | 66,128,965 0.7% | 69, male 71, female | 79% (1999) | $6,300 |
| United States | 278,058,881 0.9% | 74, male 80, female | 97% (1994) | $36,200 |

**Sources:** Central Intelligence Agency, *The World Factbook 2001*; U.S. Census Bureau

**Interpreting the Chart** How many times greater is the U.S. per capita GDP than Afghanistan's?

# Section Review 4

**Define and explain:** shah, theocracy

**Working with Sketch Maps** On the map you created in Section 3, label Tehran, Khyber Pass, and Kabul. What physical features do Tehran and Kabul have in common?

## Reading for the Main Idea

**1.** ( *Places and Regions* ) What ethnic and religious groups live in Iran?

**2.** ( *Human Systems* ) How have Afghanistan's recent wars affected the country?

Homework Practice Online
Keyword: SK3 HP17

## Critical Thinking

**3. Making Generalizations and Predictions** What challenges might the Iranian government face in the future?

**4. Drawing Inferences and Conclusions** How might Afghanistan's political problems be affected by its rugged physical geography?

## Organizing What You Know

**5. Sequencing** Copy the following graphic organizer. Use it to show the main events in Iran in recent decades.

# Reviewing What You Know

## Building Vocabulary

On a separate sheet of paper, write sentences to define each of the following words.

1. exotic rivers
2. wadis
3. fossil water
4. Muslims
5. Sunni
6. Shia
7. Qur'an
8. OPEC
9. embargo
10. theocracy

## Reviewing the Main Ideas

1. (Places and Regions) What are the three landform regions that make up this part of Southwest Asia?

2. (Places and Regions) What is the most important resource of this region?

3. (Places and Regions) Which countries in this area have large reserves of oil?

4. (Places and Regions) Which small country has some of the largest natural gas reserves in the world?

5. (Places and Regions) How have wars affected politics in this region?

## Understanding Environment and Society

### Resource Use

Use the graph in Section 2 and other print sources to create a presentation on the importance of the oil industry in one or more of the countries discussed in this chapter. As you prepare your presentation you may want to think about the following:

• How the oil industry affects people's daily lives in this region.

• What might happen to this region's economy if scientists discover an inexpensive alternative to oil.

## Thinking Critically

1. Why might it be dangerous for these countries' economies to be almost entirely dependent on the sale of oil?

2. Some of the countries of Southwest Asia are trying to increase crop production. What environmental factors might make this difficult?

3. How might Iran's recent history have been different if the 1979 revolution had not taken place?

4. Why has the United States become involved in the politics of this region?

5. What is Islam, and what are some of its practices and holidays?

**Map ACTIVITY**

On a separate sheet of paper, match the letters on the map with their correct labels.

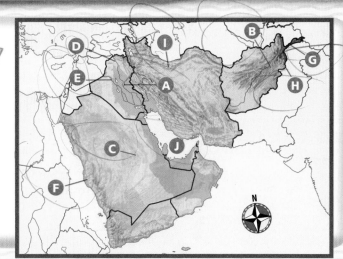

| | |
|---|---|
| Persian Gulf | Riyadh |
| Tigris River | Baghdad |
| Euphrates River | Tehran |
| Hindu Kush | Khyber Pass |
| Mecca | Kabul |

**Mental Mapping Skills ACTIVITY**

On a separate sheet of paper, draw a freehand map of the region. Make a key for your map and label the following:

| | |
|---|---|
| Afghanistan | Qatar |
| Iran | Saudi Arabia |
| Iraq | United Arab |
| Kuwait | Emirates |
| Oman | Yemen |

**WRITING ACTIVITY**

Imagine that you have been asked to write a travel brochure about one of the following countries: Afghanistan, Iran, Iraq, or Saudi Arabia. Use your textbook, the library, and the Internet to research your country. Then write a few paragraphs about its climate, attractions, and cultural events.

## Alternative Assessment

**Portfolio ACTIVITY**

**Learning About Your Local Geography**

**Individual Project** Contact your local utility company for information on where your electricity is generated and what fuel or energy source is used. Draw a diagram of your local power supply system.

**internet connect**

Internet Activity: **go.hrw.com**
KEYWORD: **SK3 GT17**

Choose a topic to explore about the Arabian Peninsula, Iraq, Iran, and Afghanistan:
- Visit Mesopotamia.
- Discover the importance of camels.
- See Arabian arts and crafts.

**go.hrw.com**

# CHAPTER 18

# The Eastern Mediterranean

*The next student we will meet lives in Turkey, a country that lies partly in Europe, partly in Asia.*

My name is Adalet, and I am in the tenth grade at Ted College, a private school in Ankara, the capital of Turkey. I live in an apartment a little outside the city with my mom and dad. We live on the twelfth floor, and have a view of the city, the distant mountains, and of course the parking lot. In the summers, my favorite time is when I can go to stay with my grandma and my grandpa in their summer house on the Aegean Sea, in Kusadasi near the ancient Greek city of Ephesus. I sleep until 11:00 A.M. or noon, then spend the day at the beach with my friends until the sun goes down.

On school days, from September to June, I get up at 8:00 A.M., put on my school uniform, and have breakfast of corn flakes or bread and cheese with milk or tea. At school we go directly to our classes. I am studying biology, physics, algebra, geometry, history, Turkish, and English. The English, science, and math classes are taught in English, the others in Turkish.

**Türkiye'den selamlar!**

Translation: Greetings from Turkey!

# Section 1 — Physical Geography

## Read to Discover

1. What are the main physical features of the eastern Mediterranean?
2. What are the climate types of the region?
3. What natural resources are found in this area?

## Define

phosphates
asphalt

## Locate

Dardanelles
Bosporus
Sea of Marmara
Jordan River
Dead Sea
Syrian Desert
Negev

An ancient temple in Petra, Jordan

### WHY IT MATTERS

The people who live in the Eastern Mediterranean region have needed irrigation and other technology to adapt to the land. Use CNNfyi.com or other current events sources to find information on ways that other people have modified their environment. Record your findings in your journal.

## The Eastern Mediterranean: Physical-Political

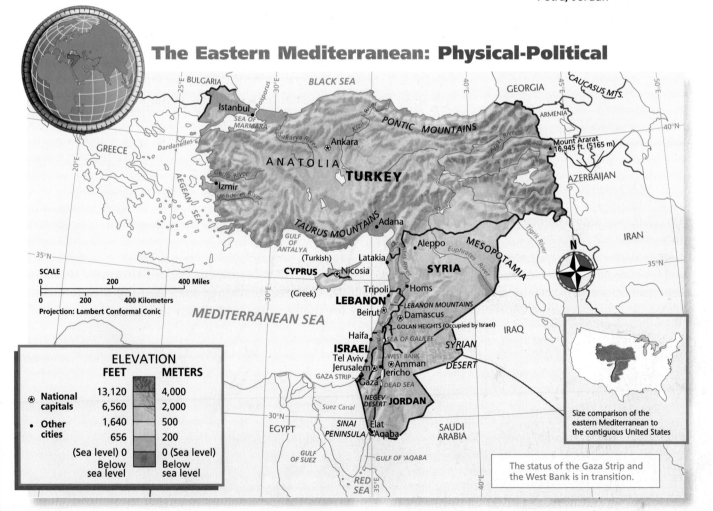

SCALE
0        200        400 Miles
0    200    400 Kilometers
Projection: Lambert Conformal Conic

ELEVATION

| | FEET | METERS |
|---|---|---|
| National capitals | 13,120 | 4,000 |
| | 6,560 | 2,000 |
| Other cities | 1,640 | 500 |
| | 656 | 200 |
| | (Sea level) 0 | 0 (Sea level) |
| | Below sea level | Below sea level |

Size comparison of the eastern Mediterranean to the contiguous United States

The status of the Gaza Strip and the West Bank is in transition.

# Physical Features

The countries of the eastern Mediterranean are Turkey, Lebanon, Syria, Jordan, and Israel. In addition to its own territory, Israel controls areas known as the Occupied Territories. These include the West Bank, the Gaza Strip, and the Golan Heights.

**On Two Continents** The eastern Mediterranean region straddles two continents. A small part of Turkey lies on Europe's Balkan Peninsula. This area consists of rolling plains and hills. A narrow waterway, made up of the Dardanelles (dahrd-uhn-ELZ), the Bosporus (BAHS-puh-ruhs), and the Sea of Marmara (MAHR-muh-ruh), separates Europe from Asia. The larger, Asian part of Turkey is mostly plateaus and highlands.

**Hills, Valleys, and Plains** Heading south from Turkey and into Syria, we cross a narrow plain. The Euphrates River, fed by precipitation in Turkey's eastern mountains, flows southeast through this plain. Farther south are more hills and plateaus. Two main ridges run north-south. One runs from southwestern Syria through western Jordan. The other, closer to the coast, runs through Lebanon, Israel, and the West Bank. The Jordan River valley separates these two ridges. A narrow coastal plain rims the region along its seacoasts. In western Turkey the coastal plain is wider.

**River and Sea** The Jordan River begins in Syria and flows south. Israel and the West Bank lie on the west side of the river. The country of Jordan lies on the east side. The Jordan River flows into the Dead Sea. This unusual body of water is the lowest point on any continent—1,312 feet (400 m) below sea level. It is so salty that swimmers cannot sink in it.

✓ **READING CHECK:** *Places and Regions* What are the region's main physical features?

**Our Amazing Planet**

The Dead Sea, which covers an area of just 394 square miles (1,020 sq km), contains approximately 12.7 billion tons of salt. Each year the Jordan River deposits 850,000 additional tons.

Istanbul lies on both sides of the waterway known as the Bosporus. This waterway divides Europe from Asia.

**Interpreting the Visual Record** Why do you think the Bosporus would be an important crossroads of trade?

# Climate

Dry climates are the rule in most of this region. However, there are important variations. Turkey's Black Sea coast and the Mediterranean coast all the way to Israel have a Mediterranean climate. Central Syria

and lands farther south have a desert climate. A small area of northeastern Turkey has a humid subtropical climate.

The Syrian Desert covers much of Syria and Jordan. It usually receives less than five inches (12.7 cm) of rainfall a year. Another desert, the Negev (NE-gev), lies in southern Israel.

✓ **READING CHECK:** ( *Places and Regions* ) What are the climates of the eastern Mediterranean?

## Resources

Unlike nearby countries in Southwest Asia, the countries of the eastern Mediterranean do not have large oil reserves. The people of this region make their living from the land in other ways.

**Limited Farming** Commercial farming is possible only where rain or irrigation provides enough water. Subsistence farming and livestock herding are common in drier areas. Desert areas support a few nomadic herders.

**Mineral Resources** Many minerals, including sulfur, mercury, and copper, are found in the region. **Phosphates**—mineral salts containing the element phosphorus—are produced in Syria, Jordan, and Israel. Phosphates are used to make fertilizers. The area also exports **asphalt**—the dark tarlike material used to pave streets. The Dead Sea is a source of mineral salts.

✓ **READING CHECK:** ( *Places and Regions* ) What natural resources are found in this area?

A shepherd in eastern Turkey watches his sheep.

**Interpreting the Visual Record** Why is livestock herding common in many parts of the eastern Mediterranean region?

▼

go.
hrw
.com

**Homework Practice Online**

Keyword: SK3 HP18

# Section Review 1

**Define and explain:** phosphates, asphalt

**Working with Sketch Maps** On a map of the eastern Mediterranean that you draw or that your teacher provides, label the following: Dardanelles, Bosporus, Sea of Marmara, Jordan River, Dead Sea, Syrian Desert, and the Negev.

### Reading for the Main Idea

1. ( *Places and Regions* ) What country lies on two continents?

2. ( *Places and Regions* ) What are the most common climates of the region?

3. ( *Places and Regions* ) How do geographic factors affect the economic activities of the region?

### Critical Thinking

4. **Drawing Inferences and Conclusions** How do you think the Dead Sea got its name?

### Organizing What You Know

5. **Categorizing** Copy the following graphic organizer. Use it to list the major landforms and bodies of water of each region.

| Country/ territory | Landforms and bodies of water |
| --- | --- |
|  |  |
|  |  |
|  |  |
|  |  |

# Section 2

## Turkey

### Read to Discover

1. What is the history of the area that is now Turkey?
2. What kind of government and economy does Turkey have?
3. How is Turkish society divided?

### WHY IT MATTERS

Turkey built dams on the Tigris and Euphrates Rivers to provide electricity and water for its people. The dams created conflict with Turkey's neighbors, Syria and Iraq. Use CNN fyi.com or other current events sources to find information about water issues around the world. Record your findings in your journal.

### Define

secular

### Locate

Ankara

Istanbul

*A replica of the legendary Trojan Horse in Turkey*

Ottoman monarchs lived in the Topkapi Palace built in 1462.

## History

Turkey, except for the small part that lies in Europe, makes up a region called Asia Minor. In ancient times this area was part of the Hittite and Persian Empires. In the 330s B.C. Alexander the Great conquered Asia Minor. Later it became part of the Roman Empire. Byzantium, renamed Constantinople, was one of the most important cities of the empire. After the fall of Rome, Constantinople became the capital of the Byzantine Empire.

In the A.D. 1000s the Seljuk Turks invaded Asia Minor. The Seljuks were a nomadic people from Central Asia who had converted to Islam. In 1453 another Turkish people, the Ottoman Turks, captured the city of Constantinople. They made it the capital of their Islamic empire.

**Ottoman Empire** During the 1500s and 1600s the Ottoman Empire was very powerful. It controlled territory in North Africa, Southwest Asia, and southeastern Europe. In the 1700s and 1800s the empire gradually weakened.

In World War I the Ottoman Empire fought on the losing side. When the war ended, the Ottomans lost all their territory outside of what is now Turkey. Greece even invaded western Asia Minor in an attempt to take more land. However, the Turkish army pushed out the invaders. Military officers

A boy holds a Turkish national flag during celebrations on Republic Day. A banner behind him shows Atatürk, the founder of modern Turkey.

then took over the government. Their leader was a war hero, Mustafa Kemal. He later adopted the name Kemal Atatürk, which means "father of the Turks." He formally dissolved the Ottoman Empire and created the nation of Turkey. He made the new country a democracy and moved the capital to Ankara. Constantinople was renamed Istanbul in 1930.

**Modern Turkey** Atatürk wanted to modernize Turkey. He believed that to be strong Turkey had to westernize. He banned the fez, the traditional hat of Turkish men, and required that they wear European-style hats. The Latin alphabet replaced the Arabic one. The European calendar and metric system replaced Islamic ones. Women were encouraged to vote, work, and hold office. New laws made it illegal for women to wear veils.

✓ **READING CHECK:** *Human Systems* What is the history of what is now Turkey?

Turkish women harvest grapes. **Interpreting the Visual Record** **What kind of climate do Turkey's coastal plains have?**

# Government and Economy

Today, Turkey has a legislature called the National Assembly. A president and a prime minister share executive power. The Turkish military has taken over the government three times. However, each time it has returned power to civilian hands.

Although most of its people are Muslim, Turkey is a **secular** state. This means that religion is kept separate from government. For example, the religion of Islam allows a man to have up to four wives. However, by Turkish law a man is permitted to have just one wife. In recent years Islamic political parties have attempted to increase Islam's role in Turkish society.

# CONNECTING TO *Literature*

*Gilgamesh is the hero of this ancient story that was popular all over Southwest Asia. In this passage Utnapishtim (oot-nuh-peesh-tuhm), whom the gods have given everlasting life, tells Gilgamesh about surviving a great flood.*

## Epic of Gilgamesh

"In those days . . . the people multiplied, the world bellowed like a wild bull, and the great god was aroused by the clamor[1]. Enlil (en-LIL) heard the clamor and he said to the gods in council, 'The uproar of mankind is intolerable[2] and sleep is no longer possible by reason of the babel[3].' So the gods agreed to exterminate[4] mankind. Enlil did this, but Ea (AY-uh) because of his oath warned me in a dream. . . . 'Tear down your house, I say, and build a boat. . . . then take up into the boat the seed of all living creatures.'

*Utnapishtim does as he is told. He builds a boat and fills it with supplies, his family, and animals. Then terrible rains come and flood Earth.*

"When the seventh day dawned the storm from the south subsided, the sea grew calm, the flood was stilled; I looked at the face of the world and there was silence, all mankind was turned to clay. . . . I opened a hatch and the light fell on my face. Then I bowed low, I sat down and I wept, . . . for on every side was the waste of water."

### Analyzing Primary Sources
1. Why did the god bring the flood?
2. Why does Utnapishtim cry?

---

**Vocabulary**   [1]clamor: noise   [2]intolerable: not bearable   [3]babel: confusing noise   [4]exterminate: kill off

---

Turkey's economy includes modern factories as well as village farming and craft making. The most important industries are clothing, chemicals, and oil processing. About 43 percent of Turkey's labor force works in agriculture. Grains, cotton, sugar beets, and hazelnuts are major crops. The Turkish economy has grown rapidly in recent years, but inflation is a problem. Large numbers of Turks have left Turkey in search of better jobs. As of 1994 an estimated 1.5 million Turks were working abroad to earn higher wages.

In the 1990s Turkey began building dams on the Tigris and Euphrates Rivers. These will provide electricity and irrigation water. However, the dams have caused concern for Syria and Iraq. They are disturbed that another country controls the sources of their water.

✓ **READING CHECK:**   *Human Systems*   What kind of government and economy does Turkey have?

# People and Culture

Turkey has more than 64 million people. Ethnic Turks make up 80 percent of the population. Kurds are the largest minority. They are about 20 percent of the population. Since ancient times the Kurds have lived in what is today southeastern Turkey. Kurds also live in nearby parts of Iran, Iraq, and Syria. In the 1980s and 1990s some Kurds fought for independence from Turkey. The Turkish government has used military force against this rebellion.

Kemal Atatürk's changes created a cultural split between Turkey's urban middle class and rural villagers. The lifestyle and attitudes of middle-class Turks have much in common with those of middle-class Europeans. Most Turks, though, are more traditional. Islam influences their attitudes on matters such as the role of women. This cultural division is a factor in Turkish politics.

Turkish cooking is much like that of the rest of the Mediterranean region. It features olives, vegetables, cheese, yogurt, and bread. Shish kebab—grilled meat on a skewer—is a favorite Turkish dish.

✓ **READING CHECK:** *Human Systems* What are the divisions in Turkish society?

▶

Crowds pass through a square near the University of Istanbul. Different styles of dress reflect the diverse attitudes that exist in Turkey today.

---

## Section Review 2

go.hrw.com
**Homework Practice Online**
Keyword: SK3 HP18

**Define and explain:** secular

**Working with Sketch Maps** On the map you created in Section 1, label Ankara and Istanbul. What are the advantages of Istanbul's location?

**Reading for the Main Idea**

1. *Human Systems* How did Atatürk try to modernize Turkey?

2. *Human Systems* What foods are popular in Turkish cooking?

**Critical Thinking**

3. **Finding the Main Idea** Why were some Turks unhappy with changes brought about by Atatürk?

4. **Analyzing Information** Why is the Turkish government building dams on the Tigris and Euphrates Rivers? How will this affect countries downriver?

**Organizing What You Know**

5. **Sequencing** Create a timeline listing major events in Turkey's history. List major people, groups, invasions, empires, and changes in government.

400 B.C.　　　　　　　　　　　A.D. 2000

# Section 3

## Israel and the Occupied Territories

### Read to Discover

1. What was the early history of Israel like?
2. What is modern Israel like?
3. What is the conflict over the Occupied Territories?

### Define

Diaspora
Zionism

### Locate

Jerusalem
Gaza Strip
Golan Heights
West Bank
Tel Aviv

#### WHY IT MATTERS

For thousands of years there has been conflict surrounding present-day Israel and the Occupied Territories. Use CNN**fyi**.com or other **current events** sources to find information about the current state of affairs in this region. Record your findings in your journal.

*A fragment of the Dead Sea Scrolls*

## Ancient Israel

The Hebrews, the ancestors of the Jews, first established the kingdom of Israel about 3,000 years ago. It covered roughly the same area as the modern State of Israel. In the 60s B.C. the Roman Empire conquered the region, which they called Palestine. After a series of Jewish revolts, the Romans forced most Jews to leave the region. This scattering of the Jewish population is known as the **Diaspora**.

During the era of Roman control, a Jewish man named Jesus began preaching a new religion. He said he was the son of God. Jesus taught that faith and love for others were more important than Judaism's many laws about daily life. His teachings particularly appealed to the poor and powerless. Both Roman and Jewish rulers saw Jesus's teachings as dangerous. Jesus was tried and executed. His followers believe he was resurrected. Christianity—Jesus's teachings and the belief in his resurrection—spread through the Roman Empire. In time, Christianity became the most common religion of the Mediterranean region.

The Arabs conquered Palestine in the mid-600s. From the 1000s to the 1200s, European armies launched a series of invasions called the Crusades. The Crusaders captured Jerusalem in 1099. In time the Crusaders were pushed out of the area altogether.

The ancient port of Caesarea lies on the coast of Israel. It was the regional capital during the time of Roman control. Today the harbor structure is partly underwater.

Israeli soldiers stand guard on a hill overlooking the Gaza Strip.

From the 1500s to World War I, Palestine was part of the Ottoman Empire. At the end of the war, it came under British control.

✓ **READING CHECK:** *Human Systems* What significant events occurred in the early history of the area of Israel?

# Modern Israel

In the late 1800s a movement called **Zionism** began among European Jews. Zionism called for Jews to establish a country or community in Palestine. Tens of thousands of Jews moved to the area.

After World War II, the United Nations recommended dividing Palestine into Arab and Jewish states. This plan created conflict among the peoples there. Fighting broke out between Israel and surrounding Arab countries. The Israeli forces defeated the Arabs.

Many Palestinians fled to other Arab states, particularly to Jordan and Lebanon. Some used terrorist attacks to strike at Israel. Israel and its Arab neighbors also fought wars in 1956, 1967, and 1973.

**Government and Economy** Israel has a prime minister and a parliament, called the Knesset. There are two major political parties and many smaller parties.

Israel has built a strong military for protection from the Arab countries around it. Terrorist attacks have also occurred. At age 18 most Israeli men and women must serve in the military.

### Eastern Mediterranean

| COUNTRY | POPULATION/ GROWTH RATE | LIFE EXPECTANCY | LITERACY RATE | PER CAPITA GDP |
|---|---|---|---|---|
| Israel* | 5,938,093 1.6% | 77, male 81, female | 95% | $18,900 |
| Jordan | 5,153,378 3% | 75, male 80, female | 87% | $3,500 |
| Lebanon | 3,627,774 1.4% | 69, male 74, female | 86% | $5,000 |
| Syria | 16,728,808 2.5% | 68, male 70, female | 71% | $3,100 |
| Turkey | 66,493,970 1.2% | 69, male 74, female | 85% | $6,800 |
| United States | 281,421,906 0.9% | 74, male 80, female | 97% | $36,200 |

*Does not include the West Bank and Gaza Strip.
**Sources:** Central Intelligence Agency, *The World Factbook 2001;* U.S. Census Bureau

**Interpreting the Chart** Which country in the region has the largest population?

## The West Bank in Transition

**SCALE**
0 5 10 Miles
0 5 10 Kilometers
Projection:
Transverse Cylindrical

Qabatiya

Tulkarm

Qalqilyah

Nablus

**West Bank**

Jordan R.

**N**

Ramallah

Jericho

Jerusalem

**ISRAEL**

Bethlehem

Dead Sea

Hebron

**Control of the West Bank:**
- Israeli
- Palestinian civil, Israeli security
- Palestinian before 1998
- Palestinian, 1998
- City of Jerusalem

The Gaza Strip is densely populated and has few natural resources. Israel captured this territory from Egypt in 1967.

▼

Israel has a modern, diverse economy. Items like high-technology equipment and cut diamonds are important exports. Tourism is a major industry. Israel's lack of water limits farming. However, using highly efficient irrigation, Israel has successfully increased food production. It imports grain but exports citrus fruit and eggs.

**Languages and Diversity** Israel's population includes Jews from all parts of the world. Both Hebrew and Arabic are official languages. When they arrive in Israel, many Jews speak English, Russian, German, Hungarian, Yiddish, or Arabic. The government provides classes to help them learn Hebrew.

About 82 percent of Israel's population is Jewish. The rest is mostly Palestinian. About three fourths of these are Muslim. The rest are Christian.

**Food and Festivals** Israeli food is influenced by Jewish religious laws. Jews are forbidden to eat pork and shellfish. They also cannot eat meat and milk products at the same meal. The country's food is as diverse as the population. Eastern European dishes are popular, as are Southwest Asian foods.

For Jews, Saturday is a holy day. Yom Kippur, the most important Jewish holiday, is celebrated in October. Passover, in the spring, celebrates the Hebrews' escape from captivity in Egypt. During Passover, people eat matzo (MAHT-suh), a special bread without yeast.

✓ **READING CHECK:** *Human Systems* What are modern Israel's government, economy, and culture like?

# The Occupied Territories

In 1967 Israel captured the Gaza Strip, the Golan Heights, and the West Bank. These are sometimes called the Occupied Territories.

**Disputed Land** The Gaza Strip is a small, crowded piece of coastal land. More than a million Palestinians live there. The area has almost no resources. The Golan Heights is a hilly area on the Syrian

border. In 1981 Israel formally declared the Golan Heights part of Israel. Syria still claims this territory.

The West Bank is the largest of the occupied areas, with a population of about 1.6 million. Since Israel took control of the West Bank, more than 100,000 Jews have moved into settlements there. The Palestinians consider this an invasion of their land. This has caused tension and violence between Arabs and Israelis.

Israel annexed East Jerusalem in 1980. Even before this, the Israeli government had moved the capital from Tel Aviv to Jerusalem. Most foreign countries have chosen not to recognize this transfer. The Palestinians still claim East Jerusalem as their rightful capital.

Control of Jerusalem is a difficult and often emotional question for Jews, Muslims, and Christians. The city contains sites that are holy to all three religions.

**The Future of the Territories** In the 1990s Israel agreed to turn over parts of the Occupied Territories to the Palestinians. In return, the Palestinian leadership—the Palestinian Authority—agreed to work for peace. Parts of the Gaza Strip and West Bank have been transferred to the Palestinian Authority. More areas of the West Bank are expected to be handed over in the future.

The future of the peace process is uncertain. Some Palestinian groups have continued to commit acts of terrorism. Some Jewish groups believe for religious reasons that Israel must not give up the West Bank. Other Israelis fear they would be open to attack if they withdrew from the territories.

✓ **READING CHECK:** **Human Systems** Why have the Occupied Territories been a source of conflict?

Muslim women gather to pray at the Dome of the Rock in Jerusalem.
▼

---

**Define and explain:** Diaspora, Zionism

**Working with Sketch Maps** On the map you created in Section 2, label Jerusalem, Gaza Strip, Golan Heights, West Bank, and Tel Aviv.

### Reading for the Main Idea

1. **Environment and Society** How has technology allowed Israel to increase its food production?

2. **Human Systems** What historical factors helped create a culturally diverse region in Israel?

### Critical Thinking

3. **Finding the Main Idea** How do political boundaries in Israel create conflicts?

4. **Summarizing** What are some difficult issues involved in the Israeli-Palestinian peace process?

### Organizing What You Know

5. **Sequencing** Copy the following graphic organizer. Use it to list the sequence of events that led to the formation of modern Israel.

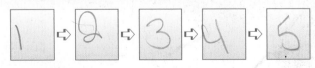

# Section 4 Syria, Lebanon, and Jordan

## Read to Discover
1. What kind of government and economy does Syria have?
2. How is Lebanese society divided?
3. What events have shaped the history of Jordan?

## Define
mandate

## Locate
Damascus
Beirut
Amman

### WHY IT MATTERS

Syria, Jordan, and Lebanon have experienced conflicts due to religious or ethnic differences of people living there. Use **CNN fyi.com** or other **current events** sources to find information about other countries struggling with such conflicts. Record your findings in your journal.

*Spices in an outdoor market*

## Syria

The capital of Syria, Damascus, is believed to be the oldest continuously inhabited city in the world. For centuries it was a leading regional trade center. Syria became part of the Ottoman Empire in the 1500s. After World War I, France controlled Syria as a **mandate**. Mandates were former territories of the defeated nations of World War I. They were placed under the control of the winning countries after the war. Syria finally became independent in the 1940s.

**Politics and Economy** From 1971 to 2000, the Syrian government was led by Hafiz al-Assad. Assad increased the size of Syria's military. He wanted to match Israel's military strength and protect his rule from his enemies within Syria. Assad's son, Bashar, was elected president after his father's death in 2000.

Syria's government owns the country's oil refineries, larger electrical plants, railroads, and some factories. Syria's key manufactured goods are textiles, food products, and chemicals. Agriculture remains important.

Roman columns still stand in the ancient city of Apamea, Syria.

Syria has only small deposits of oil and natural gas. It is rich in limestone, basalt, and phosphates.

**People** Syria's population of more than 17 million is about 90 percent Arab. The other 10 percent includes Kurds and Armenians. About 74 percent of Syrians are Sunni Muslim. Another 16 percent are Alawites and Druze, members of small branches of Islam. About 10 percent of Syrians are Christian. There are also small Jewish communities in some cities.

✓ **READING CHECK:** ( *Places and Regions* ) How is Syria's economy organized?

# Lebanon

Lebanon is a small, mountainous country on the Mediterranean coast. It is home to several different groups of people. At times these different groups have fought each other.

**History and People** During the Ottoman period many religious and ethnic minority groups settled in Lebanon. After World War I Lebanon, along with Syria, became a French mandate. Lebanon finally gained independence in the 1940s.

The Lebanese are overwhelmingly Arab, but they are divided by religion. Most Lebanese are either Muslim or Christian. Each of those groups is divided into several smaller groups. Muslims are divided into Sunni, Shia, and Druze. The Maronites are the largest of the Christian groups in Lebanon. At the time of independence, there were slightly more Christians than Muslims. Over time, however, Muslims became the majority.

▲

People must drill for water in dry areas of Syria.

**Interpreting the Visual Record**
**Judging from this photo, how has technology affected the lifestyle of people in desert areas?**

▲

This photograph from the early 1900s shows a tall cedar tree in the mountains of northern Lebanon. Lebanon's cedars have long been a symbol of the country.

A vendor in Beirut sells postcards of what the city looked like before it was scarred by war.

**Interpreting the Visual Record** What were the effects of the civil war in Lebanon?

**Civil War** For some decades after independence, Christian and Muslim politicians managed to share power. A complex system assigned certain government positions to different religious groups. For example, the president was always a Maronite. However, over time this cooperation broke down. The poorest group, the Shia, grew rapidly but were not given additional power. Tensions mounted. Adding to the divisions between Lebanese was the presence of hundreds of thousands of Palestinian refugees living in Lebanon. Ethnic and religious groups armed themselves, and in the 1970s fighting broke out. Warfare between Lebanese groups lasted until 1990. Tens of thousands of people died, and the capital, Beirut, was badly damaged.

During the 1990s Lebanon's economy slowly recovered from the civil war. The refining of crude oil brought in by pipeline is a leading industry. Other industries include food processing, textiles, cement, chemicals, and jewelry making. Lebanese farmers produce tobacco, fruit, grains, and vegetables.

✓ **READING CHECK:** ( *Human Systems* ) What is causing divisions in Lebanese society?

## Jordan

Jordan's short history has been full of conflict. Great Britain drew its borders, and Jordan's royal family is actually from Arabia. The country has few resources and several powerful neighbors. In addition, most of its people think of another country as their homeland. Yet Jordan has survived.

**History and Government** The country of Jordan (called Transjordan until 1949) was created from Ottoman territory following World War I. The British controlled the area as a mandate. They established an Arabian prince named Abdullah as the monarch of the new country. Abdullah had helped the British in World War I, but he had been driven out of Saudi Arabia. In the 1940s the country became fully independent. After the creation of Israel and the war of 1948, Jordan annexed the Arab lands of the West Bank.

At the time of its independence, Jordan's population was small. Most Jordanians lived a nomadic or seminomadic life. After each of the Arab-Israeli wars of 1948 and 1967, hundreds of thousands of Palestinian Arab refugees came to live in Jordan. These immigrants strained Jordan's resources. In addition, a cultural division arose between the Palestinians and the "original" Jordanian Arabs. After 1967 Palestinians actually made up a majority of Jordan's people.

From 1952 to 1999 Jordan was ruled by King Hussein. Most observers, both inside and outside Jordan, considered him one of the

Jordanian children play with a camel. At one time a majority of Jordanians were nomads. Today most of Jordan's people live in urban areas.

A truck crosses the Jordan River near the Dead Sea. The river is a key source of water for agriculture and other uses.

**Interpreting the Visual Record** What countries and territories border the Jordan River?

best rulers in the region. Hussein's popularity allowed him to begin some democratic reforms in the 1980s and 1990s. Today, the division between Palestinian and Jordanian Arabs causes less conflict.

**Economy and Resources** Jordan is a poor country with limited resources. The country does produce phosphates, cement, and potash. Tourism and banking are becoming important industries. Jordan depends on economic aid from the oil-rich Arab nations and the United States. Amman, the capital, is Jordan's only large city.

Jordanian farmers raise fruits and vegetables in the Jordan River valley, using irrigation. Some highland areas receive enough winter rainfall to grow grains. Raising sheep and goats is an important source of income. However, overgrazing has caused soil erosion. A crucial resource issue for Jordan is its shortage of water.

✓ **READING CHECK:** *Human Systems* How did King Hussein affect Jordan's history?

**BUILD on WHAT You Know**

**D**o you remember what you learned about uneven resource distribution? See Chapter 5 to review.

## Section Review 4

go.hrw.com **Homework Practice Online**
Keyword: SK3 HP18

**Define and explain:** mandate

**Working with Sketch Maps** On the map you created in Section 3, label Damascus, Beirut, and Amman.

### Reading for the Main Idea

1. *Human Systems* How did Hafiz al-Assad affect Syria?

2. *Human Systems* What divisions led to conflict in Lebanon?

3. *Places and Regions* Which of the countries discussed in this section does not border the Mediterranean Sea?

### Critical Thinking

4. **Finding the Main Idea** How have foreign countries influenced Jordan?

### Organizing What You Know

5. **Categorizing** Use the graphic organizer to gather information about Syria, Lebanon, and Jordan.

|  | Syria | Lebanon | Jordan |
|---|---|---|---|
| Major religion(s) |  |  |  |
| Type of government |  |  |  |
| Major problem(s) |  |  |  |
| Greatest strength(s) |  |  |  |

# Reviewing What You Know

## Building Vocabulary

On a separate sheet of paper, write sentences to define each of the following words.

1. phosphates
2. asphalt
3. secular
4. Diaspora
5. Zionism
6. mandate

## Reviewing the Main Ideas

1. **Human Systems** People and customs from what three continents have influenced the eastern Mediterranean region?

2. **Human Systems** What three major religions have holy sites in Jerusalem?

3. **Human Systems** How has westernization changed Turkey's government, economy, and culture?

4. **Human Systems** What is the conflict over the Occupied Territories?

5. **Environment and Society** How do people in this area make their living from the land?

## Understanding Environment and Society

### Conflicts over Water

Freshwater is a scarce resource throughout much of the eastern Mediterranean. Create a presentation and model on issues of water supply and demand. Consider the following:

- Ways people in this region obtain freshwater.
- Human activities that consume water.
- Problems between countries when water supplies are strained.

Create a five-question quiz, with answers, about your model that you can use to challenge your classmates.

## Thinking Critically

1. **Drawing Inferences and Conclusions** Why do you think Atatürk moved Turkey's capital from Istanbul to Ankara?

2. **Finding the Main Idea** How has human migration to Israel affected its population?

3. **Analyzing Information** How is the Dead Sea unusual? What are its commercial uses?

4. **Analyzing Information** How did refugees from Palestine affect Jordan?

5. **Drawing Inferences and Conclusions** Why did attempts to balance religious groups' participation in Lebanon's government fail?

## Map ACTIVITY

On a separate sheet of paper, match the letters on the map with their correct labels.

| | |
|---|---|
| Dardanelles | Negev |
| Bosporus | Istanbul |
| Sea of Marmara | Tel Aviv |
| Jordan River | Jerusalem |
| Dead Sea | Damascus |

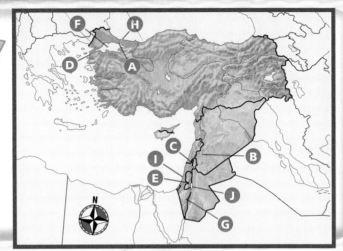

## Mental Mapping Skills ACTIVITY

On a separate sheet of paper, draw a freehand map of the eastern Mediterranean and label the following:

| | |
|---|---|
| Gaza Strip | Lebanon |
| Golan Heights | Syria |
| Israel | Turkey |
| Jordan | West Bank |

## WRITING ACTIVITY

Imagine that your family is about to travel to the eastern Mediterranean for a vacation. Your parents have asked you to help plan the trip. Write about the places you would like to visit and the reasons you would find them interesting. Be sure to use standard grammar, spelling, sentence structure, and punctuation.

# Alternative Assessment

## Portfolio ACTIVITY

### Learning About Your Local Geography

**Individual Project**  For thousands of years the eastern Mediterranean has been a crossroads between Europe, Asia, and Africa. Show how your community is linked to other towns and cities in a graphic organizer.

☑ **internet** connect

Internet Activity: **go.hrw.com**
KEYWORD: **SK3 GT18**

Choose a topic to explore about the eastern Mediterranean:

- Visit the Dead Sea.
- Compare Israeli and Arab foods.
- Travel to historic Jerusalem.

# FOCUS ON REGIONS

## Differences and Connections

In this textbook the countries of Africa are grouped together. This has been done to emphasize the region's connections. Yet any region as large as Africa has important differences from place to place. East Africa is different from West Africa, and West Africa is different from North Africa. This is also true of other large regions. In South America, for example, Brazil is different from Argentina in many important ways.

**North Africa and Southwest Asia** One subregion of Africa that geographers often include in another region is North Africa. These geographers see more connections between North Africa and Southwest Asia than between North Africa and the rest of the continent. For example, in both areas Arabic is the main language. The major religion is Islam. Political issues also tie North Africa to its eastern neighbors, as does physical geography. The countries of North Africa and Southwest

▲
The Muhammad Ali Mosque is one of many beautiful places of worship for Muslims in Cairo, Egypt. Although various religions, including Judaism and Christianity, are practiced in North Africa and Southwest Asia, most people in the two regions are Muslim.

Asia are part of a vast desert region. These countries face common issues such as water conservation and water management.

**The African Continent** There are also many reasons for placing North Africa in a region with the rest of Africa. People in Africa share some important historical, cultural, and economic ties. For example, ancient Egyptians had close contact with other peoples in Africa. In turn, cultures south of the Sahara contributed to the development of Egypt's great Nile Valley civilizations. Farther west, Mediterranean peoples have long traded with West African kingdoms south of the Sahara. Such contact helped spread

◄
This sign in Morocco is in both Arabic and French. Arabic is spoken throughout North Africa and many parts of Southwest Asia.

# Regional Links

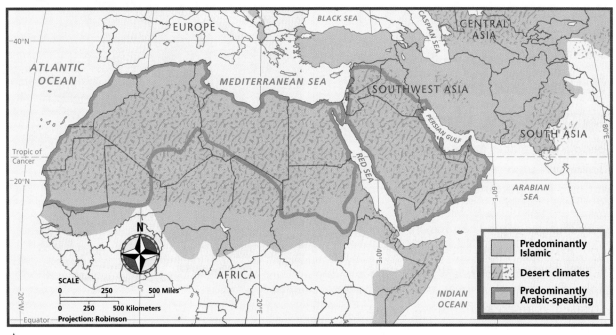

Language, religion, and climate are some of the ties between North Africa and Southwest Asia. Arabic speakers, Muslims, and desert climates are dominant throughout much of the two regions and in parts of the surrounding transition zones.

Islam among the peoples of North Africa and the rest of the continent. Today, there are mosques as far south as Nigeria and Tanzania.

North Africa also has political connections to the rest of Africa. Many African countries face similar political and economic challenges. In part, these issues arise from their shared colonial history. To resolve some of these issues, the countries of North Africa are working with other African countries. They have formed associations such as the Organization of African Unity.

**Transition Zones** There are many differences and connections between North Africa and the rest of the continent. Perhaps they are most evident in a band of countries that lie just south of the Sahara. These countries stretch from Mauritania in the west to Ethiopia and Sudan in the east. They form a transition zone. In other words, they resemble both North Africa and Africa south of the

Sahara. In Chad and Sudan, for example, strong political and cultural differences separate north and south. The northern regions of these countries are tied closely to North Africa. The southern regions of these countries are tied closely to African countries to the south.

North Africa and the countries in the transition zone have important connections to two major world regions. Which region they are placed in depends on the geographer's point of view. Understanding the differences among countries and their connections to other areas of the world is important. It is more important than deciding where on a map a region begins or ends.

## Understanding What You Read

1. What ties are there between North Africa and Southwest Asia?

2. What ties are there between North Africa and the rest of the African continent?

# Building Skills for Life: Interpreting the Past

▲
Ancient ruins in Petra, Jordan, can provide clues to the region's past.

Both people and places are a product of the past. Therefore, understanding the geography of past times is important. It gives us a more complete understanding of the world today.

History and geography can hardly be separated. All historical events have to happen somewhere. These events are affected by local geography. For example, wheat and barley were domesticated in an area of Southwest Asia called the Fertile Crescent. This region received enough rainfall for these crops to grow.

Geographers who specialize in studying the past are called historical geographers. Historical geographers are interested in where things used to be and how they developed. They also try to understand how people's beliefs and values influenced historical events. In other words, why did people do what they did?

All geographers must be skilled at interpreting the past. Cultural geographers might study how old buildings and houses reflect earlier times. Physical geographers may need to reconstruct past landscapes. For example,

many rivers have changed their course. Understanding where a river used to flow could help explain its present course.

In your study of geography, think about how a place's history has shaped the way it is today. Look for clues that can tell you about its past. Ask yourself how people may have thought about a place in earlier times. No matter where you are, the evidence of the past is all around!

## THE SKILL

**1.** Look at some of the buildings in your community. How old do you think they are? Do some look older than others? Can you describe how building styles in your community have changed over time? Why do you think styles have changed?

**2.** Analyze an important historical event that occurred in your state. What happened? Where did it happen? How was the event influenced by local geography?

**3.** Interpret the settlement history of your state or community. When was it settled? What attracted people to it? How do you think they felt about the place at the time?

# HANDS on GEOGRAPHY

One way to interpret the past is by studying old travel accounts. They often have detailed information about the people, places, and daily life of past times.

One famous travel account describes the journeys of Ibn Battuta. Ibn Battuta was one of the greatest travelers in history. During the mid-1300s he traveled about 75,000 miles (120,700 km) throughout parts of Asia and Africa. Near the end of his travels, he gave a long account of the many places he visited. This account is a valuable historical document today.

The following passage is taken from Ibn Battuta's travel account. In this passage, Ibn Battuta is visiting the Sultan of Birgi, a town in what is now western Turkey. Read the passage, and then answer the Lab Report questions.

❝ *In the course of this audience the sultan asked me this question: "Have you ever seen a stone that fell from the sky?" I replied, "I have never seen one, nor ever heard tell of one." "Well," he said, "a stone did fall from the sky outside this town of ours," and then called some men and told them to bring the stone. They brought in a great black stone, very hard and with a glitter in it—I reckoned its weight to amount to a hundredweight. The sultan ordered the stonebreakers to be summoned, and four of them came and on his com-mand to strike it they beat upon it as one man four times with iron hammers, but made no impression on it. I was astonished at this phenomenon, and he ordered it to be taken back to its place.* ❞

▲ This painting shows Ibn Battuta during his travels in the mid-1300s.

# Lab Report

1. What did the "stone that fell from the sky" look like? What do you think it was?

2. Why do you think Ibn Battuta was "astonished" by what he saw?

3. What can this story tell us about the historical geography of this region?

# UNIT 6

## Africa

Holding back the desert in Morocco

Cape Town, South Africa

## A Physician in Sierra Leone

*Dr. James Li went to Africa fresh out of medical school to work as a general practice physician. Here he describes what it was like to work at a hospital in Sierra Leone.* **WHAT DO YOU THINK?** *What might Dr. Li's patients think about health care in the United States?*

Malaria, tuberculosis, and leprosy were widespread in our hospital population. We often saw patients who had walked over 100 miles for treatment. None of the patients in our area had access to clean water. Phone lines installed by the British had been cut down and the copper wires melted to make cooking pots. Our hospital was in the remote jungle, about six hours by dirt road from the nearest major city. It had 140 beds. In the clinic, we saw several hundred other patients each day. Food for the staff and patients was grown on the hospital grounds.

I came to love the people who were our patients, particularly the very young and the very old. In the midst of shortages, I met people who lived happily and suffered the tragedies of utter poverty with a dignity that would have failed me. These reflections fill me with a strange combination of awe, sadness, humility, and excitement.

Hospital in Butare, Rwanda

Masai dancers, Kenya

### Understanding Primary Sources

**1.** What were conditions like at Dr. Li's hospital?

**2.** How does Dr. Li describe the culture of Sierra Leone?

Giraffe

# Africa

## Elevation Profile

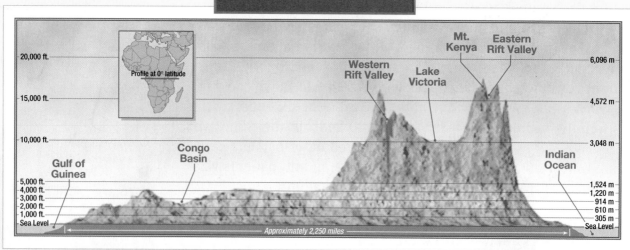

Profile at 0° latitude

20,000 ft. — 6,096 m
15,000 ft. — 4,572 m
10,000 ft. — 3,048 m
5,000 ft. — 1,524 m
4,000 ft. — 1,220 m
3,000 ft. — 914 m
2,000 ft. — 610 m
1,000 ft. — 305 m
Sea Level — Sea Level

Gulf of Guinea · Congo Basin · Western Rift Valley · Lake Victoria · Mt. Kenya · Eastern Rift Valley · Indian Ocean

Approximately 2,250 miles

### The United States and Africa:
## Comparing Sizes

### GEOSTATS:

World's longest river:
Nile River—4,160 miles
(6,693 km)

World's largest hot desert:
Sahara—about 3,500,000 sq. mi.
(9,065,000 sq km)

World's highest recorded
temperature: 136°F (58°C)
in Al Azizyah, Libya on
September 13, 1992

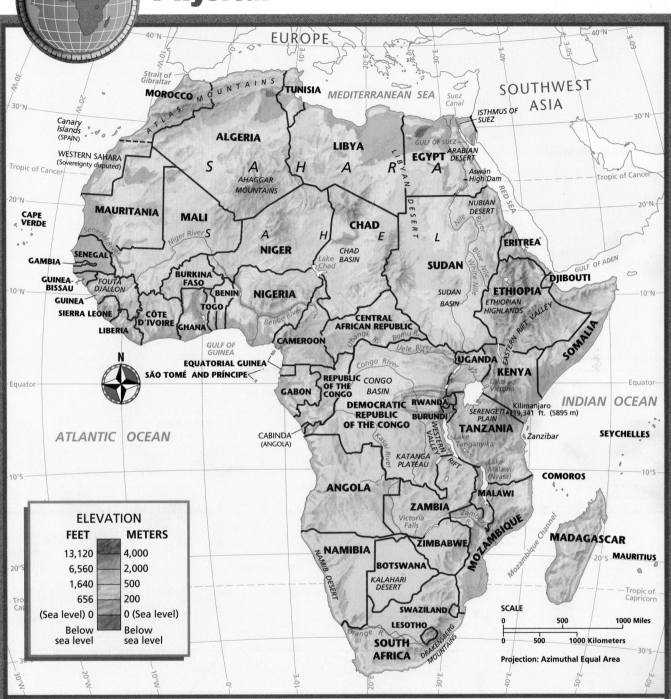

EUROPE

40°N · 10°E · 10°E · 20°E · 30°E · 40°E · 50°E · 60°E

Strait of Gibraltar
MOROCCO
ATLAS MOUNTAINS
TUNISIA
MEDITERRANEAN SEA
Suez Canal
SOUTHWEST ASIA
ISTHMUS OF SUEZ
30°N

Canary Islands (SPAIN)
ALGERIA
LIBYA
EGYPT
GULF OF SUEZ
ARABIAN DESERT

WESTERN SAHARA (Sovereignty disputed)
S          A          H          A          R          A
Aswān High Dam
Tropic of Cancer

CAPE VERDE
MAURITANIA
MALI
AHAGGAR MOUNTAINS
NIGER
CHAD
LIBYAN DESERT
NUBIAN DESERT
RED SEA
ERITREA
20°N

GAMBIA
SENEGAL
Senegal River
Niger River
BURKINA FASO
CHAD BASIN
Lake Chad
SUDAN
Blue Nile
White Nile
DJIBOUTI
GULF OF ADEN
10°N

GUINEA-BISSAU
FOUTA DJALLON
GUINEA
SIERRA LEONE
LIBERIA
CÔTE D'IVOIRE
BENIN
TOGO
GHANA
NIGERIA
Benue River
SUDAN BASIN
ETHIOPIA
ETHIOPIAN HIGHLANDS
SOMALIA

N
GULF OF GUINEA
EQUATORIAL GUINEA
SÃO TOMÉ AND PRÍNCIPE
CAMEROON
CENTRAL AFRICAN REPUBLIC
Ubangi R.
Bomu R.
Uele River
EASTERN RIFT VALLEY
UGANDA
KENYA
Lake Victoria
Equator

GABON
REPUBLIC OF THE CONGO
Congo River
CONGO BASIN
RWANDA
BURUNDI
SERENGETI PLAIN
Kilimanjaro 19,341 ft. (5895 m)
INDIAN OCEAN
SEYCHELLES
Equator

ATLANTIC OCEAN
CABINDA (ANGOLA)
DEMOCRATIC REPUBLIC OF THE CONGO
Kasai River
WESTERN RIFT VALLEY
TANZANIA
Zanzibar
Lake Tanganyika
10°S

KATANGA PLATEAU
Lake Malawi (Nyasa)
COMOROS
10°S

ANGOLA
ZAMBIA
Victoria Falls
Zambezi R.
MALAWI
MOZAMBIQUE
Mozambique Channel
MADAGASCAR
MAURITIUS

NAMIBIA
ZIMBABWE
BOTSWANA
KALAHARI DESERT
NAMIB DESERT
20°S
Tropic of Capricorn

**ELEVATION**

| FEET | METERS |
|------|--------|
| 13,120 | 4,000 |
| 6,560 | 2,000 |
| 1,640 | 500 |
| 656 | 200 |
| (Sea level) 0 | 0 (Sea level) |
| Below sea level | Below sea level |

SWAZILAND
LESOTHO
Orange R.
SOUTH AFRICA
DRAKENSBERG MOUNTAINS

SCALE
0 · 500 · 1000 Miles
0 · 500 · 1000 Kilometers
Projection: Azimuthal Equal Area
30°S

---

**1.** *Places and Regions*  Which region of Africa has the highest mountains? Which country appears to have the largest number of high mountains?

**2.** *Places and Regions*  Which countries have areas that lie below sea level? Where is the highest point in Africa?

## Critical Thinking

**3. Analyzing Information**  Which North African mountains might create a rain-shadow effect?

**4. Comparing**  Compare this map to the **climate map** of the region. Which areas might have tropical rain forests?

# Africa:
# Political

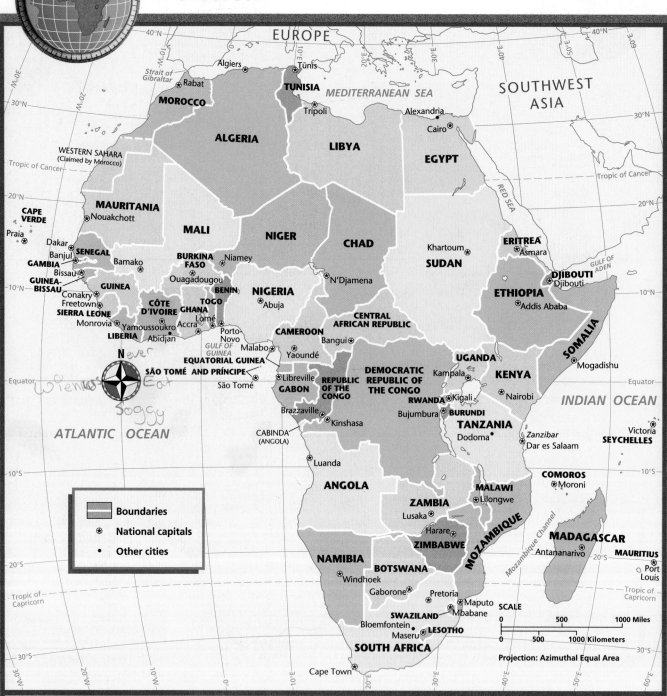

EUROPE

Strait of Gibraltar
Rabat
Algiers
Tünis
TUNISIA
Tripoli
MEDITERRANEAN SEA
Alexandria
Cairo

SOUTHWEST ASIA

MOROCCO
ALGERIA
LIBYA
EGYPT

WESTERN SAHARA (Claimed by Morocco)
Tropic of Cancer

Tropic of Cancer

MAURITANIA
Nouakchott

CAPE VERDE
Praia

RED SEA

MALI
NIGER
CHAD
Khartoum
SUDAN
ERITREA
Asmara

GULF OF ADEN

Dakar
Banjul
SENEGAL
GAMBIA
Bissau
GUINEA-BISSAU
GUINEA
Conakry
Freetown
SIERRA LEONE
Monrovia
LIBERIA
Bamako
BURKINA FASO
Niamey
Ouagadougou
BENIN
TOGO
GHANA
CÔTE D'IVOIRE
Yamoussoukro
Accra
Lomé
Abidjan
Porto-Novo
NIGERIA
Abuja
N'Djamena
CAMEROON
CENTRAL AFRICAN REPUBLIC
Bangui
DJIBOUTI
Djibouti
ETHIOPIA
Addis Ababa

GULF OF GUINEA
Malabo
EQUATORIAL GUINEA
SÃO TOMÉ AND PRÍNCIPE
São Tomé
Yaoundé
Libreville
GABON
REPUBLIC OF THE CONGO
Brazzaville
Kinshasa
DEMOCRATIC REPUBLIC OF THE CONGO
RWANDA
Kigali
Bujumbura
BURUNDI
UGANDA
Kampala
KENYA
Nairobi
SOMALIA
Mogadishu

Equator
Never Eat Soggy
Wienkes
N

ATLANTIC OCEAN

CABINDA (ANGOLA)
Luanda

TANZANIA
Dodoma
Zanzibar
Dar es Salaam

INDIAN OCEAN

SEYCHELLES
Victoria

Equator

ANGOLA
ZAMBIA
Lusaka
MALAWI
Lilongwe
COMOROS
Moroni

Boundaries
National capitals
Other cities

NAMIBIA
Windhoek
BOTSWANA
Gaborone
ZIMBABWE
Harare
MOZAMBIQUE
Mozambique Channel
MADAGASCAR
Antananarivo
MAURITIUS
Port Louis

Tropic of Capricorn
Tropic of Capricorn

Pretoria
Maputo
Mbabane
SWAZILAND
Bloemfontein
Maseru
LESOTHO
SOUTH AFRICA
Cape Town

SCALE
0    500    1000 Miles
0    500    1000 Kilometers
Projection: Azimuthal Equal Area

---

1. **Places and Regions** Which country is completely surrounded by another country?

2. **Places and Regions** Which country lies mostly on the mainland but has its capital on an island?

3. **Places and Regions** What is the largest African island country? What are the other island countries?

## Critical Thinking

4. **Comparing** Compare this map to the **climate map** of the region. Why do you think the capitals of Algeria, Tunisia, and Libya all lie on the Mediterranean Sea?

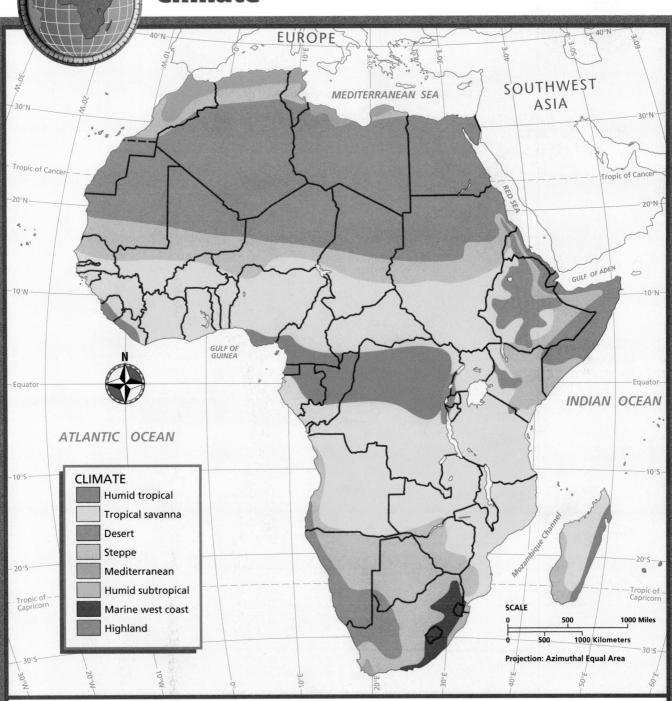

EUROPE

MEDITERRANEAN SEA

SOUTHWEST ASIA

40°N

30°N

Tropic of Cancer

20°N

RED SEA

10°N

GULF OF ADEN

GULF OF GUINEA

N

Equator

INDIAN OCEAN

ATLANTIC OCEAN

10°S

**CLIMATE**
- Humid tropical
- Tropical savanna
- Desert
- Steppe
- Mediterranean
- Humid subtropical
- Marine west coast
- Highland

20°S

Mozambique Channel

Tropic of Capricorn

SCALE

0        500      1000 Miles

0        500      1000 Kilometers

30°S

Projection: Azimuthal Equal Area

---

1. *Physical Systems*  Where are humid tropical climates found in Africa?

2. *Places and Regions*  Compare this map to the **land use and resources map** of the region. Which climate region in North Africa has limited economic activity?

## Critical Thinking

3. **Comparing**  Compare this map to the **land use and resources** and **population maps** of the region. Why might the eastern part of South Africa be more densely populated than the western part?

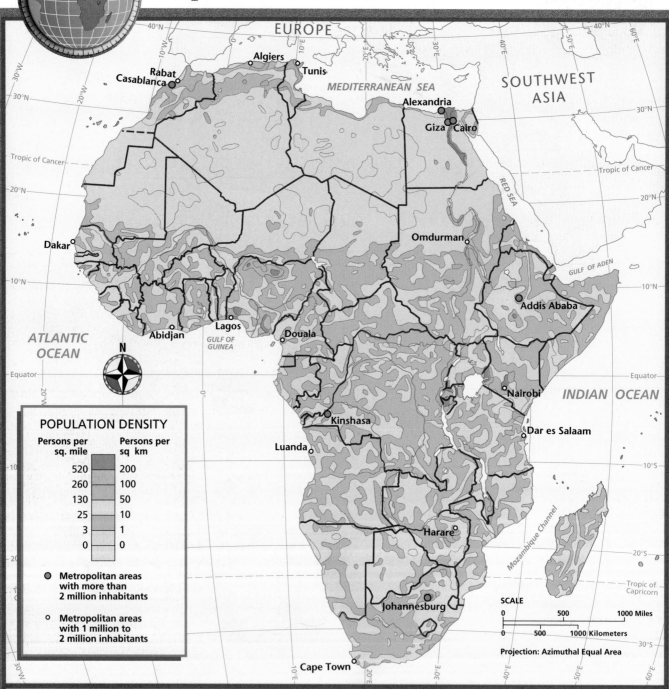

EUROPE

SOUTHWEST ASIA

MEDITERRANEAN SEA

Algiers
Tunis
Rabat
Casablanca

Alexandria
Giza  Cairo

RED SEA

Tropic of Cancer

GULF OF ADEN

Dakar

Omdurman

Addis Ababa

ATLANTIC
OCEAN

N

Lagos
Abidjan
Douala
GULF OF
GUINEA

Nairobi

INDIAN OCEAN

Equator

Kinshasa
Luanda

Dar es Salaam

**POPULATION DENSITY**

| Persons per sq. mile | Persons per sq km |
|---|---|
| 520 | 200 |
| 260 | 100 |
| 130 | 50 |
| 25 | 10 |
| 3 | 1 |
| 0 | 0 |

● Metropolitan areas with more than 2 million inhabitants

○ Metropolitan areas with 1 million to 2 million inhabitants

Harare

Mozambique Channel

Tropic of Capricorn

SCALE
0        500        1000 Miles
0     500    1000 Kilometers
Projection: Azimuthal Equal Area

Johannesburg

Cape Town

---

**1.** (*Places and Regions*) Which country has the most cities with more than 2 million people? Compare this map to the **physical map** of the region. Which river flows through or near these cities?

**2.** (*Places and Regions*) What are the two largest African cities shown south of the equator?

## Critical Thinking

**3. Analyzing Information** Use the map on this page to create a chart, graph, database, or model of population centers in Africa.

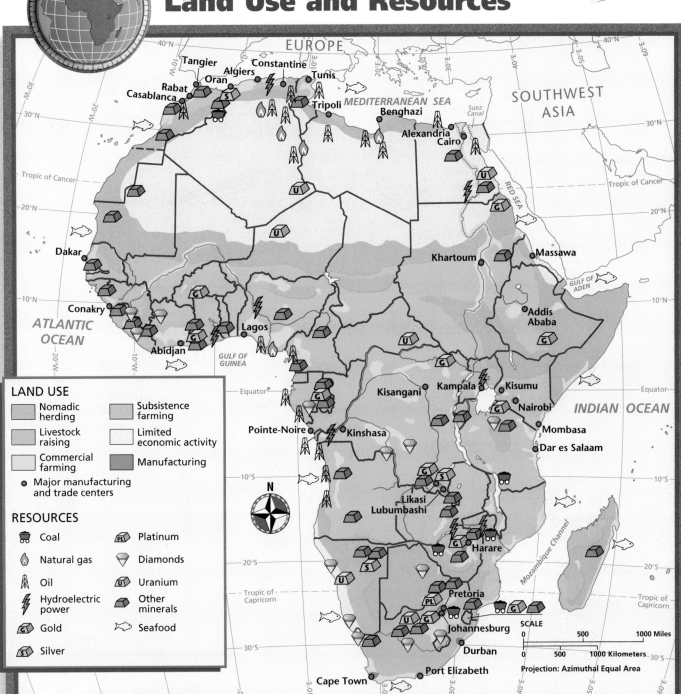

**LAND USE**

- Nomadic herding
- Livestock raising
- Commercial farming
- Subsistence farming
- Limited economic activity
- Manufacturing
- ● Major manufacturing and trade centers

**RESOURCES**

- Coal
- Natural gas
- Oil
- Hydroelectric power
- Gold
- Silver
- PL Platinum
- Diamonds
- U Uranium
- Other minerals
- Seafood

SCALE
0 — 500 — 1000 Miles
0 — 500 — 1000 Kilometers
Projection: Azimuthal Equal Area

1. **Places and Regions** Which region of Africa seems to have the most mineral resources?

2. **Environment and Society** What type of farming is the most common in Africa?

3. **Environment and Society** Compare this map to the **physical map** of the region. Which rivers support commercial farming in dry areas?

Which river in southeastern Africa provides hydroelectric power to the region?

## Critical Thinking

4. **Analyzing Information** Use the map on this page to create a chart, graph, database, or model of economic activities in Africa.

# Africa

## Algeria

**CAPITAL:**
Algiers

**AREA:**
919,590 sq. mi.
(2,381,740 sq km)

**POPULATION:**
31,736,053

**MONEY:**
Algerian dinar (DZD)

**LANGUAGES:**
Arabic (official), French, Berber

**PEOPLE PER DOCTOR:**
1,066

## Angola

**CAPITAL:**
Luanda

**AREA:**
481,351 sq. mi.
(1,246,700 sq km)

**POPULATION:**
10,366,031

**MONEY:**
kwanza (AOA)

**LANGUAGES:**
Portuguese (official), Bantu languages

**PEOPLE PER DOCTOR:**
data not available

## Benin

**CAPITAL:**
Porto-Novo

**AREA:**
43,483 sq. mi.
(112,620 sq km)

**POPULATION:**
6,590,782

**MONEY:**
CFAF*

**LANGUAGES:**
French (official), Fon, Yoruba, other ethnic languages

**PEOPLE PER DOCTOR:**
14,216

## Botswana

**CAPITAL:**
Gaborone

**AREA:**
231,803 sq. mi.
(600,370 sq km)

**POPULATION:**
1,586,119

**MONEY:**
pula (BWP)

**LANGUAGES:**
English (official), Setswana

**PEOPLE PER DOCTOR:**
4,395

## Burkina Faso

**CAPITAL:**
Ouagadougou

**AREA:**
105,869 sq. mi.
(274,200 sq km)

**POPULATION:**
12,272,289

**MONEY:**
CFAF*

**LANGUAGES:**
French (official), ethnic languages

**PEOPLE PER DOCTOR:**
27,158

## Burundi

**CAPITAL:**
Bujumbura

**AREA:**
10,745 sq. mi.
(27,830 sq km)

**POPULATION:**
6,223,897

**MONEY:**
Burundi franc (BIF)

**LANGUAGES:**
Kirundi (official), French (official), Swahili

**PEOPLE PER DOCTOR:**
16,667

## Cameroon

**CAPITAL:**
Yaoundé

**AREA:**
183,567 sq. mi.
(475,440 sq km)

**POPULATION:**
15,803,220

**MONEY:**
CFAF*

**LANGUAGES:**
English (official), French (official), 24 ethnic language groups

**PEOPLE PER DOCTOR:**
14,286

## Cape Verde

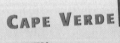

**CAPITAL:**
Praia

**AREA:**
1,557 sq. mi. (4,033 sq km)

**POPULATION:**
405,163

**MONEY:**
Cape Verdean escudo (CVE)

**LANGUAGES:**
Portuguese, Crioulo

**PEOPLE PER DOCTOR:**
3,448

*Communaute Financiere Africaine franc

Countries not drawn to scale.

# CENTRAL AFRICAN REPUBLIC

**CAPITAL:** Bangui

**AREA:**
240,534 sq. mi.
(622,984 sq km)

**POPULATION:** 3,576,884

**MONEY:** CFAF*

**LANGUAGES:** French (official), Sangho (national language), Arabic, Hunsa, Swahili

**PEOPLE PER DOCTOR:** 18,660

# CHAD

**CAPITAL:**
N'Djamena

**AREA:**
495,752 sq. mi.
(1,284,000 sq km)

**POPULATION:**
8,707,078

**MONEY:**
CFAF*

**LANGUAGES:**
French (official), Arabic (official), Sara and Sango

**PEOPLE PER DOCTOR:** 27,765

# COMOROS

**CAPITAL:**
Moroni

**AREA:**
838 sq. mi.
(2,170 sq km)

**POPULATION:**
596,202

**MONEY:**
Comoran franc (KMF)

**LANGUAGES:**
Arabic (official), French (official), Comoran

**PEOPLE PER DOCTOR:**
10,000

# CONGO, DEMOCRATIC REPUBLIC OF THE

**CAPITAL:**
Kinshasa

**AREA:**
905,563 sq. mi.
(2,345,410 sq km)

**POPULATION:**
53,624,718

**MONEY:**
Congolese franc (CDF)

**LANGUAGES:**
French (official), Lingala, Kingwana, Kikongo, Tshiluba

**PEOPLE PER DOCTOR:**
data not available

# CONGO, REPUBLIC OF THE

**CAPITAL:** Brazzaville

**AREA:**
132,046 sq. mi.
(342,000 sq km)

**POPULATION:** 2,894,336

**MONEY:** CFAF*

**LANGUAGES:**
French (official), Lingala, Monokutuba

**PEOPLE PER DOCTOR:** 3,704

# CÔTE d'IVOIRE

**CAPITAL:**
Yamoussoukro

**AREA:**
124,502 sq. mi.
(322,460 sq km)

**POPULATION:** 16,393,057

**MONEY:** CFAF*

**LANGUAGES:**
French (official), Dioula, ethnic languages

**PEOPLE PER DOCTOR:**
data not available

# DJIBOUTI

**CAPITAL:**
Djibouti

**AREA:**
8,494 sq. mi.
(22,000 sq km)

**POPULATION:**
460,700

**MONEY:**
Djiboutian franc (DJF)

**LANGUAGES:**
French (official), Arabic (official), Somali, Afar

**PEOPLE PER DOCTOR:**
5,000

# EGYPT

**CAPITAL:**
Cairo

**AREA:**
386,660 sq. mi.
(1,001,450 sq km)

**POPULATION:**
69,536,644

**MONEY:**
Egyptian pound (EGP)

**LANGUAGES:**
Arabic (official), English, French

**PEOPLE PER DOCTOR:**
472

**Sources:** Central Intelligence Agency, *The World Factbook 2001; The World Almanac and Book of Facts 2001; United Nations Development Programme: Health Profile,* pop. figures are 2001 estimates.

## EQUATORIAL GUINEA

**CAPITAL:** Malabo

**AREA:**
10,830 sq. mi.
(28,051 sq km)

**POPULATION:** 486,060

**MONEY:** CFAF*

**LANGUAGES:**
Spanish (official), French
(official), Fang, Bubi, Ibo

**PEOPLE PER DOCTOR:** 4,762

## GHANA

**CAPITAL:** Accra

**AREA:**
92,100 sq. mi.
(238,540 sq km)

**POPULATION:**
19,894,014

**MONEY:** new cedi (GHC)

**LANGUAGES:**
English (official), Akan,
Moshi-Dagomba, Ewe, Ga

**PEOPLE PER DOCTOR:**
22,970

## ERITREA

**CAPITAL:** Asmara

**AREA:**
46,842 sq. mi.
(121,320 sq km)

**POPULATION:**
4,298,269

**MONEY:** nafka (EKN)

**LANGUAGES:**
Afar, Amharic, Arabic, Tigre,
Kunama, Tigrinya

**PEOPLE PER DOCTOR:**
36,000

## GUINEA

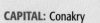

**CAPITAL:** Conakry

**AREA:**
94,925 sq. mi.
(245,857 sq km)

**POPULATION:**
7,613,870

**MONEY:**
Guinean franc (GNF)

**LANGUAGES:**
French (official), ethnic
languages

**PEOPLE PER DOCTOR:** 6,667

## ETHIOPIA

**CAPITAL:** Addis Ababa

**AREA:**
435,184 sq. mi.
(1,127,127 sq km)

**POPULATION:**
65,891,874

**MONEY:** birr (ETB)

**LANGUAGES:**
Amharic, Tigrinya, Orominga,
Guaraginga, Somali, Arabic

**PEOPLE PER DOCTOR:**
25,000

## GUINEA-BISSAU

**CAPITAL:** Bissau

**AREA:**
13,946 sq. mi.
(36,120 sq km)

**POPULATION:** 1,315,822

**MONEY:** CFAF*

**LANGUAGES:**
Portuguese (official), Crioulo,
ethnic languages

**PEOPLE PER DOCTOR:** 5,556

## GABON

**CAPITAL:** Libreville

**AREA:**
103,346 sq. mi.
(267,667 sq km)

**POPULATION:**
1,221,175

**MONEY:** CFAF*

**LANGUAGES:**
French (official), Fang,
Myene, Bateke,
Bapounou/Eschira, Bandjabi

**PEOPLE PER DOCTOR:** 5,263

## KENYA

**CAPITAL:**
Nairobi

**AREA:**
224,961 sq. mi.
(582,650 sq km)

**POPULATION:** 30,765,916

**MONEY:**
Kenyan shilling (KES)

**LANGUAGES:**
English (official), Kiwahili
(official), ethnic languages

**PEOPLE PER DOCTOR:** 5,999

## GAMBIA

**CAPITAL:** Banjul

**AREA:**
4,363 sq. mi.
(11,300 sq km)

**POPULATION:**
1,411,205

**MONEY:** dalasi (GMD)

**LANGUAGES:**
English (official), Mandinka,
Wolof, Fula

**PEOPLE PER DOCTOR:**
50,000

## LESOTHO

**CAPITAL:** Maseru

**AREA:**
11,720 sq. mi.
(30,355 sq km)

**POPULATION:**
2,177,062

**MONEY:** loti (LSL)

**LANGUAGES:**
English (official), Sesotho,
Zulu, Xhosa

**PEOPLE PER DOCTOR:**
14,306

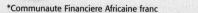

*Communaute Financiere Africaine franc

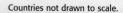

Countries not drawn to scale.

## LIBERIA

**CAPITAL:** Monrovia

**AREA:**
43,000 sq. mi.
(111,370 sq km)

**POPULATION:**
3,225,837

**MONEY:**
Liberian dollar (LRD)

**LANGUAGES:**
English (official), many ethnic languages

**PEOPLE PER DOCTOR:** 8,333

## LIBYA

**CAPITAL:** Tripoli

**AREA:**
679,358 sq. mi.
(1,759,540 sq km)

**POPULATION:**
5,240,599

**MONEY:** Libyan dinar (LYD)

**LANGUAGES:**
Arabic, Italian, English

**PEOPLE PER DOCTOR:**
data not available

## MADAGASCAR

 ←Flag

**CAPITAL:** Antananarivo

**AREA:**
226,656 sq. mi.
(587,040 sq km)

**POPULATION:**
15,982,563

**MONEY:**
Malagasy franc (MGF)

**LANGUAGES:**
French (official), Malagasy (official)

**PEOPLE PER DOCTOR:** 4,167

## MALAWI

**CAPITAL:** Lilongwe

**AREA:**
45,745 sq. mi.
(118,480 sq km)

**POPULATION:**
10,548,250

**MONEY:**
Malawian kwacha (MWK)

**LANGUAGES:** English (official), Chichewa (official), many ethnic languages

**PEOPLE PER DOCTOR:** 50,000

## MALI

**CAPITAL:** Bamako

**AREA:**
478,764 sq. mi.
(1,240,000 sq km)

**POPULATION:** 11,008,518

**MONEY:** CFAF*

**LANGUAGES:**
French (official), Bambara, many ethnic languages

**PEOPLE PER DOCTOR:** 25,000

## MAURITANIA

**CAPITAL:**
Nouakchott

**AREA:**
397,953 sq. mi.
(1,030,700 sq km)

**POPULATION:**
2,747,312

**MONEY:**
ouguiya (MOR)

**LANGUAGES:**
Hasaniya Arabic (official), Wolof (official), Pular, Soninke, French

**PEOPLE PER DOCTOR:** 11,085

## MAURITIUS

**CAPITAL:**
Port Louis

**AREA:**
718 sq. mi.
(1,860 sq km)

**POPULATION:**
1,189,825

**MONEY:**
Mauritian rupee (MUR)

**LANGUAGES:**
English (official), Creole, French, Hindi, Urdu, Hakka, Bojpoori

**PEOPLE PER DOCTOR:** 1,182

## MOROCCO

**CAPITAL:**
Rabat

**AREA:**
172,413 sq. mi.
(446,550 sq km)

**POPULATION:**
30,645,305

**MONEY:**
Moroccan dirham (MAD)

**LANGUAGES:**
Arabic (official), Berber, French

**PEOPLE PER DOCTOR:** 2,923

## MOZAMBIQUE

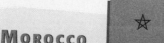

**CAPITAL:**
Maputo

**AREA:**
304,494 sq. mi.
(801,590 sq km)

**POPULATION:**
19,371,057

**MONEY:**
metical (MZM)

**LANGUAGES:**
Portuguese (official), ethnic languages

**PEOPLE PER DOCTOR:**
131,991

**Sources:** Central Intelligence Agency, *The World Factbook 2001*; *The World Almanac and Book of Facts 2001*; *United Nations Development Programme: Health Profile*; pop. figures are 2001 estimates.

## NAMIBIA

**CAPITAL:**
Windhoek

**AREA:**
318,694 sq. mi.
(825,418 sq km)

**POPULATION:**
1,797,677

**MONEY:**
Namibian dollar (NAD),
South African rand

**LANGUAGES:**
English (official), Afrikaans,
German, Oshivambo, Herero,
Nama

**PEOPLE PER DOCTOR:** 4,594

## NIGER

**CAPITAL:** Niamey

**AREA:**
489,189 sq. mi.
(1,267,000 sq km)

**POPULATION:**
10,355,156

**MONEY:** CFAF*

**LANGUAGES:**
French (official), Hausa,
Djerma

**PEOPLE PER DOCTOR:**
35,141

## NIGERIA

**CAPITAL:** Abuja

**AREA:**
356,667 sq. mi.
(923,768 sq km)

**POPULATION:**
126,635,626

**MONEY:**
naira (NGN)

**LANGUAGES:**
English (official), Hausa,
Yoruba, Ibo, Fulani

**PEOPLE PER DOCTOR:** 4,496

## RWANDA

**CAPITAL:**
Kigali

**AREA:**
10,169 sq. mi.
(26,338 sq km)

**POPULATION:**
7,312,756

**MONEY:**
Rwandan franc (RWF)

**LANGUAGES:**
Kinyarwanda (official),
French (official), English (official), Kiwahili

**PEOPLE PER DOCTOR:** 50,000

## SÃO TOMÉ AND PRÍNCIPE

**CAPITAL:** São Tomé

**AREA:**
386 sq. mi. (1,001 sq km)

**POPULATION:**
165,034

**MONEY:**
dobra (STD)

**LANGUAGES:**
Portuguese (official)

**PEOPLE PER DOCTOR:** 3,125

## SENEGAL

**CAPITAL:** Dakar

**AREA:**
75,749 sq. mi.
(196,190 sq km)

**POPULATION:** 10,284,929

**MONEY:** CFAF*

**LANGUAGES:**
French (official), Wolof,
Pulaar, Diola, Mandinka

**PEOPLE PER DOCTOR:** 14,285

## SEYCHELLES

**CAPITAL:**
Victoria

**AREA:**
176 sq. mi. (455 sq km)

**POPULATION:** 79,715

**MONEY:**
Seychelles rupee (SCR)

**LANGUAGES:** English (official),
French (official), Creole

**PEOPLE PER DOCTOR:** 906

## SIERRA LEONE

**CAPITAL:** Freetown

**AREA:**
27,699 sq. mi. (71,740 sq km)

**POPULATION:** 5,426,618

**MONEY:** leone (SLL)

**LANGUAGES:**
English (official), Mende,
Temne, Krio

**PEOPLE PER DOCTOR:** 10,832

## SOMALIA

**CAPITAL:**
Mogadishu

**AREA:**
246,199 sq. mi.
(637,657 sq km)

**POPULATION:**
7,488,773

**MONEY:**
Somali shilling (SOS)

**LANGUAGES:**
Somali (official), Arabic,
Italian, English

**PEOPLE PER DOCTOR:**
data not available

## SOUTH AFRICA

**CAPITAL:**
Pretoria

**AREA:**
471,008 sq. mi.
(1,219,912 sq km)

**POPULATION:** 43,586,097

**MONEY:** rand (ZAR)

**LANGUAGES:** 11 official
languages, including Afrikaans,
English, Ndebele, Pedi, Sotho,
Swazi, Tsonga, Tswana, Venda,
Xhosa, Zulu

**PEOPLE PER DOCTOR:** 1,742

*Communaute Financiere Africaine franc

Countries not drawn to scale.

## SUDAN

**CAPITAL:** Khartoum

**AREA:**
967,493 sq. mi.
(2,505,810 sq km)

**POPULATION:**
36,080,373

**MONEY:**
Sudanese dinar (SDD)

**LANGUAGES:** Arabic (official), Nubian, Ta Bedawie, English, many ethnic languages

**PEOPLE PER DOCTOR:** 11,300

## SWAZILAND

**CAPITAL:** Mbabane

**AREA:**
6,704 sq. mi. (17,363 sq km)

**POPULATION:**
1,104,343

**MONEY:** lilangeni (SZL)

**LANGUAGES:**
English (official), siSwati

**PEOPLE PER DOCTOR:**
data not available

## TANZANIA

**CAPITAL:**
Dar es Salaam

**AREA:**
364,898 sq. mi.
(945,087 sq km)

**POPULATION:**
36,232,074

**MONEY:**
Tanzanian shilling (TZS)

**LANGUAGES:**
Kiwahili (official), English (official), Arabic, many ethnic languages

**PEOPLE PER DOCTOR:** 20,511

## TOGO

**CAPITAL:** Lomé

**AREA:**
21,925 sq. mi.
(56,785 sq km)

**POPULATION:** 5,153,088

**MONEY:** CFAF*

**LANGUAGES:**
French (official), Ewe, Mina, Kabye, Dagomba

**PEOPLE PER DOCTOR:** 16,667

## TUNISIA

**CAPITAL:**
Tunis

**AREA:**
63,170 sq. mi.
(163,610 sq km)

**POPULATION:** 9,705,102

**MONEY:**
Tunisian dinar (TND)

**LANGUAGES:**
Arabic (official), French

**PEOPLE PER DOCTOR:**
1,640

## UGANDA

**CAPITAL:**
Kampala

**AREA:**
91,135 sq. mi.
(236,040 sq km)

**POPULATION:**
23,985,712

**MONEY:**
Ugandan shilling (UGX)

**LANGUAGES:**
English (official), Luganda, Swahili, Arabic

**PEOPLE PER DOCTOR:**
25,000

## ZAMBIA

**CAPITAL:**
Lusaka

**AREA:**
290,584 sq. mi.
(752,614 sq km)

**POPULATION:**
9,770,199

**MONEY:**
Zambian kwacha (ZMK)

**LANGUAGES:**
English (official), Bemba, Kaonda, Lozi, Lunda, Luvale, many ethnic languages

**PEOPLE PER DOCTOR:** 10,917

## ZIMBABWE

**CAPITAL:**
Harare

**AREA:**
150,803 sq. mi.
(390,580 sq km)

**POPULATION:** 11,365,366

**MONEY:**
Zimbabwean dollar (ZWD)

**LANGUAGES:**
English (official), Shona, Sindebele

**PEOPLE PER DOCTOR:** 6,909

---

**internet connect**

**go.hrw.com**

**COUNTRY STATISTICS**
GO TO: go.hrw.com
KEYWORD: SK3 FACTSU6
FOR: more facts about Africa

**Sources:** Central Intelligence Agency, *The World Factbook 2001*; *The World Almanac and Book of Facts 2001*; *United Nations Development Programme: Health Profile*; pop. figures are 2001 estimates.

# CHAPTER 19

# North Africa

The first region in Africa we will study is North Africa. Before we do that, we will meet Shaimaa. She and nearly all other Egyptians live along the Nile River or in the Nile Delta.

*A*hlan! (Hi!) My name is Shaimaa, and I am 18. I live with my mother and my little sister in an apartment. We live about an hour from downtown Cairo. My father lives in the United States but visits us every year.

Every day but Friday, I get up at 7:00 A.M., drink a glass of milk, and then meet my friends. School is about 15 minutes away on the metro (subway). We go to an all-girls school. We all have religious education in school. I study Islam with the other Muslim girls. The Christian girls meet with their religious teacher.

At about 3:00 P.M., I get home from school. I eat a big lunch of chicken and vegetables and sleep for a couple of hours. When I wake up, I have a lot of homework. At 10:00 P.M. we have a small meal of cheese, yogurt, or beans before bedtime.

On Fridays I usually go to movies with my girlfriends and walk along the Nile. Sometimes I stay home and listen to music.

أنا طالبة في القاهرة،
في شمال افريقيا.
أهلاً وسهلاً بكم

Translation: I am a student in Cairo, in North Africa. Welcome to all of you.

# Section 1 · Physical Geography

## Read to Discover

1. What are the major physical features of North Africa?
2. What climates, plants, and wildlife are found in North Africa?
3. What are North Africa's major resources?

## Define

ergs
regs
depressions
silt

## Locate

Red Sea
Mediterranean Sea
Sahara
Nile River
Sinai Peninsula
Ahaggar Mountains
Atlas Mountains
Qattara Depression
Nile Delta
Lake Nasser
Suez Canal

### WHY IT MATTERS

Most Egyptians live along the banks of the Nile River. The river's flooding is both beneficial and destructive. Use CNN**fyi**.com or other **current events** sources to find out how Egyptians are affected by the river. Record your findings in your journal.

A tomb painting from ancient Egypt

## North Africa: Physical-Political

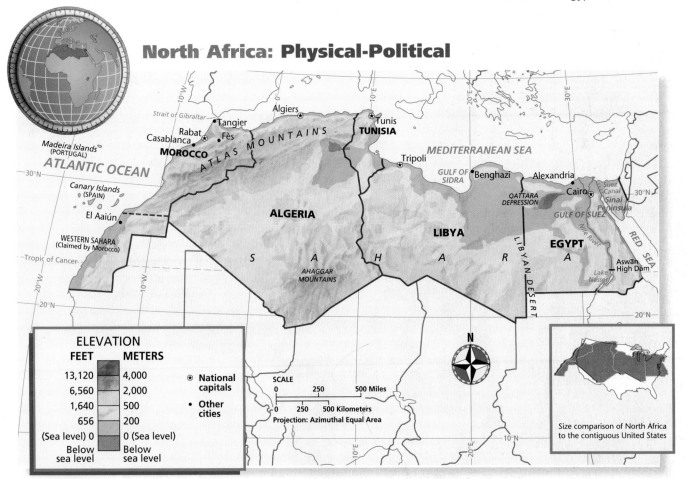

ELEVATION

| FEET | METERS |
|---|---|
| 13,120 | 4,000 |
| 6,560 | 2,000 |
| 1,640 | 500 |
| 656 | 200 |
| (Sea level) 0 | 0 (Sea level) |
| Below sea level | Below sea level |

⊛ National capitals
• Other cities

SCALE
0   250   500 Miles
0   250   500 Kilometers
Projection: Azimuthal Equal Area

Size comparison of North Africa to the contiguous United States

**internet** connect

GO TO: go.hrw.com
KEYWORD: SK3 CH19
FOR: Web sites about North Africa

# Physical Features

North Africa includes Morocco, Algeria, Tunisia, Libya, and Egypt. The region stretches from the Atlantic Ocean to the Red Sea. Off the northern coast is the Mediterranean Sea. In the south is the Sahara (suh-HAR-uh), a vast desert. The region also has mountains, the northern Nile River valley, and the Sinai (SY-ny) Peninsula.

**The Sahara** The huge Sahara covers most of North Africa and stretches southward. The name *Sahara* comes from the Arabic word for "desert." The Sahara is the largest desert in the world. It is so big that nearly all of the United States would fit into it.

Large areas of this very dry region have few people or none at all. Great "seas" of sand dunes called **ergs** cover about a quarter of the desert. Much of the rest of the Sahara is made up of broad, windswept gravel plains. These gravel plains are called **regs**.

**Mountains** Do you think of deserts as flat regions? Well, the Sahara is not flat. Some sand dunes and ridges rise as high as 1,000 feet (305 m). The Sahara also has mountain ranges. For example, the Ahaggar (uh-HAH-guhr) Mountains are located in the central Sahara. Their highest peak is 9,842 feet (3,000 m). The Atlas Mountains on the northwestern side of the Sahara are higher. Mountains there rise to 13,671 feet (4,167 m).

There also are very low areas in the Sahara. These low areas are called **depressions**. The Qattara (kuh-TAHR-uh) Depression in western Egypt is 440 feet (134 m) below sea level. Other low areas often have large, dry lake beds. Water from rare rain storms collects there.

Oases like this one in Algeria are scattered throughout the vast Sahara.

**Interpreting the Visual Record How do these trees survive in the desert's harsh, dry climate?**

The Nile The world's longest river, the Nile, flows northward through the eastern Sahara. The Nile empties into the Mediterranean Sea. It is formed by the union of two rivers, the Blue Nile and the White Nile. They meet in Sudan, south of Egypt.

The Nile River valley is like a long oasis in the desert. Water from the Nile irrigates surrounding farmland. The Nile fans out near the Mediterranean Sea, forming a large river delta. About 99 percent of Egypt's population lives in the Nile River valley and the Nile Delta.

For centuries rain far to the south caused annual floods along the northern Nile that left rich **silt** in surrounding fields. Silt is finely ground soil good for growing crops. The Aswān High Dam, which was completed in 1971, was built to control flooding. Water trapped by the dam formed Lake Nasser in southern Egypt. However, the dam also traps silt, preventing it from being carried downriver. Today Egypt's farmers must use fertilizers to enrich the soil.

The Sinai and Suez Canal East of the Nile is the triangular Sinai Peninsula. Barren, rocky mountains and desert cover the Sinai. Between the Sinai and the rest of Egypt is the Suez Canal. The canal was built by the French in the 1860s. See the Case Study about the Suez Canal in this chapter.

✓ READING CHECK:  *Places and Regions*  What are the major physical features of North Africa?

# Climate, Vegetation, and Animals

There are three main climates in North Africa. A desert climate covers most of the region. Temperatures range from mild to very hot. How hot can it get? Temperatures as high as 136°F (58°C) have been recorded in Libya! However, the humidity is very low. As a result, temperatures can drop quickly after sunset.

Water from the Nile River irrigates rich farmlands along the river and in its delta. You can clearly see the Nile Delta in the satellite photograph. The irrigated farmlands of the delta are shown in red.

Interpreting the Visual Record
**Why do you think most Egyptians live near the Nile River?**

The Arabian camel has long been used for transportation in the Sahara. It can store water in the fat of its hump. Camels have survived for more than two weeks without drinking.

Do you remember what you learned about climate regions? See Chapter 3 to review.

Olives like these in Morocco are an important agricultural product in North Africa. Olives and olive oil are common ingredients in many foods around the Mediterranean.

▼

In some areas there has been no rain for many years. However, rare storms can cause flash floods. In places these floods as well as high winds have carved bare rock surfaces out of the land. Storms of sand and dust can also be severe.

Hardy plants and animals live in the desert. Grasses, small shrubs, and even trees grow where there is enough water. Usually this is in oases. Gazelles, hyenas, baboons, foxes, and weasels are among the region's mammals.

Much of the northern coast west of Egypt has a Mediterranean climate. Winters there are mild and moist. Summers are hot and dry. Plant life includes grasses, shrubs, and even a few forests in the Atlas Mountains. Areas between the Mediterranean climate and the Sahara have a steppe climate. Shrubs and grasses grow there.

✓ **READING CHECK:** *Physical Systems* How does climate affect the plants and wildlife of North Africa?

## Resources

Good soils and rain or river water aid farming in coastal areas and the Nile River valley. Common crops are wheat, barley, olives, grapes, citrus fruits, and cotton. The region also has good fishing waters.

Oil and gas are important resources, particularly for Libya, Algeria, and Egypt. Morocco mines iron ore and minerals used to make fertilizers. The Sahara has minerals such as copper, gold, and silver.

✓ **READING CHECK:** *Places and Regions* What are North Africa's major resources?

## Section Review 1

**Define and explain:** ergs, regs, depressions, silt

**Working with Sketch Maps** On a map of North Africa that you draw or that your teacher provides, label the following: Red Sea, Mediterranean Sea, Sahara, Nile River, Sinai Peninsula, Ahaggar Mountains, Atlas Mountains, Qattara Depression, Nile Delta, Lake Nasser, and the Suez Canal. In a box in the margin, identify the dam that created Lake Nasser.

### Reading for the Main Idea

**1.** *Places and Regions* What two mountain ranges are found in North Africa?

**2.** *Places and Regions* What part of Egypt is east of the Suez Canal?

**3.** *Environment and Society* How did the Nile affect farming in the river valley?

### Critical Thinking

**4. Drawing Inferences and Conclusions** Where would you expect to find most of North Africa's major cities?

### Organizing What You Know

**5. Summarizing** Use this graphic organizer to describe the physical features of North Africa.

| Climates | Plants and Animals | Resources |
|----------|--------------------|-----------|
|          |                    |           |

# Section 2 History and Culture

## Read to Discover

1. What are the major events in the history of North Africa?
2. What are some important facts about the people and culture of North Africa?

## Define

pharaohs

hieroglyphs

Bedouins

## Locate

Alexandria

Cairo

Fès

Western Sahara

*Woven carpet from Morocco*

### WHY IT MATTERS

Egypt was home to one of the world's earliest and most complex civilizations. Use **CNNfyi.com** or other **current events** sources to find examples of new archaeological finds from Egypt. Record your findings in your journal.

## History

The Nile River valley was home to some of the world's oldest civilizations. Sometime after 3200 B.C. lands along the northern Nile were united into one Egyptian kingdom.

The early Egyptians used water from the Nile to grow wheat, barley, and other crops. They also built great stone pyramids and other monuments. Egyptian **pharaohs**, or kings, were buried in the pyramids. How did the Egyptians build these huge monuments? See Connecting to Technology on the next page.

The Egyptians also traded with people from other places. To identify themselves and their goods, the Egyptians used **hieroglyphs** (HY-ruh-glifs). Hieroglyphs are pictures and symbols that stand for ideas or words. They were the basis for Egypt's first writing system.

West of Egypt were people who spoke what are called Berber languages. These people herded sheep and other livestock. They also grew wheat and barley in the Atlas Mountains and along the coast.

**Invaders** Because of North Africa's long coastline, the region was open to invaders over the centuries. Those invaders included people from the eastern Mediterranean, Greeks, and Romans. For example, one invader was the Macedonian king Alexander the Great. He founded the city of Alexandria in Egypt in 332 B.C. This city became an important seaport and trading center on the Mediterranean coast.

Beginning in the A.D. 600s, Arab armies from Southwest Asia swept across North Africa. They brought the Arabic language and Islam to the

▲

The tombs of early Egyptian pharoahs were decorated with paintings, crafts, and treasures. You can see hieroglyphs across the top of this wall painting.

## Egyptian Monuments

The monuments of ancient Egypt are among the great wonders of the world. They are thousands of years old. These pyramids, temples, and other structures reflect the power of Egyptian rulers. They also show the skills of Egyptian engineers.

The most famous of Egypt's monuments are the huge stone pyramids at Giza. Giza is near Cairo. The pyramids there were built more than 4,000 years ago as tombs for Egyptian rulers. The largest structure is the Great Pyramid. At its base the pyramid's sides are each about 755 feet (230 m) long. The pyramid rises nearly 500 feet (152 m) above the desert floor.

Another famous set of monuments is found farther south at the Valley of the Kings. The Valley of the Kings lies along the Nile River. Between 1500 B.C. and 1000 B.C., the Egyptians built tombs into the sides of cliffs there. They also carved huge sculptures and columns on the cliff faces. Near the tombs they built giant stone temples.

How did the Egyptians build these giant monuments? Workers had to cut large blocks of stone far away and roll them on logs to the Nile. From there the blocks could be moved on barges. At the building site, the Egyptians finished carving the blocks with special tools. Then they built dirt and brick ramps on the sides of the structures. They hauled the blocks up the ramps.

The average weight of each of the 2.3 million blocks in the Great Pyramid is 2.5 tons (2.25 metric tons). It is estimated that many thousands of workers were needed to move the heavy blocks into place. Together, these workers and Egyptian engineers built amazing monuments that have stood for thousands of years.

### Understanding What You Read

1. What kinds of monuments did the Egyptians build and why?
2. How did the Egyptians' belief systems affect their use of technology in building monuments?

*The Sphinx and pyramids at Giza, Egypt*

region. Today most North Africans are Muslim and speak Arabic. Under Muslim rule, North African cities became major centers of learning, trade, and craft making. These cities included Cairo in Egypt and Fès in Morocco.

**European Control** In the 1800s European countries began to take over the region. By 1912 they controlled all of North Africa. In that year Italy captured Libya from the Ottoman Empire. Spain already controlled northern Morocco. France ruled the rest of Morocco as well as Tunisia and Algeria. Egypt was under British control.

Egypt gained limited independence in 1922. The British kept military bases there and maintained control of the Suez Canal until 1956. During World War II the region was a major battleground. After the war, North Africans pushed for independence. Libya, Morocco, and Tunisia each won independence in the 1950s.

Algeria was the last North African country to win independence. Many French citizens had moved to the country. They considered Algeria part of France. Algeria finally won independence in 1962, after a long, bitter war. Most French residents of Algeria then moved to France.

**Modern North Africa** Since independence, the countries of North Africa have tried to build stronger ties with other Arab countries. For example, Egypt led other Arab countries in several wars against Israel. However, in 1979 Egypt signed a peace treaty with Israel.

In 1976 Morocco took over the former Spanish colony of Western Sahara. Western Saharan rebels have been trying to win independence from Morocco since then.

✔ **READING CHECK:** ( *Places and Regions* ) What were some major events in the history of North Africa?

▲

The ruins of an old Roman amphitheater remain in Alexandria, Egypt.

The inset photograph shows the beautiful doors of the royal palace in Fès, Morocco.

**Interpreting the Visual Record** **What interesting architectural features do you see in the photograph?**

▼

447

The floor of the beautiful Muhammad Ali mosque in Cairo is covered with carpet. Muslim men kneel and bow with their faces to the ground to pray.

**Interpreting the Visual Record** Why do you think there are no chairs in this picture?

A variety of vegetables and meat surround a large serving of couscous.

**Interpreting the Visual Record** What does this food tell you about agricultural products of the region?

# Culture

As you have read, the histories of the North African countries have much in common. You will also find many cultural similarities among those countries.

**Language and Religion** Egyptians, Berbers, and **Bedouins** make up nearly all of Egypt's population. Bedouins are nomadic herders who travel throughout deserts of Egypt and Southwest Asia. Most people in the countries to the west are of mixed Arab and Berber ancestry. Arabic is the major language. Some people speak Berber languages.

Most ethnic Europeans left North Africa after the region's countries became independent. However, French, Italian, and English still are spoken in many areas.

Most North Africans are Muslims. Of the region's countries, Egypt has the largest number of non-Muslims. About 6 percent of Egyptians are Christians or practice other religions.

**Food and Festivals** What kind of food would you eat on a trip to North Africa? Grains, vegetables, fruits, and nuts are common there. Many meals include couscous (koos-koos). Couscous is made from wheat and looks like small pellets of pasta. It is steamed over boiling water or soup. Often it is served with vegetables or meat, butter, and olive oil. Some people mix their couscous with a fiery hot sauce called *harissa*.

A popular dish in Egypt is *fuul*. It is made from fava beans mashed with olive oil, salt, pepper, garlic, and lemons. The combination is then served with hard-boiled eggs and bread.

Important holidays in North Africa include the birthday of the prophet of Islam, Muhammad. The birthday is marked with lights, parades, and special sweets of honey, nuts, and sugar. During the holy month of Ramadan, Muslims abstain from food and drink during the day.

**Art and Literature** North Africa has long been known for its beautiful architecture, wood carving, and other crafts. Women weave a variety of textiles. Among these are beautiful carpets that feature geometric designs and bright colors.

The region has also produced important writers and artists. For example, Egyptian poetry and other writing date back thousands of years. One of Egypt's most famous writers is Naguib Mahfouz. In 1988 he became the first Arab writer to win the Nobel Prize in literature. Egypt also has a growing movie industry. Egyptian films in Arabic have become popular throughout Southwest Asia and North Africa.

Many North Africans also enjoy popular music based on singing and poetry. The musical scale there has many more notes than are common in Western music. As a result, North African tunes seem to wail or waver. Musicians often use instruments such as the three-stringed *sintir* of Morocco.

▲

This Algerian woman and her daughter are using a loom to weave a rug. The loom allows a rug maker to weave horizontal and vertical threads together.

✓ **READING CHECK:** ( *Human Systems* ) What are some important facts about the people and culture of North Africa?

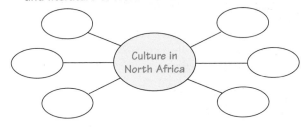

go.hrw.com **Homework Practice Online** Keyword: SK3 HP19

# Section Review 2

**Define and explain:** pharaohs, hieroglyphs, Bedouins

**Working with Sketch Maps** On the map you drew in Section 1, label Alexandria, Cairo, Fès, and Western Sahara. In a box in the margin, identify the country that claims Western Sahara.

## Reading for the Main Idea

**1.** ( *Places and Regions* ) What early civilization thrived along the northern Nile River about 3200 B.C.?

**2.** ( *Human Systems* ) How did Islam and the Arabic language come to North Africa?

**3.** ( *Human Systems* ) Which European countries controlled countries in North Africa by 1912?

## Critical Thinking

**4. Drawing Inferences and Conclusions** Look at the world map in the textbook's Atlas. Why do you think the Suez Canal is an important waterway for world shipping?

## Organizing What You Know

**5. Summarizing** Copy the following graphic organizer. Use it to identify at least six important facts about the languages, religions, food, festivals, art, and literature of North Africa.

Culture in North Africa

# CASE STUDY

## THE SUEZ CANAL: A STRATEGIC WATERWAY

The movement of goods and people around the world has increased dramatically during the past 100 years. In the world's oceans, more ships are sailing from port to port through busy shipping lanes. Just as highways can get crowded with cars, shipping lanes can get crowded with ships. These crowded areas are called choke points. Choke points are narrow routes that ships must pass through to get to other areas. The Suez Canal, Panama Canal, Strait of Malacca, Strait of Hormuz, and Strait of Gibraltar are all examples of important choke points around the world.

Choke points often have great strategic importance. In times of war, they can be important for moving ships and troops to other parts of the world. During peacetime, ships must pass through them to transport goods to world markets.

The Suez Canal in Egypt is an important choke point in the world's shipping lanes. It is also a very strategic waterway. Opened in 1869, the Suez Canal connects the Mediterranean Sea with the Red Sea. This shortens the journey for ships sailing between Europe and Asia by about 6,000 miles (9,654 km).

The history of the Suez Canal is closely tied to the growth of world trade and ocean shipping. Before World War II, the canal linked Great Britain to its colonies in East Africa, Asia, and the Pacific. Beginning in the 1930s, the development of the oil industry in the Persian Gulf made the canal even more important. It became a major shipping route for tankers carrying oil to Europe and North America.

The Suez Canal was built mainly to serve international trade. However, it has also been used by military ships. In 1905 Russian navy ships used the canal during the Russo-Japanese War. In the 1930s Italy moved troops through the canal to eastern Africa before invading Ethiopia.

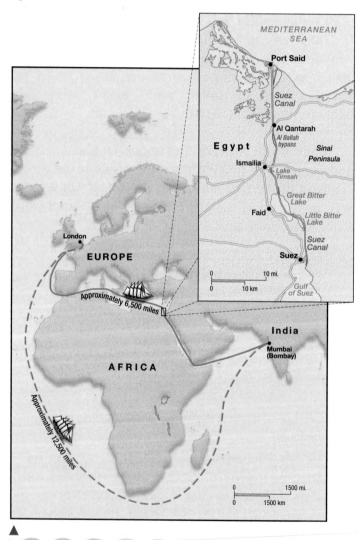

▲ A ship traveling from London to Mumbai has a much shorter journey if it travels through the Suez Canal.

**Interpreting the Map** How do you think the Suez Canal affected trade between Great Britain and India?

An important test for the Suez Canal involved relations between Egypt and Israel. In the 1950s Egypt refused to allow ships from Israel to use the canal. Even ships from countries that traded with Israel were prevented from using it. In 1956–57 the Suez Canal was closed after Israeli and Egyptian forces began fighting. It was closed again during 1967–75 after more fighting between the two countries. For several years the canal was the front line between the Israeli and Egyptian armies. While it was closed, ships were forced to make the much longer journey around Africa. This created a demand for larger ships that could carry more cargo.

Israeli troops look across the Suez Canal in 1967.

A French newspaper shows a warship crossing the Suez Canal in 1904 (left). Today, the canal is an important shipping lane (below).

Today, the Suez Canal is one of the busiest shipping lanes in the world. Each day, about 55 ships make the 15-hour journey through the canal. Ships heading north carry oil, coal, metals, and other goods to Europe and North America. Ships heading south carry wheat, corn, barley, manufactured goods, and other products to Asia.

Many modern ocean ships are now too big to use the Suez Canal. As a result, the canal's economic importance has declined in recent years. However, the Suez Canal is still an important waterway to many countries.

## Understanding What You Read

**1.** What are choke points? Why are they important?

**2.** How has the strategic importance of the Suez Canal changed since the 1930s?

### Read to Discover

1. What are the people and cities of Egypt like today?
2. What are Egypt's important economic activities?
3. What challenges does Egypt face today?

**WHY IT MATTERS**

An ongoing debate in Egypt is the place of Islam in society and the government. Use **CNNfyi.com** or other **current events** sources to find out how Egyptians view this debate. Record your findings in your journal.

### Define

fellahin

### Locate

Egypt

A gold mask from the tomb of King Tutankhamen

## People and Cities

Egypt is North Africa's most populous country. More than 67 million people live there.

**Rural Egypt**  More than half of all Egyptians live in small villages and other rural areas. Most rural Egyptians are farmers called **fellahin** (fel-uh-HEEN). They own very small plots of land. Most fellahin also work large farms owned by powerful families. Many also depend on money sent home by family members working abroad. Many Egyptians work in Europe or oil-rich countries in Southwest Asia.

**Cities**  Egypt's capital and largest city is Cairo. More than 10 million people live there. Millions more live in surrounding cities.

A muezzin (moo-E-zuhn) calls Muslims to prayer in Cairo. A muezzin often makes his calls from the door or the minaret, or tower, of a mosque. His calls—or recordings played through speakers—can be heard throughout Islamic communities five times daily.

Cairo

Libya    Saudi Arabia

Egypt

Sudan

Tourist ships sit on the Nile River in Luxor. Tourists visit the ruins of a beautiful temple built there more than 2,300 years ago. These and other historical sites make tourism an important part of Egypt's economy.

Cairo was founded more than 1,000 years ago along the Nile. Its location at the southern end of the delta helped it grow. The city lies along old trading routes between Asia and Europe. Later it was connected by railroad to Mediterranean ports and the Suez Canal.

Today Cairo is a mixture of modern buildings and small, mud-brick houses. People continue to move there from rural areas. Many live in makeshift housing. Traffic and pollution are serious problems.

Alexandria has more than 4 million people. It is located in the Nile Delta along the Mediterranean coast. The city is a major seaport and home to many industries.

✓ **READING CHECK:** *Places and Regions* What are Egypt's people and cities like today?

**Our Amazing Planet**

**F**ish is an important food for people living along the Nile. One fish, the giant Nile perch, can grow to a weight of 300 pounds (136 kg).

# Economy

To provide for its growing population, Egypt is working to expand its industries. Textiles, tourism, and oil are three of the most important industries. The Suez Canal is another source of income. Ships pay tolls to pass through it. Ships use the canal to avoid long trips around southern Africa. This makes the canal one of the world's busiest waterways.

About 40 percent of Egyptian workers are farmers. A warm, sunny climate and water for irrigation make the Nile Delta ideal for growing cotton. Farmlands along the Nile River are used for growing vegetables, grain, and fruit.

✓ **READING CHECK:** *Places and Regions* How does the Suez Canal affect Egypt's economy?

**Egypt**

| COUNTRY | POPULATION/ GROWTH RATE | LIFE EXPECTANCY | LITERACY RATE | PER CAPITA GDP |
|---------|-------------------------|-----------------|---------------|----------------|
| Egypt | 69,536,644 1.7% | 62, male 66, female | 51% | $3,600 |
| United States | 281,421,906 0.9% | 74, male 80, female | 97% | $36,200 |

**Sources:** Central Intelligence Agency, *The World Factbook 2001;* U.S. Census Bureau

**Interpreting the Chart How does the growth rate of Egypt compare to that of the United States?**

These Bedouin students attend a modern school in the Sinai. Improving education for all Egyptians is an important challenge facing the country. Among North African countries, only Morocco has a lower literacy rate than Egypt.

# Challenges

Egypt faces important challenges today. For example, the country's farmland is limited to the Nile River valley and delta. To keep the land productive, farmers must use more and more fertilizer. This can be expensive. In addition, overwatering has been a problem. It has brought to the surface salts that are harmful to crops. These problems and a rapidly growing population have forced Egypt to import much of its food.

In addition, Egyptians are divided over their country's role in the world. Many want their country to remain a leader among Arab countries. However, others want their government to focus more on improving life for Egyptians at home.

Many Egyptians live in severe poverty. Many do not have clean water for cooking or washing. The spread of disease in crowded cities is also a problem. In addition, about half of Egyptians cannot read and write. Still, Egypt's government has made progress. Today Egyptians live longer and are much healthier than 50 years ago.

Another challenge facing Egyptians is the debate over the role of Islam in the country. Some Muslims want to shape the country's government and society along Islamic principles. However, some Egyptians worry that such a change would mean fewer personal freedoms. Some supporters of an Islamic government have turned to violence to advance their cause. Attacks on tourists in the 1990s were particularly worrisome. A loss of tourism would hurt Egypt's economy.

✓ **READING CHECK:** *Places and Regions* What are some of the challenges Egypt faces today?

Homework Practice Online
Keyword: SK3 HP19

## Section Review 3

**Define and explain:** fellahin

**Working with Sketch Maps** On the map you drew in Section 2, label Egypt. In a box in the margin, identify the capital of Egypt.

### Reading for the Main Idea

1. *Human Systems* What is the relationship between religion and culture in Egypt today?

2. *Places and Regions* What industries and crops are important to Egypt's economy?

### Critical Thinking

3. **Analyzing Information** Why do so many Egyptians live along the Nile and in the Nile Delta?

4. **Finding the Main Idea** How has Cairo's location shaped its development?

### Organizing What You Know

5. **Summarizing** Copy the following graphic organizer. Use it to describe some of the challenges facing Egypt today.

Challenges

**Read to Discover**

1. What are the region's people and cities like today?
2. What are the countries' important economic activities?
3. What challenges do the countries face today?

**Define**

Casbah
souks
free port
dictator

**Locate**

Libya
Tunisia
Algeria
Morocco
Tripoli
Benghazi

Algiers
Casablanca
Rabat
Tunis
Strait of Gibraltar

**WHY IT MATTERS**

Libya has been ruled by a dictator. Use CNNfyi.com or other **current events** sources to find out more about Libya's dictatorship. Record your findings in your journal.

*Moroccan pottery*

## People and Cities

Western Libya, Tunisia, Algeria, and Morocco are often called the Maghreb (MUH-gruhb). This Arabic word means "west" or "the direction of the setting sun." Most of the Maghreb is covered by the Sahara. There you will find sandy plains and rocky uplands. Cities and farmland are located in narrow coastal strips of land. These strips lie between the Atlantic and Mediterranean coasts in the north and the Sahara and Atlas Mountains farther inland.

Libya is almost completely desert. Fertile land is limited to small areas along the coast. Cities and most of the population are found in those coastal areas. Libya is the most urbanized country in the region. More than 85 percent of Libya's more than 5 million people live in cities. The largest cities are Benghazi and the capital, Tripoli.

Algiers is a large city and is Algeria's capital. The central part of Algiers is a maze of winding alleys and tall walls. This old district is called the **Casbah**. The Casbah is basically an old fortress. **Souks**, or marketplaces, are found there today. The centers of other North African cities also have Casbahs.

Other large cities include Casablanca and Rabat in Morocco and Tunis in Tunisia. Another Moroccan city, Tangier, overlooks the Strait of Gibraltar. This beautiful city was once a Spanish territory. Today tourists can take a quick ferry ride from Spain across the strait to Tangier, a **free port**. A free port is a city in which almost no taxes are placed on goods sold there.

✓ **READING CHECK:** *Places and Regions* What geographic factors explain the region's population patterns?

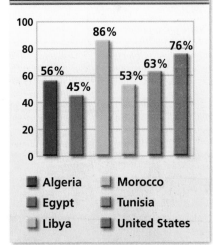

**Urbanization in North Africa**

- Algeria — 56%
- Egypt — 45%
- Libya — 86%
- Morocco — 53%
- Tunisia — 63%
- United States — 76%

**Source:** *The World Almanac and Book of Facts 2001*
Percentages of population living in urban areas

**Interpreting the Chart** Which country is the most urbanized?

## Libya, Tunisia, Algeria, and Morocco

| COUNTRY | POPULATION/ GROWTH RATE | LIFE EXPECTANCY | LITERACY RATE | PER CAPITA GDP |
|---------|-------------------------|-----------------|---------------|----------------|
| Algeria | 31,736,053 1.7% | 69, male 71, female | 62% | $5,500 |
| Libya | 5,240,599 2.4% | 74, male 78, female | 76% | $8,900 |
| Morocco | 30,645,305 1.7% | 67, male 72, female | 44% | $3,500 |
| Tunisia | 9,705,102 1.7% | 72, male 76, female | 67% | $6,500 |
| United States | 281,421,906 0.9% | 74, male 80, female | 97% | $36,200 |

**Sources:** Central Intelligence Agency, *The World Factbook 2001;* U.S. Census Bureau

**Interpreting the Chart** **According to the data in the chart, which country is the least economically developed?**

Marrakech (muh-RAH-kish) is a popular tourist resort in central Morocco. It sits in the foothills of the Atlas Mountains.

▼

# Economy

Oil, mining, and tourism are important industries in these countries. Oil is the most important resource, particularly in Libya and Algeria. Money from oil pays for schools, health care, other social programs, and military equipment. The region's countries also have large deposits of natural gas, iron ore, and lead.

Morocco is the only North African country with little oil. However, the country is an important producer and exporter of fertilizer.

About 20 percent of the workers in Libya, Tunisia, and Algeria are farmers. In Morocco farmers make up about half of the labor force. North Africa's farmers grow and export wheat, other grains, olives, fruits, and nuts. However, the region's desert climate and poor soils limit farming, particularly in Libya. Libya imports most of its food.

The Maghreb countries have close economic relationships with European countries. This is partly because of old colonial ties between North Africa and Europe. In addition, European countries are located nearby, lying just across the Mediterranean Sea. Formal agreements between North African countries and the European Union (EU) also have helped trade. Today about 80 percent of Tunisia's trade is with EU countries. The largest trade partners of Algeria, Libya, and Morocco are also EU members. Many European tourists visit North Africa.

✔ **READING CHECK:** ( *Places and Regions* ) How does the oil industry affect Libya's and Algeria's schools, health care, and other social programs?

# Challenges

The countries of the Maghreb have made much progress in health and education. However, important challenges remain. Among these challenges is the need for more economic freedom. Each of these countries has had elements of a command economy, in which government owns and operates industry. However, in recent years the region's governments have moved to loosen that control. They have sold some government-owned businesses. They have also taken other steps to help private industry grow.

Political freedoms are limited for many North Africans. Many have little say in their governments. For example, since 1969 Libya has been ruled by a **dictator**, Mu'ammar al-Gadhafi. A dictator is someone who rules a country with complete power. Gadhafi has supported bombing, kidnapping, and other acts of violence against Israel and Israel's supporters. As a result, countries have limited their economic relationships with Libya.

As in Egypt, another challenge is conflict over the role of Islam in society. For example, in Algeria some groups want a government based on Islamic principles and laws. In 1992 the government canceled elections that many believed would be won by Islamic groups. Violence between Algeria's government and some Islamic groups has claimed thousands of lives since then.

✓ **READING CHECK:** *Places and Regions* What are some of the challenges the region's countries face today?

These Islamic students at a religious school in Libya are reciting verses from the Qur'an. Religious education is important in this mostly Islamic region.

▼

**Homework Practice Online**
Keyword: SK3 HP19

---

# Section Review 4

**Define and explain:** Casbah, souks, free port, dictator

**Working with Sketch Maps** On the map you created in Section 3, label Libya, Tunisia, Algeria, Morocco, Tripoli, Benghazi, Algiers, Casablanca, Rabat, Tunis, and the Strait of Gibraltar. In a box in the margin, identify the national capitals of the region's countries.

## Reading for the Main Idea

1. *Places and Regions* What are the old, central districts of many North African cities like?

2. *Places and Regions* What type of economy have these nations had, and how is this changing?

## Critical Thinking

3. **Finding the Main Idea** Where are the region's farms and most of its people found today? Why?

4. **Analyzing Information** How are the political rights of North Africans different from those of people in the United States?

## Organizing What You Know

5. **Summarizing** Copy the following graphic organizer. Use it to list industries, resources, farm products, and trade partners of the Maghreb countries.

| | |
|---|---|
| Industries | |
| Resources | |
| Farm products | |
| Trade partners | |

# CHAPTER 19

# Reviewing What You Know

## Building Vocabulary

On a separate sheet of paper, write sentences to define each of the following words.

1. ergs
2. regs
3. depressions
4. silt
5. pharaohs
6. hieroglyphs
7. Bedouins
8. fellahin
9. Casbah
10. souks
11. free port
12. dictator

## Reviewing the Main Ideas

1. (Places and Regions) How does geography affect settlement patterns in North Africa?
2. (Places and Regions) What are North Africa's main climates?
3. (Places and Regions) What are some important challenges facing Egypt today?
4. (Places and Regions) What are the most important industries in North Africa?
5. (Places and Regions) Which is the most urbanized country in North Africa?

## Understanding Environment and Society

### Farming and Fertilizer

Egyptian farmers must use large amounts of fertilizer. Create a presentation about the use of fertilizer. Consider the following:

- The kinds of chemicals, minerals, and other materials most commonly used as fertilizers.
- How fertilizers work.
- The positive and negative effects of using fertilizer.

## Thinking Critically

1. **Finding the Main Idea** How do you think the Sahara has influenced settlement in the region?
2. **Finding the Main Idea** Why are most of North Africa's cities and population located in coastal areas?
3. **Analyzing Information** Why is the Suez Canal important to world trade?
4. **Finding the Main Idea** In what way has Islam influenced politics in North Africa?
5. **Making Generalizations and Predictions** Based on what you have read, what kinds of challenges do you think North Africans will face in coming decades? Explain your answer.

## Map ACTIVITY

On a separate sheet of paper, match the letters on the map with their correct labels.

Sinai Peninsula    Western Sahara
Ahaggar    Tripoli
  Mountains    Algiers
Atlas Mountains    Casablanca
Nile Delta    Strait of
Cairo      Gibraltar

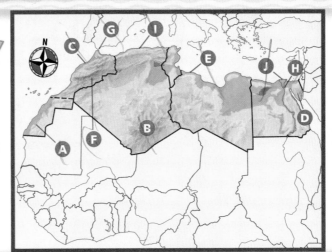

## Mental Mapping Skills ACTIVITY

On a separate sheet of paper, draw a freehand map of North Africa. Make a key for your map and label the following:

Algeria      Red Sea
Egypt      Sahara
Libya      Tunisia
Morocco

## WRITING ACTIVITY

Imagine that you are a Bedouin teenager in the Sahara. Write a one-paragraph journal entry about a typical day in your life. How do you cope with the desert heat? What is it like living without a permanent home? What religion do you practice? What do you eat? Use the library and other resources to help you. Be sure to use standard grammar, spelling, sentence structure, and punctuation.

## Alternative Assessment

## Portfolio ACTIVITY

### Learning About Your Local Geography

**Research Project** Use an almanac to identify your state's largest cities. Sketch a map of your state. Mark the three largest cities and major physical features such as rivers, mountains, and coastlines.

🖉 **internet** connect

Internet Activity: **go.hrw.com**
KEYWORD: SK3 GT19

Choose a topic to explore about North Africa:

- Journey through the Sahara.
- Examine the rich history of North Africa.
- Practice using Arabic calligraphy.

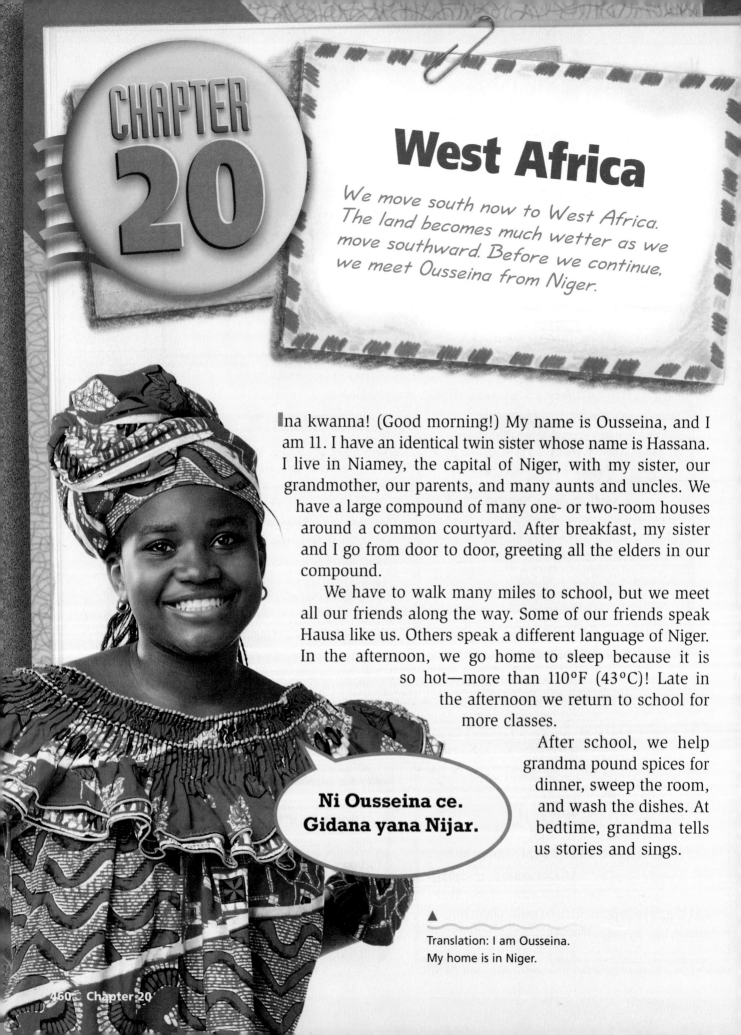

# CHAPTER 20

# West Africa

*We move south now to West Africa. The land becomes much wetter as we move southward. Before we continue, we meet Ousseina from Niger.*

Ina kwanna! (Good morning!) My name is Ousseina, and I am 11. I have an identical twin sister whose name is Hassana. I live in Niamey, the capital of Niger, with my sister, our grandmother, our parents, and many aunts and uncles. We have a large compound of many one- or two-room houses around a common courtyard. After breakfast, my sister and I go from door to door, greeting all the elders in our compound.

We have to walk many miles to school, but we meet all our friends along the way. Some of our friends speak Hausa like us. Others speak a different language of Niger. In the afternoon, we go home to sleep because it is so hot—more than 110°F (43°C)! Late in the afternoon we return to school for more classes.

After school, we help grandma pound spices for dinner, sweep the room, and wash the dishes. At bedtime, grandma tells us stories and sings.

**Ni Ousseina ce.
Gidana yana Nijar.**

Translation: I am Ousseina.
My home is in Niger.

# Section 1 Physical Geography

## Read to Discover

1. What landforms and climates are found in West Africa?
2. Why is the Niger River important to the region?
3. What resources does West Africa have?

## Define

zonal
Sahel
harmattan
tsetse fly
bauxite

## Locate

Sahara
Niger River
Gulf of Guinea

*Colorful Nigerian tapestry*

### WHY IT MATTERS

West African countries have often faced problems in managing their natural resources. Use CNN fyi.com or other current events sources to find problems faced by countries in the region regarding resources and the environment. Record your findings in your journal.

## West Africa: Physical-Political

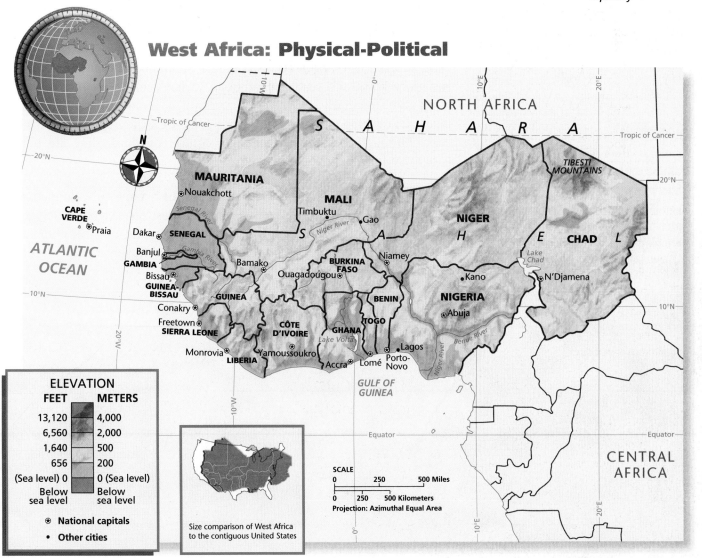

ELEVATION

| FEET | METERS |
|---|---|
| 13,120 | 4,000 |
| 6,560 | 2,000 |
| 1,640 | 500 |
| 656 | 200 |
| (Sea level) 0 | 0 (Sea level) |
| Below sea level | Below sea level |

⊛ National capitals
• Other cities

Size comparison of West Africa to the contiguous United States

SCALE
0     250     500 Miles
0   250   500 Kilometers
Projection: Azimuthal Equal Area

**internet** connect

GO TO: go.hrw.com
KEYWORD: SK3 CH20
FOR: Web sites about
West Africa

**Do you remember what you learned about desertification? See Chapter 4 to review.**

Farmers use river water to irrigate onion fields in central Mali. Farming can be difficult in the dry Sahel.

**Interpreting the Visual Record How do you think economic factors have affected the use of technology in bringing water to the fields?**

# Landforms and Climate

West Africa is largely a region of plains. There are low mountains in the southwest and high mountains in the northeast. Four major climate types stretch from east to west in bands or zones. Therefore, geographers say the region's climates are **zonal**.

**The Sahara** The northernmost parts of the region lie within the Sahara, the first climate zone. The Sahara is the world's largest desert. It stretches across northern Africa from the Atlantic Ocean to the Red Sea. Large areas of this dry climate zone have few or no people.

**The Sahel** South of the Sahara is a region of dry grasslands called the **Sahel** (sah-HEL). This second climate zone has a steppe climate. Rainfall varies greatly from year to year. In some years it never rains. During winter a dry, dusty wind called the **harmattan** (hahr-muh-TAN) blows south from the Sahara.

During the late 1960s a drought began in the Sahel. Crops failed for several years, and there was not enough grass for the herds. Animals overgrazed the land, and people cut the few large trees for firewood. Wind blew away fertile soil, and the Sahara expanded southward. Without plants for food, many animals and people died. Recent years have been rainier, and life has improved.

**The Savanna** Farther south is the savanna zone. It contains good soil, thick grass, and scattered tall trees. Farmers can do well when the rains come regularly. However, the region is home to a dangerous insect. The **tsetse** (TSET-see) **fly** carries sleeping sickness, a deadly disease. Although insecticides can help control the flies, they are too expensive for most people to buy.

**The Coast and Forest** The fourth climate zone lies along the Atlantic and Gulf of Guinea coasts. Many of West Africa's largest cities lie in this coastal zone. You will find a wet, humid tropical climate there. Plentiful rain supports tropical rain forests. However, many trees

have been cut to make room for growing populations. As a result, environmental damage is a serious problem.

✓ **READING CHECK:** ( *Places and Regions* ) What are the region's landforms and climate zones?

## The Niger River

The most important river in West Africa is the Niger (NY-juhr). The Niger River starts in low mountains just 150 miles (241 km) from the Atlantic Ocean. It flows eastward and southward for 2,600 miles (4,183 km) and empties into the Gulf of Guinea.

The Niger brings life-giving water to West Africa. In the Sahel it divides into a network of channels, swamps, and lakes. This network is known as the inland delta. The Niger's true delta on the Gulf of Guinea is very wide. Half of Nigeria's coastline consists of the delta.

✓ **READING CHECK:** ( *Environment and Society* ) Why is the Niger River important to West Africa?

▲

The hippopotamus is just one of the many animal species living in the Niger region. Hippopotamuses are good swimmers and can stay underwater for as long as six minutes.

## Resources

West Africa's mineral riches include diamonds, gold, iron ore, manganese, and **bauxite**. Bauxite is the main source of aluminum. Nigeria is a major exporter of oil. In fact, oil and related products make up about 95 percent of that country's exports.

✓ **READING CHECK:** ( *Places and Regions* ) What are some of the region's resources?

go. hrw .com **Homework Practice Online** Keyword: SK3 HP20

# Section Review 1

**Define and explain:** zonal, Sahel, harmattan, tsetse fly, bauxite

**Working with Sketch Maps** On a map of West Africa, label the following: Sahara, Sahel, Niger River, and Gulf of Guinea.

### Reading for the Main Idea

1. ( *Physical Systems* ) What effect has drought had on West Africa's vegetation?

2. ( *Places and Regions* ) What natural resources are found in West Africa?

3. ( *Places and Regions* ) What is West Africa's most important river? Describe its two delta regions.

### Critical Thinking

4. **Making Generalizations and Predictions** Where in the region would you expect to find the densest populations? Why?

### Organizing What You Know

5. **Summarizing** Copy the following graphic organizer. Use it to list and describe the region's climate zones.

| Zones | Characteristics |
|-------|-----------------|
|       |                 |
|       |                 |
|       |                 |
|       |                 |

# Section 2 History and Culture

## Read to Discover

1. What great African kingdoms once ruled the region?
2. How did contact with Europeans affect West Africa?
3. What challenges do the region's governments face?
4. What are some features of West African culture?

## Define

archaeology

oral history

animism

## Locate

Timbuktu

*Bronze figure of a hunter, lower Niger area*

### WHY IT MATTERS

Many West African countries struggled to win their independence from colonial powers and are still struggling to maintain stable governments. Use CNN fyi.com or other current events sources to find examples of political events in these countries. Record your findings in your journal.

## West Africa's History

Much of what we know about West Africa's early history is based on **archaeology**. Archaeology is the study of the remains and ruins of past cultures. **Oral history**—spoken information passed down from person to person through generations—offers other clues.

**Great Kingdoms** Ancient artifacts suggest that the earliest trading towns developed in the Niger's inland delta. Traders brought dates and salt from the desert. People from the Sahel sold animals and hides. Other trade goods were grains, fish, kola and other tropical nuts, and metals, such as gold. (Much later, kola nuts provided the flavor for cola drinks.) This trade helped African kingdoms grow. One of the earliest West African kingdoms, Ghana (GAH-nuh), had become rich and powerful by about A.D. 800.

These early West African cliff paintings illustrate features from a ceremonial ritual for young people.
**Interpreting the Visual Record What kinds of images do you see on this cliff wall?**

▼

Some 200 years later, North African merchants began crossing the Sahara to trade in Ghana. These merchants introduced Islam to West Africa. In time, Islam became the main religion practiced in the Sahel.

Later Ghana fell to Muslim warriors from Morocco. The Muslim empire of Mali (MAH-lee) replaced the kingdom of Ghana. Mali stretched from the Niger's inland delta to the Atlantic coast. Mansa Mūsā was king of Mali during the early 1300s. Famous for his wealth and wise rule, Mansa Mūsā supported artists, poets, and scholars.

The kingdom of Songhay (SAWNG-hy) came to power as Mali declined. With a university, mosques, and more than 100 schools, the Songhay city of Timbuktu was a cultural center. By about 1600, however, Moroccan invasions had weakened the kingdom.

Forested areas south of the Sahel were also home to great civilizations. In what is now Nigeria, wealthy kings were buried with brass sculptures and other treasures.

✓ **READING CHECK:** (*Human Systems*) What are some of the great African kingdoms that once ruled the region?

We might think that salt is common and cheap, but it was precious to the traders of the Sahara. At one time it was worth its weight in gold.

**The Slave Trade** During the 1440s Portuguese explorers began sailing along the west coast of Africa. The Europeans called it the Gold Coast for the gold they bought there. Once they could buy gold where it was mined, the Europeans stopped buying it from Arab traders. As a result, the trans-Sahara trade and the great trade cities faded.

For a while, both Europeans and Africans profited from trade with each other. However, by the 1600s the demand for labor in Europe's American colonies changed everything. European traders met this demand by selling enslaved Africans to colonists. The slave trade was very profitable for these traders.

The slave trade had devastating effects on West African communities. Families were broken up when members were kidnapped and enslaved. Many Africans died on the voyage to the Americas. Most who survived were sent to the West Indies or Brazil. The slave trade finally ended in the 1800s. By then millions of Africans had been forced from their homes.

**Colonial Era and Independence** In the late 1800s, many European countries competed for colonies in West Africa. France claimed most of the region's northwest. Britain, Germany, and Portugal seized the rest.

In all of West Africa only tiny Liberia remained independent. Americans had founded it in the 1820s as a home for freed slaves. Sierra Leone, a British colony, also became a home for freed slaves.

There are many reminders of the slave trade and its effects on West Africans. Performers here reenact the treatment of enslaved Africans in an old slave house in Dakar, Senegal.
**Interpreting the Visual Record** How does this photograph show slavery's effect on creative expression?

Some Europeans moved to West Africa to run the colonies. They built roads, bridges, and railroads. Teachers and missionaries set up Christian churches and schools. After World War II, Africans increasingly worked for independence. Most of the colonies gained independence during the 1950s and 1960s. Portugal, the last European country to give up its West African colonies, did so in 1974.

✔ **READING CHECK:** ( *Human Systems* ) What impact did contact with Europeans have on West Africa?

## Challenges

Independence brought a new set of challenges to the region. The borders that the Europeans had drawn ignored human geography. Sometimes borders separated members of one ethnic group. Other borders grouped together peoples that did not get along. As a result, many West Africans were more loyal to their ethnic groups than to their new countries. In addition, too few people had been trained to run the new governments. Dictators took control in many countries. Civil wars and military rulers still trouble the region. Some countries have made progress, however. For example, in 1996 Chad created its first democratic constitution.

The governments of West African countries have several difficult problems in common. Birthrates are high. As a result, more and more people must make a living from the small amount of fertile land. In addition, many people are moving to already crowded cities even though urban jobs are few. These countries must also find ways to educate more of their people. Many families cannot afford to send their children to school.

✔ **READING CHECK:** ( *Places and Regions* ) What are three challenges the region faces?

A roadside market provides a glimpse of crowded Lagos, Nigeria's largest city. More than 10 million people live in and around Lagos. Overcrowded cities are a problem throughout much of the region.

▼

# CONNECTING TO *Literature*

## *Marriage Is a Private Affair*
### *by Chinua Achebe*

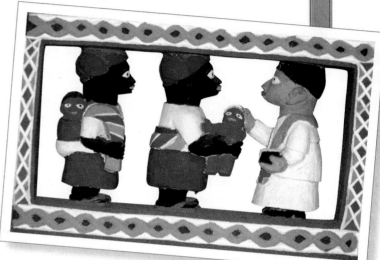

*A Nigerian church carving*

*Chinua Achebe was born in an Ibo village in Nigeria in 1930. Many of his writings explore the changes colonialism brought to Africa. They also look at the conflict between old and new ways. In this story, Achebe looks at different views a father and son have about marriage.*

"Father," began Nnaemeka suddenly, "I have come to ask for forgiveness."

"Forgiveness? For what, my son?" he asked in amazement.

"It's about this marriage question."

"Which marriage question?"

"I can't—we must—I mean it is impossible for me to marry Nweke's daughter."

"Impossible? Why?" asked his father.

"I don't love her."

"Nobody said you did. Why should you?" he asked.

"Marriage today is different . . ."

"Look here, my son," interrupted his father, "nothing is different. What one looks for in a wife are a good character and a Christian background."

Nnaemeka saw there was no hope along the present line of argument.

"Moreover," he said. "I am engaged to marry another girl who has all of Ugoye's good qualities, and who . . ."

His father did not believe his ears. "What did you say?" he asked slowly and disconcertingly[1]. . . .

"Whose daughter is she, anyway?"

"She is Nene Atang."

"What!" All the mildness was gone again. "Did you say Neneataga, what does that mean?"

"Nene Atang from Calabar. She is the only girl I can marry." This was a very rash reply and Nnaemeka expected the storm to burst.

## Analyzing Primary Sources

1. What universal theme does the passage illustrate?
2. Why do you think the father and son disagree about marriage?

**Vocabulary** [1]disconcertingly: disturbingly

These homes in Burkina Faso are made of a mixture of mud, water, and cow dung. Trees are scarce in the Sahel and savanna zones. As a result, there is little wood for construction. Women are responsible for painting and decorating the walls of the homes.

**Interpreting the Visual Record**

**For what purpose are the roofs apparently used?**

# Culture

Hundreds of ethnic groups exist in West Africa today. Hundreds of languages are spoken in the region. In some areas, using the colonial languages of French or English helps people from different groups communicate. West African languages that many people share, such as Fula and Hausa, also aid communication.

**Religion** The traditional religions of West Africa have often been forms of **animism**. Animism is the belief that bodies of water, animals, trees, and other natural objects have spirits. Animists also honor the memories of ancestors. In some isolated areas animism still forms the basis of most religious practices. Today most people of the Sahel practice Islam. Farther south live many Christians.

**Clothing and Homes** Some West Africans, particularly in cities, wear Western-style clothing. Others wear traditional robes, pants, blouses, and skirts. These are often made from colorful patterned cotton fabric. Because of the warm climate, most clothing is loose and flowing. Many women wear beautiful folded and wrapped headdresses. In the desert men often wear turbans. Both men and women may use veils to protect their faces from blowing sand.

Rural homes are small and simple. Many homes in the Sahel and savanna zones are circular. Straw or tin roofs sit atop mud, mud-brick, or straw huts. However, in cities you will find some modern buildings.

✔ **READING CHECK:** *Human Systems* What are some features of West African culture?

**Homework Practice Online**
Keyword: SK3 HP20

**Define and explain:** archaeology, oral history, animism

**Working with Sketch Maps** On the map you created in Section 1, label Timbuktu. What made Timbuktu an important Songhay city?

**Reading for the Main Idea**

1. *Human Systems* How did European contact affect West Africa's people?

2. *Human Systems* Where in West Africa are Islam and Christianity practiced?

**Critical Thinking**

3. **Drawing Inferences and Conclusions** How might shared histories and challenges lead to more cooperation among the region's countries?

4. **Drawing Inferences and Conclusions** Why do you think mud bricks are used in West Africa?

**Organizing What You Know**

5. **Summarizing** Use the following graphic organizer to summarize challenges facing West Africa.

West Africa

# Section 3  The Sahel Countries

## Read to Discover

1. What are Mauritania, Mali, and Niger like today?
2. What challenges do Chad and Burkina Faso face?

## Define

millet
sorghum
malaria
staple

## Locate

Nouakchott
Senegal River
Gao
Tibesti Mountains
Lake Chad
Ouagadougou

### WHY IT MATTERS

The shrinking of Lake Chad over the last several decades has been a major concern for the people of Chad. Many blame a changing environment and poor managing of the lake's resources. Use CNNfyi.com or other current events sources to find information about Lake Chad. Record the findings in your journal.

*Carved mask from Mauritania*

## Mauritania, Mali, and Niger

Most of the people in these three large countries are Muslim. Mauritania, in fact, has laws based on Islam. These countries are also former French colonies, and French influence remains. In Mali and Niger, the official language is French. However, the people there speak more than 60 different local languages.

Today, drought and the expanding desert make feeding the people in these countries difficult. In the Sahel nomads depend on their herds of cattle, goats, and camels. In the savanna regions farmers grow **millet** and **sorghum**. These grain crops can usually survive drought.

**Mauritania** Many Mauritanians are Moors, people of mixed Arab and Berber origin. They speak Arabic. In the past, Moors enslaved some of the black Africans. Today, tension between the two groups continues.

▶

Women carry goods for sale in a market in central Mali. Much of Mali's economic activity takes place in the Niger River's inland delta.
**Interpreting the Visual Record** Why is Mali's economic activity centered around the inland delta?

Mud and other local materials were used to build many mosques in the Sahel. This mosque is located in Djenné [je-NAY], Mali. The majority of people living in the Sahel are Muslims.

The Tuareg (TWAH-reg) people of the Sahara and Sahel pound powdered blue dye into their flowing robes. They do this rather than dip the fabric in precious water. The blue powder wears off onto the skin, where it may help hold in moisture.

Most Mauritanians were once nomadic herders. Today, the expanding Sahara has crowded more than half of the nomads into the cities. Just 40 years ago, Nouakchott (nooh-AHK-shaht), Mauritania's capital, was a small village. More than 700,000 people live there now. About half of the population lives in shacks at the city's edges.

Throughout the country, people are very poor. Only in the far south, near the Senegal River, can farmers raise crops. Fishing in the Atlantic Ocean is another source of income.

**Mali** To the east of Mauritania lies landlocked Mali. The Sahara covers much of northern Mali. In the south lies a wetter farming region. About 80 percent of Mali's people fish or farm along the Niger River. Cotton is the country's main export. Timbuktu and Gao (GOW), ancient trading cities, continue to attract tourists.

Health conditions in Mali are poor. **Malaria**, a disease spread by mosquitoes, is a major cause of death among children.

**Niger** The Niger River flows through just the southwestern corner of landlocked Niger. Only about 3 percent of Niger's land is good for farming. All of the country's farmland lies along the Niger River and near the Nigerian border. Much of the rest of Niger lies within the Sahara. Farmers raise cotton, peanuts, beans, peas, and rice. Millet and sorghum are two of the region's **staple**, or main, food crops. The grains are cooked like oatmeal. Nomads in the desert region depend on the dairy products they get from their herds for food.

## The Sahel Countries

| Country | Population/ Growth Rate | Life Expectancy | Literacy Rate | Per Capita GDP |
|---|---|---|---|---|
| Burkina Faso | 12,272,289 2.7% | 46, male 47, female | 19% | $1,000 |
| Chad | 8,707,078 3.3% | 49, male 53, female | 48% | $1,000 |
| Mali | 11,008,518 3% | 46, male 48, female | 31% | $850 |
| Mauritania | 2,747,312 2.9% | 49, male 53, female | 47% | $2,000 |
| Niger | 10,355,156 2.7% | 42, male 41, female | 14% | $1,000 |
| United States | 281,421,906 0.9% | 74, male 80, female | 97% | $36,200 |

**Sources:** Central Intelligence Agency, *The World Factbook 2001;* U.S. Census Bureau

**Interpreting the Chart** Based on the numbers in the chart, which two countries in the region are the least economically developed?

✓ **READING CHECK:** *Places and Regions* What is it like to live in Mauritania, Mali, and Niger?

# Chad and Burkina Faso

Drought has also affected the former French colonies of Chad and Burkina Faso (boohr-KEE-nuh FAH-soh). These countries are among the world's poorest and least developed. Most people farm or raise cattle.

**Chad** Chad is located in the center of Africa. The Tibesti Mountains in northern Chad rise above the Sahara. Lake Chad is in the south. Not long ago, the lake had a healthy fishing industry. It even supplied water to several other countries. However, drought has evaporated much of the lake's water. At one time, Lake Chad had shrunk to just one third its size in 1950.

The future may be better for Chad. A civil war ended in the 1990s. Also, oil reserves now being explored may help the economy.

**Burkina Faso** This country's name means "land of the honest people." Most of its people follow traditional religions. The country has thin soil and few mineral resources. Few trees remain in or near the capital, Ouagadougou (wah-gah-DOO-goo). They have been cut for firewood and building material. Jobs in the city are also scarce. To support their families many young men work in other countries. However, foreign aid and investment are starting to help the economy.

✓ **READING CHECK:** ( **Places and Regions** ) What are the challenges facing Chad and Burkina Faso?

## Major Religions of the Sahel Countries

| | Animism | Islam | Christianity |
|---|---|---|---|
| Burkina Faso | 40% | 50% | 10% |
| Chad | 25% | 50% | 25% |
| Mali | 9% | 90% | 1% |
| Mauritania | | 100% | |
| Niger | 20% | 80% | |

■ Animism   ■ Islam   ■ Christianity

Source: Central Intelligence Agency, *World Factbook 2001*

Although most people in the Sahel are Muslim, some practice forms of animism and Christianity.

**Interpreting the Graph** Which country's population is entirely Muslim? Which countries have significant numbers of Christians?

## Section Review 3

go.hrw.com **Homework Practice Online** Keyword: SK3 HP20

**Define and explain:** millet, sorghum, malaria, staple

**Working with Sketch Maps** On the map you created in Section 2, draw the boundaries of Mauritania, Mali, Niger, Chad, and Burkina Faso. Then label Nouakchott, Senegal River, Gao, Tibesti Mountains, Lake Chad, and Ouagadougou. In a box in the margin, describe what has happened to Lake Chad in recent decades.

### Reading for the Main Idea

1. ( **Places and Regions** ) Why has Nouakchott grown so rapidly?

2. ( **Places and Regions** ) Which European language is most common in the Sahel countries? Why?

### Critical Thinking

3. **Drawing Inferences and Conclusions** How do the typical foods of Niger relate to the country's water resources?

4. **Comparing** What do Chad and Burkina Faso have in common with the other Sahel countries?

### Organizing What You Know

5. **Comparing** Copy the following graphic organizer. Label each of the star's points with one of the Section 3 countries. In the center, list characteristics the countries share.

**Read to Discover**

1. What is life in Nigeria like today?
2. What economic challenges do the region's other countries face?

**Define**

secede
griots
cacao

**Locate**

Abuja          Monrovia
Lagos          Lake Volta
Dakar

**WHY IT MATTERS**

Nigeria has made a great deal of economic progress but there are problems that still hurt the nation's economy. Use CNN fyi.com or other current events sources to find examples of Nigerian social, economic, and political affairs. Record your findings in your journal.

*A gold ornament from Ghana*

The faces of Nigeria are very young. About 45 percent of all Nigerians are younger than 15 years old. Only about 22 percent of all Americans are that young.

**Interpreting the Visual Record**

**How is the clothing shown here similar to clothing worn by students in your school?**

# Nigeria

The largest country along West Africa's coast is Nigeria. With more than 113 million people, it has Africa's largest population.

**Nigeria's People** Nigeria was once an important British colony. Like many other colonies, Nigeria's borders included many ethnic groups. Today, a great variety of ethnic groups live in Nigeria. The Yoruba, Fula, Hausa, and Ibo are four of the largest ethnic groups. More than 200 languages are spoken there.

Nigeria's ethnic groups have not always gotten along. In the 1960s the Ibo tried to **secede**. That is, they tried to break away from Nigeria and form their own country. They called it Biafra (bee-AF-ruh). However, the Ibo lost the bloody war that followed.

Avoiding ethnic conflicts has continued to be an issue in Nigeria. It was important in choosing a site for a new Nigerian capital in the late 1970s. Leaders chose Abuja (ah-BOO-jah) because it was centrally located in an area of low population density.

**Nigeria's Economy** Nigeria has some of the continent's richest natural resources. Oil is the country's most important resource. Major oil fields are located in the Niger River delta and just off the coast. Oil accounts for 95 percent of the country's export earnings. Nigeria also

Oil drilling rigs like this one are common in areas of southern Nigeria. Oil accounts for about 20 percent of Nigeria's GDP. Oil revenues pay for about 65 percent of the government's budget.

The headdresses and patterned clothing worn by these women in Dakar are common in Senegal.

has good roads and railroads. Lagos (LAY-gahs), the former capital, is the country's largest city. The city is a busy seaport and trade center.

Although the country has rich resources, many Nigerians are poor. A major cause of the poverty there is a high birthrate. Nigeria can no longer feed its growing population without importing food. Another cause is the economy's dependence on oil. When prices are low, the whole country suffers. A third cause of Nigeria's poverty is a history of bad government. Corrupt government officials have used their positions to enrich themselves.

✓ READING CHECK: *Places and Regions* What are Nigeria's people and economy like today?

# Other Coastal Countries

Several small West African countries lie along the Atlantic Ocean and the Gulf of Guinea. They are struggling to develop their economies.

**Senegal and Gambia** Senegal (se-ni-GAWL) wraps around Gambia (GAM-bee-uh). The odd border was created by French and British diplomats. Senegal, a former French colony, is larger and richer than Gambia, a former British colony. Dakar (dah-KAHR) is Senegal's capital and an important seaport and manufacturing center. Senegal and Gambia have many similarities. Peanuts are their most important crop. Common foods include chicken stew and fish with a peanut sauce. Tourism is growing slowly.

## The Coastal Countries

| Country | Population/ Growth Rate | Life Expectancy | Literacy Rate | Per Capita GDP |
|---|---|---|---|---|
| Benin | 6,590,782 / 3% | 49, male / 51, female | 38% | $1,030 |
| Cape Verde | 405,163 / 0.9% | 66, male / 73, female | 72% | $1,700 |
| Côte d'Ivoire | 16,393,221 / 2.5% | 44, male / 46, female | 49% | $1,600 |
| Gambia | 1,411,205 / 3% | 52, male / 56, female | 48% | $1,100 |
| Ghana | 19,894,014 / 1.8% | 56, male / 59, female | 65% | $1,900 |
| Guinea | 7,613,870 / 2% | 44, male / 48, female | 36% | $1,300 |
| Guinea-Bissau | 1,315,822 / 2.2% | 47, male / 52, female | 54% | $850 |
| Liberia | 3,225,837 / 1.9% | 50, male / 53, female | 38% | $1,100 |
| Nigeria | 126,635,626 / 2.6% | 51, male / 51, female | 57% | $950 |
| Senegal | 10,284,929 / 2.9% | 61, male / 64, female | 33% | $1,600 |
| Sierra Leone | 5,426,618 / 3.6% | 43, male / 49, female | 31% | $510 |
| Togo | 5,153,088 / 2.6% | 52, male / 56, female | 52% | $1,500 |
| United States | 281,421,906 / 0.9% | 74, male / 80, female | 97% | $36,200 |

**Sources:** Central Intelligence Agency, *The World Factbook 2001;* U.S. Census Bureau

**Interpreting the Chart Which country in the region has the highest life expectancy?**

Many of the people speak a language called Wolof (WOH-lawf). **Griots** (GREE-ohz) are important to the Wolof-speakers and other West Africans. Griots are storytellers who pass on the oral histories of their tribes or peoples. Sometimes the griots combine music with their stories, which may take hours or days to tell. Wolof women wear complex hairstyles and gold jewelry.

**Guinea, Guinea-Bissau, and Cape Verde** Guinea's main natural resource is a huge supply of bauxite. Its small neighbor to the east, Guinea-Bissau (GI-nee bi-SOW), has undeveloped mineral resources. Cape Verde (KAYP VUHRD) is a group of volcanic islands in the Atlantic. It is West Africa's only island country. Farming and fishing bring in the most money there.

**Liberia and Sierra Leone** Liberia is Africa's oldest republic. Monrovia, Liberia's capital, was named for U.S. president James Monroe. The freed American slaves who settled Liberia and their descendants lived in coastal towns. They often clashed with the Africans already living there. Those Africans and their descendants were usually poorer and lived in rural areas. In the 1980s conflicts led to a bitter civil war. Sierra Leone (lee-OHN) has also experienced violent civil war. The fighting has wrecked the country's economy. Now, both Liberia and Sierra Leone must rebuild. They do have natural resources on which to build stronger economies. Liberia produces rubber and iron ore. Sierra Leone exports diamonds.

Flowers color the countryside on Santa Antão island in Cape Verde. However, farming can be difficult because droughts are common in the island country.

**Interpreting the Visual Record What kinds of vegetation do you see on the island?**

**Ghana and Côte d'Ivoire** The countries of Ghana and Côte d'Ivoire (koht-dee-VWAHR) have rich natural resources. Those resources may help them build strong economies. Ghana is named for the ancient kingdom, although the kingdom was northwest of the modern country. Ghana has one of the largest human-made lakes in the world—Lake Volta. Gold, timber, and **cacao** (kuh-KOW) are major products. Cocoa and chocolate are made from the seeds of the cacao tree. The tree came originally from Mexico and Central America.

Côte d'Ivoire is a former French colony whose name means "Ivory Coast" in English. It is a world leader in cacao and coffee exports. Côte d'Ivoire also boasts Africa's largest Christian church building.

**Togo and Benin** Unstable governments have troubled both Togo and Benin (buh-NEEN) since independence. Both have experienced periods of military rule. Their fragile economies have contributed to their unstable and sometimes violent politics. These long, narrow countries are poor. The people depend on farming and herding for income. Palm tree products, cacao, and coffee are the main crops in Togo and Benin.

✓ **READING CHECK:** *Places and Regions* What are characteristics of the economies of the coastal countries?

▲

A storyteller passes on a legend to children in Côte d'Ivoire. Oral storytellers use facial expressions, gestures, and even music and dance. Those techniques help draw listeners into a story.

**Interpreting the Visual Record** What role might oral storytellers like the one shown here play in a place where many people cannot read?

---

# Section Review 4

**Define and explain:** secede, griots, cacao

**Working with Sketch Maps** On the map that you drew in Section 3, draw the boundaries for the coastal countries. Label Abuja, Lagos, Dakar, Monrovia, and Lake Volta. In a box in the margin, identify the largest and most populous country on West Africa's coast.

### Reading for the Main Idea

1. *Places and Regions* How is Cape Verde different from the other countries in the region?

2. *Places and Regions* What is Nigeria's most important natural resource? Why?

**Critical Thinking**

3. **Finding the Main Idea** Why must Liberia and Sierra Leone rebuild their economies?

4. **Analyzing Information** Why was choosing a new capital important to Nigeria's future?

### Organizing What You Know

5. **Summarizing** Copy the following graphic organizer. Use it to list three main causes of poverty in Nigeria today.

Causes of poverty in Nigeria

# CHAPTER 20 Reviewing What You Know

## Building Vocabulary

On a separate sheet of paper, write sentences to define each of the following words.

1. zonal
2. Sahel
3. harmattan
4. tsetse fly
5. bauxite
6. archaeology
7. oral history
8. animism
9. millet
10. sorghum
11. malaria
12. staple
13. secede
14. griots
15. cacao

## Reviewing the Main Ideas

1. ( *Places and Regions* )  What are the four climate zones of West Africa?
2. ( *Places and Regions* )  How do the Niger River's two delta regions differ?
3. ( *Human Systems* )  How did Islam come to West Africa?
4. ( *Environment and Society* )  How has drought affected the countries of the Sahel?
5. ( *Environment and Society* )  On what natural resource does Nigeria's economy depend?

## Understanding Environment and Society

### Health

Prepare a presentation, including a chart, graph, database, or model, about disease in West Africa. Consider the following:

- The parts of West Africa in which the tsetse fly, mosquitoes, and other dangerous insects are common.
- What diseases the insects spread.
- How these insects have affected human settlement and activities.

Then create a five-question quiz, with answers, about your presentation to challenge fellow students.

## Thinking Critically

1. **Drawing Inferences and Conclusions** Why are many of West Africa's largest cities located in the coastal and forest zone?

2. **Finding the Main Idea** What role did trade play in the early West African kingdoms and later European colonies in the region?

3. **Analyzing Information** What are three cultural features of West Africa influenced by Europeans?

4. **Drawing Inferences and Conclusions** How have borders set by European colonial powers led to conflicts such as Nigeria's war in Biafra in the late 1960s?

5. **Contrasting** How is Liberia's history different from that of other West African countries?

### Map ACTIVITY

On a separate sheet of paper, match the letters on the map with their correct labels.

Niger River
Gulf of Guinea
Timbuktu
Nouakchott
Senegal River

Tibesti Mountains
Lake Chad
Abuja
Lagos
Lake Volta

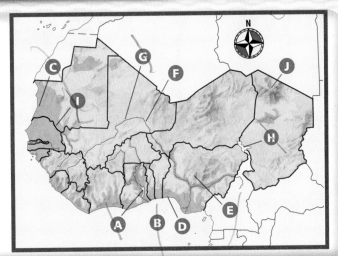

### Mental Mapping Skills ACTIVITY

On a separate sheet of paper, draw a freehand map of West Africa. Label the following:

Burkina Faso
Chad
Liberia
Mali

Mauritania
Niger
Nigeria
Sahel

### WRITING ACTIVITY

Imagine that you are an economic adviser to a West African country of your choice. Use print resources to prepare a short economic report for your country's leader. Identify the country's important natural resources and what can be done with them. In addition, describe economic advantages or disadvantages of the country's climate, location, and physical features. Be sure to use standard grammar, spelling, sentence structure, and punctuation.

## Alternative Assessment

### Portfolio ACTIVITY

**Learning About Your Local Geography**

**Group Project** The borders of today's African countries were largely drawn by Europeans. With your group, research how the borders of your state were decided.

### internet connect

Internet Activity: go.hrw.com
KEYWORD: SK3 GT20

Choose a topic to explore about West Africa:
• Find out about giant baobab trees.
• Meet the people of West Africa.
• Learn about the history of the slave trade.

# CHAPTER 21

# East Africa

East Africa has been identified by historians as the cradle of the human race. It has made great contributions to the development of world civilization.

My name is Tsiyon. I am 13, and I live in Addis Ababa, the capital of Ethiopia. My house is very far from the city center. I live with my parents and my brothers. We have a servant who helps my mother with the housework. My mother stays at home. My father works for the game department, doing research on the wild animals of Ethiopia.

After a breakfast of bread and tea with milk, I ride to school in a city taxi—a small blue and white minibus—with my brother, Wondemagegn, who works in a garage. I am in the seventh grade at Freyhewat Number Two Junior Secondary School. There are 82 kids in my class! I am in school from 8:00 A.M. to 3:00 P.M. I am studying Amharic—an Ethiopian language—English, math, science, and sports. When I grow up, I want to be a doctor.

At noon, I eat a lunch I brought from home. When I get home, I help my mother sweep the house. Then I watch television. In the evenings, I do my homework.

**Indemin adderu?**

▲

Translation: How did you pass the night?

# Section 1 Physical Geography

## Read to Discover

1. What are the major landforms of East Africa?
2. Which rivers and lakes are important in this region?
3. What are East Africa's climate types and natural resources?

## Define

rifts

## Locate

Great Rift Valley
Mount Kilimanjaro
Lake Victoria
White Nile
Blue Nile

### WHY IT MATTERS

Many scientists believe that the first humans on Earth lived on the land that we now call East Africa. Use CNNfyi.com or other current events sources to learn about recent discoveries related to the beginnings of humankind. Record your findings in your journal.

*A bat-eared fox from Tanzania*

## East Africa: Physical-Political

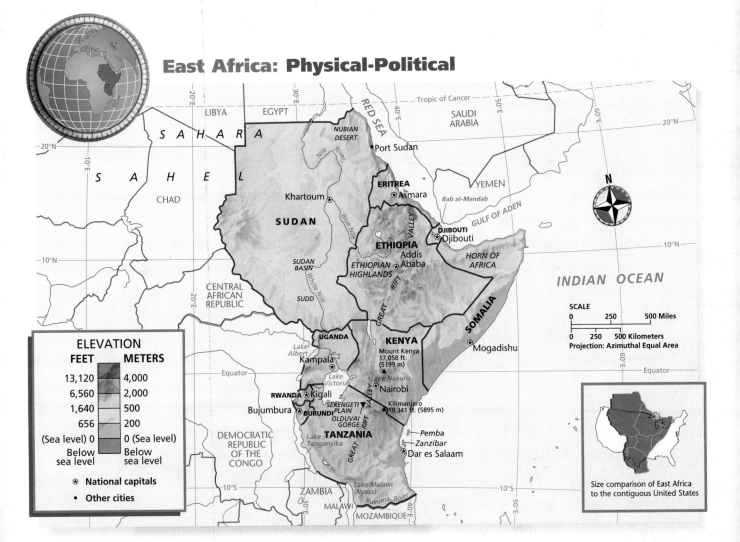

ELEVATION

| FEET | METERS |
| --- | --- |
| 13,120 | 4,000 |
| 6,560 | 2,000 |
| 1,640 | 500 |
| 656 | 200 |
| (Sea level) 0 | 0 (Sea level) |
| Below sea level | Below sea level |

⊛ National capitals
• Other cities

SCALE
0   250   500 Miles
0   250   500 Kilometers
Projection: Azimuthal Equal Area

Size comparison of East Africa to the contiguous United States

## Our Amazing Planet

**B**aobab (BOW-bab) trees are one of the few kinds of trees on the African savanna. It is also one of the largest trees in the world. It can grow as large as 30 feet (9 m) in diameter and to a height of 60 feet (18 m). The trunks are often used to store water or as temporary shelters.

This is a crater rim view of Mount Kilimanjaro. Another name for this volcano is Kilima Njaro—"shining mountain" in Swahili.

**Interpreting the Visual Record** Why do you think this region is a major tourist attraction?

# The Land

East Africa is a land of high plains and plateaus. In the north, deserts and dry grasslands define the landscape. In the southwest, large lakes dot the plateaus. In the east, sandy beaches and beautiful coral reefs run along the coast. East Africa's most striking features are its great **rifts**. They cut from north to south across the region. Rifts are long, deep valleys with mountains or plateaus on either side. Rifts form when Earth's tectonic plates move away from each other.

**The Rift Valleys** Deep beneath East Africa's surface, Earth's mantle is churning. This movement causes the land to arch and split along the rift valleys. If you look at the Great Rift Valley from the air, it looks like a giant scar. The Great Rift Valley is made up of two rifts—the eastern rift and the western rift. The rift walls are usually a series of steep cliffs. These cliffs drop an average of about 9,000 feet (2,743 m) to the valley floor. The eastern rift begins north of the Red Sea. The rift continues south through Eritrea (er-uh-TREE-uh) and Ethiopia (ee-thee-OH-pee-uh) into southern Tanzania (tan-zuh-NEE-uh). The western rift extends from Lake Albert in the north to Lake Malawi (mah-LAH-wee), also known as Lake Nyasa, in the south.

**Mountains and Plains** East Africa also has many volcanic mountains. Mount Kilimanjaro (ki-luh-muhn-JAHR-oh), at 19,341 feet (5,895 m), is Africa's tallest mountain. Although this part of Africa is along the equator, the mountain is so high that snow covers its two volcanic cones. Plains along the eastern rift in Tanzania and Kenya are home to famous national parks.

✔ **READING CHECK:** *Places and Regions* What are the major landforms of East Africa?

# Rivers and Lakes

East Africa is the site of a number of rivers and large lakes. The Nile is the world's longest river. It begins in East Africa and flows north to the Mediterranean Sea. Water from small streams collects in Lake Victoria, the source of the White Nile. Waters from Ethiopia's highlands form the Blue Nile. These two rivers meet at Khartoum, Sudan, to create the mighty Nile. The Nile provides a narrow, fertile lifeline through Sudan by providing irrigation in the desert.

Lake Victoria is Africa's largest lake in area, but it is shallow. Along the western rift is a chain of great lakes. Many of the lakes along the drier eastern rift are quite different. Heat from Earth's interior makes some of these eastern lakes so hot that no human can swim in them. Others, like Lake Nakuru, are too salty for most fish. However, algae in Lake Nakuru provides food for more than a million flamingos.

✓ **READING CHECK:** ( *Places and Regions* ) Which rivers and lakes are most important in this region?

▲ Lake Nakuru is known in part for the many flamingos that gather there.

# Climate and Resources

Northern Sudan and the northeast coast have desert and steppe climates. The climate changes to tropical savanna as you travel south. However, the greatest climate changes occur along the sides of the rift valleys. The rift floors are dry, with grasslands and thorn shrubs. In contrast, the surrounding plateaus and mountains have a humid highland climate and dense forests. Rain falls at the high elevations, but the valleys are in rain shadows.

Most East Africans are farmers or herders. However, the region does have mineral resources such as coal, copper, diamonds, gold, iron ore, and lead.

✓ **READING CHECK:** ( *Places and Regions* ) What are East Africa's climate types and natural resources?

## BUILD on WHAT You Know

**D**o you remember what you learned about rain shadows? See Chapter 3 to review.

**go. hrw .com** **Homework Practice Online**

Keyword: SK3 HP21

## Section Review 1

**Define and explain:** rifts

**Working with Sketch Maps** On a map of East Africa that you draw or that your teacher provides, label the following: Great Rift Valley, Mount Kilimanjaro, Lake Victoria, White Nile, and Blue Nile. How do the mountains help support the river systems?

### Reading for the Main Idea

1. ( *Places and Regions* ) What are the major landforms of East Africa?

2. ( *Places and Regions* ) Which rivers and lakes are located in this part of Africa?

3. ( *Physical Systems* ) Why are volcanic mountains found in parts of East Africa?

### Critical Thinking

4. **Drawing Inferences and Conclusions** How do you think the climate types found in East Africa influence what grows there?

### Organizing What You Know

5. **Summarizing** Copy the following graphic organizer. Use it to describe what you know about East Africa's physical geography.

| | Vegetation | Climates |
|---|---|---|
| Coasts | | |
| Rift Valleys | | |
| Plateaus/mountains | | |

**Read to Discover**

1. What important events and developments influenced the history of East Africa?

2. What is the culture of East Africa like?

**Define**

Swahili

*A Turkana woman*

## History

Several early civilizations developed at the site known as Meroë, near where the branches of the Nile come together. These civilizations had their own forms of writing. Each controlled a major trade route. East Africans traded ivory and gold, among other things.

This statue depicts a prince from the early Nubian civilization of northern Sudan.

**Christianity and Islam** Like Egypt, Ethiopia was an early center of Christianity. In the A.D. 500s Christianity spread into neighboring Nubia, which is now part of Egypt and Sudan. In Nubia, Christian kingdoms lasted until about 1500. Ethiopia still has a large Christian population today.

Arab armies conquered Egypt and North Africa by about A.D. 700. However, these armies were not able to keep control of East Africa. Gradually, Arabic-speaking nomads spread into northern Sudan from Egypt. They brought their Islamic faith with them. At the same time, Islam spread to the coastal region of what is now Somalia. Christianity is believed to have been introduced in Ethiopia as early as the A.D. 300s. Christian kingdoms, particularly in Ethiopia, have fought wars with Muslim leaders. Religion continues to be a source of conflict in this East African region.

**The Slave Trade** The east coast slave trade dates back more than 1,000 years. Most slaves went to Islamic countries in Africa and Asia. The Portuguese had begun setting up forts and settlements on the East African coast by the early 1500s. At first, the Europeans made little

This sketch shows a slave market in Zanzibar. Arab traders took advantage of local rivalries and encouraged powerful African leaders to capture their enemies and sell them into slavery.

**Interpreting the Visual Record**
**What does this piece of art tell us about the historical culture of this region?**

effort to move into the interior. However, in the late 1700s the East African island of Zanzibar became an international slave-trading center. Later, plantations like those of the Americas were set up with slave labor to grow cloves and sugarcane.

**Africa Divided** In the mid-1800s European adventurers traveled into the African interior searching for the source of the Nile. Here they found rich lands well suited for agriculture. In the 1880s the European powers divided up most of the continent. Most of Africa's modern borders resulted from this process. Control over much of East Africa went to the British. Germany colonized Tanzania, Rwanda, and Burundi. After World War I, with the defeat of Germany, the British took over Tanzania. Belgium gained control of Rwanda and Burundi.

**Conflict** Within East Africa, just Kenya was settled by large numbers of Europeans. The colonial rulers usually controlled their countries through African deputies. Many of these deputies were traditional chiefs, who often favored their own peoples. This tended to strengthen ethnic rivalries. These ethnic divisions have made it hard for governments to create feelings of national identity.

**Independence** Ethiopia was never colonized. Its mountains provided natural protection, and its peoples and emperors resisted colonization. It was, however, annexed by Italy from 1936 to 1941. Most East African countries were granted independence by European colonizers in the early 1960s. More recently, East Africa has become headquarters for some international companies and organizations.

✓ **READING CHECK:** ( **Human Systems** ) Which European countries influenced the history of East Africa?

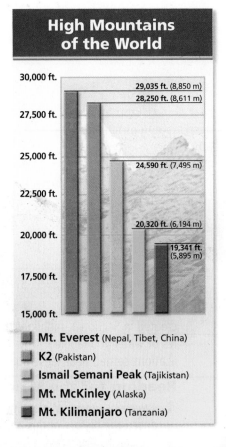

**High Mountains of the World**

30,000 ft.

29,035 ft. (8,850 m)
28,250 ft. (8,611 m)

27,500 ft.

25,000 ft.

24,590 ft. (7,495 m)

22,500 ft.

20,320 ft. (6,194 m)

20,000 ft.

19,341 ft. (5,895 m)

17,500 ft.

15,000 ft.

■ **Mt. Everest** (Nepal, Tibet, China)
■ **K2** (Pakistan)
■ **Ismail Semani Peak** (Tajikistan)
■ **Mt. McKinley** (Alaska)
■ **Mt. Kilimanjaro** (Tanzania)

**Interpreting the Graph How much taller is Mt. Everest than K2?**

Afar nomads stop for rest in a desert region of northern Ethiopia.

# Culture

East Africa has the world's longest history of human settlement. Gradually, the region developed the continent's greatest diversity of people and ways of life. The **Swahili** language is widely spoken in East Africa. This Bantu language has been greatly influenced by Arabic. In fact, the word Swahili comes from the Arabic word meaning "on the coast."

East Africa shares many challenges with other African regions. One challenge is that populations are growing faster than the economies that support them. Many jobless people have crowded into the cities. Another challenge is religious and ethnic conflict. Such conflict and other political problems have slowed economic progress. Often a country's wealth is spent on weapons rather than helping people.

The ethnic conflicts have roots in the region's history. Colonial borders drawn by Europeans often lumped different ethnic groups into one country. Differences between groups have led to conflict in some countries since independence.

The worst ethnic conflict has been in Rwanda and Burundi. Thousands of Tutsi were killed by the Hutu in Rwanda in the 1990s. There also has been fighting between Muslims and Christians in the northern part of the region.

✔ **READING CHECK:** *Human Systems* What conflicts have occurred between groups in East Africa?

go.hrw.com

**Homework Practice Online**

Keyword: SK3 HP21

## Section Review 2

**Define and explain:** Swahili

**Working with Sketch Maps** On the map you created in Section 1, highlight the location of the bodies of water you labeled. Why do you think early civilizations settled near these bodies of water?

### Reading for the Main Idea

1. *Human Systems* Which European countries influenced the history of this area?

2. *Human Systems* What are the main religions practiced in East Africa?

### Critical Thinking

3. **Finding the Main Idea** What conflicts have occurred because of political boundary lines?

4. **Drawing Inferences and Conclusions** Why might Swahili be a particularly important language in East Africa?

### Organizing What You Know

5. **Sequencing** Create a time line listing historical events in East Africa from the A.D. 400s to the 1990s. Be sure to include the adoption of Christianity, the slave trade, exploration, colonial rule, independence, and ethnic conflict.

A.D. 400 ——————————————— 1990s

# Section 3   The Countries of East Africa

## Read to Discover

1. Why did settlers come to Kenya?
2. How was Tanzania created?
3. What are Rwanda and Burundi like?
4. What is Uganda like?
5. What are the physical features of Sudan?

## Define

gorge

## Locate

Kenya
Tanzania
Rwanda
Burundi
Uganda
Sudan

### WHY IT MATTERS

Thousands of tourists enjoy the beautiful wildlife preserves and national parks of Kenya, Uganda, and Tanzania each year. Use CNNfyi.com or other current events sources to find out about travel and sightseeing opportunities in these countries. Record your findings in your journal.

Sudanese jar from the A.D. 100s

## Kenya

Kenya's first cities were founded along the coast of the Indian Ocean by Arab traders. Beginning in the 1500s Portugal controlled this coast for about 200 years. Arabs then recaptured it.

During the 1800s British merchants began trading on the coast. They built a railway from Mombasa to Lake Victoria. British settlers then came to take advantage of the fertile highlands. People from India and Pakistan also came to work on the Europeans' farms. Many of the local people, particularly the Kikuyu, moved out of their traditional areas. They became farmworkers or took jobs in the cities. After World War II many Africans protested British colonial rule. There were peaceful demonstrations as well as violent ones.

One conflict was over land. The British and the Kikuyu viewed land differently. The British considered land a sign of personal wealth, power, and property. The Kikuyu saw land as a source of food rather than something to be bought or sold. This caused conflict because the British wanted the land. Kenya gained independence from Britain in the 1960s, and its government has been quite stable ever since.

Kenya is a popular tourist destination. Tourism is a major source of income for the country. Kenya's greatest challenge is its rapidly increasing population. There is no empty farmland left in most areas. Much of Kenya has been set aside as national parkland.

As in the rest of Africa, Europeans once ruled colonies in East Africa. Fort Jesus, founded in 1593 by the Portuguese, is a national monument in Kenya.

East Africa    485

## East Africa

| Country | Population/ Growth Rate | Life Expectancy | Literacy Rate | Per Capita GDP |
|---|---|---|---|---|
| Burundi | 6,223,897 2.4% | 45, male 47, female | 35% | $720 |
| Kenya | 30,765,916 1.3% | 47, male 48, female | 78% | $1,500 |
| Rwanda | 7,312,756 1.2% | 38, male 40, female | 48% | $900 |
| Sudan | 36,080,373 2.8% | 56, male 58, female | 46% | $1,000 |
| Tanzania | 36,232,074 2.6% | 51, male 53, female | 68% | $710 |
| Uganda | 23,985,712 2.9% | 43, male 44, female | 62% | $1,100 |
| United States | 281,421,906 0.9% | 74, male 80, female | 97% | $36,200 |

**Sources:** Central Intelligence Agency, *The World Factbook 2001;* U.S. Census Bureau

**Interpreting the Chart Which country has the lowest literacy rate?**

These giraffe feed on the tree-studded grasslands of the Serengeti. This reserve was opened in 1974 and is Kenya's most famous and popular animal reserve.

▼

Many people would like to farm these lands. If the national parks are converted to farmland, however, African wildlife would be endangered. In addition, the tourism industry would likely suffer.

✔ **READING CHECK:** *Human Systems* Why did settlers come to Kenya?

## Tanzania

South of Kenya is the large country of Tanzania. It was created in the 1960s when Tanganyika and the island of Zanzibar united. Today many tourists come to explore numerous national parks and Mount Kilimanjaro. The mountain's southern slopes are a rich agricultural region that provides coffee and tea for exports. Also in Tanzania is the Serengeti Plain. On this plain, herds of antelope and zebras still migrate freely, following the rains. Nearby is a famous archaeological site, Olduvai Gorge. A **gorge** is a narrow, steep-walled canyon. Evidence of some of the earliest humanlike fossils have been found in Olduvai Gorge.

Tanzania is a country of mainly poor subsistence farmers. Poor soils and limited technology have restricted productivity. This country has minerals, particularly gold and diamonds. Although the Tanzanian government has tried to make the country more self-sufficient, it has not yet succeeded.

✔ **READING CHECK:** *Places and Regions* How was the country of Tanzania created?

# CONNECTING TO Science

*Olduvai Gorge, Tanzania*

Many scientists believe the human species has its origins in Africa. Archaeologists there have discovered fossil remains of humans and humanlike animals several million years old. Some of the most important finds have occurred at a site known as Olduvai Gorge.

Located in Tanzania, Olduvai is a steep-sided canyon some 30 miles (48 km) long. It is up to 300 feet (90 m) deep. The exposed sides of this gorge contain fossil deposits estimated to be more than 4 million years old. Along with the fossils, scientists found stone tools and the remains of numerous humanlike animals.

Archaeologists Louis and Mary Leakey played a key role in uncovering Olduvai's secrets. In 1931 Louis Leakey found remains of ancient tools and bones in the gorge. Then in 1959 Mary Leakey found the skeleton of an *Australopithecus*, the first humanlike creature to walk upright. Several years later, the

## OLDUVAI GORGE

Leakeys found the remains of a more advanced species. The new find was known as *Homo habilis*. The species could make stone tools.

These discoveries helped provide some of the missing links between humans and their ancestors. Today archaeological work at Olduvai Gorge continues to add to our understanding of human origins.

**Understanding What You Read**
1. What is Olduvai Gorge?
2. What part has Olduvai played in the search for human origins?

# Rwanda and Burundi

These two countries in fertile highlands were once German colonies. After World War I the Belgians ruled them. In the 1960s, after they gained independence, they were divided into two countries. Both countries are mostly populated by two ethnic groups—the Tutsi and the Hutu. Violence between the groups has killed thousands. Rwanda and Burundi have the densest rural settlement in Africa. Foreign aid has helped improve farming and health care.

✓ **READING CHECK:** ( *Human Systems* ) Why did the creation of Rwanda and Burundi create conflict?

Our Amazing Planet

Red colobus monkeys of Zanzibar eat charcoal, which absorbs poisons in the fruit-tree leaves the monkeys sometimes eat.

# Uganda

Uganda, another site of an ancient empire, is found on the plateau north and west of Lake Victoria. Economic progress has been slow. Foreign investment stopped as a result of a violent dictatorship. In the 1970s the country's economy collapsed. Limited peace and democracy were achieved in the late 1980s.

✔ **READING CHECK:** ( *Human Systems* ) What is Uganda like today?

▲ Alfred Louis Sargent created this engraving of Khartoum, Sudan, in the 1800s.

# Sudan

Sudan is Africa's largest country. It has three physical regions. The Sahara makes up the northern half of the country. Dry savannas extend across the country's center. Much of southern Sudan is taken up by a swamp called the Sudd. Sudan is mainly an agricultural country, but it is also developing some of its mineral resources. Oil reserves have not yet been developed.

Modern Sudanese culture shows influences of Arab and traditionally African cultures. Arab Muslims make up about 40 percent of the population and have political power. They dominate northern Sudan. Khartoum, the capital, is located in this area. During the last several decades there has been a civil war between northern Muslims and southerners who practice Christianity or traditional African religions.

✔ **READING CHECK:** ( *Human Systems* ) What conflict has been occurring in Sudan?

go.
hrw
.com
**Homework Practice Online**
Keyword: SK3 HP21

## Section Review 3

**Define and explain:** gorge

**Working with Sketch Maps** On the map you created in Section 2, label Kenya, Tanzania, Rwanda, Burundi, Uganda, and Sudan. Why are some of the countries of this region agriculturally fertile while others are not?

### Reading for the Main Idea

1. ( *Places and Regions* ) What makes the highlands of Kenya important?

2. ( *Places and Regions* ) Which areas of East Africa are tourist attractions?

### Critical Thinking

3. **Making Generalizations and Predictions** How might irrigation help a region's economic development?

4. **Finding the Main Idea** How has unrest hurt Rwanda and some other East African countries?

### Organizing What You Know

5. **Summarizing** Copy the following graphic organizer. Use it to list each country in this section. In one column list resources important to its development, and in the next column list obstacles that could prevent the country's economic success.

| Country | Resources | Obstacles |
|---------|-----------|-----------|
|         |           |           |
|         |           |           |

# Section 4  The Horn of Africa

## Read to Discover

1. What are the main physical features of Ethiopia?
2. What is Eritrea like?
3. What is Somalia like?
4. What are the physical and cultural characteristics of Djibouti?

## Define

droughts

## Locate

Ethiopia
Eritrea
Somalia
Djibouti
Bab al-Mandab

### WHY IT MATTERS

The United States sent food aid and 15,000 troops to Somalia in the 1990s to try to bring peace to the war-torn nation. Use CNN fyi.com or other current events sources to investigate current conditions in Somalia. Record your findings in your journal.

*A classic Swahili sailing dhow*

## Ethiopia

Ethiopia is one of the world's poorest countries. The rugged mountain slopes and upland plateaus have rich volcanic soil. Agriculture is Ethiopia's chief economic activity. It exports coffee, livestock, and oilseeds. However, during the last 30 years the region has experienced serious **droughts**. Droughts are periods when little rain falls and crops are damaged. Drought, combined with war and ineffective government policies, caused the starvation of several million people in the 1980s.

Except for a time when Ethiopia was at war with Italy, the Ethiopian highlands have never been under foreign rule. The mountains protected the interior of the country from invasion. Most of the highland people are Christian, while most of the lowland people are Muslim.

✓ **READING CHECK:** *Places and Regions* What physical features are found in Ethiopia?

As Afar nomads in Ethiopia move their encampment, they are continually challenged by the environment. **Interpreting the Visual Record How important are these camels for the Afar? What purpose do they serve?**

▼

| The Horn of Africa | | | | |
|---|---|---|---|---|
| COUNTRY | POPULATION/ GROWTH RATE | LIFE EXPECTANCY | LITERACY RATE | PER CAPITA GDP |
| Djibouti | 460,700 2.6% | 49, male 53, female | 46% | $1,300 |
| Eritrea | 4,298,269 3.8% | 54, male 59, female | 25% | $710 |
| Ethiopia | 65,891,874 2.7% | 44, male 46, female | 36% | $600 |
| Somalia | 7,448,773 3.5% | 45, male 48, female | 24% | $600 |
| United States | 281,421,906 0.9% | 74, male 80, female | 97% | $36,200 |

**Sources:** Central Intelligence Agency, *The World Factbook 2001*; U.S. Census Bureau

**Interpreting the Chart** Which country in the region has the highest level of economic development, and why?

The main mosque, Khulafa el Rashidin, was built in 1937 with Italian Carrara marble in Asmara, Eritrea.

**Interpreting the Visual Record** What architectural elements of this building have you seen in other regions you have studied?

# Eritrea

Eritrea, located on the Red Sea, was once part of Ethiopia. In the late 1800s the Italians made this area a colony. In the 1960s it became an Ethiopian province. After years of war, Eritrea broke away from Ethiopia in 1993. The economy has slowly improved since then. The population is made up of Muslims and Christians.

✔ **READING CHECK:** *Places and Regions* What is Eritrea like today?

# Somalia

Somalia is a land of deserts and dry savannas. Most Somalis are nomadic herders. Livestock and bananas are the main exports. Somalia is less diverse than most other African countries. Most residents of Somalia are members of the Somali people. Most Somali share the same culture, religion (Islam), language (Somali), and way of life (herding). Somalia has been troubled by civil war. In the 1990s widespread starvation caused by the war and a severe drought attracted international attention. The United Nations sent aid and troops to the country. U.S. troops were sent to Somalia to assist with this operation.

✔ **READING CHECK:** *Environment and Society* How have drought and conflict affected Somalia?

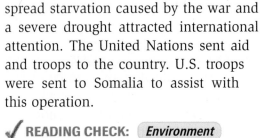

# Djibouti

Djibouti is a small desert country. It lies on the Bab al-Mandab. This is the narrow strait that connects the Red Sea and the Indian Ocean. The strait lies along a major shipping route. This has helped Djibouti's economy. In the 1860s Djibouti came under French control. It gained independence in 1977. The French government still contributes economic and military support to the country. Its port, which serves landlocked Ethiopia, is a major source of income. Djibouti is heavily dependent on food imports.

The people of Djibouti include the Issa and the Afar. The Issa are closely tied to the people of Somalia. The Afar are related to the people of Ethiopia. Members of both groups are Muslim. Somalia and Ethiopia have both wanted to control Djibouti. So far the country has maintained its independence.

✓ **READING CHECK:** ( *Places and Regions* ) What are Djibouti's physical and cultural features?

▲ Djibouti's Lake Assal has one of the lowest surface levels on the planet. It lies 515 feet (157 m) below sea level. The only way to reach this area is by use of a four-wheel drive vehicle.

**Interpreting the Visual Record** What about the surrounding physical geography would appear to limit access to this lake?

**Define and explain:** droughts

**Working with Sketch Maps** On the map you created in Section 3, label Ethiopia, Eritrea, Somalia, Djibouti, and Bab al-Mandab. What physical features help the economies of the region?

### Reading for the Main Idea

1. ( *Places and Regions* ) What physical features have helped protect Ethiopia from foreign invasion?

2. ( *Places and Regions* ) What country was part of Ethiopia until it broke away in 1993?

go.
hrw
.com
**Homework Practice Online**
Keyword: SK3 HP21

### Critical Thinking

3. **Drawing Inferences and Conclusions** Why do you think France remains interested in Djibouti?

4. **Finding the Main Idea** Why have foreign aid agencies been involved in East Africa?

### Organizing What You Know

5. **Analyzing Information** Copy the following graphic organizer. Use it to show the major religions of these countries. Add boxes as needed.

| Country | Religion |
|---------|----------|
|         |          |
|         |          |

# Reviewing What You Know

On a separate sheet of paper, write sentences to define each of the following words.

1. rifts
2. Swahili
3. gorge
4. droughts

## Reviewing the Main Ideas

1. ( Places and Regions ) What are East Africa's main natural resources?

2. ( Physical Systems ) What caused the formation of the Great Rift Valley of East Africa?

3. ( Human Systems ) How have Arabs, Portuguese, the British, and the Kikuyu affected Kenya?

4. ( Environment and Society ) What factors have slowed Tanzania's economic growth?

5. ( Environment and Society ) How have droughts in the Horn of Africa affected its people and their relationship with the rest of the world?

## Understanding Environment and Society

### Environmental Issues

Many East African countries have endured ethnic, religious, and political conflicts. Sometimes environmental issues can cause conflict. Prepare a presentation, including a graph, database, or model, comparing conflicts in East Africa over environmental issues. You may want to think about the following:

- Specific conflicts about environmental issues.
- Steps East Africans might take to eliminate these conflicts.

You may want to compare your data to facts you have learned about other regions in Africa for more ideas.

## Thinking Critically

1. **Finding the Main Idea** What is the significance of the Nile River in this region's human history?

2. **Analyzing Information** Why are foreign investors hesitant to invest in many countries of this region?

3. **Summarizing** Why do most East Africans make their living by farming and herding?

4. **Making Generalizations and Predictions** What problems have resulted in part from the boundary lines drawn by European powers, and how might the countries of East Africa overcome these problems?

5. **Analyzing Information** How has Ethiopia avoided falling under foreign rule for most of its history?

**Map ACTIVITY**

On a separate sheet of paper, match the letters on the map with their correct labels.

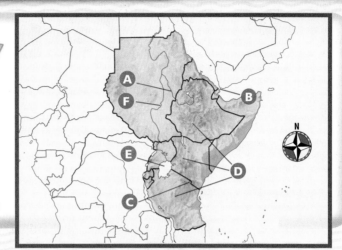

| | |
|---|---|
| Great Rift Valley | White Nile |
| Mount Kilimanjaro | Blue Nile |
| Lake Victoria | Bab al-Mandab |

**Mental Mapping Skills ACTIVITY**

On a separate sheet of paper, draw a freehand map of East Africa. Make a key for your map and label the following:

| | |
|---|---|
| Burundi | Rwanda |
| Djibouti | Somalia |
| Eritrea | Sudan |
| Ethiopia | Tanzania |
| Kenya | Uganda |

**WRITING ACTIVITY**

Imagine that you have been awarded an all-expenses-paid vacation to East Africa. Write a letter to your travel agent explaining what you want to do on your trip. List and describe physical features you want to see and African wildlife and historical sites you would like to explore. Be sure to use standard grammar, spelling, sentence structure, and punctuation.

## Alternative Assessment

**Portfolio ACTIVITY**

**Learning About Your Local Geography**

**Cooperative Project** Much of Africa's precolonial history was memorized by elders, rather than written down. Prepare an oral history of how older people in your community recall a certain historical event.

**internet connect**

Internet Activity: **go.hrw.com**
KEYWORD: SK3 GT21

Choose a topic to explore about East Africa:
- Hike Mount Kilimanjaro.
- Learn about cultural groups in East Africa.
- Travel back to ancient Nubian kingdoms.

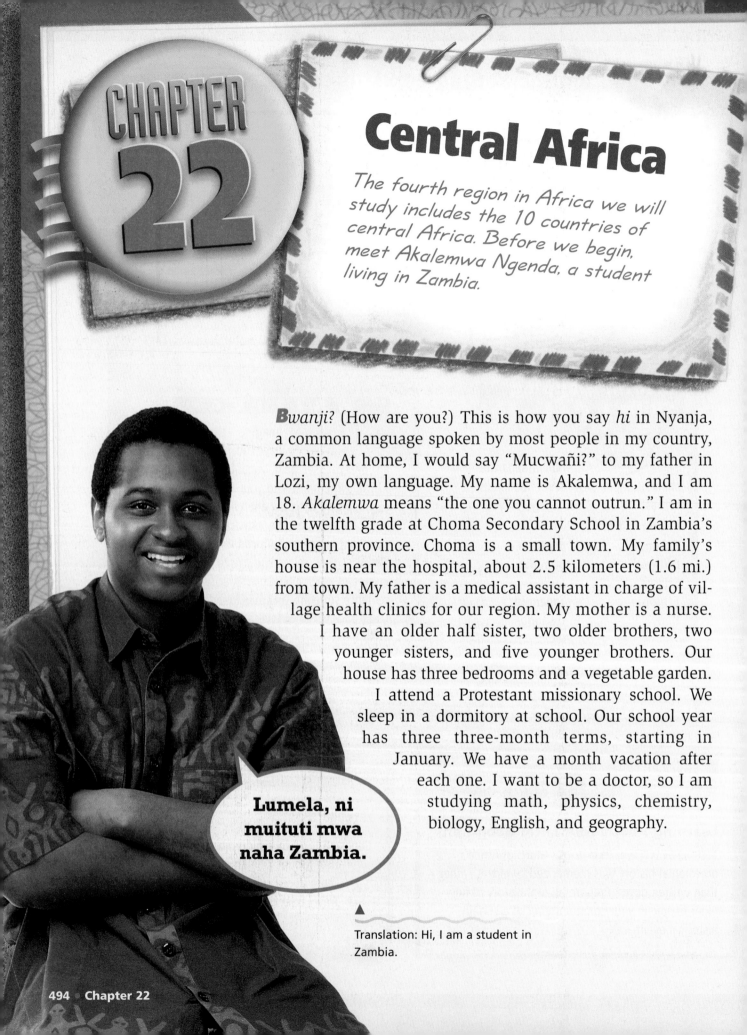

# CHAPTER 22

# Central Africa

The fourth region in Africa we will study includes the 10 countries of central Africa. Before we begin, meet Akalemwa Ngenda, a student living in Zambia.

**B**wanji? (How are you?) This is how you say *hi* in Nyanja, a common language spoken by most people in my country, Zambia. At home, I would say "Mucwañi?" to my father in Lozi, my own language. My name is Akalemwa, and I am 18. *Akalemwa* means "the one you cannot outrun." I am in the twelfth grade at Choma Secondary School in Zambia's southern province. Choma is a small town. My family's house is near the hospital, about 2.5 kilometers (1.6 mi.) from town. My father is a medical assistant in charge of village health clinics for our region. My mother is a nurse. I have an older half sister, two older brothers, two younger sisters, and five younger brothers. Our house has three bedrooms and a vegetable garden.

I attend a Protestant missionary school. We sleep in a dormitory at school. Our school year has three three-month terms, starting in January. We have a month vacation after each one. I want to be a doctor, so I am studying math, physics, chemistry, biology, English, and geography.

**Lumela, ni muituti mwa naha Zambia.**

Translation: Hi, I am a student in Zambia.

# Section 1 Physical Geography

## Read to Discover

1. What are the major physical features of central Africa?
2. What climates, plants, and animals are found in the region?
3. What major natural resources does central Africa have?

## Define

basin
canopy
copper belt
periodic markets

## Locate

Congo Basin
Western Rift Valley
Lake Tanganyika
Lake Malawi
Congo River
Zambezi River

### WHY IT MATTERS

The rain forests of Central Africa are home to many plant and animal species. Use CNNfyi.com or other current events sources to find information about rain forests around the world. Record your findings in your journal.

A copper and wood religious artifact from Gabon

## Central Africa: Physical-Political

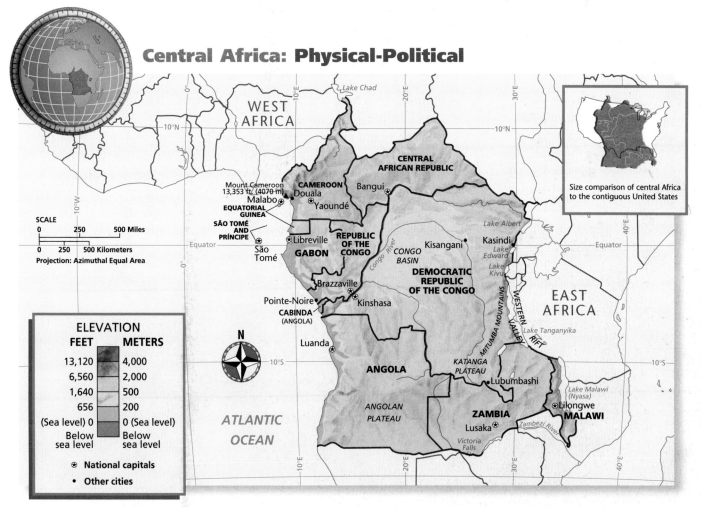

Size comparison of central Africa to the contiguous United States

SCALE
0    250    500 Miles
0    250    500 Kilometers
Projection: Azimuthal Equal Area

ELEVATION

| FEET | METERS |
|------|--------|
| 13,120 | 4,000 |
| 6,560 | 2,000 |
| 1,640 | 500 |
| 656 | 200 |
| (Sea level) 0 | 0 (Sea level) |
| Below sea level | Below sea level |

⊛ National capitals
• Other cities

WEST AFRICA
Lake Chad
CENTRAL AFRICAN REPUBLIC
Mount Cameroon 13,353 ft. (4070 m)
CAMEROON
Bangui
Douala
Malabo
Yaoundé
EQUATORIAL GUINEA
SÃO TOMÉ AND PRÍNCIPE
Libreville
GABON
REPUBLIC OF THE CONGO
São Tomé
Equator
Lake Albert
Kisangani
Kasindi
Lake Edward
CONGO BASIN
Congo River
Lake Kivu
DEMOCRATIC REPUBLIC OF THE CONGO
Brazzaville
Pointe-Noire
Kinshasa
CABINDA (ANGOLA)
MITUMBA MOUNTAINS
WESTERN RIFT VALLEY
EAST AFRICA
Lake Tanganyika
Luanda
KATANGA PLATEAU
ANGOLA
Lubumbashi
Lake Malawi (Nyasa)
ANGOLAN PLATEAU
ZAMBIA
Lusaka
Lilongwe
MALAWI
Zambezi River
Victoria Falls
ATLANTIC OCEAN

📶 internet connect 🌐go.hrw.com

GO TO: **go.hrw.com**
KEYWORD: **SK3 CH22**
FOR: **Web sites about central Africa**

**Our Amazing Planet**

**O**ne of the Congo River's most common animals is the crocodile. This sharp-toothed reptile can grow to about 20 feet (6 m) in length. It swims by sweeping its long tail from side to side.

Local people call Victoria Falls *Mosi-oa-Tunya*, which means "the smoke that thunders." The Zambezi River plunges 355 feet (108 m) over a cliff between Zambia and Zimbabwe.

# Physical Features

Central Africa stretches southward from Cameroon and the Central African Republic to Angola and Zambia. The Atlantic Ocean lies off the western coast.

Think of the region as a big soup bowl with a wide rim. Near the middle of the bowl is the Congo Basin. A **basin** is a generally flat region surrounded by higher land such as mountains and plateaus.

In northwestern Cameroon are volcanic mountains. The highest is 13,353 feet (4,070 m). Central Africa's highest mountains lie along the Western Rift Valley. Some of these snow-capped mountains rise to more than 16,700 feet (5,090 m). The Western Rift Valley stretches southeastward from the Democratic Republic of the Congo. Lake Tanganyika (tan-guhn-YEE-kuh) and Lake Malawi are found there.

Two major river systems drain the region. In the north the Congo River flows westward to the Atlantic Ocean. Hundreds of smaller rivers flow into the Congo. In the south the Zambezi (zam-BEE-zee) River flows eastward to the Indian Ocean. The Zambezi is famous for its great falls, hydroelectric dams, and lakes.

✔ **READING CHECK:** *Places and Regions* What are the major physical features of central Africa?

# Climates, Plants, and Animals

Central Africa lies along the equator and in the low latitudes. The Congo Basin and much of the Atlantic coast have a humid tropical climate. It is wet and warm all year. This climate supports a large, dense tropical rain forest.

The many different kinds of trees in the tropical rain forest form a complete **canopy**. This is the uppermost layer of the trees where the limbs spread out. Leaves block sunlight to the ground below.

Small antelopes, hyenas, elephants, and okapis live in the rain forest region. The okapi is a short-legged relative of the giraffe. Many insects also live in the forest. However, few other plants or creatures

live on the forest floor. This is because little sunlight shines through the canopy. Many animals live in the trees. They include birds, monkeys, bats, and snakes. Large areas of the tropical rain forest are being cleared rapidly for farming and timber. This threatens the plants, animals, and people who live there.

North and south of the Congo Basin are large areas with a tropical savanna climate. Those areas are warm all year, but they have distinct dry and wet seasons. There are grasslands, scattered trees, and shrubs. Only in the high eastern mountains is there a highland climate. Dry steppe and even desert climates are found in the far south.

✓ **READING CHECK:** ( *Places and Regions* ) What are the region's climates, plants, and animals?

## Resources

Central Africa's rivers are among the region's most important natural resources. They are used for travel, trade, and producing hydro-electricity. Other energy resources are oil, natural gas, and coal.

Central Africa has many minerals, including copper, uranium, tin, zinc, diamonds, gold, and cobalt. Most of Africa's copper is found in an area called the **copper belt**, which includes northern Zambia and the southern Democratic Republic of the Congo.

Central African countries have mostly traditional economies. Most people in central Africa are subsistence farmers. However, an increasing number of farmers are growing crops for sale. Common crops include coffee, bananas, and corn. In rural areas, people trade their products in **periodic markets**. A periodic market is an open-air trading market. It is set up regularly at a crossroads or in a town.

✓ **READING CHECK:** ( *Places and Regions* ) What is central Africa's most important natural resource, and why?

▲ Elephants have created a network of trails and clearings throughout the tropical rain forest. Many animals will gather at forest clearings.

**go. hrw .com** **Homework Practice Online** Keyword: SK3 HP22

## Section Review 1

**Define and explain:** basin, canopy, copper belt, periodic markets

**Working with Sketch Maps** On a map of central Africa that you draw or that your teacher provides, label the following: Congo Basin, Western Rift Valley, Lake Tanganyika, Lake Malawi, Congo River, and Zambezi River. In a box in the margin, describe the location of the highest mountains.

### Reading for the Main Idea

1. ( *Places and Regions* ) What major landforms and rivers are found in the region?

2. ( *Physical Systems* ) Why do few plants and animals live on the floor of the tropical rain forest?

3. ( *Places and Regions* ) For the most part, what type of economy do Central African countries have?

### Critical Thinking

4. **Making Generalizations and Predictions** How might central Africa become a rich region?

### Organizing What You Know

5. **Summarizing** Copy the following graphic organizer. Use it to describe the region's climates, plants and animals, and major resources.

| Climates | Plants and Animals | Resources |
|---|---|---|
|  |  |  |

## Read to Discover

1. What is the history of central Africa, and what challenges do the people there face today?
2. What are the people and cultures of central Africa like?

## Define

ivory
dialects

## Locate

Brazzaville
Kinshasa

Bag made from raffia palm fibers, Cameroon

# History

Early humans lived in central Africa many thousands of years ago. They had different languages and cultures. About 2,000 years ago new peoples began to move into the region from western Africa. Those new peoples spoke what are called Bantu languages. Today, Bantu languages are common in most of the region.

This carved mask was created by a Bantu-speaking people called the Fang. Most live in Cameroon, Equatorial Guinea, and Gabon. Their ancestors moved there in the 1800s.

**Early History** Several early Bantu-speaking kingdoms formed in central Africa. Among the most important was the Kongo Kingdom. It was located around the mouth of the Congo River. The Kongo and other central Africans traded with peoples in western and eastern Africa.

Some of the early kingdoms used slaves. In the late 1400s, Europeans came to the region. They began to trade with some African kingdoms for slaves. The Europeans took many enslaved Africans to the Americas. Europeans also wanted the region's forest products and other resources, such as **ivory**. Ivory is a cream-colored material that comes from elephant tusks. It is used in making fine furniture, jewelry, and crafts.

Some African kingdoms became richer by trading with Europeans. However, all were gradually weakened or destroyed by the Europeans. European countries divided all of central Africa into colonies in the late 1800s. The colonial powers were France, the United Kingdom, Belgium, Germany, Spain, and Portugal.

The Europeans drew colonial borders that ignored the homelands of central Africa's ethnic groups. Many groups were lumped together in colonies. These groups spoke different languages and had different ways of life. These differences resulted in conflicts, particularly after the colonies won independence.

**Modern Central Africa** African colonies did not gain independence until after World War II. The largest central African colony was the Belgian Congo. It is now the Democratic Republic of the Congo. That country won independence in 1960. Angola won independence from Portugal in 1975. It was the last European colony in central Africa.

Independence for some African countries came after bloody wars. After independence, fighting between some ethnic groups continued within the new countries. The region also became a battleground in the Cold War. The United States and the Soviet Union supported their allies in small wars throughout Africa. The region's wars killed many people and caused great damage. Some fighting continues off and on in the region.

**Challenges Today** Ending these wars is one of central Africa's many challenges today. The region's countries must also develop their natural resources more effectively. This would help the many poor people who live there. Another great challenge is stopping the spread of diseases such as malaria and AIDS. These diseases are killing millions of people and leaving many orphans.

✓ **READING CHECK:** *Human Systems* What role did Europeans play in central Africa's history?

# Culture

Today, about 100 million people live in central Africa. They belong to many different ethnic groups with varying customs.

Our Amazing Planet

In 1986 a cloud of carbon dioxide killed many people and animals near Cameroon's Lake Nyos. The lake is located in the center of a volcanic mountain. An earthquake may have allowed the gas to escape from deep in the lake.

Zambian women are grinding wheat to prepare it for cooking. They are using rods called pestles. The container is called a mortar. This technique is used for grinding many ingredients.

**Interpreting the Visual Record** **How and why is the technology used to grind wheat different from what people in other places might use?**

# CONNECTING TO *History*

A headrest from early Luanda, a Bantu kingdom

About 2,000 years ago, the movement of groups of people began to change Africa. Traders, farmers, and other people moved across the southern third of Africa. Experts believe these people came from areas that are now part of Nigeria and Cameroon. Their movement across Africa lasted many centuries. During this period new languages developed. We call them Bantu languages. The grammar and root sounds of the different Bantu languages remain similar.

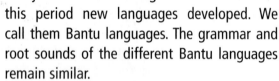

## BANTU LANGUAGES

Some Bantu speakers moved southward along the Atlantic coast. Others moved eastward to Kenya and then turned southward. Over time they reached the tip of southern Africa. The Bantu speakers mixed with peoples who already lived in these lands.

The migration of Bantu speakers had important effects on African life. They brought new ways for growing food. They used tools made of iron, which others also began to use. The Bantu-speakers of course brought their languages. Today, many Africans speak Swahili, Zulu, and other Bantu languages.

### Understanding What You Read

1. From where did the Bantu peoples come?
2. How did their movement shape Africa?

**D**o you remember what you learned about world religions? See Chapter 5 to review.

**Peoples and Languages** As you have read, many central Africans speak Bantu languages. However, those languages can be very different from each other. In fact, hundreds of different languages and **dialects** are spoken in the region. A dialect is a variation of a language.

Many people in the region speak African languages in everyday life. However, the official languages of the central African countries are European. French is the official language of the former French colonies in the north. It is also the official language of the Democratic Republic of the Congo. English is the official language in Zambia and Malawi. Portuguese is spoken in Angola and the island country of São Tomé and Príncipe. Spanish and French are the official languages of tiny Equatorial Guinea.

**Religion** Many people in the former French, Spanish, and Portuguese colonies are Roman Catholic. Protestant Christianity is most common in former British colonies. Many people practice traditional African religions. In some cases Christian and African practices have been combined.

These Cameroon juju dancers are calling attention to the destruction of the tropical rain forest. Note the headpieces that represent some of the forest's animals.

Many Muslims live near the mostly Muslim countries of the Sahel in the north. Zambia also has many Muslims as well as Hindus. The Hindus are the descendants of immigrants from southern Asia.

**Food** In most central African countries, corn, rice, grains, and fish are common foods. In the tropical rain forest, plantains, cassava, and various roots are important foods. For example, in Cameroon you might eat a dish called *fufu*. *Fufu*, a thick, pasty ball of mashed cassava, yams, or plantains, is served with chicken, fish, or a beef gravy.

**The Arts** *Makossa* dance music from Cameroon has become popular throughout Africa. It can be played with various instruments, including guitars and electric keyboards. The cities of Brazzaville and Kinshasa on the Congo River are the home of *soukous* music.

The region is also famous for carved masks, sculpture, and beautiful cotton gowns. The gowns are dyed in bright colors. They often show pictures that represent things important to the wearer.

The *likembe*, or thumb piano, was invented in the lower Congo region. Today its music is heard in many African countries.

**Interpreting the Visual Record**
**How is the *likembe* played?**

✔ **READING CHECK:** ( *Human Systems* ) What are some characteristics of the people and culture of central Africa?

# Section Review 2

**Homework Practice Online**
Keyword: SK3 HP22

**Define and explain:** ivory, dialects

**Working with Sketch Maps** On the map you created in Section 1, label Brazzaville and Kinshasa.

**Reading for the Main Idea**

1. ( *Human Systems* ) Why are many languages that are spoken today in central Africa related?

2. ( *Human Systems* ) What have been some of the causes of wars in central Africa?

3. ( *Human Systems* ) What arts are popular in the region?

**Critical Thinking**

4. **Finding the Main Idea** How did Europeans influence the culture of the region?

**Organizing What You Know**

5. **Summarizing** Copy the following graphic organizer. Use it to identify central Africa's challenges.

Challenges

# The Democratic Republic of the Congo

## Read to Discover

1. What is the history of the Democratic Republic of the Congo?
2. What are the people and culture of the country like?
3. What is the economy of the country like?

## Define

civil war

## Locate

Lubumbashi

### WHY IT MATTERS

The Democratic Republic of the Congo faces many challenges. Use CNNfyi.com or other current events sources to find out more about some of the challenges facing the nation today. Record your findings in your journal.

*A wooden cup of the Congo region*

# History

Portuguese sailors made contact with the Kongo Kingdom in 1482. Over time the slave trade and other problems weakened the Kongo and other African kingdoms.

**A Belgian Colony** In the 1870s King Leopold II of Belgium took control of the Congo Basin. The king ruled the Congo Free State as his personal colony until 1908. His soldiers treated the Africans harshly. They forced people to work in mines and on plantations. These policies brought international criticism.

The Belgian government took control of the colony from the king in 1908. Many Belgian businesses and people moved there. They mined copper and other resources. The giant colony won independence from tiny Belgium in 1960.

**A New Country** Many Belgians fled the country after 1960. There were few teachers, doctors, and other professionals left in the former colony. In addition, people from different areas and ethnic groups fought each other. These problems were partly to blame for keeping the country poor.

A dictator, who later changed his name to Mobutu Sese Seko, came to power in 1965. He was an ally of the United States during the Cold War. Mobutu changed the country's name to Zaire in 1971. During his rule, the country suffered from economic problems and government corruption.

A dancer performs in a coming-of-age ceremony for young people. Many such African traditions have survived the period of colonial rule by Europeans.

A new government took over in 1997 after a **civil war**. A civil war is a war between two or more groups within a country. The new government changed the country's name to the Democratic Republic of the Congo. However, fighting between ethnic groups has continued.

✓ **READING CHECK:** ( *Human Systems* ) What has the history of the Democratic Republic of the Congo been like?

### The Democratic Republic of the Congo

| Country | Population/ Growth Rate | Life Expectancy | Literacy Rate | Per Capita GDP |
|---------|------------------------|-----------------|---------------|----------------|
| Democratic Republic of the Congo | 53,624,718 3.1% | 47, male 51, female | 77% | $600 |
| United States | 281,421,906 0.9% | 74, male 80, female | 97% | $36,200 |

**Sources:** Central Intelligence Agency, *The World Factbook 2001;* U.S. Census Bureau

## The People

More than 50 million people live in the Democratic Republic of the Congo today. The population is very diverse. It is divided among more than 200 ethnic groups. The Kongo people are among the largest groups. These groups speak many different languages, but the official language is French. About half of the country's people are Roman Catholic. Protestant Christians, Muslims, and people who practice traditional African religions also live in the country.

More than 4 million people live in Kinshasa, the capital and largest city. Kinshasa is a river port located along the Congo River near the Atlantic coast. The crowded city has some modern buildings. However, most of the city consists of poor slums.

✓ **READING CHECK:** ( *Human Systems* ) What are the people and culture of the Democratic Republic of the Congo like?

**Interpreting the Chart** How does the literacy rate of the Democratic Republic of the Congo compare to that of the United States?

A family sells charcoal along a road in the northern Democratic Republic of the Congo. Charcoal is a major fuel source. In many rural areas there is no electricity.

▼

The Congo River lies in the distance in this photograph of Kinshasa.

## Major World Copper Producers

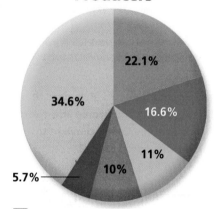

22.1%

34.6%

16.6%

11%

10%

5.7%

■ Chile

■ United States

■ Zambia, Democratic Republic of the Congo

■ Former Soviet republics

■ Peru

■ Rest of the world

Source: *Europa Book of the Year 1998*

**Interpreting the Chart** How much of the world's copper do Zambia and the Democratic Republic of the Congo produce?

## The Economy

The Democratic Republic of the Congo is a treasure chest of minerals and tropical resources. For example, the south is part of central Africa's rich copper belt. Much of the copper from the area is shipped through the city of Lubumbashi (loo-boom-BAH-shee). The country also has gold, diamonds, and cobalt. The country's tropical rain forest also supplies wood, food, rubber, and other products.

However, the country's people are very poor. Most people live in rural areas. They must farm and trade for food. Civil war, bad government, and crime have scared many foreign businesses away. As a result, the country's rich resources have helped few of its people.

For the economy to improve, the country needs peace and a stable government. Schools must be improved and better health care provided. The country also must repair and expand roads and railways. If its challenges are met, the country's resources can make the future brighter.

✓ **READING CHECK:** *Environment and Society* How might the economy of the country improve?

go.hrw.com
**Homework Practice Online**
Keyword: SK3 HP22

**Define and explain:** civil war

**Working with Sketch Maps** On the map you created in Section 2, label the Democratic Republic of the Congo and Lubumbashi. Why is Lubumbashi economically important?

**Reading for the Main Idea**

1. *Places and Regions* What European country ruled what is now the Democratic Republic of the Congo as a colony until 1960?

2. *Places and Regions* What were some problems the country faced after independence?

**Critical Thinking**

3. **Finding the Main Idea** In what ways is the Democractic Republic of the Congo a culturally diverse country? What ethnic group is among the largest?

4. **Drawing Inferences and Conclusions** How might better schools and transportation help the country's economy?

**Organizing What You Know**

5. **Sequencing** Copy the following time line. Use it to identify important groups and individuals in the history of the present-day Democratic Republic of the Congo.

1482 ———————————————— 2000

**Read to Discover**

1. What are the people and economies of the northern central African countries like?
2. What are the people and economies of the southern central African countries like?

**Define**

exclave

**Locate**

Douala
Yaoundé
Luanda

**WHY IT MATTERS**

Poverty is a serious problem for the people of northern central Africa. Use CNNfyi.com or other current events sources to find information about poverty and other challenges in the region. Record your findings in your journal.

*Fruit and nuts from the tropical rain forest*

## Northern Central Africa

Six countries make up northern central Africa. Four are Cameroon, the Central African Republic, Gabon, and the Republic of the Congo. They gained independence from France in 1960. Cameroon had been a German colony until after World War I. Tiny Equatorial Guinea gained independence from Spain in 1968. The island country of São Tomé and Príncipe won independence from Portugal in 1975.

**The People** Cameroon is by far the most populous country in this region. About 15.8 million people live there. The Central African Republic has the second-largest population, with 3.5 million. Tiny São Tomé and Príncipe has only about 165,000 people.

A large variety of ethnic groups are found in northern central Africa. Many people are moving from rural areas to cities to search for jobs. Governments are struggling to provide basic services in those crowded cities.

Douala (doo-AH-lah) and Yaoundé (yown-DAY) in Cameroon are the largest cities. Each has more than 1 million people. Douala is an important seaport on the Atlantic coast. Yaoundé is Cameroon's capital. Brazzaville, the capital of the Republic of the Congo, also has 1 million people. The city is a major Congo River port.

**The Economy** Most of the area's countries are very poor. Most people are farmers. Gabon has the strongest economy

Although the region's cities are growing rapidly, most people still live in rural areas. This small village is located in northern Cameroon. As in much of rural Africa, several buildings make up a family's home. **Interpreting the Visual Record** **What is similar about the construction of these houses?**

## Northern Central Africa

| Country | Population/Growth Rate | Life Expectancy | Literacy Rate | Per Capita GDP |
|---|---|---|---|---|
| Cameroon | 15,803,220 2.4% | 54, male 55, female | 63% | $1,700 |
| Central African Republic | 3,576,884 1.9% | 42, male 46, female | 60% | $1,700 |
| Congo, Republic of the | 2,894,336 2.2% | 44, male 51, female | 75% | $1,100 |
| Equatorial Guinea | 486,060 2.5% | 52, male 56, female | 78% | $2,000 |
| Gabon | 1,221,175 1.0% | 49, male 51, female | 63% | $6,300 |
| São Tomé and Príncipe | 165,034 3.2% | 64, male 67, female | 73% | $1,100 |
| United States | 281,421,906 0.9% | 74, male 80, female | 97% | $36,200 |

**Sources:** Central Intelligence Agency, *The World Factbook 2001;* U.S. Census Bureau

**Interpreting the Chart** Which country in the region has the smallest population? the largest?

in central Africa. More than half of the value of its economy comes from the oil industry. Oil is important in Cameroon as well as in the Republic of the Congo.

The mighty Congo River is also a vital trade and transportation route. As a result, it plays a major role in the region's economy. Many of the region's goods and farm products are shipped down river to Brazzaville. Brazzaville lies across the Congo River from Kinshasa. From Brazzaville, goods are shipped by railroad to a port on the Atlantic coast.

✓ **READING CHECK:** *Human Systems* What are the people and economies of northern central Africa like?

## Southern Central Africa

Zambia, Malawi, and Angola make up the southern part of central Africa. The British gave Zambia and Malawi independence in 1964. Angola won independence from Portugal in 1975.

**The People** The populations of the three southern countries are nearly the same size. They range from about 9.7 million in Zambia to more than 11 million in Angola. Angola and Zambia are much larger in area than Malawi. Large parts of Angola and Zambia have few people. Most people in the region live in rural areas. They grow crops and herd cattle and goats.

Riverboats carry the king of Zambia's Lozi people to a dryland home during the flooding season. This event is an annual ritual for the Lozi, who live in western Zambia. As in other central African countries, many different ethnic groups live in Zambia.

**Interpreting the Visual Record** How can you tell these people are taking part in a formal tradition?

Angola's capital, Luanda, is the southern region's largest city. More than 2 million people live there. Seen from the sea, Luanda looks like a modern city. The city has many high-rise buildings and factories. Unfortunately, Luanda and its people have suffered from poverty and years of war. Rebels fought the Portuguese in the 1960s and early 1970s. After independence, the country plunged into civil war. Fighting has continued off and on since then. Many people have been killed or injured by land mines.

**The Economy** In peacetime, the future of Angola could be bright. There are many places with fertile soils. The country has large deposits of diamonds and oil. The oil is found offshore north of Luanda and in the **exclave** of Cabinda. An exclave is part of a country that is separated by territory of other countries. Cabinda is separated from the rest of Angola by the Democratic Republic of the Congo.

Much of Zambia's income comes from rich copper mines. However, 85 percent of Zambia's workers are farmers. Most of the country's energy comes from hydroelectric dams and power plants along rivers.

Almost 90 percent of Malawi's people live in rural areas. Nearly all of them are farmers. The building of factories and industries has been slow. Aid from other countries and religious missionaries has been important to the economy.

## Southern Central Africa

| COUNTRY | POPULATION/ GROWTH RATE | LIFE EXPECTANCY | LITERACY RATE | PER CAPITA GDP |
|---|---|---|---|---|
| Angola | 10,366,031 2.2% | 37, male 40, female | 42% | $1,000 |
| Malawi | 10,548,250 1.5% | 37, male 38, female | 56% | $900 |
| Zambia | 9,770,199 1.9% | 37, male 38, female | 78% | $880 |
| United States | 281,421,906 0.9% | 74, male 80, female | 97% | $36,200 |

**Sources:** Central Intelligence Agency, *The World Factbook 2001*; U.S. Census Bureau

**Interpreting the Chart** Which country in the region has the highest literacy rate?

✓ **READING CHECK:** ( *Human Systems* ) What are the people and economies of the southern central African countries like?

Homework Practice Online
go.hrw.com
Keyword: SK3 HP22

# Section Review 4

**Define and explain:** exclave

**Working with Sketch Maps** On the map you created in Section 3, label the countries of northern and southern central Africa, and Douala, Yaoundé, and Luanda. In a box in the margin, describe Luanda.

## Reading for the Main Idea

1. ( *Places and Regions* ) Which country has the strongest economy in central Africa?

2. ( *Environment and Society* ) What significance does oil have in the economies of many countries in the region?

3. ( *Human Systems* ) What has happened in Angola since that country won its independence?

## Critical Thinking

4. **Analyzing Information** Why is Brazzaville important to the region's economy?

## Organizing What You Know

5. **Summarizing** Copy the following graphic organizer. Divide it into nine rows below the headings. Use it to list the countries discussed in this section. Then identify the European country that colonized each central African country. Finally, list the date each country won independence.

| Country | European colonial ruler | Year of independence |
|---|---|---|
| | | |

# Reviewing What You Know

## Building Vocabulary

On a separate sheet of paper, write sentences to define each of the following words.

1. basin
2. canopy
3. copper belt
4. periodic markets
5. ivory
6. dialects
7. civil war
8. exclave

## Reviewing the Main Ideas

1. (Places and Regions) What two river systems are most important in central Africa? Where are the region's highest mountains found?
2. (Human Systems) How were the Bantu languages introduced to central Africa?
3. (Human Systems) What religions are practiced by people in the Democratic Republic of the Congo?
4. (Human Systems) What European countries once colonized central Africa?
5. (Environment and Society) How important has oil been to Gabon's economy?

## Understanding Environment and Society

### Health

Malaria has been a problem for thousands of years. Create a presentation about malaria. In preparing your presentation, consider the following:
• What malaria is and how it is spread.
• Where malaria is most common.
• What health experts have done to fight malaria.

## Thinking Critically

1. **Drawing Inferences and Conclusions** Why do few large animals live on the floor of central Africa's tropical rain forests?
2. **Finding the Main Idea** How have borders drawn by European colonial powers contributed to ethnic conflicts in central Africa?
3. **Analyzing Information** How have their locations on major rivers or near important natural resources aided the growth of cities such as Brazzaville and Lubumbashi?
4. **Drawing Inferences and Conclusions** Why do you think European languages are still the official languages in the countries of central Africa?
5. **Finding the Main Idea** How did the Cold War contribute to problems in central Africa?

## Map ACTIVITY

On a separate sheet of paper, match the letters on the map with their correct labels.

Congo Basin

Western Rift
 Valley

Lake
 Tanganyika

Lake Malawi

Congo River

Zambezi River

Kinshasa

Lubumbashi

Douala

Luanda

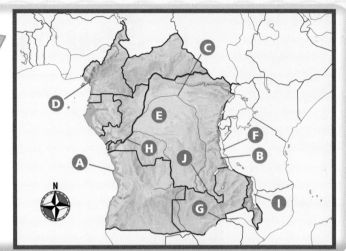

## Mental Mapping Skills ACTIVITY

On a separate sheet of paper, draw a freehand map of central Africa. Make a key for your map and label the following:

Angola

Democratic
 Republic of the
 Congo

Malawi

Republic of
 the Congo

Zambia

## WRITING ACTIVITY

Imagine that you have been hired to write a magazine article describing challenges facing central Africans. Write a descriptive headline and a brief summary for your proposed article. The article should cover the region's economic, political, and health challenges. Be sure to use standard grammar, spelling, sentence structure, and punctuation.

# Alternative Assessment

## Portfolio ACTIVITY

**Learning About Your Local Geography**

**Group Project** Plan a periodic market. List items grown or produced locally. Then design an advertisement to persuade farmers or craft makers to sell at the market.

### internet connect

Internet Activity: **go.hrw.com**
KEYWORD: **SK3 GT22**

Choose a topic to explore about central Africa:
- Identify threats to the Congo Basin.
- Visit the people of central Africa.
- Learn the importance of African cloth.

# Southern Africa

*Southern Africa is a region going through many changes. Some people in the area have a comfortable lifestyle, but others live in severe poverty.*

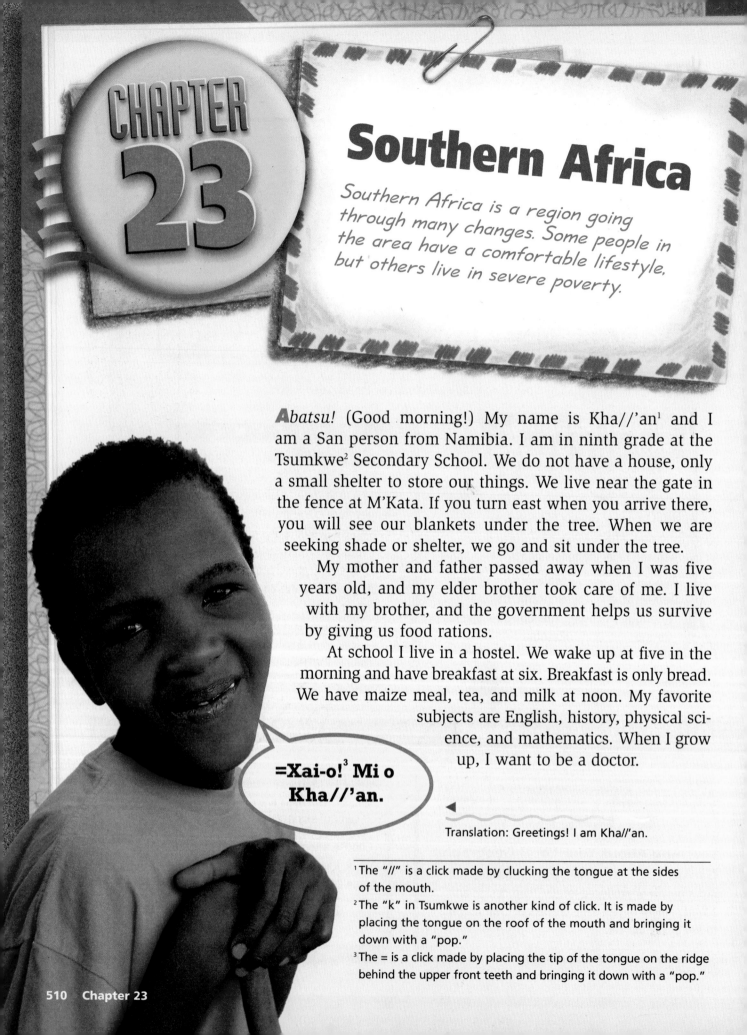

**A**batsu! (Good morning!) My name is Kha//'an[1] and I am a San person from Namibia. I am in ninth grade at the Tsumkwe[2] Secondary School. We do not have a house, only a small shelter to store our things. We live near the gate in the fence at M'Kata. If you turn east when you arrive there, you will see our blankets under the tree. When we are seeking shade or shelter, we go and sit under the tree.

My mother and father passed away when I was five years old, and my elder brother took care of me. I live with my brother, and the government helps us survive by giving us food rations.

At school I live in a hostel. We wake up at five in the morning and have breakfast at six. Breakfast is only bread. We have maize meal, tea, and milk at noon. My favorite subjects are English, history, physical science, and mathematics. When I grow up, I want to be a doctor.

**=Xai-o![3] Mi o Kha//'an.**

◄

Translation: Greetings! I am Kha//'an.

[1] The "//" is a click made by clucking the tongue at the sides of the mouth.

[2] The "k" in Tsumkwe is another kind of click. It is made by placing the tongue on the roof of the mouth and bringing it down with a "pop."

[3] The = is a click made by placing the tip of the tongue on the ridge behind the upper front teeth and bringing it down with a "pop."

# Section 1 Physical Geography

## Read to Discover

1. What are the major physical features and climates of southern Africa?
2. What resources are found in the region?

## Define

enclaves
the veld
pans

## Locate

Drakensberg
Inyanga Mountains
Cape of Good Hope
Kalahari Desert
Namib Desert
Orange River
Aughrabies Falls
Limpopo River

### WHY IT MATTERS

The rich mineral resources of southern Africa, such as gold, diamonds, and platinum, are important to international economic stability. Use CNN fyi.com or other current events sources to find examples of how this region is using its resources. Record your findings in your journal.

*Pygmy mouse lemur*

## Southern Africa: Physical-Political

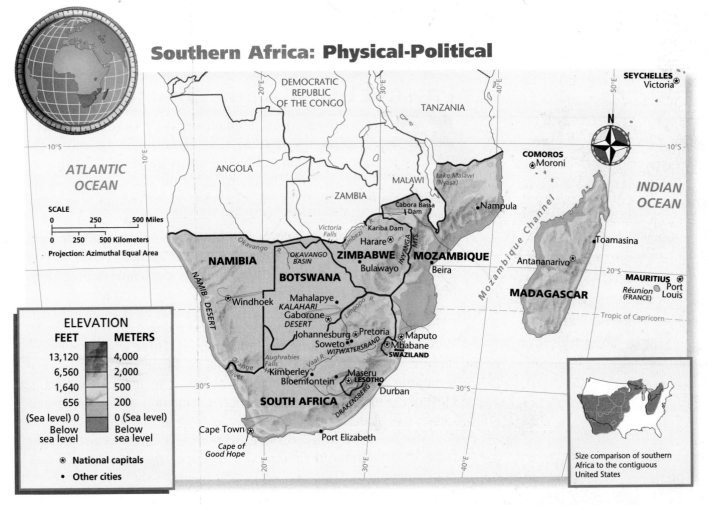

ELEVATION

| FEET | METERS |
|------|--------|
| 13,120 | 4,000 |
| 6,560 | 2,000 |
| 1,640 | 500 |
| 656 | 200 |
| (Sea level) 0 | 0 (Sea level) |
| Below sea level | Below sea level |

⊛ National capitals
• Other cities

Size comparison of southern Africa to the contiguous United States

The Drakensberg range rises sharply in eastern South Africa.

**Interpreting the Visual Record** Why do you think tourists are attracted to this region?

**D**rakensberg means "dragon mountain" in the Afrikaans language. The Zulu, one of the peoples of the region, call it Kwathlamba, meaning "barrier of pointed spears" or "piled-up rocks."

# Countries of the Region

Lining southern Africa's coasts are Namibia (nuh-MI-bee-uh), South Africa, and Mozambique (moh-zahm-BEEK). Botswana (bawt-SWAH-nah), Zimbabwe (zim-BAH-bway), and the two tiny countries of Lesotho (luh-SOH-toh) and Swaziland (SWAH-zee-land) are all land-locked. Lesotho and Swaziland are **enclaves**—countries surrounded or almost surrounded by another country. Madagascar (ma-duh-GAS-kuhr), off the east coast, is the world's fourth-largest island.

# Physical Features and Climate

The surface of southern Africa is dominated by a large plateau. The southeastern edge of this plateau is a mountain range called the Drakensberg (DRAH-kuhnz-buhrk). The steep peaks rise as high as 11,425 feet (3,482 m) from the plains along the coast. Farther north, another mountain range, the Inyanga (in-YANG-guh) Mountains, forms the plateau's eastern edge.

The open grassland areas of South Africa are known as **the veld** (VELT). Kruger National Park covers 7,523 square miles (19,485 sq km) of the veld. The park contains lions, leopards, elephants, rhinoceroses, hippos, baboons, and antelope.

**Climate** The region's climates range from desert to cool uplands. Winds carry moisture from the Indian Ocean. These winds are forced upward by the Drakensberg and Inyanga Mountains. The eastern slopes are rainy, but climates are drier farther inland and westward. Most of the interior of southern Africa is semiarid and has steppe and savanna vegetation.

Near the Cape of Good Hope, winter rains and summer drought create a Mediterranean climate. Off the Cape, storms and rough seas are common.

**Deserts and Rivers** In the central and western parts of the region, savanna and steppe give way to two major deserts. The Kalahari (ka-luh-hahr-ee) occupies most of Botswana. Here ancient streams have drained into low, flat areas, or **pans**. Minerals left behind when the water evaporated form a glittering white layer.

The Namib (NAH-mib) Desert lies along the Atlantic coast. Inland, the Namib blends into the Kalahari and steppe. Almost no rain falls, but at night fog rolls in from the ocean. Some plants and animals survive by using the fog as a source of water.

Southern Africa has some of the world's most spectacular rivers and waterfalls. The Orange River passes through the Aughrabies (oh-KRAH-bees) Falls as it flows to the Atlantic. When the water is highest, the Aughrabies Falls are several miles wide. The water tumbles down 19 separate waterfalls. The Limpopo (lim-POH-poh) River is the region's other major river. It flows into the Indian Ocean.

✓ **READING CHECK:** *Places and Regions* What are southern Africa's physical features and climate?

⌨ internet connect

GO TO: go.hrw.com
KEYWORD: SK3 CH23
FOR: Web sites about southern Africa

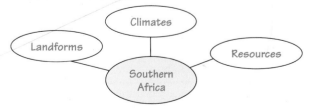

▲ The Orange River flows down the spectacular Aughrabies Falls. The falls are near the Namibian border in northwestern South Africa.

## Resources

Southern Africa is very rich in mineral resources. Gold, diamonds, platinum, copper, uranium, coal, and iron ore are all found in the region. Where rain is plentiful or irrigation is possible, farmers can grow a wide range of crops. Ranchers raise livestock on the high plains. Some nomadic herders still live in desert areas.

✓ **READING CHECK:** *Places and Regions* What are the main resources of southern Africa?

go.hrw.com **Homework Practice Online**

Keyword: SK3 HP23

# Section Review 1

**Define and explain:** enclaves, the veld, pans

**Working with Sketch Maps** On a map of southern Africa that you draw or that your teacher provides, label the following: Drakensberg, Inyanga Mountains, Cape of Good Hope, Kalahari Desert, Namib Desert, Orange River, Aughrabies Falls, and Limpopo River. The Orange River forms part of the border between what two countries?

### Reading for the Main Idea

1. *Places and Regions* What are the major landforms of southern Africa?

2. *Places and Regions* What are the main natural resources of the region?

3. *Physical Systems* How do physical processes affect southern Africa's climate?

### Critical Thinking

4. **Drawing Inferences and Conclusions** How do you think the climate off the Cape of Good Hope has affected shipping in the area?

### Organizing What You Know

5. **Summarizing** Copy the following graphic organizer. Use it to list the landforms, climates, and resources of southern Africa.

Climates

Landforms

Resources

Southern Africa

### Read to Discover

**1.** What was the early history of southern Africa like?

**2.** How did Europeans gain control of southern Africa, and what changes did this cause?

### Define
Boers

### Locate
Cape Town

*Modern sculpture from Zimbabwe*

#### WHY IT MATTERS

Among the many problems facing southern Africa are frequent natural disasters. Use CNN fyi.com or other **current events** sources to find examples of these disasters and how officials work to deal with them. Record your findings in your journal.

▲

Ancient rock art of southern Africa often includes hunters and animals.

**Interpreting the Visual Record** What do these images suggest about the people who made them?

## Early History

Southern Africa's landscape and climate have influenced the region's history. For example, monsoon winds blow from the Indian Ocean to southern Africa from November to February. From May to September the wind blows the other way, from Africa to Asia. Ancient ships used these winds to make regular trading voyages between the two continents.

**The Khoisan** Some of the oldest human fossils have been found in southern Africa. By about 18,000 B.C., groups of hunter-gatherers were living throughout the mainland region. They left distinctive paintings of people and animals on rock surfaces. Some descendants of these people still live in certain desert regions. They speak languages of the Khoisan language family, which share unusual "click" sounds. However, most Khoisan people were absorbed into groups that moved into the region later.

**Bantu Migrations** Some 1,500–2,000 years ago a different group of people spread from central Africa into southern Africa. They spoke another family of languages known as Bantu. Today, most southern Africans speak one of the more than 200 Bantu languages. Scholars believe the early Bantu people introduced the use of iron to make tools. The Bantu are also thought to have introduced cattle herding to the region.

**Shona and Swahili** By about A.D. 1000 one Bantu group, the Shona, had built an empire. It included much of what is now Zimbabwe and Mozambique. They farmed, raised cattle, and traded gold with other groups on the coast. They also constructed stone-walled towns called *zimbabwe*. The largest town, now called Great Zimbabwe, may have had 10,000 to 20,000 residents. Great Zimbabwe was abandoned in the 1400s.

Among Great Zimbabwe's trading partners were the Swahili-speaking people of the east coast. These were Africans who had adopted Islam and many Arab customs by the A.D. 1100s. The Swahili-speakers were sailors and traders. Archaeologists have found Chinese porcelain at Great Zimbabwe. This suggests that Africa and East Asia were connected by an Indian Ocean trade network.

People fish with nets in the Indian Ocean. Fishing is an important industry in Mozambique and Madagascar.

**Madagascar** Madagascar's early history is quite different from the rest of southern Africa. Madagascar's first settlers came from Asia, rather than Africa, about A.D. 700. The island's culture shows the influence of both Africa and Asia. Malagasy, Madagascar's official language, is related to languages spoken in Indonesia. Malagasy also includes many words from the Bantu language family.

**Mozambique** In the early 1500s the Portuguese set up forts in Mozambique. They hoped to take over the region's gold trade from the Swahili-speakers and Arabs. The Portuguese also established large estates along the Zambezi River that used slave labor. In the 1700s and 1800s Mozambique became an important part of the slave trade. Africans were captured there and sent as slaves to Brazil and other parts of the world.

✔ **READING CHECK:** ( *Human Systems* ) What were some key events in the early history of southern Africa?

The Portuguese built this prison in Mozambique in the 1800s.

**Interpreting the Visual Record**
**How might this architecture reflect European influences?**

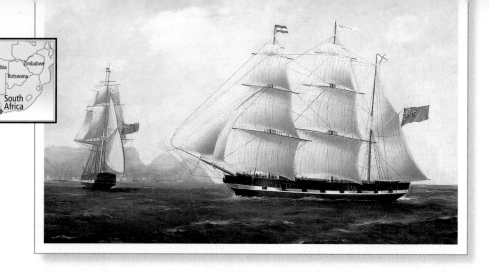

In this painting, British ships sail past the Cape of Good Hope. The distinctively shaped Table Mountain is visible in the distance.
**Interpreting the Visual Record How are these ships propelled?**

**M**uch of southern Africa was a malaria zone. Quinine, a medicine made from a South American tree, could combat malaria. Using this medicine, Europeans were able to move into lowland areas where malaria was common.

In this 1935 photograph, elephant tusks and rhino horns are inspected in a London warehouse.

# The Dutch, British, and Portuguese in South Africa

The land around the Cape of Good Hope lacked the gold and copper of the Zambezi Valley. However, it had a Mediterranean climate. It also was free of the mosquitoes and tsetse flies that spread tropical diseases. In 1652 the Dutch set up a trade station at a natural harbor near the Cape. This small colony would eventually become known as Cape Town. It provided supplies to Dutch ships sailing between the Dutch East Indies and Europe. The Dutch brought in slaves to work in the colony. Some were Malays from Southeast Asia. Others were Africans bought at slave markets in other parts of Africa.

**Afrikaners and Afrikaans** The main language spoken in the colony was Dutch. Over time, Khoisan, Bantu, and Malay words were added, creating a new language called Afrikaans. White descendants of the original colonists are called Afrikaners. Some European men married Khoisan or Malay women. People descended from Malays, Khoisan, or a mixture of these with Europeans are called Coloureds.

**A British Colony** Afrikaner frontier farmers called **Boers** gradually spread out from the original colony. Then, in the early 1800s, Great Britain took over the area of the Cape. The Boers resisted the British colonial government. Many Boers packed all their belongings into wagons and moved farther east and north. This movement was called the Great Trek.

At about the same time, a Bantu-speaking group, the Zulu, became a powerful fighting force. They conquered the surrounding African peoples, creating their own empire. When the Boers moved into the northern plains, they entered Zulu territory. The two sides clashed over control of the land. Eventually the Zulu were challenged by the British and defeated after a series of battles.

**Trade in Slaves and Ivory** The British banned slavery in their empire in 1833. The Portuguese colonies of Angola and Mozambique remained as Africa's main slave markets. The slave trade eventually ended in the late 1800s. African trade began to focus on ivory—the tusks of elephants. Hunters wiped out the entire elephant population in some parts of southern Africa.

**Diamonds, Gold, and Colonies** In the 1860s diamonds were discovered in the northern part of the Cape Colony. In 1886 gold was discovered in the Transvaal, an area controlled by the Boers. Thousands of British and others came to South Africa. Railroads were built to connect the interior with the coast.

As the British moved north from the Cape Colony, some Boers moved into what is now Botswana. Afraid that the Boers would take over his country, Botswana's ruler asked for British protection. In 1885 Botswana (then known as Bechuanaland) came under British control. What is now Namibia became German South-west Africa—a German colony. In 1889 what is now Zimbabwe came under control of the British South Africa Company as part of Rhodesia. It became a self-governing British colony in 1923.

**South Africa** In 1899 tensions over land and mineral wealth led to war between the Boers and the British. The Boers were greatly outnumbered, but held off the British army for three years. In the end the Boers were defeated. Their territory was added to the British colony of South Africa. In 1920, following Germany's defeat in World War I, Namibia was placed under South Africa's control.

This old steam train still operates in South Africa. The British built this and other railroads during the colonial period.

**Interpreting the Visual Record**
**Why did the Europeans connect the interior with the coast?**

✓ **READING CHECK:** ( *Human Systems* ) How did Europeans gain control of southern Africa, and what changes did this cause?

---

Homework Practice Online
Keyword: SK3 HP23

**Define and explain:** Boers

**Working with Sketch Maps** On the map you created in Section 1, label Cape Town. What were the advantages of Cape Town's location?

**Reading for the Main Idea**

1. ( *Human Systems* ) How did the Bantu affect the history of southern Africa?

2. ( *Human Systems* ) How do archaeologists believe Chinese porcelain came to Great Zimbabwe?

**Critical Thinking**

3. **Finding the Main Idea** How did the slave trade affect southern Africa?

4. **Analyzing Information** What European groups settled in southern Africa? How did these groups interact with each other?

**Organizing What You Know**

5. **Sequencing** Copy the following time line. Use it to mark important events in the history of southern Africa from 18,000 B.C. to 1920.

|—————————————————————————|
18,000 B.C.                                              1920

## Section 3: South Africa Today

### Read to Discover

1. What was South Africa's policy of apartheid?
2. What factors led to the end of apartheid?
3. What is South Africa's economy like?
4. What are South Africa's prospects for the future?

### Define

apartheid
townships
sanctions

### Locate

Witwatersrand
Johannesburg
Durban
Port Elizabeth

Zulu in traditional warrior's clothing

Nelson Mandela was sentenced to life imprisonment in 1964 but was released in 1990. In 1994 he was elected president of South Africa.

## Racial Divisions

In the early 1900s South Africa's government, which was dominated by Afrikaners, became increasingly racist. Some black South Africans opposed the government. They formed the African National Congress (ANC) in 1912 to defend their rights. However, the trend toward racial division and inequality continued.

After World War II South Africa became an independent country. The South African government set up a policy of separation for its different peoples. This policy was called **apartheid**, meaning "apartness." The government divided people into three groups: whites, coloureds and Asians, and blacks—the overwhelming majority. Coloureds and Asians were only allowed to live in certain areas. Each African tribe or group was given its own rural "homeland."

The whites owned most of the good farmland. They also owned the mines and other natural resources. Black Africans had no rights in white areas. Blacks' land, housing, and health care were poor compared to those for whites. Education for blacks was limited, and classes were often taught in Afrikaans. Coloureds' facilities were poor but slightly better than those for blacks. People who protested these rules were sent to prison. One of those imprisoned was a lawyer named Nelson Mandela, a leader of the ANC.

Many blacks found work in white-owned industries, mines, shops, and farms. They had to live in separate areas called **townships**. These were often crowded clusters of tiny homes. They were far from the jobs in the cities and mines.

✓ **READING CHECK:** *Human Systems* What was apartheid?

## Pressure against South Africa

Many people around the world objected to South Africa's apartheid laws. Some countries banned trade with South Africa. Some companies in the United States and Europe refused to invest their money in South Africa. Many international scientific and sports organizations refused to include South Africans in their meetings and competitions. These penalties, called **sanctions**, were intended to force South Africa to end apartheid.

**South Africa and Its Neighbors** During the 1960s, 1970s, and 1980s other countries in southern Africa gained their independence from colonial rule. British colonists in Rhodesia protested Britain's decision to grant independence. They declared their own white-dominated republic in 1970. This break resulted in years of violence and civil war. Finally the white government agreed to hold elections. They turned the country over to the black majority. The new government renamed the country Zimbabwe.

Mozambique was granted independence in 1975 after 10 years of war against Portuguese rule. However, rebels backed by Rhodesia and South Africa plunged Mozambique into another long war. Despite violent resistance, Namibia continued to be ruled by South Africa until independence in 1990.

**The End of Apartheid** As other countries in southern Africa gained independence, South Africa became more and more isolated. Protest within the country increased. The government outlawed the ANC. Many ANC members were jailed or forced to leave the country. Antiapartheid protesters turned increasingly to violence. South African

In townships like Kayalitsha, black workers lived in crude shacks.

**Interpreting the Visual Record** **How did the apartheid system affect the roles and responsibilities of South Africans?**

Members of the African National Congress lead a rally celebrating Nelson Mandela's release from prison.

These are uncut, or rough, diamonds. Diamonds are the hardest mineral. This makes them useful for certain types of cutting and drilling.

Interpreting the Visual Record

**Why do you think some diamonds are more suitable for industrial uses than for jewelry?**

forces attacked suspected rebel bases in neighboring countries like Botswana and Zimbabwe.

Finally, in the late 1980s South Africa began to move away from the apartheid system. In 1990 the government released Nelson Mandela from prison. Mandela was elected president in 1994 after all South Africans were given the right to vote.

Today all races have equal rights in South Africa. Public schools and universities are open to all, as are hospitals and transportation. However, economic equality has been slow in coming. White South Africans are still wealthier than the vast majority of black South Africans. Also, divisions between different black ethnic groups have caused new tensions. Still, South Africans now hope for a better future.

✔ **READING CHECK:** *Human Systems* Why and how did South Africa do away with apartheid?

## South Africa's Economy

South Africa's government is trying to create jobs and better conditions for black workers and farmers. However, South Africa's mineral wealth and industries are still mostly owned by white people. Even officials who favor reform are afraid that too-rapid change will weaken the economy. They fear it will drive educated and wealthy whites to leave the country. The government has avoided taking white-owned farmland to divide among black farmers.

South Africa's energy resources include coal and hydroelectric power. Rich uranium mines provide fuel for nuclear power plants. In addition to gold and diamonds, mineral resources include copper, platinum, iron ore, and chromium.

The Witwatersrand region around Johannesburg is the continent's largest industrial area. South African and foreign companies build computers, cars, televisions, and many other products needed for modern life. The major port is Durban on the Indian Ocean coast. Cape Town and Port Elizabeth are other important ports.

✔ **READING CHECK:** *Human Systems* How has apartheid continued to affect South Africa's economy today?

## South Africa's Future

South Africa has more resources and industry than most African countries but faces severe problems. It must begin to deliver equal education and economic opportunities to the entire population.

◄ Cape Town has grown into a large industrial city. In this photograph, the harbor is visible beyond the tall buildings of the business district.

New problems have arisen since the end of apartheid. Crime has increased in the large cities. Also, South Africa, like the rest of the region, is facing a terrible AIDS epidemic.

There are 11 official languages in South Africa, although English is used in most areas. South Africa produces fine wines from the region around Cape Town. It has a unique cooking style combining Dutch, Malay, and African foods. The country also has a lively tradition of literature and the arts. Today, traditional ethnic designs are used in clothing, lamps, linens, and other products. These are sold to tourists and locals alike.

### South Africa

| COUNTRY | POPULATION/ GROWTH RATE | LIFE EXPECTANCY | LITERACY RATE | PER CAPITA GDP |
|---------|------------------------|-----------------|---------------|----------------|
| South Africa | 43,586,097 0.3% | 48, male 49, female | 82% | $8,500 |
| United States | 281,421,906 0.9% | 74, male 80, female | 97% | $36,200 |

**Sources**: Central Intelligence Agency, *The World Factbook 2001*; U.S. Census Bureau

✓ **READING CHECK:** *Places and Regions* What are the challenges faced by South Africa?

**Interpreting the Visual Record** **What is South Africa's per capita GDP?**

go.hrw.com **Homework Practice Online** Keyword: SK3 HP23

## Section Review 3

**Define and explain:** apartheid, townships, sanctions

**Working with Sketch Maps** On the map you created in Section 2, label Witwatersrand, Johannesburg, Durban, and Port Elizabeth.

### Reading for the Main Idea

**1.** *Human Systems* What was the system of apartheid, and how did it affect the roles and responsibilities of South Africans?

**2.** *Human Systems* How did people around the world protest apartheid?

**3.** *Places and Regions* What challenges remain for South Africa?

### Critical Thinking

**4. Analyzing Information** Why is South Africa the continent's most economically developed country?

### Organizing What You Know

**5. Summarizing** Use this graphic organizer to list information about life in South Africa during apartheid and since the system ended.

| During apartheid | Since apartheid ended |
|------------------|----------------------|
| | |

# Section 4

## The Other Southern African Countries

### Read to Discover

1. What groups have influenced Namibia's culture?
2. What factors have helped Botswana's economy?
3. What is Zimbabwe's economy like?
4. Why has Mozambique remained so poor?
5. What events have marked Madagascar's recent history?

### Define

Organization of African Unity (OAU)

### Locate

Windhoek
Gaborone
Harare
Maputo

#### WHY IT MATTERS

Like many African countries, Madagascar has suffered in recent years from environmental problems. Use CNNfyi.com or other **current events** sources to find examples of how Madagascar is coping with its environmental problems. Record your findings in your journal.

*Grilled shrimp from Mozambique*

## Namibia

Most Namibians live in the savannas of the north or in the cooler central highlands. Windhoek, the capital, is located in these highlands. About 7 percent of the population is white, mainly of German descent. The rest of the population is divided among several different ethnic groups. Most Namibians are Christian. English is the official language. However, schooling was in Afrikaans until recently.

At independence in 1990, white farmers held most of the productive land. Most of Namibia's income comes from the mining of diamonds, copper, lead, zinc, and uranium. Fishing in the Atlantic Ocean and sheep ranching are also important sources of income.

Namibian culture shows many different influences. In many rocky areas, ancient rock engravings and paintings of the Khoisan are preserved. Beer and pastries reflect the period of German colonization.

✓ **READING CHECK:** *Human Systems* What are Namibia's cultural influences?

A San grandmother and child drink water from an ostrich egg. The San people traditionally lived by hunting and gathering. However, just a few live this way today.

**Interpreting the Visual Record** **What factors do you think might lead many San people to give up their traditional way of life?**

▼

## Botswana

Botswana is a large, landlocked, semiarid country. Thanks to mineral resources and stable political conditions, Botswana is one of Africa's success stories. Cattle ranching and mining of copper and diamonds are the principal economic activities. Recently, international companies have set up factories here. A new capital,

Gaborone, was built after independence. Like the other countries of the region, Botswana belongs to the **Organization of African Unity (OAU)**. The OAU, founded in 1963, tries to promote cooperation between African countries.

Botswana's population is less than 1.6 million. About 79 percent belong to a single ethnic group, the Tswana. Most of the population live in the savanna and steppe areas of the east and south. The San and other minority groups mostly live in the northern swamps and the Kalahari Desert. About half of Botswana's people are Christian. The rest follow traditional African religions.

Botswana's major river, the Okavango, flows from Angola into a huge basin. The swamps of this basin are home to elephants, crocodiles, antelope, lions, hyenas, and other animals. Many tourists travel to Botswana to see these wild animals in their habitat.

Traditional crafts of Botswana include ostrich-eggshell beadwork and woven baskets with complex designs. People there also produce colorful wool tapestries and rugs.

✔ **READING CHECK:** ( *Places and Regions* ) Why might Botswana be considered a success story?

▲

The Okavango River spreads out to form a large swampy area. Dense vegetation allows only small boats to move through the narrow channels.

## Zimbabwe

Zimbabwe's capital is Harare. Zimbabwe gained independence in 1980. Since then, the country has struggled to create a more equal distribution of land and wealth. White residents make up less than 1 percent of the population. However, they still own most of the large farms and ranches.

Zimbabwe exports tobacco, corn, sugar, and beef. It now manufactures many everyday items, including shoes, batteries, and radios. Exports of gold, copper, chrome, nickel, and tin are also important to Zimbabwe's economy.

The AIDS epidemic threatens to kill hundreds of thousands of Zimbabwe's people, leaving many orphans behind. These effects will make economic growth harder. Other diseases such as malaria and tuberculosis are often deadly. There are also tensions between the majority Shona people and the minority Ndebele.

Artists in Zimbabwe have revived the tradition of stone sculpture found at Great Zimbabwe. Some of the larger pieces are among the most striking examples of modern art in the world.

✔ **READING CHECK:** ( *Places and Regions* ) What is Zimbabwe's economy like?

### Other Southern African Countries

| COUNTRY | POPULATION/ GROWTH RATE | LIFE EXPECTANCY | LITERACY RATE | PER CAPITA GDP |
|---|---|---|---|---|
| Botswana | 1,586,119 0.5% | 37, male 38, female | 70% | $6,600 |
| Madagascar | 15,982,563 3% | 53, male 58, female | 80% | $800 |
| Mozambique | 19,371,057 1.3% | 37, male 36, female | 42% | $1,000 |
| Namibia | 1,797,677 1.4% | 42, male 39, female | 38% | $4,300 |
| Zimbabwe | 11,365,366 0.2% | 39, male 36, female | 85% | $2,500 |
| United States | 281,421,906 0.9% | 74, male 80, female | 97% | $36,200 |

**Sources:** Central Intelligence Agency, *The World Factbook 2001;* U.S. Census Bureau

**Interpreting the Chart Which countries are the least economically developed in the region, according to the chart?**

# CONNECTING TO *History*

In 1884–85, representatives of Europe's colonial countries met in Berlin. These countries included Belgium, France, Germany, Great Britain, Italy, Portugal, and Spain. Each was conquering areas in Africa. Their claims to territory were beginning to overlap. Leaders began to worry that a rivalry in Africa might trigger a war in Europe.

The Berlin conference was called to agree to boundaries for these African colonies. No Africans were invited to the conference. The European representatives divided up Africa among themselves. The new borders sometimes followed physical features, such as lakes and mountains. Many simply followed straight lines of latitude or longitude. Often people from the same ethnic group were separated by the new borders. In other places, ethnic groups hostile to each other were grouped together.

Most of the European colonies in Africa became independent after 1960. However, the leaders of the new African countries have

## AFRICA'S BORDERS

Cartoon of France and Britain dividing Africa

mostly avoided drawing new boundary lines. So these countries still struggle with the borders they inherited from the Berlin Conference. These borders have made it hard for many African countries to build national loyalty among their citizens.

**Understanding What You Read**

1. How were Africa's borders established?
2. What consequences have these borders had for modern Africa?

## BUILD on WHAT You Know

**D**o you remember what you learned about uneven resource distribution? See Chapter 5 to review.

## Mozambique

Mozambique is one of the world's poorest countries. Its economy was badly damaged by civil war after independence from Portugal. Today, Mozambique's ports of Maputo—the capital—and Beira once again ship many products from interior Africa. The taxes collected on these shipments are an important source of revenue. Energy sources include coal and new hydroelectric dams on the Zambezi River. Plantations grow cotton, cashews, sugar, and tea.

Most of Mozambique's people belong to various Bantu ethnic groups. Each group has its own language. However, the country's official language is Portuguese. About 30 percent of the people are Christian, and 20 percent are Muslim.

Mozambique is famous for its fiery pepper or *peri-peri* sauces. They are often served on shrimp and rice.

✓ **READING CHECK:** ( *Places and Regions* ) What factor limited Mozambique's economic development?

# Madagascar

Madagascar is a former French colony. It was ruled by a socialist dictator until the early 1990s. At that point the people demanded a new political system. The optimism that came with democracy faded as the new leaders struggled with poverty. Surprisingly, in 1996 the people voted the former dictator back into power.

Nearly all of Madagascar's people are still very poor. There is little industry. Most of the country's income comes from exports of coffee, sugar, vanilla, and cloves. Most of the people depend on subsistence farming.

Madagascar has many animals found nowhere else. This is because the island has been separated from the African mainland for millions of years. Some 40 species of lemurs, relatives of apes, live only on this island. However, destruction of the rain forests threatens many of Madagascar's animals with extinction.

Malagasy and French are spoken throughout Madagascar. About 55 percent of the people follow traditional African religions. Some 40 percent are Christian, and about 5 percent are Muslim.

✓ **READING CHECK:** ( *Places and Regions* ) What has Madagascar's recent history been like?

▲

Remnants of French culture can still be seen in Madagascar.

**Interpreting the Visual Record** **Which of these vendors' foods suggests a connection to French culture?**

Homework Practice Online
Keyword: SK3 HP23

**Define and explain:** Organization of African Unity (OAU)

**Working with Sketch Maps** On the map you created in Section 3, label Windhoek, Gaborone, Harare, and Maputo. Which cities are located on the plateau of the southern African interior?

### Reading for the Main Idea

**1.** ( *Human Systems* ) How have diseases affected Zimbabwe's people and economy?

**2.** ( *Human Systems* ) How did civil war affect Mozambique?

**3.** ( *Environment and Society* ) What minerals does Namibia have, and how do they affect its economy?

## Critical Thinking

**4. Drawing Inferences and Conclusions** How do you think the fact that Botswana's population is almost entirely of a single ethnic group has affected its politics?

## Organizing What You Know

**5. Summarizing** Copy the following graphic organizer. Use it to list information about southern African cultures.

| Country | Culture |
|---|---|
| Namibia | |
| Botswana | |
| Zimbabwe | |
| Mozambique | |
| Madagascar | |

# Reviewing What You Know

## Building Vocabulary

On a separate sheet of paper, write sentences to define each of the following words.

1. enclaves
2. the veld
3. pans
4. Boers
5. apartheid
6. townships
7. sanctions
8. Organization of African Unity (OAU)

## Reviewing the Main Ideas

1. **Places and Regions** What are southern Africa's two deserts like?

2. **Environment and Society** What made it possible for early southern Africans to trade with Asians?

3. **Human Systems** What did the original Bantu migrants bring to southern Africa?

4. **Environment and Society** How have mineral resources affected South Africa?

5. **Human Systems** What three racial groups were defined and separated by apartheid? Which group made up the majority of the population?

## Understanding Environment and Society

### City Location

Johannesburg grew because of gold deposits nearby. Cape Town's location is excellent for a port. Create a presentation on why cities are located where they are. As you prepare your presentation you may want to think about the following:

- What physical features seem to contribute to the growth of cities around the world?
- Which major cities of southern Africa owe their locations to deposits of minerals?

## Thinking Critically

1. **Drawing Inferences and Conclusions** In what parts of southern Africa do you think most farming takes place? Why?

2. **Analyzing Information** What finally motivated the South African government to end the apartheid system?

3. **Summarizing** Who were the Afrikaners, and what role did they play in the history of southern Africa?

4. **Summarizing** What factors have slowed the economic development of the countries in this region?

5. **Finding the Main Idea** How did the discovery of diamonds and gold affect the settlement of Europeans in southern Africa?

## Map ACTIVITY

On a separate sheet of paper, match the letters on the map with their correct labels.

Drakensberg

Inyanga Mountains

Cape of Good Hope

Kalahari Desert

Namib Desert

Orange River

Limpopo River

Harare

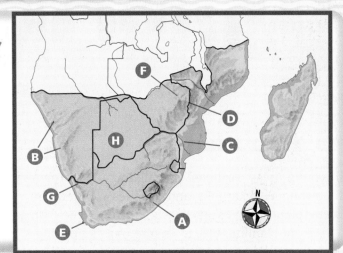

## Mental Mapping Skills ACTIVITY

On a separate sheet of paper, draw a freehand map of southern Africa. Make a key for your map and label the following:

Botswana

Madagascar

Mozambique

Namibia

South Africa

Zimbabwe

## WRITING ACTIVITY

Write a brief essay in which you compare and contrast Botswana and Mozambique. How are the physical features of these two countries similar or different? How do these features affect the economies of Botswana and Mozambique? What are the major industries? Be sure to use standard grammar, spelling, sentence structure, and punctuation.

# Alternative Assessment

## Portfolio ACTIVITY

**Learning About Your Local Geography**

**Mineral Resources** Southern Africa is rich in minerals. Working in a group, list mineral resources found in your area. Then create a display about local mineral resources.

### internet connect

Internet Activity: go.hrw.com
KEYWORD: SK3 GT23

Choose a topic to explore about southern Africa:

- Explore the Namib Desert.
- Go on a South African safari.
- Investigate apartheid.

# ENVIRONMENT

## Kenya's Tree Planters

Ten million young trees scattered throughout Kenya offer new hope to farmers and families. The trees were planted by women who farm these lands. "We are planting trees to ensure our own survival," says Wangari Maathai. She is the founder of Kenya's Green Belt Movement.

### Deforestation

Like many other developing countries, Kenya is a country of farmers and herders. The most productive farmlands are in the highlands. This area was once green with trees and plants. Over the past century, however, much of this land has been cleared. Today, less than 10 percent of the original forests remain. Many trees were cut for firewood, which people use for cooking.

Without tree roots to hold the soil in place, the land eroded. The land was losing its fertility.

Farmers moved to the savannas in search of better land.

Wangari Maathai recognized what was happening. "When I would visit the village where I was born," she says, "I saw whole forests had been cleared for cultivation and timber. People were moving onto hilly slopes and riverbeds and marginal areas that were only bush when I was a child." Maathai was shocked to find children suffering from malnutrition. People were no longer eating foods such as beans and corn. Instead, they were eating refined foods such as rice. They were doing this because these foods need less cooking—and thus less firewood.

### The Green Belt Movement

On June 5, 1977, in honor of World Environment Day, Maathai and a few supporters planted seven trees in Nairobi, Kenya's capital. Thus began the Green Belt Movement. This movement then spread through the Kenyan highlands and captured people's attention around the world.

From the beginning, Maathai knew that the success of her efforts depended mainly on women. In Kenya, men tend cash crops such as coffee and cotton. Women collect firewood and grow corn, beans, and other food crops. It is the women who grow the food their families eat. The women were the first to see the connection between poor soil and famine.

◄

Many of the trees in Kenya's highlands have been cleared for crops.

The movement's workers encouraged women in Kenya to plant trees. They pointed out that women would not have to walk miles to collect firewood. They would have wood available nearby for fires, fences, and buildings. If the tree seedlings survived, the women would also be paid a small sum of money.

First, a few small nurseries were started to give out free seedlings. The nurseries are staffed by local women who are paid for their work. Nurseries also train and pay local people known as Green Belt Rangers. The Rangers visit farms, check on seedlings, and offer advice.

Before long, nurseries were appearing in communities throughout the highlands. Kenyan women talked to friends and neighbors about the benefits of planting trees. Neighbors encouraged Esther Wairimu to plant seedlings. Five years later, her fields were surrounded by mango, blue gum, and other trees. "I have learned that a tree… is life," she says.

Today, the advantages of planting trees are clear. Farmers now have fuel and shade. Even

▲

Workers from the Green Belt Movement teach schoolchildren in Kenya how to care for tree seedlings.

more important, the soil is being protected from erosion. The number of Green Belt nurseries has grown to 3,000. Most are run by women.

### Expanding the Movement

Maathai believes that local people must work together to protect the environment. She stresses that the Green Belt Movement relies on farmers. The movement receives little government support. Most of the money comes from small personal donations.

Now Maathai dreams of spreading her movement to other African countries. "We must never lose hope…," she says. "One person *can* make a difference."

Wangari Maathai (right) has encouraged Kenyan women to plant millions of trees. Women are paid for the seedlings they plant that survive.

▼

## Your Turn

Working in small groups, think of an environmental issue facing your community or state.

1. Develop a plan that demonstrates how "one person can make a difference."

2. Present your group's plan to the rest of the class.

# Building Skills for Life: Understanding Ecosystems

Elephants have adapted to the ecosystem of Africa's Namib Desert.

The plants and animals in an area, together with the nonliving parts of their environment, form an ecosystem. An important thing to remember about ecosystems is that each part is interconnected.

Life on Earth depends on the energy and nutrients flowing through ecosystems. Energy and nutrients move between plants, animals, and soils through food chains and food webs.

Most ecosystems involve three groups of organisms: producers, consumers, and decomposers. Producers make their own food. Plants are producers. They make food by combining carbon dioxide, nutrients from the soil, sunlight, and water. Consumers are unable to make food. They have to get food from producers or from other consumers. Humans are consumers. We eat plants (producers) and animals (consumers). Decomposers get food from dead organisms and wastes. Bacteria and fungi are decomposers.

Like all forms of life, humans depend on ecosystems for survival. Knowing how ecosystems work helps us understand how we are connected to both living and nonliving things. It can also help us manage, protect, and use our environments wisely.

## THE SKILL

1. Describe an ecosystem in the region where you live. What plants and animals live there? How are they connected?

2. Make a table showing some of the producers, consumers, and decomposers in an ecosystem. What do you think would happen if one of these groups suddenly disappeared?

3. Try to identify some ways that human activities have changed ecosystems in your community. Have some plants or animals disappeared?

# HANDS on GEOGRAPHY

Like all organisms, lions are part of an ecosystem. Lions survive by killing and eating other animals, such as zebras and gazelles. After lions have killed an animal, they eat their fill. Then other animals such as vultures and hyenas eat what is left.

The lion itself is food for other organisms. Small animals like ticks, fleas, and mosquitoes drink the lion's blood. The lion's waste serves as food for organisms that live in the soil. When the lion dies, it will be eaten by other animals.

How does the lion fit into its ecosystem? You can answer this question by drawing a connections web. These guidelines will help you get started.

1. Draw a picture of a lion.

2. Think of interactions that lions have with other parts of their environment.

3. Include these interactions in your drawing. For example, lions eat zebras, so you could add a zebra to your drawing.

4. Draw lines connecting the lion to other parts of its environment. For example, you could draw a line connecting the lion and the zebra.

5. Be sure to extend the connections to include nonliving parts of the environment as well. For example, lions eat zebras, zebras eat grass, and grass depends on sunlight.

6. Continue making connections on your diagram. When you are done, answer the Lab Report questions.

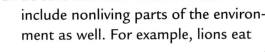

# Lab Report

1. Label the producers, consumers, and decomposers on your connections web. To which group do lions belong?

2. How are lions dependent on nonliving parts of their environment?

3. Imagine there are no more lions. How do you think the ecosystem shown in your connections web would be affected?

# UNIT 7

## East and Southeast Asia

Shwedagon Pagoda, Yangon, Myanmar

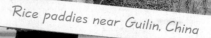
Rice paddies near Guilin, China

# A Peace Corps Volunteer in Mongolia

*Matt Heller served as a Peace Corps volunteer in Mongolia. He worked as an English teacher and coordinated a greenhouse reconstruction project.* **WHAT DO YOU THINK?** *What kinds of changes would you have to make in your life to live in Mongolia?*

I've been a Peace Corps volunteer in Mongolia for eighteen months. I live in a *ger*, a tent with a small wood stove in the center. It is strong and practical, perfect for a nomadic herder. I, however, am an English teacher in a small school in rural Mongolia. *Ger* life is hard. It makes twenty-year-olds look thirty-five. It makes your soul hard.

Mongolians are very proud of their history. Once, while sitting on the train going from Ulaanbaatar to my own town, Bor-Undur, a Mongolian pointed to his arm and said, "In here is the blood of Genghis Khan. Beware." There is no argument to that statement. I responded, "Yes, older brother (a respectful title addressed to elders), your country is beautiful. Mongolians are lucky."

Along with many other things, I'm learning how Mongolians live. In the steppe there is very little snow, only biting wind and dust. It gets as cold as −50 degrees, not counting the wind chill factor. If I leave tea in a mug, it will freeze by morning. I've broken three mugs that way.

A Mongolian outside his home

*Festival of Ages parade, Kyoto, Japan*

## Understanding Primary Sources

**1.** What conclusion does Matt Heller make about Mongolians and their past?

**2.** How does Matt Heller describe the climate in Mongolia?

*Giant panda*

# East and Southeast Asia

## Elevation Profile

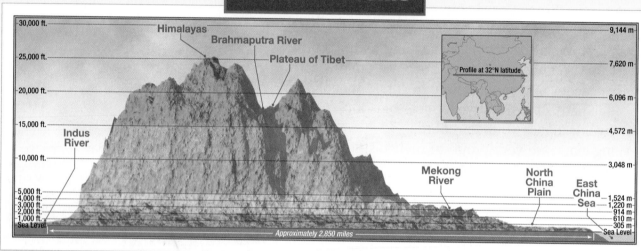

- 30,000 ft. — 9,144 m
- 25,000 ft. — 7,620 m
- 20,000 ft. — 6,096 m
- 15,000 ft. — 4,572 m
- 10,000 ft. — 3,048 m
- 5,000 ft. — 1,524 m
- 4,000 ft. — 1,220 m
- 3,000 ft. — 914 m
- 2,000 ft. — 610 m
- 1,000 ft. — 305 m
- Sea Level — Sea Level

Himalayas
Brahmaputra River
Plateau of Tibet
Indus River
Mekong River
North China Plain
East China Sea

Profile at 32°N latitude

Approximately 2,850 miles

## The United States and East and Southeast Asia:
## Comparing Sizes

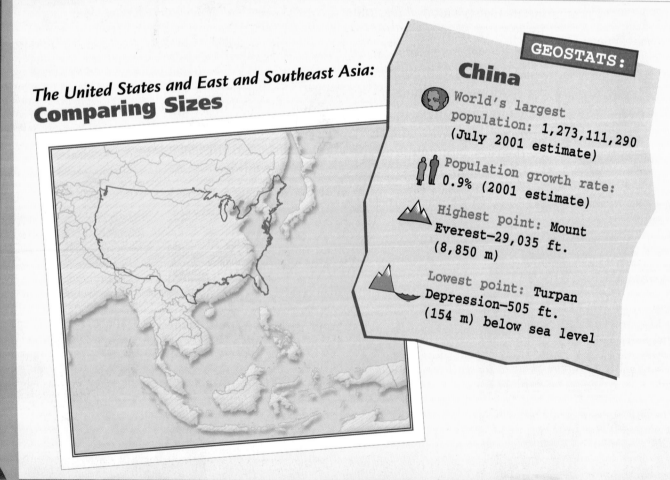

### GEOSTATS:
### China

World's largest population: 1,273,111,290 (July 2001 estimate)

Population growth rate: 0.9% (2001 estimate)

Highest point: Mount Everest—29,035 ft. (8,850 m)

Lowest point: Turpan Depression—505 ft. (154 m) below sea level

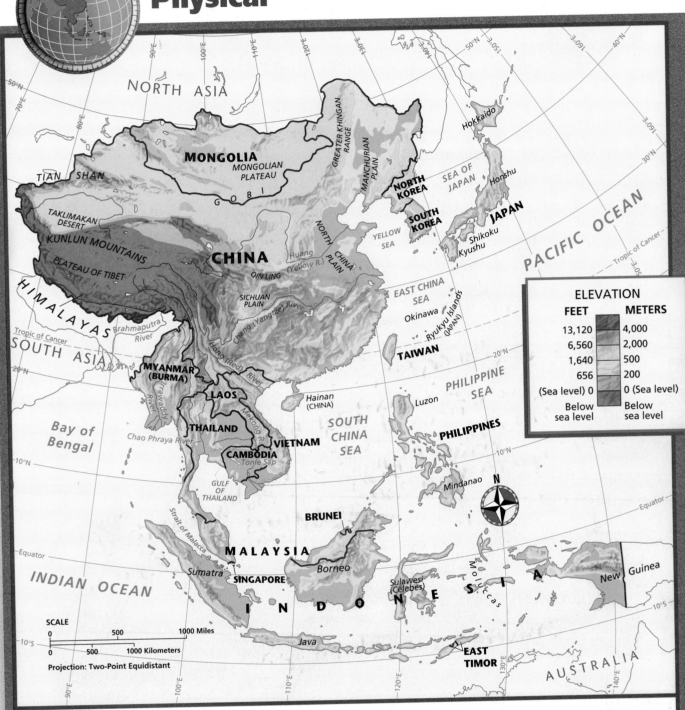

NORTH ASIA

MONGOLIA
MONGOLIAN PLATEAU

TIAN SHAN

TAKLIMAKAN DESERT

KUNLUN MOUNTAINS

PLATEAU OF TIBET

HIMALAYAS

Brahmaputra River

Tropic of Cancer

SOUTH ASIA

GOBI

GREATER KHINGAN RANGE

MANCHURIAN PLAIN

NORTH CHINA PLAIN

CHINA

Huang (Yellow R.)

QIN LING

SICHUAN PLAIN

Chang (Yangtze) River

NORTH KOREA

SOUTH KOREA

SEA OF JAPAN

Hokkaido

Honshu

JAPAN

Shikoku

Kyushu

YELLOW SEA

EAST CHINA SEA

Okinawa

Ryukyu Islands (JAPAN)

TAIWAN

PACIFIC OCEAN

Tropic of Cancer

MYANMAR (BURMA)

Irrawaddy River

LAOS

THAILAND

Chao Phraya River

Mekong R.

VIETNAM

CAMBODIA

Tonle Sap

GULF OF THAILAND

Hong (Red) River

Hainan (CHINA)

SOUTH CHINA SEA

Luzon

PHILIPPINE SEA

PHILIPPINES

Mindanao

Bay of Bengal

BRUNEI

MALAYSIA

Strait of Malacca

Sumatra

SINGAPORE

Borneo

INDONESIA

Sulawesi (Celebes)

Moluccas

New Guinea

INDIAN OCEAN

Java

EAST TIMOR

AUSTRALIA

Equator

**ELEVATION**

| FEET | METERS |
|---|---|
| 13,120 | 4,000 |
| 6,560 | 2,000 |
| 1,640 | 500 |
| 656 | 200 |
| (Sea level) 0 | 0 (Sea level) |
| Below sea level | Below sea level |

SCALE
0 — 500 — 1000 Miles
0 — 500 — 1000 Kilometers
Projection: Two-Point Equidistant

1. *Places and Regions* Which of the region's physical features could make travel and trade difficult?

2. *Places and Regions* What are the region's three largest island countries?

3. *Places and Regions* Which countries have territory on the mainland and on islands?

## Critical Thinking

4. **Comparing** Compare this map to the **population map**. What physical features might prevent western China from becoming densely populated? Why might eastern China be so densely populated?

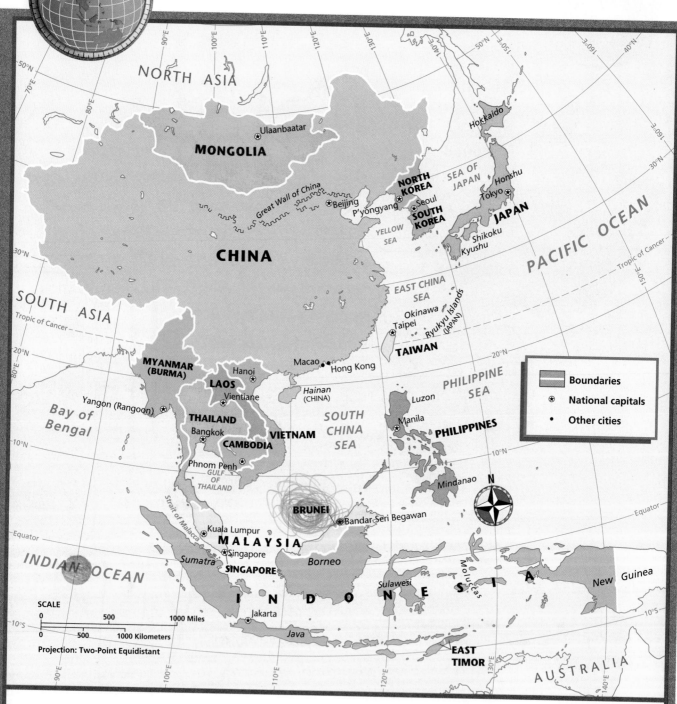

1. **Places and Regions** Which country entirely on the mainland shares a border with just one of the region's other countries?

2. **Places and Regions** What is the only landlocked country in Southeast Asia? Which country in East Asia is landlocked?

## Critical Thinking

3. **Comparing** Compare this map to the **physical map** of the region. Which physical feature forms the border of southwestern China? Which other physical features form natural borders in the region?

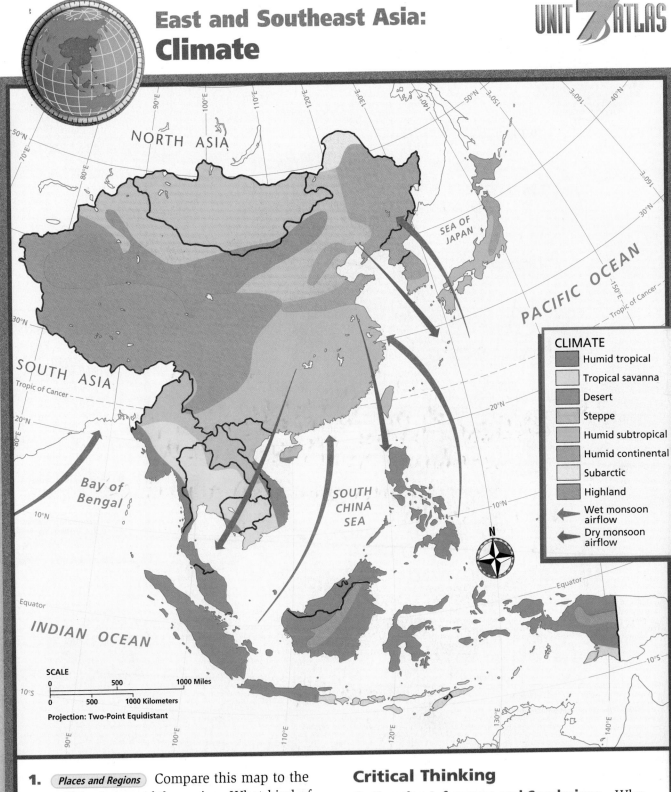

CLIMATE
- Humid tropical
- Tropical savanna
- Desert
- Steppe
- Humid subtropical
- Humid continental
- Subarctic
- Highland
- ← Wet monsoon airflow
- ← Dry monsoon airflow

NORTH ASIA

SOUTH ASIA

Tropic of Cancer

Bay of Bengal

INDIAN OCEAN

Equator

SEA OF JAPAN

PACIFIC OCEAN

Tropic of Cancer

SOUTH CHINA SEA

Equator

SCALE
0        500        1000 Miles
0        500        1000 Kilometers
Projection: Two-Point Equidistant

1. **Places and Regions** Compare this map to the **political map** of the region. What kind of climate does most of Mongolia have?

2. **Physical Systems** Study the monsoon airflow patterns shown on this map. In which directions do the wet and dry monsoons flow?

## Critical Thinking

3. **Drawing Inferences and Conclusions** Why might this region have such a variety of climate types?

4. **Drawing Inferences and Conclusions** Why might the South China Sea be stormy?

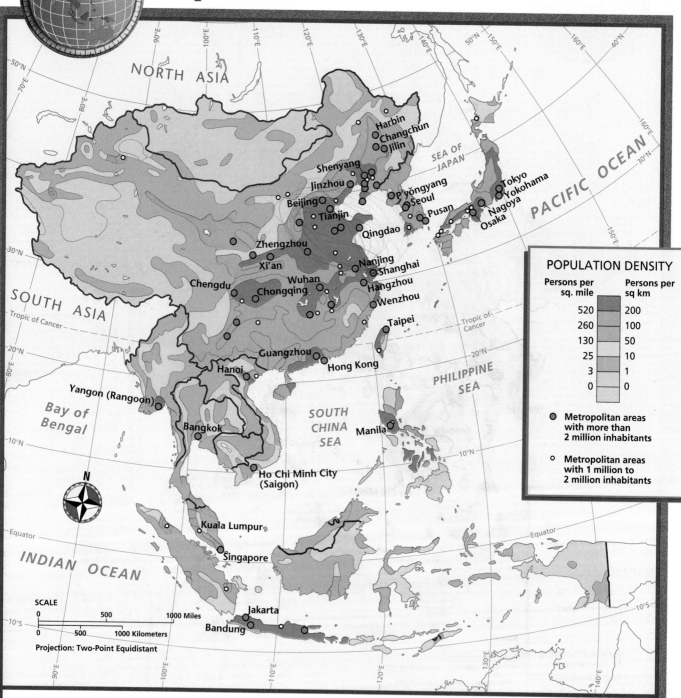

NORTH ASIA

SEA OF
JAPAN

PACIFIC OCEAN

Harbin
Changchun
Jilin
Shenyang
Jinzhou
Beijing
Tianjin
P'yŏngyang
Seoul
Pusan
Qingdao
Tokyo
Yokohama
Nagoya
Osaka

SOUTH ASIA

Zhengzhou
Xi'an
Chengdu
Wuhan
Chongqing
Nanjing
Shanghai
Hangzhou
Wenzhou

Tropic of Cancer

Taipei

Tropic of Cancer

Guangzhou
Hanoi
Hong Kong

PHILIPPINE
SEA

Yangon (Rangoon)

Bay of
Bengal

Bangkok

SOUTH
CHINA
SEA

Manila

Ho Chi Minh City
(Saigon)

Kuala Lumpur
Singapore

Equator                                                 Equator

INDIAN OCEAN

Jakarta
Bandung

SCALE
0          500        1000 Miles
0     500      1000 Kilometers
Projection: Two-Point Equidistant

## POPULATION DENSITY

| Persons per sq. mile | Persons per sq km |
|---|---|
| 520 | 200 |
| 260 | 100 |
| 130 | 50 |
| 25 | 10 |
| 3 | 1 |
| 0 | 0 |

● Metropolitan areas with more than 2 million inhabitants

○ Metropolitan areas with 1 million to 2 million inhabitants

**1.** *Places and Regions* What is the population density in the area between Shanghai and Beijing?

**2.** *Environment and Society* Compare this map to the **physical map** of the region. Which physical features help explain the low population density in western China?

## Critical Thinking

**3. Analyzing Information** Use the map on this page to create a chart, graph, database, or model of population centers in East and Southeast Asia.

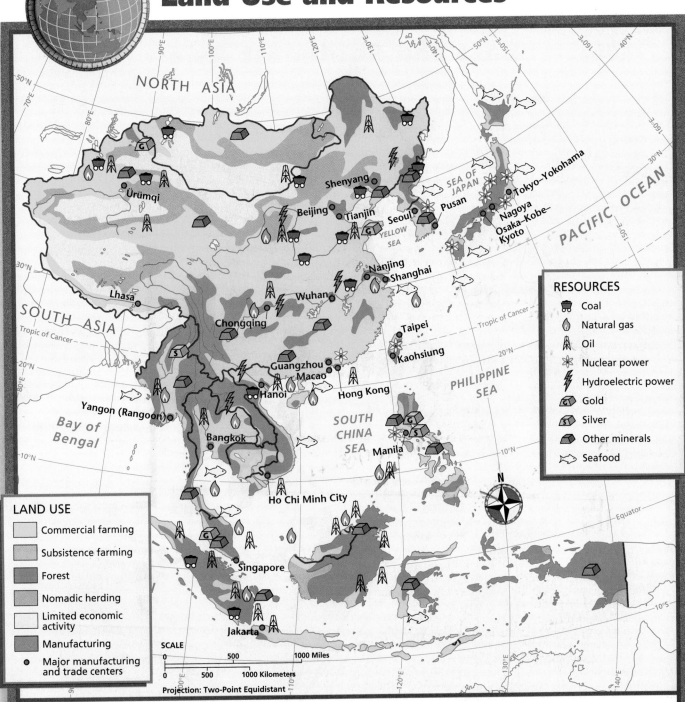

LAND USE
- Commercial farming
- Subsistence farming
- Forest
- Nomadic herding
- Limited economic activity
- Manufacturing
- ● Major manufacturing and trade centers

RESOURCES
- Coal
- Natural gas
- Oil
- Nuclear power
- Hydroelectric power
- G Gold
- S Silver
- Other minerals
- Seafood

SCALE
0        500        1000 Miles
0    500    1000 Kilometers
Projection: Two-Point Equidistant

**1.** (Places and Regions) Which two countries have large areas where nomadic herding is common?

**2.** (Places and Regions) Where in China is most commercial farming found? In which countries is subsistence farming common?

## Critical Thinking

**3. Analyzing Information** Use the map on this page to create a chart, graph, database, or model of economic activities in East and Southeast Asia.

# Fast FACTS

# East and Southeast Asia

## BRUNEI

**CAPITAL:**
Bandar Seri Begawan

**AREA:**
2,228 sq. mi. (5,770 sq km)

**POPULATION:**
343,653

**MONEY:**
Bruneian dollar (BND)

**LANGUAGES:**
Malay (official), English, Chinese

**NUMBER OF TELEVISIONS:**
201,900 (1998)

## JAPAN

**CAPITAL:**
Tokyo

**AREA:**
145,882 sq. mi. (377,835 sq km)

**POPULATION:**
126,771,662

**MONEY:**
yen (JPY)

**LANGUAGES:**
Japanese

**NUMBER OF TELEVISIONS:**
86,500,000 (1997)

## CAMBODIA

**CAPITAL:**
Phnom Penh

**AREA:**
69,900 sq. mi. (181,040 sq km)

**POPULATION:**
12,491,501

**MONEY:**
riel (KHR)

**LANGUAGES:**
Khmer (official), French

**NUMBER OF TELEVISIONS:**
94,000 (1997)

## LAOS

**CAPITAL:**
Vientiane

**AREA:**
91,428 sq. mi. (236,800 sq km)

**POPULATION:**
5,635,967

**MONEY:**
kip (LAK)

**LANGUAGES:**
Lao (official), French, English, ethnic languages

**NUMBER OF TELEVISIONS:**
52,000

## CHINA

**CAPITAL:**
Beijing

**AREA:**
3,705,386 sq. mi. (9,596,960 sq km)

**POPULATION:**
1,273,111,290

**MONEY:**
yuan (CNY)

**LANGUAGES:**
Mandarin, Yue, other forms of Chinese

**NUMBER OF TELEVISIONS:**
400,000,000 (1997)

## MALAYSIA

**CAPITAL:**
Kuala Lumpur

**AREA:**
127,316 sq. mi. (329,750 sq km)

**POPULATION:**
22,229,040

**MONEY:**
ringgit (MYR)

**LANGUAGES:** Bahasa Melayu (official), English, Chinese dialects, ethnic languages

**NUMBER OF TELEVISIONS:**
10,800,000 (1999)

## INDONESIA

**CAPITAL:**
Jakarta

**AREA:**
741,096 sq. mi. (1,919,440 sq km)

**POPULATION:**
228,437,870

**MONEY:**
Indonesian rupiah (IDR)

**LANGUAGES:**
Bahasa Indonesia (official), English, Dutch, Javanese

**NUMBER OF TELEVISIONS:**
13,750,000

## MONGOLIA

**CAPITAL:**
Ulaanbaatar

**AREA:**
604,247 sq. mi. (1,565,000 sq km)

**POPULATION:**
2,654,999

**MONEY:**
togrog/tugrik (MNT)

**LANGUAGES:**
Khalkha Mongol, Turkic, Russian

**NUMBER OF TELEVISIONS:**
168,800 (1999)

Countries not drawn to scale.

## MYANMAR
## (Burma)

**CAPITAL:**
Yangon (Rangoon)

**AREA:**
261,969 sq. mi.
(678,500 sq km)

**POPULATION:**
41,994,678

**MONEY:**
kyat (MMK)

**LANGUAGES:**
Burmese, many ethnic
languages

**NUMBER OF TELEVISIONS:**
320,000 (2000)

## NORTH KOREA

**CAPITAL:**
P'yŏngyang

**AREA:**
46,540 sq. mi.
(120,540 sq km)

**POPULATION:**
21,968,228

**MONEY:**
North Korean won (KPW)

**LANGUAGES:**
Korean

**NUMBER OF TELEVISIONS:**
1,200,000 (1997)

## PHILIPPINES

**CAPITAL:**
Manila

**AREA:**
115,830 sq. mi.
(300,000 sq km)

**POPULATION:**
82,841,518

**MONEY:**
Philippine peso (PHP)

**LANGUAGES:**
Filipino, English

**NUMBER OF TELEVISIONS:**
3,700,000

## SINGAPORE

**CAPITAL:**
Singapore

**AREA:**
250 sq. mi. (648 sq km)

**POPULATION:**
4,300,419

**MONEY:**
Singapore dollar (SGD)

**LANGUAGES:**
Chinese, Malay, Tamil,
English

**NUMBER OF TELEVISIONS:**
1,330,000

## SOUTH KOREA

**CAPITAL:**
Seoul

**AREA:**
38,023 sq. mi.
(98,480 sq km)

**POPULATION:** 47,904,370

**MONEY:**
South Korean won (KRW)

**LANGUAGES:**
Korean, English

**NUMBER OF TELEVISIONS:**
15,900,000 (1997)

## TAIWAN

**CAPITAL:**
Taipei

**AREA:**
13,892 sq. mi.
(35,980 sq km)

**POPULATION:**
22,370,461

**MONEY:**
New Taiwan
dollar (TWD)

**LANGUAGES:** Mandarin,
Taiwanese (Min), Hakka
dialects

**NUMBER OF TELEVISIONS:**
8,800,000

## THAILAND

**CAPITAL:**
Bangkok

**AREA:**
198,455 sq. mi.
(514,000 sq km)

**POPULATION:** 61,797,751

**MONEY:**
baht (THB)

**LANGUAGES:** Thai, English,
ethnic languages

**NUMBER OF TELEVISIONS:**
15,190,000

## VIETNAM

**CAPITAL:**
Hanoi

**AREA:**
127,243 sq. mi.
(329,560 sq km)

**POPULATION:**
79,939,014

**MONEY:**
dong (VND)

**LANGUAGES:** Vietnamese
(official), Chinese,
English, French,
Khmer, ethnic languages

**NUMBER OF TELEVISIONS:**
2,900,000

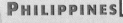

**internet connect**

**COUNTRY STATISTICS**
**GO TO: go.hrw.com**
**KEYWORD: SK3 FactsU7**
**FOR: more facts about East
and Southeast Asia**

**Sources:** Central Intelligence Agency, *The World Factbook 2001; The World Almanac and Book of Facts 2001;* pop. figures are 2001 estimates.

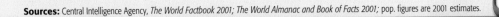

# CHAPTER 24

# China, Mongolia, and Taiwan

*This region of Asia with its varied landscape and cultures is home to one of the world's oldest living civilizations.*

Hello! My name is Lu Hua. Lu is my family name, and Hua is my given name. In China the family name comes first. I am 16 and live in Jin Shan County, outside of Shanghai, with my parents and my brother. My father is a clerk in a Volkswagen factory. My ancestors have lived in this village for hundreds of years. All 200 people in this village are named Lu.

I am in my last year at Jin Shan County High School. To get into this school, which is the best in the county, I had to pass a very difficult exam when I was 11. I had the best score that year. The school goes from seventh to twelfth grade. Each grade has four classes with 50 kids in each class. Now I am hoping to go on to a university. In China only one or two out of a hundred kids can go to college.

Most of my friends want to be scientists. I think I would like to be a diplomat, to travel, and have adventures. My family are common people, though, not Chinese Communist Party members, so I may not get into the diplomatic college.

你好嗎?

Translation: How are you?

# Section 1 Physical Geography

## Read to Discover

1. What are the physical features of China, Mongolia, and Taiwan?
2. What types of climate are found in China, Mongolia, and Taiwan?
3. What natural resources do China, Mongolia, and Taiwan have?

## Define

dikes
arable

## Locate

Himalayas
Mount Everest
Kunlun Mountains
Tian Shan
Plateau of Tibet
Taklimakan Desert
Tarim Basin

Gobi
North China Plain
Huang He
Chang River
Sichuan (Red) Basin
Xi River

## WHY IT MATTERS

China was once one of the most isolated countries in the world. Today, however, it plays a major role in the world community. Use CNNfyi.com or other current events sources to find out more about China's role in world affairs. Record your findings in your journal.

*Mask made of gold*

## China, Mongolia, and Taiwan: Physical-Political

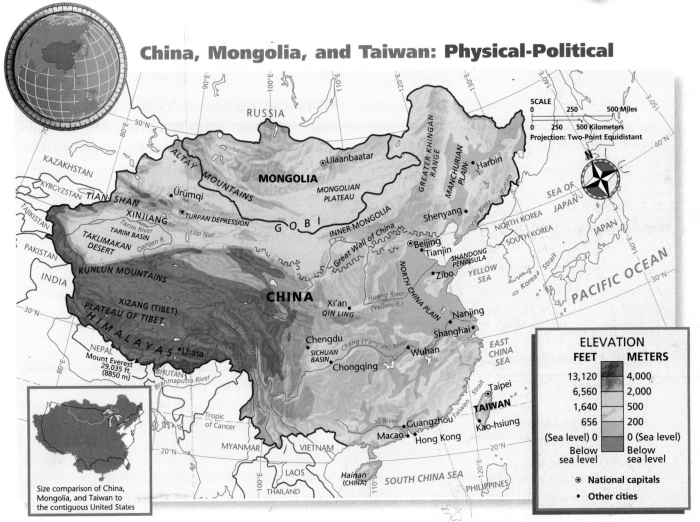

SCALE
0    250    500 Miles
0    250    500 Kilometers
Projection: Two-Point Equidistant

**ELEVATION**

| FEET | | METERS |
|---|---|---|
| 13,120 | | 4,000 |
| 6,560 | | 2,000 |
| 1,640 | | 500 |
| 656 | | 200 |
| (Sea level) 0 | | 0 (Sea level) |
| Below sea level | | Below sea level |

⊛ National capitals
• Other cities

Size comparison of China, Mongolia, and Taiwan to the contiguous United States

These snow-covered mountains are in the Wolong Nature Reserve in central China.

**Interpreting the Visual Record** What climate types would you expect to find in this area of the reserve?

**internet** connect

GO TO: go.hrw.com
KEYWORD: SK3 CH24
FOR: Web sites about China, Mongolia, and Taiwan

**D**o you remember what you learned about plateaus? See Chapter 2 to review.

# Physical Features

China has some of the world's tallest mountains, driest deserts, and longest rivers. Mongolia (mahn-GOHL-yuh) is China's neighbor to the north. It is a large, rugged, landlocked country. Burning hot summers and bitter cold winters are common there. In contrast, Taiwan (TY-WAHN) is a green tropical island just off the coast of mainland China.

**Mountains** The towering Himalayas (hi-muh-LAY-uhz), the world's tallest mountain range, run along China's southwestern border. Mount Everest lies in the Himalayas on China's border with Nepal. At 29,035 feet (8,850 m), it is the world's tallest mountain. If you move north from the Himalayas, you will find several other mountain ranges. These are the Kunlun Mountains (KOON-LOON), the Tian Shan (TYEN SHAHN), and the Altay Mountains (al-TY). To the east, on Mongolia's eastern border with China, you will see the Greater Khingan (KING-AHN) Range.

Mountains stretch the length of Taiwan and cover the eastern half of the island. In some places, the mountains end in steep cliffs at the edge of the Pacific Ocean. To the west of the mountains is a fertile coastal plain.

**Plateaus, Basins, and Deserts** Isolated plateaus and basins separate the region's mountain ranges. The huge Plateau of Tibet lies between the Himalayas and the Kunlun Mountains. With an average elevation of 16,000 feet (4,877 m), it is the world's highest plateau. The Taklimakan (tah-kluh-muh-KAHN) Desert is a huge expanse of sand. It occupies the central part of the Tarim (DAH-REEM) Basin in western China. In the northeastern corner of the basin, the Turpan (toohr-PAHN) Depression drops about 505 feet (154 m) below sea level.

The Mongolian Plateau covers most of the country of Mongolia. The Gobi (GOH-bee) takes up much of the central and southeastern sections of the plateau. The Gobi is the coldest desert in the world and covers more than 500,000 square miles (1,295,000 sq km). Much of the Gobi is gravel and bare rock.

**Plains** China and Mongolia have few areas of lowlands made up of coastal and river floodplains. However, these fertile plains support the major population centers. Millions of people live in the North China Plain. It is the largest plain in China and is crossed by major rivers.

**Rivers** The river known as the Huang (HWAHNG) rises on the eastern edge of the Plateau of Tibet. It flows eastward through the North China Plain and empties into the Yellow Sea. It takes its name, which means "yellow river," from the yellowish mud it carries. Winds carry loess, a yellowish-brown soil, from the Gobi to northern China. The Huang picks up the loess as the river flows through the region. On its way to the sea the river dumps the loess, raising the river bottom. This can lead to flooding. Floodwaters deposit a layer of rich silt that is good for farming but also cause great damage and loss of life. As a result, the Huang has long been known as China's Sorrow. The Chinese have tried to control the Huang by building **dikes**. These high banks of earth or concrete help reduce flooding.

The Chang (CHAHNG), or Yangtze (YAHNG-TSE), River also rises in the Plateau of Tibet. It flows eastward for 3,434 miles (5,525 km) across central China through the fertile Sichuan (SEE-CHWAHN), or Red, Basin. The Chang is China's—and Asia's—longest river. In fact, its name means "long river." The Chang is one of China's most important transportation routes. It is connected to the Huang by the world's oldest and longest canal system, the Grand Canal. The Xi (SHEE) River is southern China's most important river and transportation route.

✓ **READING CHECK:** *Places and Regions*  What are the major physical features of this region?

# Climate

China, Mongolia, and Taiwan are part of a huge region with several different climates. China's precipitation varies. The southeastern coastal region is the country's most humid area. As you move northwestward the climate becomes steadily drier. The extreme northwest has a true desert climate.

Seasonal monsoon winds greatly affect the climate of the region's southern and eastern parts. In winter, winds from Central Asia bring dry, cool-to-cold weather to eastern

China has greater potential for hydroelectric power than any other country in the world. When completed in 2009, the Three Gorges Dam on the Chang River will be the world's largest dam.

The Gobi is the world's third-largest desert. Herders ride Bactrian camels. **Interpreting the Visual Record** What characteristics of a desert environment can be seen in this photo?

## China, Mongolia, and Taiwan

| Country | Population/ Growth Rate | Life Expectancy | Literacy Rate | Per Capita GDP |
|---------|------------------------|-----------------|---------------|----------------|
| China | 1,273,111,290 0.9% | 70, male 74, female | 82% | $3,600 |
| Mongolia | 2,654,999 1.5% | 62, male 67, female | 83% | $1,780 |
| Taiwan | 22,370,461 0.8% | 74, male 80, female | 94% | $17,400 |
| United States | 281,421,906 0.9% | 74, male 80, female | 97% | $36,200 |

**Sources:** Central Intelligence Agency, *The World Factbook 2001;* U.S. Census Bureau

**Interpreting the Chart Which country has the fastest rate of population growth?**

This bronze vessel dates to the A.D. 1000s. Found in a tomb, it is just over a foot long (30 cm) and is covered with detailed animal designs.

**Interpreting the Visual Record What features of this object suggest animal characteristics?**

Asia. In summer, winds from the Pacific bring warm, wet air. This creates hot, rainy summers. Typhoons sometimes hit the coastal areas during the summer and fall. Typhoons are violent storms with high winds and heavy rains similar to hurricanes. They often bring flooding and cause a great deal of damage.

✓ **READING CHECK:** *Places and Regions* What are the climates of China, Mongolia, and Taiwan like?

## Resources

China has a wide range of mineral resources. These include gold, iron ore, lead, salt, uranium, and zinc, as well as energy resources such as coal and oil. China has greater coal reserves than any other country. At the present rate of use, these reserves will last another 1,000 years. China also produces enough oil to meet most of its own needs.

Mongolia has deposits of coal, copper, gold, iron ore, and oil. Taiwan's most important natural resource is its **arable** land, or land that is suitable for growing crops.

✓ **READING CHECK:** *Places and Regions* What are the region's resources?

Homework Practice Online

Keyword: SK3 HP24

## Section Review 1

**Define and explain:** dikes, arable

**Working with Sketch Maps** On a map of China, Mongolia, and Taiwan that you draw or that your teacher provides, label the following: the Himalayas, Mount Everest, Kunlun Mountains, Tian Shan, Plateau of Tibet, Taklimakan Desert, Tarim Basin, Gobi, North China Plain, Huang He, Chang River, Sichuan Basin, and Xi River. Where do you think the most fertile areas of the region are located?

### Reading for the Main Idea

1. *Places and Regions* What and where is the world's largest plateau? What is the world's tallest mountain? Where is it located?

2. *Environment and Society* What are three major rivers in eastern and southern China? How does the Huang affect China's people?

3. *Places and Regions* What is the region's driest area?

### Critical Thinking

4. **Drawing Inferences and Conclusions** What do you think might be the major factors that influence this region's climate?

### Organizing What You Know

5. **Summarizing** Summarize the natural environments of China, Mongolia, and Taiwan.

| Country | Physical Features | Climates | Resources |
|---------|-------------------|----------|-----------|
| | | | |
| | | | |

# Section 2 China's History and Culture

## Read to Discover

1. What are some of the major events in the history of China?
2. What are some features of China's culture?

## Define

emperor
dynasty
porcelain
martial law
pagodas

## Locate

China
Great Wall

### WHY IT MATTERS

The Chinese government has been criticized by much of the world community for its political system. Use CNN**fyi**.com or other **current events** sources to find out more about efforts to encourage the Chinese government to enact democratic political reforms. Record your findings in your journal.

*A bronze flying horse from the Han dynasty*

## History

Farmers have cultivated rice in southern China for some 7,000 years. Warm, wet weather made the region ideal for growing rice. Rice remains one of the region's main sources of food. Farmers in drier northern China grew a grain called millet and other crops. The early Chinese also grew hemp for fiber for clothing and spun silk from the cocoons of silkworms. Various cultures developed, particularly along the region's rivers.

**The Qin Dynasty and the Great Wall** Beginning about 2000 B.C. northern Chinese living in the Huang valley formed kingdoms. As Chinese civilization began to develop, peoples from various regions organized into large states. Each state was governed by an **emperor**—a ruler of a large empire. An emperor is often a member of a **dynasty**. A dynasty is a ruling family that passes power from one generation to the next. Beginning in about 500 B.C., the Chinese began building earthen

The Great Wall of China, including its branches and curves, stretches more than 2,000 miles (3,218 km).

▼

Archaeologists have discovered 6,000 of these uniquely crafted soldiers near Xi'an. Each of these figures from the Qin dynasty has different facial features.

This vase from the Ming dynasty is an example of early Chinese art.
**Interpreting the Visual Record** How does this vase compare to artifacts left by other early cultures you have studied?

walls hundreds of miles long. These walls separated the kingdoms from the northern nomads and from each other. Records show that the first emperor of the Qin, also spelled Ch'in (CHIN), dynasty ordered the building of the Great Wall along China's northern border. People began to connect the sections of walls about 200 B.C.

The Qin dynasty is well known for its contributions to China's culture. It left behind many historical artifacts. For example, when the first emperor died, he was buried with thousands of life-sized warriors and horses made of clay. You might wonder why someone would want their tomb filled with clay figures. It was an ancient Chinese funeral tradition to bury masters with clay soldiers for protection. Since the Qin emperor had made many enemies during his life, he wanted protection after his death.

During the Qin dynasty the Chinese used a writing system to record their history. This system was similar to the one used in China today. China's name also dates from this time period. In Chinese, China means "Qin kingdom" or "middle kingdom." This name may refer to the Chinese belief that China was the center, or middle, of the world.

**The Han Dynasty** The Han dynasty came after the Qin dynasty. From the 200s B.C. to the A.D. 200s, the Han dynasty expanded its kingdom southward. The Han also extended the Great Wall westward to protect the Silk Road. This road was originally used by trading caravans taking silk and other Chinese goods to regions west of China. During the Han dynasty the Chinese invented the compass, which aided travel. The dynasties that followed the Han made China even more powerful. The Chinese continued to make important contributions to society. Later contributions include paper and **porcelain** (POHR-suh-luhn), a type of very fine pottery.

**Mongols, Ming Dynasty, and the Manchu** In the 1200s Mongol armies led by Genghis Khan conquered China. *Khan* is a title that means "ruler." The Mongols were feared and known for spreading terror throughout the region. Their use of horses added to their military advantage.

Within 100 years the Ming dynasty seized control of China. After several battles with the Mongols, the Ming emperors closed China to outsiders. These emperors strengthened the Great Wall and focused on the development of their own culture.

In the 1600s a group called the Manchu began expanding from their home in Manchuria. Manchuria is located in far northeastern China. The Manchus conquered Inner Mongolia, Korea, and all of northern China. Led by the Qing (CHING) dynasty, the Manchu controlled China for more than 260 years. The dynasty's strong government slowly weakened, however, and was overthrown in the early 1900s.

**Outside Influences** Marco Polo was one of the few Europeans to visit China before the 1500s. Europeans reached China by following the Silk Road. None came by sea before the 1500s. In the 1500s Portuguese sailors established a trade colony at Macao (muh-KOW) in south China. French and British sailors and traders followed. The Chinese believed that foreigners had little to offer other than silver in return for Chinese porcelain, silk, and tea. Even so, Europeans introduced crops like corn, hot chili peppers, peanuts, potatoes, sweet potatoes, and tobacco. By the 1800s the European countries wanted to control China's trade. A series of conflicts caused China to lose some of its independence. For example, during this period the British acquired Hong Kong. The British, Germans, and French also forced China to open additional ports. China did not regain total independence until the mid-1900s.

**The Republics of China** In 1912 a revolutionary group led by Sun Yat-sen (SOOHN YAHT-SUHN) forced the last emperor to abdicate, or give up power. This group formed the first Republic of China. Mongolia and Tibet each declared their independence.

After Sun Yat-sen's death the revolutionaries split into two groups, the Nationalists and the Communists. A military leader named Chiang Kai-shek (chang ky-SHEK) united China under a Nationalist government. The Communists opposed him, and a civil war began. During

The Catalan Atlas from the 1300s shows Marco Polo's family traveling by camel caravan.

**Interpreting the Visual Record** **What kind of information might this atlas provide?**

This time line reviews major events in China's rich history. The last Chinese dynasty was overthrown in 1912.

**Interpreting the Time Line**

**What events have shaped China's government in the 1900s?**

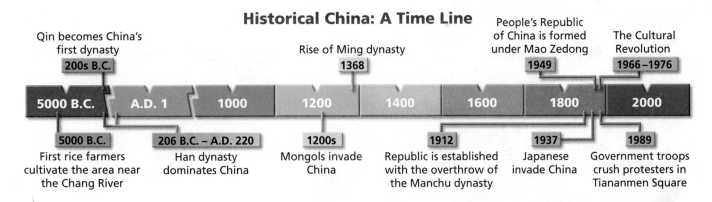

## Historical China: A Time Line

Qin becomes China's first dynasty
**200s B.C.**

Rise of Ming dynasty
**1368**

People's Republic of China is formed under Mao Zedong
**1949**

The Cultural Revolution
**1966–1976**

| 5000 B.C. | A.D. 1 | 1000 | 1200 | 1400 | 1600 | 1800 | 2000 |

**5000 B.C.**
First rice farmers cultivate the area near the Chang River

**206 B.C. – A.D. 220**
Han dynasty dominates China

**1200s**
Mongols invade China

**1912**
Republic is established with the overthrow of the Manchu dynasty

**1937**
Japanese invade China

**1989**
Government troops crush protesters in Tiananmen Square

World War II both groups fought the Japanese. The Communists finally defeated the Nationalists in 1949. Led by Mao Zedong (MOW ZUH-DOOHNG), the Communists set up the People's Republic of China. Mao's version of communism is known as Maoism. Only one political party—the Communist Party—was allowed.

Chiang Kai-shek and his Nationalists retreated to Taiwan. There they created a government for what they called the Republic of China. This government maintained its control through **martial law**, or military rule, for many years.

This image of Mao Zedong is a recognizable symbol of the Cultural Revolution.

**Mao's China** Under Mao the government took over the country's economy. His government seized private land and organized it into large, government-run farms. Factories were also put under state control. The central government decided the amount and type of food grown on a farm. It also regulated the production of factory goods, owned all housing, and decided where people should live. Sometimes families were separated or forced to relocate. Women were given equal status and assigned equal work duties. To control China's huge population, the government tried to restrict couples to one child per family. Religious worship was prohibited. Despite the efforts to organize the economy, there were planning errors. In the 1960s a famine killed about 30 million people.

**The Cultural Revolution** In 1966 Mao began a movement called the Cultural Revolution. The Revolution was an attempt to make everyone live a peasant way of life. Followers of Mao were known as Red Guards. They closed schools and universities. Millions of people were sent to the countryside to work in the fields. Opponents were imprisoned or executed.

The Potala Palace in Tibet was built in the A.D. 600s. Today, it has more than 1,000 rooms and is used for religious and political events.

After Mao's death in 1976, the new Chinese communist leadership admitted some past mistakes. It tried to modernize the government. Today, farmers can grow and market their own crops on a portion of their rented land. Almost every inch of productive land is used. China is able to meet most of its food needs. The Chinese enjoy a more varied diet of chicken, fish, fruits, meat, and vegetables. Many of China's large, inefficient state-run factories are being closed or turned over to private industries. Millions of Chinese have started small businesses.

A few Chinese have become wealthy. Some business owners can afford to build private homes and to buy cars, computers, and televisions. However, most Chinese are poor. State employees are paid low wages, live in tiny apartments, and cannot afford cars.

Although the government has allowed individuals some economic freedom, it restricts freedom of speech and religion. In 1989 the Chinese army was called in to attack pro-democracy student demonstrators in Tiananmen Square in Beijing (BAY-JING). Many students were injured or killed. Other rebellions among China's ethnic minorities, particularly in Tibet, have been crushed.

✓ **READING CHECK:** *Human Systems* What are some major events in China's history?

# Culture

About 92 percent of China's population consider themselves Han Chinese. Almost everyone can speak one of the seven major Chinese dialects. Mandarin Chinese is the official language and the most common.

**Values and Beliefs** Several philosophies and religions began in China. Taoism (TOW-i-zuhm), or Daoism (DOW-i-zuhm), is an ancient Chinese religion. Taoists believe that humans should try to follow a path that agrees with nature and avoids everyday concerns. The word *dào* means "the path." Each object or natural feature is thought to have its own god or spirit that may reward good deeds or bring bad luck.

The teachings of Confucius also have been important to Chinese culture. Confucius was a philosopher who lived from 551 to 479 B.C. His teachings stressed the importance of family. Confucius believed that children should

The Chinese New Year is also called the Lunar New Year. This is because the cycles of the moon are the basis for the Chinese calendar. The New Year is sometimes called the Spring Festival.

**Interpreting the Visual Record** **What object are parade participants carrying? What does it resemble?**

# CONNECTING TO *Literature*

*Confucius, a Chinese philosopher*

*This Chinese tale comes from the Hsiao Ching, or Book of Filial Piety—which means "devotion to parents." A student of a follower of Confucius is believed to have written it about 400 B.C. This story encourages children to protect their parents.*

## A Loving Son

Wu Meng was eight years old and very dutiful to his parents. His family was so poor that they could not afford to furnish their beds with mosquito-curtains. Every summer night thousands of mosquitoes attacked them, feasting upon their flesh and blood.

Wu Meng looked at his tired parents asleep on their bed as thousands of mosquitoes fiercely attacked them. Wu saw them sucking his parents' blood, which caused his heart to grieve.

To protect his parents, Wu decided that he would not drive the mosquitoes away from himself. Lying on the bed, he threw off his clothes, and soon feeling the pain of the mosquito attacks, he cried: "I have no fear of you, nor have you any reason to fear me. Although I have a fan, I will not use it, nor will I strike you with my hand. I will lie very quietly and let you gorge to the full." Such was his love for his parents!

### Analyzing Primary Sources

1. How does this tale reflect traditional Chinese philosophical beliefs?
2. Why do you think the author of the *Hsiao Ching* wrote this story?

---

respect their parents and subjects should respect their ruler. He believed people should treat those under their control justly and argued that state power should be used to improve people's lives.

The religion called Buddhism also has been important in China. It was founded by an Indian prince, Siddhartha Gautama. Gautama was born in Nepal about 563 B.C. He decided to search for truth and knowledge. Enlightenment—peace and a sense of being one with the universe—came to him while he was sitting under a Bo or Bodhi tree. As a result, he was given the name Buddha, which means "awakened or enlightened one." Buddhism reached China from India about A.D. 100. It became the country's main religion between the 300s and 500s. Indian architecture also became popular in China. Chinese **pagodas**, or Buddhist temples, are based on Indian designs. Pagodas have an upward-curving roof. Some pagodas are 15 stories tall.

**Lifestyle** Chinese culture highly values education. Chinese children are required to attend nine years of school. However, just 1 to 2 percent of students pass the difficult entrance exams to get into a university.

The Chinese government tries to control many aspects of everyday life. For example, parents are allowed to have just one child. This is because the government is trying to slow population growth.

The government also controls the newspapers and telephone system. This allows it to limit the flow of information and ideas. Satellite TV, the Internet, and e-mail are becoming more widespread, however. This makes it more difficult for the government to control communication between individuals.

Chinese food varies widely from region to region. Food in Beijing is heavily salted and flavored with garlic and cilantro. Sichuan-style cooking features hot pepper sauces. Cantonese cooking was introduced to the United States by immigrants from Guangzhou (GWAHNG-JOH).

Traditional Chinese medicine stresses herbal products and harmony with the universe. People around the world have used acupuncture. This therapy involves inserting fine needles into specific parts of the body for pain relief. Many Chinese herbal remedies have been used by American drug companies as the basis for modern medicines.

China has rich literary traditions. Painting, porcelain, sculpture, and carving of ivory, stone, and wood are also popular. Performing arts emphasize traditional folktales and stories shown in dances or operas with elaborate costumes.

✓ **READING CHECK:** *Human Systems* What is China's culture like?

▲

For more than 200 years the Beijing Opera, or Peking Opera, has been recognized worldwide for its artistic contributions. Originally performed for the royal family, it is now viewed by the public and is aired on Chinese television and radio stations.

go.
hrw
.com

**Homework Practice Online**

Keyword: SK3 HP24

**Define and explain:** emperor, dynasty, porcelain, martial law, pagodas

**Working with Sketch Maps** On the map you created in Section 1, label China and the Great Wall. Why do you think the Chinese chose to build the Great Wall where they did?

**Reading for the Main Idea**

**1.** *Human Systems* What contributions did the Qin and Han dynasties make to Chinese history?

**2.** *Human Systems* How did Mao's rule change China?

**3.** *Human Systems* How has China changed since Mao's death in 1976?

**Critical Thinking**

**4. Summarizing** What are three philosophies or religions that have been important in China? Describe them.

**Organizing What You Know**

**5. Summarizing** Copy the following graphic organizer. Use it to describe the Ming and the Manchu.

| Ming Dynasty | Manchu |
| --- | --- |
|  |  |
|  |  |
|  |  |

# Section 3 China Today

## Read to Discover

1. Where do most of China's people live?
2. What are the major cities in China, and what are they like?
3. What is China's economy like?
4. What challenges does China face?

## Define

command economy
multiple cropping
most-favored-
  nation status

## Locate

Beijing        Chongqing
Shanghai       Hong Kong
Nanjing        Macao
Wuhan

**WHY IT MATTERS**

In 1997 Hong Kong was returned to China after nearly 100 years of British rule. Use CNNfyi.com or other current events sources to find out more about developments in Hong Kong's free market economy since its return to Chinese rule. Record your findings in your journal.

*The Bei Si pagoda*

## China's Population

China has the largest population in the world—some 1.25 billion people. That number is equal to about 20 percent of the world's population. More people live in China than in all of Europe, Russia, and the United States combined. China's population is growing rapidly—by about 11 million each year. Some years ago, China's leaders took steps to bring the growth rate under control. They encouraged people to delay getting married and starting families. As you have read, they also have limited the size of families.

China's population is not evenly distributed across the land. The western half of the country, which is mostly desert and mountain ranges, is almost empty. Just 10 percent of China's people live there. The rest are crowded into the country's eastern half. In fact, more people live in the North China Plain than in the entire United States. However, this region is only about the size of Texas. Most Chinese live in the countryside. Even so, China has 40 cities with populations greater than 1 million.

✓ **READING CHECK:** *Human Systems* Where do most of China's people live?

## COMPARING POPULATIONS

**China and the United States**

*China*

*United States*

= 150,000,000 people

**Source:** Central Intelligence Agency, *The World Factbook 2001*

**Interpreting the Chart** How many people does one figure on the chart represent?

## China's Cities

Studying China's physical features helps explain why its residents live where they do. By locating rivers and river valleys, we can see where millions of people could best survive.

Several of China's most important cities are located on the Chang River. Shanghai, the country's largest city, lies on the Chang Delta. It serves as China's leading industrial center and is the major seaport. Shanghai's skyline is constantly changing. New hotels and office buildings seem to rise from the city center almost daily.

Using the map in Section 1, follow the course of the Chang River inland. Locate the cities of Nanjing and Wuhan (WOO-HAHN). These two industrial centers were built around iron-ore and coal mines. If you continue to follow the river upstream, you will reach Chongqing (CHOOHNG-CHING), located in the Sichuan Basin. It is one of the few large cities in China's interior. Guangzhou, located at the mouth of the Xi River, is southern China's largest city. Long famous as a trading center, it was known in the West as Canton. Today Guangzhou is one of China's major industrial cities.

Beijing, also known as Peking, is China's capital. It was established more than 3,000 years ago as a trading center. Beijing is the largest city in northern China and is well known for its cultural heritage. Beijing has famous tourist sites like the "Forbidden City," the great palace of the last emperor.

About 90 miles (145 km) southeast of Guangzhou is Hong Kong, a former British colony. With a population of 6.5 million, Hong Kong is one of the world's most densely populated places. It is only half as large as Rhode Island, but has more than seven times as many residents. Hong Kong is China's major southern seaport and is a center for banking and international trade. It is also a major tourist destination.

▲
Hong Kong's dragon-boat races have changed over the past 2,000 years from a cultural festival to an international sport.

Towering skyscrapers mark Shanghai's skyline.
**Interpreting the Visual Record  How can you tell this city is growing rapidly?**
▼

The British occupied the island of Hong Kong in the 1830s. In the late 1800s Hong Kong was leased to the British for 99 years. The lease ran out in 1997, and Hong Kong then became a special administrative region of China. The British left. Hong Kong has some political independence and is allowed to maintain its free-market economy. Macao, a nearby port city, was once a Portuguese colony. At the end of 1999, it was returned to China. It was the last foreign territory in China.

✔ **READING CHECK:** *Places and Regions* What are the major cities of China?

▲

In 1997 Hong Kong was returned to China. The return put an end to more than 150 years of British control.

## China's Economy

When the Chinese Communists took power in 1949 they set up a **command economy**. In this type of economy, the government owns most industries and makes most economic decisions. It set almost all production goals, prices, and wages. In the late 1970s, however, the government began to introduce some elements of free enterprise.

**Agriculture** Only about 10 percent of China's land is good for farming. Nevertheless, China is a world leader in the production of many crops. China's huge workforce makes this possible. More than 50 percent of Chinese workers earn a living from farming. Having many farmers means the land can be worked intensively to produce high yields. China's farmers have also increased production by cutting terraces into hillsides to create new farmland.

China is divided between rice-growing and wheat-growing regions. The divide lies midway between the Huang and the Chang River. To the south, rice is the main crop. Here **multiple cropping** is common because the weather is warm and wet. Multiple cropping means that two or three crops are raised each year on the same land. This practice makes southern China more prosperous than northern China. Wheat and sorghum are northern China's main crops.

Models of rice fields like these have been found in Han dynasty tombs. **Interpreting the Visual Record What resources appear to be necessary for growing rice in this region?**

▼

**Industry** When the Communists came to power, the Chinese economy was based almost entirely on farming. The Communist government introduced programs to build industry. Today, China is an industrial giant. It produces everything from satellites and rockets to toys and bicycles. Mining is also important. For example, China is a leading producer of iron ore.

✓ **READING CHECK:** ( *Human Systems* ) What kind of economy does China have?

# Future Challenges

China has enjoyed remarkable economic success in recent years. As a result, the standard of living has improved in most of China. Most Chinese are much better off than they were just a few years ago. However, by global standards China remains a relatively poor country. In addition, China's drive to industrialize has caused major problems. The smoke and waste pumped out by industries have badly polluted the air and water.

Another challenge involves the government's unwillingness to match the new economic freedoms with political reforms. China's human rights record has affected its economic relations with other countries. The U.S. government has considered canceling China's **most-favored-nation status** several times. Countries with this status get special trade advantages from the United States. China's future economic health might depend on its government's willingness to accept political reforms and join the world economic community.

✓ **READING CHECK:** ( *Human Systems* ) What challenges does China face?

By the mid-1990s clothing, electrical equipment, footwear, textiles, and other consumer goods were among China's leading exports. Employees of the Bei Bei Shoe Factory glue soles on by hand on an assembly line in Shanghai.

**Interpreting the Visual Record** Why might companies choose to use people rather than machines on this type of assembly line?

▼

# Section Review 3

**Define and explain:** command economy, multiple cropping, most-favored-nation status

**Working with Sketch Maps** On the map you created in Section 2, label Beijing, Shanghai, Nanjing, Wuhan, Chongqing, Hong Kong, and Macao. In the margin of your map, draw a box for each city. List the characteristics of each city in its box.

## Reading for the Main Idea

1. ( *Places and Regions* ) Where do most people in China live? Why?

2. ( *Places and Regions* ) Along which rivers are several of China's most important cities located? Why?

3. ( *Environment and Society* ) What farming practices have allowed the Chinese to increase production?

## Critical Thinking

4. **Finding the Main Idea** How has the Chinese government changed its economic policies since the late 1970s? What has been the impact of these changes?

## Organizing What You Know

5. **Summarizing** Copy the following graphic organizer. Use it to describe the kinds of challenges facing China today. Identify specific environmental, political, and economic challenges.

| Challenges |
|---|
|  |

# Section 4 Mongolia and Taiwan

## Read to Discover

**1.** How has Mongolia's culture developed?

**2.** What is Taiwan's culture like?

## Define

*gers*

## Locate

Mongolia       Kao-hsiung
Ulaanbaatar    Taipei
Taiwan

*Mythical animal statue at Taroka Gorge, Taiwan*

# Mongolia

Mongolia is home to the Mongol people and has a fascinating history. You will learn of invaders and conquests and a culture that prizes horses.

**Mongolia's History**  Today when people discuss the world's leading countries, they do not mention Mongolia. However, 700 years ago Mongolia was perhaps the greatest power in the world. Led by Genghis Khan, the Mongols conquered much of Asia, including China. Later leaders continued the conquests, building the greatest empire the world had seen. The Mongol Empire reached its height in the late 1200s.

It stretched from Europe's Danube River in the west to the Pacific Ocean in the east. Over time, however, the empire declined. In the late 1600s Mongolia fell under the rule of China.

In 1911, with Russian support, Mongolia declared its independence from China. Communists took control of the country 13 years later and established the Mongolian People's Republic. The country then came under the influence of the Soviet Union. Mongolia became particularly dependent on the Soviet Union for economic aid. This aid ended when the Soviet Union collapsed

This engraving shows early Mongolian soldiers.

Nomads of Mongolia live in *gers* like those shown here.
**Interpreting the Visual Record** **What in this photo suggests this would not be a permanent settlement?**

in the early 1990s. Since then, Mongolians have struggled to build a democratic government and a free-market economy.

**Mongolia's Culture** Despite years of Communist rule and recent Western influence, the Mongolian way of life remains quite traditional. Many people still follow a nomadic lifestyle. They live as herders, driving their animals across Mongolia's vast grasslands. They make their homes in **gers** (GUHRZ). These are large, circular felt tents that are easy to raise, dismantle, and move.

Since most people live as herders, horses play an important role in Mongolian life. Mongolian children learn to ride when they are very young—often before they are even five years old. In Mongolia, the most powerful piece in the game of chess is the horse, not the queen.

**Mongolia Today** Mongolia is a large country—slightly larger than Alaska. Its population numbers just over 2.5 million. Some 25 percent of Mongolians live in Ulaanbaatar (oo-lahn-BAH-tawr), the capital city. Ulaanbaatar is also Mongolia's main industrial and commercial center. Mongolia's other cities are quite small. Not one has a population greater than 100,000.

✓ **READING CHECK:** *Human Systems* What are some elements of Mongolian culture?

**Our Amazing Planet**

In the Gobi, temperatures can range from -40°F (-40°C) in January to 113°F (45°C) in July. Some areas of this desert receive little more than 2 inches (5 cm) of rain each year.

# Taiwan

For many years the island of Taiwan was known in the West as Formosa. This name came from Portuguese sailors who visited the island in the late 1500s. They thought the island was so lovely that they called it *Ilha Formosa*, or "beautiful island."

Chiang Kai-shek served in the Japanese army before returning to China to help overthrow the Manchu dynasty. He was head of the Nationalist government in China for 20 years, then moved with his followers to Taiwan.

Taiwan has good farmlands, but the island's eastern half is mountainous.
**Interpreting the Visual Record** How do the trees shown here compare to trees common where you live?

## Taiwan's History
The Chinese began settling Taiwan in the A.D. 600s. Some 600 years later the Japanese took control of eastern Taiwan. The search for spices brought European traders to Taiwan. The Dutch, Portuguese, and Spanish all tried to set up bases there. However, raiders from mainland China drove out these Europeans in the mid-1600s.

The struggle among the Chinese, Japanese, and Europeans for control of Taiwan continued until the late 1800s. In 1895 a treaty between the Chinese and the Japanese gave Taiwan to Japan. The Japanese then tried to force their way of life on the people of Taiwan. The Taiwanese rebelled against these efforts, but their revolts were crushed by the Japanese military.

After Japan's surrender at the end of World War II in 1945, China once again took command of Taiwan. In 1949 Mao Zedong established the People's Republic of China in mainland China. Chiang Kai-shek and the Nationalist Chinese government fled to Taiwan. The Nationalist government controlled Taiwan through martial law for decades. In recent years, however, the government has expanded democratic rights. China still claims that Taiwan is a province of China—not an independent country.

## Taiwan's Culture
Taiwan's history is reflected in its culture. Its population is about 85 percent native Taiwanese. They are descendants of people who migrated from China to Taiwan over hundreds of years. Chinese ways dominate Taiwan's culture. However, some building styles and certain foods reflect Japanese influences. European and American practices and customs have strongly influenced Taiwan's way of life in recent years. This is particularly true in the cities.

**Taiwan Today** Taiwan has a modern, industrial economy and a population of nearly 22 million. These people live on an island the size of Delaware and Maryland combined. Most people live on the western coastal plain of Taiwan. Population densities there can reach higher than 2,700 per square mile (1,042 per sq km). Taiwan's two largest cities, Kao-hsiung (KOW-SHYOOHNG) and Taipei (TY-PAY), are located on the coastal plain. Taipei is the capital city. It faces serious overcrowding and environmental problems. The thousands of cars, motorcycles, and trucks that clog Taipei's streets each day cause severe air pollution.

In the early 1950s Taiwan's economy was still largely based on agriculture. Today, however, only about 10 percent of workers make a living as farmers. Even so, Taiwan still produces enough rice—the country's chief food crop—to feed all of its people. Taiwan's farmers also grow fruits, sugarcane, tea, and vegetables.

Taiwan now has one of Asia's most successful economies. It is a world leader in the production and export of computers and sports equipment.

▲

Taipei, Taiwan, was founded in the 1700s and has developed into an important city for overseas trade.

**Interpreting the Visual Record** What characteristics of Taipei shown here resemble other cities?

✓ **READING CHECK:** ( *Human Systems* ) What are some elements of the culture of Taiwan?

---

## Section Review 4

**Homework Practice Online**
Keyword: SK3 HP24

**Define and explain:** *gers*

**Working with Sketch Maps** On the map you created in Section 3, label Mongolia, Ulaanbaatar, Taiwan, Kao-hsiung, and Taipei. In the border of your map, draw a box for each city. Describe each city in its box. How has the history of each city played a part in its growth?

**Reading for the Main Idea**

1. ( *Human Systems* ) How do most people earn a living in Mongolia?

2. ( *Human Systems* ) Write a brief outline of the significant individuals or groups that have influenced Taiwan's history.

3. ( *Human Systems* ) How has Taiwan's economy changed since the early 1950s?

**Critical Thinking**

4. **Analyzing Information** What are some problems Taiwan faces today?

**Organizing What You Know**

5. **Summarizing** Copy the following graphic organizer. Use it to design and write two postcards to a friend describing life in Mongolia. In your postcards, note how life follows traditional patterns yet is also undergoing changes.

# CHAPTER 24
# Reviewing What You Know

## Building Vocabulary

On a separate sheet of paper, write sentences to define each of the following words.

1. dikes
2. arable
3. emperor
4. dynasty
5. porcelain
6. martial law
7. pagodas
8. command economy
9. multiple cropping
10. most-favored-nation status
11. *gers*

## Reviewing the Main Ideas

1. ( *Places and Regions* ) What physical features separate this region's mountain ranges?

2. ( *Places and Regions* ) Why is the Huang called the Yellow River?

3. ( *Environment and Society* ) What idea did the first emperor of the Qin dynasty have that greatly affected the landscape of China?

4. ( *Human Systems* ) What country discussed in this chapter once ruled a vast empire that stretched into Europe?

5. ( *Environment and Society* ) What are Taiwan's leading exports?

## Understanding Environment and Society

### Resource Use

Growing industries and cities are taking over farmland in China. Create a presentation about potential problems caused by this situation. Consider the following:

- Actions China's government has already taken to try to solve the problem of its growing population.
- Problem in balancing population and food supply.

## Thinking Critically

1. **Drawing Inferences and Conclusions** Why do you think so few Europeans reached China before the 1500s?

2. **Drawing Inferences and Conclusions** How might Chinese history have been different if Europeans had not forced trade upon the Chinese?

3. **Finding the Main Idea** What was the Cultural Revolution and how did it affect life in China?

4. **Making Generalizations and Predictions** In what ways does modern technology threaten the Chinese government's ability to control the flow of information in the country? What changes might the free flow of information bring to China?

5. **Analyzing Information** How is Taiwan's history reflected in the island's culture today?

### Map ACTIVITY

On a separate sheet of paper, match the letters on the map with their correct labels.

Mount Everest
Plateau of Tibet
North China
  Plain
Huang

Chang River
Great Wall
Shanghai
Hong Kong
Ulaanbaatar

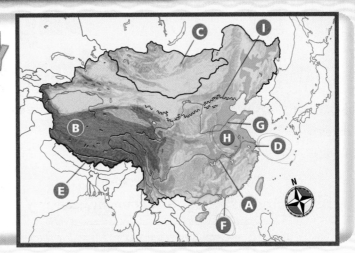

### Mental Mapping Skills ACTIVITY

On a separate sheet of paper, draw a freehand map of China, Mongolia, and Taiwan. Make a key for your map and label the following:

China
Gobi
Himalayas

Mongolia
Pacific Ocean
Taiwan

### WRITING ACTIVITY

Imagine that you are a Chinese university professor. Using the time line in section 2, the text, and other sources, write a brief lesson plan on China's history. You may want to include some visuals, such as photographs of artifacts, in your lesson plan. Be sure to use standard grammar, spelling, sentence structure, and punctuation.

## Alternative Assessment

### Portfolio ACTIVITY

**Learning About Your Local Geography**

**Cooperative Project** Fishing is an important source of food in China. Is fishing important in your community? Draw and label three types of fish available in your community.

☑ **internet** connect

Internet Activity: **go.hrw.com**
**KEYWORD: SK3 GT24**

Choose a topic to explore about China, Mongolia, and Taiwan:
- Follow the Great Wall of China.
- Visit the land of Genghis Khan.
- See the artistic treasures of China.

# CHAPTER 25

# Japan and the Koreas

*Now we continue east to North and South Korea and the island nation of Japan. First we meet Akiko, a Japanese student whose school day may be very different from yours.*

*Konichiwa!* (Good afternoon!) I'm Akiko, and I'm in the seventh grade at Yamate school. Every morning except Sunday I put on my school uniform and eat rice soup and pickles before I leave for school. The train I take is so crowded I can't move. At school, I study reading, math, English, science, and writing. I know 1,800 Japanese characters, but I need to know about 3,000 to pass the ninth grade exams. For lunch, I eat rice and cold fish my mom packed for me. Before we can go home, we clean the school floors, desks, and windows. My dad usually isn't home until after 11:00 P.M., so my mom helps me with my homework in the "big" (8 feet by 8 feet) room of our three-room apartment. In the evenings, I go to a *juku* school to study for the ninth grade exams. If I do not do well, I will not go to a good high school, and my whole family will be ashamed. On Sundays, I sometimes go with my parents to visit my grandparents, who are rice farmers. I like rock music a lot, especially U2.

こんにちは. 私は東京に 住んでいます.

Translation: Good afternoon. I live in Tokyo.

# Section 1 Physical Geography

## Read to Discover

1. What are the physical features of Japan and the Koreas?
2. What natural resources does the region have?
3. Which climate types are found in the region?

## Define

tsunamis
Oyashio Current
Japan Current

## Locate

Korean Peninsula
Sea of Japan
Hokkaido
Honshu
Shikoku
Kyushu

### WHY IT MATTERS

Weather plays an important role in Japanese life. Use CNNfyi.com or other current events sources to find examples of how weather has affected Japanese history and society. Record the findings in your journal.

*Japanese bonsai*

## Japan and the Koreas: Physical-Political

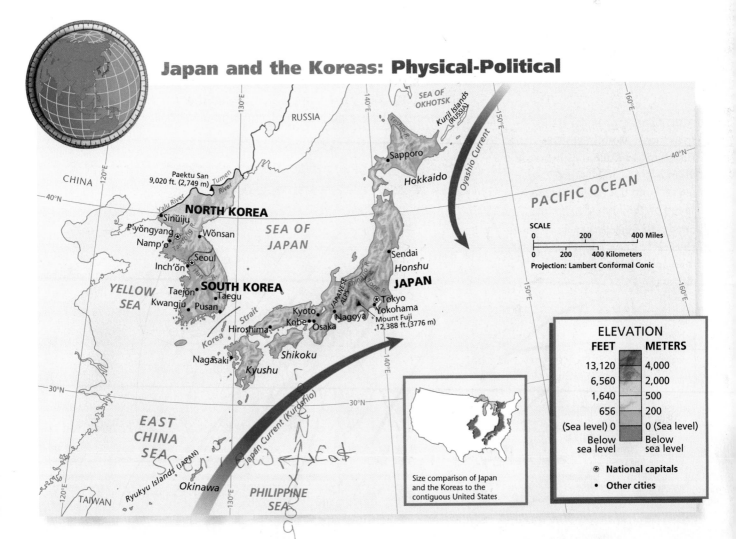

SEA OF OKHOTSK

RUSSIA

Kuril Islands (RUSSIA)

Oyashio Current

PACIFIC OCEAN

40°N

Sapporo

Hokkaido

CHINA

Paektu San 9,020 ft. (2,749 m)
Tumen River
Yalu River

40°N

NORTH KOREA
Sinŭiju
P'yŏngyang
Namp'o
Wŏnsan

Taedong R.

SEA OF JAPAN

Sendai
*Honshu*

SCALE
0      200      400 Miles
0   200   400 Kilometers
Projection: Lambert Conformal Conic

Seoul
Inch'ŏn

SOUTH KOREA
Taejŏn
Taegu

JAPANESE ALPS

Shinano R.

Tone R.

JAPAN

⊛ Tokyo
Yokohama

YELLOW SEA

Kwangju
Pusan

Kyoto
Kobe
Osaka

Nagoya

Mount Fuji
12,388 ft.(3776 m)

Korea Strait

Hiroshima

Nagasaki

*Shikoku*

*Kyushu*

EAST CHINA SEA

30°N

30°N

Japan Current (Kuroshio)

Size comparison of Japan and the Koreas to the contiguous United States

TAIWAN

Ryukyu Islands (JAPAN)

Okinawa

PHILIPPINE SEA

ELEVATION
| FEET | | METERS |
|---|---|---|
| 13,120 | | 4,000 |
| 6,560 | | 2,000 |
| 1,640 | | 500 |
| 656 | | 200 |
| (Sea level) 0 | | 0 (Sea level) |
| Below sea level | | Below sea level |

⊛ National capitals
• Other cities

**internet** connect

**GO TO: go.hrw.com**
**KEYWORD: SK3 CH25**
**FOR: Web sites about Japan and the Koreas**

**Our Amazing Planet**

The world's largest crab lives off the southeastern coast of Japan. The giant spider crab can grow larger than 12 feet (3.6 m) across (from claw to claw). It can also weigh more than 40 pounds (18 kg)!

A *shinkansen*, or bullet train, speeds past Mount Fuji. This Hiroshima-to-Kokura train travels at an average 162.3 mph (261.8 kmh) but has a maximum speed of 186 mph (300 kmh).
**Interpreting the Visual Record** What physical features might make building railroads in this region of Japan difficult?

# Physical Features

The Korean Peninsula extends southward about 600 miles (965 km) from mainland Asia. The peninsula is relatively close to southern Japan.

The Korean Peninsula is about the same size as Utah. It contains two countries, North Korea and South Korea. The Yalu and Tumen Rivers separate North Korea from China. The Tumen River also forms a short border with Russia. Off the coast of the Korean Peninsula lie more than 3,500 islands.

The Sea of Japan separates Japan from the Eurasian mainland. The narrow Korea Strait lies between South Korea and the island country of Japan. No place in Japan is more than 90 miles (145 km) from the sea. Japan is about the size of California. It is made up of four large islands called the home islands. The country also includes more than 3,000 smaller islands. The home islands from north to south are Hokkaido (hoh-KY-doh), Honshu (HAWN-shoo), Shikoku (shee-KOH-koo), and Kyushu (KYOO-shoo). South of the home islands are Japan's Ryukyu (ree-YOO-kyoo) Islands. Okinawa is the largest of these islands. Fewer than half of the Ryukyus are inhabited.

**Mountains** Rugged and heavily forested mountains are a common sight in the landscape of this region. Mountains cover about 75 percent of Japan. Many of Japan's mountains were formed by volcanic activity. The country's longest mountain range, the Japanese Alps, forms a volcanic spine through Honshu. The small amount of plains in these countries is found along the coasts and river valleys.

**The Ring of Fire** Japan lies along the Pacific Ring of Fire—a region of volcanic activity and earthquakes. Under Japan the dense

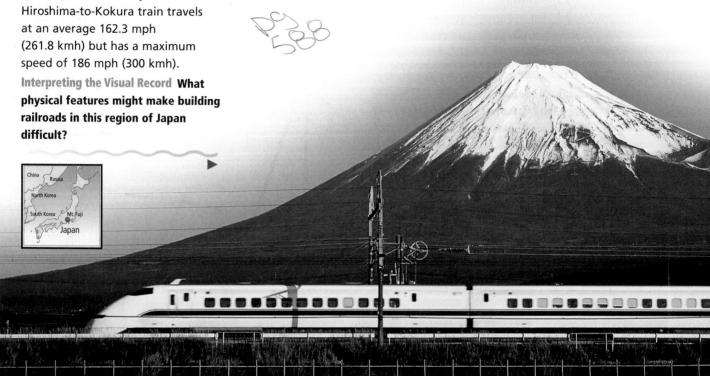

Pacific plate dives beneath the lighter Eurasian and Philippine plates. This subduction zone borders the Pacific side of the Japanese islands, forming the Japan Trench. This is one of the deepest places on the ocean floor. The movement of one tectonic plate below another builds up tension in Earth's crust. The Eurasian plate buckles and pushes up, creating mountains and fractures in the crust. Magma flows up through these fractures. Where magma rises to the surface, it forms volcanoes. Today, Japan has about 40 active volcanoes. Mount Fuji (FOO-jee), Japan's highest peak, is an inactive volcano.

Because Japan lies along a subduction zone, earthquakes are also common. As many as 1,500 occur every year. Most are minor quakes. In 1995, however, an earthquake killed more than 5,000 people in Kobe.

Underwater earthquakes sometimes create huge waves called **tsunamis** (tsooh-NAH-mees). These dangerous waves can travel hundreds of miles per hour. They can also be as tall as a 10-story building when they reach shore. In 1993 a tsunami caused terrible destruction when it struck the coast of Hokkaido.

Unlike Japan, the Korean Peninsula is not located in a subduction zone. As a result, it has no active volcanoes and is dominated by eroded mountains. Earthquakes are quite rare.

✓ **READING CHECK:** ( *Places and Regions* ) What are the physical features of Japan and the Koreas?

**D**o you remember what you learned about plateaus? See Chapter 2 to review.

## Natural Resources

Except for North Korea, the region is not rich in natural resources. It has no oil or natural gas. The Korean Peninsula's mountainous terrain and rivers, however, are good for producing hydroelectric power. North Korea also has iron ore, copper, zinc, lead, and coal.

Japan lies near one of the world's best fisheries. East of Japan the cool **Oyashio** (oh-YAH-shee-oh) **Current** dives beneath the warm, less dense **Japan Current**. The cool water scours the bottom, bringing nutrients to the surface. Fish can find plentiful food to eat in this rich marine environment.

✓ **READING CHECK:** ( *Places and Regions* ) What are the region's natural resources?

▲ Every hour an artificial volcano erupts at Ocean Dome, the world's largest indoor beach, at Miyazaki, Japan.

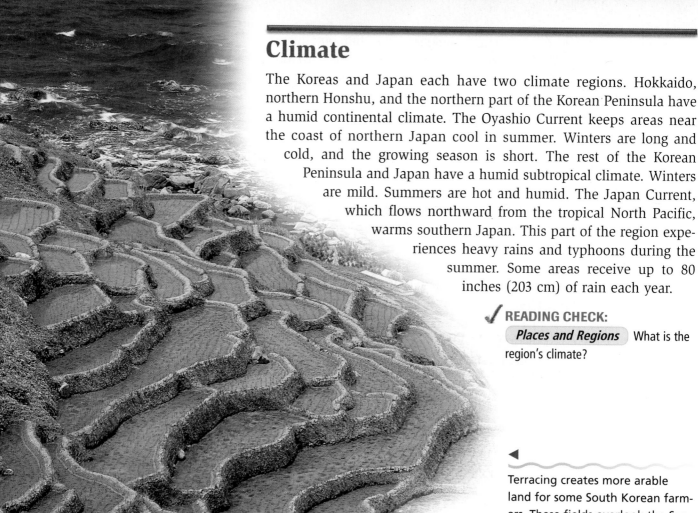

# Climate

The Koreas and Japan each have two climate regions. Hokkaido, northern Honshu, and the northern part of the Korean Peninsula have a humid continental climate. The Oyashio Current keeps areas near the coast of northern Japan cool in summer. Winters are long and cold, and the growing season is short. The rest of the Korean Peninsula and Japan have a humid subtropical climate. Winters are mild. Summers are hot and humid. The Japan Current, which flows northward from the tropical North Pacific, warms southern Japan. This part of the region experiences heavy rains and typhoons during the summer. Some areas receive up to 80 inches (203 cm) of rain each year.

✓ **READING CHECK:**

( *Places and Regions* ) What is the region's climate?

◄

Terracing creates more arable land for some South Korean farmers. These fields overlook the Sea of Japan.

**Interpreting the Visual Record How do the terraces here hold water?**

**Homework Practice Online**
Keyword: SK3 HP25

## Section Review 1

**Define and explain:** tsunamis, Oyashio Current, Japan Current

**Working with Sketch Maps** On a map of Japan and the Koreas that you draw or that your teacher provides, label the following: the Korean Peninsula, Sea of Japan, Hokkaido, Honshu, Shikoku, and Kyushu. On what physical features might Japan and the Koreas depend for their economies?

### Reading for the Main Idea

1. ( *Physical Systems* )  How has Japan's location in a subduction zone made it different from the Koreas?

2. ( *Physical Systems* )  How do ocean currents affect the climates of Japan?

### Critical Thinking

3. **Drawing Inferences and Conclusions** How do you think residents are affected by this region's mountainous terrain and the nearness of the sea?

4. **Making Generalizations and Predictions** What can you predict about South Korea's and Japan's economies?

### Organizing What You Know

5. **Summarizing** List the landforms, natural resources, and climates of Japan, North Korea, and South Korea.

|  | Landforms | Resources | Climate |
|---|---|---|---|
| Japan |  |  |  |
| South Korea |  |  |  |
| North Korea |  |  |  |

# Section 2 The History and Culture of Japan

## Read to Discover

1. What was Japan's early history and culture like?
2. How did the modernization of Japan take place?

## Define

Shintoism
shamans
samurai
shogun
Diet

**WHY IT MATTERS**

Japanese cultural traditions are important not only in Japan but also in other societies. Use CNNfyi.com or other current events sources to find information on Japanese cultural traditions. Record the findings in your journal.

A ukiyo-e, a Japanese woodblock print

## Early Japan

Japan's first inhabitants came from central Asia thousands of years ago. Rice farming was introduced to Japan from China and Korea about 300 B.C. As the population increased, farmers irrigated new land for growing rice. They also built dikes and canals to channel water into the rice paddies. Local chieftains organized the workers and controlled the flow of water. This control allowed the chieftains to extend their political power over larger areas.

**Religion** The earliest known religion of Japan, **Shintoism**, centers around the *kami*. *Kami* are spirits of natural places, sacred animals, and ancestors. Many of Japan's mountains and rivers are sacred in Shintoism. **Shamans**, or priests who communicated with the spirits, made the *kami*'s wishes known.

Buddhism and Confucianism were later introduced from China. Buddhist shrines were often located next to older *kami* shrines. Today, as in the past, most Japanese practice Shintoism and Buddhism. As you learned in Chapter 27, the principles of Confucianism include respect for elders, parents, and rulers.

▲

Todaiji Temple in Nara, Japan, contains the largest wooden hall in the world and a statue of Buddha that is more than 48 feet (15 m) tall.
**Interpreting the Visual Record** What interesting features do you see in this building's architecture?

# CONNECTING TO *Literature*

*Sadako and the Thousand Paper Cranes*
by Eleanor Coerr

*On August 6, 1945, the United States dropped an atomic bomb on Hiroshima, Japan, trying to bring an end to World War II.* Sadako and the Thousand Paper Cranes *is based on the story of a real little girl who lived in Hiroshima at the time of the bombing. Ten years later, she died as a result of the radiation from the bomb.*

## Sadako and the Thousand Paper Cranes

That afternoon Chizuko was Sadako's first visitor. She smiled mysteriously as she held something behind her back. "Shut your eyes," she said. . . . Chizuko put some pieces of paper and scissors on the bed. "Now you can look," she said.

"What is it?" Sadako asked, staring at the paper.

Chizuko was pleased with herself. "I've figured out a way for you to get well," she said proudly. "Watch!" She cut a piece of gold paper into a large square. In a short time she had folded it over and over into a beautiful crane.

Sadako was puzzled. "But how can that paper bird make me well?"

"Don't you remember that old story about the crane?" Chizuko asked. "It's supposed to live for a thousand years. If a sick person folds one thousand paper cranes, the gods will grant her wish and make her healthy again." She handed the crane to Sadako. "Here's your first one."

### Analyzing Primary Sources

1. How do the cranes reflect traditional Japanese culture?
2. How does Chizuko's visit to Sadako reflect her feelings about her friend?

**The Shoguns** In the A.D. 700s Japan began to develop a political system of its own. Many small feudal domains were each ruled by a lord. **Samurai** (SA-muh-ry) were warriors who served the lords. Rivalries were put aside when a foreign threat appeared. For example, the feudal domains united against the Mongols in the 1200s. After a victory, the emperor sometimes named the warriors **shogun**. Shogun means "great general" and is the highest rank for a warrior.

In the mid-1500s, Portuguese traders arrived in Japan. Spanish missionaries followed, introducing Christianity to Japan. Later, Europeans were forced to leave. Japanese leaders feared that foreign ideas might undermine Japanese society. Japan remained cut off from the Western world until the mid-1850s.

✓ **READING CHECK:** *Human Systems* What was early Japan like?

# Modern Japan

In 1853 U.S. commodore Matthew Perry's warships sailed into Tokyo Bay. Perry displayed U.S. naval power and brought gifts that showed the wonders of American technology. Perry's arrival convinced the Japanese that they needed to become as politically strong as the Americans and Europeans. In the 1860s Japan began to industrialize and modernize its educational, legal, and governmental systems.

Commodore Matthew Perry arrives in Japan in 1853.

**An Imperial Power** Japan needed resources in order to industrialize. As a result, it began to expand its empire around 1900. Japan annexed, or took control of, Korea in 1910. Japan also took over northeastern China and its supply of coal and iron ore. Japan continued to expand in Asia during the late 1930s.

**World War II** During World War II Japan was an ally of Germany and Italy. Japan brought the United States into the war in 1941 by attacking the U.S. naval base at Pearl Harbor, Hawaii. Japan conquered much of Southeast Asia and many Pacific islands before being defeated by U.S. and Allied forces in 1945. With the end of World War II Japan lost its empire.

**Government** After World War II the United States occupied Japan until 1952. With U.S. aid, Japan began to rebuild into a major world industrial power. Japan also established a democratic government. Today, Japan is a constitutional monarchy with several political parties. The government is made up of the **Diet** (DY-uht)—an elected legislature—and a prime minister. Japan's emperor remains a symbol of the nation, but he has no political power.

✓ **READING CHECK:** *Places and Regions* How did Japan modernize?

## Section Review 2

**Define and explain:** Shintoism, shamans, samurai, shogun, Diet

**Working with Sketch Maps** On the map you created in Section 1, label China and Korea. In a box in the margin, identify the body of water that separates Korea from Japan. Why do you think China and Korea had a strong influence on Japan's culture and history?

### Reading for the Main Idea

1. *Human Systems* What religions have been practiced in Japan, and from where did they come?

2. *Places and Regions* Why did Japan decide to trade with the United States and Europe?

### Critical Thinking

3. **Finding the Main Idea** How and why did rice farming develop in Japan?

4. **Analyzing Information** What influences do the principles of Confucianism have on the Japanese?

### Organizing What You Know

5. **Sequencing** Copy the following graphic organizer. Use it to show important developments in modern Japanese history from the 1850s to today.

☐ ⇨ ☐ ⇨ ☐ ⇨ ☐ ⇨ ☐

# Section 3

## Japan Today

### Read to Discover

1. Where do most Japanese live?
2. What are the major Japanese cities like?
3. What is life in Japan like?
4. How has the Japanese economy developed?

### Define

megalopolis
kimonos
futon
intensive cultivation
work ethic
protectionism
trade surplus

### Locate

Inland Sea
Osaka
Tokyo
Kobe
Kyoto

Small child in a traditional kimono

### WHY IT MATTERS

The Japanese economy has struggled for the last several years due to a number of factors. The health of the Japanese economy is not only important to Japan but to much of the world. Use CNN fyi.com or other current events sources to find information on the Japanese economy. Record the findings in your journal.

▲
Beyond Tokyo's Nijubashi Bridge is the Imperial Palace, the home of the emperor.

## Where People Live

Japan is one of the world's most densely populated countries. It is slightly smaller than California but has nearly four times as many people! There are an average of 863 people per square mile (333/sq km). However, Japan is very mountainous. Within its area of livable land, population density averages 7,680 people per square mile (2,964/sq km).

Most people live on the small coastal plains, particularly along the Pacific and the Inland Sea. Japan's major cities and farms compete for space on these narrow coastal plains. Only about 11 percent of Japan's land is arable, or fit for growing crops.

The Japanese have reclaimed land from the sea and rivers. In some places, they have built dikes to block off the water. They have drained the land behind the dikes so it could be used for farming or housing. They have even built artificial islands. The airport near Osaka, for example, was built on an artificial island in the early 1990s.

✓ READING CHECK:   ( *Human Systems* )  Where do most people in Japan live?

# Japan's Cities

Japan's cities, like major cities everywhere, are busy, noisy, and very crowded. Almost 30 million people live within 20 miles of the Imperial Palace in Tokyo. This densely populated area forms a **megalopolis**. A megalopolis is a giant urban area that often includes more than one city as well as the surrounding suburban areas. Yokohama is Japan's major seaport.

Most of Tokyo was built recently. An earthquake in 1923 and bombings during World War II destroyed most of the old buildings.

Tokyo is the capital and the center of government. Japan's banking, communications, and education are also centered here. Tokyo is densely populated, and land is scarce. As a result, Tokyo's real estate prices are among the world's highest.

Tokyo's Ginza shopping district is the largest in the world. Some department stores sell houses and cars and provide dental care. They also offer classes on how to properly wear **kimonos**—traditional robes—and to arrange flowers.

High rents in Ginza and elsewhere in Tokyo encourage the creative use of space. Tall buildings line the streets. However, shops are also found below the streets in the subway stations. Another way the Japanese have found to maximize space is the "capsule hotel." The guests in these hotels sleep in compartments too small to stand in upright. Businesspeople often stay in these hotels rather than commuting the long distances to their homes.

So many people commute to and from Tokyo that space on the trains must also be maximized. During peak travel periods, commuters are crammed into cars. They are helped by workers hired to push as many people into the trains as possible.

Another megalopolis in Japan is located in the Kansai region. It has three major cities: Osaka (oh-SAH-kah), Kobe (KOH-bay), and Kyoto (KYOH-toh). Industrial Osaka has been a trading center for centuries. Kobe is an important seaport. Kyoto was Japan's capital for more than 1,000 years.

√ **READING CHECK:**

*Places and Regions* What is life like in Japan's major cities?

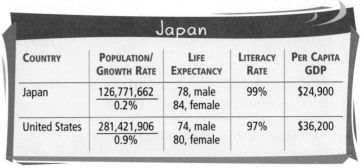

| | Japan | | | |
|---|---|---|---|---|
| **COUNTRY** | **POPULATION/ GROWTH RATE** | **LIFE EXPECTANCY** | **LITERACY RATE** | **PER CAPITA GDP** |
| Japan | 126,771,662 0.2% | 78, male 84, female | 99% | $24,900 |
| United States | 281,421,906 0.9% | 74, male 80, female | 97% | $36,200 |

**Sources:** Central Intelligence Agency, *The World Factbook 2001;* U.S. Census Bureau

**Interpreting the Chart** How does life expectancy in Japan compare to that of the United States?

Japanese workers stay focused on their responsibilities on an electronics production line.
▼

The port of Kobe is located in the central part of the Japanese islands.

Japanese and American all-star baseball teams compete in Yokohama.

**Interpreting the Visual Record** How is this scoreboard different from one in the United States?

# Life in Japan

Japan is a very homogeneous nation. In other words, almost everyone—more than 99 percent of the population—is ethnically Japanese and shares a common language and culture. Japanese society has traditionally been dominated by men, but this is changing. More Japanese women have jobs today than in the past, but most women are still expected to be dutiful wives and mothers. Many quit their jobs when they marry.

Many Japanese families live in suburbs, where housing is cheaper. As a result, many Japanese spend as much as three hours commuting to and from work.

Because land is so scarce, most Japanese homes do not have large yards. Most homes are also smaller than typical American homes. Rooms are usually used for more than one purpose. For example, a living room may also serve as a bedroom. During the day, people sit on cushions at low tables. At night, they sleep on the floor on a **futon** (FOO-tahn)—a lightweight cotton mattress. In the morning they put the mattress away, and the bedroom becomes a living room again.

For most occasions, people wear Western-style clothing. Many Japanese wear kimonos at festivals and weddings. Listening to music and playing video games are popular leisure activities. Baseball, golf, and skiing are also popular. On festival days, families may gather to enjoy the cherry blossoms or visit a local shrine or temple. They might also watch the ancient sport of sumo wrestling or traditional dramas on television. Many Japanese enjoy traditional arts such as the tea ceremony, flower arranging, growing dwarf potted trees called bonsai, and kite flying.

✓ **READING CHECK:** ( *Human Systems* ) What is life like in Japan?

# Japan's Economy

Japan has few natural resources. It therefore imports many of the raw materials it uses to run its industries. Oil is one key material that Japan must import. The country produces about one third of its energy through nuclear power.

The sea is an important source of food. Japan has the world's largest fishing industry. It also imports fish from all over the world. Fish is a major part of the Japanese diet. In fact, Tokyo's largest fish market sells about 5 million pounds of seafood each day. The average Japanese eats more than 100 pounds of fish each year. In contrast, the average American eats less than 5 pounds each year.

**Agriculture** Most Japanese farms are located on Honshu. Many farmers own their land and live in small villages. Farms in Japan are much smaller than those in the United States. The average Japanese farm is about 2.5 acres (1 hectare). Most American farms are about 150 times larger. Japan's shortage of land means that there is little pastureland for livestock. Meat is a luxury. The Japanese get most of their protein from fish and soybeans.

Farmers make the most of their land by terracing the hillsides. This means cutting the hillside into a series of small flat fields. The terraces look like broad stair steps. The terraces give farmers more room to grow crops. Japanese farmers use **intensive cultivation**—the practice of growing food on every bit of available land. Even so, Japan must import about two thirds of its food.

Farmers are encouraged to stay on the land and to grow as much rice as possible. However, many farms are too small to be profitable. To solve this problem, the Japanese government buys the rice crop. The price is set high enough to allow farmers to support their families. The government then resells it at the same price. Because this price is much higher than the world market price, the government restricts rice imports.

Seeds of the tea plant were first brought to Japan about A.D. 800. Tea is now an important product of southern Japan. Top-quality teas are harvested by hand only. Workers pick just the tender young leaves at the plant's tip.

**Interpreting the Visual Record**
**How might using machines for harvesting leaves affect the quality of the tea?**

▼

**Industry** Japan imports most of its raw resources. These resources are then used to make goods to sell in other countries. For example, Japan is known for its high-quality automobiles. Japan also makes televisions, cameras, and compact disc players.

There are many reasons for Japan's economic success. Most Japanese have a strong **work ethic**. This is the belief that work in itself is worthwhile. Most Japanese work for large companies and respect their leaders. In return, employers look after workers' needs. They offer job security, exercise classes, and other benefits.

The Japanese have also benefited from investments in other countries. For example, some Japanese companies have built automobile factories in the United States. Other Japanese companies have invested in the American entertainment and real estate industries.

**Japan and the Global Market** Japan's economy depends on trade. In the past the government set up trade barriers to protect Japan's industries from foreign competition. This practice is called **protectionism**. This has helped Japan build up a huge **trade surplus**. A trade surplus means that a nation exports more than it imports. Other countries have objected to Japan's trade practices. Some countries have even set up barriers against Japanese goods. As a result, Japan has eased some trade barriers.

Japan has other economic problems, too. Some Asian countries that pay lower wages are able to produce goods more cheaply than Japan. The most important problem Japan—and Asia—faced in the 1990s was an economic slowdown. It threatened the country's prosperity. Japan is now in a recovery and slow-growth period.

✔ **READING CHECK:** ( *Human Systems* ) How have Japan's leaders tried to protect the nation's economy?

▲
A worker in this Japanese automobile factory does his job with the help of a robot.

# Section Review 3

go.hrw.com **Homework Practice Online** Keyword: SK3 HP25

**Define and explain:** megalopolis, kimonos, futon, intensive cultivation, work ethic, protectionism, trade surplus

**Working with Sketch Maps** On the map you created in Section 2, label Inland Sea, Osaka, Tokyo, Kobe, and Kyoto. Draw a box in the margin of your map. What do the cities have in common? Write your answer in the margin box.

### Reading for the Main Idea

**1.** ( *Environment and Society* ) How does Japan's physical geography affect farming?

**2.** ( *Human Systems* ) How has Japan developed its industries without plentiful raw materials?

### Critical Thinking

**3. Drawing Inferences and Conclusions** In what ways do the daily lives of the Japanese reflect influences of Western culture?

**4. Drawing Inferences and Conclusions** Why do you suppose other countries might be concerned about Japan's surplus?

### Organizing What You Know

**5. Summarizing** Copy the following graphic organizer. Use it to list the activities and services available in Tokyo.

Tokyo

# Section 4

## The History and Culture of the Koreas

### Read to Discover

1. What was Korea's ancient history like?
2. What were the major events of Korea's early modern period?
3. Why was Korea divided after World War II, and what were the effects of the division?

### Define
demilitarized zone

### Locate
North Korea
South Korea

**WHY IT MATTERS**

The Korean War left many lingering problems for Koreans and Americans alike. Use CNN**fyi**.com or other **current events** sources to find examples of current relations between the United States and North and South Korea. Record the findings in your journal.

*A tray decorated with mother-of-pearl inlay*

## Ancient Korea

Korea's earliest inhabitants were nomadic hunters from north and central Asia. About 1500 B.C. they adopted rice farming, which had been introduced from China. Then, in 108 B.C., the Chinese invaded Korea. This invasion marked the beginning of a long period of Chinese influence on Korean culture. The Chinese introduced their system of writing and their system of examinations for government jobs. They also introduced Buddhism and Confucianism to Korea.

Korea's original religion—shamanism—continued to be practiced, along with the newer traditions introduced from China. According to shamanism, natural places and ancestors have spirits. Many mountains are particularly sacred to Koreans. Shamanism is still practiced in South Korea.

Over the centuries, Korean tribes eventually recaptured most of the peninsula. In the A.D. 600s the kingdom of Silla (SI-luh) united the peninsula. Korea's golden age began. Korea became known in Asia for its architecture, painting, ceramics, and fine jewelry.

*A weaver demonstrates his craft near Seoul.*

*This celadon vase is from the A.D. 1000s.*

Heavy fencing and explosives have kept people out of the demilitarized zone for decades. As a result, this land has provided a safe home for rare animal and plant species. Some scientists hope that in the future the DMZ can be set aside as a nature preserve, which would attract tourists while protecting the wildlife.

During the Silla period Korea began using the results of examinations to award government jobs. Generally only boys who were sons of noblemen could take the examinations. People from the lower classes could not rise to important positions by studying and passing the examinations, as they could in China.

By the early 900s a new kingdom had taken power. The modern name of Korea comes from this kingdom's name, Koryo. During the Koryo dynasty, Korean artisans invented the first movable metal type. During the following dynasty, scholars developed the Hangul (HAHN-gool) alphabet, which was officially adopted in 1446. Hangul was much easier to use with the Korean language than Chinese characters had been. Because Hangul had only 24 symbols, it was easier to learn. It had previously been necessary to memorize about 20,000 Chinese characters to read the Buddhist scriptures.

✔ **READING CHECK:** *Human Systems* How did the Chinese influence Korea's ancient history?

## Early Modern Korea

By the early 1600s China again controlled Korea. For 300 years Korea remained under Chinese control. Closed off to most other outsiders, Korea became known as the Hermit Kingdom. During this period, Catholicism was introduced into Korea through missionaries in China. Korea's Christian community was sometimes persecuted and remained small until the mid-1900s.

In the mid-1890s Japan defeated China in the Sino-Japanese War. This cleared the way for Japan to annex Korea in 1910. The Japanese ruled harshly. They took over the Korean government and many businesses and farms. Koreans were forced to take Japanese names, and

Japanese was taught in the schools. Japan ruled Korea until the end of World War II.

✓ **READING CHECK:** ( *Places and Regions* ) What were some major events in Korea's early modern period?

# A Divided Korea

At the end of World War II, U.S. and Soviet troops oversaw the Japanese departure from Korea. The Soviets helped Communist leaders take power in the north. The United States backed a democratic government in the south. The United Nations hoped that the Koreas would reunite. However, the United States and the Soviet Union could not agree on a plan. In 1948 South Korea officially became the Republic of Korea. North Korea became the Democratic People's Republic of Korea led by Korean Communist dictator Kim Il Sung.

In 1950 North Korea tried to unify the country by invading South Korea, resulting in the Korean War. The United Nations sent troops—mostly U.S.—to defend South Korea. Communist China sent forces to North Korea. A truce was declared in 1953, but Korea remains divided. The border between North Korea and South Korea is a strip of land roughly 2.4 miles (4 km) wide called the **demilitarized zone** (DMZ). This buffer zone separates the two countries. A total of about 1 million U.S., South Korean, and North Korean soldiers patrol the DMZ. It is the world's most heavily guarded border.

In the early 1970s and early 1990s North and South Korea tried to reach an agreement for reunification. The negotiations failed. Still, Koreans remain hopeful that their country will one day be reunited.

✓ **READING CHECK:** ( *Places and Regions* ) What were some events in Korea's history after World War II?

**Our Amazing Planet**

Casting bronze bells is an ancient Korean craft. The largest bell in South Korea, completed in A.D. 771, is more than 12 feet (3.6 m) tall and weighs about 25 tons (110,000 kg). When struck, it is said that the bell's tone can be heard 40 miles (64 km) away.

**go.hrw.com** **Homework Practice Online** Keyword: SK3 HP25

## Section Review 4

**Define and explain:** demilitarized zone

**Working with Sketch Maps** On the map you created in Section 3, label North Korea and South Korea. In the margin, draw a box and include in it information that explains the significance of the DMZ. When was it established?

**Reading for the Main Idea**

1. ( *Human Systems* ) What were some of the accomplishments of the early Koreans before about 1600? What dynasty gave Korea its name?

2. ( *Human Systems* ) What long-lasting effect did the Korean War have on the Korean Peninsula?

**Critical Thinking**

3. **Analyzing Information** How has the Korean Peninsula been influenced by other countries?

4. **Making Generalizations and Predictions** What might be preventing North Korea and South Korea from reuniting?

**Organizing What You Know**

5. **Sequencing** Copy the following time line. Use it to list the important events of Korean history from 1500 B.C. through the 1500s.

1500 B.C. ————————————— 1500s

### Read to Discover

1. What are South Korea's government and society like?
2. What is South Korea's economy like?
3. What is North Korea like?
4. How has North Korea's government affected the country's development?

### Define

entrepreneurs

*chaebol*

kimchi

famine

### Locate

Seoul

Pusan

P'yŏngyang

*Korean-style vegetables*

### WHY IT MATTERS

North and South Korea are still struggling to reach an understanding after some 50 years since the end of the Korean War. Use CNN**fyi**.com or other **current events** sources to find examples of the political, economic, and diplomatic relations between the two countries. Record the findings in your journal.

## North Korea and South Korea

| Country | Population/ Growth Rate | Life Expectancy | Literacy Rate | Per Capita GDP |
|---------|------------------------|-----------------|---------------|----------------|
| North Korea | 21,968,228 1.2% | 68, male 74, female | 99% | $1,000 |
| South Korea | 47,904,370 0.9% | 71, male 79, female | 98% | $16,100 |
| United States | 281,421,906 0.9% | 74, male 80, female | 97% | $36,200 |

**Sources:** Central Intelligence Agency, *The World Factbook 2001;* U.S. Census Bureau

**Interpreting the Chart How does North Korea's per capita GDP compare to that of South Korea?**

## South Korea's People and Government

South Korea is densely populated. There are 1,197 people per square mile (462/sq km). Most people live in the narrow, fertile plain along the western coast of the Korean Peninsula. Travel in the peninsula's mountainous interior is difficult, so few people live there. South Korea's population is growing slowly, at about the same rate as in most industrialized countries.

**South Korea's Cities** Because South Korea is densely populated, space is a luxury—just as it is in Japan. Most South Koreans live in small apartments in crowded cities. Seoul (SOHL) is the country's capital and largest city. The government, the economy, and the educational system are centered there. After the Korean War, the population exploded because refugees flocked to Seoul seeking work and housing. By 1994 the city had nearly 11 million residents. Today, Seoul is one of the world's most densely populated cities. It has some 7,000 people per square mile (2,703/sq km).

South Korea's second-largest city is Pusan (POO-sahn). This major seaport and industrial center lies on the southern coast. Pusan also has an important fishing industry.

The rapid growth of South Korea's cities has brought problems. Housing is expensive. The many factories, cars, and coal-fired heating systems sometimes cause dangerous levels of air pollution. Industrial waste has also polluted the water.

**Postwar Government** South Korea is technically a democracy, but it was run by military dictators until the late 1980s. More recently, South Korea introduced a multiparty democratic government. The government controls economic development but does not own businesses and property.

 **READING CHECK:** ⟨ *Human Systems* ⟩ What kind of government does South Korea have?

# South Korean Society

Like Japan's, South Korea's population is homogeneous. Most Koreans complete high school. About half go on to some form of higher education. Women are beginning to hold important jobs.

**Traditional Families** Most Koreans marry someone they meet through their parents. Most families still value sons. This is because only a son can take over the family name. Only a son can lead the ceremonies to honor the family's ancestors. Some couples who do not have a son adopt a boy with the same family name. This is not too difficult because there are few family names in Korea.

**Religion** Today, Christianity is the most common religion, followed closely by Buddhism. Whatever their religion, most Koreans take part in ceremonies to honor their ancestors. Most also follow Confucian values. Many Koreans still ask shamans for personal advice.

 **READING CHECK:** ⟨ *Human Systems* ⟩ What is South Korea's society like?

This view looks out over the busy harbor of Pusan. Travelers can take a ferry from Pusan across the Korean Strait to Japan.

**Interpreting the Visual Record** **How does this photo show the importance of shipping to this region's economy?**

## South Korea's Economy

After the war, South Korea industrialized quickly, and its market economy grew. By the 1990s it had become one of the strongest economies in Asia.

**Industry** Koreans' strong sense of family often carries over into work. Large groups of relatives may become **entrepreneurs**. This means they use their money and talents to start and manage a business. Businesses are sometimes linked through family and personal ties into huge industrial groups called **chaebol**.

The government has encouraged the use of nuclear power. It also has encouraged the growth of high-technology industries. These industries make electronic goods for export. Other important industries are steel, shipbuilding, automobiles, and textiles. In the late 1990s South Korea, like many other Asian countries, experienced an economic slowdown. It is now making a rapid recovery.

**Agriculture** South Korea has the peninsula's richest agricultural land. However, less than 20 percent of the land can be farmed. The shortage of land means that South Korea must import about half of its food.

Most South Korean farms are small and lie along the western and southern coasts. The rugged terrain makes using heavy machinery difficult. As a result, farmers must do much of their work by hand and with small tractors. Since the late 1980s there has been a shortage of farmworkers.

Farmers grow rice on about half their land. Other important crops are Chinese cabbage and soybeans. Soybeans are used to make soy sauce and tofu, or bean curd. Chinese cabbage that has been spiced and pickled is called **kimchi**. This is Korea's national dish.

✓ **READING CHECK:** *Places and Regions* What is South Korea's economy like?

## North Korea's People and Government

North Korea's Communist Party controls the government. For many years, North Korea had ties and traded mostly with other Communist countries. Since the Soviet Union's breakup in 1991, North Korea has been largely isolated from the rest of the world. In the late 1990s North Korea angered many countries by trying to develop nuclear weapons and missiles.

**Population** Like South Korea and Japan, North Korea has a homogeneous population. North Korea is not as densely populated as South Korea. In North Korea, there are 513 people per square mile (198/sq km).

This is one of many statues of Kim Il Sung in P'yŏngyang. He led North Korea from the end of World War II until his death in 1994. Although dead, Kim Il Sung was declared the "Eternal President" of North Korea in 1998.

**Interpreting the Visual Record** How does this statue compare to monuments honoring important people in the history of the United States?

**North Korea's Capital** The capital of North Korea is P'yŏngyang (pyuhng-YANG). About 2.6 million people live there. North Korea's only university is in P'yŏngyang. Few private cars can be seen on the city streets. Most residents use buses or the subway system to get around. At night, many streets are dark because the city frequently experiences shortages of electricity.

✓ **READING CHECK:** ( *Places and Regions* ) What is North Korea like?

## North Korea's Economy

North Korea has a command economy. This means that the central government plans the economy and controls what is produced. The government also owns all the land and housing and controls access to jobs.

North Korea's best farmland is along the west coast. Only 14 percent of North Korea's land can be farmed. Most of this land is owned by the state. It is farmed by cooperatives—groups of farmers who work the land together. Some people have small gardens to grow food for themselves or to sell at local markets.

North Korea does not produce enough food to feed its people. It lost its main source of food and fertilizer when the Soviet Union collapsed. Poor harvests in the mid-1990s made the situation worse. **Famine**, or severe food shortages, resulted. The government's hostility toward the West made getting aid difficult. Thousands starved.

North Korea is rich in mineral resources. It has also developed a nuclear power industry. North Korea makes machinery, iron, and steel. However, its factories use outdated technology.

✓ **READING CHECK:** ( *Human Systems* ) How has North Korea's government affected the country's economic development?

Rice farming requires large amounts of human energy for transplanting, weeding, and harvesting. These farmers are planting seedlings.

**Interpreting the Visual Record Why do you think it would be difficult to use machinery for transplanting here?**

go.hrw.com **Homework Practice Online**
Keyword: SK3 HP25

# Section Review 5

**Define and explain:** entrepreneurs, *chaebol*, kimchi, famine

**Working with Sketch Maps** On the map you created in Section 4, label Seoul, Pusan, and P'yŏngyang. Why do you think these cities remain important? Write your answer in a box in the margin.

### Reading for the Main Idea

1. ( *Places and Regions* ) How did South Korea's cities change after the Korean War?

2. ( *Environment and Society* ) How does North Korea's physical geography affect its farmers?

3. ( *Places and Regions* ) What kind of economies do North and South Korea have, and how are they different?

### Critical Thinking

4. **Finding the Main Idea** How have entrepreneurs affected South Korea's economy?

### Organizing What You Know

5. **Categorizing** List characteristics of the government, industry, and agriculture of North and South Korea since World War II. Where the circles overlap, list things the countries share.

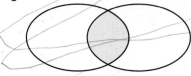

# Reviewing What You Know

## Building Vocabulary

On a separate sheet of paper, write sentences to define each of the following words.

1. tsunamis
2. shamans
3. samurai
4. shogun
5. Diet
6. kimonos
7. futon
8. intensive cultivation
9. work ethic
10. protectionism
11. trade surplus
12. demilitarized zone
13. entrepreneurs
14. kimchi
15. famine

## Reviewing the Main Ideas

1. ( *Places and Regions* ) What are the geographic features of Japan? of Korea?

2. ( *Human Systems* ) Which other Asian countries have influenced the culture of Japan? What contributions did they make?

3. ( *Places and Regions* ) What factors have contributed to Japan's economic success?

4. ( *Human Systems* ) Why were there foreign troops on the Korean Peninsula in the 1950s?

5. ( *Places and Regions* ) Why has Seoul grown rapidly since the Korean War? What is life in the city like?

## Understanding Environment and Society

### Resource Use

Japan's cultured-pearl industry is an example of how the Japanese have adapted to their limited amount of land by making creative use of the sea. Create a presentation about the pearl industry. As you create your presentation, consider the following:

- The kinds of pearls that are found there.
- Where and how pearls are produced.
- Things that could hurt Japan's role in the pearl industry.

## Thinking Critically

1. **Analyzing Information** How have geographic features affected where people live in Japan and the Korean Peninsula?

2. **Contrasting** What physical features make Japan different from the Koreas? Create a chart to organize your answer.

3. **Finding the Main Idea** How have the Japanese changed the physical landscape to meet their needs?

4. **Analyzing Information** How has Tokyo developed into a megalopolis?

5. **Contrasting** How do the economies of North and South Korea differ?

# Building Social Studies Skills

## Map ACTIVITY

On a separate sheet of paper, match the letters on the map with their correct labels.

| | |
|---|---|
| Hokkaido | Tokyo |
| Honshu | Seoul |
| Shikoku | P'yŏngyang |
| Kyushu | |

## Mental Mapping Skills ACTIVITY

On a separate sheet of paper, draw a freehand map of Japan and the Koreas. Make a key for your map and label the following:

| | |
|---|---|
| China | North Korea |
| Inland Sea | Sea of Japan |
| Japan | South Korea |

## WRITING ACTIVITY

Imagine that you are traveling in Japan, North Korea, or South Korea. Write a one-page letter to a friend describing the places you have visited and an adventure you have had during your stay. Be sure to use standard grammar, spelling, sentence structure, and punctuation.

# Alternative Assessment

## Portfolio ACTIVITY

### Learning About Your Local Geography

**Cooperative Project** Japan and South Korea are very densely populated. How densely populated is your state? With your group, research the population densities of counties within your state. Create a population density map of the area you have researched.

### internet connect

Internet Activity: **go.hrw.com**
KEYWORD: SK3 GT25

Choose a topic to explore Japan and the Koreas:

- Investigate volcanoes.
- Visit Japan and the Koreas.
- Compare your school to a Japanese school.

# Southeast Asia

*Our study of the world now takes us to Southeast Asia. This vast region stretches from Myanmar eastward to New Guinea in the Pacific Ocean.*

**S**awaddee! (May you have good fortune!) I am Chosita, and I am 14 years old. I live in Bangkok with my parents and my older sister. We get up early for school because traffic in Bangkok is very heavy. By 6:00 A.M. we are on the road. My school has an eatery where street vendors sell all kinds of food—noodles in broth with beef, stir-fried noodles with meat and greens, dessert cakes of taro, pumpkin, and sticky rice, and fruits like rambutan, mangosteen, durian, and mango.

We go to school from June to September and from November to February. Our big vacation is March through May.

Our school has 38 students and two teachers in each class. I will not learn to use the computer until next year because we are the last class under the old school policy. The new policy has all students begin learning the computer in fourth grade.

สวัสดีค่ะ ดิฉันชื่อ โชสิตา
ดิฉันอยู่ที่กรุงเทพฯ
ซึ่งเป็นเมืองหลวงของประเทศไทยค่ะ

▲
Translation: Hi! My name is Chosita. I live in Bangkok, the capital of Thailand.

# Section 1 Physical Geography

## Read to Discover

1. What are the major physical features of Southeast Asia?
2. What climates, vegetation, and wildlife are found in the region?
3. What resources does Southeast Asia have?

## Define

mainland
archipelagos

## Locate

| | |
|---|---|
| Indochina Peninsula | Irian Jaya |
| Malay Peninsula | Borneo |
| New Guinea | Java |
| Malay Archipelago | Sumatra |
| Philippines | Mekong River |

### WHY IT MATTERS

Indonesia is made up of thousands of islands. Many have their own culture. There are ongoing conflicts between these groups. Use CNNfyi.com or other current events sources to find examples of this problem. Record your findings in your journal.

*Golden statue from Thailand*

## Southeast Asia: Physical-Political

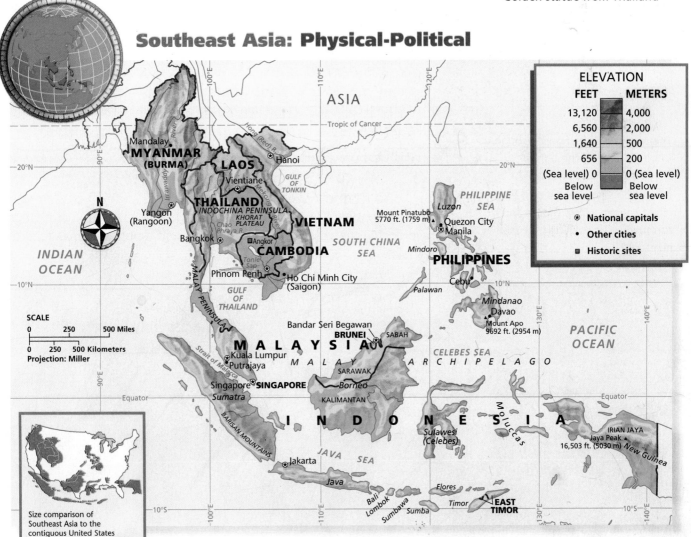

Size comparison of Southeast Asia to the contiguous United States

**internet** connect

GO TO: go.hrw.com
KEYWORD: SK3 CH26
FOR: Web sites about
Southeast Asia

**Do you remember what you learned about the Pacific Ring of Fire? See Chapter 2 to review.**

The Mekong River flows through a floodplain along the border between Thailand and Laos.
**Interpreting the Visual Record What might happen to low islands and surrounding areas during the wet monsoon?**

# Physical Features

Southeast Asia is made up of two peninsulas and two large island groups. The Indochina and Malay (muh-LAY) Peninsulas lie on the Asian **mainland**. A mainland is a region's main landmass. The two large groups of islands, or **archipelagos** (ahr-kuh-PE-luh-gohs), lie between the mainland and New Guinea. They are the Malay Archipelago—made up mostly of Indonesia—and the Philippines. The Philippines are sometimes considered part of the Malay Archipelago. Western New Guinea is called Irian Jaya. It is part of Indonesia.

**Landforms** Southeast Asia's highest mountains are on the mainland in northern Myanmar (MYAHN-mahr). Mountain ranges fan out southward into Thailand (TY-land), Laos (LOWS), and Vietnam (vee-ET-NAHM). Between the mountains are low plateaus and river floodplains. The floodplains are rich farmlands.

Some of the large islands also have high mountains. Those islands include Borneo, Java, Sumatra, New Guinea, and some in the Philippines. They are part of the Pacific Ring of Fire. Earthquakes and volcanic eruptions often shake this part of the world.

**Rivers** Five major river systems drain the mainland. Many people and the largest cities are found near these rivers. The greatest river is the Mekong (MAY-KAWNG). The Mekong River flows southeast from China to southern Vietnam. You will read about the other rivers later in this chapter.

✓ **READING CHECK:** *Places and Regions* What are Southeast Asia's major physical features?

# Climate, Vegetation, and Wildlife

The warm temperatures of this tropical region generally do not change much during the year. However, northern and mountain areas tend to be cooler.

Much of the rainfall on the mainland is seasonal. Wet monsoon winds from nearby warm oceans bring heavy rains in the summer. Dry monsoons from the northeast bring drier weather in winter. Most of the islands are wet all year. Typhoons bring heavy rains and powerful winds to the island countries.

The region's tropical rain forests are home to many kinds of plants and animals. About 40,000 kinds of flowering plants grow in Indonesia alone. Rhinoceroses, orangutans, tigers, and elephants also live in the region. However, many of these plants and animals are endangered. Southeast Asia's rain forests are being cleared for farmland, tropical wood, and mining.

◄ *Orangutan* is a Malaysian word for "man of the forest." These apes once lived in jungles throughout much of Southeast Asia. Hunting by humans has thinned the orangutan population in much of the region. Most orangutans today live on Borneo and Sumatra.

✓ **READING CHECK:** ( *Places and Regions* ) What are the region's climates, vegetation, and wildlife like?

## Resources

Southeast Asia's rain forests produce valuable wood and other products. Thailand, Indonesia, and Malaysia (muh-LAY-zhuh) are the world's largest producers of natural rubber. The rubber tree is native to South America. However, it grows well in Southeast Asia's tropical climates.

Rich volcanic soils, floodplains, and tropical climates are good for farming. Abundant water and good soils in river deltas are ideal for growing rice. Coconuts, palm oil, sugarcane, coffee, and spices are also key products. Countries here also mine tin, iron ore, oil, and gas.

**A** plant in Indonesia produces the world's largest flower —about 3 feet (1 m) across!

✓ **READING CHECK:** ( *Places and Regions* ) What are the region's important resources?

go.hrw.com **Homework Practice Online**
Keyword: SK3 HP26

# Section Review 1

**Define and explain:** mainland, archipelagos

**Working with Sketch Maps** On a map of Southeast Asia that your teacher provides or that you draw, label the following: Indochina Peninsula, Malay Peninsula, New Guinea, Malay Archipelago, Philippines, Irian Jaya, Borneo, Java, Sumatra, and the Mekong River. In a box in the margin, describe the Mekong River.

## Reading for the Main Idea

1. ( *Places and Regions* ) Where are the region's highest mountains?

2. ( *Places and Regions* ) Where are large cities found?

3. ( *Places and Regions* ) Which countries are the world's largest producers of natural rubber?

## Critical Thinking

4. **Making Generalizations and Predictions** What do you think might happen to the region's wildlife if much of the tropical rain forests continue to be destroyed?

## Organizing What You Know

5. **Summarizing** Copy the following graphic organizer. Use it to describe the region's climates, vegetation and wildlife, and resources.

| Climates | Vegetation and wildlife | Resources |
|----------|------------------------|-----------|
|          |                        |           |

# Section 2  History and Culture

## Read to Discover

1. What are some important events in the history of Southeast Asia?
2. What are the people and culture of Southeast Asia like today?

## Define

refugees

## Locate

| | |
|---|---|
| Angkor | Indonesia |
| Cambodia | Malaysia |
| Thailand | Timor |
| Vietnam | Myanmar |
| Laos | Singapore |

### WHY IT MATTERS

Sea trade routes have always been important in this region but have also created a piracy problem. Use CNNfyi.com or other current events sources to find examples of piracy in this region. Record your findings in your journal.

*Assorted peppers from Myanmar*

---

The Khmer built the beautiful Angkor Wat in the A.D. 1100s in Angkor. This vast temple in present-day Cambodia was dedicated to Vishnu, a Hindu god.

**Interpreting the Visual Record** How does this temple's architecture compare to other religious buildings you have seen?

# History

Southeast Asia was home to some of the world's earliest human settlements. Over time many peoples moved there from China and India. The Khmer (kuh-MER) developed the most advanced of the region's early societies. The Khmer Empire was based in Angkor in what is now Cambodia (kam-BOH-dee-uh). It controlled a large area from the early A.D. 800s to the mid-1200s.

**Colonial Era** Europeans began to establish colonies in Southeast Asia in the 1500s. By the end of the 1800s, the Portuguese, British, Dutch, French, and Spanish controlled most of the region. The United States won control of the Philippines from Spain after the Spanish-American War in 1898. Just Siam (sy-AM), now called Thailand, remained independent.

A Filipino official releases a dove during his country's independence celebrations in Manila. The Philippines was the largest U.S. overseas possession from 1898 to 1946.

Japan invaded and occupied most of Southeast Asia during World War II. After Japan was defeated in 1945, the United States granted the Philippines independence a year later. European countries tried to regain control of their colonies in the region. Some Southeast Asians decided to fight for independence. One of the bloodiest wars was in French Indochina. The French finally left in 1954. Their former colonies of Vietnam, Laos, and Cambodia became independent. By the mid-1960s, European rule had ended in most of the region.

**Modern Era** Unfortunately, fighting did not end in some countries when the Europeans left. Vietnam split into two countries. In the 1960s the United States sent troops to defend South Vietnam against communist North Vietnam. Civil wars also raged in Laos and Cambodia. Communist forces took power in all the countries in 1975. North and South Vietnam were then united into one country.

The region's wars caused terrible destruction. Millions died, including more than 50,000 Americans. About 1 million Vietnamese **refugees** tried to escape the communist takeover in South Vietnam. Refugees are people who flee their own country, usually for economic or political reasons. Many refugees from the region came to the United States.

In Cambodia more than 1 million people died under a cruel communist government. That government ruled from 1975 to 1978. Then Vietnam invaded Cambodia in 1978, sparking another conflict. That war continued off and on until the mid-1990s. Many Cambodian refugees fled to Thailand.

Communists and other groups also fought against governments in the Philippines, Indonesia, and Malaysia. In 1975 Indonesia invaded the former Portuguese

Hanoi's Ho Chi Minh Mausoleum honors the communist leader who fought for Vietnam's independence. He led North Vietnam from 1954 to his death in 1969. Many U.S. soldiers and Vietnamese died during the war he led against South Vietnam.

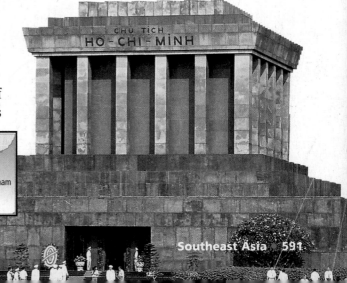

colony of East Timor. The East Timorese demanded independence. However, the Indonesian military kept a tight grip on the region. The people of East Timor voted for independence in 1999. East Timor then plunged again into violence. The United Nations sent troops to restore peace and manage the area before independence was achieved.

**Governments** The region's countries have had different kinds of governments. Many have been ruled by dictators. Some countries, such as the Philippines and Indonesia, now have governments elected by the people.

In other countries, the people still have little say in their government. For example, Myanmar is ruled by a military government. That government has jailed and even killed its opponents. Vietnam and Laos are still ruled by Communist governments. Only recently have Indonesians been allowed to vote in free elections. In some countries, such as Singapore, the same party always wins elections.

✓ **READING CHECK:** *Places and Regions* What were some key events in Southeast Asian history?

# Culture

The populations of most countries in Southeast Asia are very diverse. This is because many different peoples have moved to the area over time. Today, for example, nearly 70 percent of the people in Myanmar are Burmese. However, Chinese, Asian Indians, and many other ethnic groups also live there.

The Shwedagon Pagoda is a beautiful Buddhist shrine in Yangon, Myanmar. Pagodas are important parts of a Buddhist temple complex. **Interpreting the Visual Record** **What architectural features do you see in the photograph?**

Many ethnic Chinese live in the largest cities of most Southeast Asian countries. In Singapore they are a majority of the population—more than 75 percent. Singapore is a tiny country at the tip of the Malay Peninsula.

**Languages and Religions** The peoples of Southeast Asia speak many different languages. For example, in the former Dutch colony of Indonesia, most people speak Bahasa Indonesia. However, Javanese, other local dialects, English, and Dutch are also spoken there. European and Chinese languages are spoken in many other countries.

In addition, Indians, Chinese, Arab traders, and Europeans brought different religions to the region. For example, Hinduism is practiced in the region's Indian communities. However, Buddhism is the most common religion in the mainland countries today. Islam is the major religion in Malaysia, Brunei, and Indonesia. In fact, Indonesia has the largest Islamic population in the world. Nearly 90 percent of its more than 228 million people are Muslim.

Christians are a minority in most of the former European colonies. However, more than 80 percent of people in the Philippines, a former Spanish colony, are Roman Catholic.

**Food** Southeast Asian foods have been influenced by Chinese, South Asian, and European cooking styles. There are many spicy, mild, and sweet varieties. Rice is the most important food in nearly all of the countries. It is served with many other foods and spices, such as curries and chili peppers. Coconut is also important. It is served as a separate dish or used as an ingredient in other foods.

▲

Women in Laos sprinkle water on passing Buddhist monks during a New Year festival. This custom symbolizes the washing away of the old year. It is said to bring good luck to people in the year ahead.

**Interpreting the Visual Record**
**What kinds of clothes are the monks wearing?**

✓ **READING CHECK:** *Human Systems*  How have migration and cultural borrowing influenced the region's culture?

**Section Review 2**

**Define and explain:** refugees

**Working with Sketch Maps** On the map you created in Section 1, label the region's countries, Angkor, and Timor. In a box in the margin, describe the recent history of East Timor.

**Reading for the Main Idea**

1. *Places and Regions*  What was the Khmer Empire?

2. *Human Systems*  How did Europeans influence the region's history and culture?

**Critical Thinking**

3. **Drawing Inferences and Conclusions**  Why do you think European countries wanted to regain their Southeast Asian colonies following World War II?

4. **Finding the Main Idea**  What religion is most common in the mainland countries? in the island countries?

**Organizing What You Know**

5. **Sequencing**  Copy the following time line. Use it to identify important people, years, periods, and events in Southeast Asia's history.

A.D. 800                                    2000

# Section 3 · Mainland Southeast Asia Today

## Read to Discover

1. Where do people in the mainland countries live today?
2. What are the economies of the mainland countries like?

## Define

*klongs*

## Locate

Bangkok
Yangon
Hanoi
Ho Chi Minh City
Chao Phraya River

Irrawaddy River
Hong (Red) River
Vientiane
Phnom Penh

### WHY IT MATTERS

The region's cities are growing rapidly. This can create problems with the city's everyday functioning. Use CNNfyi.com or other **current events** sources to find examples of urbanization problems in the region. Record your findings in your journal.

*Golden door of a Buddhist temple*

## People and Cities

Most mainland Southeast Asians today live in rural areas. Many are farmers in fertile river valleys and deltas. Fewer people live in remote hill and mountain villages.

However, the region's cities have been growing rapidly. People are moving to urban areas to look for work. The cities have many businesses, services, and opportunities that are not found in rural areas. Many of the cities today are crowded, smoggy, and noisy.

Look at the chapter map. You will find that the largest cities are located along major rivers. Location near rivers places these cities near important rice-growing areas. Access to rivers also makes them key

A Vietnamese man sells incense sticks in Ho Chi Minh City.

**Interpreting the Visual Record** **Why might people in warm, sunny climates wear hats like the one in this photo?**

shipping centers for farm and factory products. The largest cities are Bangkok, Yangon, Hanoi, and Ho Chi Minh City.

**Bangkok** The mainland's largest city is Bangkok, Thailand's capital. Bangkok lies near the mouth of the Chao Phraya (chow PRY-uh) River. More than 7 million people live there. Much of Bangkok is connected by **klongs**, or canals. The *klongs* are used for transportation and for selling and shipping goods. They also drain water from the city.

**Other Cities** The region's second-largest city is Yangon, formerly known as Rangoon. It is Myanmar's capital and major seaport. The city is located in the Irrawaddy River delta on the coast of the Andaman Sea. To the east, Vietnam's largest cities are also located in major river deltas. The capital, Hanoi (ha-NOY), is located in the Hong (Red) River delta in the north. Ho Chi Minh City is located in the Mekong River delta in the south. Ho Chi Minh City was once known as Saigon and was South Vietnam's capital. Today it is an important seaport and business center with more than 4.6 million people.

▲
Boat traffic can be heavy along Bangkok's *klongs*. These canals have been part of the city's original transportation system for centuries.

✓ **READING CHECK:** ( *Places and Regions* ) Where do most people in mainland Southeast Asia live today and why?

# Economy

War, bad governments, and other problems have slowed progress in most of the mainland countries. However, rich resources could make the future brighter for the people there.

**Vietnam** Vietnam's economy has been slowly recovering since the end of the war in 1975. In recent years, the Communist government has begun moving from a command economy to a more market-oriented one. Some people are now allowed to own private businesses. Most Vietnamese remain farmers.

Most of Vietnam's factories, coal, oil, and other resources are in the north. The Hong and Mekong River deltas are major farming areas. Rice is the most important crop and food. In many places it is planted twice each year.

**Laos** This mountainous, landlocked country has few good roads, no railroads, and few telephones and televisions. Only some cities have

## Mainland Southeast Asia

| Country | Population/ Growth Rate | Life Expectancy | Literacy Rate | Per Capita GDP |
|---|---|---|---|---|
| Cambodia | 12,491,501 2.3% | 55, male 59, female | 35% | $1,300 |
| Laos | 5,635,967 2.5% | 52, male 55, female | 57% | $1,700 |
| Myanmar | 41,994,678 0.6% | 54, male 57, female | 83% | $1,500 |
| Thailand | 61,797,751 0.9% | 66, male 72, female | 94% | $6,700 |
| Vietnam | 79,939,014 1.5% | 67, male 72, female | 94% | $1,950 |
| United States | 281,421,906 0.9% | 74, male 80, female | 97% | $36,200 |

**Sources:** Central Intelligence Agency, *The World Factbook 2001;* U.S. Census Bureau

**Interpreting the Chart According to the data in the chart, which country in the region is the most economically developed?**

## Major Producers of Natural Rubber

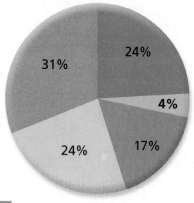

- 24%
- 31%
- 4%
- 17%
- 24%

■ Thailand
■ Indonesia
■ Malaysia
■ Rest of Southeast Asia
■ Rest of the world

**Source:** United Nations, *Monthly Bulletin of Statistics*, July 1999

*Interpreting the Chart* **Which country is the largest producer of natural rubber?**

▶

Trees like these in Thailand make the region the world's largest producer of natural rubber.

electricity. The economy is mostly traditional—most people are subsistence farmers. They produce just enough food for themselves and their families. The Communist government in Vientiane (vyen-TYAHN), the capital, has also recently begun allowing more economic freedom.

**Cambodia** Economic progress in Cambodia has been particularly slow because of war and political problems. Agriculture is the most important part of the economy. The capital and largest city, Phnom Penh (puh-NAWM PEN), is located along the Mekong River. It lies in Cambodia's southern rice-growing area.

**Thailand** Thailand's economy has had problems but is the strongest of the mainland countries. This is partly because Thailand has rich resources. These resources include timber, natural rubber, seafood, rice, many minerals, and gems. Factories produce computers and electronics. Many Thai operate small businesses. Tourism is also important.

**Myanmar** This former British colony is also called Burma. It gained independence in 1948 and was officially renamed Myanmar in 1989. It has rich resources, including copper, tin, iron ore, timber, rubber, and oil. However, a harsh military government has limited political freedom. This has slowed economic progress.

✓ **READING CHECK:** *Places and Regions*
What are the mainland economies like?

## Section Review 3

go.hrw.com **Homework Practice Online**
Keyword: SK3 HP26

**Define and explain:** *klongs*

**Working with Sketch Maps** On the map you created in Section 2, label Bangkok, Yangon, Hanoi, Ho Chi Minh City, Chao Phraya River, Irrawaddy River, Hong (Red) River, Vientiane, and Phnom Penh. Describe the mainland's largest city.

### Reading for the Main Idea

1. ( *Places and Regions* ) Where do most mainland Southeast Asians live and why?

2. ( *Human Systems* ) Why are many people moving to cities?

3. ( *Places and Regions* ) Which country has the strongest economy and why?

### Critical Thinking

4. **Finding the Main Idea** What kinds of problems appear to have slowed economic progress in the region?

### Organizing What You Know

5. **Summarizing** Copy the following graphic organizer. Use it to describe the mainland's major cities. In each of its six circles, write the name of a city. In the circles, write important facts about the cities.

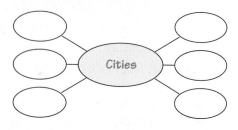

Cities

# Section 4  Island Southeast Asia Today

## Read to Discover

1. What are the major cities of the island countries?
2. What are the economies of the island countries like?

## Define

kampongs
sultan

## Locate

Jakarta
Manila
Kuala Lumpur
Luzon
Bali

A decorative Indonesian fabric called a batik (buh-TEEK)

### WHY IT MATTERS

Some countries in this region have higher per capita GDPs as a result of their growing economies. Use CNN**fyi**.com or other **current events** sources to check economic growth in this region. Record your findings in your journal.

## People and Cities

Indonesia is the largest of the island countries and the world's fourth-most-populous country. The country's more than 17,000 islands were known as the Dutch East Indies until 1949. Malaysia, Singapore, and Brunei were British colonies. The British granted independence to Malaysia in 1963. Singapore split from Malaysia in 1965. In 1984 Brunei became the region's last European colony to gain independence. As you have read, the Philippines gained independence from the United States in 1946. More than 7,000 islands make up that country.

Many people live in rural areas in the island countries. However, the island countries are more urbanized than the mainland countries. As on the mainland, many people are moving to cities in search of jobs. One country, Singapore, is simply a large city on a small island.

Modern skyscrapers tower over colonial-era buildings in Singapore. The city has one of the world's busiest ports.

**Interpreting the Visual Record** What does Singapore's architecture tell you about its economy and culture?

# CONNECTING TO Art

Wayang *puppets*

## Shadow Puppets

Puppetry is an art form with roots in ancient civilizations, including Greece, Rome, China, and India. On the Indonesian island of Java, one of the world's great puppet traditions is known as *wayang*. This shadow puppet theater still entertains audiences.

*Wayang* puppets are beautiful works of art. The puppets are made from thin sheets of painted leather. They are pierced with holes so that light can shine through them. Then they are mounted on sticks. The performance takes place behind a screen. A light source is placed behind the puppets. The puppet's shadows fall on the screen and are visible to the audience on the other side.

*Wayang* performances tell stories from the *Ramayana* and the *Mahabharata*. These are two long poems of the Hindu religion. Hinduism came to Java from India hundreds of years ago. The puppets play the parts of gods, heroes, and villains. A performance usually lasts all night and includes the traditional music of Java. The music is played by an orchestra that includes gongs and other traditional instruments.

Over the years, *wayang* artists have developed other types of puppets. Some puppets are wooden forms. A new generation of artists is even creating computerized stories for *wayang* theater.

### Understanding What You Read
1. Where did puppetry originate?
2. What is a *wayang* performance like?

### Our Amazing Planet

In 1883 a huge volcanic eruption on the Indonesian island of Krakatau killed thousands. Ash in the atmosphere colored sunsets around the world for months.

**Jakarta** The region's largest city is Jakarta, Indonesia's capital. More than 11 million people live there. It is located on Java, which is by far Indonesia's most populous island. Many Indonesians live in **kampongs** around Jakarta. A kampong is a traditional village. It has also become the term for the crowded slums around large cities.

**Singapore** If you traveled from Jakarta to Singapore, you would find two very different cities. Singapore is one of the most modern and cleanest cities in the world. Crime rates also are very low. How has Singapore accomplished this?

Its government is very strict. For example, fines for littering are stiff. People caught transporting illegal drugs can be executed. The government even bans chewing gum and certain movies and music.

Is the lack of some individual freedoms a good trade-off for less crime, a clean city, and a strong economy? Some people in Singapore say yes. Others believe Singapore can be just as successful with less government control.

**Other Cities** The region's other large cities include Manila and Kuala Lumpur. More than 10 million people live in Manila, the capital of the Philippines. The city is a major seaport and industrial center on Luzon. Luzon is the country's largest and most populated island.

Kuala Lumpur is Malaysia's capital as well as its cultural, business, and transportation center. It is a modern city with two of the world's tallest buildings, the twin Petronas Towers.

✔ **READING CHECK:** *Places and Regions* What are some of the major cities of the island countries?

## Economy

The economies of the island countries grew rapidly until the mid-1990s. Then economic and political problems slowed growth for a while. However, rich resources are helping the economies there to recover. In addition, wages and labor costs are low in many of the countries. This means that companies there can manufacture many products more cheaply for export.

**Indonesia** Europeans once called Indonesia the Spice Islands because of its cinnamon, pepper, and nutmeg. Today, its rich resources include natural rubber, oil, natural gas, and timber. Indonesia also has good farmlands for rice and other crops. Busy factories turn out clothing, electronics, and furniture. Some islands, such as Bali, are popular with tourists.

### Island Southeast Asia

| COUNTRY | POPULATION/ GROWTH RATE | LIFE EXPECTANCY | LITERACY RATE | PER CAPITA GDP |
|---------|------------------------|-----------------|---------------|----------------|
| Brunei | 343,653 2.1% | 71, male 76, female | 88% | $17,600 |
| Indonesia | 228,437,870 1.6% | 66, male 71, female | 84% | $2,930 |
| Malaysia | 22,229,040 2.4% | 68, male 74, female | 84% | $7,900 |
| Philippines | 82,841,518 1.7% | 65, male 71, female | 95% | $3,600 |
| Singapore | 4,300,419 1.7% | 77, male 83, female | 94% | $26,500 |
| United States | 281,421,906 0.9% | 74, male 80, female | 97% | $36,200 |

**Sources:** Central Intelligence Agency, *The World Factbook 2001;* U.S. Census Bureau

**Interpreting the Chart According to the chart, which country's economic development is closest to that of the United States?**

Farming is an important economic activity in the Philippines. In mountain areas, farmers plant rice and other crops in terraced fields. These flat terraces hold water and slow erosion along mountainsides.

▼

Bali dancers are popular tourist attractions in Indonesia, a country with many different dance styles. This *Barong* dancer uses her hands, arms, and eyes to help tell a traditional story.

Large areas of Indonesia's tropical rain forests are often burned for farming. Smoke from the fires can spread for hundreds of miles. The smoke sometimes blots out sunlight, smothering cities in haze.

**The Philippines** The Philippines is mostly an agricultural country today. A big problem is the gap between rich and poor Filipinos. A few very rich Filipinos control most of the land and industries. Most farmers are poor and own no land.

The economy has improved in recent years. Companies sell many electronics and clothing products to overseas customers, particularly in the United States. The country also has rich resources, including tropical forests, copper, gold, silver, and oil. Farmers grow sugarcane, rice, corn, coconuts, and tropical fruits.

**Singapore** Singapore is by far the most economically developed country in all of Southeast Asia. The British founded the city at the tip of the Malay Peninsula in 1819. This location along major shipping routes helped make Singapore rich. Goods are stored there before they are shipped to their final stop. In addition, many foreign companies have opened banks, offices, and high-technology industries there.

**Malaysia** Malaysia is made up of two parts. The largest part lies on the southern Malay Peninsula. The second part lies on the northern portion of Borneo. Well-educated workers and rich resources make Malaysia's future look bright. The country produces natural rubber, electronics, automobiles, oil, and timber. The government is trying to attract more high-technology companies to the country. Malaysia is also the world's leading producer of palm oil.

Electronics and technology products are increasingly important to the region's economies. This Filipino is working at a semiconductor manufacturing plant.
**Interpreting the Visual Record** Why do you think the person in the photograph is dressed this way?

**Brunei** Large deposits of oil have made Brunei rich. This small country on the island of Borneo is ruled by a **sultan**. A sultan is the supreme ruler of a Muslim country. Brunei shares the island of Borneo with Indonesia and Malaysia.

This beautiful mosque in Brunei's capital reflects the country's oil wealth. Money from oil and natural gas production pays for many social services there.

✓ **READING CHECK:** *Places and Regions* How do rich resources affect the economies of the island countries?

# Section Review 4

**Define and explain:** kampongs, sultan

**Working with Sketch Maps** On the map you created in Section 3, label Jakarta, Manila, Kuala Lumpur, Luzon, and Bali. In a box in the margin, identify the most heavily populated islands in Indonesia and the Philippines.

## Reading for the Main Idea

1. *Places and Regions* What is the region's largest city? What is the importance of Manila and Kuala Lumpur to their countries?

2. *Places and Regions* Why was Indonesia once called the Spice Islands? What European country once controlled nearly all of Indonesia?

go. hrw .com **Homework Practice Online**
Keyword: SK3 HP26

## Critical Thinking

3. **Analyzing Information** Some Singaporeans say that limiting some individual freedoms is a good trade-off for less crime and a better economy. Do you agree? Why or why not?

4. **Comparing/Contrasting** How have Singapore and Brunei become rich countries?

## Organizing What You Know

5. **Summarizing** Copy the following graphic organizer. Use it to list the nine Southeast Asian countries that are former European colonies. Next to each country's name, write the name of the European country that once controlled it.

| Southeast Asian country | European colonial power |
|---|---|
|  |  |

# CASE STUDY

## MULTIETHNIC INDONESIA

Indonesia is a multiethnic country—a country with many different ethnic groups. The national motto of Indonesia is *Bhinneka Tunggal Ika*, which means "the many are one." This motto comes from the many different ethnic groups that live there.

More than 300 different ethnic groups live in Indonesia. Most of these groups speak their own language and have their own way of life. No single ethnic group holds a majority. The largest are the Javanese, Sundanese, Madurese, and Coastal Malays. The country also has many smaller ethnic groups, such as the Dayaks and the Balinese. Why does Indonesia have so many different ethnic groups? Part of the answer lies in the country's diverse physical geography.

Indonesia is a very large country. It is made up of more than 17,000 islands. About 228 million people live on these islands. Indonesia's islands, mountains, and dense rain forests have served as boundaries between different ethnic groups. Many small ethnic groups lived in isolation and had very little contact with other peoples. Over time, these groups developed their own cultures, languages, and ways of life.

The modern country of Indonesia has its roots in the early 1600s. About this time, Dutch traders built forts in the area. They wanted to protect the trade routes used by Dutch ships to transport spices and other goods. The Dutch remained an important force in the region until Indonesia became independent in 1949. The long history of

Most Indonesians are related to the peoples of East Asia. However, in the eastern islands, most people are of Melanesian origin. Over the centuries, many Arabs, Indians, and Europeans have added to the country's ethnic diversity.

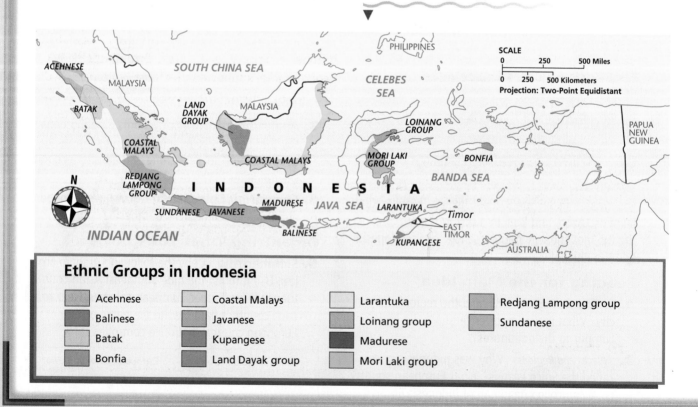

### Ethnic Groups in Indonesia

- Acehnese
- Balinese
- Batak
- Bonfia
- Coastal Malays
- Javanese
- Kupangese
- Land Dayak group
- Larantuka
- Loinang group
- Madurese
- Mori Laki group
- Redjang Lampong group
- Sundanese

The Balinese are one of Indonesia's many ethnic groups. Unlike most other Indonesians, Hinduism is their main religion.

Dutch control helped unify the islands into the modern country of Indonesia.

In addition to this shared past, several other factors have helped unify Indonesia. For example, Indonesia's government has promoted the country's official language, Bahasa Indonesia. Although most Indonesians speak more than one language, Bahasa Indonesia is used in schools and government. The use of this language has been an important force in uniting the country. The government has also tried to develop a common Indonesian culture. It has promoted national holiday celebrations, education, popular art, and television and radio programs.

A shared history, a common education system, and an official language help give isolated ethnic groups an Indonesian identity. However, the country's multiethnic society still faces some important challenges. In certain parts of Indonesia, people want independence. For example, in 1999 people in East Timor voted for independence from Indonesia. This caused a great deal of unrest. Most people there supported the vote, but others did not. When some groups rioted, many Timorese left the area for their own safety. The Acehnese, an ethnic group on the island of Sumatra, have also been seeking independence.

## Ethnic Groups in Indonesia

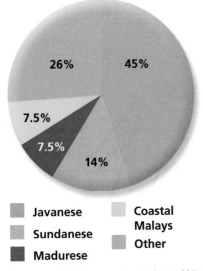

26%
45%
7.5%
7.5%
14%

- Javanese
- Sundanese
- Madurese
- Coastal Malays
- Other

**Source:** Central Intelligence Agency, *The World Factbook 2001*

## Understanding What You Read

1. How diverse is Indonesia's society? What has helped to promote cooperation among the different ethnic groups that live in the country?

2. What are some important challenges facing Indonesia today?

# Reviewing What You Know

## Building Vocabulary

On a separate sheet of paper, write sentences to define each of the following words.

1. mainland
2. archipelagos
3. refugees
4. *klongs*
5. kampongs
6. sultan

## Reviewing the Main Ideas

1. ( Places and Regions )  What peninsulas and archipelagos make up Southeast Asia?

2. ( Places and Regions )  Where will you find the highest mountains in Southeast Asia?

3. ( Places and Regions )  What factors have slowed economic progress in mainland Southeast Asia?

4. ( Places and Regions )  What resources are important to the economies of the region?

5. ( Human Systems )  How did European countries influence Southeast Asia?

## Understanding Environment and Society

### Rice Farming

Rice is the main crop and most common food in Southeast Asia. Develop a presentation about rice farming. In developing your presentation, consider the following:

• How rice is grown.
• What growing conditions are needed.
• Where rice is grown in Southeast Asia.

## Thinking Critically

1. **Drawing Inferences and Conclusions** Why are some cities located near river deltas so large?

2. **Finding the Main Idea** What outside cultures have strongly influenced the development of Southeast Asian culture?

3. **Analyzing Information** How did the Philippines and Vietnam gain independence?

4. **Finding the Main Idea** How do the climates of mainland countries differ from those in the island countries? What natural disasters are a danger in the region?

5. **Analyzing Information** How do labor costs affect the island countries' economies?

### Map ACTIVITY

On a separate sheet of paper, match the letters on the map with their correct labels.

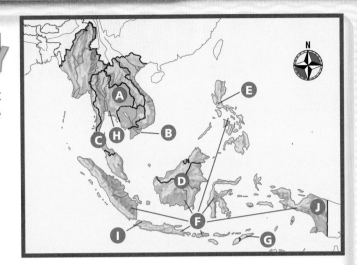

Indochina Peninsula

Malay Peninsula

Malay Archipelago and the Philippines

Irian Jaya

Borneo

Mekong River

Timor

Bangkok

Jakarta

Manila

### Mental Mapping Skills ACTIVITY

On a separate sheet of paper, draw a freehand map of Southeast Asia. Make a key for your map and label the following:

Andaman Sea

Hanoi

Java

Kuala Lumpur

Philippines

Singapore

Sumatra

Yangon

### WRITING ACTIVITY

Imagine that you are an economic adviser for a poor Southeast Asian country. Write a one-paragraph summary explaining how some countries in the region built stronger economies. Use the report to suggest policies your chosen country might adopt to build its economy. Be sure to use standard grammar, spelling, sentence structure, and punctuation.

## Alternative Assessment

### Portfolio ACTIVITY

**Learning About Your Local Geography**

**Individual Project** Find out how your local community was affected by the Vietnam War. Interview community members, locate and read old newspapers or firsthand accounts, and present an oral report.

📄 **internet** connect

Internet Activity: go.hrw.com
KEYWORD: SK3 GT26

Choose a topic to explore about Southeast Asia:

- Explore an Indonesian rain forest.
- Learn about shadow puppets.
- See buildings of Southeast Asia.

## Indonesia's Threatened Rain Forests

### Why Are Rain Forests Important?

Do you know where bananas, pineapples, and oranges originally came from? Each of these plants first grew in a tropical rain forest.

Tropical rain forests are considered by many to be the most important forests in the world. It is estimated that about half of all species of plants, animals, and insects on Earth live in tropical rain forests. Rain forest trees and plants help maintain global temperatures. They also help hold rain-drenched soil in place. This prevents it from washing away and clogging rivers. About one fourth of all medicines currently found in drugstores come from tropical rain forests.

Tropical rain forests can be found in many countries along the equator and between about 20° north and south latitude. One of the largest rain forests is in Brazil's Amazon Basin. In Africa, rain forests are found in many countries, such as Gabon and the Democratic Republic of the Congo. In Southeast Asia, rain forests are found in countries such as Thailand, Vietnam, and Indonesia.

**Deforestation in Indonesia** Indonesia has large areas of tropical rain forest in Borneo, Sumatra, and Irian Jaya. These areas are home to many unusual species of plants and animals. For example, the largest flower in the world, the *Rafflesia arnoldii*, is found there.

Indonesia's tropical rain forests are being rapidly cut down. About 4,700 square miles (12,170 sq km) of rain forest are lost each year. This rate of deforestation is second only to Brazil's. Some people have predicted that much of Indonesia's

▲

Found in the rain forests of Sumatra, the *Rafflesia arnoldii* is the largest known flower in the world. It can weigh up to 24 pounds (11 kg) and can measure about 3 feet (1 meter) across.

rain forests will be gone in just 10 years. When the rain forests are cleared, animals such as the endangered orangutan do not have a home.

There are many reasons that Indonesia's tropical rain forests are being cleared. Trees from tropical rain forests produce beautiful woods. They are used to make furniture, boats, and houses. The demand for special trees and wood has made logging a profitable business. Much of the logging is done by large corporations that do not replant the areas that are cut.

Deforestation in Indonesia also occurs because people need land to farm and raise animals. They also need wood for fuel. People clear the land using a method called slash-and-burn. Large trees are cut, or slashed, and left on the ground. Then the land is burned during the dry season. This clears the land of vegetation and prepares it for farming. In 1997 large areas of land in Indonesia were cleared. Huge fires burned out of control. The fires burned an area roughly the size of Denmark. Smoke filled the sky and caused some airplanes and ships to crash.

## Protecting Indonesia's Rain Forests

Some people in Indonesia are trying to protect the rain forests. Parks and nature reserves have been set up that are off-limits to logging companies. Some groups are finding ways to earn money without cutting down trees. Selling fruits and nuts from the rain forest is one way. Also, international organizations such as the Rainforest Action Network are helping to protect the forests. Some environmental groups are even pressuring countries to stop buying trees that come from tropical rain forests.

Much of the timber cut in Indonesia and other Southeast Asian countries is exported to Japan. Indonesia exports about 2 million tons of plywood and 145,000 tons of lumber to Japan each year.

Orangutans live in the tropical rain forests of Borneo and Sumatra. Deforestation has seriously reduced their habitat. The word *orangutan* means "man of the forest."

## Understanding What You Read

**1.** Why are Indonesia's tropical rain forests being cut down?

**2.** What is being done to protect Indonesia's tropical rain forests?

# Geo SKILLS

## Building Skills for Life: Interpreting Cultural Landscapes

Cultural landscapes are the forms put on the land by people. For example, buildings, field patterns, and roads are all a part of cultural landscapes. Cultural landscapes show a people's way of life.

Different cultures create distinctive cultural landscapes. For example, a village in China looks very different from a village in France. By comparing how the two villages look, we can begin to see how their cultures are different.

Geographers interpret cultural landscapes. They observe a landscape, describe what they see, and try to explain how it reflects the culture of the place. This is called reading the cultural landscape.

You can read cultural landscapes too. To read a cultural landscape, start by describing what you see. What kinds of buildings are there? What are they used for? What kinds of clothing are people wearing? Then, think about how what you see relates to the place's culture. What would it be like to live there? What do people there do for fun?

Cultural landscapes tell a story. By reading and interpreting these stories, you can learn a lot about people and geography.

Architecture is an important part of the cultural landscape at the Black Dragon Pool in southern China.

## PRACTICING THE SKILL

1. Try to read the cultural landscapes of your community. What forms have people put on the land? What do they tell you about the daily life of the people who live there?

2. Watch a television show or movie and interpret the cultural landscapes you see. What is distinctive about them? How are they different from the cultural landscapes you are used to? Can you guess where the program was filmed?

3. Look carefully at the pictures in a newspaper or magazine without reading the captions. Do the pictures tell a story? Is culture a part of this story?

# HANDS on GEOGRAPHY

The photographs below show two very different cultural landscapes. What can these photographs tell us about each place's culture and way of life? Look closely at each photograph and then answer the Lab Report questions.

◄ ～～～
A cultural landscape in East Asia

▲ ～～～
A cultural landscape in

## Lab Report

1. What do these two photographs show? On a separate sheet of paper, write a short description of each photograph.

2. Do these two photographs tell you something about each place's culture and way of life? On a separate sheet of paper, describe what you think the culture of these two places is like.

3. Are there some things about a place's culture that you cannot learn from just looking at a photograph? What are they? If you took a trip to these two places, what else could you learn about their cultures?

# UNIT 8

## South Asia

**CHAPTER 27**
*India*

**CHAPTER 28**
*The Indian Perimeter*

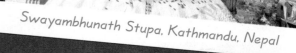

Swayambhunath Stupa, Kathmandu, Nepal

Karakoram Range, Pakistan

## A Scholar in India

*Emily K. Bloch coordinates educational programs at the South Asia Outreach center at the University of Chicago. Her special area of interest is South Asian children's literature. Here she describes the many types of transportation she has used in India.* **WHAT DO YOU THINK?** *Which type of transportation would you enjoy the most?*

In my travels throughout India, I've had the good fortune to ride on a variety of vehicles. I've ridden in buses and cycle-rickshaws, taxis and three-wheeled scooters, on a motorcycle through Calcutta and on the crossbar of a bicycle. I rode in a howdah [seat] on the back of an elephant in a wildlife sanctuary. I even had an uncomfortable, but very welcome, lift in a bullock cart.

But my favorite mode of travel is also one of the most popular in India—riding the great trains. The railway, with more than 1.5 million employees, is the largest employer in the world. It has nearly 40,000 miles of track. Eleven thousand trains, connecting more than 7,000 stations, carry about 12 million people daily. Though the luxury of the princely rail lines beckons, and the first-class cars provide food and bed-linens, I love the crowded, second-class, wooden-benches experience and look forward to my next journey side by side with my fellow Indian and foreign travelers.

Polo players at elephant festival, Jaipur, India

*Women in festival dress, Rajasthan, India*

## Understanding Primary Sources

**1.** What do Emily Bloch's transportation experiences illustrate about the use of technology in India?

**2.** Which method of travel does Emily Bloch prefer? Why?

*White Bengal tiger*

# South Asia

## Elevation Profile

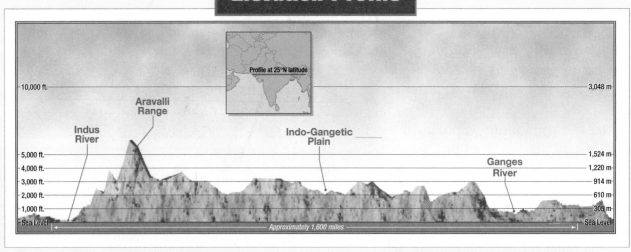

Profile at 25°N latitude

| | |
|---|---|
| 10,000 ft. | 3,048 m. |

Aravalli Range

Indus River

Indo-Gangetic Plain

Ganges River

5,000 ft. — 1,524 m.
4,000 ft. — 1,220 m.
3,000 ft. — 914 m.
2,000 ft. — 610 m.
1,000 ft. — 305 m.
Sea Level — Sea Level

*Approximately 1,600 miles*

*The United States and South Asia:*
## Comparing Sizes

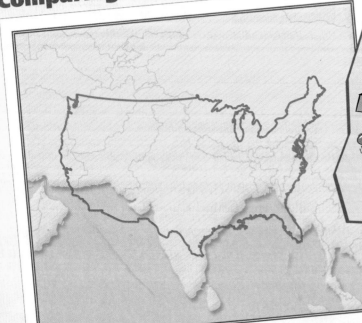

## GEOSTATS:

### India

World's second-largest population:
1,029,991,145 (July 2001 estimate)

Predicted population in 2025:
1,415,274,000

World's most populous democracy

World's greatest recorded total rainfall in one month:
366 in. (930 cm) in Cherrapunji, in July 1861

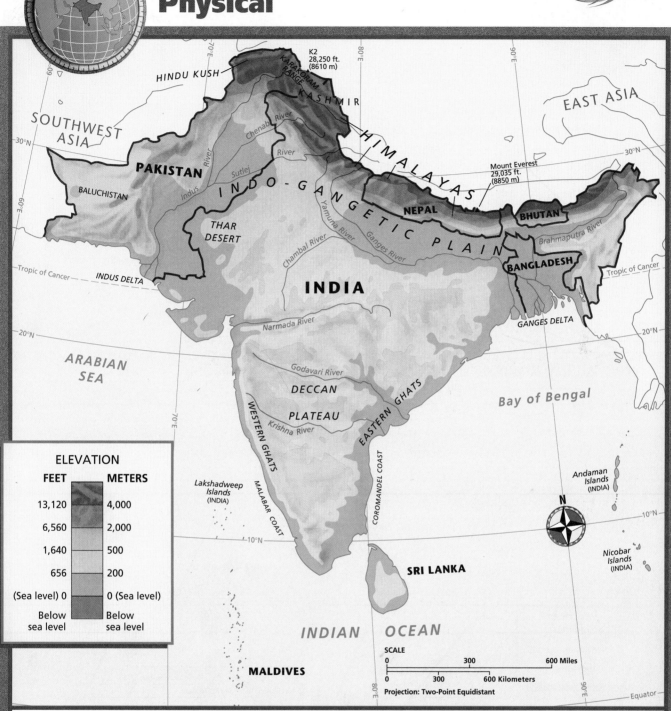

ELEVATION

| FEET | METERS |
|------|--------|
| 13,120 | 4,000 |
| 6,560 | 2,000 |
| 1,640 | 500 |
| 656 | 200 |
| (Sea level) 0 | 0 (Sea level) |
| Below sea level | Below sea level |

SCALE

0 — 300 — 600 Miles

0 — 300 — 600 Kilometers

Projection: Two-Point Equidistant

**1.** ( *Places and Regions* ) Which country has the lowest overall elevation? Which countries have mountains that stretch from their western to eastern borders?

**2.** ( *Places and Regions* ) Which two rivers that drain the Deccan Plateau flow directly into the Bay of Bengal?

## Critical Thinking

**3. Drawing Inferences and Conclusions** Based on the map, do you think it would be easier for travelers or invaders to come to northern India by land or by sea? Why might this be the case?

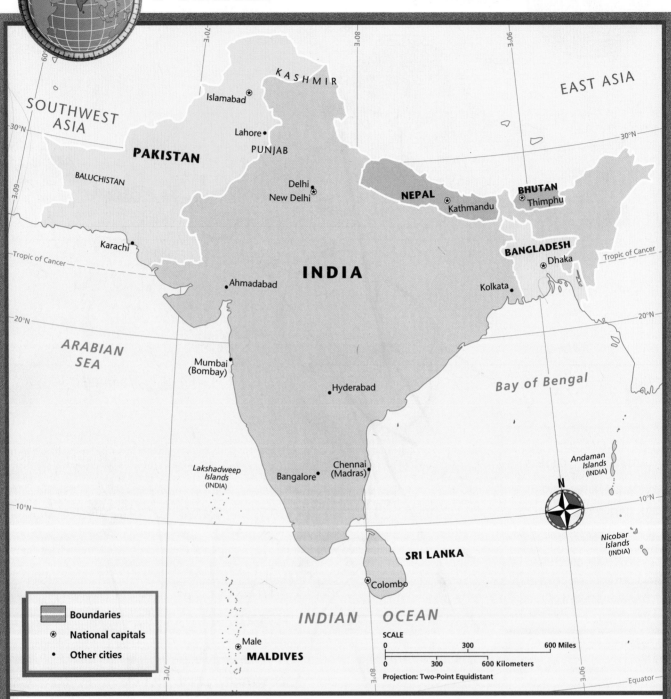

SOUTHWEST ASIA

KASHMIR

Islamabad ⊛

30°N

PAKISTAN

Lahore •

PUNJAB

BALUCHISTAN

Delhi •
New Delhi ⊛

EAST ASIA

30°N

NEPAL ⊛
Kathmandu

BHUTAN
⊛ Thimphu

Karachi •

Tropic of Cancer

BANGLADESH
⊛ Dhaka

Tropic of Cancer

INDIA

• Ahmadabad

Kolkata •

20°N

20°N

ARABIAN SEA

Mumbai
(Bombay) •

• Hyderabad

Bay of Bengal

Lakshadweep
Islands
(INDIA)

Bangalore •

Chennai
(Madras) •

Andaman
Islands
(INDIA)

N

10°N

10°N

SRI LANKA

⊛ Colombo

Nicobar
Islands
(INDIA)

INDIAN OCEAN

SCALE

0          300          600 Miles

• Male
MALDIVES

0      300      600 Kilometers

Projection: Two-Point Equidistant

Equator

**Legend:**
- Boundaries
- ⊛ National capitals
- • Other cities

1. **Places and Regions** What are the region's two island countries? Which is larger?

2. **Places and Regions** Which country is almost completely surrounded by India?

3. **Places and Regions** Compare this map to the **physical map**. Which small countries might be called the "Mountain Kingdoms?"

## Critical Thinking

4. **Drawing Inferences and Conclusions** Bangladesh was once part of Pakistan. What role do you think Bangladesh's location may have played in its drive for independence?

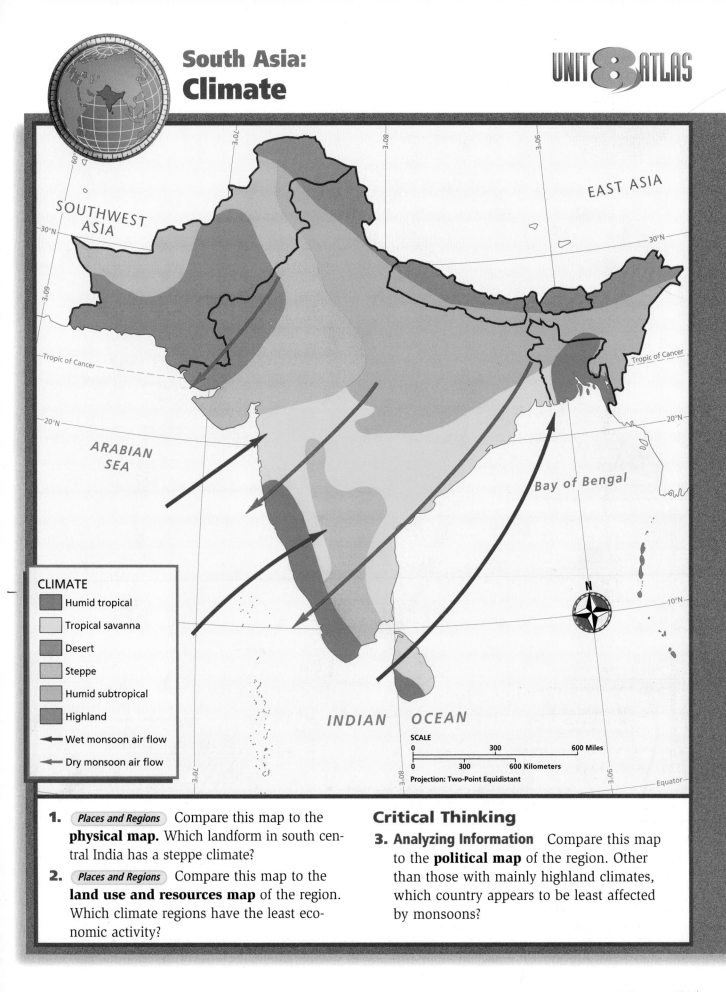

**CLIMATE**

- Humid tropical
- Tropical savanna
- Desert
- Steppe
- Humid subtropical
- Highland
- ← Wet monsoon air flow
- ← Dry monsoon air flow

SOUTHWEST ASIA

EAST ASIA

ARABIAN SEA

Bay of Bengal

INDIAN OCEAN

Tropic of Cancer

Tropic of Cancer

Equator

N

SCALE
0        300        600 Miles
0    300    600 Kilometers
Projection: Two-Point Equidistant

---

1. *Places and Regions*  Compare this map to the **physical map.** Which landform in south central India has a steppe climate?

2. *Places and Regions*  Compare this map to the **land use and resources map** of the region. Which climate regions have the least economic activity?

**Critical Thinking**

3. **Analyzing Information**  Compare this map to the **political map** of the region. Other than those with mainly highland climates, which country appears to be least affected by monsoons?

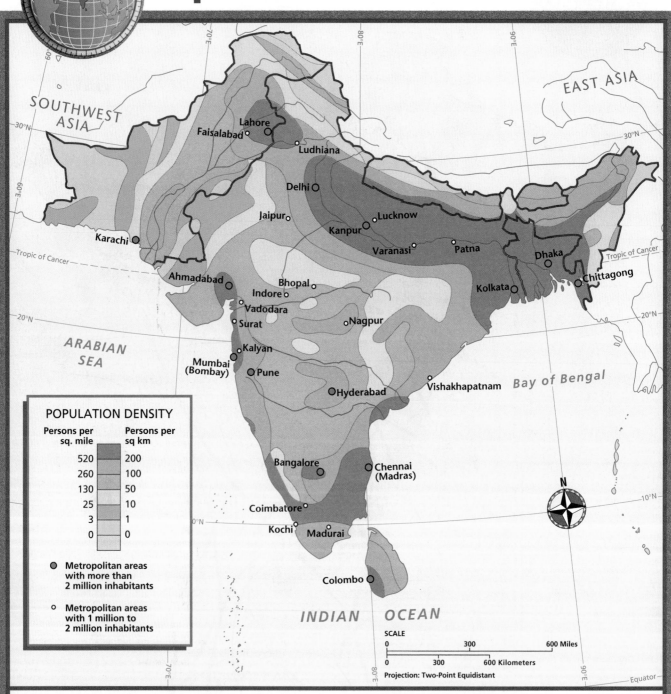

POPULATION DENSITY

| Persons per sq. mile | Persons per sq km |
|---|---|
| 520 | 200 |
| 260 | 100 |
| 130 | 50 |
| 25 | 10 |
| 3 | 1 |
| 0 | 0 |

● Metropolitan areas with more than 2 million inhabitants

○ Metropolitan areas with 1 million to 2 million inhabitants

SCALE
0        300        600 Miles
0        300        600 Kilometers
Projection: Two-Point Equidistant

1. ( Places and Regions ) Compare this map to the **physical map**. Which large Indian city is located on the Ganges Delta?

2. ( Places and Regions ) Compare this map to the **physical map** of the region. What is the name of the large densely populated area in the northeastern part of the region?

## Critical Thinking

3. **Analyzing Information** Use the map on this page to create a chart, graph, database, or model of population centers in South Asia.

# South Asia:
# Land Use and Resources

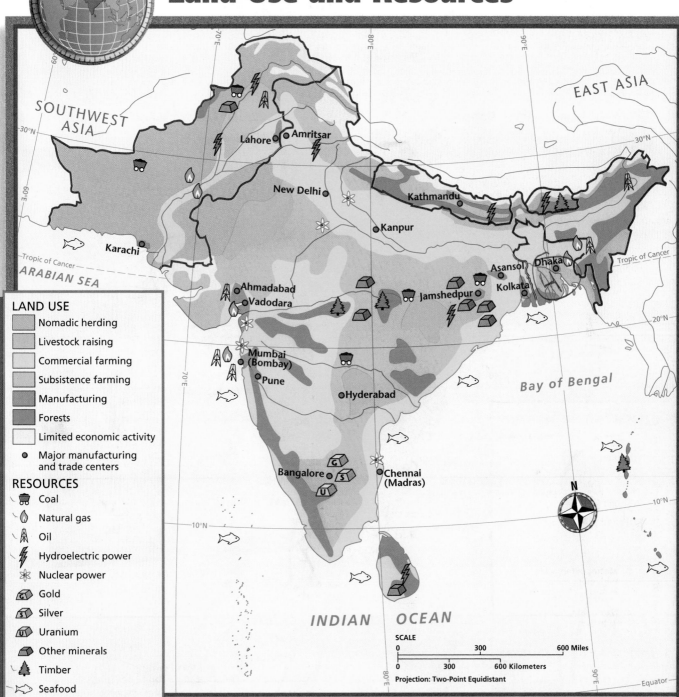

**1.** *Places and Regions* Which country has the largest area used for nomadic herding?

**2.** *Places and Regions* Which country has the largest area used for manufacturing?

**3.** *Places and Regions* Which city is near the region's gold, silver, and uranium mines?

**4.** *Places and Regions* Which country does not produce hydroelectric power?

## Critical Thinking

**5. Analyzing Information** Use this map to create a chart, graph, database, or model of economic activities in South Asia.

# South Asia

## BANGLADESH

**CAPITAL:**
Dhaka

**AREA:**
55,598 sq. mi.
(144,000 sq km)

**POPULATION:**
131,269,860

**MONEY:**
taka (BDT)

**LANGUAGES:**
Bangla (official), English

**ARABLE LAND:**
73 percent

## BHUTAN

**CAPITAL:**
Thimphu

**AREA:**
18,147 sq. mi.
(47,000 sq km)

**POPULATION:**
2,049,412

**MONEY:**
ngultrum (BTN),
Indian rupee (INR)

**LANGUAGES:**
Dzongkha

**ARABLE LAND:**
2 percent

Crystal clear waters in the Maldives

## INDIA

**CAPITAL:**
New Delhi

**AREA:**
1,269,338 sq. mi.
(3,287,590 sq km)

**POPULATION:**
1,029,991,145

**MONEY:** Indian rupee (INR)

**LANGUAGES:**
Hindi (official), English (associate official), 14 other official languages, many ethnic languages

**ARABLE LAND:** 56 percent

## MALDIVES

**CAPITAL:**
Male

**AREA:**
116 sq. mi.
(300 sq km)

**POPULATION:**
310,764

**MONEY:**
rufiyaa (MVR)

**LANGUAGES:**
Maldivian Divehi, English

**ARABLE LAND:**
10 percent

Countries not drawn to scale.

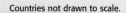

Buddhist monks in Kandy, Sri Lanka

# NEPAL

**CAPITAL:**
Kathmandu

**AREA:**
54,363 sq. mi.
(140,800 sq km)

**POPULATION:**
25,284,463

**MONEY:**
Nepalese rupee (NPR)

**LANGUAGES:**
Nepali (official), other ethnic languages

**ARABLE LAND:**
17 percent

# SRI LANKA

**CAPITAL:** Colombo

**AREA:**
25,332 sq. mi.
(65,610 sq km)

**POPULATION:**
19,408,635

**MONEY:**
Sri Lankan rupee (LKR)

**LANGUAGES:**
Sinhalese, Tamil, English

**ARABLE LAND:**
14 percent

**internet** connect

**COUNTRY STATISTICS**
**GO TO:** go.hrw.com
**KEYWORD:** SK3 FactsU8
**FOR:** more facts about South Asia

# PAKISTAN

**CAPITAL:**
Islamabad

**AREA:**
310,401 sq. mi.
(803,940 sq km)

**POPULATION:**
144,616,639

**MONEY:**
Pakistani rupee (PKR)

**LANGUAGES:**
Punjabi, Sindhi, Siraiki, Pashtu, Urdu (official), Balochi, Hindko, Brahui, English, many ethnic languages

**ARABLE LAND:**
27 percent

**Sources:** Central Intelligence Agency, *The World Factbook 2001*; *The World Almanac and Book of Facts 2001*; pop. figures are 2001 estimates.

# CHAPTER 27

# India

India is a huge country with an ancient culture and a population of a billion people. However, you might find you have quite a bit in common with a student from India.

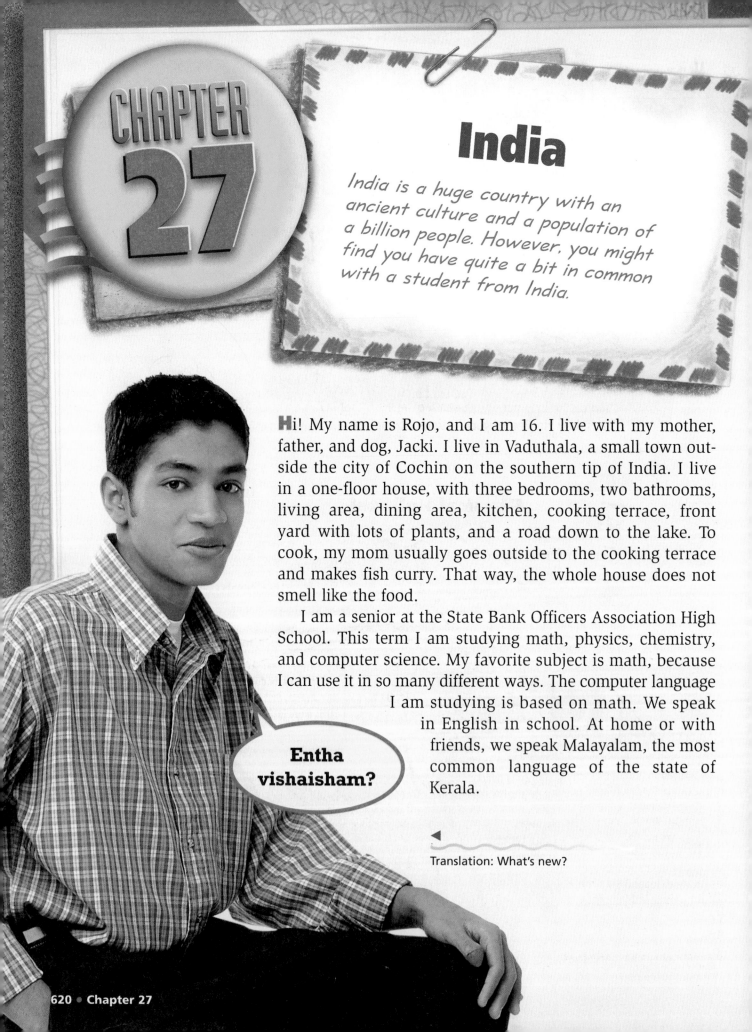

Hi! My name is Rojo, and I am 16. I live with my mother, father, and dog, Jacki. I live in Vaduthala, a small town outside the city of Cochin on the southern tip of India. I live in a one-floor house, with three bedrooms, two bathrooms, living area, dining area, kitchen, cooking terrace, front yard with lots of plants, and a road down to the lake. To cook, my mom usually goes outside to the cooking terrace and makes fish curry. That way, the whole house does not smell like the food.

I am a senior at the State Bank Officers Association High School. This term I am studying math, physics, chemistry, and computer science. My favorite subject is math, because I can use it in so many different ways. The computer language I am studying is based on math. We speak in English in school. At home or with friends, we speak Malayalam, the most common language of the state of Kerala.

**Entha vishaisham?**

Translation: What's new?

# Section 1 Physical Geography

## Read to Discover

1. What are the three main landform regions of India?
2. What are the major rivers in India?
3. What climate types does India have?
4. What natural resources does India have?

## Define

teak

## Locate

Gangetic Plain
Deccan
Eastern Ghats
Western Ghats

Ganges River
Bay of Bengal
Brahmaputra River
Thar Desert

### WHY IT MATTERS

India is the largest country of the Indian Subcontinent. Its climate helps to create its fertile soil. Use CNN fyi.com or other current events sources to find information about other ways that India's climate affects daily life. Record your findings in your journal.

*An Indian black cobra*

## India: Physical-Political

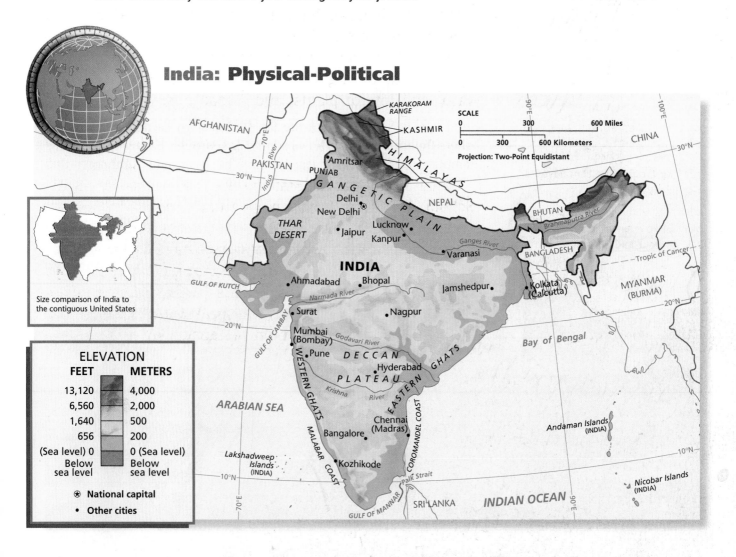

Size comparison of India to the contiguous United States

### ELEVATION

| FEET | METERS |
|---|---|
| 13,120 | 4,000 |
| 6,560 | 2,000 |
| 1,640 | 500 |
| 656 | 200 |
| (Sea level) 0 | 0 (Sea level) |
| Below sea level | Below sea level |

⊛ National capital
• Other cities

internet connect

GO TO: go.hrw.com
KEYWORD: SK3 CH27
FOR: Web sites about India

BUILD on WHAT You Know

**D**o you remember what you learned about plate tectonics? See Chapter 2 to review.

A farmer plows rice fields in northern India. The Himalayas rise in the distance.

**Interpreting the Visual Record**
**Why do so many of India's people live on the Gangetic Plain?**

# Landforms

India has three main landform regions: the Himalayas, the Gangetic (gan-JE-tik) Plain, and the Deccan (DE-kuhn). The Himalayas run along the country's northern border and were created when two tectonic plates collided and pushed Earth's crust up.

The vast Gangetic Plain lies to the south of the Himalayas. It stretches about 1,500 miles (2,415 km) across northern India. About half of India's population lives there.

South of the Gangetic Plain is the triangular peninsula known as the Deccan. Most of its area is a plateau, which is divided by many hills and valleys. The plateau's edges are defined by the Eastern Ghats (GAWTS) and Western Ghats. These low mountain ranges separate the plateau's eastern and western edges from narrow coastal plains.

✓ **READING CHECK:** *Places and Regions* What are the three main landform regions of India?

# Rivers

India's most important river, the Ganges (GAN-jeez), begins on the southern slopes of the Himalayas. It then flows southeastward across northern India. It spreads into a huge delta before flowing into the Bay of Bengal. Hindus call the Ganges the "Mother River" and consider it sacred. Rich silt left by the Ganges has made the Gangetic Plain India's farming heartland.

The Brahmaputra (brahm-uh-POO-truh) River starts in the Plateau of Tibet. It flows through the far northeastern corner of India. From there the Brahmaputra flows southward through Bangladesh, where it empties into the Ganges Delta. The Narmada (nuhr-MUH-duh), Godavari (go-DAH-vuh-ree), and Krishna (KRISH-nuh) Rivers drain the Deccan. A large irrigation project along the Narmada River is under construction. It will include more than 40 branch canals.

✓ **READING CHECK:** *Places and Regions* What are India's most important rivers?

# Climate

India has a variety of climate types. Areas in the Himalayas have highland climates with snow and glaciers. The Thar Desert near the border with Pakistan is hot and dry year-round. The Gangetic Plain has a humid tropical climate. Farther south in the Deccan there are tropical savanna and steppe climates.

Seasonal winds—monsoons—bring moist air from the Indian Ocean in summer. In winter the wind brings dry air from the Asian interior. The timing of the monsoons is very important to farmers in India. If the summer rains come too soon or too late, food production suffers.

✓ **READING CHECK:** *Places and Regions* What are India's climates?

The city of Cherrapunji (cher-uh-POOHN-jee), in northeastern India, holds the world's record for rainfall in one year: almost 87 feet (26.5 m)!

# Resources

India's fertile farmlands are important to its economy. Most of India's people work in agriculture. The country also produces cash crops for export. These include cashew nuts, cotton, jute, spices, sugarcane, tea, and tobacco.

Large deposits of iron ore, bauxite, uranium, and coal are among India's mineral resources. There are some oil reserves, but not enough to meet the country's needs. Gemstones are a valuable export.

India's forests are an important resource, as well as home to wildlife. **Teak**, one of the most valuable types of wood, grows in India and Southeast Asia. Teak is very strong and durable and is used to make ships and furniture.

✓ **READING CHECK:** *Places and Regions* What are India's natural resources?

go.hrw.com **Homework Practice Online** Keyword: SK3 HP27

## Section Review 1

**Define and explain:** teak

**Working with Sketch Maps** On a map of India that you draw or that your teacher provides, label the following: Gangetic Plain, Deccan, Eastern Ghats, Western Ghats, Ganges River, Bay of Bengal, Brahmaputra River, and Thar Desert. How would you describe the relative location of India?

### Reading for the Main Idea

1. *Places and Regions* What is the main mountain range of India?

2. *Places and Regions* What are some of India's most important cash crops? What type of wood is a valuable forest product?

### Critical Thinking

3. **Making Generalizations and Predictions** What do you think happens to India's crops if the monsoon rains come too soon? too late?

4. **Summarizing** How does the Ganges affect economic activities in India?

### Organizing What You Know

5. **Summarizing** Copy the following graphic organizer. Use it to list the landforms, climates, and resources of India.

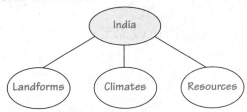

# Section 2 India's History

## Read to Discover
1. What outside groups affected India's history?
2. What was the Mughal Empire like?
3. How did Great Britain gain control of India?
4. Why was India divided when it became independent?

## Define
Sanskrit
sepoys
boycott

## Locate
Delhi
Kolkata
Mumbai

### WHY IT MATTERS

India's history has been shaped by invasions, conquests, and colonization. Use CNN**fyi**.com or other **current events** sources to find information about how daily life in India has been shaped by its history. Record your findings in your journal.

*Coat of arms of the East India Company*

## Early Indian Civilizations

Mohenjo Daro was one of the largest cities of the Harappan civilization.

**Interpreting the Visual Record** **How might you tell from this photo that Harappan cities were well planned?**

▼

The first urban civilization on the Indian Subcontinent was centered around the Indus River valley. Its territory was mainly in present-day Pakistan but also extended into India. Scholars call this the Harappan civilization after one of its cities, Harappa. By about 2500 B.C. the people of this civilization were living in large, well-planned cities. Scholars believe the Harappans traded by sea with the peoples of Mesopotamia. The Harappans had a system of writing, but scholars have not been able to read it. As a result, very little is known about Harappan religion and customs.

**The Indo-Aryans** By about 1500 B.C. a new group of people had come into northern India. Scholars call these people Indo-Aryans. Their language was an early form of **Sanskrit**. Sanskrit is still used in India in religious ceremonies.

The Indo-Aryans took control of northern India. These new arrivals mixed with Indian groups that were already living there. Their religious beliefs and customs mixed as well, forming the beginnings of the Hindu religion.

Hills and mountains prevented the Indo-Aryans from conquering southern India. However, Sanskrit and other Indo-Aryan cultural traits spread to the south.

**The Coming of Islam** About A.D. 1000, Muslim armies began raiding northwestern India. In the early 1200s a Muslim kingdom was established at Delhi. Because the monarch was known as a sultan, this kingdom was called the Delhi sultanate. The Delhi sultanate eventually gained control over most of northern India. It also became a leading center of Islamic art, culture, and science. Most Indians, however, kept their own religions and did not convert to Islam.

Over the next two centuries the Delhi sultanate expanded into the Deccan. However, in the early 1500s a new invasion from Central Asia swept into India. This new conquest marked the beginning of the Mughal (MOO-guhl) Empire.

✓ **READING CHECK:** *Human Systems* How did outside groups affect early Indian history?

This carved-lion pillar comes from Sarnath, an ancient city in northern India. The pillar was created in the 200s B.C. and is now the state emblem of India.

# The Mughal Empire

The founder of the Mughal Empire was Babur, whose name meant "the Tiger." Babur was descended from Mongol emperor Genghis Khan. He was not only a brilliant general, but also a gifted poet. Babur defeated the last sultan of Delhi and took over most of northern India. After his death, however, Babur's lands were divided among his sons. They fought each other for years.

Babur's grandson, Akbar, finally emerged to reunite the Mughal Empire. He recaptured northern India and then expanded his empire into central India. Akbar was a good ruler as well as a successful conqueror. He reorganized the government and the tax system to make them more efficient. The fertile farmland and large population of the Gangetic Plain made the Mughal Empire rich. It quickly became one of the most powerful states in the world. The reign of Akbar and his successors was a golden age of architecture, painting, and poetry.

This illustration is from a book of the life of Babur, the first Mughal emperor. It shows Babur surrounded by servants and nobles.

# CONNECTING TO Literature

*Indian writer R.K. Narayan's* My Days: A Memoir *describes the author's childhood in the early 1900s. In the following passage Narayan recalls traveling from boarding school to his parents' new home. At that time, travel was complicated and sometimes dangerous.*

At the proper time, I was awakened and put into a huge mat-covered wagon drawn by a pair of bullocks; I sat on a bed of straw covered over with a carpet; a stalwart[1] peon[2] from Hassan high school was seated beside the driver. Manja was his name . . . Part of the way as we traveled along, Manja got off and walked ahead of the caravan, carrying a staff menacingly. Some spots in that jungle and

## My Days: A Memoir

mountain country were well-known retreats of highway robbers; one form of protection was to travel in a closely moving caravan with Manja waving a staff at the head of the column, uttering blood-curdling challenges. That was enough to keep off robbers in those days.

We passed along miles and miles of tree-shaded highway, gigantic mango and blueberry trees and lantana[3] shrubs in multicolored bloom stretching away endlessly. A couple of times the bullocks were rested beside a pond or a well. The road wound up and down steep slopes—the sort of country I had never known before. . . . The overpowering smell of straw in the wagon and the slow pace of the bullocks with their bells jingling made me drowsy . . . After hours of tossing on straw, we came to a bungalow[4] set in a ten-acre field. [It was my parents' new home.] . . . The moment I was received into the fold at the trellised ivy-covered porch, I totally ignored Manja, and never looked in his direction, while he carried my baggage in.

## Analyzing Primary Sources

1. What are some of the words the author uses to describe the countryside?
2. How do you think Manja's description of this journey might be different from the author's?

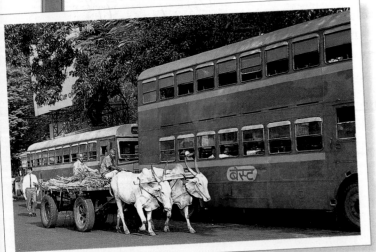

*A bullock cart and a double-decker bus in India*

---

**Vocabulary**   [1]stalwart: strong and reliable   [2]peon: a menial laborer   [3]lantana: shrub with colorful flowers
[4]bungalow: one-story house with low roof that originated in Bengal, India

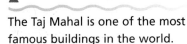

The Taj Mahal is one of the most famous buildings in the world.

The ruling Mughals were Muslim, but Islam remained a minority religion in India. Most people continued to practice Hinduism. Akbar himself was tolerant and curious about other religions. He invited religious scholars and priests—including Christians, Hindus, Jains, and Muslims—to his court. He even watched them debate.

Akbar's grandson, Shah Jahan, is remembered for the impressive buildings and monuments he had built. These include the famous Taj Mahal. This grand building contains the tomb of Shah Jahan's beloved wife, Mumtaz Mahal.

In the 1600s and 1700s the Mughal Empire slowly grew weaker. Wars in the Deccan and revolts in many parts of the empire drained Mughal resources. At about this time, Europeans became an important force in Indian history.

✓ **READING CHECK:** ( *Human Systems* ) What was the Mughal Empire like?

Construction of the Taj Mahal began in 1631 and was not completed until 1653. Almost 20,000 people worked on the building.

# The British

During the 1700s and 1800s the British slowly took control of India. At first this was done by the English East India Company. This company won rights to trade in the Mughal Empire in the 1600s. The East India Company first took control of small trading posts. Later the British gained more Indian territory.

**Company Rule** As the Mughal Empire grew weaker, the British East India Company expanded its political power. The company also built up its own military force. This army was made up mostly of

In September 1857, British and loyal Sikh troops stormed the gate of Delhi, defended by rebel sepoys. Bloody fighting continued until late 1858.

**Interpreting the Visual Record**
**How did the Indian Mutiny lead to a change in the way India was governed?**

**sepoys**, Indian troops commanded by British officers. The British used the strategy of backing one Indian ruler against another in exchange for cooperation. By the mid-1800s the company controlled more than half of India. The rest was divided into small states ruled by local princes.

The British changed the Indian economy to benefit British industry. India produced raw materials, including cotton, indigo—a natural dye—and jute. These materials were then shipped to Britain for use in British factories. Spices, sugar, tea, and wheat were also grown in India for export. Railroads were built to ship the raw materials to Calcutta (now Kolkata), Bombay (now Mumbai), and other port cities. India also became a market for British manufactured goods. Indians, who had woven cotton cloth for centuries, were now forced to buy British cloth.

**The Indian Mutiny** British rule angered and frightened many Indians. In 1857, the sepoy troops revolted. They killed their British officers and other British residents. The violence spread across northern India. Large numbers of British troops were rushed to India. In the end the British crushed the rebellion.

The Indian Mutiny convinced the British government to abolish the British East India Company. The British government began to rule India directly, and India became a British colony.

**Anti-British Protest** During the late 1800s Indian nationalism took a different form. Educated, middle-class Indians led this movement. In 1885 these Indian nationalists created the Indian National Congress to organize their protests. At first they did not demand independence. Instead, they asked only for fairer treatment, such as a greater share of government jobs. The British refused even these moderate demands.

After World War I more and more Indians began demanding the end of British rule. A lawyer named Mohandas K. Gandhi became the most important leader of this Indian independence movement.

Mohandas Gandhi was known to his followers as the Mahatma, or the "great soul."

**Gandhi and Nonviolence** Gandhi reached out to the millions of Indian peasants. He used a strategy of nonviolent mass protest. He called for Indians to peacefully refuse to cooperate with the British. Gandhi led protest marches and urged Indians to **boycott**, or refuse to buy, British goods. Many times the police used violence against marchers. When the British jailed Gandhi, he went on hunger strikes. Gandhi's determination and self-sacrifice attracted many followers. Pressure grew on Britain to leave India.

✓ **READING CHECK:** *Human Systems* What role did the British play in India?

# Independence and Division

After World War II the British government decided to give India independence. The British government and the Indian National Congress wanted India to become one country. However, India's Muslims demanded a separate Muslim state. Anger and fear grew between Hindus and Muslims. India seemed on the verge of civil war.

Finally, in 1947 the British divided their Indian colony into two independent countries, India and Pakistan. India was mostly Hindu. Pakistan, which then included what is today Bangladesh, was mostly Muslim. However, the new boundary left millions of Hindus in Pakistan and millions of Muslims in India. Masses of people rushed to cross the border. Hundreds of thousands were killed in rioting and panic.

In the chaotic days of August 1947, millions of people left their homes to cross the new border between India and Pakistan. These Muslims are preparing to leave New Delhi by train.

✓ **READING CHECK:** *Places and Regions* Why was India divided when it became independent?

Homework Practice Online
Keyword: SK3 HP27

**Define and explain:** Sanskrit, sepoys, boycott

**Working with Sketch Maps** On the map you created in Section 1, label Delhi, Kolkata, and Mumbai. What bodies of water are important to each of these cities?

**Reading for the Main Idea**

1. *Human Systems* What made the Mughal Empire one of the most powerful states in the world?

2. *Human Systems* How did the British East India Company gain control of most of India?

3. *Human Systems* Who was the most important leader of the Indian independence movement, and what was his strategy?

**Critical Thinking**

4. **Finding the Main Idea** Why was the British colony of India divided into two countries?

**Organizing What You Know**

5. **Sequencing** Copy the following time line. Use it to mark important events in Indian history from 2500 B.C. to A.D. 1947.

|————————————————————|
2500 B.C.                                    A.D. 1947

**Read to Discover**

1. What four major religions originated in India?
2. What is the caste system?
3. What languages are important in India?
4. What kind of government does India have, and what is India's economy like?

**Define**

reincarnation
karma
nirvana
caste system
Dalits
green revolution

**Locate**

Kashmir

**WHY IT MATTERS**

Religion has played a tremendous role in both the past and present culture of India. Use CNN fyi.com or other **current events** sources to find information about religion in India. Record your findings in your journal.

Masala dosa, *a rice and lentil dish from India*

This bronze statue depicts the Hindu god Siva.

Cows mingle with pedestrians and bicyclists in the street of an Indian town.

# Religions of India

Religion is an important part of Indian culture. Four major religions—Hinduism, Buddhism, Jainism, and Sikhism—originated in India. Christianity and Islam, both of which originated elsewhere, also have millions of followers in India. About 81 percent of India's people are Hindu. About 12 percent of Indians are Muslim, and 2.3 percent are Christian. Around 2 percent are Sikh, and 2.5 percent are Buddhist, Jain, Parsi, or followers of another religion. Remember that 1 percent of India's population is about 10 million people!

**Hinduism** Hinduism is one of the oldest religions in the world. Hindus worship many gods. These include Brahma the Creator, Vishnu the Preserver, and Siva the Destroyer. Hinduism teaches that all gods and all living beings are part of a single spirit.

Two beliefs central to the Hindu religion are **reincarnation** and **karma**. Reincarnation is the belief that the soul is reborn again and again in different forms. Karma is the positive or negative force caused by a person's actions. Hindus believe that a person with good karma may be reborn as a person of higher status. A person with bad karma may be reborn with lower status, or as an animal or insect.

Hinduism also teaches a special respect for cows. Hindus do not eat beef. Even today, cows can be seen roaming cities and villages.

**Buddhism** Buddhism was founded in northern India in the 500s B.C. by a man named Siddhartha Gautama. Gautama became known as the Buddha, or "Enlightened One."

The Buddha taught his followers they could avoid sorrow if they followed certain rules. For example, he told them not to lie, steal, or be greedy. By following these rules, Buddhists believe they can escape from the suffering of life. This escape from suffering is known as **nirvana**.

Buddhism spread from India to other parts of Asia. Buddhism is no longer widely practiced in India. However, the religion is very important in Sri Lanka, China, Japan, and Southeast Asia.

**Jainism** Jainism was founded at about the same time as Buddhism. It teaches that all things in nature—animals, plants, and stones—have souls. Jains reject all forms of violence against any living thing. They are strict vegetarians. Some even cover their noses with cloth to avoid breathing in insects and thus killing them.

Jains make up only a small minority. However, they have made many contributions to Indian art, mathematics, and literature.

**Sikhism** Sikhism was founded in the late 1400s. It combines elements of Hinduism and Islam. Members of this religion are called Sikhs. Traditionally, many Sikh men have become soldiers. They continue to play an important role in India's army.

▲

The Buddha is often depicted in poses of meditation.

**Interpreting the Visual Record**

**What elements of this statue could show examples of meditation?**

Jain women worship at a temple in Kolkata.

◄

A Sikh guards the Golden Temple, the center of the Sikh religion, in Amritsar, India. Sikh men can be recognized by their beards and special turbans.

**Interpreting the Visual Record** Do you know of any other religious or cultural groups whose members have a distinctive way of dressing?

Most Sikhs live in the state of Punjab in northern India. Some Sikhs want to break away from India and form an independent country. The Indian government has refused to allow this, and violent clashes have resulted.

✓ **READING CHECK:** ( *Human Systems* ) What four religions originated in India?

## Castes

Another key feature of Indian society is the **caste system**. Castes are groups of people whose birth determines their position in society. The castes are ranked in status, from highest to lowest. People from a higher caste cannot marry or even touch people of lower castes.

Many Dalits, like this woman in Goa, still perform jobs that Indians consider dirty or impure. Despite government efforts, most Dalits still live in poverty.

**Interpreting the Visual Record** What factors might keep most Dalits from getting better jobs?

The people at the bottom, called **Dalits**, do work that higher castes consider unclean. They wash and cremate dead bodies, process cow hides into leather goods, and sweep up trash.

Gandhi tried to improve people's attitudes toward the Dalits. He called them "Children of God." After independence, the Indian government officially ended the caste system. However, it is still a strong force in Indian society. The government also tried to improve economic conditions for the Dalits. Today some Dalits are educated and have good jobs. The majority, though, are still poor.

✓ **READING CHECK:** *Human Systems* How does the caste system create conflict in Indian society?

| India | | | | |
|---|---|---|---|---|
| **COUNTRY** | **POPULATION/ GROWTH RATE** | **LIFE EXPECTANCY** | **LITERACY RATE** | **PER CAPITA GDP** |
| India | 1,029,991,145 1.7% | 62, male 64, female | 52% | $2,200 |
| United States | 281,421,906 0.9% | 74, male 80, female | 97% | $36,200 |

**Sources:** Central Intelligence Agency, *The World Factbook 2001;* U.S. Census Bureau

**Interpreting the Chart** **How does India's economic development compare with that of the United States?**

## Languages

India's people speak an amazing number of different languages. There are 24 languages with a million or more speakers, plus hundreds of other languages. Hindi is the main language of about 30 percent of the people, mostly in northern India. In 1965 it became the official national language. However, the states of southern India have resisted the push to adopt Hindi. English is still commonly used in government, business, and higher education throughout India.

✓ **READING CHECK:** *Human Systems* What languages are important in India?

## Government and Economy

India has made a great deal of economic progress since gaining independence, but the country remains poor. Rapid population growth strains the country's resources, and the divisions among India's people make it difficult to govern.

**Government** India is ruled by a democratic government. With more than 1 billion people, the country is the world's largest democracy. The structure of the government is based on Britain's parliamentary system. However, as in the United States, India's central government shares power with state governments.

Indian politics have sometimes been marked by violence and assassinations. The government used force to defeat Sikh rebels in 1984. There have also been outbreaks of

Parliament House, New Delhi, is the home of India's legislative branch.

**Interpreting the Visual Record** **What form of government does India have? What is one feature that India's government shares with the U.S. government?**

India has stationed large numbers of troops in Kashmir.

violence between Hindus and Muslims. In 1992 a mob of Hindus tore down a mosque that stood on a Hindu holy site. Riots broke out in many parts of India as a result.

India's border with Pakistan has been in dispute since 1947. Both countries claim a mountainous region called Kashmir. Before India gained independence, Kashmir was ruled by a Hindu prince. Most of its people were Muslim, however. India and Pakistan have fought over Kashmir several times. Today, both countries have nuclear weapons, making the prospect of a future war even more frightening.

**Economy** India's economy is a mixture of the traditional and the modern. In thousands of villages, farmers work the fields just as they have for centuries. At the same time, modern factories and high-tech service industries demonstrate India's potential for wealth. However, the country still does not have enough good roads and telecommunications systems.

Close to 60 percent of India's workforce are farmers. Farming makes up 25 percent of India's GDP. Most farmers work on small farms less than 2.5 acres (1 hectare) in size. Many grow barely enough to feed themselves and their families. In recent years, the government has worked to promote commercial farming.

India's leading crops include rice, wheat, cotton, tea, sugarcane, and jute. Cattle and water buffalo are raised to pull plows and to provide milk.

Peppers are harvested in northern India.

**Interpreting the Visual Record** **What is one way agricultural products are transported in India?**

Beginning in the 1960s, the Indian government started agricultural programs known as the **green revolution**. This effort encouraged farmers to adopt more modern methods. It promoted greater use of fertilizers, pesticides, and new varieties of wheat and rice. Crop yields increased. In years with good weather, India is self-sufficient in food and can export farm products.

India is considered a developing country. However, its economy is large enough to rank among the world's top 10 industrial countries. India's industries include textiles, jewelry, cars, bicycles, oil products, chemicals, food processing, and electronics.

India's moviemaking industry is one of the world's largest. Mumbai is a major moviemaking center. Movies are an incredibly popular form of entertainment, as millions of Indians cannot read. Many Indian movie stars have gone into politics. Indian movies have a distinctive style. They usually feature music and dancing and often draw on themes from Indian myths. Indian movies are popular in many other countries as well.

India now has a large, well-educated middle class. These people have enough money for luxuries like cable television and personal computers. Some Indians are very rich. Yet the majority of Indians are still poor.

▲
Red-hot steel is poured into molds in a foundry near Kolkata.

**Interpreting the Visual Record**
**Which of India's industries might use the steel produced here?**

✓ **READING CHECK:** *Places and Regions* What are India's government and economy like?

## Section Review 3

**Homework Practice Online**
Keyword: SK3 HP27

**Define and explain:** reincarnation, karma, nirvana, caste system, Dalits, green revolution

**Working with Sketch Maps** On the map that you created in Section 2, label the Kashmir region of India. What other country claims Kashmir?

### Reading for the Main Idea

1. *Human Systems* What are the main religions practiced in India? Which religion has the largest number of followers?

2. *Environment and Society* How did India's government increase agricultural output in the 1960s?

### Critical Thinking

3. **Drawing Inferences and Conclusions** Why might India's government find it difficult to improve the economic situation of the Dalits?

4. **Finding the Main Idea** Why are movies such a popular form of entertainment in India?

### Organizing What You Know

5. **Categorizing** Copy the following graphic organizer. Use it to list the leading crops and industries of India.

| Leading crops | Leading industries |
|---|---|
|  |  |

# Reviewing What You Know

## Building Vocabulary

On a separate sheet of paper, write sentences to define each of the following words.

1. teak
2. Sanskrit
3. sepoys
4. boycott
5. reincarnation
6. karma
7. nirvana
8. caste system
9. Dalits
10. green revolution

## Reviewing the Main Ideas

1. (Places and Regions) How were the Himalayas formed?
2. (Human Systems) What was the first urban civilization on the Indian Subcontinent?
3. (Human Systems) Who brought Sanskrit to India?
4. (Human Systems) What are the Hindu ideas of reincarnation and karma?
5. (Human Systems) What factors divide Indian society?

## Understanding Environment and Society

### Cows in India

The Hindu respect for cows has influenced the way Indians interact with their environment. Create a presentation about cows in India. As you prepare your presentation, consider the following:

• How Hindus' respect for cows has affected cattle populations in India.
• What cows eat, and whether humans ever have to compete with cows for food in India.
• How Hindu ideas of reincarnation and karma affect Indians' treatment of cows.

## Thinking Critically

1. **Drawing Inferences and Conclusions** Why do you think Hindi has not become the language of all of India?

2. **Summarizing** How do India's natural resources affect its economy?

3. **Finding the Main Idea** How did the Indian government's promotion of new farming technology affect India's farming culture?

4. **Drawing Inferences and Conclusions** Why do you think the Mughal Empire under Akbar and his successors was considered a "golden age"?

5. **Drawing Inferences and Conclusions** How might the growth of a well-educated, high-tech workforce affect India's economy?

**Map** ACTIVITY

On a separate sheet of paper, match the letters on the map with their correct labels.

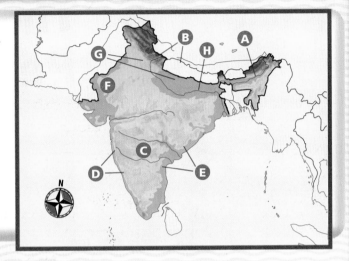

Himalayas
Gangetic Plain
Deccan
Eastern Ghats
Western Ghats

Ganges River
Brahmaputra River
Thar Desert

## Mental Mapping Skills ACTIVITY

On a separate sheet of paper, draw a freehand map of the Indian Subcontinent. Make a key for your map and label the following:

Bangladesh
Bay of Bengal
India
Indian Ocean

Kashmir
Nepal
Pakistan

## WRITING

ACTIVITY Write a one- to two-page report about how religion influences life in India. List and describe India's major religions, then write about how they relate to politics, border disputes, social classes, daily life, languages, the economy, and so on. Be sure to use standard grammar, spelling, sentence structure, and punctuation.

## Alternative Assessment

## Portfolio ACTIVITY

### Learning About Your Local Geography

**The Seasons**  The change of the seasons is important to daily life in India. Create a poster on how temperature and precipitation of all four seasons affect daily life in your area.

☑ internet connect

Internet Activity: **go.hrw.com**
KEYWORD: SK3 GT27

Choose a topic to explore about India:
- Tour the regions of India.
- Travel to ancient India.
- Learn about Mohandas Gandhi.

go. hrw .com

# CHAPTER 28

# The Indian Perimeter

*The countries of this region, along with the Himalayas, help create India's border. After you meet Rehan you will learn that this land is one of majestic beauty with a rich heritage.*

I am Rehan, and I am 14. I am an only child and live with my parents in Karachi, a big sprawling city like Los Angeles. On one side is the sea, on the other is the desert.

If you came to visit me in Pakistan, I would take you to the beach to watch the beautiful sunsets and ride on a camel. My parents used to take me there for camel rides when I was very little. Next I would take you to see the old colonial architecture in the city center. Then we would go and have a meal in a roadside cafe—grilled beef or lamb kabobs on a stick. I usually get up very early for school. By 7:10 A.M. I have breakfast—cereal and toast—and leave for school with my father. He is a doctor with an office near my school. I am in the second year (equivalent to grade 10) of a boys' private school styled after the British public school system.

Next year, I am going to America with my mother. My parents want me to have a chance to go to a world-class university.

السلام عليكم!

Translation: God's peace be upon you!

# Section 1 Physical Geography

## Read to Discover

1. What major physical features are located in the Indian Perimeter?
2. What climates and natural resources are found in this region?
3. What are the physical features of the island countries?

## Define

cyclones

storm surges

## Locate

Brahmaputra River
Ganges River
Himalayas
Mount Everest
Tarai
Karakoram Range

Hindu Kush
Khyber Pass
Indus River
Thar Desert

### WHY IT MATTERS

In 2001 Pakistan played an important role in world events when the United States asked to use its airspace to conduct military actions against terrorist leader Osama bin Laden. Use CNNfyi.com or other **current events** sources to find the latest information on Pakistan's role in world affairs. Record your findings in your journal.

*A relief sculpture of a Bodhi tree*

## The Indian Perimeter: Physical-Political

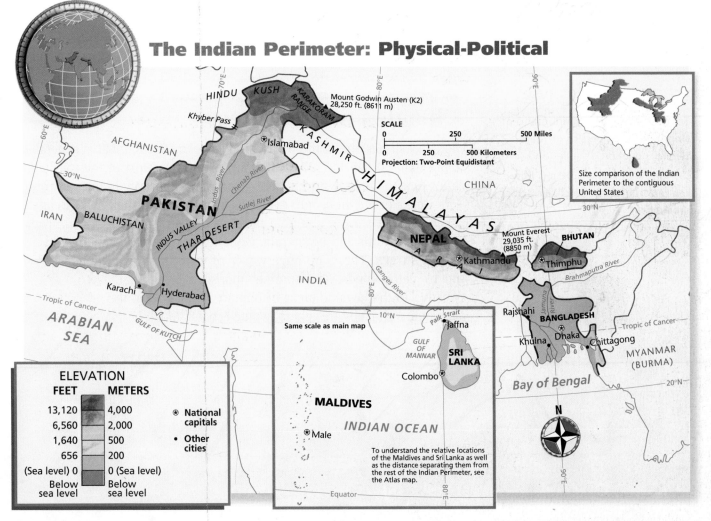

SCALE
0 — 250 — 500 Miles
0 — 250 — 500 Kilometers
Projection: Two-Point Equidistant

Size comparison of the Indian Perimeter to the contiguous United States

Mount Godwin Austen (K2) 28,250 ft. (8611 m)

Mount Everest 29,035 ft. (8850 m)

HINDU KUSH
KARAKORAM RANGE
Khyber Pass
AFGHANISTAN
⊛ Islamabad
KASHMIR
CHINA
IRAN
BALUCHISTAN
PAKISTAN
Indus River
Chenab River
Sutlej River
HIMALAYAS
NEPAL
⊛ Kathmandu
BHUTAN
⊛ Thimphu
INDUS VALLEY
THAR DESERT
INDIA
Ganges River
T A R A I
Brahmaputra River
Jamuna River
Rajshahi
BANGLADESH
Karachi
Hyderabad
Khulna
Dhaka
Chittagong
Tropic of Cancer
ARABIAN SEA
GULF OF KUTCH
MYANMAR (BURMA)
Bay of Bengal

**ELEVATION**

| FEET | METERS |
|---|---|
| 13,120 | 4,000 |
| 6,560 | 2,000 |
| 1,640 | 500 |
| 656 | 200 |
| (Sea level) 0 | 0 (Sea level) |
| Below sea level | Below sea level |

⊛ National capitals
• Other cities

Same scale as main map

Palk Strait
Jaffna
GULF OF MANNAR
SRI LANKA
Colombo ⊛

**MALDIVES**

INDIAN OCEAN
⊛ Male

To understand the relative locations of the Maldives and Sri Lanka as well as the distance separating them from the rest of the Indian Perimeter, see the Atlas map.

Tropic of Cancer

Equator

N

**D**o you remember what you learned about deltas? See Chapter 2 to review.

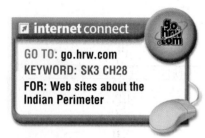

**internet** connect

GO TO: go.hrw.com
KEYWORD: SK3 CH28
FOR: Web sites about the Indian Perimeter

Terraced fields in the mountains of Nepal allow farmers to increase their production of millet and corn. **Interpreting the Visual Record** How can terracing lead to increased crop production?

# Physical Features

The broad delta formed by the Brahmaputra (brahm-uh-POO-truh) and Ganges (GAN-jeez) Rivers covers most of Bangladesh. Some 200 rivers and streams crisscross this eastern part of the Indian Subcontinent. These numerous waterways, the low elevation of the land, and heavy monsoon rains combine to bring frequent floods to Bangladesh. Although these floods cause great damage, they leave behind a layer of fertile soil.

North of Bangladesh is Bhutan. This tiny country lies high in the mountain range known as the Himalayas (hi-muh-LAY-uhz). To the west is Nepal. The Himalayas occupy some 75 percent of Nepal's land area. Mount Everest, Earth's highest mountain, is located on Nepal's border with China. The Tarai (tuh-RY) is a low plain along Nepal's southern border. It is the country's main farming area. West of the Himalayas is the Karakoram (kah-rah-KOHR-oohm) Range. To the west the Karakorams merge into another mountain range, the Hindu Kush.

On Pakistan's western border is the Khyber (KY-buhr) Pass. For centuries, invaders and traders have traveled through this high mountain pass to India. East of the Khyber Pass is the Indus River. The Indus Valley lies mostly to the east of the river. This valley is Pakistan's main farming region and its most heavily populated area. East of these fertile lands is the Thar (TAHR) Desert, or the Great Indian Desert. A barren, hilly, and dry plateau in western Pakistan joins the plateaus of Iran.

✓ **READING CHECK:** *Places and Regions* What are the major physical features of this region?

# Climate and Resources

Bangladesh has one of the world's wettest climates. Rainfall is generally more than 60 inches (127 to 152 cm) each year. Most of the rain falls from June to October, during the wet summer monsoon. In the early and late weeks of the monsoon, **cyclones** sweep in from the Bay of Bengal. These violent storms resemble the hurricanes of the Caribbean. They bring high winds and heavy rain. Cyclones are often accompanied by **storm surges**. These are huge waves of water that are whipped up by fierce winds. The summer monsoon brings hot, wet weather to the lowland areas of Bhutan and Nepal. In the mountains climates are generally much cooler. Much of

Pakistan has a desert climate, receiving less than 10 inches (25 cm) of rain each year. Summer temperatures can reach as high as 120°F (49°C).

Bangladesh's most important resource is its fertile farmland. About 15 percent of Bangladesh is forested, so it has some timber supplies. However, severe deforestation and soil erosion have plagued the region, particularly in Nepal. Bhutan and Nepal have farmland in lowland areas. Both countries have some minerals, but few are mined. Pakistan has large natural gas reserves but limited oil supplies. It has to import oil to meet its energy needs. Pakistan's other natural resources include coal, limestone, and salt.

✓ **READING CHECK:** ( *Places and Regions* ) What are the natural resources of the region?

## The Island Countries

The Indian Perimeter region also includes Sri Lanka and the Maldives. Sri Lanka is a large island located just off the southeastern tip of India. Plains cover most of the island's northern half and coastal areas. Mountains and hills rise in the south-central part of the island.

About 1,200 tiny tropical islands in the Indian Ocean make up the Maldives. The island group stretches from south of India to the equator. Only about 200 of the islands are inhabited. None rises more than 6 feet (1.8 m) above sea level.

✓ **READING CHECK:** ( *Places and Regions* ) What are the physical features of the island countries?

**Our Amazing Planet**

In May 1997 a cyclone and storm surges devastated Bangladesh. More than 1.5 million people were left homeless.

go.hrw.com
**Homework Practice Online**
Keyword: SK3 HP28

# Section Review 1

**Define and explain:** cyclones, storm surges

**Working with Sketch Maps** On a map of India and the Indian Perimeter that you draw or that your teacher provides, label the following: Brahmaputra River, Ganges River, Himalayas, Mount Everest, Tarai, Karakoram Range, Hindu Kush, Khyber Pass, Indus River, and Thar Desert. Where is Earth's highest mountain located? What plains area is Nepal's main farming region?

### Reading for the Main Idea

1. ( *Places and Regions* ) Why has the Khyber Pass been important in the history of Pakistan and India?

2. ( *Places and Regions* ) How have erosion and deforestation affected the region? Which country has been most affected by these problems?

3. ( *Places and Regions* ) What island countries are found in the region? How are they different from each other?

### Critical Thinking

4. **Drawing Inferences and Conclusions** How do you think climate affects life in Pakistan and Bangladesh?

### Organizing What You Know

5. **Summarizing** Copy the following graphic organizer. Use it to describe the landforms, climates, and resources of the region.

| | Major Landforms | Climates | Resources |
|---|---|---|---|
| Pakistan | | | |
| Bangladesh | | | |
| Bhutan | | | |
| Nepal | | | |